D0762727

Handbook of College Reading and Study Strategy Research

Handbook of College Reading and Study Strategy Research

⇜ɰɰ⇝

Edited by

Rona F. Flippo
Fitchburg State College
David C. Caverly
Southwest Texas State University

LAWRENCE ERLBAUM ASSOCIATES, PUBLISHERS
2000   Mahwah, New Jersey   London

Lawrence Erlbaum Associates, Inc., Publishers
10 Industrial Avenue
Mahwah, NJ 07430

Cover design by Kathryn Houghtaling Lacey

Library of Congress Cataloging-in-Publication Data

Handbook of college reading and study strategy research / editors, Rona F. Flippo,
    David C. Caverly.
        p. cm.
    Includes bibliographical references and indexes.
        ISBN 0-8058-3003-0 (cloth : alk. paper). — ISBN 0-8058-3004-9 (paper : alk. paper).
    1. Reading (Higher education)—United States—Handbooks, manuals, etc. 2. Study
    skills—United States—Handbooks, manuals, etc. I. Flippo, Rona F. II. Caverly, David
    C.
    LB2395.3.H36   1999
    428.4'071'1—dc21   99-12747
                                                                          CIP

Books published by Lawrence Erlbaum Associates are printed on acid-free paper,
and their bindings are chosen for strength and durability.

Printed in the United States of America
10 9 8 7 6 5 4 3 2 1

Contents

∽§§∽

Foreword

⤳§§⤳

Martha Maxwell
Founder, Student Learning Center,
University of California Berkeley

The *Handbook of College Reading and Study Strategy Research* will be welcomed by professionals in the field as it is the only current volume that describes in depth the theories and research on which college reading and study strategy programs are based. In addition, it offers researchers and scholars important solutions to problems and suggestions about areas that need to be further explored and better understood.

Graduate students, their professors, and decision makers who determine policies for developmental programs will profit from reading this volume. Experienced practitioners, too, will appreciate the opportunity to review the recent evidence and be brought up to date in a field where both the basic concepts of the field and the students are changing.

Although college administrators and faculty agree that good reading and study strategies are essential for success in college, there are strong differences in opinions about what strategies are necessary and where and how they should be taught. In fact, as the authors in this handbook point out, there are disagreements about both the definition of reading and study strategies and the nature of its theories. For example, in chapter 8, Allgood, Risko, Alvarez, and Fairbanks describe the confusion and conflict over whether reading should be defined as a process, product, or discipline. Certainly these different views affect the perception of how students learn and how they should be taught.

The lack of success of many college reading and study strategy courses is also at issue. Some states are currently mandating that these courses be removed from 4-year public institutions and that students with weaker skills be sent to community colleges. Their rationale comes from studies like Adelman's (1996) research for the National Center for Educational Statistics. In a 10-year longitudinal study of high school students, Adelman concluded that 4-year colleges are not very efficient in helping students with the comprehensive literacy problems that force students to take remedial reading courses, and that we are defrauding students if we pretend otherwise. He adds that these students require solutions far more comprehensive than even community college can provide and urges that high schools assume more responsibility for preparing students for college reading. He maintains that we cannot let high school students continue to feel they have a good chance of completing college if they leave high school with poor reading skills. Other researchers have supported Adelman's finding and confirm that many college developmental reading courses do not do what they promise (Bohr, 1994–1995; Dimon, 1993; Keimig, 1983; Maxwell, 1979, 1997). On the other hand, the extensive research provided within this handbook counters these critics. College reading and study strategy programs that use the sound instructional practices summarized by this handbook have demonstrated success.

Mandated reading courses have many shortcomings. In addition to stigmatizing students who take remedial courses, they have other undesirable side effects. They have been shown to increase dropout rates, lower self-confidence and slow students' progress toward graduation. Students academically at risk who did not take required reading courses often did not suffer these problems (Dimon, 1993; Maxwell, 1997). The question arises as to whether this is an artifact of misplaced instruction, or college reading instructors who have good intentions but are ill-prepared to handle the rigors of developmental reading students at the college level.

Many factors limit the effectiveness of college reading and study strategy courses including the lack of training and experience of the teachers; the course goals, design, and strategies; and the nature of the placement tests. As this handbook points out, there are only four universities in the United States that offer a graduate major in developmental reading and study strategies; so, teaching college reading and study strategy courses has traditionally involved on-the-job-training. This was true 30 years ago when a demographic study of members of the College Reading Association found that 50% were teaching college reading and study strategies for the first time and only about 60 % had taken courses in how to teach reading or study strategies (Maxwell, 1965).

Yet even today, hundreds of new, inexperienced, and minimally trained people accept college reading and study strategy positions each year. If they have taken any graduate courses in reading and study strategies, they have usually been trained to teach in the primary grades. Many are left to their own devices to learn about how to teach college students, to select texts and appropriate materials, to develop teaching strategies, and to find ways to help individual students read their college textbooks and study in their courses. Thus underprepared teachers remain a problem for college reading and study strategy instruction as much as underprepared students do. Often educational supervisors are equally limited in their knowledge about the field of college reading and study strategies and cannot help. This handbook improves the skills and knowledge base of those teachers who are new to the field by summarizing sound instructional practice based on research relevant to the college age population.

Another factor that strongly influences where and how college reading and study strategy courses are taught is the vast number of high school students representing the "baby boom echo" who are entering college. Nationally, the pool of new freshmen is expected to increase by at least 15% over the next 15 years. Colleges will have no increase in funding or resources to handle the additional load of students. Undoubtedly, accepting students with weaker skills and poor preparation who need intensive help will be a lower priority for public colleges when faced with rejecting qualified students for whom they have no room.

On the other hand, even if the reading and study strategies of entering freshman greatly improve, there will still be a need for reading and study strategy programs. Even the best students need help in reading and learning in content areas that are outside their specialty. Hopefully, what will happen is that future college reading and study strategy instructors will offer more effective programs instead of preserving today's simplistic solution of mandated testing and assignment to required courses. There are many working alternatives as this handbook points out. Indeed, we already recognize the positive benefits of such approaches as adjunct skills classes, supplemental instruction, or paired courses where reading and study strategies are integrated with content courses often supplemented by tutoring. Individualized services, online computer programs and other technological solutions show the promise of becoming cost-effective ways to help students improve their reading and study strategies under the right conditions. Programs in which reading and study strategies are integrated with other needed support services can provide students with information to make informed choices about the programs and enable them to volunteer for the courses they need.

This handbook also provides a guide for future researchers because it suggests many issues that need further investigation to help practitioners improve their teaching strategies. Here are some of the questions and issues that the chapter authors raise:

- Because we expect more and better prepared students to enter college in the future, and college courses will become more challenging, how can we improve our teaching of higher level reading and thinking skills?
- Which teaching strategies are effective in aiding students to improve their metacognitive strategies?
- How can teachers make students aware of their own metacognitive strategies, see that they guide themselves in continuing to develop and improve their strategies, and efficiently monitor their own work?
- Are there social, ethnic, or other differences that affect a student's ability to become an active participant in his or her own learning? If so, are there methods that can help students overcome these blocks?
- Teachers can model strategies, but how can they make these activities generative?
- How can technology incorporate constructivist strategies in learning programs—that is, introduce collaborative group processes or actively involve other people so that a student working on a computer program is not simply being exposed to another teacher-directed activity?
- Under what conditions is discipline-specific reading training better than general reading training for students?
- How can we show professors and textbook authors how to weave effective study approaches into their presentation of content and into the textbooks they write for college courses?
- No one yet has satisfactorily answered the question of why so many of our students come to college with poor reading skills and an aversion to reading and

learning. Is it our competitive culture, our family values, or is it just the school experience that turns them off? What are the reasons so many have motivational problems? Wouldn't finding ways to prevent motivational problems be cheaper and more effective than the intensive work it takes to cure them?

- How can we improve program evaluation? College reading and study strategy program directors have been urged, cajoled, criticized, and condemned for decades because they do not routinely evaluate their programs. Yet even today, systematic evaluations are rarely done and even when programs are evaluated, the recommendations are often ignored. Perhaps as Boylan, Bonham, White, and George suggest in chapter 13, college reading programs need a new evaluation paradigm and some simpler models so reading professionals can do more effective follow-up studies routinely.
- This handbook should help researchers avoid some lines of research that have proved unproductive in the past. For example, many researchers have tried to discover the best way to teach vocabulary, when, in truth, there is no one best way to learn new words. It takes many approaches and requires intensive practice.
- We need further descriptive studies that provide longitudinal information on how average students develop their own reading and study skills as they adapt to college demands.

In this ever-changing world of higher education, where new theories of knowledge and new technologies are emerging, this handbook helps keep educators abreast of the developments that have occurred and helps focus expectations on those changes yet to come.

In chapter 1, Stahl and King exhort us to become the historians of our field and not rely on others to do this for us. Similarly, if the research questions that have been raised are to be answered, more college reading and study strategy specialists must become involved in research. This handbook guides future teachers and college reading and study strategy researchers to ask more appropriate questions and develop new strategies for finding answers that will help produce better teachers, better programs, and better college learners.

REFERENCES AND SUGGESTED READINGS

Adelman, C. (1996, October 4). The truth about remedial work: It's more complex than windy rhetoric and simple solutions suggest. *Chronicle of Higher Education, 43*(6), A56.

Bohr, L. (1994–1995). College courses which attract and generate good readers. *Journal of College Reading and Learning, 26*(2) 30–44.

Dimon, M. G. (1993). *The effect of reading/study skills courses on high-risk students.* Doctoral dissertation, The Claremont Graduate School, Claremont, CA.

Keimig, R. T. (1983). *Raising academic standards: A guide to learning improvement.* Washington, DC: ASHE-ERIC. Clearing House for Higher Education/Association for the Study of Higher Education.

*Maxwell, M. (1979). *Improving student learning skills.* San Francisco: Jossey-Bass.

Maxwell, M. J. (1967). *Characteristics of members of the College Reading Association.* Unpublished paper, Reading and Study Skills Laboratory, Counseling Center, University of Maryland.

*Maxwell, M. (1997). *The dismal status of required developmental reading programs: Roots, causes and solutions.* (ERIC Document Reproduction No. ED 415 501)

Preface

❧§§❧

The discipline of college reading and study strategy instruction is as old as college it-self. Historical evidence suggests remedial Latin was taught to students developing their strategies to read texts and listen to lectures within the first organized colleges of the 12th century. As higher education emerged in the United States so did what came to be called "developmental education" in the most prestigious universities and colleges. During the rapid growth of junior and community colleges in the early 1960s, college reading and study strategy research gained new attention.

Today, developmental education can be found in all forms of postsecondary schools around the world: medical and law schools, universities, baccalaureate colleges, junior and community colleges, and technical schools. Conservatively, it is estimated that more than 104,000 higher education personnel currently teach more than 3.8 million students (or 30% of those enrolled in higher education) in some form of reading and study strategy developmental educational program (National Center for Education Statistics [NCES], 1996). These personnel range from college reading and study strategy instructors, graduate professors training these instructors, administrators directing such programs, and decision makers directing the efforts of all of these educators. These personnel call their efforts developmental, remedial, college preparatory, or basic skills instruction. We prefer the term *developmental* as it connotes the students have developed in their strategic ability to read and study to a certain extent, but still need to develop further their strategies to succeed with the task demands placed on them for college work (cf. Pugh, Pawan, & Antommarchi, chap. 2, this volume). However, the contributors to this volume had latitude in their choice of terminology.

Still, with all this need and effort, college reading and study strategies have historically been under scrutiny from those who argue remedial education does not belong at the college level (cf. Stall & King, chap. 1, this volume). We have seen a resurgence to phase out of higher education long-standing programs considered "remedial." This has been done by reshuffling these programs to other institutions or relying on commercial, outside services as substitutes. An example of these program struggles for justification have taken place recently in the state of New York.

The City University of New York's (CUNY) Board of Trustees decided to do away with most remedial classes at its 11 four-year colleges. This decision ended that institution's historic commitment to open admission and access to public higher education. Applicants who fail one or more of CUNY's tests in reading, writing, or mathematics will have to successfully complete a summer program, attend a CUNY community college, or go elsewhere for their education. Roughly two thirds of the prospective students affected will be Asian, African American, or Hispanic (Healy, 1998). As of this writing, the CUNY community college programs have been left intact; however, the mayor formed a panel, dominated by proponents of privatization, to examine and recommend the "best means" to take remediation out of CUNY's hands (Healey & Schmidt, 1998).

The issues, of course, involve a clash of values: calls for quality and standards versus pleas to consider the needs and dreams of the poor and racially diverse minority populations (Schmidt, 1998. See Pintozzi & Valeri-Gold, chap. 10, this volume, for information regarding linguistically diverse populations served and the magnitude of this needed service.) Data released by the U.S. Department of Education indicates that the total number of minority students in U.S. colleges and universities has increased by 3.2 %, to about 3,609,300 in 1996, the latest year for which the data was available. Minority students then represented more than one fourth of the enrolled U.S. citizens (Gose, 1998). Gose is recommended for a breakdown, state by state of the various minority populations. A similar press for higher standards has taken place in the State University of New York (SUNY) system (Healy & Schmidt, 1998). While as of this writing, no dismantling of reading and study strategy programs in the SUNY schools have been mentioned, we project that it may eventually come to this.

Obviously, decisions to eliminate remedial courses indicate an undervaluing of these courses and of the programs that offer them. This is a shame because evidence suggests that the quality and costs of these programs are a very good buy (Breneman, 1998). Although, as Breneman and others who commented on his review (Abraham, 1998; Hoxby, 1998) indicated, it is extremely difficult to calculate the national cost of remedial education at the college level; Breneman's calculation of approximately $1 billion annually is a very modest cost (he calculated less than 1%) of the national expenditure of the public higher education budget.

In fact, Hoxby (1998) argued that remedial courses and their expenses should not be calculated *against* the colleges at all because many of the students who did not learn basic skills in public high schools are being better served by the colleges' remedial programs. Rather than cut college programs and budgets, or negatively affect colleges' images, colleges should instead be praised, recognized, and rewarded for the exemplary jobs they are doing for students who have thus far not learned enough in the K–12 systems! The high schools, said Hoxby, who failed in their responsibilities to educate these students, should instead pay the colleges for their reeducation, and, implied Hoxby, public high schools could learn how to do a better job with these students by studying college remedial course strategies and programs.

We, of course, do not believe that high schools should be blamed, but we do agree with Hoxby (1998), neither should the colleges. Rather, we see remedial course offerings as part of the amenities and services that open-access institutions of higher education *should be offering*. Certainly, many other amenities and services are offered by colleges for students that are just as or more costly (e.g., sports, music, art, dance, counseling, as well as disabilities services and alcohol and drug abuse programs). Although not all students need or use all of these programs, they are still offered at comprehensive institutions for those that do. We argue that students, who were not prepared or motivated to learn in K–12 settings, may very well be prepared and highly motivated to learn in college. If so, they deserve the second chance that developmental programs (our preference over the term "remedial") offer them. Additionally, students new to our societies and cultures, who have come to learn and study, should not be excluded because of language barriers. These students do offer additional challenges, but they also offer a rich diversity to our institutions.

Breneman (1998) reviewed the 1995 NCES survey and indicated the following findings:

1. About 78% of higher education institutions that enrolled freshman included at least one remedial reading, writing, or mathematics course. Remedial courses are offered at virtually all (100% of) 2-year public colleges, and 94% of colleges with high minority enrollments. Eighty-one percent of public 4-year colleges offered at least one remedial course, and 63% of private 4-year colleges did the same.

2. Overall, remedial reading courses were offered by 57% of the institutions, and almost all 2-year colleges.

3. Overall, the average number of courses offered was 2.1 for reading and 2.0 for writing, with public 2-year colleges offering a much higher average.

4. Twenty-nine percent of first-time freshmen were enrolled in at least one remedial reading, writing, or mathematics course in fall 1995. (Remedial courses in mathematics were taken more than for reading or writing.)

5. Most institutions reported that students do not take remedial courses for long periods of time: two thirds reported less than 1 year, 28% indicated 1 year, and 5% indicated more than 1 year (pp. 361–362).

So, what happens if more and more institutions shed their remedial course obligations, as has happened in New York City? One possibility that has been employed elsewhere involves contracting with private corporations to provide remedial courses for students. For example, it has been reported (Gose, 1997) that Kaplan Education Centers are providing courses for Greenville Technical College and Chattanooga State Technical Community College; and that another company, Sylvan Learning Systems, is doing the same for Columbia College Chicago, Howard Community College, and Towson University. Gose reports that dozens more, in Connecticut, Ohio, South Carolina, and in other states, are considering hiring Kaplan or Sylvan.

Although it is too soon to examine results, as reading professionals we are skeptical of any programs that are likely to decontextualize reading and study strategy work from required college content courses. In other words, we advocate programs that involve students reading, writing, and studying the actual texts and other materials required for the college courses they are taking concurrently with developmental reading and study strategy programs. We advocate more, not less, integration between developmental courses and content courses, and we fail to see how outside private companies can provide this integration better than knowledgeable insiders with more control over college curriculum and staffing. We further agree with Breneman (1998) and others (Abraham, 1998; Hoxby, 1998); college "developmental" (our word, not theirs) courses are a good buy and *should be continued by colleges* who know the students, know their needs, and can best provide the context and motivation for the various student populations to succeed.

Still, this debate cannot be quelled by logic alone. Rather, we must also answer these basic questions through reviewing the research. Indeed, does developmental/remedial education effectively improve the reading and study strategies of the underprepared? If so, what are the best recommendations of experts on how to teach these strategies and organize for this instruction? This volume addresses and explores the issues surrounding these questions.

We have learned a great deal about how students learn at the college level, as well as the best practices for instruction to improve that learning. In previous work, we began collecting this knowledge into a review of the theoretical, empirical, and instructional research present in the field of college reading and study strategies (Flippo & Caverly, 1991a, 1991b). Now, as we begin a new millennium, we have updated and expanded this review to help those who theorize, research, and teach developmental reading and study strategies in colleges and universities make sound instructional decisions. This handbook brings together notable scholars of college reading and study strategies to provide an introduction and rationale for each of their topics, summarize the theoretical foundations of the topic, synthesize the qualitative and quantitative research surrounding their topic, present implications for teaching and further research, and collect a bibliography of references and suggested readings to extend learning beyond this book, the most relevant of which are indicated by asterisks (*).

In chapter 1, Stahl and King begin with a historical overview of the field of college reading and study strategies. Their overview provides a heritage for the field and verifies its existence. Next, Pugh, Pawan, and Antommarchi (chap. 2) explore the literacy demands of postsecondary reading. These two chapters put into perspective the rationale for developmental reading and study strategy instruction and set the stage for the topics discussed in the remaining chapters of the volume.

Simpson and Randall begin in chapter 3 by reviewing vocabulary development among postsecondary readers. In so doing, they suggest practical teaching and programmatic guidelines. In chapter 4, Nist and Holschuh examine how college reading and study strategy instruction has moved from teacher-directed to student-generative comprehension strategies. They argue any comprehension instruction should include strategies that have cognitive, metacognitive, and affective components, as well as purposeful shifting from the teacher to the student. In chapter 5, Caverly, Orlando, and Mullen extend this discussion on comprehension to review the research on textbook study reading strategies. These strategies include underlining, notetaking from text, outlining, cognitive mapping, and Survey, Question, Read, Recite, Review (SQ3R). Connecting the research on reading and writing, in chapter 6, Valeri-Gold and Deming review the meaning-making processes of both reading and writing. They then discuss the value of integrating instruction for these two, very important, and interrelated college tools.

In chapter 7, Armbruster shifts the focus to begin exploring study strategies, specifically notetaking from lectures. Critiquing the research, she examines the value of taking notes, and concludes with implications for instruction and research. In chapter 8, Allgood, Risko, Alvarez, and Fairbanks discuss those study factors that separate students who succeed in postsecondary education versus those who do not succeed. Specifically, they examine what developmental educators can do to improve students' ability to understand course expectations, motivate themselves, and develop self-efficacy toward improving their performance. Next, in chapter 9, Flippo, Becker, and Wark review test preparation and test taking at the college level. Examining test-wiseness, test-taking strategies, test coaching, and text anxiety, they make recommendations for teaching students how to prepare for and take tests. Considering the special needs and issues of English as a second language (ESL) students, Pintozzi and Valeri-Gold (chap. 10) review both the theoretical and instructional literature of these special populations. They provide research-based instructional strategies for the cultural verities of ESL students. In chapter 11, Caverly and Peterson explore the role of technology in college developmental reading. Presenting a theoretical model for integrating technology, they review the research on the instructional effectiveness of technology as a tutor, as a tool, and as a tutee, and make recommendations for instruction.

The focus shifts next to instructional program issues. Beginning in chapter 12, Johnson and Carpenter connect reading and study strategy instruction with the broader concept of learning assistance as they review various program organizational structures. They conclude with ingredients for creating a successful program. In chapter 13, Boylan, Bonham, White, and George discuss the principles, research, and practice of evaluating college reading and study strategy programs. After presenting an overview of the changing role of evaluation over the last 50 years, they critique the various evaluation models, provide exemplars of applications of these models, and offer recommendations for the practitioner. Flippo and Schumm, in chapter 14, conclude this handbook with a discussion and complete review of reading tests that could be used in college programs, as well as present conclusions, implications, and recommendations for the use of these instruments. There is also an accompanying appendix of current reading tests.

This book is the most comprehensive and up-to-date source available for the college reading and study strategy practitioner. Providing a thorough examination of theory, research, and practice, college reading teachers will find information to make better instructional decisions, administrators will find justification for programmatic implementations, and professors will find in one book both theory and practice to better prepare graduate students to understand the parameters and issues of this field. We believe it will serve you well as we all continue to study, research, learn, and share more about college reading and study strategy issues and instruction.

—*Rona F. Flippo*
—*David C. Caverly*

REFERENCES AND SUGGESTED READINGS

*Abraham, A. A. (1998). Comment on remediation in higher education: Its extent and cost. In D. Ravitch (Ed.), *Brookings papers on education policy 1998* (pp. 371–376). Washington, DC: Brookings Institution Press.

*Breneman, D. W. (1998). Remediation in higher education: Its extent and cost. In D. Ravitch (Ed.), *Brookings papers on education policy 1998* (pp. 359–383). Washington, DC: Brookings Institution Press.

*Flippo, R. F., & Caverly, D. C. (Eds.). (1991a). *College reading & study strategy programs.* Newark, DE: International Reading Association.

*Flippo, R. F., & Caverly, D. C. (Eds.). (1991b). *Teaching reading & study strategies at the college level.* Newark, DE: International Reading Association.

Gose, B. (1997, September 19). Tutoring companies take over remedial teaching at some colleges. *The Chronicle of Higher Education, 44*(4), A44–A45.

Gose, B. (1998, June 5). Minority enrollment rose 3.2% in 1996. *The Chronicle of Higher Education, 44*(39), A32–A43.

Healy, P. (1998, June 5). CUNY's 4-year colleges ordered to phase out remedial education. *The Chronicle of Higher Education, 44*(39), A26–A27.

Healy, P., & Schmidt, P. (1998, July 10). In New York, a "standards revolution" or the gutting of public colleges? *The Chronicle of Higher Education, 44*(44), A21–A23.

*Hoxby, C. M. (1998). Comment on remediation in higher education: Its extent and cost. In D. Ravitch (Ed.), *Brookings papers on education policy 1998* (pp. 376–381). Washington, DC: Brookings Institution Press.

National Center for Education Statistics (1996). *Remedial education at higher education institutions in fall 1995.* [Online]. Available at http:// nces.ed.gov/pubs/97584.html

Schmidt, P. (1998, March 10). A clash of values at CUNY over remedial education. *The Chronicle of Higher Education, 44*(28), A33–A34.

Acknowledgments

༄❦❦༄

Undertaking a project like this can be overwhelming. Fortunately for us, our task was made much easier because of our broad network of professional contacts. These contacts have developed over the years through our membership in and activities with several key reading and developmental education organizations. Therefore, we wish to acknowledge these organizations for providing us with a forum to meet, interact, and form lifelong professional contacts with other reading and study strategy professionals with an interest in college students. We especially thank the American Reading Forum (ARF), College Reading Association (CRA), College Reading and Learning Association (CRLA), International Reading Association (IRA), National Association of Developmental Education (NADE), and National Reading Conference (NRC). Likewise, we thank and acknowledge the many members of these organizations who tirelessly attend, make presentations at, and serve on the committees of these groups year after year. We could not have completed this book without all of them.

Both of us have had the good fortune to be mentored and advised by great minds in the field of college reading and study strategies. Out of respect for what you have taught us, thank you A. Garr Cranney, Alton L. Raygor, Larry Mikulecky, and Sharon Pugh. We also wish to acknowledge and thank all the other college reading teachers and researchers who came before us; we have built our knowledge on what you have taught.

Special recognition is given to two graduate students in education at Fitchburg State College, Sherri L. Borreson and Charlene C. Cormier, who each worked diligently on different aspects of this book. Thank you both for your important contributions.

Of course, we owe our greatest thanks to the excellent researchers and writers who authored the chapters included here. They were invited to contribute because of their expertise in both the specific area covered in their chapter and the field of college reading and study strategies in general.

Finally, a very special thanks must be given to Naomi Silverman, our wonderful editor, as well as to Lawrence Erlbaum Associates for their foresight in recognizing the need for this handbook and for their dedication to this project. Thank you for making the *Handbook of College Reading and Study Strategy Research* a reality for us and the many readers who appreciate a handbook for our field, at long last.

—*Rona F. Flippo*
—*David C. Caverly*

1

A History of College Reading

‿❧❧‿

Norman A. Stahl
Northern Illinois University

James R. King
University of South Florida

What is an academic discipline? As a field it is either granted or proclaims for itself the status of a discipline, empowering its members. Can the field of reading be said to be a discipline? Perhaps it is; perhaps it is not. What is clear, however, is that within any field or any discipline there are subgroups, some of which have high status and some of which are marginalized. For instance, when you converse with colleagues in the field of English or read the work of Robert Scholes, it is evident that the study of literature has enjoyed greater status than the study of written composition in the discipline. Similar hierarchic status relations exist in reading research and reading pedagogy as well.

It can be argued that college reading has been an established subfield in reading research and reading pedagogy for at least 100 years. Manzo (1983) also noted that college reading is both a generator of new ideas and a repository of considerable wisdom. Cranney (1983a, 1983b) provided valuable bibliographies of the field's contributions. Still, many individuals agree that the field does not receive the same respect that comes to other subfields of literacy pedagogy such as elementary reading, remedial/corrective reading, secondary reading, or more recently, adult reading coupled with family literacy. It is rather ironic that many of the greatest scholars in reading research and pedagogy wrote about college readers and/or college reading and study strategy instruction (e.g., Guy Buswell, William S. Gray, Ernest Horn, Constance McCullough, Nila B. Smith, Ruth M. Strang, Miles A. Tinker, Paul A. Witty, George Spache, Francis P. Robinson) to the extent that much of our historical, if not foundational understandings of basic reading processes rest on work conducted with college readers. It is equally ironic that all of our professional organizations—the International Reading Association (IRA), the National Reading Conference (NRC), the College Reading Association (CRA), the College Reading and Learning Association (CRLA), and the American Reading Forum (ARF)—were founded with the major input of college reading professionals. Given this legacy, it is an enigma why the specialization of college reading remains somewhat of a pariah within the overall field or discipline.

One way to unshackle any field from the chains of a pariah status is to fully document and disseminate a rich and an important history to both internal and external audiences. Even more so, it is imperative to have each professional in the field develop a sense of one's own place in the history of the academic speciality. The field of college reading and learning instruction has, to varying degrees, undertaken the historiography and the dissemination of its own legacy. However, the lack of formal and specific training of developmental reading and learning assistance specialists over the years coupled with the intense day-to-day demands of conducting a college reading program or learning assistance center, have mitigated against most members of the field knowing much about our historical roots.

In the quest for parity in the reading profession, it is time for current and future developmental educators and learning assistance personnel to learn of the field's contributions to reading research and pedagogy. The purpose of this chapter is to provide future postsecondary reading specialists as well as more established professionals an opportunity to review the specialization's heritage. In addition, the chapter discusses one's responsibility for helping the field grow in stature through undertaking what is called *nearby history* and more nationally oriented historical work.

LEARNING HISTORY: RESOURCES FOR HISTORICAL STUDY OF COLLEGE READING INSTRUCTION

The history of any field can be viewed through a multitude of lenses by examining a range of primary and secondary historical sources. Reading educators tend to overrely on the classic *American Reading Instruction* by Smith (1934b, 1965, 1986). This overreliance is a case of academic tunnel vision. Such an action begs the question of whether there has been a lack of scholarship or a lack of professional preparation across the field. One cannot question the level of professional awareness if there does not exist a corpus of sources available to the individual seeking a deeper understanding of the reading field's history.

Does a body of historical resources exist for the overall field of literacy? The answer to this question is yes. Does such a body of historical resources exist for the more specific area of college reading and study strategy programs? The answer here must be a qualified yes.

In an article dealing with the need to undertake historical research pertaining to college reading instruction, Stahl, Hynd, and Henk (1986) proposed that three categories of historical materials could be found in various repositories. The first category included extensive chronicles integrating numerous primary and secondary sources. The second category was comprised of summaries or timelines that highlighted major events or trends in the field. The third category was made up of monographs and texts that had earned a place of historical importance in the field. The authors reviewed the available historical writings that fell into each of the categories, but within each category, it was obvious that the literature was sparse. Furthermore, these writers suggested that this dearth of materials might have provided a partial understanding of why college reading specialists overlooked the history of the field when designing curriculum, developing programs, writing worktexts, and conducting research.

Now more than a decade later, it is useful to revisit the corpus of resources available to students of the history of reading and study strategy instruction at the postsecondary level. In reviewing these works, two of the categories (historical chronicles, and historical summaries and timelines) that were used by Stahl, Hynd, and Henk (1986) are employed with the addition of a new category for those historically focused studies that investigate specific topics (e.g., study techniques, reading and writing instruction) or specific historical eras. Such an addition to the categorization scheme reflects the greater breadth in studies now comprising the body of historical knowledge, and a concomitant coming of age of the field as well.

Historical Chronicles

The first category of historical sources is comprised of documents that draw on an extensive number of primary and secondary sources. It was not surprising to discover that all of the sources included here were dissertation projects, but it is interesting to note that the historical work is usually but one component in each of these dissertations. Five of the studies (Bailey, 1982, Blake, 1953, Heron, 1989, Leedy, 1958, Straff, 1985) focus directly on college reading instruction while a sixth study (Brier, 1983) looks at academic preparedness for higher education.

The seminal historical work for the field is the dissertation undertaken by Leedy (1958). Through the extensive use of primary sources along with secondary sources ($N = 414$), Leedy traced the role of reading, readers, reading materials, and reading programs in U.S. higher education from 1636 to 1958. From this massive undertaking, Leedy (1958) put forth two important conclusions pertaining to the field's history. First, he noted that the college reading improvement programs of 1958 were the result of a slow but orderly evolution in the recognition of the importance of reading's role in postsecondary education. Second, reading programs were implemented over the years because students and representatives of the institutions recognized that ineffective reading and study skills created problems in academic achievement. Leedy's historical work is to college reading as what *American Reading Instruction* is to the overall field of literacy—a fact that is not overly surprising since Nila B. Smith served on Leedy's dissertation committee. (A more detailed analysis of this historical research and the national survey that accompanied it can be found in Stahl, 1988.)

There are three other dissertations that provide major historical reviews, or historical analyses of the literature in the field. Blake (1953) examined the historical, social, and educational forces that promoted the growth of college reading and study skills programs during the first 50 years of the 20th century. This work was part of an analysis of the program at the University of Maryland and a national survey. Although this dissertation does not provide the depth of historical coverage as found in

Leedy's work (1958), it does give a somewhat alternative view of reading activities in pre-1950 postsecondary education.

Straff (1985) undertook a critical historical analysis of a selected literature base ($N = 74$ sources) to determine what research, theory, and practice in college reading instruction was available from 1900 to 1980. The intent was to provide a foundation for future program development. His overall conclusions were not unlike those derived by Leedy (1958). Straff noted that college reading programs grew at a slow and deliberate pace and that this growth reflected local needs as opposed to a coordinated national movement. He also offered the opinion that the field had grown in quantity and in quality. The critical analysis led to the conclusion that the literature base had matured from the simple acknowledgment of reading/study problems in higher education, to the discussion of the implementation of programs, to research on the effectiveness of programs. Still, the literature reviewed led Straff to conclude that across the century there was little data from acceptable research concerning program rationale, instructional objectives, student populations, curricula, staffing, student reading behaviors, funding sources, and shifts in societal priorities on which to base recommendations for future program development. (For an era-focused meta-analysis of the research of the 1960s and 1970s, see Sanders, 1979.)

Heron (1989) completed dissertation research that considered the historical context for postsecondary reading requirements, the needs of at-risk college readers, and the instructional level and approach used by selected college reading programs ($N = 89$). Heron's research used resources that dated back to 1927, and she reviewed the documents through the lens of Chall's developmental reading theory (Chall, 1983). The study led to several conclusions including:

1. The reading requirements in higher education had increased dramatically across the history of American higher education.
2. College reading was dependent on reading skills and strategies as well as domain specific knowledge.
3. Reading problems of college students spanned Chall's developmental stages, and these deficiencies are compounded by the lack of knowledge and language of the academic discourse.
4. Reading programs were categorized by attention to Chall's development levels.
5. Historically, lower level programs emphasizing diagnosis and skills (Stages 1–3) were decreasing in number, higher level programs emphasizing content strategies and critical reading (Stages 3 and 4) were increasing, and bridge programs such as the developmental education model (Stages 1–4) were also increasing in number but more slowly than those Heron designated as the higher level programs.

Heron also noted published reports that contained appropriate qualitative descriptions of instructional techniques and acceptable quantitative measures of the effectiveness of instructional methods were not common. This situation made it nearly impossible to evaluate the effectiveness of methods of instruction. It is interesting to note how this point parallels Straff's statement about the dearth of quality research in the field.

Within this category of historical chronicles, we include the dissertation under-taken by Bailey (1982). Bailey's critical analysis summarized, classified, and evaluated 170 research studies from 31 different journals published between 1925 and 1980. Although this work cannot be called a true historical study, it does serve as a most extensive annotated bibliography and it is an important reference source for the historian of our field. Furthermore, researchers in the areas of reading rate, reading technology (precomputer), teaching methods, test-taking skills, notetaking, textbook study methods, listening, instructional materials, vocabulary, physical factors, reading comprehension, or combined methods will find Bailey's analysis of the research in each category to be of interest.

Finally, we add to this category a study that expands the boundary of historical research beyond college reading and study strategy instruction. Brier (1983) undertook a historical narrative that explored the actions undertaken by the newly formed Vassar College and the equally new Cornell University between 1865 to 1890 to meet the academic needs of underprepared students. This dissertation draws widely from primary sources to document the controversy that developed when both institutions enrolled a sizable number of students who required preparatory instruction, often in the basic skills, in order to meet with academic success in the academic program. Vassar College responded by developing a preparatory program, whereas Cornell University referred students elsewhere for assistance. This study demonstrates conclusively that issues associated currently with open door (i.e., all students are admitted) and special admissions programs have been of concern in the field of higher education for more than 100 years. The findings from this dissertation and the article that evolved from it (Brier, 1984) have been referenced regularly in the literature on the history of developmental education—in which college reading and study strategy programs have been but one important component.

Before moving on to another classification of texts, there is a sixth dissertation (Smith, 1934a) that later evolved into several editions of a classic text (Smith, 1934b, 1965, 1986) that should be mentioned as a resource. Indeed, Smith's *American Reading Instruction* was a most important contribution for the era in which it was released, and its revisions continue to have great importance even if the sophistication of historical method is not up to current standards. Although this text provides broad coverage of U.S. reading instruction since the earliest years of the 17th century, it does not focus specifically on college reading instruction. Still, college reading instruction is integrated into Smith's discussions of the field. Unfortunately finding information about the history of college reading often requires a working knowledge of each era's scholarship on college reading and also the field's historical relationship to other reading specializations, such as secondary school reading and adult reading or to shared topics such as eye movement research or developmental reading. This is not to demean Smith's historical work, rather it is important to put it in proper perspective for the writer and researcher in college reading.

The strength of the documents in the historical chronicles category is found in the depth and breadth of coverage by each author on the particular topic of focus. As a whole, the documents draw from a range of primary sources from the eras defined in each work. Researchers of historical topics and the historical roots of current topics will find these sources most useful. The Smith (1934a) text is readily available in research libraries in book form (Smith, 1934b, 1965, 1986) as it has been previously distributed by IRA. It is likely that the dissertations mentioned here are available most readily for a fee through University Microfilms International. Older dissertations are occasionally available through interlibrary loan. Unfortunately, this lack of easy availability at a reasonable cost or within a speedy time frame may be one reason why these dissertations are not utilized by writers to the same degree as are the historical summaries and timelines covered in the following section.

Historical Summaries and Timelines

The sources contained in this category provide the college reading specialist with chronological presentations of watershed events in the field's history. This work appears as chapters or sections in comprehensive books or edited texts focusing on the fields of learning assistance, college reading, or developmental education as well as in yearbook chapters and journal articles that are more specific in nature. These chapters and articles cannot be expected to contain the same depth of coverage for each historical era as that found in the previously mentioned dissertation studies. Another issue to consider is that a number of these works, such as Spache (1969), were written with the multiple purposes of providing a historical survey along with being a state-of-the-art review and a speculative discussion about the future of the profession. These multipurpose articles often use the historical discussion as a necessary avenue to get to the discussion of the present or to offer a prophecy of the future and they do not generally utilize sound historical method. These works can be placed in three categories: college reading, learning assistance, and developmental education. Each is now covered in turn.

College Reading.   During the height of the NRC's and the CRA's interest postsecondary reading instruction in the 1960s and early 1970s, Lowe authored two papers that provide college reading professionals with concise histories of the field. In his first paper, Lowe (1967b) analyzed 49 surveys of college reading programs undertaken between Parr's survey (1930) and Thurstone, Lowe, and Hayden's (1965) work. Lowe noted that during the period under review, public, private, gender-specific, historically African American, sectarian, and professional junior and senior postsecondary institutions had been surveyed. He pointed out that across the years, the number of programs had grown in number and size, and this growth paralleled an emergence of greater professionalism in the field. Lowe's (1970) second paper, which evolved from his dissertation (Lowe, 1967a), traces the college reading field's history from the founding of the Harvard University program of 1915 to the late 1960s by using each decade as the historical marker. The professional growth of college reading programs as well as the field in its entirety is covered along with the curricular trends and instructional innovations introduced during each decade.

It took 20 years for another wide-ranging historical chronicle of the college reading field (Wyatt, 1992) to appear in a professional journal. Wyatt draws on many of the most widely referenced secondary historical sources as well as selected primary sources in the fields of college reading, developmental education, learning assistance, and higher education to provide a linear and chronological discussion of the underprepared reader and writer in postsecondary education since the early 1800s. Woven throughout the chronology is the description of how a number of *prestigious* institutions (e.g., Harvard University, Yale University, the University of California, Stanford University) responded to the reading needs of their students. Wyatt pointed out that given the field's longevity and the current population projections for the years ahead, college reading programs may prove to be most important for the future.

Learning Assistance.   The development of the learning assistance movement has been covered by a number of writers. Enright (1975) provided a frequently referenced history of the origins of the learning assistance center in which she proposed that the movement went through five eras:

1. the age of clinical aspiration: programs become scientific (1916–1940)
2. the age of disenchantment: remedial reading is not the answer (1940–1950)
3. the age of integration: programs treat the whole student (1950–1960)
4. the age of actualization: good ideas become realities (1960–1970)
5. the age of systematization: the learning assistance center is organized (1970–1980).

This work, based on extensive literature review, shows the degree to which the roots of the learning assistance center are intertwined with the history of college reading instruction as well as how the learning assistance center movement evolved a broader orientation in which college reading was an intricate component.

Enright and Kerstiens (1980) revisited the history of learning assistance centers in the historically important but short-lived *New Directions for College Learning Assistance* sourcebook series. Again, it is evident from the literature covered in this article that it is very difficult to separate the history of learning assistance centers from that of college reading and study strategy instruction, and developmental education. The authors provide an overview of historical events from 1850 to 1940 and then move into a decade-by-decade review of the evolvement of the learning assistance center. The authors demonstrate effectively how across the decades the terminology describing the reading–learning programs evolved along with changes in philosophy and instructional method.

Drawing heavily from secondary sources, Lissner (1990) discussed the learning assistance center's evolution from 1828 through the latter 1980s. The 19th century is described as the prehistory of the learning assistance center movement because it focused on compensatory designs such as preparatory programs and tutoring schools. The 20th century is presented as an evolvement of postsecondary learning assistance programs during the depression, World War II, the GI Bill era, the Sputnik era, the open admissions era, and the learning center movement. An important conclusion is that learning centers originated as one of a long series of responses to two themes in higher education: the recurring perception that entering students were less prepared for college level work than the preceding academic generation, and the greater opportunities for higher education provided to broader segments of the population.

Maxwell's (1979) classic text, *Improving Student Learning Skills*, contained a detailed outline of events and trends that demonstrated that postsecondary institutions had been concerned with students' qualifications for college work since the 1850s.

Given the importance of Maxwell's work to the field of learning assistance, it is not surprising that many of the historical works published after its publication used Maxwell's outline as a foundation for these works. Maxwell's (1997) much revised edition of this text provides rich narratives combined with personal anecdotes based on 50 years of leadership in the field. Included as well is information from historical sources on topics such as at-risk students, tutoring, learning centers, writing instruction, and reading instruction. It can be expected that the individuals who comprise the next generation of college reading specialists and learning assistance professionals will receive their introductions to the history of the field through Maxwell's text.

   Developmental Education.   Cross (1976) provided one of the first historical discussions with a focus on the field of developmental education. Indeed, the tenuousness of the new developmental education label is observed in Cross' use of the term *remedial* in juxtaposition in the title of the chapter. The historical discussion is directed at two themes: (a) causes of poor academic performance, and (b) historical trends in evaluation of remediation in higher education. In discussing how poor academic performance was viewed, Cross proposed there was a predominant vantage held by educators in each of five eras respectively defined and roughly delimited as (a) poor study habits—pre 1935, (b) inadequate mastery of basic academic skills—late 1930s through the early 1940s, (c) low academic ability or low intelligence—postwar 1940s through early 1960s, (d) psychological and motivational blocks to learning—mid 1960s, and (e) sociocultural factors relating to deprived family and school backgrounds —latter 1960s through 1976. Cross pointed out that specialists in each succeeding era saw the problems associated with lack of success in college as having greater complexity than in the preceding era and that solutions tended to be additive across the years. In looking at the the trends in evaluation of remedial programs, she noted that the time spanning the 1940s and 1950s was a period of relatively unsophisticated methodological analysis of the effectiveness of programs. The evaluation of the 1960s focused on emotional defenses of both the programs of the era and the students entering higher education through such programs. In the 1970s, evaluation was concerned with the degree to which programs actually helped students meet academic goals.
   Several articles (Boylan, 1988, 1990; Boylan & White, 1987, 1994) on the history of developmental education have been released through the work of individuals associated with the National Center for Developmental Education (NCDE). These articles show how developmental education services have been provided to students in U.S. education from 1630 to the present. Specific attention is directed toward each academic generation's version of the nontraditional student as they were served by the new categories of postsecondary institutions or institutions with evolving missions. This work argues convincingly that it is the American way to bring new groups of students into higher education, label them in some pejorative manner, and then watch them overcome the stereotypes and their mispreparation to become functional members of the ever-evolving traditional class of college students. Then the cycle then begins once again with a new group of nontraditional students.
   Both Robert's (1986) and Tomlinson's (1989) summaries of the trends in the developmental education movement from the mid-1800s to the modern era parallel many of the other historical sources mentioned in this section. Both authors concur that pro-

grams have grown from being isolated, narrowly conceived, and inadequately funded to being more integrated, broadly conceptualized, and regularly funded campus entities. Tomlinson also provided a most useful historical contribution through the graphic presentation of the changes in the terminology used to identify developmental education style programs as well as the labels for the students receiving such services during three different eras (1860s–1890s, 1900s–1940s, 1950s–1989). Carpenter and Johnson (1991) provided another brief historical summary that closely mirrors the discussions provided by Robert and Tomlinson.

Bullock, Madden, and Mallery (1990) covered the growth of the developmental studies field beginning with the pre-open admissions era (before 1965). They then moved to the equality and access era (1965–1980), and continued through the accountability era (1980–1989). So as to adequately situate the field in the larger milieu, each section is divided into subsections that cover (a) the social milieu for the time, (b) the era's impact on U.S. education, (c) the university setting, and (d) the place of developmental education in the university setting. The authors also provided a chronological outline of the civil rights legislation and judicial decisions that impacted higher education in this century. This outline is particularly useful for the college reading professionals serving in states where affirmative action-oriented special admissions programs are under political attack in the late 1990s.

The last of the historical surveys available for consideration is the work by Casazza and Silverman (1996), which combines events common to the fields of learning assistance and developmental education with events shaping higher education within designated eras. The authors argued that the tension created between traditionalist viewpoints and reformist philosophies have promoted gradual change in education. Given this premise, three eras were identified. The first era (1700–1862) is characterized by the tensions that evolved from the development of a new U.S. system built on democratic ideals, while the educational touchstones for those times were the classical colleges of the old world. A second era (1862–1960) stressed the tensions that evolved as higher education continued to open, or be forced to open its portals to a more diverse clientele. Finally, the third era (1960–2000) looks at the tensions that existed in the movement to provide support services to an increasingly diverse body of students. As Casazza and Silverman review each era, they strive to answer three key questions: What is the purpose of postsecondary education, who should attend college, and what should the curriculum look like? The authors show that the learning assistance and developmental education fields do not operate in a vacuum. Rather, they are intertwined intricately into the culture and events shaping higher education.

The set of articles in this category provide well-written summaries of where the field has been, and in several cases, interesting theories that speculate where the field is going. Given that the outlets used were largely publications, a college reading specialist should have little difficulty in obtaining and then referring to any or all of these historical summaries although interlibrary loan services may need to be utilized for sources that do not have wide distribution. Many of the sources mentioned here can be found in academic libraries both as an originally published text and as a prepress or archive version in the ERIC document collection.

The weakness of the materials in this category is that from article to article, there is a degree of redundancy. Because of this redundancy, there is a blurring of the distinctions among college reading instruction, learning assistance programs, and developmental education. It is true there is much common history among the fields, and it is also true that there are modern interrelationships among the fields. Still, there are differences in breadth of mission and in underlying philosophy. Reaching common ground is important, but so is the systematic identification of differences. Perhaps this redundancy, particularly in the more recent articles, is due to an overreliance on the common use of certain secondary sources (e.g., Brier 1984; Brubacher & Rudy, 1976; Maxwell, 1979) and also in the borrowing of interesting primary sources from one article to another. The bottom line, however, may very well be that the field is saturated with historical surveys and that writers should turn to more focused historical topics such as those found in the next category.

Historical Topics and Eras

As a field reaches a developmental stage where its history is valued and there is an academic commitment to more fully understand specific contributions of individuals and institutions within historical contexts, the studies begin to focus on topics or specific eras. In the case of the topical papers, these articles were often logical historical outgrowths of popular research trends or theoretical postulates from the era in which the piece was authored. In other instances, the papers were part of an ongoing line of historical work by an author or an authoring team. In the case of era-focused articles, the authors tend to present works that define the era(s) when organized into a concerted whole. Comparisons to other eras, historical and present, may be integrated into the work as well. In the paragraphs that follow, we address studies that are of a topical nature and follow with work focused on historical eras.

Topical Studies.   During the latter 1980s and early 1990s the interest in the relationship of reading and writing as modes of learning was evidenced by numerous professional publications (e.g., Bartholomae & Petrosky, 1986; Pugh & Pawan, 1991). Quinn's (1995) article traced the impact of important pedagogical influences, instructional trends, theories, and research on the integration of reading and writing instruction in higher education from the turn of the century to the mid-1990s. In undertaking this project the author drew on historical work in the fields of writing across the curriculum (WAC), reading and writing instruction in Grades K–12, college reading instruction, content field reading instruction, and reading research. Quinn demonstrated that interest in the reading–writing connection arose on several occasions during the 20th century, but it is with the current discussions of reading and writing as powerful tools for promoting thinking and learning that the integration of the two fields could evolve into an important instructional model.

Learning strategies, also known as work methods, work study methods, study methods, study skills, and study strategies during different eras, have been the topic of several historical texts. Stahl (1983) and Stahl and Henk (1986) traced the growth of textbook study systems through the development of Survey Q3R (Survey, Question, Read, Recite, Review [SQ3R]). Specific attention was given to the development of study systems through their relationship to the scientific management theory up to the advent of World War II. In addition, these texts covered the initial research underlying the design of SQ3R and analyzed the research undertaken with the system through the late 1970s. Finally, more than 100 clones of SQ3R, developed between the postwar period and the 1980s, were detailed. It was found that at the time of its introduction in the postwar period, SQ3R was a most effective sobriquet and organizing mechanism for a set of rather well-accepted reading strategies based on era appropriate theory (i.e., scientific management theory better known as *Taylorism*) and reading research.

In another historical text Stahl, King, and Eilers (1996) looked at learning strategies such as the inductive outline procedure, the self-recitation study method, Survey Q3R, the block method, and the Bartusch active method which have been lost to varying degrees from the literature. The authors suggested that a study strategy must be perceived as efficient by the user regardless of the innovative theory or research validation underlying it, be associated with advocates or originators viewed as professional elites by the reading instructors in the field, and be in line with the tenor of the times, past or present, so as to be accepted by students and instructors.

Textbooks and workbooks published for the field of college reading and study strategy instruction also merit historical analysis. Two articles provide an initial focus on this topic. The first article (Stahl, Simpson, & Brozo, 1988) used a historical context to examine content analyses of college reading texts published since 1921. The data from specific-content analyses and the observed trends in the body of professional literature suggested that no consensus existed across texts as to what constituted effective study strategies. Research evidence for most of the techniques advocated was not present. Both scope and validity of the instructional methods and the practice activities were limited. The transfer value of many practice activities was questionable. Overall, the content analyses issued since 1941 suggested that there had been a reliance on impressionable evidence rather than research in designing college reading textbooks.

The task of conducting a historical analysis of instructional materials for college reading instruction has been limited because an authoritative compilation of instructional materials was not available. Early attempts at developing such a resource (Bliesmer, 1957; Narang, 1973) provide an understanding of two historical eras, but both were rather limited in breadth across the years as well as in depth across editions for specific texts. Stahl, Brozo, and Hynd (1990) undertook the compilation of an exhaustive list of texts pertaining to college reading instruction. These authors also detailed their archival activities that were undertaken to develop the list. By employing texts published in the 1920s as an example, the authors explained how the college reading specialist might use the resource list in conducting research or in designing curriculum. On completion of the task, the list contained 593 bibliographic entries for books printed between 1896 and 1987. Each entry also contained the dates for each of the identified editions of the respective text. The full bibliographic list is available in the technical report that accompanied the article (Stahl, Brozo, & Hynd, 1989).

Walvekar (1987) approached trends impacting college reading and learning assistance in relation to evolving practices in program evaluation throughout the 30 years that preceded the release of the article. For instance, Walvekar shows how three forms of program evaluation, humanistic evaluation, systematic evaluation, and research were responses to larger issues associated with the open door policy at community colleges, the expanded diversity in students at 4-year institutions, and the call for greater retention of students at all institutions in the 1970s. Overall, she felt that evaluation was undeveloped in the 1960s, inadequate through the early 1980s, and still evolving as of 1987.

Mason (1994) provided a comparative study in a historical context of seven college reading programs, founded in most cases in the 1920s or 1930s at elite institutions—Harvard University, Hamline University, Amherst College, the University of Chicago, Syracuse University, the University of Pennsylvania, and the University of Iowa. In comparing and contrasting instructional programs, institutional mandates, academic homes, assessment procedures, and staff qualifications across the institutions, the author reports as much variation existed as did commonality in programs.

Era Studies.   There are several era-focused studies that can be found in the literature. These works cover the post-World War II college reading scene. One valuable era-focused work is Kingston's (1990) discussion of the programs of the late 1940s through the 1960s. This narrative rests in part on the insights, experiences, and knowledge of an important leader in the field during the time frame in question. Kingston covered changes and innovations in assessment, elements of the curriculum, and instructional programs. Finally, Kingston briefly covered the birth of professional organizations (the Southwest Reading Conference—SRC, the CRA) and journals (*Journal of Developmental Reading, Journal of the Reading Specialist*) that were to serve the field during the period and the years after.

Another study that overlaps the periods covered in the previous article by Kingston is the work by Mallery (1986), which compared two periods of college reading and study skills programs: the 1950s through the mid-1960s; and the period from 1965 to 1980. The period before 1965 was characterized by program orientation and organization being dependent on home department and instructional methods. The demarcation point between the two eras was the point when the *new students* began to make their presence felt in the college reading and study skills programs with the advent of the War on Poverty. The influx of federal dollars into higher education led to underrepresented student populations gaining admission to postsecondary institutions in numbers not seen before. Issues about the open door becoming a revolving door gained in importance in the 1970s. During this time, questions also arose as to the training that was desirable for college reading specialists. Instructional philosophies differed from college to college, and instructional activities included diagnosis, individualization, content area reading, and study skills instruction. The previously discussed work by Bullock, Madden, and Mallery (1990) is an outgrowth of this article.

Within the category of era studies, it is practical to include two studies that discuss respectively the contributions of the NRC and the CRLA as organizations that each in its own historical time provided fundamental leadership for the field. Van Gilder's (1970) dissertation traced the evolvement of the NRC from its first meeting as the SRC for Colleges and Universities in April 1952 to April 1970. Through his use of historical research and content analysis of the organization's conference yearbooks and journal articles, Van Gilder was able to conclude that NRC's origins and maturity reflected the growth and development of college reading in the nation. The content of the yearbooks during the organization's first 5 years focused on administrative procedures, student selection processes, and mechanical equipment for college reading programs. During the next 4 years, the papers grew in sophistication, as the presenters began to focus on research, evaluation, and the interaction of college reading with other academic fields. Speed of reading became less a topic of importance as greater interest was directed at comprehension and reading flexibility. During the 1960s, the membership was beginning to face a crisis that was both developmental and generational between those who were interested in the pedagogy of college reading and those who were more concerned with the research on the psychology of reading and learning. The outcome, with hindsight, was rather predictable. In the past few years, the NRC has become the world's premier forum for reading research. Although topics on college reading and learning assistance can still be found on the yearly program, the proportion of presentations on these topics does not approach the number found during the organization's formative years when a dedicated group of college reading professionals met to discuss the practical problems associated with the postsecondary reading programs of the early and mid 1950s.

Although unknown to the field at the very time Van Gilder was writing his dissertation in 1970, the onus of leadership in college reading was being assumed by another group still in its formative years—the CRLA. O'Hear (1993), writing in the 25th anniversary edition of the *Journal of College Reading and Learning*, examined what has been learned about the field through the articles published in the journal and in the earlier conference yearbooks of the CRLA (known first as the Western College Reading Association [WCRA] and then as the Western College Reading and Learning Association [WCRLA]). O'Hear proposed that following the enrollment of the *new students* in the late 1960s, the field evolved from its blind reliance on a deficit model that was driven by standardized tests and borrowed secondary school instructional techniques and materials. It evolved to a model where students' needs were better understood and more likely to be approached by instruction based on current learning theory and reading research. This article, along with works by Kerstiens (1993) and Mullen and Orlando (1993) in the same anniversary edition, provide an important historical perspective of CRLA's many contributions that often go unnoticed because of the group's earlier regional membership focus.

The yearbooks of the SRC and NRC, the North Central Reading Association (NCRA), and the CRA provided the foundational resources for the field in the 1950s, 1960s and parts of the 1970s. The yearbooks and journal volumes for the CRLA and the National Association for Developmental Education (NADE) provide the measure of the field as we begin the 21st century.

The Field in History.   A logical question naturally comes forward at this point in the discussion of the topic. What does the body of historical scholarship say about the field? The answer as one might expect is multifaceted. First and foremost, there is a documented history, particularly at the the survey level, of the field of college developmental reading and its kindred fields of learning assistance and developmental education. There is little excuse today for the college reading instructor not to have a sense of the field's history through the reading of the many readily available texts. Furthermore, we should expect that the more seasoned professionals, particularly those students in doctoral programs as well as those individuals in master's degree programs that focus specifically on developmental education, will have read widely and critically a number of the varied historical chronicles, historical summaries and timelines, topical studies, and era studies that comprise the historical literature for the field.

Second, it is evident that the number of historically oriented texts is growing both in number and in sophistication. In 1986, Stahl, Hynd, and Henk were able to identify nine texts that covered historical topics about the field of developmental reading and learning assistance. This chapter includes more than 55 resources with the same historical mission (admittedly several are pre-1986 texts). The interest in history is due in part to the field coming of age with a committed cadre of scholars who have not abandoned college reading for what had often been considered the greener pastures in teacher education, elementary reading education, or content field reading. Also with an established as well as graying professoriate in college reading and learning assistance, there has been a growing desire to know one's place and roots in a profession and perhaps as well to define one's role or legacy in the history of the field.

The sophistication in the research has grown. There are now a number of studies that attempt to be more than simple chronological surveys of past events. Although the work available currently might not always stand the test of a trained historian, it is becoming more focused on specific topics and defined eras. Still there are numerous opportunities for members of the profession to become involved in preserving the historical legacy of the field. We now turn to the role each of us play in the history of the field.

DOING HISTORY

Although we all make history and are part of history on a day-to-day basis, most individuals take a naive view of history as representing only the greater scope of events at the national or the international levels. Hence, the history of our profession is generally viewed as nothing short of the broad historical chronicles as authored by Smith (1965, 1986) or Shannon (1989) that pay scant attention to the field of college developmental reading and learning assistance. History is also erroneously thought of as the story of men of wealth and taste. The thought of being a historian and undertaking historiography at a personal or a local level can seem to be a most daunting task. Still, we believe that each college reading specialist can be and certainly should be a historian of what Kyvig and Marty (1982) called *nearby history.*

Nearby History

What then is *nearby history* and what is its value to our profession? As an outgrowth of the turbulence and social upheavals of the 1960s, there came to be an academic and practical value for the detailed study of specific institutions and communities through the advent of social history. We hold that the college reading program and the learning assistance center are intricate parts of a larger institution, and that the professionals delivering services along with the students receiving those services are part of a defined community in a postsecondary institution, and thus worthy of concerned and careful study.

In asking questions about the conditions that lead to the origins of the program, the purposes of the program at various stages in its life, the dynamics of the relationships with other academic units, the milestones across the years, the unique program

features, and the traditions incorporated into the design of the unit, the distinctive nature of the reading program comes to be known, pride of community is promoted, and
we gain information on the history of that program. Furthermore, we then have a more
solid foundation on which to build a future or to handle current pedagogical issues and
institutional situations currently facing the program. There is reason that the methods
of the historian should be utilized to preserve the accomplishments and the heritage of
specific college reading programs and learning assistance centers in postsecondary institutions across the land. Two good examples of historical narratives of specific programs are Christ's (1984) account of the development of the Learning Assistance
Center at California State University–Long Beach and Spann's (1996) historical perspective of the National Center for Developmental Education at Appalachian State
University.

Although it is not the purpose of this chapter to cover the methods and techniques of historiography, we would be remiss if we did not note there exists a range of
documents at the disposal of the college reading program and academic learning center that open the doors to the study of an academic unit's history. These documents include published texts of wide circulation (e.g., scholarly books, institutional histories,
journal and yearbook articles, course texts and workbooks, dissertations, published
tests, government reports), documents of local distribution (e.g., campus newspapers,
college catalogs, campus brochures, recruitment posters, training manuals), unpublished documents (e.g., yearly reports, accreditation documents, formative and
summative evaluation reports, faculty service reports), and media products (e.g., pho-
tographs, videos, movies, software) from the program's files or the institutional archives. Artifacts such as tachistoscopes, controlled readers, reading films, reading
accelerators, and so on may seem like obsolete junk forgotten in storage closets, yet
these artifacts have as much historical value in learning of a program's history as old
texts or archives of students' work from past generations.

The history of a college reading program as an entity, along with the history of the
academic community that comprises that program, can be preserved through the collection of autobiographies and life history or oral history narratives of current and former
faculty, administrators, as well as current and former students. Autobiography can begin
simply enough through the process of keeping a reflective journal. Then, as recollections
from across the life span are cued by critical incidents impacting one's current personal
or professional life, new narratives can be written down and folded into the accounts in
the autobiographical portfolio.

Autobiography need not be an exercise in solitude. For instance, through the use of
a professional writing circle, colleagues in a learning center might assist each other in the
development of the autobiography and begin, in due time, to analyze the various stories
to determine whether there are kindred events or themes that emerge across the circle.
The language from the accounts themselves as well as the language of the discussions of
those accounts have much to say about the conduct and culture of the program in which
the participants have served the institution. The autobiographic account can have impact in understanding the self as a professional. It can have impact on the workings of an
entire program.

The autobiographic account can also have a tremendous impact on the field of developmental education. *Lives of the Boundary* by Rose (1989) is a good example of autobi-

ography as we see him overcome the effects of being branded a *remedial* learner as a youngster in South Los Angeles, and later become a leading advocate of quality education for all students. It is through his exploration of the self that we as readers are able to participate vicariously as to understand and become sympathetic for the argument Rose put forward.

First, life history and oral history can play an equally important role in preserving the history of a college reading or learning assistance program. Projects can be undertaken from several different vantages. With the more established programs, current faculty might undertake oral history interviews with retired faculty or staff members who served with the program or were served by the program during the years they were employed at the institution. Second, life history interviews with former students might provide interesting narratives that suggest the ways in which the program played a part in their development as college students and mature readers. Finally, life history narratives of current faculty or staff members provide an interesting picture of the personal histories that underlie the current pedagogical philosophy of the program.

The history of a program can be disseminated in a number of ways. The audience for the dissemination activity may be internal to the institution or it may be an external body of reading professionals, legislators, or community members. Traditional written forms of dissemination include both scholarly and trade books, historical articles in both state and national level journals or yearbooks, and chapters in an institutional history. The historical study of a program (e.g., Walker, 1980) or an oral history project focusing on individuals associated with a program or professional organization (Stahl, King, Dillon, & Walker, 1994) can be a most appropriate but often overlooked thesis or dissertation topic. Program histories can also find avenues for dissemination through conference presentations. Other forms of media can be used to highlight the program's history including videotapes, slide or tape shows, cassette lectures, Internet homepage presentations, artifact or document displays, and so on. Useful references for undertaking and disseminating program histories include Caunce (1994), Kyvig and Marty (1982), and Thompson (1988).

Historical Research for the Profession.   We now shift the discussion to

historical topics that have more nationally oriented foci. In 1986 Stahl, Hynd, and Henk suggested that there were 10 avenues that might provide fruitful options for undertaking historical research of the college reading profession. These topics, detailed in Table 1.1 with some modifications, continue to serve as important options for the field's historical endeavors for several reasons. First, given the depth of each topic, there are many valid and valuable opportunities for research by either the neophyte or more experienced literacy historian. Second, given the breadth of the field, there is still a need to undertake historical research in each of the areas. Third, the avenues have been laid out in such a manner that by undertaking any of the suggestions, history becomes immediately relevant for the researcher and equally relevant for the individual who later reads the articles or attends a conference session that is the product of the historian's endeavors.

Given the premise that the suggestions put forth by Stahl, Hynd, and Henk (1986) for the study of the history of college reading are valid for the field as it enters the new millennium, these 10 avenues for historical study are presented with some modifications in Table 1.1. Each of the topics is followed by a respective focus question. In the third column, there are references presented for the historical research published on the topic, historical studies providing guidance for future research, or research covering resources for historical work with the topic.

An example of how one of the avenues may be followed is useful at this juncture. A number of currently available study strategy texts have gone through multiple editions over the years. It would be valuable to conduct a historical case study combining content analysis methodology as in the manner used by Stahl and Fisher (1992) to determine how texts such as *How to Study in College, Developing Textbook Thinking,* or *Bridging the Gap: College Reading* have evolved across editions. Such a case study would tell the field much about how research, theory, and pedagogical trends for an era were integrated into the instructional materials used by students. For instance, how did the process and product research of the 1980s influence such texts? How did research and theory on student intent find its way into the texts as it was added to the study strategy mix? Each of the suggested avenues provide rich opportunities for research.

The historical works of the college reading profession can be disseminated through a range of activities. Conferences sponsored by CRLA, CRA, NRC, and ARF have included the presentation of historical papers or workshops on conducting historical work. The latter three have yearbooks where refereed articles based on the respective presentations can be published. All of the journals in the field of reading research and pedagogy or developmental education have published historical works, including works pertaining to college reading. The *Journal of Developmental Education* publishes interviews on a regular basis, and recently, the excellent interview with Walter Pauk (Kerstiens, 1998) had an oral history flavor to it. Still, it must be noted that historically focused manuscripts are not submitted for review to journal editors on a regular basis, and because of this fact such work cannot be published with regular frequency. Finally, the History of Reading Special Interest Group of the IRA has supported individuals concerned with the history of the college reading field through its sessions at the annual IRA Convention and its promotion of the historical agenda for all areas of literacy.

Final Thoughts. The value of studying literacy history is great (Moore, Monaghan, & Hartman, 1997). The options for historical research are many, yet the desire to undertake such work is most singular. Each of us must be a historian and each of us must also be a student of history. Although the conduct of historical work in the field of college reading instruction is alive and growing—although slowly, it is as marginalized within the field of college reading as the field of college reading is marginalized in the overall field of reading research and instruction. In an era where the future of many a program is at best tenuous, it is important for the professionals in the field to understand that we have been making history for at least 100 years; we should be learning and interpreting our history through classes, journal articles, and conference presentations; and we should be doing history at both the nearby and national levels on a regular basis. Simply put, we should remain cognizant that our understanding of our past defines our future.

TABLE 1.1
Doing the History of College Reading

Avenues for Research	Questions for Research	Research Examples
Judging the impact of historical events	How have pedagogical, sociological, and economic events and trends at the national and international levels impacted the field?	Bullock, Madden, & Mallery (1990)
Focusing on an era	What was the impact of influential research, theories, individuals, institutions, instructional texts for a defined era?	Brier (1983); Christ (1984); Kingston (1990); Mallery (1986); Van Gilder (1970)
Assessing the impact of influential individuals	What were the critical contributions and influences of key leaders over the years (e.g., Francis Robinson, Alton Raygor, Frances Triggs)?	Flippo, Cranney, Wark, & Raygor (1990); Heron (1989); Stahl (1983); Stahl & Henk (1986)
Consulting the experienced	What can we learn about the history of the field through oral histories and autobiographies of leaders (e.g., Walter Pauk, Martha Maxwell, Frank Christ)?	Kerstiens (1998); Rose (1989); Stahl, King, Dillon, & Walker (1994)
Noting trends in programs	What can we learn about reading programs by collecting, chronicling, and summarizing descriptions and surveys from across the years?	Enright (1975); Leedy (1958); Lowe (1967b)
Tracing changes in materials	How have published instructional materials changed or evolved across the years due to theory, research, or pedagogical trends?	Leedy (1958); Stahl, Simpson, & Brozo (1988)
Observing changes across textbook editions	What can a historical case study of a particular text across multiple editions inform us about the field (e.g. *How to Study in College* by Walter Pauk)?	Stahl, Brozo, & Hynd (1989, 1990)
Judging innovation	How do innovations in instruction or curriculum measure versus the record of precursors? How do innovations stand the test of time?	Stahl, King, & Eilers (1996)

TABLE 1.1 (continued)

Avenues for Research	Questions for Research	Research Examples
Appraising elements of instrumentation	How have formal and informal measures of assessment changed or influenced practice over the years?	Flippo, Hanes, & Cashen (1991); Kerstiens (1993)
Creating archives and preserving a legacy	What is the best way of preserving texts, tests, hardware, and software of instruction from previous generations for future generations?	

REFERENCES AND SUGGESTED READINGS

Bailey, J. L. (1982). *An evaluation of journal published research of college reading study skills, 1925–1980.* Unpublished doctoral dissertation, University of Tennessee, Knoxville. (University Microfilms #8215369)

Bartholomae, D., & Petrosky, A. (1986). *Facts, artifacts, and counterfacts.* Upper Montclair, NJ: Boynton Cook.

Blake, W. S. (1953). *A survey and evaluation of study skills programs at the college level in the United States and possessions.* Unpublished doctoral dissertation, University of Maryland, College Park.

Bliesmer, E. P. (1957). Materials for the more retarded college reader. In O. S. Causey (Ed.), *Techniques and procedures in college and adult reading programs: 6th yearbook of the Southwest Reading Conference.* Fort Worth: Texas Christian University Press.

Boylan, H. R. (1988). The historical roots of developmental education. *Research in Developmental Education, 5*(3), 1–4.

Boylan, H. R. (1990). The cycle of new majorities in higher education. In A. M. Frager (Ed.), *College reading and the new majority: Improving instruction in multicultural classrooms* (pp. 3–12). Oxford, OH: College Reading Association.

Boylan, H. R., & White, W. G. (1987). Educating all the nation's people: The historical roots of developmental education. *Research in Developmental Education, 4*(4), 1–4.

Boylan, H. R., & White, W. G. (1994). Educating all the nation's people: The historical roots of developmental education—condensed version. In M. Maxwell (Ed.), *From access to success* (pp. 3–7). Clearwater, FL: H & H Publishing.

*Brier, E. (1984). Bridging the academic preparation gap: An historical view. *Journal of Developmental Education, 8*(1), 2–5.

Brier, E. M. (1983). *Bridging the academic preparation gap at Vassar College and Cornell University, 1865–1890.* Unpublished doctoral dissertation, Columbia University Teachers College, New York. (University Microfilms #8322180)

Brubacher, J. S., & Rudy, W. (1976). *Higher education in transition: A history of American colleges and universities*. New York: Harper and Row.

Bullock, T. L., Madden, D. A., & Mallery, A. L. (1990). Developmental education in American universities: Past, present, and future. *Research & Teaching in Developmental Education, 6*(2), 5–74.

Carpenter, K., & Johnson, L. L. (1991). Program organization. In R. F. Flippo & D. C. Caverly (Eds.), *College reading & study strategy programs* (pp. 28–69). Newark, DE: International Reading Association.

*Casazza, M. E., & Silverman, S. L. (1996). *Learning assistance and developmental education: A guide for effective practice*. San Francisco, CA: Jossey-Bass.

Caunce, S. (1994). *Oral history and the local historian*. London: Longman.

Chall, J. S. (1983). *Stages of reading development*. New York: McGraw-Hill.

Christ, F. L. (1984). Learning assistance at California State University-Long Beach, 1972–1984. *Journal of Developmental Education, 8*(2), 2–5.

Cranney, A. G. (1983a). Two decades of adult reading programs: Growth, problems, and prospects. *Journal of Reading, 26*(5), 416–423.

Cranney, A. G. (1983b). Two decades of college-adult reading: Where to find the best of it. *Journal of College Reading and Learning, 16*(1), 1–5.

*Cross, K. P. (1976). *Accent on learning*. San Francisco: Jossey-Bass.

*Enright, G. (1975). College learning skills: Frontierland origins of the learning assistance center. In R. Sugimoto (Ed.) *College learning skills: Today and tomorrowland. Proceedings of the eighth annual conference of the Western College Reading Association*. Las Cruces, NM: Western College Reading Association. (ERIC Document Reproduction Service No. ED 105–204)

Enright, G., & Kerstiens, G. (1980). The learning center: Toward an expanded role. In O. T. Lenning & R. L. Nayman (Eds.), *New directions for college learning assistance: New roles for learning assistance* (pp. 1–24). San Francisco: Jossey-Bass.

Flippo, R. F., Cranney, A. G., Wark, D., & Raygor, B. R. (1990). From the editor and invited guests—In dedication to Al Raygor: 1922–1989. *Forum for Reading, 21*(2), 4–10.

Flippo, R. F., Hanes, M. L., & Cashen, C. J. (1991). In R. F. Flippo & D. C. Caverly (Eds.), *College reading & study strategy programs* (pp. 118–173). Newark, DE: International Reading Association.

Heron, E. B. (1989). *The dilemma of college reading instruction: A developmental analysis*. Unpublished doctoral dissertation, Harvard University, Cambridge, MA. (University Microfilms #9014298)

Kerstiens, G. (1993). A quarter-century of student assessment in CRLA publications. *Journal of College Reading and Learning, 25*(2), 1–9.

*Kerstiens, G. (1998). Studying in college, then & now: An interview with Walter Pauk. *Journal of Developmental Education, 21*(3), 20–24.

Kingston, A. J. (1990). A brief history of college reading. *Forum for Reading, 21*(2), 11–15.

Kyvig, D. E., & Marty, M. A. (1982). *Nearby history*. Nashville, TN: American Association for State and Local History.

*Leedy, P. D. (1958). *A history of the origin and development of instruction in reading improvement at the college level*. Unpublished doctoral dissertation, New York University, New York. (University Microfilms #59–01016)

Lissner, L. S. (1990). The learning center from 1829 to the year 2000 and beyond. In R. M. Hashway (Ed.), *Handbook of developmental education* (pp. 127–154). New York: Praeger.

Lowe, A. J. (1967a). *An evaluation of a college reading improvement program.* Unpublished doctoral dissertation, University of Virginia, Charlottesville. (University Microfilms #68–03139)

Lowe, A. J. (1967b). Surveys of college reading improvement programs: 1929–1966. In G. B. Schick & M. May (Eds.), *Junior college and adult reading—expanding fields, 16th yearbook of the National Reading Conference* (pp. 75–81). Milwaukee, WI: National Reading Conference. (ERIC Document Reproduction Service No. ED 011–230)

*Lowe, A. J. (1970). *The rise of college reading, the good and bad and the indifferent: 1915–1970.* Paper presented at the College Reading Association Conference, Philadelphia. (ERIC Document Reproduction Service No. ED 040–013)

Mallery, A. L. (1986). College reading programs 1958–1978. In D. Lumpkin, M. Harshberger, & P. Ransom (Eds.), *Evaluation in reading: Learning teaching administering, Sixth Yearbook of the American Reading Forum* (pp. 113–125). Muncie, IN: Ball State University. (ERIC Document Reproduction Service No. ED 290–136)

Manzo, A. V. (1983). College reading: Past and presenting. *Forum for Reading, 14,* 5–16.

Mason, R. B. (1994). *Selected college reading improvement programs: A descriptive history.* New York: Author. (ERIC Document Reproduction Service No. ED 366–907)

Maxwell, M. (1979). *Improving student learning skills.* San Francisco, CA: Jossey-Bass.

*Maxwell, M. (1997). *Improving student learning skills: A new edition.* Clearwater, FL: H&H Publishers.

Moore, D. W., Monaghan, E. J., & Hartman, D. K. (1997). Conversations: Values of literacy history. *Reading Research Quarterly, 32*(1), 90–102.

Mullen, J. L. & Orlando, V. P. (1993). Reflections on 25 years of the *Journal of College Reading and Learning. Journal of College Reading and Learning, 25*(2), 25–30.

Narang, H. L. (1973). Materials for college and adult reading improvement programs. *Reading World, 12*(3), 181–187.

O'Hear, M. (1993). College reading programs: The last 25 years. *Journal of College Reading and Learning, 25*(2), 17–24.

Parr, F. W. (1930). The extent of remedial reading work in state universities in the United States. *School and Society, 31,* 547–548.

Pugh, S. L., & Pawan, F. (1991). Reading, writing, and academic literacy. In R. F. Flippo & D. C. Caverly (Eds.), *College reading & study strategy programs* (pp. 1–27). Newark, DE: International Reading Association.

*Quinn, K. B. (1995). Teaching reading and writing as modes of learning in college: A glance at the past; A view to the future. *Reading Research and Instruction, 34*(4), 295–314.

Roberts, G. H. (1986). *Developmental education: An historical study.* (ERIC Document Reproduction Service No. 276–395.)

Rose, M. (1989). *Lives on the boundary.* New York: Penguin.

Sanders, V. A. (1979). *A meta-analysis: The relationship of program content and operation factors to measured effectiveness of college reading-study.* Unpublished doctoral dissertation, University of the Pacific, Stockton. (University Microfilms #7923975)

Shannon, P. (1989). *Broken promises: Reading instruction in the twentieth-century America.* Granby, MA: Bergin & Garvey.

Smith, N. B. (1934a). *A historical analysis of American reading instruction.* Unpublished doctoral dissertation, Teachers College, Columbia University. New York.

Smith, N. B. (1934b). *American reading instruction.* New York: Silver, Burdett.

Smith, N. B. (1965). *American reading instruction.* (rev. ed.). Newark, DE: International Reading Association.

Smith, N. B. (1986). *American reading instruction.* Prologue by L. Courtney, FSC, and epilogue by H. A. Robinson. Newark, DE: International Reading Association.

Spache, G. D. (1969). College—adult reading: Past, present, and future. In G. B. Schick & M. May (Eds.), *The psychology of reading behavior, 18th Yearbook of the National Reading Conference* (pp. 188–194). Milwaukee, WI: National Reading Conference.

Spann, M. G. (1996). National Center of Developmental Education: The formative years. *Journal of Developmental Education, 20*(2), 2–6.

Stahl, N. A. (1983). *A historical analysis of textbook-study systems.* Unpublished doctoral dissertation, University of Pittsburgh. (University Microfilms #8411839)

Stahl, N. A. (1988, January–March). Historical titles in reading research and instruction: A history of the origin and development of instruction in reading improvement at the college level. *Reading Psychology, 9,* 73–77.

Stahl, N. A., & Fisher, P. J. L. (1992). RT remembered: The first 20 years. *Reading Teacher, 45*(5), 370–377.

Stahl, N. A., & Henk, W. A. (1986). Tracing the roots of textbook-study systems: An extended historical perspective. In J. A. Niles (Ed.), *Solving problems in literacy: Learner, teachers and researchers—35th yearbook of the National Reading Conference* (pp. 366–374). Rochester, NY: National Reading Conference.

Stahl, N. A., Brozo, W. G., & Hynd, C. R. (1989). *The development and validation of a comprehensive list of primary sources in college reading instruction with full bibliography.* (College Reading and Learning Assistance Tech. Rep. No. 88–03.) DeKalb: Northern Illinois University. (ERIC Document Reproduction Service No. ED 307–597)

Stahl, N. A., Brozo, W. G., & Hynd, C. R. (1990, October). The development and validation of a comprehensive list of primary sources in college reading instruction. *Reading Horizons, 31*(1), 22–34.

*Stahl, N. A., Hynd, C. R., & Henk, W. A. (1986). Avenues for chronicling and researching the history of college reading and study skills instruction. *Journal of Reading, 29*(4), 334–341.

Stahl, N. A., King, J. R., & Eilers, V. (1996). Postsecondary reading strategies: Rediscovered. *Journal of Adolescent and Adult Literacy, 39*(5), 368–379.

Stahl, N. A., King, J. R., Dillon, D., & Walker, J. (1994). The roots of reading: Preserving the heritage of a profession through oral history projects. In E. G. Sturtevant & W. Linek (Eds.), *Pathways for literacy: 16th yearbook of the College Reading Association* (pp. 15–24). Commerce, TX: College Reading Association.

*Stahl, N. A., Simpson, M. L., & Brozo, W. G. (1998, Spring). The materials of college reading instruction: A critical and historical perspective from 50 years of content analysis research. *Reading Research and Instruction, 27*(3), 16–34.

Straff, W. W. (1985). *Comparisons, contrasts, and evaluation of selected college reading programs*. Unpublished doctoral dissertation, Temple University, Philadelphia. (University Microfilms #8611937)

Thompson, P. (1988). *The voice of the past—Oral history*. New York: Oxford University Press.

Thurstone, E. L., Lowe, A. J., & Hayden, L. (1965). A survey of college reading programs in Louisiana and Mississippi. In E. L. Thurston & L. E. Hafner (Eds.), *The philosophical and sociological bases of reading—14th Yearbook of the National Reading Conference* (pp. 110–114). Milwaukee, WI: National Reading Conference.

Tomlinson, L. M. (1989). *Postsecondary developmental programs: A traditional agenda with new imperatives* (ASHE-ERIC Higher Education Report 3). Washington, DC: Clearinghouse on Higher Education.

Van Gilder, L. L. (1970). *A study of the changes within the National Reading Conference*. Uunpublished doctoral dissertation, Marquette University, Milwaukee, WI. (University Microfilms #71–20742)

Walker, J. (1980). *The reading and study skills program at Northern Illinois University, 1963–1976*. Unpublished doctoral dissertation, Northern Illinois University, DeKalb.

Walvekar, C. C. (1987). Thirty years of program evaluation: Past, present, and future. *Journal of College Reading and Learning, 20*(1), 155–161.

*Wyatt, M. (1992). The past, present, and future need for college reading courses in the U.S. *Journal of Reading, 36*(1), 10–20.

2

Academic Literacy
and the New College Learner

࿔ᔇᔇ࿔

Sharon L. Pugh
Faridah Pawan
Carmen Antommarchi
Indiana University

I t is a truism to say that the 21st century is bringing more to read, more ways to read it, and more reasons to be an effective reader than ever before. Two trends in particular affect postsecondary learners: (a) the accelerated evolution of knowledge in all fields, which implies the necessity of extensive reading to keep up; and (b) growing awareness of the importance of multiple perspectives and dialogical reasoning (Paul, 1987), which necessitates the reading of multiple texts on a given issue. In addition, the changing nature of work and the likelihood of several career changes in a working life emphasize the importance of facility in acquiring and synthesizing new information and concepts. Compounding all of these realities is the technology revolution, which has made the proliferation of information, most of it in written form, an issue for everyone.

In short, reading is the platform from which critical thinking, problem solving, and effective expression are launched. Reading, moreover, cannot be narrowly defined simply as the ability to decode and comprehend written language. Rather, *literacy* involves the ability to understand and make use of information provided in a variety of forms and entailing a variety of sign systems. In a culture that may be described as hyperliterate, individuals with poor literacy skills face formidable barriers to success, beginning with their postsecondary education.

This chapter explores a number of strands that seem essential in understanding the nature and demands of academic literacy in postsecondary institutions today and in the future. First, we discuss the nature of academic literacy. Second, we look at key reading and literacy theories that show a basic paradigm shift from conceptualizing reading as an interactional to a transactional process. Third, we consider student development theories that have strongly influenced thinking about postsecondary learning. Following these theoretical discussions, we examine the nature of texts, both print and electronic, in college courses today, and project the future trends that will figure significantly in the lives of postsecondary learners. Finally, we meaningfully draw these strands together and discuss implications for providers of postsecondary academic support.

NATURE OF ACADEMIC LITERACY

Although this discussion focuses largely on texts, we do not confine literacy to a narrow definition of reading written language. Rather, we subscribe to a complex concept of literacy requiring definition from at least four angles: (a) the relationship of literacy to its traditional components, reading and writing, and the print cultures that have dominated Western thought for the past few centuries; (b) the mindset that has grown out of these cultures, particularly the rational, analytical thinking that is characteristic of academic thought and inquiry; (c) electronically mediated literacy, which requires not only the ability to read and write but also skill in searching and evaluating information in large databases and the proliferation of information-rich sources placed at one's fingertips by the Internet; and (d) the multiple ways of encoding and expressing information that converge in most media today and have encouraged consideration of different kinds of intelligence. Within this framework, we distinguish *academic literacy* as it pertains specifically to the kinds of knowing characteristic of educational settings. Williams and Snipper (1990) defined academic literacy as

> the ability to process and interact with a body of artifacts and ideas preserved within the specific domains of educational institutions. It is a set of behaviors peculiar to the formally educated. Academic literacy reflects the notion that literate people are those who read literature, philosophy, history, and contemporary essays, the very sort of texts college students face during their first two years of undergraduate work. It reflects the notion that they can also write about these texts in some fashion. And it reflects the belief that they can comprehend such texts within the larger context of Western cultural traditions. (p. 8)

This definition is noteworthy because of its emphasis on texts and genres of knowledge traditional in education. Although we are witnessing fundamental changes in how higher education is perceived and delivered, as noted, for example, in the rapid growth of so-called "virtual universities," institutions that operate without traditional campuses and feature a much greater emphasis on practical and applied knowledge (Traub, 1997), this definition of academic literacy still has great currency. In the discussion that follows, we deal with literacy in more general terms, but we do not lose touch with the stricter notion of academic literacy as the ability to operate within the texts and genres of Western traditions, and to engage in certain reading and writing processes reflective of these texts and genres.

Even when construed as relating to uses of written language, literacy is a complex phenomenon. Eisenstein (1979) pointed out that Western society lives, breathes, and thrives on printed matter. As print technologies have advanced, the availability of printed material has progressed from abundant to overwhelming. In the early 1980s, when the World Wide Web (WWW) as we know it had not been formalized, Kozol (1985) was already arguing for a literacy that enables us to bring order and meaning not only to this superabundance of print but also to life amid the information explosion. As we discuss further under reading and student development theories, literacy involves the ability to navigate purposely and critically through a network of information connections that become denser by the day.

The Literate Mindset

What holds constant over changing technologies is the Western academic definition of *literate individuals* as those who are able to synthesize, organize, and interpret ideas as well as apply information gained from reading to new situations (Clifford, 1984). Such high-level literacy abilities are the means by which individuals become *informed readers* (Fish, 1980), or those guided by awareness of their own prior knowledge and its contribution to the new meanings they construct from texts. Such readers attend not only to what texts say but to what they say to texts. In a similar vein, Freire and Macedo's (1987) concept of literacy includes the claim that "the very act of learning to read and write has to start from a very comprehensive act of reading the world, something which humans do before reading the words" (p. xiii). "Reading the world" includes taking a conscious approach toward learning and the acquisition of knowledge. Readers of the world (and therefore of themselves) focus on knowledge relevant to their future needs as well as those of the present. This "power of envisagement," as Freire termed it, results in hypothetical thinking and experimentation to test the truth and usefulness of theoretically conceived ideas.

We have come a long way since the debate surrounding "cultural literacy," fueled by Hirsch's (1987) controversial book, which to many readers reduced literacy to its lowest denominator, a list of allusions and metaphors that signify exposure to a few key texts and items of knowledge. As useful as such knowledge might be in games and on admissions exams, we generally agree that our minds are more like active agents than storage containers. Knowing who Ophelia was may satisfy the test of cultural literacy in the narrow sense. But to understand why Pipher (1994) used the title *Reviving Ophelia* for her book about the perils of being a female adolescent in the United States today requires the ability to process the allusion metaphorically, encode a whole theoretical stance into an image that symbolizes the experience of a major segment of the population, infer the argument implicit in the concept of "reviving" the person who was decidedly past revival in Shakespeare's play, and, finally, critically evaluate the theory and the argument in relation to other knowledge and experience. Quite an order for two words! But this example illustrates the complexity and sophistication of the literacy that has evolved over centuries of cumulative, interrelated text production.

READING AND LITERACY THEORY

One of the reasons for the controversy surrounding the publication of Hirsch's *Cultural Literacy* was its timing, coming out just when reading and literacy theories were abandoning the premises in that Hirsch's argument was based on the theory that comprehension is an interaction between what is in the reader's mind and the object of comprehension. This change is clearly illustrated in the disenchantment with Rumelhart's (1985) interactional theory of reading in favor of Rosenblatt's (1978, 1993, 1994) transactional theory. Rumelhart's theory of reading assumes that knowledge exists outside the reader and the text. Input from the two interact to create meaning (Grabe, 1991). Input from print, however, is emphasized, so that the goal of successful reading is as close an alignment as possible with the text author's intended message.

Rosenblatt's transactional theory differs from Rumelhart's theory in that it situates knowledge creation within the reader's mind, putting greater emphasis on the reader's input while rejecting the idea that knowledge must be justified in terms of external standards (Shelton, 1994). The symbols on the page "evoke" meaning contextualized by the reader's social and cultural contexts (Cunningham & Fitzgerald, 1996). Rosenblatt's (1994) continuum of efferent reading (for information)—aesthetic reading (as an experience)—calls for the reader to pay attention to elements within him or herself that could range from the logical to the affective (Peregoy & Boyle, 1992). The walls separating reader and text are dismantled as the "inside" world of the reader and the "outside" world of the text are unified in the process of knowledge construction.

STUDENT DEVELOPMENT THEORY

Another way of looking at college literacy is through the lenses provided by the various models of epistemological development that have appeared over the past 40 years. These models represent different perspectives on postsecondary learning because of the particular characteristics of the populations, institutions, and times on which their research is based. Taken together, however, they describe a general sequence of development that seems plausible to most educators. Perhaps more to the point, these models can be read as stories that the college tells about itself and reveal the values, ideals, and expectations of a postsecondary learning community. They also share the assumption that intellectual development represents an increasing convergence of the knower and the known.

Perry (1970); Belenky, Clinchy, Goldberger, and Tarule (1986); King and Kitchner (1994); and Baxter-Magolda (1992) developed models that all place students who depend on authorities for validation of knowledge at the lower end of intellectual development, and students who see themselves as constructors of knowledge, at the higher end. These researchers generally agree that at the most sophisticated levels of development, students have a sense that knowledge is ever-evolving and contextualized within students' own perspectives (Hofer & Pintrich, 1997).

Table 2.1 indicates how these models conceptualize learner epistemologies at different points of development.

TABLE 2.1
Ways of Knowing in College: A Metaphorical Interpretation

About Knowledge	About Instructors	Assumptions — About Students and Self	About Texts	About Studying and Learning
Level 1: Knowledge is contained in books and the minds of experts.	Instructors are sovereigns who hold and control valid knowledge.	Students are subjects. They obtain what they need from those with sovereign authority.	Texts are the sovereigns' tools of authority.	Memorize; follow formulas and models exactly; take what is given and make it one's own.
Level 2: Knowledge is elusive but "out there" to be discovered.	Instructors are guides. They lead planned expeditions to find knowledge.	Students are scouts. They should follow their leader and the rules of the expeditions.	Texts are the maps of the expeditions.	Follow directions; get lots of explanation and feedback to stay on track.
Level 3: Knowledge is a myth; everything is relative, so all we have are different opinions.	Instructors are bosses whom students must learn to please.	Students are subordinates who must leave their own opinions at the door and do as they are told.	Texts are the manuals that govern the job.	Figure out what the instructor wants and do it as well as possible.
Level 4: Knowledge is incomplete and in the making.	Instructors are technicians in the great laboratory of knowledge.	Students are laboratory apprentices.	Texts are changing repositories of knowledge.	Learn procedures and operations; become skilled in the work of the domain.
Level 5: Knowledge is uncertain and controversial.	Instructors are detectives trying to unravel mysteries	Students are problem solvers helping the master detective.	Texts are the source of vital clues and evidence to be examined critically.	Use information, procedures, and understanding to solve problems.
Level 6: Knowledge is constructed systematically within frameworks that vary and are constructions themselves.	Instructors are judges determining valid structures of knowledge within their disciplines.	Students are interns who help construct knowledge.	Texts belong to a universe of knowing and derive their value from the communities or genres in which they are written.	Use information, procedures, understanding, and problem solving to form intelligent but flexible positions.

Developmental educators may look at Table 2.1 and think how far a student must go to move beyond the initial stages of depending on authorities for knowledge that is conceived as outside the self. Or they may look at a conventional textbook and wonder how a student may engage with it transactionally. These are valid concerns. New college learners are not likely to be functioning at higher levels of developmental stages or negotiating their learning in transactional terms. Conventional texts, lectures, and exams are still the rule in the majority of classes, and these tend to emphasize demonstration rather than construction of knowledge. One may even argue that students today are in the awkward position of having each foot in a different realm—one in the familiar world of texts, lectures, and exams, the other in the emerging universe of electronic networks and communications, the setting of greatest relevance to the future. To put it another way, they need parallel literacies.

Accordingly, academic support must attend to the immediate tasks at hand—the reading, listening, and test taking that have always been our concern—while helping students develop the cognitive sophistication and skills that current technologies demand. In the next part of our discussion, we consider the nature of both the printed texts that still predominate postsecondary classes and of electronically based information sources such as databases and the Internet.

THE NATURE OF COLLEGE TEXTS

So far, we have considered contemporary postsecondary learning from theoretical perspectives that might not have a great deal of reality to actual learners or those who provide academic support. Although electronic media are rapidly achieving predominance, most students today still purchase texts, attend lectures, and take exams over material that has been delivered by these means.

Any kind of reading material can be assigned in a college class, but most introductory courses use a traditional comprehensive textbook that provides foundational knowledge in the discipline. In addition, supplemental readings in the form of instructor-composed readers and trade books are common in many courses. If we compare reading to traveling, learning from conventional introductory textbooks is like flying in a small plane, in which one sees a lot but from a distance; reading trade books is like traveling by car or train, moving along at the level of the scene one is seeing; and reading professional articles is like traveling on foot, working carefully through a small piece of a larger terrain, often with effort but with more opportunity to interact.

Large, comprehensive textbooks represent the kind of reading least likely to be associated with transactional reading or the higher levels of student development charts. They do not invite reader construction of meaning, honor the knowledge the reader brings to the text, or lend themselves to critical reading. This is not to say that the necessity of learning from such texts precludes critical reading or epistemological development, but that they must be dealt with on their own terms, as a kind of scaffolding for building structures of new knowledge, while other kinds of learning and development are also supported. These textbooks usually have most if not all of the following characteristics: high conceptual density; compression of information: a paragraph may represent a volume of research; use of special terminology, often as the object of learning;

multiple ways of presenting information through print, including prose, tables and graphs, photos and illustrations, boxed anecdotes, advance organizers, and summaries; organization that reflects the logic of the discipline represented or patterns that dominate thinking in the field.

To illustrate the last characteristic, we may look at discussions by representatives of four disciplines, chemistry, biology, psychology, and history, concerning the nature of texts in their introductory courses.

Little (1995) described chemistry texts as built of "macrostructures," which are composed of main ideas or concepts. Within these macrostructures or main concepts, the reading material reinforces ways of thinking that are associated with chemistry as a process as well as a body of knowledge. Besides *definition structures* and *comparison structures*, which are self-explanatory, Little named *solution pathways*, which are strategies formed from applying examples of problem solving to new problems of a similar type; *sequence structures*, lists or formulas for carrying out processes in which the order of items or steps is crucial; *enumeration structures*, in which order is also crucial; *response structures*, in which questions are posed and then answered in the text; *causal relationships*, which are the focus of experimental science; and *the scientific method*, chief tool for determining causality, involving relationships among dependent and independent variables.

This description emphasizes the importance of precision reading, in which the text is followed closely like a complex set of directions. The text is a model for the kind of thinking that emphasizes scrupulous accuracy and quantitative logic, the habits of mind that will lead learners to the next levels of work in chemistry. Memorizing at both macro- and microlevels may be necessary as a means to assemble a kind of "tool kit" to support the development of scientific reasoning. However, memorizing and internalizing macrostructures are not sufficient for success in beginning chemistry. Of greatest importance in reading is to understand and learn to use the reasoning of the field.

Lawson (1995) described two kinds of organization used in most introductory biology texts: from the small and simple to the complex and large, or the opposite. Both reflect basic organization of biological phenomena on the basis of size and complexity. Lawson outlined the first, or "micro to macro," approach as follows: "atoms → molecules →organelles → cells → tissues → organs → organ systems → organisms → populations → biological communities → ecosystems → organ systems → organisms → populations → biological communities → ecosystems → biomes → biosphere" (p. 7). An introductory text following this "building block" organization typically begins with cells, moves through genetics and evolution to the physiology of plants and animals, and then covers ecology. Alternatives to this approach may attempt a more conceptual organization, such as one text that starts with ecology, moves through evolution and diversity, and then deals with cells, plants, and animals in that order. Another uses the metaphors of "sphere" for the big picture of ecology, "language" for genetics, and "systems" for a number of different kinds of phenomena inclusive of most of the traditional "building block" sequence.

With regard to psychology texts, Mealey and McIntosh (1995) described seven major areas of psychology: biological, experimental, cognitive, developmental, clinical, social, and personality. These generally constitute the macrostructure of psychology texts, often in that order, so that at the beginning, the study of psychology is close to the study of biology, and the field is presented as a natural science. This order is often counter to popular conceptions of psychology, which tend to focus on self-analysis, abnormalities, and therapies. Because many students do not consider psychology as remote a field as either chemistry or biology, the textbook may actually negate reader experience by forefronting such technical material as nervous system structure and animal experimentation. This content may help reorient new learners to the field before they reach material that may be more like the articles they read in magazines and self-help books. Boxed material may apply scientifically presented concepts to narrative situations, but these accounts are illustratory and tangential to the main text.

Almost inevitably, a history will be organized chronologically, with a macrostructure scheme composed of major eras of time being covered. History is narrative by nature, but involves as much interpretation as reporting. Introductory history texts tend to emphasize the latter, however, so that the basic argumentative structure of history may not be evident to the reader, who sees pages packed densely with "facts." Pace and Pugh (1996) recommended an architectural metaphor for readers so that they build meaningful structures out of what may seem like masses of details. They also offered the metaphors of acting as a detective, a lawyer, and a judge to convey what historians do and how they think, but the student learning from a textbook rather than doing inquiry may find only the first of these applicable. As a junior detective, the student sorts through levels of information to separate concepts from supporting details, a common kind of analytical reading.

In an analysis of textbooks used in development reading courses, Schumm, Ross, and Walker (1992) presented a modified versions of Singer's Friendly Text Inventory (Dreher & Singer, 1989), with five basic categories for evaluating textbooks on the basis of user-friendliness: (a) organization, including macrostructures, transitional devices, consistency of writing style, and text overviews and summaries; (b) explication, which includes uses of definitions and examples written clearly to make concepts comprehensible; (c) conceptual density, which refers to number of concepts presented in a given amount of space and the accessibility of the vocabulary used in the presentation; (d) metadiscourse, in which the author gives cues to the reader as to the level of importance of information; and (e) instructional devices, referring to the layout and apparatus of the textbook such as a well-organized table of contents, glossary, index, headings, and subheadings; questions to aid self-testing; and so on. Interestingly, only about 22% of the items of the modified version of the inventory refer to content, and 78% to text organization, cues, and apparatus.

READING A TRADE BOOK

Although a *textbook* is written specifically for a particular kind of course in a particular discipline and therefore intended exclusively for a student audience, a *trade book* is intended for a broad range of readers. The term means, simply, books for sale, or the kind one finds on the shelves of bookstores and libraries. In college classes, assigned trade books include ethnographies, historical accounts of specific periods or events, analyses of social or political topics, or literary works, such as long essays or biographies. Table 2.2 illustrates the complementary nature of the two kinds of texts.

To further illustrate the nature of trade book reading, we analyze one that has often been assigned in introductory courses at Indiana University, Stack's (1974) *All Our Kin:*

TABLE 2.2
Characteristic Comparison of Trade Books and Textbooks

Characteristics	
Trade Book	*Textbook*
1. Generally presents information and concepts in an argumentative structure, with issues, positions, and support for positions. The overall argument or perspective is usually composed of many constituent arguments. Students need to read on multiple levels of comprehension to grasp the main and supporting arguments of the book, and, in the end, may take away quite different senses of it, depending on their own perspective and background knowledge.	1. Generally presents information and concepts in a straightforward manner with some explanation and supporting evidence but not in great depth. Great compression of content and a heavy concept load along with little invitation to critical reading.
2. Organization is idiosyncratic to its topic and represents the logic of its focused argument, not the larger domain of a discipline.	2. Organization attempts to represent the logic of its discipline or topical domain.
3. Typographically conservative, employing for the most part the usual devices found in any book or magazine, such as chapter headings, subheadings, and occasional marks of emphasis such as italics or boldface. Drawings, photos, charts, and other illustrative material may be included but are usually subordinate or supplementary.	3. Makes use of a variety of typographical devices to cue the reader and present content in different forms.
4. Attempts to engage active reading by being interesting, lucid, and persuasive in its argument. Has a distinct authorial voice (or voices).	4. Attempts to engage active reading by posing questions and problems or by suggesting activities. Style is relatively voiceless.
5. May provide vocabulary development contextually and occasionally in glossaries, but expanding terminology is not an explicit purpose of the book.	5. May provide vocabulary development in the form of glossaries or end-of-chapter summaries of terms. Special terms are often italicized for emphasis when they first appear.
6. Attempts to draw readers into a critical consideration of its topic by drawing inferences, evaluating arguments, relating material to their own prior knowledge, and reaching conclusions.	6. Attempts to accommodate readers in the learning of its specific content in the fashion presented. Readers are not necessarily invited to impose their own order, draw inferences, or reach conclusions.

Strategies for Survival in a Black Community. Although not as widely used at the present, during the past 10 years it has been required in some sections of introductory sociology and anthropology and was, for several years, used in a summer bridge course in reading for entering college students.

All Our Kin is a relatively short book, 175 pages including chapter notes, bibliography, index, and several appendices. Students flipping through probably decide it is 129 pages, the length of the actual text. It is the author's account of kinship networks in the poor, urban minority neighborhood in which she lived as a participant observer for several months. Short as it is, it is a detailed account of a phenomenon which might be covered in a paragraph or two in a conventional textbook. The book illustrates the list of characteristics of trade books as follows:

1. *Argument structure*: Stack set out the gist of her argument at the beginning, that behaviors and coping strategies exhibited by the urban poor are appropriate and effective in their situation. Within that general argument she presented subanalyses and arguments relating to specific aspects of domestic and community life.

2. *Topic-specific organization*: As an ethnography, the book combines narrative and expository modes of writing. Throughout the book, the story of the researcher's experiences in the community is narrated, but the narrative is heavily laden with her sociological analyses and concepts.

3. *Typography and format*: These are fairly conventional, with primary reliance on prose and little emphasis on graphics. The book has the typical scholarly apparatus of glossary, extensive bibliography, and appendices that unpack certain aspects of her analysis.

4. *Authorial voice and identifiable perspective*: The author is personally present in the text, which is written with a first-person point of view. Being female and pregnant at the time of her study were prominent features in her experiences in the community and are embedded in the narrative she tells.

5. *Vocabulary*: A glossary helps the reader decode both special terms used by the researcher and the special language of the participants in her study. The writing assumes some knowledge of the concepts and language of kinship relationships, which she maps as part of her analysis.

6. *Critical reading*: The book invites critical response, not only in presenting an argument from an identifiable and personalized perspective but also in taking on controversial issues, such as race relations (the researcher was not the same race as her participants) and the insider–outsider controversy in sociology. Anyone witnessing a discussion of this book by a multiracial group of students would realize just how critical the response to it can be.

Increasingly, courses that once relied on a single comprehensive text now assign one or more supplementary trade books, sometimes as many as five or six. Students whose reading consists of a combination of textbook and trade book assignments experience a major mindset shift going from one kind of text to the other, yet they may not be aware that a shift of perspectives is appropriate. A formal textbook is a didactic instrument intended to help the learner construct a scaffold for learning in a discipline. A trade book, by contrast, may assume that the scaffold is in place.

READING PROFESSIONAL ARTICLES

Although professional articles are not likely to be assigned at introductory levels, some-times they are, and in these cases students may run into special problems that may be invisible to the assigning instructor. Such problems are often due to the high level of background knowledge assumed in this format, which does not provide room for contextual explanation. Such articles often begin with a brief and specialized review of the literature that is opaque to the novice to the field. In other cases, the article is a chapter of a larger work and assumes information and concepts that were presented earlier in the text.

Students confronted with these kinds of text, often presented in an instructor-composed reader that further fragments the information for the novice, are best advised to consult with the instructor and extract as much explanation as possible for the reading. Instructors who compose such readers may be well advised to take the students' perspective into account and provide advance organizers and other aids, follow-up questions that can be used for class discussion, and vocabulary definitions where needed. Instructors should also make sure that students with little background knowledge can reasonably comprehend these texts, perhaps by having readers at this level preview them before including them in a reader.

This much said, it should also be noted that professional articles do invite critical, transactional reading and involve the reader directly in the current genre knowledge of the discipline they represent. They are also similar to reading for professional and career purposes in that they are shorter pieces reporting on current developments and presenting interpretations and arguments that must be evaluated in the context of the standing knowledge in the field. As demonstrated in the next section on electronic media, more reading assigned in college courses will be of this nature.

ELECTRONIC MEDIA

Well before Hirsch's *Cultural Literacy*, a kind of homage to the texts of the past, Rifkin (1984) dramatically characterized a human cultural shift from "pyrotechnology" to "biotechnology" as we trade fire for computers as our primary technological tool. During the decade in which computers became ubiquitous in most work and learning sites, Rifkin asserted that generations following his were growing up in a different realm on the other side of a closed border, one in which "all physical phenomena are reduced, reorganized, and redefined to meet the operating requirements of the computer" (p. 20). That is, thinking, and literacy, are hereafter fundamentally changed. Whether or not we embrace Rifkin's more apocalyptic projections, we can certainly agree that in the last 10 years we have seen changes that have permanently altered our experiences with information and learning.

Learning on the Internet

The Internet is rapidly becoming an important instructional tool. Web-based instruction seems to have no limits to its possibilities, and the long-ignored and frequently disdained distance education format has been revitalized by the Web to the point of becoming one of the most rapidly expanding fields in higher education. Not only is the list of institutions extending access to their programs using the Web growing exponentially, but a new kind of institution, called the "virtual" university, is challenging established universities by providing universal access to online courses that can lead to valid undergraduate and graduate degrees (Traub, 1997). Existing in cyberspace, these programs do not need expensive campus facilities or require learners to leave their home communities, and so they promise to make higher education affordable to a broader range of people. Although traditionally printed materials are still used, a lot of reading materials are available on the Web while interactions among students and teachers occur mainly online.

The idea of text as data to be read in the form of hypertext or nonlinear links is the result of an idea computer scientist Nelson had in the 1960s and 1970s. He argued that traditional texts could be scrolled into a computer database and then be retrieved through the use of algorithmic combinations. These combinations would provide the reader with choices to follow according to interest or need (Nelson, 1974). This was a revolutionary way of looking at text. A reading text could be created through different combinations of links rather than following the traditional linear model of printed text that assumes the reader starts at the beginning and follows through to the conclusion. Written texts provide tables of content and indexes that function as organizing maps, but the reader has always had the option to jump around and pick and choose (Lemke, 1993). Hypertext increases this possibility.

This new way of reading texts has entered our educational institutions through the increasing use of the WWW for publication and for research. Now written sources seem limitless to the reader. Links presented in a document can lead to other relevant sections, selections, and authors and weave a seamless net of interconnectedness that ends only when the reader consciously decides to put a stop to it. Each link can lead to a complex and sometimes chaotic set of directions, but it also allows for the kind of exploration and critical, independent thinking that we want to encourage on the part of our students. Maneuvering hypertext may well define what it means to be literate in the next century.

This nonlinear characteristic makes it the ultimate constructivist learning environment where multiple perspectives can be shared through an active environment of hypermedia and other asynchronic or synchronic discussion facilities, an ideal setting for ill-structured problem solving. In *The Structure of Scientific Revolutions*, Kuhn (1970) called for a radical paradigm shift in the understanding of knowledge building. Learning takes place not through absorption but through active interaction between the learner and the "world's richness" (Brooks & Brooks, 1993). Brown, Collins, and Duguid (1989) referred to this world-embedded learning activity as a "cognitive apprenticeship." By entering the culture of the target subject domain, the student participates in a culture-specific activity that allows participation in the "distributed cognition" (Salomon, 1993) of that content community. The Internet is the tool for facilitating this active distribution of knowledge.

Another important aspect of Web-based learning is the potential it offers for intercultural experiences that go beyond reading texts about settings different from one's own. The Web is already a major vehicle for promoting global perspectives, and some have suggested that it can level the playing field between male and female participation in collaborative activities and discussion, although some, like feminist scholar Bonnell, warn that men tend to be socialized more toward technology and may still dominate on the Internet (Blumenstyk, 1997).

To obtain these and other benefits from the ultimate network of networks that the Web is, however, one must learn to navigate in a labyrinth as challenging as the one in ancient Crete, but without a Daedalus to build wings for escape or an Ariadne to trail a guiding thread. Fortunately, there are other guides, known as *search engines*, but students must learn to use and evaluate these too.

Most search engines use what are called Boolean strategies, which allow users to link words together in phrases rather than search the database for each one of the words separately. Some of the available search engines are better than others, not just because the results are more precise, but because they are continually being revised and updated. Four that have proved especially useful to us are the following:

> *Metacrawler*: This search engine, managed by Indiana University Bloomington, allows for simultaneous searches on eight major search engines or any selection of these eight.
>
> *Alta Vista*: This is a huge and fast Web index of more than 30 million homepages, especially useful for academically related searches using keyword strategies.
>
> *Yahoo*: Developed by graduate students at Stanford University, Yahoo facilitates searches that begin with large categories to more focused ones. The large categories include art, business, education, entertainment, environment, government, and so forth.
>
> *Lycos:* Developed by the Carnegie Mellon Foundation, it is often called "The Catalog" of the Internet. Lycos searches more than 5 million Web pages and is kept up to date by robotic technology.

As students enter higher education with increasingly sophisticated experiences with the Internet in earlier stages of education, college instructors find themselves pushed to utilize this medium for developing critical thinking, problem- solving, and collaborative abilities. For example, on the Web, students find all kinds of information of varying quality. One major problem is that, unlike printed materials, which usually undergo a review and selection process, information on the Web is unfiltered. It is important for students to learn to critically evaluate the information they obtain, and teachers need to help them hone such skills as considering evidence, judging authenticity of data, comparing different stances on issues, analyzing and synthesizing information judged useful, and constructing their own understanding of issues. The Web now offers support for such learning.

READING AND HYPERMEDIA

In addition to the vast resources of the Internet, *hypertext* and *hypermedia* programs enable learners to connect various sources of information with a text at hand. Hypertext provides connections to other texts, while hypermedia link nonprint forms such as video, audio, and still pictures to the text. Readers can also manipulate the mechanical and linguistic elements of text by requesting reduction of reading rate, changing the style and size of print, calling for help with pronunciation, and, if needed, requesting a second language translation of a text.

Dixon (1993) and Farmer (1992) found that programs based on hypertext and hypermedia are useful to learners with reading difficulties. For example, the Responsive Text Program enables readers who have trouble decoding information to use the computer to listen to a spoken version of the written text.

By facilitating the incorporation of multiple-sign systems in reading, these programs encourage readers to engage actively in nonlinear, weblike processes in meaning construction. The learning principles just discussed—the integration of the knower and the known, flexibility among multiple perspectives, transactional reading, contextual and committed knowing, and construction as opposed to absorption of knowledge—are all supported by new technologies in a way that provides a wide range of media for utilizing information and changes the way in which we use and produce conventional printed materials. (For a further discussion on hypermedia, see Caverly & Peterson, chap. 11, this volume.)

CONCLUSIONS

Literacy is the means by which postsecondary learners can attain academic success. Central to their success is an academic literacy that enables students to work effectively with texts and genres, not only of Western but also of varied traditions. It is a form of literacy that encompasses both a multiperspectival approach to knowing and the utilization of personal knowledge and background (Pugh & Pawan, 1991). We described and compared different kinds of texts that postsecondary learners encounter, namely, textbooks, trade books, journal articles, and information presented on the Internet. We included analyses of the types of content, organizational framework, and the types of reader engagement and responses expected in the reading of each text.

Developments in the way information is presented and transmitted have introduced new dimensions to academic literacy. Among other things, the superabundance of printed materials necessitates the ability to manage, synthesize, and organize information. The advent of the electronic revolution brought about by computers facilitates the incorporation of multiple sources of information to the text at hand. Many computer programs provide readers with the ability to access information in a nonhierarchical manner, making information in varied forms and platforms simultaneously available.

These developments suggest several ways in which functional academic literacy has already started to change. One is that readers are increasingly able to access and customize their reading outside boundaries set by assigned texts. Another is that readers move beyond a language-centered approach as they are encouraged to integrate music, art, video, and drama with text, a process known as *transmediation*. Collaboration among learners takes on new significance with growing awareness of a multitude of resources available and of meanings to be constructed.

Research in theories of students' intellectual development and reading has responded to changes in information presentation and transmission. For example, as readers must navigate meaningfully through the overwhelming sea of information available to them, greater importance is given to students' abilities to utilize their background experience and personal knowledge to select, interpret, and critically evaluate ideas. In student development theory, emphasis is placed on learners' internal validation of information rather than on outside authority, while in reading theory, focus is on the readers' creative output from merging their experiences with the information they read. In general, the focus is on the construction of new meaning from reading rather than the discovery of meaning found within texts.

The new dimensions of literacy that have come into play for individuals who are academically literate have implications for providers of postsecondary academic support. For one thing, college-level instructors need to include field-specific and content-specific approaches in their reading instruction. Each area of study dictates the type of organizational patterns and rhetorical styles used in texts. Students need to be taught to anticipate, recognize, and utilize the styles effectively in their reading.

The variety of texts college students encounter requires that students apply a variety of reading strategies, those that are very field-specific and those that are adaptable to a variety of texts or what Mayer (1983) called *near-transfer* and *far-transfer* skills. In the acquisition of both skills, readers need to be flexible with their use of strategies. They also need to be introduced to critical thinking strategies early in reading instruction to be able to evaluate effectively the continuous flow of information from all sources.

Given an increasing focus on the experiences that they bring to a reading event, readers need to be encouraged to see the utility of their background experience and personal knowledge in reading. However, as students may have had their experiences discredited in the past and therefore fear this process as disempowering. Students may see knowledge as separate from personal feelings and experiences (Johnston & Nicholls, 1995) and also refuse to accept the experiences of their fellow students as viable sources of information (Edelsky, 1991). Likewise, King (1992) reported that when a professor attempted to engage in reflective activities, there was discomfort and resentment among students. However, helping students go beyond this prejudice against personal knowledge can be one of the most effective ways of helping them negotiate meaning for themselves in an era of information overload.

We strongly agree with Hynds' (1990) assertion that the location of meaning in reading events rests in interpersonal connection making and meaning construction. In simpler terms, meaning is socially constructed, a concept that increases in significance in an environment of ever-evolving electronically generated information with the nonsequential and nonhierarchical processing the environment demands. Collaboration allows for information to be gathered simultaneously from different sources, in a multiperspective and multidisciplined way. This approach is also most relevant to students' future careers and lifelong learning needs. Belenky et al. (1986) suggested the metaphor of the midwife to characterize teaching that empowers students as active builders of their own knowledge in collaboration with peers. The midwife teacher, whose gender is irrelevant, is he or she who acknowledges students as creative agents who engage actively and mutually, not only with fellow learners but also with information that comes to them from a multitude of sources.

REFERENCES AND SUGGESTED READINGS

*Baxter-Magolda, M. B. (1992). *Knowing and reasoning in college: Gender related patterns in students' intellectual development.* San Francisco, CA: Jossey Bass.

*Belenky, M. F., Clinchy, B., Goldberger, N., & Tarule, J. (1986). *Women's ways of knowing.* New York: Basic Books.

Blumenstyk, G. (1997). A feminist scholar questions how women fare in distance education. In *The Chronicle of Higher Education* [Online]. Available: http://www.chronicle.com/colloquy/97/distanceed/background.htm.

Brooks, J. G., & Brooks, M. G. (1993). *The search of understanding: The case for constructivist classrooms.* Alexandria, VA: Association for Supervision and Curriculum.

Brown, J. S., Collins, A., & Duguid, P. (1989). Situated cognition and the culture of learning. Institute for Learning Technologies. [Online]. Available: http://www.ilt.columbia.edu/ilt/papers/JohnBrown.html.

Clifford, G. J. (1984). Buch und Lesen: Historical perspectives on literacy and schooling. *Review of Educational Research, 54,* 472–500.

*Cunningham, F. W., & Fitzgerald, J. (1996). Epistemology and reading. *Reading Research Quarterly, 31,* 36–60.

Dixon, R. A. (1993). *Improved reading comprehension: A key to university retention?* Paper presented at the annual Midwest Regional Reading and Study Skills conference, Kansas City, MO. (ERIC document Reproduction Service No. ED 359 498)

Dreher, M. J., & Singer, H. (1989). Friendly texts and text-friendly teachers. *Theory into Practice, 28,* 98–104.

Edelsky, C. (1991). *With literacy and justice for all: Rethinking the social in language and education.* London: Falmer.

Eisenstein, E. (1979). *The printing process as an agent of change: Communications and cultural transformation in early modern Europe* (2 vols.). New York: Cambridge University Press.

Farmer, M. E. (1992). Computer-assisted reading: Effects of whole-word feedback on fluency and comprehension in readers with severe disabilities. *Remedial and Special Education, 13,* 50–60.

Fish, S. (1980). *Is there a text in this class?* Cambridge, MA: Harvard University Press.

*Freire, P., & Macedo, D. (1987). *Literacy: Reading the word and the world.* Granby, MA: Bergin & Garvey.

Grabe, W. (1991). Current developments in second language reading research. *TESOL Quarterly, 25,* 375–406.

Hirsch, E. D., Jr. (1987). *Cultural literacy: What every american needs to know.* Boston: Houghton Mifflin.

*Hofer, B. K., & Pintrich, P. R. (1997). The development of epistemological theories: Beliefs about knowledge and knowing and their relation to knowing. *Review of Educational Research, 67,* 88–140.

*Hynds, S. (1990). Reading as a social event: Comprehension and response in text, classroom and world. In D. Bodgdan & S. B. Straw (Eds.), *Beyond communication: Reading comprehension and criticism* (pp. 237–256). Portsmouth, NH: Boynton/Cook.

Johnston, P. H., & Nicholls, J. G. (1995). Voices we want to hear and voices we don't want to hear. *Theory into Practice, 34*(2), 94-100

King, J. R. (1992). *Professing and post modernity: Social constructions of teaching selves.* (ERIC Document Reproduction Service, No. 353 580)

King, P. M., & Kitchener, K. S. (1994). *Developing reflective judgment: Understanding and promoting intellectual growth and critical thinking in adolescents and adults.* San Francisco, CA: Jossey Bass.

*Kozol, J. (1985). *Illiterate America.* New York: New American Library.

Kuhn, T. S. (1970). *The structure of scientific revolutions* (2nd ed.). Chicago: University of Chicago Press.

Lawson, A. (1995). *Studying for biology.* New York: HarperCollins.

Leland, C. H., & Harste, J. C. (1994). Multiple ways of knowing: Curriculum in a new key. *Language Arts, 1,* 337–346.

*Lemke, J. L. (1993). "Hypermedia and higher education." *Interpersonal Computing and Technology, 1*(2) [Online serial]. Available: http://www.lib.ncsu.edu/stacks/i/ipct/ipct-v1n02-lemke-hypermedia.txt

Little, L. (1995). *Studying for chemistry.* New York: HarperCollins.

Mayer, R. E. (1983). *Thinking, problem solving and cognition.* New York: W. H. Freeman.

Mealey, D. L., & McIntosh, W. D. (1995). *Studying for psychology.* New York: HarperCollins.

Nelson, T. H. (1974). *Dream machines/Computer lib.* Redmond, WA: Tempus.

Pace, D., & Pugh, S. L. (1996). *Studying for history.* New York: HarperCollins.

Paul, R. (1987). Dialogical thinking: Critical thought essential to the acquisition of rational knowledge and passions. In J. B. Baron & R. Sternberg (Eds.), *Teaching thinking skills: Theory and practice* (pp. 152–160). New York: W. H. Freeman.

Peregoy, S. F., & Boyle, O. F. (1992). *Writing, reading and learning in ESL: A resource book for K-8 teachers.* New York: Longman.

*Perry, W. (1970). *Forms of intellectual and ethical development in the college years.* Orlando, FL: Holt, Rinehart & Winston.

Pipher, M. B. (1994). *Reviving Ophelia: Saving the selves of adolescent girls.* New York: Putnam.

Pugh, S., & Pawan, F. (1991). Reading, writing and academic literacy. In R. F. Flippo & D. C. Caverly (Eds.), *College reading & study strategy programs* (pp. 1–27). Newark, DE: International Reading Association.

Rifkin, J. (1984). *Algeny.* New York: Penguin Books.

Rosenblatt, L. M. (1978). *The reader, the text, the poem : The transactional theory of the literary work.* Carbondale: Southern Illinois University Press.

Rosenblatt, L. M. (1993). The transactional theory: Against dualisms. *College English, 55,* 377–386.

*Rosenblatt, L. M. (1994). The transactional theory of reading and writing. In H. Singer & R. B. Ruddell (Eds.), *Theoretical models and processes of reading* (4th ed., pp. 1057–1092). Newark, DE: International Reading Association.

Rumelhart, D. E. (1985). Toward an interactive model of reading. In H. Singer & R. B. Ruddell (Eds.), *Theoretical models and processes of reading* (4th ed., pp. 722–750). Newark, DE: International Reading Association.

Salomon, G. (1993). *Distributed cognitions: Psychological and educational considerations.* New York: Cambridge University Press.

Schommer, M. (1990). Effects of beliefs about the nature of knowledge on comprehension. *Journal of Educational Psychology, 82,* 498–504.

Schumm, J. S., Ross, G., & Walker, S. (1992). Considerateness of Postsecondary Reading Textbooks: A content analysis. *Journal of Developmental Education, 15,* 16–23.

Shelton, K. Y. (1994). *Reader response theory In the high school English Classroom.* Paper presented at the 84th annual meeting for the National Council of Teachers of English, Orlando, Florida. (ERIC Document Reproduction Service No. ED 379 655)

*Siegel, M. (1995). More than words: The generative power of transmediation for learning. *Canadian Journal of Education, 20,* 455–475.

Stack, C. (1974). *All our kin: Strategies for survival in a black community.* New York: Harper & Row.

Tierney, R. J. (1992). *Computer acquisition: A longitudinal study of the influence of high computer access on students' thinking, learning and interactions.* (ERIC Document Reproduction Service No. ED 393 668)

Traub, J. (1997, October 20). Drive-thru U. *New Yorker,* 114–123.

Williams, J. D., & Snipper, G. C. (1990). *Literacy and bilingualism.* New York: Longman.

3

Vocabulary Development
at the College Level

꙳৯৯꙳

Michele L. Simpson
Sally N. Randall
University of Georgia

The importance of vocabulary is daily demonstrated in schools and out. In the classroom, the achieving students possess the most adequate vocabularies. Because of the verbal nature of most classroom activities, knowledge of words and ability to use language are essential in these activities.

—Petty, Herold, and Stoll (1968, p. 7)

For a variety of theoretical and pragmatic reasons, researchers and practitioners have supported vocabulary development for college students. Words are important because they are the visual and auditory symbols that individuals use in communication to represent important ideas and concepts. When individuals have an understanding of these words, they increase their perceptions of the world, expand and reorganize their prior knowledge, and facilitate their ability to use appropriate words in expressive communication situations (Kibby, 1995). More specifically, college students must understand the discipline-specific, general, and technical words they read in their assigned texts and hear in lectures or discussions if they hope to succeed. They also need extensive and varied expressive vocabularies in order to write essays and research papers and deliver oral presentations during class.

Many college students, however, possess neither the receptive and expressive vocabularies nor the strategies necessary to cope with the demands of independent learning in an academic discipline. We know from previous research that at-risk students have qualitatively and quantitatively different vocabularies from their more successful counterparts (Beck & McKeown, 1991; Curtis, 1987; Marshelek, 1981). We also know that most college freshmen have a limited number of learning strategies for dealing with difficult text and concepts (Pressley, 1995; Simpson, Hynd, Nist, & Burrell, 1997). Sartain et al. (1982) traced the learning difficulties of college students enrolled in philosophy, physics, psychology, and English composition. The students were asked to keep logs and attend weekly seminars conducted by graduate assistants to discuss the problems they were having in their classes. During those 2 years, the most common difficulty reported by students across all four content areas was technical vocabulary. Hopper and Wells (1981) reached similar conclusions in a study involving 600 college students.

In summary, if college students are to succeed, they need an extensive vocabulary and a variety of strategies for understanding the words and language of an academic discipline. College reading professionals who work with students need to be aware of research-validated and effective approaches and strategies for vocabulary development. This chapter reviews the research and theory related to vocabulary and offers practical teaching and programmatic guidelines.

This chapter is organized into three major sections. In the first section we address the issues underlying vocabulary development and instruction. Then we review and highlight selected studies that have addressed the question of how best to develop college students' vocabulary knowledge. In the third section, we describe effective vocabulary practices. We conclude with an outline of future directions and recommendations for college reading professionals.

ISSUES UNDERLYING VOCABULARY KNOWLEDGE AND INSTRUCTION

Before teachers or researchers make a decision on a commercial material, vocabulary program, or strategy to be used in the classroom or validated in an empirical study, they should first acknowledge some theoretical and methodological issues concerning vocabulary development. Perhaps the most important theoretical issue is what constitutes "knowing" a word. Closely related to this first issue is the troublesome methodological issue that considers how to measure word knowledge and vocabulary growth in our students. The third issue addresses the role of students as they attempt to acquire vocabulary knowledge.

Although these issues may seem somewhat routine, their impact on the results of various vocabulary studies has been significant (Beck & McKeown, 1991; Mezynski, 1983). This section lays the groundwork for analyzing and interpreting the extant literature on vocabulary.

What Does It Mean To Know a Word?

What factors determine whether a student has learned a new word? Although this question is difficult to answer, we do know that knowing a word is "not an all-or-nothing proposition" (Baumann & Kameenui, 1991; Beck & McKeown, 1991). Rather, students' understanding of a word probably exists in degrees or on a differential continuum much like the one described by Dale (1965). He suggested that word knowledge follows four stages: (a) I've never seen the word; (b) I've heard of it, but I don't know what it means;

(c) I recognize it in context, it has something to do with....; and (d) I know the word in one or several of its meanings. Dale's fourth stage comes the closest to capturing what most people believe best constitutes what is involved in knowing a word. That is, students understand a word when they recognize it, provide appropriate and precise definitions that fit the context, and use it in expressive language situations.

Kameenui, Dixon, and Carnine (1987) described three levels of word knowledge: *full conceptual word knowledge, partial word knowledge,* and *verbal associational knowledge.* According to Kameenui et al., full conceptual word knowledge is defined by a set of critical features (those common to all examples) and variable features (those demonstrated by some examples but not all). When a student's knowledge of a concept is limited to the critical features, variable features, or various combinations of such features, that student has partial concept knowledge. Obviously, partial knowledge exists in several degrees. A student's verbal association word knowledge is not an indication of any conceptual knowledge; rather, it is the pairing of a label to its meaning, a one-dimensional rote activity. For example, a student with a verbal associational knowledge of a word such as **exacerbate** would probably write a sentence similar to this:" John always **exacerbated** his sister, which made his mother angry." In this situation, the student has substituted the dictionary definition, **irritated**, a word familiar to the student, for the unknown word **exacerbated**. As a result of this definition substitution, he has created a meaningless sentence.

But what does it mean to know a word conceptually? What cognitive and metacognitive processes should instructors emphasize with their students? Using the ideas of Tennyson and Park (1980), who reviewed the literature on the teaching of concepts, and the suggestions of other researchers, we offer the following key processes that seem to be essential to knowing a word fully or conceptually. Students should be able to

1. Recognize and generate critical attributes, examples, nonexamples of a concept (Beck, McCaslin, & McKeown, 1980; Graves, 1985; Tennyson & Park, 1980).
2. Sense and infer relationships between concepts and their own backgrounds (Ausubel, 1963; Beck, McKeown, & Omanson, 1987; Henry, 1974; O'Rourke, 1974).
3. Recognize and apply the concept to a variety of contexts (Carnine, Kameenui, & Coyle, 1984; Mezynski, 1983; Stahl, 1983).
4. Generate novel contexts for the targeted concept (Beck, McCaslin, & McKeown, 1980; Stahl, 1983, 1985).

With such a perspective of word knowledge, the issue is not whether students know the word but in what way they know the word. We should also point out that it is not always imperative for students to know at a full conceptual level all words that they encounter in their reading or listening. However, if instructors want to improve their students' reading comprehension or affect their expressive vocabularies, then full conceptual understanding is probably necessary (Baumann & Kameenui, 1991; Beck & McKeown, 1991).

For whatever reason, researchers rarely strive to develop full concept knowledge with their participants. Moreover, only a few researchers have explicitly stated their criteria for word knowledge (Beck, Perfetti, & McKeown, 1982; Stahl, 1983), relying instead on their assessment instruments to create that criteria implicitly. Consequently, the type of vocabulary assessment used in research or in the classroom becomes critical to the entire process of vocabulary development.

How Can Vocabulary Knowledge Be Measured?

The type of format used to measure students' understanding of a word should be closely related to the instructor's philosophy of what it means to know a word (Baumann & Kameenui, 1991; Kameenui, Carnine & Freschi, 1982). If there is not a match among the philosophy, instruction, and test format, then there is a strong possibility that the format will mask, overestimate, or provide inaccurate data about students' vocabulary understanding and achievement. For example, if a matching test is used to measure the effectiveness of an instructional lesson that emphasized word classification or categorization, some students may do poorly on the test because the instruction did not focus on the strict memorization of definitions. If, however, the researcher selects an analogy test format, the students would have a better opportunity to demonstrate what they have learned.

Curtis' (1987) research clearly demonstrated the importance of acknowledging the type of information assessed by test or practice formats. She found that when fifth-grade students were given a checklist and asked to respond yes if they knew a word, they did so 80% of the time. However, when asked to provide an example or partial explanation of the word, the students could do so only 50% of the time. Moreover, only 20% of the students' answers were correct when the testing format asked them to provide synonyms and complete explanations.

The most common practice and testing format appears to be the multiple-choice question (Beck & McKeown, 1991; Stahl, Brozo, & Simpson, 1987). High school reading textbooks continue the tradition of the basals by providing students lists of words that they eventually look up in the dictionary, practice in a definition or synonym exercise, and then test in a multiple-choice format (Stahl, 1985). This trend does not change at the college level. When Stahl et al. (1987) conducted a content analysis of 60 vocabulary textbooks, they found that multiple-choice questions were the predominate method for measuring students' vocabulary understanding. There are many limitations to recognition formats such as multiple-choice and matching items. Kameenui et al. (1987) argued that multiple-choice vocabulary tasks are "useless at best and dangerous at worst" because they cannot reveal the dimensions of students' conceptual understanding (p. 15). Beck and McKeown (1991) suggested that most multiple-choice formats make vocabulary knowledge appear "flat, as if all words are either known to the same level or unknown" (p. 796). Perhaps the most important factor to be remembered about the multiple-choice test format is the influential role that distractors play in a test item. Anderson and Freebody (1981) pointed out that distractors, especially poorly constructed ones, can actually confuse students who understand a word or permit students who do not understand a word to guess correctly at the meaning of a word.

What is needed are formats that are more sensitive to the dimensions and levels of students' vocabulary knowledge. Although some attempts have been made (e.g., Nagy, Herman, & Anderson, 1985; Nist & Simpson, 1997; Simpson, 1987), these alternative formats have not been systematically researched or incorporated into everyday practice.

College reading professionals need to carefully define which level of word knowledge they wish to stress, select vocabulary strategies that will help students learn at that level, and then create tests that are sensitive to the effects of those instructional strategies.

What Is the Student's Role in Vocabulary Acquisition?

The third issue concerns the role of students during vocabulary instruction. Theory and research have suggested that students who actively try to make sense of what they see and hear are those who learn more (Craik & Lockhart, 1972; Mayer, 1996; Wittrock, 1990). The activity of the learner has been theoretically defined by Craik (1979) and Craik and Lockhart (1972), who proposed that deeper, more elaborate and distinctive processing of stimuli results in better performance, all other things being equal. Because the levels of processing model has been criticized (Eysenck, 1979), other researchers have suggested modifications. For example, Tyler, Hertel, McCallum, and Ellis (1979) proposed that the amount of cognitive effort required by a task is an important determinant of later recall performance, with greater cognitive effort leading to greater recall. Strategy research with college-level learners supports this concept (Mayer, 1996; Simpson & Nist, 1997; Simpson, Olejnik, Tam, & Supattathum, 1994).

Within these theoretical frameworks, which are speculative, vague, and somewhat difficult to quantify, Stahl (1985) attempted to describe the tasks of the active learner. He suggested that, depending on the instructional methods used, a student learning new vocabulary should be involved in *associative processing, comprehension processing*, and *generative processing*. Associative processing requires the learner to make an association or connection between a word and its synonym or definition within a particular context. This level of activity might involve the learners in dictionary study or programmed learning. Associative processing is the lowest level of involvement, requiring the least amount of processing (Craik, 1979; Craik & Lockhart, 1972) and the least amount of effort (Tyler et al., 1979), but it is the basis for the next two levels of processing.

The second level, comprehension processing, requires the learner to apply word associations to a new situation in a meaningful and correct manner. The learner could be asked to complete analogy or categorization exercises, fill in the blanks in cloze exercises, or judge whether a word has been used correctly. The third level, generative processing, asks the learner to create or generate a novel context for the targeted word. Generative processing engages students in activities such as creating original sentences using the vocabulary word, creating semantic maps, studying definitional characteristics, or participating in discussions. Beck, McKeown, and colleagues (see Beck & McKeown, 1983) created a comprehensive program of vocabulary research and development that involves students in a variety of generative processing activities. For example, students were asked to answer questions using the words they had been taught (e.g., Would a *glutton* tend to be *obese?*) rather than simply matching definitions to the words they were studying.

When researchers compare different vocabulary strategies to determine which is more effective, they often fail to define adequately or to keep equivalent the processing requirements (or involvement) of the learners (Mezynski, 1983; Stahl & Fairbanks, 1986). Consequently, a strategy that actively engages the learner in solving problems, answering questions, or producing applications in new situations may be compared directly with another strategy that asks the learner to fill in blanks or to match words with definitions. Not surprisingly, the more active strategy involving the learner in generative processing appears to be the superior method of vocabulary instruction. Researchers and teachers should thoroughly address these three issues before they draw conclusions about the effectiveness of any vocabulary approach.

RESEARCH ON VOCABULARY DEVELOPMENT AT THE COLLEGE LEVEL

This section examines the research on vocabulary development at the college level. Most of the research studies focus on intermediate-aged students and these studies were conducted in the 1980s. Moreover, many of the studies, especially earlier ones in the 1970s, seemed to have inherent limitations that we felt had to be acknowledged. For example, a plethora of studies have been conducted in which one strategy is compared to another in order to determine a superior strategy for vocabulary development. However, in many of these studies the students received minimal, if any, training in the vocabulary strategy. We did not find it surprising when we read the results of these studies that indicated the students' vocabulary or comprehension did not significantly improve as a result of "using" the strategy. Many other vocabulary studies have compared one strategy that involved students in considerable cognitive processing (e.g., making a semantic map) to another strategy that involved students in repeating definitions to words. Again, as we read the results we were not surprised to learn that students using a strategy that demanded only rote memory processing learned fewer vocabulary words than those students using strategies that demanded their active processing. In addition to these inherent flaws in the extant literature, many researchers have not addressed the issues of what it means to know a word, how their assessment instruments reflect this orientation, the limitations of using artificially constructed text, and the role of students' prior knowledge.

Although the picture we paint appears grim, there is a small body of research on vocabulary development at the college level that should provide reading professionals with some guidance and direction as they evaluate commercial materials and design their programs for improving their students' vocabulary. There are several ways to structure a review of the literature, but we have chosen to organize the research studies in this manner: (a) traditional word knowledge approaches, (b) content-specific vocabulary strategies, (c) alternative delivery modes, and (d) student-centered approaches. We acknowledge that, as with any organizing schema, some of these studies could be included in more than one of these categories. We also note that the majority of the studies reviewed were conducted with college students; however, in some situations, we have included studies conducted with secondary-aged or elementary-aged students because they were particularly noteworthy and applicable to college students.

Studies on Traditional Word Knowledge Approaches

Practitioners and researchers who believe that systematic instruction should focus on general vocabulary improvement probably favor the instrumentalist position outlined by Anderson and Freebody (1981). The instrumentalist hypothesis maintains that word knowledge is a direct causal link affecting text comprehension. Thus, the more individual word meanings taught, the better students comprehend any new or difficult expository material they read. Anderson and Freebody stressed that the most distinguishing characteristic of the instrumentalist hypothesis is the emphasis on direct and generic vocabulary-building exercises.

Studies from the late 1960s and early 1970s emphasized master word lists, with words taught by repetitive associations with synonyms or brief dictionary definitions; standardized reading tests were used to measure vocabulary acquisition. In contrast, studies in the late 1970s and early 1980s emphasized more active and generative strategies, words taught within context, and informal assessment procedures. Many of the more recent studies reflect a continued interest in these deeper levels of processing vocabulary, often concluding that no one method is best but that many can be used effectively as complements to one another.

Because of the vast methodological differences in earlier and later general vocabulary improvement studies, it is not surprising that the findings tend to be highly equivocal. Nevertheless, we will analyze these traditional word knowledge studies using this organizational schema: (a) morphemic analysis, (b) dictionary definitions and synonyms, (c) contextual analysis, and (d) keyword studies.

Morphemic Analysis.

One prevalent instructional practice in college reading programs is the training in morphemic analysis as a method for helping students unlock the meaning of unknown words they encounter. A *morpheme* is the smallest meaning unit in a language. *Free morphemes* are what have traditionally been called root words; they can function independently or they can be combined with bound morphemes. *Bound morphemes* have meaning but must be combined with free morphemes; bound morphemes include prefixes and suffixes. Morphemic analysis requires knowledge of prefixes and suffixes and their meanings, knowledge of associated spelling and pronunciation changes, and extensive knowledge of root words. Theoretically, if a student knows many affixes, with the learning of each new free morpheme or root word, the student can actually generate several more new words by adding bound morphemes. Morphemic analysis is sometimes termed *internal contextual analysis* as opposed to an external analysis of the context surrounding a word (Jenkins, Matlock, & Slocum, 1989).

Morphemic analysis and the use of affixes might be considered a college reading tradition. Of the 60 vocabulary workbooks analyzed by Stahl et al. (1987), 44 (80%) heavily emphasized morphemic analysis. Although teaching affixes and morphemic analysis has been widely recommended for all ages and levels of students (Dale, 1965; Deighton, 1960; O'Rourke, 1974), little empirical research exists at any age level to support the practice as a method of developing general vocabulary (Graves & Hammond, 1979). However, Baumann and Kameenui (1991) summarized the findings of recent research and concluded that although the research is limited, it appears that training in morphemic analysis for upper elementary and older students can improve their ability to infer the meaning of a word from morphologically related words.

We could find only three training studies that focused on using morphemic analysis with college students. Of the three researchers, only Albinski (1970) found that the preteaching of affixes was effective with college students. Einbecker (1973) instructed students in root words and Strader and Joy (1980) presented instruction in affixes. In both studies researchers found no significant differences in word knowledge when instruction in morphemic analysis was compared to other methods of instruction. Strader and Joy did find that such instruction improved the students' ability to combine morphemes.

White, Power, and White (1989) indirectly assessed the value of teaching morphological analysis by evaluating the probability that students could successfully analyze affixed words. They used a random sample of target words that contained the four most commonly occurring prefixes (re-, un-, dis-, and in-) found in an intermediate grades dictionary. White et al. concluded that readers who had knowledge of the most common meanings of each root word could use knowledge of affixes to determine the meaning of about 80% of the words in the original sample. Their recommendations were that along with instruction in affixes, students should also be trained to attempt to determine possible meanings of root words from context.

On the theoretical level, student knowledge of affixes as a generative strategy for unlocking the meaning of new words has some appeal. On the other hand, the lack of empirical research supporting this practice invites caution. Several important issues and questions could be addressed in future research studies: (a) Would an analysis of the words in a beginning college dictionary parallel the results found by White et al.? (b) How can morphemic analysis be paired with other instructional methods for college students? (c) Do at-risk college students have adequate knowledge of root words? What is the best way to increase that knowledge? (d) Can students be trained to transfer their knowledge of morphemic analysis to their independent reading?

Dictionary Definitions and Synonyms.

Teaching dictionary definitions and synonyms for words that are grouped together, independent of any specific context, is perhaps the oldest and most prevalent instructional method in secondary and postsecondary education. In experimental studies using such word lists, subjects receive a list of words and their definitions or synonyms or are told to consult a dictionary for comprehensive definitions and synonyms. The words to be learned generally come from commercial workbooks, standardized tests, or high-frequency word lists and share no common theme or focus. Both the control group (usually with no instruction) and the experimental group are given a standardized test to measure the effects of the instruction. In general, this type of study, conducted in the 1950s and 1960s, found no significant differences favoring the subjects who learned definitions and synonyms to improve their general vocabulary (Crump, 1966; Fairbanks, 1977; McNeal, 1973).

Baumann and Kameenui (1991) explained that this kind of associative learning requires the pairing of two ideas. Learning a definition requires the pairing of a concept with its label; learning a synonym requires the pairing of a previously known label with a new label. This learning involves drill and rote memorization. We agree with Baumann and Kameenui and the early researchers cited earlier that a definition approach to vocabulary study must be seen as merely a first instructional step in learning new vocabulary. Students at all ages should be guided to move beyond the definition to a deeper level of word knowledge if the objective is for students to be able to understand and use the words effectively in academic contexts.

Two recent studies have examined the effects of the quality of definitions on students' vocabulary understanding. McKeown (1993) and Nist and Olejnik (1995) found that "adequate" definitions, as opposed to typical dictionary definitions, improved performance on generative measures of vocabulary knowledge by fifth graders and developmental college students, respectively. As defined by the researchers, adequate definitions included: a clear differentiation from related words, a broad enough context to make correct interpretation likely, specific language, logical connections between the components of the definition, and examples.

In their study, Nist and Olejnik (1995) found that adequate definitions had a significant impact on students' performance on four levels of vocabulary knowledge, independent of the strength of the context. They concluded that a dictionary can be a useful tool for college students but suggested that students may need training in how to distinguish adequate from inadequate definitions. Future research might examine the adequacy of definitions found in a variety of dictionaries using the criteria outlined by McKeown and Nist and Olejnik. With the results from such research, college reading professionals could then guide their students toward dictionaries that would allow them to work independently on vocabulary improvement.

Other studies have compared the efficacy of teaching students definitions and synonyms with teaching students contextual analysis. These studies are discussed later.

Contextual Analysis. The use of context clues for vocabulary improvement has long been highly recommended because of its purported advantages over other strategies. The theory is that students need not be dependent on a dictionary or glossary; instead, when confronted with unknown words, students can independently use the information in the surrounding context to unlock the meaning. Proponents suggest that students can be trained to "scrutinize the semantic and syntactic cues in the preceding and following words, phrases, and sentences" (Baumann & Kameenui, 1991, p. 620). Many secondary and postsecondary reading method textbooks instruct teachers to tell their students to use contextual clues when they come across a word they do not know, and most commercial vocabulary materials for college students emphasize the use of contextual analysis.

Many factors influence a student's ability to use context clues to discover the meaning of an unknown word. Both Baumann and Kameenui (1991) and Sternberg (1987) outlined some of the textual variables that they believe aid or hinder the process of contextual analysis. The variables that seem most pertinent to college learning include the density of unknown words in the selection, the importance of the word's meaning to the comprehension of the selection, the proximity and specificity of the clues, and the overall richness of the context. Individual student characteristics such as prior knowledge in the domain, general vocabulary knowledge, and ability to make inferences also impact a student's ability to use contextual analysis. Sternberg's theory of the three processes involved in contextual analysis underscores the importance of these individual variables and the complexity of the task of contextual analysis. He proposed that contextual analysis involves the selective encoding of only relevant information from the context, the combining of multiple cues into one definition, and the comparison of this new information with the reader's prior knowledge. These are certainly complex cognitive tasks.

The issue of the richness of the context deserves separate discussion because of the significance of this variable on the research that has been conducted. In much early research on contextual analysis, passages were developed specifically for research purposes with artificially rich contexts containing unusually explicit cues. McDaniel and Pressley (1989) referred to these as "embellished contexts." Raphael (1987) and Schatz and Baldwin (1986) suggested that, at best, natural contexts are not as rich as those developed by researchers and, at worst, are even misleading to the reader. It is very unlikely that students trained using artificially enriched contexts will be able to transfer contextual analysis to their own reading tasks in natural contexts.

The most promising studies are those that have trained students to use contextual analysis. Most of these studies have been conducted with students in the intermediate or middle school grades. Both Jenkins et al. (1989) and McKeown (1985) taught fifth graders in similar multistep procedures for deriving meaning from context. Students tried out possible meanings, evaluated their guesses by checking context, and revised guesses as needed. Jenkins et al. found that the training did not help the students master the words under study, but it did improve their ability to determine meaning for words they encountered subsequent to the training. McKeown found that students with high verbal ability were much more successful with the task of contextual analysis. She concluded that deriving meaning from context requires a level of semantic maturity and verbal ability that is not fully developed in all students. Buikema and Graves (1993) trained middle school students to find different types of context cues and found that they were better able to derive meaning independently on posttests than their counterparts who received no training.

We located only one study in which older students were trained to use contextual analysis. Sternberg (1987) investigated whether or not adults who were taught his theoretical framework of contextual analysis and trained to use it when reading, would improve their ability to derive meaning from context. The subjects were assigned to three teaching/training conditions: (a) the three processes involved in contextual analysis, (b) the individual variables that effect contextual analysis, or (c) the kinds of contextual clues. All of the trained subjects showed significantly greater posttest gains in their ability to derive meaning from context than the controls who received no training.

Sternberg's (1987) research findings would seem to suggest that training in the processes, the mediating variables, and the types of context clues can be valuable to students. Although these training procedures have not been yet been demonstrated as a long-term method for vocabulary development, they do seem to offer students specific approaches for initially unlocking the meanings of words encountered in their independent readings. However, it should be noted that the skills involved in contextual analysis require a fairly high level of verbal ability and inferential thinking. Whether at-risk students could master the processes involved in Sternberg's model is questionable.

In an attempt to find the one "best" method of vocabulary instruction, many studies have compared the effects of contextual analysis with other methods of vocabulary learning. In a review of these studies, Stahl and Fairbanks (1986) suggested than an emphasis on contextual information is more effective than an emphasis on definitions. Weiss, Mangrum, and Llabre's study (1986) typified the type of comparative strategy research conducted with college students. In their study, one group of students studied only the definitions of pseudowords, while the second group studied both definitions and two sentences that provided contexts. The two groups did not differ on either a multiple-choice posttest or a subsequent recall measure.

Rather than strictly compare one strategy to another, Nist and Olejnik (1995) studied the effects of strong and weak contexts and adequate and inadequate definitions on college students' vocabulary acquisition. They constructed both the weak and strong contexts to reflect authentic reading tasks in college texts. Nist and Olejnik concluded from their study that the strength of the context had very little effect on students' performance, but the quality of the definitions did. The researchers concluded that college students do not usually search the context to help determine word meanings, possibly because the contexts of typical college texts are not rich enough to be useful to students. Other variables that might discourage college students from searching the context are the density of unknown words in texts and the students' prior knowledge in the domain.

Once again, it is difficult to draw a single conclusion from such disparate results. Contextual analysis does not appear to be an effective method for mastering, even in the short term, the meanings of new words. However, it appears that training in contextual analysis, as outlined by several researchers, can provide many students with a valuable tool for initially unlocking the meaning of a new word encountered in independent readings. Students would then have to take further steps to learn the word so it became part of their working vocabulary.

Future researchers might consider addressing these two questions about contextual analysis: (a) How do average and at-risk college students differ in their ability to benefit from this type of training? (b) How can we teach students to transfer contextual analysis skills to their independent reading of texts? As researchers tackle these questions, they should attempt to use naturally occurring contexts that have not been embellished with explicit clues, including those found in college science and history texts.

Keyword Studies.   Considerable interest and research have focused on mnemonic strategies such as the keyword approach. The majority of the research has been on the *keyword method*, which was originally designed for learning a foreign language (Raugh & Atkinson, 1975). In this strategy, students are trained either to find a keyword or clue within the unknown target word and then develop a mental image of that keyword or to use the keyword and mental image provided by the researcher or trainer. The variation of this method asks the learner to place the keyword and definition in a meaningful sentence. For example, if the target word to be learned was *acrophobia*, a student might focus on the clue of *acro* and then develop the image of an acrobat who was afraid of heights walking on a tightrope high in the sky. The learner could then generate a sentence such as: "The acrobat, who has always been afraid of high places, suffered from acrophobia."

Paivio (1971) stated that mental imagery is important in facilitating long-term retention for adults because of the dual coding of organizational factors. Advocates of the dual-coding theory maintain that two different but interconnected symbolic processing systems exist for encoding information—one verbal and the other nonverbal. They propose that information is encoded in verbal, nonverbal, or both systems depending on the task and the concreteness or abstractness of the words read. Abstract words are more likely to activate verbal codings and concrete words are more likely to activate either nonverbal codings or a combination of both verbal and nonverbal systems. Other re-

searchers have suggested that the associative imagery of the keyword mnemonic operates by linking or relating items so they form unified wholes or higher order units. Thus,
when one item is recalled, that item acts as a retrieval cue for the other items to regener-
ate the whole (Begg, 1972, 1973; Bower, 1970, 1972).

Several authors (e.g., Levin, 1993; McCarville, 1993) have stressed the importance of understanding the appropriate uses of the keyword approach. Levin emphasized
that a mnemonic is a memory device only, and that it must serve as a base for future
deeper processing of the word. McCarville agreed with Levin in her discussion of college
learners, stating that the keyword approach is a "precomprehension strategy" (p. 2) that
allows students to initially recall newly learned words; however, they must develop more
complex and elaborative understandings of those words.

In general, the research studies have concluded that college students who use the
keyword method perform significantly better than their counterparts on various kinds of
vocabulary measures. For example, Pressley, Levin, and Miller (1981, 1982) found that
students who used the keyword strategy performed better than students using a ver-
bal-contextual strategy or controls who received no instruction. In a study of at-risk college students, Roberts and Kelly (1985) found only modest differences favoring the
keyword method in an immediate recall test, but much greater differences on a measure
of delayed recall. Smith, Stahl, and Neel (1987) reported similar findings. McDaniel and
Pressley (1989) concluded from their study that the keyword approach was superior to
contextual analysis for their subjects' definitional recall.

In two experiments with regularly admitted college students, Hall (1988) attempted to replicate a natural learning environment; he avoided choosing only words
which were conducive to keyword associations and he required students to generate
their own keywords. In his first study, Hall controlled the rate of presentation of words
and their definitions and found that when the rate of presentation was slow, students
were more likely to use the keyword approach but obtained lower scores than when the
rate of presentation was faster. He concluded that multiple short exposures to words are
more effective than fewer long exposures and that use of the keyword approach for some
words is not a help in learning word meanings. In a second experiment, students learned
one "easy" list (words that obviously suggested possible keywords) and a "typical" list
(words that did not readily suggest keywords). Hall found little difference between the
students and controls on learning the easy words, but the controls actually outperformed
the subjects on the typical words. After the experiment subjects reported that they preferred semantically linked mnemonic devices and would use the keyword method more
selectively in the future.

Although the findings appear impressive, keyword method studies do have some
limitations. The most evident is the lack of applicability to actual classrooms. The words
that college professionals typically select to teach their students and those that students
encounter in their course texts are not like those used in the keyword studies. Keyword
researchers usually use concrete, three syllable, low-frequency nouns with concise definitions (Pressley et al., 1981, 1982). A second limitation is the need to factor in the time
variable. If the strategy is to be effective, students must be able to use it independently
and quickly. However, Stahl, Brozo, Smith, Henk, and Commander (1991) reported
that students had difficulty generating keywords for vocabulary they were learning in a
college class. Remembering that Hall (1988) found greater vocabulary learning with

shorter spaced exposures to words and meanings, the trade-off for spending significant periods of time generating keywords may not be advantageous. A final limitation to keyword studies is a failure to investigate whether or not students can and will transfer the keyword system to their own learning tasks.

In the future researchers need to apply the keyword method in a realistic setting to answer the question, "What would happen if college students were given a list of words without the corresponding keywords and asked to learn the words as efficiently as possible for application in a specific task?" Researchers should also query students about their evaluation of the keyword strategy and its utility in their academic lives.

Studies on Content-Specific Vocabulary Strategies

Although most of the earlier studies focused on how to increase students' general vocabulary, the more recent studies have investigated teacher-directed or student-initiated strategies for learning difficult but important content area words. This latter orientation is similar to the knowledge hypothesis proposed by Anderson and Freebody (1981). This hypothesis suggests that vocabulary should be taught within the context of learning new concepts so that new words can be related to one another and to prior knowledge. Thus, the source for words to be taught or studied is not teacher-made word lists, but the difficult or unknown words that are critical for students' comprehension of specific content area reading assignments.

Some of the strategies previously discussed—particularly those related to contextual or morphemic analysis—could be used by students to understand key vocabulary encountered while learning from text. However, the strategies examined in this section differ from traditional word knowledge approaches because the primary concern is for developing students' understanding of content area information and concepts.

Many of the research studies that have examined content-specific vocabulary strategies have focused on college students' comprehension improvement rather than their vocabulary improvement. Of the studies we located that focused on vocabulary improvement, there seemed to be a trend supporting the argument that these strategies can assist students in learning vocabulary and concepts across a variety of content areas. These content-specific strategies include visual organizers and the Node Acquisition and Integration Technique (NAIT; Diekhoff, Brown, & Dansereau, 1982).

Visual Organizers. Visual organizers graphically display vocabulary terms to show the interrelationship of new concepts and previously learned concepts. Some visual organizers highlight text structure or help students understand main ideas. Although a variety of names have been given to these visual organizers—structured overviews, concept maps, semantic maps, semantic feature analysis, graphic organizers, matrix outlines—they generally can trace their origins to Ausubel's (1963) theory of meaningful receptive learning. Ausubel proposed that students can learn more effectively if new vocabulary in a content area is related to their background or prior knowledge. He proposed the advance organizer as one strategy for organizing and strengthening students' existing cognitive structure. In general, these visual organizers can be totally teacher-directed or student-initiated and can be used either before reading, or following reading.

Numerous studies have been conducted to measure the effects of visual organizers on students' learning from text. Moore and Readence (1980) concluded from their meta-analysis of 16 of these studies that only 2% of the variability in text learning could be explained by the use of organizers. The researchers noted, however, that the advantages of organizers were stronger when they were used as a postreading activity and when vocabulary was included as the criterion variable. We should note that since Moore and Readence's meta-analysis in 1980, several studies have demonstrated that students' comprehension significantly improved with the use of visual organizers such as concept maps (e.g., Bernard & Naidu, 1992; McCagg & Dansereau, 1991; Ruddell & Boyle, 1989).

In the limited number of studies we found on visual organizers and vocabulary development, college students were either provided a completed organizer or asked to complete a partially constructed organizer after they had read a text excerpt. Pyros (1980), however, examined the impact of researcher-provided advance organizers on students' vocabulary understanding. The college students in the experimental group were given 1 hour of training on the purpose and function of the advance organizer, whereas the control group received a list of technical terms with definitions that related to the same unit. Both groups then read 2,500-word selections from psychology and economics. Analysis of the data revealed no significant differences between the groups on the immediate and delayed vocabulary measures.

Barron and Schwartz (1984) and Dunston and Ridgeway (1990) provided their subjects with either partially completed or researcher-constructed visual organizers as a postreading strategy. In Barron and Schwartz's study, the graduate students who had completed the skeletal organizers performed significantly better on the vocabulary relationship test than the control group who had studied teacher-provided definitions of the words. Dunston and Ridgeway (1990) examined the impact of researcher-constructed organizers and partially constructed organizers on college freshmen's performance on a test over a chapter taken from a speech course. They found no significant differences between the treatment conditions on the multiple-choice or free recall task. Given that no training was provided in the Dunston and Ridgeway study and that the students had only 70 minutes to read, fill in the visual organizer, and study it in preparation for the test, their findings were not surprising.

Some researchers have examined the effect of combining visual organizers with other types of student activities. Carr and Mazur-Stewart (1988), for example, studied the usefulness of the Vocabulary Overview Guide (VOG), which involved students in developing personal clues for a set of semantically related words and monitoring their understanding of the concepts. Students were also given a four-step procedure for studying the targeted words contained in the VOG. The control group read the same passages, underlined and listed unknown vocabulary words, and then used context clues to define them. A vocabulary posttest and an unannounced delayed test 4 weeks later were administered to measure students' retention of the targeted words. The VOG group scored significantly higher on both the immediate and the delayed vocabulary tests.

Bean, Wells, and Yopp (1981) took a different approach to the study of visual organizers in that they examined students' reactions to the strategy. In their study they found that freshmen in philosophy and history courses rated organizers as either excellent or superior. The students' evaluation led the researchers to conclude that the graphic postorganizer, when accompanied by small group discussion, "appears to increase deep semantic processing" (p. 9).

Of these studies, only Carr and Mazur-Stewart (1988) provided the intensive training necessary for college students to learn how to independently develop a visual organizer and then use that organizer as a study strategy for an upcoming examination. In fact, the students in their study received training with eight practice passages before they even participated in the study. Given that Carr and Mazur-Stewart used passages they had written for the study, it would be useful for future studies to investigate the effectiveness of the organizer strategy using student's textbooks and other forms of naturally occurring prose.

NAIT.   NAIT (Diekhoff et al., 1982), is based primarily on network models of long-term memory structure (Collins & Loftus, 1975; Rumelhart, Lindsey, & Norman, 1972) and the depths of processing approach described by Craik and Tulving (1975). The NAIT strategy was designed to help students systematically select and define key concepts, consider examples and applications, and identify existing relationships among the concepts.

The strategy has four basic stages. In Stage 1, the students are asked to identify key concepts or important terms they need to learn within a text. During the second stage, students use relationship-guided definitions to construct a semantic network around each of the selected key concepts. The authors suggested using a definition worksheet to help students locate the various relationships. In Stage 3, the elaboration stage, students think of examples or potential applications of the key concepts and record these examples on the definition worksheet. During the final stage students identify meaningful similarities and differences among the different concepts being studied.

Diekhoff et al. (1982) tested NAIT for effectiveness with undergraduate students. The experimental group received 3 hours of NAIT training that utilized passages from biology, physics, geography, and geology. Two days after the training, both the experimental and the control groups received two passages from an introductory psychology textbook to study for 60 minutes. The experimental group was told to use NAIT in studying the passages, whereas students in the control group were told to use any of their own learning techniques. Following the study period, all passages and worksheets were collected from both groups. One week later, both groups were given a 30-minute essay test on the passages. The test required the students to define and discuss five experimenter-selected key concepts in as much depth and detail as possible and to make comparisons among pairs of words selected by the researchers. The experimental subjects performed significantly better than the untrained control group on both measures, supporting the effectiveness of the NAIT approach.

The NAIT strategy appears to be promising in that it actively involves the students in the selection of key vocabulary terms and then provides a format that encourages their elaborative processing. As the authors suggested, research should be undertaken to determine the effectiveness of the approach where the test format differs from NAIT's format. The researchers, who have recently studied matrix outlining, a strategy very similar to NAIT, appear to have capitalized on Diekhoff et al.'s findings and recommendations (e.g., Dubois, Staley, Guzy, & DiNardo, 1995; Kiewra, 1994). Their research studies have suggested that matrix outlines can strongly affect students' comprehension of expository text.

Studies on Alternative Delivery Modes

Although there are a variety of alternative delivery modes for teaching vocabulary, we focus on two modes that have been examined in studies with college students: computer-assisted instruction (CAI) and cooperative learning.

CAI.   CAI as a delivery medium seems to have great potential for supplementing college programs designed to promote vocabulary development. That is, CAI could give students increased time on task, accommodate different levels of ability, offer practice on words not yet mastered and avoid repetition of mastered words, and provide a variety of formats to motivate students. These are all positive attributes of CAI. However, unless college reading professionals are selective, there is a danger that the same inherent limitations of some commercial vocabulary materials might also be present in CAI.

We found only three studies that directly examined CAI in the area of vocabulary development. Reinking and Rickman (1990) found a definite advantage for sixth graders who used computers in reading difficult science texts. In their study, students who read science passages on computers received higher scores on a vocabulary measure than either of the groups who read the passages on paper. Also, students who were required to view the definition of each target word before moving on to the next computer screen scored higher than those who were given the option of reading the definition.

Balajthy's (1988) findings are significant to college instructors who wish to use computer instruction as program supplements. He examined the variables of interest, effectiveness, rate of presentation, and achievement and found that students could not accurately evaluate their own learning and confused interest with effectiveness. Each student worked in a traditional vocabulary workbook and with two different computer programs. Overall, the students rated the two computer formats as most effective; however, the workbook format achieved the highest posttest scores with the least time on task. Interestingly, there was no difference in achievement or time on task between students who rated a format effective as opposed to those who rated the same format ineffective. Also, for each format there was a correlation between interest and effectiveness rating. Balajthy suggested that instructors must maintain some degree of control over student choices.

Wheatley, Muller, and Miller (1993) described a computer program they developed for use with at-risk college freshmen. Their instructional foci were contextual analysis and morphology. They found that the computer program allowed most students to reach 90% mastery of target words but did not enhance their ability to derive meaning from context. They outlined the following guidelines for a college computer- assisted vocabulary program:

- The program should be flexible enough that instructors can add and delete words.
- Words must be taken from the texts that students are using in content courses.
- Words should appear in context.
- Students should receive class credit for their work on the computer.
- Corrective tutorials should be specific to errors made by individuals.
- Assessment should be periodic and cumulative.

From the conclusions reached by Reinking and Rickman (1990) and Balajthy (1988), we would add that instructors should carefully decide how much choice students should exercise within the program.

Future researchers might address the following questions: What is the optimal format for CAI (games or text)? Which vocabulary approaches adapt most effectively to CAI delivery? What is the ideal rate of presentation and the number of exposures for new words? How can students be trained to independently monitor their own level of achievement? What is the optimal level of instructor control over the CAI? (Also see Caverly & Peterson, this volume.)

Cooperative Learning.   Neither of the two studies of vocabulary instruction that we examined showed a significant advantage for cooperative learning. Levin, Levin, Glasman, and Nordwall (1992) compared vocabulary instruction across the four treatment conditions of the keyword approach learned either individually or in small groups or contextual analysis learned either individually or in small groups. The intermediate grade students took immediate and delayed tests of definition recall and a cloze measure of sentence comprehension. Although the researchers observed active participation within the small groups, they found no significant difference between the individual and small group treatment for either vocabulary approach.

The research of Hodge, Palmer, and Scott (1993) found no advantage for at-risk college students who were trained to use reciprocal teaching in small groups. Student group leaders helped the members develop summaries, generate and answer questions, clarify concepts and words, and make predictions as they discussed readings. Other students completed traditional skills activities. There was no significant difference in gains on the Nelson–Denny Reading Test (1976) between the groups.

Cooperative learning as a medium of delivery has been used widely in middle and secondary grades in recent years. However, we did not locate enough research on vocabulary acquisition to be able to judge the effectiveness of the medium at the college level. Researchers should address the following questions: What are the attributes of cooperative learning that make it a unique delivery mode? How do the discussions among college students in cooperative groups enhance metacognitive awareness of language learning? Can cooperative learning, as a supplement to other approaches to vocabulary instruction, increase vocabulary acquisition?

Studies on Student-Centered Approaches

A limited number of research studies have examined the impact of capitalizing on students' prior knowledge and interests in order to develop their vocabulary. The studies we located either emphasized the importance of providing concrete, direct background experiences for college students as they learn new words or the importance of involving students in determining what new vocabulary they would learn. We examine both types of studies.

Concrete, Direct Experiences.   The basic assumption in this approach is that students can best understand and remember new vocabulary after they have developed or enhanced their background for the concept the word represents. Manzo (1982) indicated that teachers can enhance students' background through the provision of on-the-spot experiences with follow-up discussions. Tulving (1983) suggested that this type of experience can become a part of a student's *episodic memory*—that is, memory for events. Tulving's theory suggests that vocabulary acquisition must begin in the episodic memory. Once additional contexts for a word are learned, the word, with all its related contexts, becomes a part of the *semantic memory*—the memory for general meanings that can be applied in numerous situations. This should be the ultimate goal of vocabulary instruction.

Petty et al. (1968) concluded from a review of 50 different vocabulary studies that providing experiences in using a word is extremely important in a learner's vocabulary acquisition. Few researchers, however, have experimentally explored this concept with college learners. In the one study found in this area, Duffelmeyer (1980) reported positive results. Duffelmeyer tested the impact of providing experiences with new vocabulary by requiring 56 college students to act out investigator-prepared skits. The skits were built around words taken from passages in the comprehension section of the Nelson–Denny Reading Test (1976). After each dramatization, the investigator asked the class several questions about the targeted word. Then the students were asked to volunteer a personal experience that would convey the meaning of the word. The subjects in the comparative group used a traditional approach that emphasized context clues, structural analysis, and dictionary use. The experience-based group significantly outperformed the traditional group on the exam, supporting Duffelmeyer's hypothesis that college students can benefit from an experience-based approach to general vocabulary growth. However, this method is limited because of the considerable expenditure of time that is required and the improbability that independent transfer will occur.

Students' Input in Selecting Words.   Some researchers propose that a student's vocabulary increases more when the motivation is intrinsic than when it is extrinsic (Goodman, 1976; Haggard, 1980, 1984; Herber, 1978). Haggard concluded from her research on vocabulary acquisition that during their elementary and secondary years, students learned new words because the words had some immediate usefulness or particular significance. She later replicated the study with college-age students to determine if the same motivations for learning new words existed. Over a 6-week period, 42 college sophomores and juniors logged their own vocabulary development in a journal. The most commonly cited reason for learning new words was to be able to use them immediately in order to be more successful in class. The second most commonly reported reason for selecting a particular word was the need to clarify meaning. Of the total number of words learned, 40% were related to courses the students were taking—that is, content-specific words. Haggard concluded that the process of collecting words can definitely enhance a college student's interest in expanding vocabulary, in both course content and general use.

We found only one study that experimentally investigated the value of asking college students to select the words they wish to learn. Whereas Haggard's study was descriptive, Gnewuch (1974) conducted a 12-week empirically based study with 407 college students. Those in the experimental groups (students enrolled in reading classes) skimmed their reading assignments to find words that they knew vaguely but felt they could not define adequately. Then they were asked to write the words in the context in which they were found, make a guess at the meaning, and check that guess against a dictionary definition. Those in the control group (students enrolled in study skills classes) were given no special vocabulary instructions or guidance. The experimental subjects scored significantly higher than the control subjects in vocabulary growth on a standardized reading test. A limitation of this research is the failure to compare the students to controls who were presented word lists developed by instructors. Nevertheless, Gnewuch's findings are sufficiently intriguing to encourage the undertaking of other studies of this type. Future researchers should, however, collect data beyond standardized test scores. For example, it would be informative to interview the students participating in such a project to discover their opinions about this approach and their strategies for learning unknown words.

More research on student-centered vocabulary approaches should be conducted with college students. Of particular interest would be attempts to validate approaches like Haggard's (1982) self-collection strategy.

EFFECTIVE VOCABULARY PRACTICES

Although the extant literature cannot describe a comprehensive program of vocabulary instruction, we rely on some seminal research studies and our own practical teaching experiences with college students to describe some effective vocabulary practices. These seven characteristics, which are not mutually exclusive, include: (a) an emphasis on definitional and contextual knowledge, (b) students' active and elaborative processing, (c) vocabulary in context, (d) students' interest, (e) intense instruction, (f) a language-rich environment, and (g) wide reading.

An Emphasis on Definitional and Contextual Knowledge

From reviews of research on vocabulary acquisition, Stahl (1983, 1985) suggested that a student who really knows a word has both definitional and contextual knowledge about that word. Stahl described *definitional knowledge* as knowledge of the relationships between a word and other known words, such as those that appear in a dictionary definition or a network model of semantic memory (Collins & Loftus, 1975). Because most readers do not break words into their definitional parts during reading, Stahl maintained that another type of information, *contextual knowledge*, is necessary to account for a reader's full knowledge of words. Contextual knowledge is the knowledge of a core concept, first acquired in a specific context, that becomes generalized or decontextualized through a number of exposures in different situations.

What does this research suggest for vocabulary development at the college level? Most important, instruction that emphasizes memorization and pairing of labels to synonyms imparts only definitional knowledge. Such knowledge is likely to have a negligible impact on a student's subsequent reading comprehension or expressive language abilities (Kameenui et al., 1987). Students can easily memorize definitions of words from lists (they have done it all through the elementary and secondary grades), but they quickly forget those verbal associations. Thus, the best vocabulary instruction should emphasize both definitional and contextual information about a word, but with an emphasis on the latter.

Students' Active and Elaborative Processing

Researchers who required students to process new words actively and elaboratively found that these students performed significantly better than their counterparts who were involved in rote memorization and repetition (Beck & McKeown, 1991; Carr & Mazur-Stewart, 1988; Diekhoff et al., 1982). From their reviews, Stahl (1983, 1985), Stahl and Fairbanks (1986), and Mezynski (1983) likewise concluded that active and elaborative processing is critical to students' vocabulary development.

Unfortunately, it appears that most commercial materials do not actively engage students in their own learning; rather, they tend to treat learners as passive recipients of knowledge. In a content analysis of 60 college-level vocabulary texts, Stahl et al. (1987) found that sentence completion and sentence fill-in exercises predominated in 82% of the books, whereas matching exercises appeared in 70% of the texts. Furthermore, these exercises seemed to be designed so students could complete them in environments where they would correct their own work and probably never interact with another individual regarding the new words.

If commercial materials must be used with college students, they could be modified or supplemented in several ways. For example, students could be invited to discuss workbook answers in small or large group settings. Such discussion might engage the students in elaborative processing by encouraging them to justify their answers. Another approach would be to ask students to write their own sentences. Such activities would ensure that both definitional and contextual knowledge of a word is emphasized.

College reading professionals could also examine the numerous activities and assessment formats outlined by Simpson (1987). These activities and formats actively involve students in deeper and more elaborative processing through such activities as imaging, finding examples, applying words to new contexts, comparing and contrasting, and determining interrelationships among words. Moreover, strategies such as the vocabulary overview guide (Carr & Mazur-Stewart, 1988) or NAIT (Diekhoff et al., 1982) could easily be integrated within an existing college reading program whether supplementary vocabulary workbook exercises were used or not.

Vocabulary in Context

The main instructional approach in earlier vocabulary research involved giving students a list of words and requiring them to manipulate and memorize appropriate definitions. The long-term benefits of such an approach on a student's expressive and receptive vocabulary, and on reading comprehension, appear very limited (Baumann & Kameenui, 1991; Beck & McKeown, 1991). Although there are numerous reasons for this lack of effectiveness, one important explanation needs to be emphasized: vocabulary should be taught from a unifying context (Jenkins & Dixon, 1983; Mezynski, 1983). Words taught in the context of a subject area are learned more effectively than words learned in isolation or studied from unrelated lists because context allows words to become integrated with previously acquired knowledge.

Thus, college reading professionals should select or have the students select targeted words from what the students are reading, whether that be textbook chapters, newspapers, magazines, or novels. For example, if students are reading a chapter from a communication arts textbook, words such as *arbitrary, connotation, denotation,* or *syntax* could be studied. Another alternative is to group target words into semantic categories (Beck et al., 1982). One such category could be adjectives that negatively describe a person's actions: *lax, infantile, obsequious, narcissistic.* Whatever approach is used to provide the context and organizing schema, we need to remember that long term vocabulary learning occurs within realistic school-related or life-coping tasks, not within artificially contrived word lists. This is true whether such words come from locally produced or commercially prepared materials.

Students' Interest

We all know the role that student interest plays in our classrooms. That is, when students are interested in what they hear in class or read about in an assignment, this interest significantly impacts their attention, effort, persistence, thinking processes, and performance (Hidi, 1990). Unfortunately, the history of vocabulary instruction does not seem to acknowledge this obvious fact. The common routine of asking students to look up words in a dictionary and write a sentence using the words can be a tedious and mindless task. Most students view such tasks as drudgery, counter to what we want students to believe about word learning. What we need to do as college reading professionals is to create situations where learning new words is fun and intriguing.

One reason student interest may be lacking with current approaches or materials is that someone else (the teacher or the producer of commercial materials) has made the decision concerning the words students are to study and learn. When college students are encouraged to select their own words, greater interest is ensured. Although there are a variety of approaches that encourage and reward students for learning new words of interest to them, Haggard's (1982) vocabulary self-collection strategy (VSS) can easily be incorporated into any college vocabulary program.

VSS capitalizes on these conditions by asking students to bring from their own environments (television, peers, reading) two words that they believe the whole class could benefit from learning. The teacher also selects two words. When the students enter the classroom, they immediately write the words on the chalkboard. Once the class officially begins, the students identify their words and tell what they mean (with a formal or informal definition), where they found the words, and why they feel the class should learn them. After all the words on the board (including the teacher's) have been explained, the class narrows the list to a predetermined number of words. During the next phase, the students who introduced the words selected for study again define their words. The teacher facilitates the discussion by clarifying, redefining, and extending student definitions. At this point, all the students record the selected words and their definitions in their vocabulary journals. By the end of the session, each student has a class list of words in addition to the two words he or she brought in.

We have modified and streamlined VSS to fit our instructional program and students. That is, as a homework assignment students select 10 words a week from articles they have read in the *Newsweek* or other unit-related articles and list those words on a vocabulary ballot, which they hand in to us on Fridays. During the weekend we tally their suggested words, selecting the top 10 words that students wish to learn. On Mondays we distribute a list of those words and where they can be found in the *Newsweek* articles. Those 10 words are the words we study for the week.

In addition to involving students in selecting the words to be studied, we should constantly model and demonstrate our personal excitement about words. As Manzo and Sherk (1971) suggested, "the single most significant factor in improving vocabulary is the excitement about words which teachers can generate" (p. 78). During class discussions, in conversations with students before or after class, or when responding to students' journals or e-mail messages, we should use words that we want our students to consider and eventually integrate into their own expressive and receptive vocabularies. In short, we need to be playful with words so that students regain the excitement about learning that is inherent in all individuals.

Intense Instruction

Researchers have consistently concluded that effective vocabulary instruction needs to be intense. Intense instruction has been characterized as being teacher-directed with the use of multiple examples and repeated exposures to the words, cumulative review in differing contexts, and a variety of expressive activities that require the students' active involvement. Such instruction obviously occurs over a sustained period of time and is recursive in nature (Beck & McKeown, 1991; Stahl & Fairbanks, 1986). Although brief practices can have some effect on students' performance on vocabulary tests, there is considerable memory loss over time. That is, the words students memorized on Friday for a test will likely be forgotten by Monday if the instruction was brief and cursory. Stahl and Fairbanks (1986) suggested that there is little decline in words learned through intense instruction because multiple repetition leads to decontextualized knowledge of word meanings. Moreover, they concluded that students involved in intense vocabulary study tend to have fewer comprehension difficulties caused by a slowness in lexical access.

We need to remember, however, that duration is not the critical characteristic of vocabulary instruction. Mere repetition of a word and its definition over time is not beneficial unless the student is actively involved in processing. Moreover, intense instruction without active student involvement can be boring and counterproductive to the goals of an effective vocabulary development program. An intense model of vocabulary development implies that fewer words should be taught, but in more depth. The words selected for direct instruction, either by the students or the teacher, should be of high utility and relevance to learning across the academic disciplines. When students see or hear the words they have studied in contexts such as their psychology lectures or assigned textbook readings for history, they actually are surprised and excited. This excitement and sensitivity to words is something we need to capture and cultivate.

Language-Rich Environments

Researchers have agreed that word learning should occur within a context that supports literacy and language development (Beck &McKeown, 1991; Cunningham, 1992; Kibby, 1995). College reading professionals can best promote vocabulary growth by working with students to create an environment where learning new words and strategies can be done through genuine communication processes. That is, students should be involved in using all the language systems for learning new words. For example, they should be given opportunities to "try out" words in low-risk situations, to discuss new words daily, and to talk freely and openly about how words relate to their real-world concerns. Because these oral language activities are essential to building students' confidence in using new words, we need to allot sufficient time for them. Once students have acquired this oral language facility, we then can ask them to use their new words in writing assignments and practice activities (Rubin & Dodd, 1987).

In addition, we should make sure we include dialogues and discussions about word learning (Nist & Simpson, 1997). During discussion, teachers and students should work together to determine which generative strategies would be most appropriate for specific words. Discussion might also include *why* certain strategies are appropriate or inappropriate for a given word or group of words. If, for example, students have a difficult time evoking an image or keyword for an unknown word, then another strategy such as a visual organizer might be a better choice. We should always encourage students to consider a variety of vocabulary strategies because there is no one best way to learn new words. However, students can only learn this fact through classroom dialogues and discussions.

Wide Reading

According to Nagy (1988), a proponent of incidental word learning, "increasing the volume of students' reading is the single most important thing a teacher can do to promote large-scale vocabulary growth" (p. 32). Although the merits of wide reading are occasionally debated, most individuals would agree that wide reading can increase students' depth of vocabulary knowledge, their background knowledge, their reading fluency, and their sensitivity or awareness of new words (Baumann & Kameenui, 1991; Carver, 1994; Kibby, 1995). Students who read widely and frequently are the students who have the depth of word knowledge necessary for success in school and in life. They are also the students who perform better on standardized achievement tests such as the Scholastic Aptitude Tests (SAT). We know one SAT review book that tells students that the verbal section of the SAT is nothing more than a test of their vocabulary.

Just as second-language learners are told to read extensively and intensively in order to build their language facility, we need to encourage our students to read beyond what they are assigned to read for classes. The students we encounter in college reading programs are not illiterate, they are aliterate. That is, as high school students they have not read what they were assigned to read nor have they acquired the habit of reading for pleasure. In fact, we have been told by many of our students that they never finished a novel until they came to college. College reading professionals should also keep in mind that what students read is not as important as the fact that they are reading. Forcing students to read the "important" works or classics will not instill a love of reading, and may, in fact, cause negative reactions. Rather than the classics, we like to encourage students to read newspapers, magazines, and popular novels on a daily basis.

These seven effective vocabulary development practices should assist the college reading professional in designing a systematic and comprehensive vocabulary program for students rather than relying on commercial materials to dictate their program. In the next section we offer some final recommendations.

FUTURE DIRECTIONS AND RECOMMENDATIONS

College reading professionals face three major challenges. The first, and perhaps most important, requires that they objectively scrutinize their present programs with the following questions in mind:

1. Does the present vocabulary program offer a balance between more additive approaches designed to encourage general vocabulary development and generative strategies designed to encourage student-initiated, content-oriented, vocabulary growth? Does the program offer a variety of strategies appropriate for individual learning styles?
2. Does the present vocabulary program help students develop an appreciation and sensitivity to words so that they will continue to develop their personal vocabularies on a long-term basis?
3. Does the present vocabulary program provide direct instruction that takes into consideration what it means to know a word at the conceptual level?
4. Does the present vocabulary program use a variety of activities and evaluation measures? Are these supported by theory and research?
5. Most important, does the present vocabulary program have specific goals that match the characteristics of the students? Does this program reflect the academic literacy tasks that students will encounter during their college career?

A second major challenge for college reading professionals is to provide ongoing feedback to the editors and writers of commercial materials concerning the relevance and quality of their products. College reading teachers must not accept without question what publishers present. The need to examine materials in light of their own specific needs, keeping in mind what research has said about effective vocabulary instruction. As

Stahl et al. (1987) concluded, the materials on the market today tend to be based on tradition rather than on research-supported principles. The critical link between researchers and publishers is the teacher; consequently, it is vital that college reading professionals offer their objective and constructive opinions on commercial materials.

The final challenge for college reading professionals is to conduct action-oriented, applied, and empirical research with their own students. The process could begin with valuable descriptive studies, such as Haggard's (1980, 1984), which ask students to share their perceptions of how they learn new words and what strategies they use. A fruitful step is to conduct single-subject research, as Crist (1981) did, or to utilize a quasi-experimental design in an actual classroom setting, like that of Beck et al. (1980). As to the research questions that should be addressed, our main suggestion is to avoid studies that seek to determine a superior strategy. After suffering through countless studies comparing one strategy to another, we should acknowledge what theory and research has already told us—there is no magic answer to long-term and lasting vocabulary development.

ACKNOWLEDGMENT

The authors would like to acknowledge the contributions of Ed Dwyer on an earlier version of this chapter (Simpson & Dwyer, 1991).

REFERENCES AND SUGGESTED READINGS

Albinski, E. E. (1970). Part, whole, and added parts learning of same-stem words and the effect of stem learning on acquisition and retention of vocabulary. *Dissertation Abstracts International, 31,* 1609A.

Anderson, R. C., & Freebody, P. (1981). Vocabulary knowledge. In J. T. Guthrie (Ed.), *Comprehension and teaching: Research reviews* (pp. 77–117). Newark, DE: International Reading Association.

Ausubel, D. P. (1963). *The psychology of meaningful verbal learning.* New York: Grune & Stratton.

Balajthy, E. (1988). An investigation of learner-control variables in vocabulary learning using traditional instruction and two forms of computer-based instruction. *Reading Research and Instruction, 27,* 15–24.

Barron, R. F., & Schwartz, R. N. (1984). *Spatial learning strategies: Techniques, applications and related issues.* San Diego, CA: Academic Press.

*Baumann, J. F., & Kameenui, E. J. (1991). Research on vocabulary instruction: Ode to Voltaire. In J. F. Flood, J. M. Jensen, D. Lapp, & J. R. Squire (Eds.), *Handbook of research on the teaching the English language arts* (pp. 604–632). New York: Macmillan.

Bean, T. L., Wells, J., & Yopp, H. (1981). *University students' perceptions of critical reading guides in history and philosophy.* (ED 211 956)

*Beck, I., & McKeown, M. (1991). Conditions of vocabulary acquisition. In R. Barr, M. L. Kamil, P. B. Mosenthal, & P. D. Pearson (Eds.), *Handbook of reading research* (Vol. II, pp. 789–814). White Plains, NY: Longman.

Beck, I. L., McCaslin, E., & McKeown, M. (1980). *The rationale and design of a program to teach vocabulary to fourth-grade students.* Pittsburgh: University of Pittsburgh, Learning Research Center.

Beck, I. L., & McKeown, M. G. (1983). Learning words well: A program to enhance vocabulary and comprehension. *The Reading Teacher, 36,* 622–625.

*Beck, I. L., McKeown, M. G., & Omanson, R. C. (1987). The effects and uses of diverse vocabulary instructional techniques. In M. G. McKeown & M. E. Curtis (Eds.), *The nature of vocabulary acquisition* (pp. 147–163). Hillsdale, NJ: Lawrence Erlbaum Associates.

Beck, I. L., Perfetti, C. A., & McKeown, M. G. (1982). The effects of long term vocabulary instruction on lexical access and reading comprehension. *Journal of Educational Psychology, 74,* 506–521.

Begg, I. (1972). Recall of meaningful phrases. *Journal of Verbal Learning and Verbal Behavior, 11,* 431–439.

Begg, I. (1973). Imagery and integration in the recall of words. *Canadian Journal of Psychology, 27,* 159–167.

Bernard, R. M., & Naidu, S. (1992). Post-questioning, concept mapping, and feedback: A distance education field experiment. *British Journal of Educational Technology, 23,* 48–60.

Bower, G. H. (1970). Imagery as a relational organizer in associative learning. *Journal of Verbal Learning and Verbal Behavior, 9,* 529–533.

Bower, G. H. (1972). Mental imagery and associative learning. In L. W. Gregg (Ed.), *Cognition in learning and memory* (pp. 51–87). New York: Wiley.

Brown, J. I., Nelson, M. J., & Denny, E. C. (1976). *Nelson–Denny Reading Test* Boston: Houghton-Miflin.

Buikema, J. L., & Graves, M. F. (1993). Teaching students to use context cues to infer word meanings. *Journal of Reading, 36,* 450–457.

Carnine, D., Kameenui, E. J., & Coyle, G. (1984). Utilization of contextual information in determining the meaning of unfamiliar words. *Reading Research Quarterly, 19,* 188–204.

Carr, E. M., & Mazur-Stewart, M. (1988). The effects of the vocabulary overview guide on vocabulary comprehension and retention. *Journal of Reading Behavior, 20,* 43–62.

Carver, R. P. (1994). Percentage of unknown vocabulary words in text as a function of the relative difficulty of the text: Implications for instruction. *Journal of Reading Behavior, 26,* 413–437.

Collins, A. M., & Loftus, E. A. (1975). A spreading-activation theory of semantic processing. *Psychological Review, 82,* 407–428.

Craik, F. I. M. (1979). Levels of processing: Overview and closing comments. In L. S. Cermak & F. I. M. Craik (Eds.), *Levels of processing in human memory* (pp. 447–461). Hillsdale, NJ: Lawrence Erlbaum Associates.

Craik, F. I. M., & Lockhart, R. S. (1972). Levels of processing: A framework for memory research. *Journal of Verbal Learning and Verbal Behavior, 11,* 671–684.

Craik, F. I. M., & Tulving, E. (1975). Depth of processing and the retention of words in episodic memory. *Journal of Experimental Psychology: General, 104,* 268–294.

Crist, R. L. (1981). Learning concepts from contexts and definitions: A single subject replication. *Journal of Reading Behavior, 13,* 271–277.

Crump, B. M. (1966). Relative merits of teaching vocabulary by a direct and an incidental method. *Dissertation Abstracts International, 26,* 901A–902A.

Cunningham, P. (1992). Content area vocabulary: Building and connecting meaning. In E. K. Dishner, T. W. Bean, J. E. Readence, & D. W. Moore (Eds.), *Reading in the content areas: Improving classroom instruction* (3rd ed., pp. 182–189). Dubuque, IA: Kendall/Hunt.

Curtis, M. E. (1987). Vocabulary testing and instruction. In M. G. McKeown & M. E. Curtis (Eds.), *The nature of vocabulary acquisition* (pp. 37–51). Hillsdale, NJ: Lawrence Erlbaum Associates.

Dale, E. (1965). Vocabulary measurement: Techniques and major findings. *Elementary English, 42,* 895–901.

Deighton, L. D. (1960). Developing vocabulary: Another look at the problem. *English Journal, 49,* 82–88.

Diekhoff, G. M., Brown, P. J., & Dansereau, D. F. (1982). A prose learning strategy training program based on network and depth-of-processing models. *Journal of Experimental Education, 50,* 180–184.

DuBois, N., Staley, R., Guzy, L., & DiNardo, P. (1995, April). *Durable effects of a study skills course on academic achievement.* Paper presented at the annual meeting of the American Educational Research Association, Washington DC.

Duffelmeyer, F. A. (1980). The influence of experience-based vocabulary instruction on learning word meanings. *Journal of Reading, 24,* 35–40.

Dunston, P. J., & Ridgeway, V. G. (1990). The effect of graphic organizers on learning and remembering information from connected discourse. *Forum for Reading, 22,* 15–23.

Einbecker, P. G. (1973). *Development of an audiovisual program based upon the acquisition of perceptual knowledge to increase college students' vocabulary.* (ED 101 303)

Eysenck, M. W. (1979). Depth, elaboration, and distinctiveness. In L. S. Cermak & F. I. M. Craik (Eds.), *Levels of processing in human memory* (pp. 89–118). Hillsdale, NJ: Lawrence Erlbaum Associates.

Fairbanks, M. M. (1977, March). *Vocabulary instruction at the college/adult level: A research review.* (ED 134 979).

Gnewuch, M. M. (1974). The effect of vocabulary training upon the development of vocabulary, comprehension, total reading, and rate of reading of college students. *Dissertation Abstracts International, 34,* 6254A.

Goodman, K. S. (1976). Behind the eye: What happens in reading. In H. Singer & R. Ruddell (Eds.), *Theoretical models and processes of reading* (2nd ed., pp. 470–496). Newark, DE: International Reading Association.

Graves, M. F. (1985). *A word is a word...Or is it?* New York: Scholastic.

Graves, M. F., & Hammond, H. K. (1979). A validated procedure for teaching prefixes and its effect on students' ability to assign meaning to novel words. In M. L. Kamil & A. J. Moe (Eds.), *Perspectives on reading research and instruction* (pp. 184–188). Washington, DC: National Reading Conference.

Haggard, M. R. (1980). Vocabulary acquisition during elementary and post-elementary years: A preliminary report. *Reading Horizons, 21,* 61–69.

Haggard, M. R. (1982). The vocabulary self-collection strategy: An active approach to word learning. *Journal of Reading, 26,* 203–207.

Haggard, M. R. (1984, December). *A study of university student vocabulary acquisition: Motivation, sources, and strategies.* Paper presented at the National Reading Conference, St. Petersburg, FL.

Hall, J. W. (1988). On the utility of the keyword mnemonic for vocabulary learning. *Journal of Educational Psychology, 80,* 554–562.

Henry, G. H. (1974). *Teaching reading as concept development: Emphasis on affective thinking.* Newark, DE: International Reading Association.

Herber, H. L. (1978). *Teaching reading in the content areas* (2nd ed.). Englewood Cliffs, NJ: Prentice Hall.

Hidi, S. (1990). Interest and its contribution as a mental resource for learning. *Review of Educational Research, 60,* 549–572.

Hodge, E. A., Palmer, B. C., & Scott, D. (1993). Effects of metacognitive training in cooperative groups on the reading comprehension and vocabulary of at-risk college students. *Research and Training in Developmental Education, 10,* 31–42.

Hopper, J., & Wells, J. C. (1981, April). *The specific vocabulary needs of academic disciplines.* (ED 207-000)

Jenkins, J. R., & Dixon, R. (1983). Vocabulary learning. *Contemporary Educational Psychology, 8,* 237–260.

Jenkins, J. R., Matlock, B., & Slocum, T. A. (1989). Two approaches to vocabulary instruction: The teaching of individual word meanings and practice in deriving word meaning from context. *Reading Research Quarterly, 24,* 215–235.

Kameenui, E. J., Carnine, D. W., & Freschi, R. (1982). Effects of text construction and instruction procedures for teaching word meanings on comprehension and recall. *Reading Research Quarterly, 17,* 367–388.

Kameenui, E. J., Dixon, R. C., & Carnine, D. W. (1987). Issues in the design of vocabulary instruction. In M. G. McKeown & M. B. Curtis (Eds.), *The nature of vocabulary acquisition* (pp. 129-145). Hillsdale, NJ: Lawrence Erlbaum Associates.

*Kibby, M. W. (1995). The organization and teaching of things and the words that signify them. *Journal of Reading, 39,* 208–223.

Kiewra, K. A. (1994). The matrix representation system: Orientation, research, theory, and application. In J. Smart (Ed.), *Higher education: Handbook of theory and research* (pp. 331–373). New York: Agathon.

Levin, J. R. (1993). Mnemonic strategies and classroom learning: A twenty-year report card. *Elementary School Journal, 94,* 235–244.

Levin, J. R., Levin, M. E., Glasman, L. D., & Nordwall, M. B. (1992). Mnemonic vocabulary instruction: Additional effectiveness evidence. *Contemporary Educational Psychology, 17,* 156–174.

Manzo, A. V. (1982). Subjective approach to vocabulary acquisition. *Reading Psychology, 3,* 155-160.

Manzo, A. V., & Sherk, J. K. (1971). Some generalizations and strategies for guiding vocabulary learning. *Journal of Reading Behavior, 4,* 78–89.

Marshalek, B. (1981). *Trait and process aspects of vocabulary knowledge and verbal ability* (Tech. Rep. No. 15). Stanford, CA: Stanford University, School of Education.

Mayer, R. E. (1996). Learning strategies for making sense out of expository text: The SOI model for guiding three cognitive processes in knowledge construction. *Educational Psychology Review, 8,* 357–371.

McCagg, E. C., & Dansereau, D. F. (1991). A convergent paradigm for examining knowledge mapping as a learning strategy. *Journal of Educational Research, 84,* 317–324.

McCarville, K. B. (1993). Keyword mnemonic and vocabulary acquisition for developmental college students. *Journal of Developmental Education, 16,* 2–6.

McDaniel, M. A., & Pressley, M. (1989). Keyword and context instruction of new vocabulary meanings: Effects on text comprehension and memory. *Journal of Educational Psychology, 81,* 204–213.

McKeown, M. G. (1985). The acquisition of word meaning from context by children of high and low ability. *Reading Research Quarterly, 20,* 482–496.

McKeown, M. G. (1993). Creating effective definitions for young word learners. *Reading Research Quarterly, 28,* 17–31.

McNeal, L. D. (1973). Recall and recognition of vocabulary word learning in college students using mnemonic and repetitive methods. *Dissertation Abstracts International, 33,* 3394A.

Mezynski, K. (1983). Issues concerning the acquisition of knowledge: Effects of vocabulary training or reading comprehension. *Review of Educational Research, 53,* 253–279.

Moore, D. W., & Readence, J. E. (1980). Meta-analysis of the effect of graphic organizers on learning from text. In M. L. Kamil & A. J. Moe (Eds.), *Perspectives on reading research and instruction* (pp. 213–218). Washington, DC: National Reading Conference.

*Nagy, W. E. (1988). *Teaching vocabulary to improve reading comprehension.* Newark, DE: International Reading Association.

Nagy, W. E., Herman, P. A., & Anderson, R. C. (1985). Learning words from context. *Reading Research Quarterly, 20,* 233–253.

Nist, S. L., & Olejnik, S. (1995). The role of context and dictionary definitions on varying levels of word knowledge. *Reading Research Quarterly, 30,* 172–193.

Nist, S. L., & Simpson, M. L. (1997). *Developing vocabulary concepts for college thinking* (2nd ed.). Boston: Houghton Mifflin.

O'Rourke, J. P. (1974). *Toward a science of vocabulary development.* The Hague: Mouton.

Paivio, A. (1971). *Imagery and verbal process.* New York: Holt, Rinehart & Winston.

Petty, W. T., Herold, C. P., & Stoll, E. (1968). *The state of knowledge about the teaching of vocabulary.* Champaign, IL: National Council of Teachers of English.

Pressley, M. (1995). More about the development of self-regulation: Complex, long-term, and thoroughly social. *Educational Psychologist, 30,* 207–212.

Pressley, M., Levin, J. R., & Miller, G. E. (1981). How does the keyword method affect vocabulary, comprehension, and usage? *Reading Research Quarterly, 16,* 213–225.

Pressley, M., Levin, J. R., & Miller, G. E. (1982). The keyword method compared to alternative vocabulary-learning strategies. *Contemporary Educational Psychology, 7,* 50–60.

Pyros, S. W. (1980). Graphic advance organizers and the learning of vocabulary relationships. *Dissertation Abstracts International, 41,* 3509A.

Raphael, T. E. (1987). Research on reading: But what can I teach on Monday? In V. Richardson-Koehler (Ed.), *Educator's handbook: A research perspective* (pp. 26–48). New York: Longman.

Raugh, M. R., & Atkinson, R. C. (1975). A mnemonic method for learning a second-language vocabulary. *Journal of Educational Psychology, 67*, 1–16.

Reinking, D., & Rickman, S. S. (1990). The effects of computer-mediated texts on the vocabulary learning and comprehension of intermediate-grade readers. *Journal of Reading Behavior, 22*, 395–408.

Roberts, J., & Kelly, N. (1985). The keyword method: An alternative strategy for developmental college readers. *Reading World, 24*, 34–39.

Rubin, D. L., & Dodd, W. M. (1987). *Talking into writing: Exercises for basic writers.* ERIC Clearinghouse on Reading and Communication Skills: National Council of Teachers of English.

Ruddell, R. B., & Boyle, O. F. (1989). A study of cognitive mapping as a means to improve summarization and comprehension of expository text. *Reading Research and Instruction, 29*, 12–22.

Rumelhart, D. E., Lindsey, P. H., & Norman, D. A. (1972). A process model of long term memory. In E. Tulving & W. Donaldson (Eds.), *Organization of memory* (pp. 198–246). San Diego, CA: Academic Press.

Sartain, H. W., Stahl, N., Ani, U. N., Bohn, S., Holly, B., Smoleski, C. S., & Stein, D. W. (1982). *Teaching techniques for the languages of the disciplines.* Pittsburgh, PA: University of Pittsburgh.

Schatz, E. K., & Baldwin, R. S. (1986). Context clues are unreliable predictors of word meaning. *Reading Research Quarterly, 21*, 439–453.

Simpson, M. L. (1987). Alternative formats for evaluating content area vocabulary understanding. *Journal of Reading, 31*, 20–27.

Simpson, M. L., & Dwyer, E. J. (1991). Vocabulary acquisition and the college student. In R. F. Flippo & D. C. Caverly (Eds.), *Teaching reading & study strategies at the college level* (pp. 1–41). Newark, DE: International Reading Association.

Simpson, M. L., & Nist, S. L. (1997). Perspectives on learning history: A case study. *Journal of Literacy Research, 29*, 363–395.

Simpson, M. L., Hynd, C. R., Nist, S. L., & Burrell, K. I. (1997). College academic assistance programs and practices. *Educational Psychology Review, 9*, 39–87.

Simpson, M. L., Olejnik, S., Tam, A. Y., & Supattathum, S. (1994). Elaborative verbal rehearsals and college students' cognitive performance. *Journal of Educational Psychology, 86*, 267–278.

Smith, B. D., Stahl, N. A., & Neel, J. H. (1987). The effect of imagery instruction on vocabulary development. *Journal of College Reading and Learning, 22*, 131–137.

*Stahl, N. A., Brozo, W. G., & Simpson, M. L. (1987). A content analysis of college vocabulary textbooks. *Reading Research and Instruction, 26*(4), 203–221.

Stahl, N. A., Brozo, W. G., Smith, B. D., Henk, W. A., & Commander, N. (1991). Effects of teaching generative vocabulary strategies in the college developmental reading program. *Journal of Research and Development in Education, 24*, 24–32.

Stahl, S. A. (1983). Differential word knowledge and reading comprehension. *Journal of Reading Behavior, 15*, 33–50.

Stahl, S. A. (1985). To teach a word well: A framework for vocabulary instruction. *Reading World, 24,* 16–27.

Stahl, S. A., & Fairbanks, M. M. (1986). The effects of vocabulary instruction: A model-based meta-analysis. *Journal of Educational Research, 56,* 72–110

Sternberg, R. B. (1987). Most vocabulary is learned from context. In M. G. Mckeown & M. E. Curtis (Eds.), *The nature of vocabulary acquisition* (pp. 89–105). Hillsdale, NJ: Lawrence Erlbaum Associates.

Strader, S. G., & Joy F. (1980, November). *A contrast of three approaches to vocabulary study for college students.* (ED 197 330)

Tennyson, R. D., & Park, O. (1980). The teaching of concepts: A review of instructional design literature. *Review of Educational Research, 50,* 55–70.

Tulving, E. (1983). *Elements of episodic memory.* New York: Oxford University Press.

Tyler, S. W., Hertel, P. T., McCallum, M. C., & Ellis, H. C. (1979). Cognitive effort and memory. *Journal of Experimental Psychology: Human Learning and Memory, 5,* 607–617.

Weiss, A. S., Mangrum, C. T., & Llabre, M. M. (1986). Differential effects of differing vocabulary presentations. *Reading Research and Instruction, 25,* 265–276.

Wheatley, E. A., Muller, D. H., & Miller, R. B. (1993). Computer-assisted vocabulary instruction. *Journal of Reading, 37,* 92–102.

White, T. G., Power, M. A., & White, S. (1989). Morphological analysis: Implications for teaching and understanding vocabulary growth. *Reading Research Quarterly, 24,* 283–304.

Wittrock, M. C. (1990). Generative processes of comprehension. *Educational Psychologist, 24,* 345–376.

4

Comprehension Strategies
at the College Level

↫§§↬

Sherrie L. Nist
Jodi L. Holschuh
University of Georgia

In previous research, Nist and Mealey (1991) described a variety of teacher-directed comprehension strategies based on theories that were prevalent at the time—metacognitive theory, schema theory, and text structure theory. However, the thinking of the field has evolved since then thus causing a reevaluation of the role and theoretical base of teacher-directed comprehension strategies at the college level.

Many of the comprehension strategies Nist and Mealey described as strategic or generative were neither because they were not strategies that students could eventually use on their own. *Strategic* implies a purposive and deliberate selection from a repertoire of strategies (Paris, Lipson, & Wixson, 1983; Pressley, 1986; Winne, 1995). Moreover, generative strategies involve four processes: (a) attention, (b) motivation, (c) knowledge and preconceptions, and (d) generation (Wittrock, 1986, 1990, 1992). The implication of these definitions is that strategies should have cognitive, metacognitive, and affective components and that teacher-directed comprehension strategies should, at some point, lead to and foster students' generative strategy use at the college level. This chapter approaches the topic in a decisively different manner. That is, we discuss the role of teacher-directed comprehension strategies as they are related to the idea that (a) strategies should have cognitive, metacognitive and affective components; and (b) teacher-directed strategies should eventually lead to students' use of generative strategies (Weinstein, 1994; Wittrock, 1986, 1990, 1992).

THEORETICAL RATIONALE

Teacher-directed comprehension strategies that lead to the use of generative strategies appear to have three major elements: metacognitive, cognitive, and affective. Each of these theoretical bases are discussed here.

Metacognitive

Although some aspects of how we currently define *metacognition* are anything but new (e.g., Dewey, 1910; Thorndike, 1917), the term was not directly related to reading comprehension until the late 1970s. At that time, Flavell (1978) defined metacognition as "knowledge that takes as its subject or regulates any aspect of any cognitive endeavor" (p. 8). More recently, Baker and Brown (1984); Brown, Armbruster, and Baker (1986); Garner (1987a); and Garner and Alexander (1989) defined metacognition in more precise terms. These theorists delineate two (not necessarily independent) aspects of metacognition: knowledge about cognition and self-regulation of cognition.

The first key aspect of metacognition, knowledge about cognition, concerns what readers know about their cognitive resources and the regulation of those resources. *Regulation* includes the ability to detect errors or contradictions in text, knowledge of different strategies to use with different kinds of texts, and the ability to separate important from unimportant information. According to Baker and Brown (1984), knowledge about cognition is stable in that learners understand their own cognitive resources, including information about themselves as thinkers. It is also statable in that readers can reflect on their cognitive process and explain what they have done to others. Moreover, knowledge about cognition is domain-specific and can differ depending on the type of material with which students are interacting (Alexander, 1992).

The second key aspect of metacognition is readers' ability to control or self-regulate their actions during reading. *Self-regulation* includes planning and monitoring, testing, revising, and evaluating the strategies employed when reading and learning from text (McWhorter, 1993). In short, metacognition involves the regulation and control of learning, or more specific to this chapter, the regulation and control of the reading process and the strategies employed during this process. Knowledge of cognition also includes having declarative, procedural, and conditional knowledge (Paris et al., 1983). Because of its importance, metacognition has become an integral part of models of reading, studying, and learning (McCombs, 1996; Paris et al., 1983; Thomas & Rohwer, 1986; Weinstein, 1997). In fact, we view metacognition as the foundation of understanding text. Students must be able to judge whether they understand the information presented in a written text, by the instructor during lecture, or some other vehicle as well as the manner in which it was presented.

Research indicates that there are major differences between the metacognitive abilities of good and poor readers (Baker, 1985; Schommer & Surber, 1986; Simpson & Nist, 1997). Nowhere is this discrepancy more clearly seen than in college students. At the same time, by the time students enter college, they are expected to possess metacognitive skills. Professors have little sympathy for students who say they did poorly because they thought they understood the materials but did not, studied the wrong information, or felt ready for a test when they really were not. Moreover, in an environment where 85% of all learning comes from independent reading (Baker, 1974) and texts are central to learning (Voss & Silfries, 1996), college students who are not aware metacognitively probably will experience academic problems (Baker & Brown, 1984).

Although considerable research has been conducted in the area of metacognition, much of it has focused on younger children (e.g., Corkill, 1996). Studies carried out with either high school or college students are more difficult to synthesize because of their smaller numbers and diverse nature. In addition, the college-age participants in these studies were enrolled in regular undergraduate courses (generally introductory psychology), and therefore did not necessarily typify students who would be enrolled in a college developmental or academic assistance reading program. Thus generalizability is something of a problem. Given this caveat, however, we can still draw some useful conclusions.

Recent metacognitive studies involving older students and adults seem to break down into three main classifications: (a) those that compare the metacognitive abilities of skilled and unskilled readers (Baker, 1985; Gambrell & Heathington, 1981; Maki & Berry, 1984; Simpson & Nist, 1997); (b) those that attempt to improve metacognitive abilities with strategic intervention (Larson et al., 1985; Pressley, Snyder, Levin, Murray, & Ghatala, 1987; Thiede & Dunlosky, 1994); and (c) those that attempt to determine how metacognition can be measured in college students (Pintrich, Smith, Garcia, & McKeachie, 1991).

In the comparison studies, differences surfaced in the metacognitive abilities of skilled and unskilled readers at all age levels. Poor readers generally lacked knowledge of comprehension strategies, had misconceptions about the reading process, and did not know what to do about comprehension failures (Gambrell & Heathington, 1981; Simpson & Nist, 1997). In addition, poor readers used different standards by which to judge their understanding (Baker, 1985).

Although research indicates that even college students lack the necessary metacognitive skills (Baker & Brown, 1984; Garner & Alexander, 1989), the results of the intervention studies suggest that college students can better monitor their level of text understanding and test preparedness by employing a variety of strategies. Pressley et al. (1987) found that when adjunct questions were inserted into reading passages on which participants were tested, the students' perceived readiness for examination (PREP) improved. Elaborative devices such as cooperative learning pairs (Larson et al., 1985) have also been found to improve metacognition. Moreover, others have examined accuracy of judgments about learning as a way of examining metacognitive strategies (Dumais, 1992; Thiede & Dunlosky, 1994; Vesonder & Voss, 1985) For example, Thiede and Dunlosky (1994) found that when examining college students' accuracy of judgments about learning (JOL), students had better JOLs for delayed than immediate tests. Accuracy of JOLs was also better for recall than for recognition tasks. Thus training seems to pay off in improving college students' metacognitive abilities.

Effective use of reading and learning strategies implies metacognitive awareness, especially in students' ability to monitor their own learning (Dole, Duffy, & Pearson, 1991). Moreover, strategies that have a metacognitive component and promote thinking about "what" and "how" students know will enable them to perform better (Nist, Simpson, Olejnik, & Mealey, 1991; Pressley et al., 1987; Simpson, Olejnik, Tam, & Supattathum, 1994).

Cognitive

In addition to having a metacognitive component, generative strategies also have a cognitive component. This section addresses the issue of knowledge and the degree to which one's knowledge influences strategic learning.

Cognitive strategies engage students in activities that lead to understanding, knowing, or "making cognitive progress" (Garner, 1988). Currently, when we think about the role that cognition plays in strategic learning, knowledge research comes to mind, particularly research focusing on prior knowledge or schema (Anderson, 1978; Anderson & Pichert, 1978; Anderson, Spiro, & Anderson, 1978) and research focusing on domain knowledge (Alexander, 1992).

Alexander (1996) separates the knowledge research into two categories: *first generation knowledge* and *second generation knowledge*. First generation knowledge focused on knowledge as "pervasive, individualistic, and modifiable" (p. 90). Such studies focused on the importance of prior knowledge in learning (e.g., Anderson, Reynolds, Schallert & Goetz, 1977; Bransford & Franks, 1971), how the knowledge possessed by experts and novices differ (e.g., Chi, Feltovich, & Glaser, 1981; Wineburg, 1991), and how students' knowledge can be impacted through strategy training (e.g., Nist & Simpson, 1988). Alexander referred to what we learned from first generation knowledge as "guiding premises" and suggested that this information has formed a solid foundation on which to build second generation knowledge. According to Alexander, second generation knowledge "has given way to an increased complexity and conditionality" (p. 90) where knowledge is seen as multidimensional and multifaceted.

First Generation Knowledge.   *Schema theory* is rooted in the first generation knowledge studies. Schema theory relates to the effect of prior knowledge on a new learning situation. Like metacognition, schema theory is not new. It emerged in the early 1930s with Bartlett's (1932) somewhat ambiguous definition of schema, although it has been suggested that Bartlett was at least partially influenced by Gestalt psychologists (Anderson & Pearson, 1984).

Since then, schema theory has been defined more specifically as an abstract framework that organizes knowledge in memory by putting information into the correct "slots," each of which contains related parts (Anderson & Pearson, 1984; Just & Carpenter, 1987; Wilson & Anderson, 1986). When new information enters memory, it not only must be compatible with one of the slots, but it must actually be entered into the proper slot before comprehension can occur. Some researchers (e.g., Ausubel, 1963) believe that this knowledge is structured hierarchically, with the most abstract features of a concept at the top and the most concrete features at the bottom.

According to schema theory, comprehension is an interactive process between the text and the reader. Wilson and Anderson (1986) compared this interaction with putting together a jigsaw puzzle. If each piece of incoming information fits perfectly into a slot, if each slot contains important information, and if the text is coherently interpreted (much like the pieces of a puzzle fitting snuggly together), the text has been satisfactorily comprehended. The puzzle analogy breaks down after this, however, because even with a well-written text, the author expects readers to make inferences, and therefore does not provide information for every slot in a schema.

The importance of schema theory and the activation of prior knowledge as it relates to reading comprehension can be seen in the five functions of a schema. These functions affect both the learning and the remembering of textual information (Anderson, 1978; Anderson & Pichert, 1978; Anderson et al., 1978):

1. A schema provides ideational scaffolding. Schemata provide a framework for organizing incoming information and retrieving stored information.
2. A schema permits selective attention. Schemata help readers select the important information from the text.
3. A schema permits inference making. As noted earlier, no text is completely explicit; a reader will always have to make inferences. Schemata allow such inferences by enabling readers to fill in the gaps with preexisting knowledge and to generate hypotheses about missing information.
4. A schema allows orderly memory searches. Because schemata have slots for certain pieces of information, the reader can be guided to the kinds of information that need to be retrieved.
5. A schema facilitates editing and summarizing. This function also relates to readers' abilities to determine key ideas. Because a schema allows readers to distinguish important from unimportant information, it also facilitates the formulation of graphic organizers or questions containing important information.

A considerable amount of the research on schema theory and prior knowledge focuses on various theoretical aspects (Barlett, 1932; Just & Carpenter, 1980; Sanford & Garrod, 1981). In addition, other studies have focused on the practical classroom applications and implications of schemata and prior knowledge. These studies can be grouped into three main categories: (a) manipulation studies, (b) cross-cultural studies, (c) expert–novice studies.

In manipulation studies, participants are asked to call up schemata based on manipulated texts or purposes (e.g., Anderson, Pichert, & Shirey, 1983; Pichert & Anderson, 1977). The overall results of the manipulation research indicate that it is important for college readers to activate the proper schema. But it also suggests that when related but different schema are activated, students may be better able to problem solve and make inferences, although comprehension may be more difficult. Although it is probably safe to say that few texts will be ambiguous as those used in some of the manipulation studies, it is still important for college reading instructors to have a theoretical understanding of why students may have difficulty when they encounter ambiguous texts.

Cross-cultural studies examine how students' cultural familiarity with a topic affects the way they learn and interpret information about that topic. Although these studies were actually few in number and were conducted in the late 1970s and the 1980s, they have considerable implications for reading and understanding at the college level. Cross-cultural studies have compared individuals expected to be familiar with or majoring in particular areas of an ambiguous topic. Depending on their backgrounds, the groups interpreted the passages differently. Similarly, cross-cultural studies have compared students from different cultures or subcultures in terms of their ability to read, comprehend, and interpret culturally related passages (Steffensen, Joag-dev, & Anderson, 1979). The results provided strong evidence for the role that schemata play in reading comprehension. Participants spent more reading time on the culturally unfamiliar passage and made more distortions when recalling that passage. In addition, participants recalled more culturally important propositions from the culturally familiar passage.

Expert–novice studies, which can be found in both first and second generation research present a topic and then compare the learning strategies of participants who have little knowledge about that topic with the strategies of knowledgeable participants. Furthermore, both the experts and the novices are equivalent in terms of intelligence, verbal ability, and reading ability. Studies such as those by Spilich, Vesonder, Chiesi, and Voss (1979), and Chiesi, Spilich, and Voss (1979) suggested that those who know a lot about a topic can remember and synthesize important information better than those with little topic knowledge.

Second Generation Knowledge.   Although there is some overlap in the types of studies conducted over the two generations of knowledge research, one of the major differences between the two is that early research studied knowledge as one dimensional (Alexander, 1992). Second generation knowledge, however, focuses more on the interactive nature of knowledge, taking into consideration other factors such as beliefs, strategies, and task. For example, recent studies examined the interaction of knowledge and task (Simpson & Nist, 1997), knowledge and beliefs (Alexander & Dochy, 1995; Schommer, 1990), and knowledge and strategies (Alexander & Judy, 1988). Of particular importance in this chapter, is the interaction between domain and strategy knowledge, which Alexander (1992) believed helps researchers better address complex problems such as how transfer can be achieved. In addition, knowledge is no longer viewed as operating independently of the affective or motivational components (Alexander, 1996). These interactions are most clearly evident in current theories of learning and studying (e.g., McCombs, 1996; Thomas & Rohwer, 1986; Weinstein, 1997), which portray the interactive nature of knowledge as a combination of metacognitive, cognitive, and affective components.

Another difference between the two generations of knowledge is that second generation knowledge is domain-specific. That is, knowledge is seen as situational and is studied within a particular context (Alexander, 1996). Because the structure of domains differ, strategies to understand information differ as well (Alexander & Judy, 1988; Simpson & Nist, 1997). Researchers initially believed that if students knew some general learning strategies they would be able to transfer these skills to a variety of domains. However, this does not seem to be the case.

Finally, domain knowledge is currently viewed as a body of knowledge that is outside of an individual as an acknowledged corpus of knowledge. As such, because it is always evolving, domain knowledge is never complete. Furthermore, the acquisition of domain knowledge progresses in stages, from acclimation, to competence, and finally to proficiency/expertise (Alexander, 1998). But domain knowledge is also defined as the declarative, conditional, and procedural knowledge that individuals have about a specific field of study (Alexander, 1992). Declarative knowledge is "knowing that," procedural knowledge is "knowing how," and conditional knowledge is knowing "when and where." For example, in selecting strategies to use to learn history, declarative knowledge would be "Text marking would be an appropriate strategy to use," procedural knowledge would be "I know how to pull the information out in the form of a time line in the margins of my book," and conditional knowledge would be "I know that time lines would help me learn the chronology, but I will need to select another strategy in order to see the relationships among key events."

Over these two generations of research, we have learned much about the nature of knowledge. The first generation provided a solid framework, especially in helping us gain an understanding of the role of schema in learning. The second generation portrays knowledge in a more interactive way suggesting that students are neither cognitively or affectively inert (Pintrich & Garcia, 1994). And as Alexander (1996) aptly pointed out, one's prior knowledge includes beliefs, attitudes, and values, not just domain information. Both generations of knowledge research have certainly influenced strategy instruction at the college level.

Affective

In addition to having metacognitive and cognitive components, generative strategies also have an affective component. Affective influences have been described as related to self-schemas (Pintrich & Garcia, 1994). In general, an individual strives to achieve positive self-schemas and to avoid or prevent negative self-schemas. In this sense, affective influences can provide the motivation for self-regulated learning and strategy use. Although there are many dimensions of the affective component, we will address three major influences on comprehension that are often influenced by instruction: motivation, beliefs about text, and epistemological beliefs.

Motivation. Motivation is one affective component that is influenced by instruction. Motivation is a function of students' perceptions of the value of information (McCombs, 1996). Wittrock (1986) defined motivation as the process of initiating, sustaining, and directing activity. In an alternate view of motivation, Paris and Turner (1994) coined the term *situated motivation*, which is dependent on specific situations. Situated motivation is based on the framework of self-regulated learning because it involves evaluating, monitoring, and directing one's learning. Motivation is situated based on personal beliefs, instructors, materials, and task. According to this definition, motivation, like metacognition, is unstable because an individual's goals are not the same in all settings and may vary as a consequence of the learner's assessment of expectations, values, goals, and rewards in a particular setting. Thus, it is an appropriate model for college learning where tasks, expectations, rewards, and goals vary greatly.

There are four characteristics that influence situated motivation (Paris & Turner, 1994). First, choice or intrinsic value plays a role. This is consistent with Schiefele (1991) who found that students who had a personal interest in the text information used appropriate learning strategies to process text more deeply and reported a higher quality of experience. Second, challenge is important because students are not motivated when they experience success at tasks that did not require effort. A third important characteristic is control; students who have control over their learning situations tend to be more highly motivated. Most of the tasks involved in college learning are not under students' control nor can teachers grant total freedom or control to their students, but students do have volitional control over the strategies they choose to learn material. Finally, collaboration, or social interaction with peers affects motivation. Social interaction is motivational because talking to peers can enhance students' interests. Also feedback provided by peers is often more meaningful than the feedback provided by instructors (Paris & Turner, 1994). However, unlike secondary schools, reading and studying in college is often done in isolation (Winne, 1995).

Academic performance depends on the ways that motivation and the use of learning strategies are influenced based on the characteristics of the instructor, the task, and the class (Collins-Eaglin & Karabenick, 1994; Pokay & Blumenfeld, 1990). Learning strategies are typically viewed as an aid to motivation because using effective learning strategies can create a sense of control over achievement. This is a cyclical process because a sense of control may raise a students' sense of self-efficacy, which can lead to using more effective learning strategies (Corno, 1989; Pintrich & DeGroot, 1990; Schunk, 1991; Zimmerman, Bandura, & Martinez-Pons, 1992).

Students' self-efficacy is also related to motivation and to the types of strategies used by learners. Students with low self-efficacy often use less effective strategies such as memorization of facts, whereas students with higher self-efficacy rely on more elaborative learning strategies (McCombs, 1988). The ability to select and use appropriate learning strategies for a task are characteristics of an "expert learner" (Nolen, 1988), however, some students report rarely use learning strategies although they know about the benefits (Schiefele, 1991). This could be because of skill and will issues. Researchers have found that students will not use learning strategies if they do not feel that the task is challenging enough to warrant strategy use (McCombs, 1996; Paris et al., 1983).

College instructors often feel frustrated by their apparent inability to "motivate" students to learn (Svinicki, 1994). McCombs (1996) stated that the key to understanding motivation is the realization that students are naturally motivated to learn. By examining the relationship among motivation, cognition, strategy use, and self-regulated learning, educators find common conclusions about enhancing students natural motivation. First, students learn best in classrooms that encourage a mastery approach to learning (Dweck & Leggett, 1988; Nolen, 1988). Second, motivation can affect the use of effective learning strategies (Pintrich & DeGroot, 1990). Students need to feel that the task is challenging enough to warrant strategy use and they will use deeper processing strategies if they have a mastery approach to learning. Third, motivation is unstable and varies from content to content (Paris & Turner, 1994). Students' self-efficacy varies based on their perceived ability (Schunk, 1991). Finally, although research has indicated that motivation is domain-specific, perhaps the factors that lead to students' motivation are not. Student motivation for learning seems to be based on the factors of goal orientation, use of effective strategies, and self-regulated learning (McCombs, 1996). Motivation also appears to be related to strategy selection and epistemological beliefs (Pintrich & Garcia, 1994).

Beliefs About Text.   The idea that students bring an array of beliefs about specific concepts or even complete domains to a learning situation is not particularly new. We know that students' prior knowledge, of which beliefs are a part, influences comprehension at all levels. Some students believe that everything they read in text is truth. Even if we know better, it is somehow difficult not to be drawn into the printed page (Williams, 1994). How such beliefs influence students' interactions with text is a topic of interest to researchers and practitioners alike.

Several generalizations can be made about what research has shown about text beliefs. First, epistemological beliefs seem to influence text beliefs (Schommer, 1994a). Whether or not beliefs cut across texts within domains or the domains themselves is yet to be determined (e.g., Jehng, Johnson, & Anderson, 1993; Schommer, 1994b). Second, mature learners approach texts from different disciplines in different ways (Carson, Chase, & Gibson, 1992). That is, effective learners believe that science text is approached differently than history text. Third, even when text is persuasive, it is very difficult to change one's beliefs (Chambliss, 1994). Finally, experts and novices have beliefs about text that cause them to respond to and interpret text in different ways (Wineburg, 1991).

For example, Wineburg's (1991) research concerning students' beliefs about history text suggests that *subtexts*, or underlying texts, supplement the more explicit meaning of the text. Wineberg had college history professors and bright college-bound high school seniors think aloud as they read seven different historical texts, asking both groups to verbalize their thoughts about the content (not the processes). Although his results were not particularly shocking—historians knew more history than the students did—students rarely saw the subtexts in what they were reading. Wineburg suggested that this inability to understand a writer's point of view is based on what he calls "an epistemology of text" (p. 510). That is, in order to be able to detect subtexts, students must believe that they actually exist. Moreover, he also concluded that students treat their texts as indisputable sources of information and suggests that reading should be taught as a way to "engage in new kinds of thinking" rather than simply as a way to learn new information (p. 515).

Although research in the area of text beliefs is in relatively early stages, it is clear that such beliefs do influence text understanding and approaches that students use to comprehend text information. Moreover, such beliefs seem to spill over into strategies that students select to learn text information as well as the more general beliefs that students possess about what constitutes knowledge and learning.

Epistemological Beliefs.

Epistemological beliefs also play a role in the affective component. *Epistemological beliefs* are defined as a set of beliefs about the nature of knowledge and the process of knowing (Hofer & Pintrich, 1997; Schommer 1990, 1994b). Because there is a growing body of research suggesting their influence on comprehension, thinking, and reasoning (Hofer & Pintrich, 1997; Schommer 1994b), epistemological beliefs have current interest to educators. Research on epistemological beliefs began as an attempt to determine some of the contributing factors to difficulties students face in learning (Perry, 1970; Schommer, 1994a).

Historically, epistemological beliefs were thought of as a system of complex unidimensional beliefs. Perry (1968, 1970) believed that students progressed through fixed stages of development. The college student begins in a naïve position and moves through a series of nine fixed positions on the way to a mature cognitive understanding. In the initial position, called *basic dualism*, the student views the world in polar terms: right or wrong, good or bad. Right answers exist for every question, and a teacher's role is to fill students' minds with those answers. The student then moves through a series of middle positions to a position of *multiplicity*, in which a student begins to understand that answers may be more opinion than fact and that not all answers can be handed down by authority. From this position, a student may move to a position of *relativism*. In this position, a student understands that truth is relative and that it depends on the context and the learner. A student who has moved to the position of relativism believes that knowledge is constructed.

More recently, Schommer's research has examined a system of more or less independent, multidimensional epistemological beliefs that may influence students' performance (Schommer, 1990, 1994b; Schommer & Walker, 1995). Schommer and others have defined epistemological beliefs about learning as an individual's beliefs about the certainty of knowledge, the organization of knowledge, and the control of knowledge acquisition (Schoenfeld, 1988; Schommer & Hutter, 1995). Moreover, these beliefs are thought to develop over time and can change depending on content, experience, and task (Schommer, Calvert, Gariglietti, & Bajaj, 1997). Research has indicated that students' epistemological beliefs are most obvious in higher order thinking, because students need to take on multiple perspectives and process information deeply rather than memorize information (Schommer & Hutter, 1995).

According to Hammer (1995), in order to develop mature beliefs, teachers must assign classroom tasks that encourage such beliefs. This view is supported by Jehng et al. (1993) who reasoned that students' epistemological beliefs are shaped by their schooling. As students obtain more education, their beliefs about learning become more sophisticated. It appears, then, that the early school years do have an effect in shaping a student's beliefs about the nature of knowledge (e.g., Schoenfeld, 1985).

Evidence of the importance of instruction on the development of epistemological beliefs can be found in Hammer's research. Hammer (1995) extended his research on the influence of epistemological beliefs about physics to the teaching of physics by including activities in his own teaching that would promote more mature epistemological beliefs. To promote the belief that knowledge is complex, Hammer required a three-part structure for answering questions about the text. First, students chose what they thought was the correct answer and explained why. Second, students identified the tempting wrong answer and explained why someone might think it was correct. Third, students explained why the way of thinking in the second part did not work for this problem. Thus, to answer all three parts of each problem, students needed to understand the concept well enough to explain alternate conceptions. A student who learned isolated pieces of information would not be able to respond to the second and third parts of the problem. If teachers hope to promote certain epistemological beliefs, Hammer concluded that these beliefs needed to be integrated into classroom instruction.

Oldfather and Dahl (1994) viewed *epistemological empowerment* as an extension of metacognition. Epistemological empowerment has to do with an individual's beliefs in his or her ability to construct meaning or to know something. Students who are epistemologically empowered believe that knowledge comes from within, not from external sources, they make sense of things from their own standpoint, and they understand that there are multiple viewpoints on many issues. However, those who are not epistemologically empowered believe that knowledge lies with external authority. They may view knowledge as consisting of independent facts that they must absorb. This impacts instruction because epistemological empowerment is facilitated in classes where teachers give students a sense of ownership in the construction of knowledge (Belenky, Clinchy, Goldberger, & Tarule, 1986; Thomas & Oldfather, 1997). One way to encourage epistemological empowerment is through creating a classroom environment of respect for student opinions and by giving students a voice in the classroom. In addition, instructors' beliefs about knowledge influence their instruction (Thomas & Oldfather, 1997). Teachers who believe that knowledge is based on a static, objective reality that develops over time, will use classroom assessments that reflect that belief (i.e., assessments based on right and wrong answers). This type of assessment places emphasis on the content of knowledge rather than on the process of knowing. However, when teaching students to use comprehension strategies for college learning, alternate assessments that emphasize process and direct instruction of strategies for learning may be more effective.

It is apparent from the current research that there is a relationship between students' beliefs and their comprehension of text. But it is less clear as to how strategy selection is related to students' beliefs. However, based on our current understanding of both epistemological beliefs and strategy use, we know that both can be enhanced through direct instruction.

DIRECT INSTRUCTION

A discussion of teacher-directed comprehension strategies would be incomplete without a review of the importance and elements of direct instruction. The relevance of direct instruction emerged from the teacher effectiveness research that received attention in the late 1970s and early 1980s (Berliner, 1981; Rosenshine, 1979). The emergence in the early 1970s of cognitive psychology, which emphasized the reading process rather than the product, also has contributed to recognition of the important role direct instruction plays in the reading process. As a result, educators have realized that when students get 5 out of 10 items correct it does not necessarily mean that they know only 50% of the information. It means that instruction should consider the kinds of items students are missing and why they are missing them. These ideas are slowly beginning to penetrate college reading programs and general college classrooms today.

Chiseri-Strater (1991) stated that "extensive and demanding reading is at the heart of most liberal arts classes as well as coursework in other disciplines. ... What we learn is embedded in how we learn" (p. 160). Anyone who is a strategic learner knows this to be true. Hence, students need to be taught explicitly a repertoire of strategies and receive instruction on how to apply them (Pressley, Symons, Snyder, & Cariglia-Bull, 1989). Most students, however, do not receive direct training in application of comprehension strategies (McKeachie, 1988).

Nonetheless, research does indicate that students who receive direct strategy instruction perform better than students who did not (Brown, Campione, & Day, 1981). For example, Nist and Simpson (1988) found that students who received direct instruction in how to annotate text increased their studying efficiency and their performance. In addition, Casazza (1993) found that students taught to write summaries using the direct instruction model of explanation, modeling, questioning, and application (EMQA; Irwin, 1986), were more successful in learning to write summaries than students who were not taught using EMQA. It appears that direct instruction can do more than just improve recall of information; it can show students ways to enhance their own knowledge (Brown et al., 1981).

Several researchers suggest that strategy training should include three components (Brown et al., 1981; Pressley & Harris, 1990; Pressley et al., 1989). First, students should become familiar with a definition or description of the strategy. Researchers believe that it is important to give a concrete and complete explanation of the strategy at the onset of training because students will be more likely to use the strategies effectively if they understand what the strategies are and why they work (Nist & Kirby, 1989; Pressley et al., 1989). Second, an explanation of why the strategy should be learned must be addressed because providing this explanation is important for facilitating students' self-control of the strategy (Jones, 1988; Pressley & Harris, 1990). Moreover, students will apply the strategy more effectively if they understand why it is important (Brown et al., 1981; Garner, 1987b). Third, providing instruction on how to use a strategy, including both teacher modeling and direct instruction, will facilitate learning (Hare & Borchardt, 1984; Pressley et al., 1989).

Direct instruction includes the following interrelated steps:

1. *Modeling the Process.* The instructor must show the "how" of learning. Instructors think aloud, showing students how a mature learner thinks through an idea or solves a problem. Modeling the strategy should be done through concrete examples and explicit verbal elaboration. According to Pressley and Harris (1990), teacher modeling of strategy and self-regulated use of the strategy are what constitutes good instruction.
2. *Providing Examples.* During this phase the instructor shows students examples of how the strategy has been used in a variety of contexts. Providing examples of the strategy helps students understand how the strategy works (Pressley et al., 1989).
3. *Practicing Strategy Use.* Strategy practice should be guided at first, where students repeat the instructor's strategy using new situations or problems. Instructors should be available to help students and to provide feedback. Eventually, students should practice independently outside the classroom (Nist & Kirby, 1989; Pressley et al., 1989).
4. *Evaluating Strategy Use.* Evaluation that includes both teacher-provided feedback and self-monitoring techniques will help students become independent learners (Pressley et al., 1989). In addition, students need to become familiar with the appropriate circumstances for strategy use.

Another configuration of direct instruction is the *cognitive apprenticeship* method (Brown, Collins, & Duguid, 1989). In this model the instructor (a) *models* the strategy in an authentic activity, (b) supports the students doing the task through *scaffolding*, (c) allows the students to *articulate* their knowledge and monitor the effectiveness of the strategy on their learning, and (d) gradually *fades* or withdraws support so the students become proficient. This model was developed to illustrate how students best learn mathematics, but it has implications for other content classrooms.

Pressley et al. (1989) found that the more explicit the level of instruction, the greater the effects of the training. Direct instruction is essential for students to become aware of the strategic nature of reading and to utilize strategies independently (Grant, 1994). It has also been shown that using explicit instruction for strategy training aids both high- and low-ability students, although low-ability students require extended instruction (Jones, 1988). With both of these models for direct instruction, the responsibility for learning shifts from the instructor to the student. When students become responsible for their own learning the transfer of strategic knowledge occurs.

Every college reading instructor strives to get students to the point of transfer, but this is a difficult goal to accomplish, especially with at-risk students (Mealey & Frazier, 1992). Research on strategy instruction offers substantial evidence that students need direct instruction on strategy selection and use, especially at-risk learners. The next section discusses teacher-directed comprehension strategies that can be used to help students become self-regulated learners and to transfer information to new learning situations.

STRATEGIES

This section discusses teacher-directed comprehension strategies that lead toward generative use. Furthermore, the strategies presented have metacognitive, cognitive, and affective components. To review, generative strategies are behaviors and thoughts used to influence comprehension (Wittrock, 1986, 1990, 1992). In this model, then, strategies are active and their use requires effort. Furthermore, college students must be able to generate meaning by building relations between the text and what they already know. They may assimilate the knowledge into their existing schemata or may construct a new schema to incorporate the new information. This active learning model implies that the mind is not passive while reading; rather it is actively organizing, isolating, and elaborating on key information (Wittrock, 1990).

We also focus on strategies that are flexible. Strategies should be flexible in order to be utilized in a variety of contexts and must eventually be self-selected by the learner to attain a specific goal (Nist et al., 1991; Weinstein, 1994). Effective comprehension strategies should allow students to actively interact, elaborate, and rehearse the text information in order to retain it for later use (Nist & Simpson, 1988). In addition, strategy selection necessitates a deliberate decision and effort by the learner (Paris et al., 1983). However, before many students are able to self-select appropriate learning strategies they need a good deal of direct instruction and scaffolding. The ultimate goal is for students to use the strategy or modifications of a strategy without guidance from the instructor.

We need to make one final comment about strategy use. The results of research examining the efficacy of strategy use has not been consistent. Many studies did not allow students to self-select strategies; instead, the studies focused on comparing one strategy with another in a horse race—the best strategy wins in the end. Another reason for inconsistent results occurred is because the studies did not portray normal reading/studying conditions by imposing time constraints or by employing extremely short, easy passages (Wade & Trathen, 1989). In addition, many strategies used in college reading classes do not have support in research. Even fewer have been researched using at-risk students enrolled in college reading courses. Instead, these strategies are found in content reading texts or other methods resources.

For these reasons we concentrate on the processes underlying strategy use than on specific strategies, and we offer suggestions of strategies that embody those processes.

Where possible we cite research that has been used with high school and college students. We narrowed our focus to strategies that met two basic criteria. First, the strategies had to possess metacognitive, cognitive, and affective components. Second, they had to be strategies that can be scaffolded. In other words, they must be strategies that students can eventually generate themselves. We discuss specific strategies within the processes of organizing information, isolating key ideas, and elaborating on information.

Organizing Strategies

The purpose of organizing strategies is to build and activate students' background knowledge, cue awareness of the quality and quantity of that knowledge, and focus attention before reading. Many types of organizing activities are presented in content area reading texts, but only some of these strategies are generative in nature and have cognitive, metacognitive, and affective elements. For example, early work in organizing strategies focused on advanced organizers (Ausubel, 1963, 1968), which would not be considered generative. However, teaching students how to create graphic organizers, concept maps, and how to preview texts would be generative because students would be able to eventually use these strategies on their own.

Graphic Organizers.   Graphic organizers (Barron, 1969, also called *structured overviews*) are hierarchically arranged tree diagrams of a text's key terms and concepts. In a revealing meta-analysis, Moore and Readence (1984) found that graphic organizers were more effective than the advance organizers from which they derive (Moore & Readence, 1980).

Graphic organizers are generative in that they can be used in a variety of learning and studying situations. Although they were originally used as a teacher-directed prereading activity, and can be introduced as such, the effectiveness of graphic organizers is more pronounced when students devise them as a postreading strategy, expanding them to take the form of concept maps (Moore & Readence, 1984). Moore and Readence also suggested that student involvement may be the reason for graphic organizers' reported effectiveness. This idea supports Dinnel and Glover's (1985) finding that student encoding of graphic organizers may be a key factor in their effectiveness.

Teaching college students to use graphic organizers in a generative way can begin with instructors using graphic organizers as an overview of a text or to introduce new vocabulary or terms. Indeed, there is some evidence from the Moore and Readence (1984) meta-analysis to suggest that the construction of graphic organizers enhances the teacher's feeling of preparation. However, instruction can also show students how graphic organizers can be useful in helping to visualize text structure by indicating cause–effect, problems–solution, compare–contrast, chronology, and other patterns (for guidance in developing text structure graphic organizers, see Readence, Bean, & Baldwin, 1985). Hence, graphic organizers contain strong cognitive and metacognitive elements. Visual representations of key concepts often enable students to see these organizational patterns, thus making the text's structure more explicit. They encourage students to see how knowledge in a particular domain is structured and can provide students with a guide as they talk through important text information.

One of the drawbacks of graphic organizers is that students may need strong verbal skills for the graphic organizer to be effective, especially as a prereading strategy (Tierney & Cunningham, 1984). On the positive side, the form that graphic organizers take can be varied according to the desired purpose. In addition, training in this strategy may indeed facilitate transfer to new texts (Dansereau, Holley, & Collins, 1980). Moreover, more recent studies on mapping, a type of graphic organizer (Bernard & Naidu, 1992; Briscoe & LaMaster, 1991), conclude that mapping can be effective especially in classes where synthesis, rather than memorization of facts, is required. Students who benefit most are those who are persistent in using the strategy and those who have high content knowledge in a particular domain (Hadwin & Winne, 1996).

Concept Mapping.   Concept maps allow students to create a visual representation of information (Hadwin & Winne, 1996). Maps sometimes look like flow charts, depicting a hierarchy or linear relationship, or they can be created in such a way to represent complex interrelationships among ideas. Mapping helps students link concepts together and also increases their metacognitive awareness of their comprehension of text information. Research has found that at-risk college learners perform better on exams when they have received direct instruction on the use of mapping (Lipson, 1995). Mapping has been shown to facilitate learning in many content areas because this strategy helps students organize information, relate it to their prior knowledge, and elaborate on the relationships between ideas by providing personal examples (Lipson, 1995). Lipson (1995) described mapping in the following manner. First, students identify key concepts, then they identify supporting concepts, then they identify relationships between the key and supporting concepts.

One of the drawbacks of concept mapping is that students who are having difficulty with the information will have trouble constructing maps by themselves. Research has indicated that students with low content knowledge may feel insecure about concept mapping (Hadwin & Winne, 1996). One of the benefits of concept mapping is that it helps students identify relationships among ideas (Lipson, 1995). In addition, concept mapping helps students process information at deeper levels.

As previously mentioned, students must have fairly well-honed metacognitive skills in order to organize the relationships between and among ideas. Therefore, in order for graphic organizers to be generative, instructors need to provide students initially with a great deal of direct instruction, practice, and feedback. Then instruction needs to be scaffolded as students grapple with more lengthy texts, become familiar with various organizational patterns, and detect key concepts and their interrelationships.

Previews.   Another organizer that can become generative in nature is the *preview* (Graves & Cooke, 1980). Previews are more than just introductory statements. Rather they are somewhat lengthy descriptions that provide upcoming information about a piece of text students will read. The major purpose of previewing is to activate knowledge, to aid in organization, and to provide purposes for reading. In addition, previewing allows time for reflection on what is to be read (Nist & Diehl, 1998). As such, previewing also has metacognitive, cognitive, and affective components.

Initially, instructors might try to link students' existing knowledge with new information that will be encountered. Instead of simply assigning a section to read, the instructor builds anticipation and interest in the content, directs students' attention, and reminds them, through discussion, of what they already know about the topic at hand. In addition, previewing allows instructors to "plant" purpose-setting questions and thoughts in order to give students direction when they read. Finally, because previewing allows for reflection, it can also lead to increased metacognitive awareness.

Although some research exists that validates the effectiveness of previewing, especially with difficult materials (Alvarez, 1983; Graves & Cooke, 1980; Graves & Prenn, 1984; Risko & Alverez, 1986), much of what has been written about the process is written in college reading and studying texts (e.g., Nist & Diehl, 1998; Nist & Simpson, 1996; Pauk, 1994). Such texts provide students with guidelines on how to preview and the role that previewing plays in overall text understanding. Yet, our own experience shows that it is difficult to get students to take this step on their own before they begin to interact with text. Worse yet, it is often difficult to convince students that previewing can be used to their advantage in instances where they just do not have time to read the entire chapter before attending a lecture. Thus, getting college students to the point where they have the will to engage in previewing on their own, although they might have obtained the skill, can be a challenge.

Isolating Key Information

In addition to organizing, students must also be able to isolate key information. The purpose of isolating key information is to reduce the amount of information that a student must remember. Thus, teaching isolation is crucial and difficult because the inability to identify important information can lead to academic frustration and failure.

Research has indicated that many students encounter difficulty in isolating important material (Anderson & Armbruster, 1984; Nist & Kirby, 1989). That is, many students are unable to distinguish between important and unimportant information. Some of the most widely used strategies for isolating key ideas are text-marking strategies. As students read and mark they isolate and concentrate on the information at the time of reading, thereby engaging in deeper processing of the information (Nist & Hogrebe, 1987). However, because high school students are not permitted write in their books, students may come to college without appropriate text-marking strategies and will not be able to effectively use these strategies without explicit training (Nist & Kirby, 1989).

Underlining and Highlighting.   Although the research on underlining and highlighting is extensive, the findings are very inconsistent. Some researchers found no difference when comparing underlining with other strategies (Hoon, 1974; Stordahl & Christensen, 1956). Other researchers found underlining less effective than other strategies such as note taking (Kulhavy, Dyer, & Silver, 1975). Still other studies found underlining to be more effective compared with other text-marking techniques such as starring key ideas or bracketing important concepts (Rickards & August, 1975). In addition, a majority of these studies used very short passages in a laboratory setting, which does not accurately reflect how students mark text in natural settings with college-level material. Furthermore, because studies used different research methodologies and statistical analyses to reach their results, the best generalization we can make concerning the research on underlining and highlighting is that, as a strategy, it appears not to be harmful (Nist & Hogrebe, 1987). Although underlining and highlighting are popular methods of isolating information, they do not meet Wittrock's (1990) definition of generative learning because they do not require students to organize, transform, or elaborate on the material. We include them here, however, because instructors can teach these strategies as a beginning point, moving on to more generative strategies such as annotation.

One of the drawbacks of underlining or highlighting is that neither method actively engages students in selecting the key ideas. In other words, underlining is passive. Students often mark text that appears to be important but may not be (Nist & Kirby, 1989). In addition, because students need fairly well-developed metacognitive skills to be able to monitor their understanding as they underline, many simply underline or highlight material that they do not comprehend. But underlining does have its benefits. One benefit is that it is a strategy that students spontaneously select and thus, is one that they will be likely to transfer to many different learning situations. (For further discussion of underlining and highlighting, see Caverly, Orlando, & Mullen, chap. 5, this volume.)

Annotation.   Another text-marking strategy for isolating key ideas is text *annotation.* Annotation, which, unlike underlining and highlighting is generative in nature, and has metacognitive, cognitive, and affective components. Annotation is a logical "next step" or additional step in the teaching students how to isolate key information.

Annotating text includes the following components: (a) writing brief summaries in the text margins in the students' own words, (b) enumerating multiple ideas (e.g., cause–effect relations, characteristics), (c) noting examples in the margins, (d) putting information on graphs and charts if appropriate, (e) marking possible test questions, (f) noting confusing ideas with a question mark in the margins, and (g) selectively underlining key words or phrases (Nist & Simpson, 1988). Students are not only responsible for pulling out the main points of the text, but also the other key information (e.g., examples and details) that they need to comprehend for exams. In this way annotation goes beyond the process of isolation. Students are actually transforming information by changing or personalizing it in some way.

Teaching students to use annotation is a process that requires time and practice before students become fluent and effective annotators (Frazier, 1993). Therefore, teacher-directed instruction is imperative when students learn how to annotate. According to Simpson and Nist (1990), this direct instruction should include: (a) motivational activities, (b) an explanation of strategy rationale and processes, (c) strategy modeling using a talk-through method, (d) guided practice with feedback, and (e) independent practice with feedback.

The benefits of annotation are numerous. First, students are actively reading and monitoring their understanding. When students encounter information that they cannot put into their own words, they know that they do not comprehend the information. Second, students using annotation are actively constructing ideas and making connections to what they know (Simpson & Nist, 1990). In this way, the strategy is flexible (Nist et al., 1991) and should facilitate deeper processing (Anderson & Armbruster, 1984) and metacognitive awareness. Third, annotation can be motivating for students because they are approaching the text with a purpose (Nist & Diehl, 1998). Fourth, annotating helps students organize the information so that they can see links between the main points and supporting details.

But annotation does have drawbacks. One possible drawback is that its usefulness depends on the depth of processing. If students are simply copying the text verbatim, there is little benefit (Anderson & Armbruster, 1984). For deeper processing and comprehension, students must annotate in their own words (Nist & Simpson, 1988; Strode, 1991). Another drawback, especially from students' perspectives, is that it takes longer to read and interact with texts. This may be especially troublesome for at-risk learners who may already read laboriously. Finally, as previously mentioned, annotation instruction also takes a good deal of time. Research has indicated that mastering this strategy may necessitate more than one semester of instruction and practice (Holschuh, 1995; Mealey & Frazier, 1992).

Elaborating

Although organizing and isolating key information are important elements in being academically successful, students also need to know and use elaborative strategies. Of the three strategic processes, *elaboration* is the final step. In other words, students cannot elaborate on information without first organizing and isolating key information in some way. College students are often in learning situations where they are required to synthesize and analyze information, situations where rote memorization strategies not suffice (Pressley, Ghatala, Woloshyn, & Pirie, 1990). Moreover, tasks that require elaboration of information across texts often cause frustration (Simpson, 1994).

Elaborative strategies allow students to relate new information to what they already know (Wittrock, 1986). When students elaborate, they add information that is not explicit in the text they are studying (Hamilton, 1997; Simpson et al., 1994). However, research has indicated that adults do not spontaneously elaborate as they read (Pressley et al., 1992). Elaboration is often covert and difficult to observe (McWhorter, 1993) and thus may prove difficult to teach.

There are many different strategies students can use to go about the difficult task of elaboration. These comprehension strategies include elaborative interrogation, elaborative verbal rehearsals, and self-testing.

Elaborative Interrogation. Pressley and colleagues (Menke & Pressley, 1994; Pressley et al., 1992; Willoughby, Wood, & Kahn, 1994) posited that using elaborative interrogation by inserting "why" questions into text enhances student learning because it encourages students to use prior knowledge to make relationships between ideas. Elaborative interrogation is related to schema theory because the student is tying existing knowledge to new information (Willoughby et al., 1994). The instructor poses questions that support the ideas that students need to learn (Menke & Pressley, 1994). This strategy is most effective when students already have some knowledge about a topic because when students are faced with unfamiliar material, they usually access inappropriate schemata (Willoughby et al., 1994). Because the instructor is responsible for inserting the elaborative questions, this strategy does not meet Wittrock's definition of a generative strategy. However, elaborative questions can be the basis for students to learn the types of questions they should be asking themselves as they read. By making explicit ties between elaborative questions used in class and questions that students should ask themselves when they read on their own, instructors can help students monitor their understanding of text.

Self-questioning has many purposes as a way of elaborating on information from prompting the retrieval of prior knowledge and focusing attention to checking comprehension of information and predicting possible test items. Self-questioning has been shown to improve comprehension and performance on exams (King, 1992; Tierney & Cunningham, 1984). It also has drawbacks. Teaching students how to question is often difficult, but it is imperative because students need to be instructed on what types of questions are effective. For example, Foos (1989) found that students often asked themselves questions that called for specific facts when they did not receive instruction on how to self-question.

Elaborative Verbal Rehearsals.   Elaborative verbal rehearsal is a strategy that provides an important means of monitoring understanding of text (Nist & Diehl, 1998). This strategy has been shown to have an impact on at-risk students' exam performance (Simpson et al., 1994). When students use this strategy, they are rehearsing aloud the important information as if they were teaching it to an audience (Simpson, 1994). A good elaborative verbal rehearsal consists of the following processes: (a) relating ideas across text and to prior knowledge, (b) incorporating personal reactions or opinions about the ideas, (c) summarizing key ideas in students' own words, (d) including appropriate text examples, and (e) including appropriate text examples (Simpson, 1994). Research has indicated that the quality of the talk-through played a major role in its effectiveness, so students need explicit instruction on how to conduct an effective elaborative verbal rehearsal (Simpson et al., 1994). This instruction should include modeling a good example, explaining the rationale for strategy use, and providing feedback on students use of the strategy (Simpson et al., 1994). Elaborative verbal rehearsals are metacognitive because they help students distinguish what they know from what they do not know.

One of the drawbacks to elaborative verbal rehearsal is that students must have a good understanding of the information before it can be used. Simpson (1994) suggested that this strategy only be used by students who can decode the text material. One of the benefits of this strategy is that it facilitates students' active and elaborative understanding of text information.

Self-Testing.   Self-testing allows students to determine whether or not they are comprehending information so that they can modify their strategies if necessary (Weinstein, 1994). By monitoring their understanding, students identify gaps or errors in their comprehension. This metacognitive check is important for strategic learning because students must be aware of comprehension problems before they can do something about them (Weinstein, 1994). Often students do not even realize that there are holes in their understanding until they receive a score on an exam (Weinstein, Meyer, & Van Mater Stone, 1994).

Self-testing can be done individually or through cooperative learning. Research has indicated that students seem to both consolidate and integrate their knowledge of new information in collaborative settings (Dansereau, 1988). Using the direct instruction model, teachers can help students become able to self-test individually by first using self-testing collaboratively. For example, instructors can allow class time for small group review and self-testing of information. One good strategy for instructors is to allow time for students to brainstorm and solve possible test questions.

Summary

One of the most important elements of teacher-directed comprehension strategies is to make students aware of how to select task-appropriate strategies. This can be accomplished by modeling the strategy in a variety of contexts and discussing it with peer groups. Students should be encouraged to modify strategies in such a way that they have ownership of the strategy. In addition to providing scaffolding on strategy use so that students can eventually use the strategy on their own, instructors should be sure that the strategy possesses metacognitive, cognitive, and affective elements.

Research on comprehension strategies and their use has progressed dramatically in the past 20 years from a focus on specific strategies to a focus on the processes involved in strategy use. Thus, currently, it is safe to conclude that it is not so much the strategy that makes the difference, but the processes that underlie that strategy.

CONCLUSION AND RECOMMENDATIONS

For Instruction

In this chapter, we have taken the stance that any teacher-directed strategy presented to students should have the potential of becoming generative in nature. For example, when teaching organizing strategies, instructors may begin by introducing the idea of graphic overviews or teacher-directed prereading activities. But instruction does not stop here. Instructors need to scaffold instruction to the point where students can create concept maps or engage in a variety of useful prereading activities independently as a way of generatively processing information and creating meaning by building relationships between parts of the text (Wittrock, 1990).

For isolating key ideas, instructors can build on the strategies that students already use, such as underlining or highlighting by introducing the more active strategy of annotation. Moreover, in teaching students elaborating strategies, instructors can teach elaborative interrogation as a means of showing students how to generate their own higher level questions.

Because we are moving in the direction of a better understanding of the processes that underlie effective strategy use, it is important for instructors to explain these processes to students so that students can make decisions about which strategies meet their needs. Rather than just teaching specific strategies, teaching students about the processes that underlie strategy use is more worthwhile. Also, making sure that students understand the declarative, procedural, and conditional knowledge about a strategy leads to greater transfer of knowledge.

We have also suggested that getting students to the point where they can transfer strategies to new situations takes time. The specific comprehension strategies discussed in this chapter rely heavily on initial teacher instruction and direction, but then allow students to modify the strategies for any number of situations. We strongly believe that teacher-directed comprehension strategies that do not lead to generative use on the part of students serve little purpose in helping students become active, self-regulated learners.

In addition, we believe that affect is important in strategy use. Students must possess not only the skill, but the will to use a variety of strategies (Weinstein, 1997). It is more than being motivated to learn. Successful strategy use also depends on students' epistemological beliefs and beliefs about text. Moreover, college students need to possess a repertoire of organizing, isolating, and elaborating strategies from which they can select in a variety of situations. That is the skill part. They also need to have the will to make deliberate choices about which strategies to use and follow through with their use as they learn, study, and prepare for exams.

For Research

Our review of the theory and research related to teacher-directed comprehension strategies at the college level points to several conclusions and recommendations. Because we know that studying is usually an isolated activity (Thomas & Rohwer, 1986) we need to arm college students, particularly at-risk college students, with generative strategies that they can use independently. But the question still remains, which strategies are best? Unless college students can move beyond teacher dependence and apply strategies on their own, they will have a difficult time being academically successful in college. Studies must be devised that indicate alternative methods instructors can employ to move students toward becoming independent learners. For example, graphic overviews can push students to call up existing knowledge and to begin thinking differently about a topic. However, we know that once students leave the confines of college reading and studying classes, they are not going to sit down and construct their own graphic overview. Rather, we want to provide students with the resources to understand the processes underlying the effectiveness of graphic overviews and then show them how to use these processes in the privacy of their own studying. Currently, researchers are only beginning to explore the processes underlying specific strategies rather than the strategies themselves, thus making this an area that needs continued exploration.

In addition, more long-term studies need to be conducted that focus on a variety of questions. Just how much scaffolding is necessary in order for transfer to occur? How long and what kind of instruction leads to transfer? How can we get students to use strategies? Because much of the research on specific strategies, especially those that have traditionally been termed "teacher-directed" have been short in duration, there are many questions left to answer.

Third, alternative methodologies help researchers gain greater insight into students' strategy use. Descriptive studies, in addition to paving the way for more well-planned quantitative investigations, can help researchers better understand the processes involved in strategy knowledge.

Additionally, more research that ties together the cognitive and affective components of strategy use is important. Students must not only have the skill but also the will to engage in strategy use. Research that investigates how the affective component can be used to engage students in strategy selection and use is needed. Moreover, we have only minimal knowledge of the role of epistemologies, particularly as to how they relate to strategy use (Hofer & Pintrich, 1997). Finally, we also need additional research on the situational nature of strategy use.

REFERENCES AND SUGGESTED READINGS

*Alexander, P. A. (1992). Domain knowledge: Evolving themes and emerging concerns. *Educational Psychologist, 27,* 33–51.

Alexander, P. A. (1996). The past, present, and future of knowledge research: A reexamination of the role of knowledge in learning and instruction. *Educational Psychologist, 31,* 89–92.

Alexander, P. A. (1998). The nature of disciplinary and domain learning: The knowledge, interest, and strategic dimensions of learning subject-matter text. In C. A. Hynd (Ed.), *Learning from text across conceptual domains.* Mahwah, NJ: Lawrence Erlbaum Associates.

Alexander, P. A., & Dochy, F. J. R. C. (1995). Conceptions of knowledge and beliefs: A comparison across varying cultural and educational communities. *American Educational Research Journal, 32,* 413–442.

*Alexander, P. A., & Judy, J. E. (1988). The interaction of domain-specific and strategic knowledge in academic performance. *Review of Educational Research, 58,* 375–404.

Alvarez, M. C. (1983). Using a thematic preorganizer and guided instruction as aids to concept learning. *Reading Horizons, 24,* 51–58.

Anderson, R. C. (1978). Schema-directed processes in language comprehension. In A. Lesgold, J. Pelligreno, S. Fokkema, & R. Glaser (Eds.), *Cognitive psychology and instruction* (pp. 67–82). New York: Plenum.

*Anderson, R. C., & Pearson, P. D. (1984). A schemata-theoretic view of basic processes in reading. In P. D. Pearson (Ed.), *Handbook of reading research* (pp. 255–291). New York: Longman.

Anderson, R. C. & Pichert, J. W. (1978). Recall of previously unrecallable information following a shift in perspective. *Journal of Verbal Learning and Verbal Behavior, 17,* 1–13.

Anderson, R. C., Pichert, J. W., & Shirey, L. L. (1983). Role of reader's schema at different points in time. *Journal of Educational Psychology, 75,* 271–279.

*Anderson, R. C., Reynolds, R. E., Schallert, D. L., & Goetz, E. T. (1977). Frameworks for comprehending discourse. *American Educational Research Journal, 14,* 367–382.

Anderson, R. C., Spiro, R., & Anderson, M. C. (1978). Schemata as scaffolding for representation of information in connected discourse. *American Educational Research Journal, 15,* 433–440.

*Anderson, T. H., & Armbruster, B. B. (1984). Studying. In P. D. Pearson (Ed.), *Handbook of reading research* (pp. 657–679). New York: Longman.

Ausubel, D. P. (1963). *The psychology of meaningful verbal learning.* New York: Grune & Stratton.

Ausubel, D. P. (1968). *Educational psychology: A cognitive view.* New York: Holt, Rinehart & Winston.

*Baker, L. (1985). Differences in the standards used by college students to evaluate their comprehension of expository prose. *Reading Research Quarterly, 20,* 297–313.

*Baker, L., & Brown, A. L. (1984). Metacognitive skills and reading. In P. D. Pearson (Ed.), *Handbook of reading research* (pp. 353–394). New York: Longman.

Baker, W. E. (1974). *Reading skills* (2nd ed.). Englewood Cliffs, NJ: Prentice-Hall.

Barron, R. F. (1969). The use of vocabulary as an advance organizer. In H. L. Herber & P. L. Sanders (Eds.), *Research on reading in the content areas: First year report* (pp. 29–39). Syracuse, NY: Syracuse University, Reading and Language Arts Center.

*Bartlett, F. C. (1932). *Remembering: A study in experimental and social psychology*. New York: Cambridge University Press.

Belenky, M. F., Clinchy, B. M., Goldberger, N. R., & Tarule, J. M. (1986). *Women's ways of knowing: The development of self, voice, and mind*. New York: Basic Books.

Berliner, D. C. (1981). Academic learning time and reading achievement. In J. T. Guthrie (Ed.), *Comprehension and teaching: Research reviews* (pp. 203–226). Newark, DE: International Reading Association.

Bernard, R. M., & Naidu, S. (1992). Post-questioning, concept mapping, and feedback: A distance education field experiment. *British Journal of Educational Technology, 23,* 48–60.

Bransford, J. D., & Franks, J. J. (1971). The abstraction of linguistic ideas. *Cognitive Psychology, 2,* 331–350.

Brisco, C., & LaMaster, S. U. (1991). Meaningful learning in college biology through concept mapping. *The American Biology Teacher, 53,* 214–219.

*Brown, A. L., Armbruster, B. B., & Baker, L. (1986). The role of metacognition in reading and studying. In J. Orasanu (Ed.), *Reading comprehension: From research to practice* (pp. 49–76). Hillsdale, NJ: Lawrence Erlbaum Associates.

Brown, A. L., Campione, J. C., & Day, J. D. (1981). Learning to learn: On training students to learn from texts. *Educational Researcher, 10,* 14–21.

*Brown, J. S., Collins, A., & Duguid, P. (1989). Situated cognition and the culture of learning. *Educational Researcher, 18,* 32–42.

Carson, J. G., Chase, N. D., & Gibson, S. U. (1992). *Literacy analyses of high school and university courses: Summary descriptions of selected courses*. Atlanta, GA: Center for the Study of Adult Literacy, Georgia State University.

Casazza, M. E. (1993). Using a model of direct instruction to teach summary writing in a college reading class. *Journal of Reading, 37,* 202–208.

Chambliss, M. J. (1994). Why do readers fail to change their beliefs after reading persuasive text? In R. Garner & P. A. Alexander (Eds.), *Beliefs about text and instruction with text* (pp. 75-89). Hillsdale, NJ: Lawrence Erlbaum Associates.

Chi, M. T. H., Feltovich, P., & Glaser, R. (1981). Categorization and representation of physics problems by experts and novices. *Cognitive Science, 5,* 121–152.

Chiesi, H. L., Spilich, G. J., & Voss, J. F. (1979). Acquisition of domain-related information in relation to high and low domain knowledge. *Journal of Verbal Learning and Verbal Behavior, 18,* 254–274.

*Chiseri-Strater, E. (1991). *Academic literacies: The public and private discourse of university students*. Portsmouth, NH: Boynton/Cook.

Collins-Eaglin, J., & Karabenick, S. A. (1994, April). *Motivation in college classes: Are goal orientations and incentive structures likely to facilitate or impede academic performance?* Paper presented at the meeting of the American Educational Research Association, New Orleans, LA.

Corkill, A. J. (1996). Individual differences in metacognition. *Learning and Individual Differences, 8,* 275–304.

*Corno, L. (1989). Self-regulated learning: A volitional analysis. In B. J. Zimmerman & D. H. Schunk (Eds.), *Self regulated learning and academic achievement* (pp. 111–141). New York: Springer-Verlag.

Dansereau, D. F. (1988). Cooperative learning strategies. In C. E. Weinstein, E. T. Goetz, & P. A. Alexander (Eds.), *Learning and study strategies: Issues in assessment, instruction, and evaluation* (pp. 103–120). New York: Academic Press.

Dansereau, D. F., Holley, C. D., & Collins, K. W. (1980, April). *Effects of learning strategy training on text processing.* Paper presented at the annual meeting of the American Educational Research Association, Boston.

Dewey, J. (1910). *How we think.* Lexington, MA: D. C. Heath.

Dinnel, D., & Glover, J. H. (1985). Advance organizers: Encoding manipulations. *Journal of Educational Psychology, 77,* 514–521.

Dole, J., Duffy, G., & Pearson, P. D. (1991). Effects of two types of prereading instruction on the comprehension of narrative and expository text. *Reading Research Quarterly, 26,* 142–159.

Dumais, S. (1992). Editorial statement. *Memory and Cognition, 20,* 326.

*Dweck, C. S., & Leggett, E. L. (1988). A social-cognitive approach to motivation and personality. *Psychological Review, 95,* 256–273.

Flavell, J. H. (1978). Metacognitive development. In J. M. Scandura & C. J. Brainerd (Eds.), *Structural/process theories of complex human behavior* (pp. 8–19). Alphen as. Rijn, The Netherlands: Sijthoff and Noordhoff.

Foos, P. W. (1989). Effects of student-written questions on student test performance. *Teaching of Psychology, 16,* 77–78.

Frazier, D. W. (1993). Transfer of college developmental reading students' textmarking strategies. *Journal of Reading Behavior, 25,* 17–41.

Gambrell, L. B., & Heathington, B. S. (1981). Adult disabled readers' metacognitive awareness about reading tasks and strategies. *Journal of Reading Behavior, 13,* 215–222.

*Garner, R. (1987a). *Metacognition and reading comprehension.* Norwood, NJ: Ablex.

*Garner, R. (1987b). Strategies for reading and studying expository text. *Educational Psychologist, 22,* 299–312.

Garner, R. (1988). Verbal -report data on cognitive and metacognitive strategies. In C. E. Weinstein, E. T. Goetz, & P. A. Alexander (Eds.), *Learning and study strategies* (pp. 63–76). San Diego, CA: Academic Press.

*Garner, R., & Alexander, P. A. (1989). Metacognition: Answered and unanswered questions. *Educational Psychologist, 24,* 143–158.

Grant, R. (1994). Comprehension strategy instruction: Basic considerations for instructing at-risk college students. *Journal of Reading, 38,* 42–48.

Graves, M. F., & Cooke, C. L. (1980). Effects of previewing difficult stories for high school students. *Research on Reading in the Secondary Schools, 6,* 38–54.

Graves, M. F., & Prenn, M. C. (1984). Effects of previewing expository passages on junior high school students' comprehension, recall, and attitudes. In J. A. Niles & L. A.

Harris (Eds.), *Changing perspectives on research in reading/language processing and instruction* (pp. 173–177). Rochester, NY: National Reading Conference.

*Hadwin, A. F., & Winne, P. H. (1996). Study strategies have meager support. *Journal of Higher Education, 67,* 692–715.

Hamilton, R. J. (1997). Effects of three types of elaboration on learning concepts from text. *Contemporary Educational Psychology, 22,* 229–318.

Hammer, D. (1995). Epistemological considerations in teaching introductory physics. *Science Education, 79,* 393–413.

Hare, V. C., & Borchardt, K. M. (1984). Direct instruction of summarization skills. *Reading Research Quarterly, 20,* 62–78.

*Hofer, B. K., & Pintrich, P. R. (1997). The development of epistemological theories: Beliefs about knowledge and knowing and their relation to learning. *Review of Educational Research, 67,* 88–140.

Holschuh, J. L. (1995, November). *The effect of feedback on annotation quality and test performance.* Paper presented at the annual meeting of the College Reading Association, Clearwater, FL.

Hoon, P. W. (1974). Efficacy of three common study methods. *Psychological Reports, 35,* 1057–1058.

Irwin, J. (1986). *Teaching reading comprehension processes.* Englewood Cliffs, NJ: Prentice-Hall.

*Jehng, J. J., Johnson, S. D., & Anderson, R. C. (1993). Schooling and students' epistemological beliefs about learning. *Contemporary Educational Psychology, 18,* 23–35.

Jones, B. F. (1988). Text learning strategy instruction: Guidelines from theory and practice. In C. E. Weinstein, E. T. Goetz, & P. A. Alexander (Eds.), *Learning and study strategies: Issues in assessment, instruction, and evaluation* (pp. 223–260). San Diego, CA: Academic Press.

Just, M. A., & Carpenter, P. A. (1980). A theory of reading: From eye fixations to comprehension. *Psychological Review, 87,* 329–354.

Just, M. A., & Carpenter, P. A. (1987). *The psychology of reading and language comprehension.* Boston: Allyn & Bacon.

*King, A. (1992). Facilitating elaborative learning through guided student-generated questioning. *Educational Psychologist, 27,* 111–126.

Kulhavy, R. W., Dyer, J. W., & Silver, L. (1975). The effects of notetaking and test expectancy on the learning of text material. *Journal of Educational Research, 68,* 363–365.

Larson, C. O., Dansereau, D. F., O'Donnell, A. M., Hythecker, V. I., Lambiotte, J. G., & Rocklin, T. R. (1985). Effects of metacognition and elaborative activity on cooperative learning and transfer. *Contemporary Educational Psychology, 10,* 342–348.

*Lipson, M. (1995). The effect of semantic mapping instruction on prose comprehension of below-level college readers. *Reading Research and Instruction, 34,* 367–378.

Maki, R. H., & Berry, S. L. (1984). Metacomprehension of text material. *Journal of Experimental Psychology: Learning, Memory, and Cognition, 10,* 663–697.

McCombs, B. L. (1988, April). *What is the relationship between motivation and self-regulated learning?* Paper presented at the annual meeting of the American Educational Research Association, New Orleans.

*McCombs, B. L. (1996). Alternative perspectives for motivation. In L. Baker, P. Afflerbach, & D. Reinking (Eds.), *Developing engaged readers in school and home communities* (pp. 67–87). Mahwah, NJ: Lawrence Erlbaum Associates.

*McKeachie, W. (1988). The need for strategy training. In C. E. Weinstein, E. T. Goetz, & P. A. Alexander (Eds.), *Learning and study strategies: Issues in assessment, instruction, and evaluation* (pp. 3–9). Orlando, FL: Academic Press.

McWhorter, J. Y. (1993). *The effects of postsecondary learning strategy use on performance.* Unpublished doctoral dissertation, University of Georgia, Athens, GA.

Mealey, D. L., & Frazier, D. W. (1992). Directed and spontaneous transfer of textmarking: A case study. In N. D. Paduk, T. Rasinski, & J. Logan (Eds.), *Literacy research and practice: Foundations for the year 2000* (pp. 153–164). Pittsburg, KS: CRA Yearbook.

Menke, D. J., & Pressley, M. (1994). Elaborative interrogation: Using "why" questions to enhance the learning from text. *Journal of Reading, 37,* 642–645.

*Moore, D. W., & Readence, J. E. (1980). A metaanalysis of graphic organizers on learning from text. In M. L. Kamil & A. J. Moe (Eds.), *Perspectives on reading research and instruction* (pp. 213–218). Washington, DC: National Reading Conference.

Moore, D. W., & Readence, J. E. (1984). A quantitative and qualitative review of graphic organizer research. *Journal of Educational Research, 78,* 11–17.

Nist, S. L., & Diehl, W. (1998). *Developing textbook thinking* (4th ed.). Boston: Houghton Mifflin.

Nist, S. L., & Hogrebe, M. C. (1987). The role of underlining and annotating in remembering textual information. *Reading Research and Instruction, 27,* 12–25.

Nist, S. L., & Kirby, K. (1989). The text marking patterns of college students. *Reading Psychology, 10,* 321–338.

Nist, S. L., & Mealey, D. L. (1991). Teacher-directed comprehension strategies. In R. F. Flippo & D. C. Caverly (Eds.), *Teaching reading & study strategies at the college level* (pp. 42–85). Newark, DE: International Reading Association.

*Nist, S. L., & Simpson, M. L. (1988). The effectiveness and efficiency of training college students to annotate and underline text. In J. E. Readence, R. S. Baldwin, J. Konopak, & W. O'Keefe (Eds.), *Dialogues in literacy research* (pp. 251–257). Chicago: National Reading Conference.

Nist, S. L., & Simpson, M. L. (1996). *Developing textbook fluency.* Boston: Houghton Mifflin.

*Nist, S. L., Simpson, M. L., Olejnik, S., & Mealey, D. L. (1991). The relation between self-selected study processes and test performance. *American Educational Research Journal, 28,* 849–874.

*Nolen, S. B. (1988). Reasons for studying: Motivational orientations and study strategies. *Cognition and Instruction 5,* 269–287.

Oldfather, P., & Dahl, K. (1994). Toward a social constructivist reconceptualization of intrinsic motivation for literacy learning. *Journal of Reading Behavior, 26,* 139–158.

*Paris, S. G., Lipson, M. Y., & Wixson, K. K. (1983). Becoming a strategic reader. *Contemporary Educational Psychology, 8,* 293–316.

*Paris, S. G., & Turner, J. C. (1994). Situated Motivation. In P. R. Pintrich, D. R. Brown, & C. E. Weinstein (Eds.), *Student motivation, cognition, and learning: Essays in honor of Wilbert J. McKeachie* (pp. 213–238). Hillsdale, NJ: Lawrence Erlbaum Associates.

Pauk, W. (1989). *How to study in college.* Boston: Houghton Mifflin.

Perry, W. G., Jr. (1968). *Patterns of development in thought and values of students in a liberal arts college: A validation of a scheme* (ERIC Document Reproduction Service No. ED 024 315). Cambridge, MA: Harvard University.

*Perry, W. G., Jr. (1970). *Forms of intellectual and ethical development in the college years: A scheme.* New York: Holt, Rinehart, & Winston.

Pichert, J. W., & Anderson, R. C. (1977). Different perspectives on a story. *Journal of Educational Psychology, 69,* 309–315.

*Pintrich, P. R., & DeGroot, E. (1990). Motivational and self-regulated learning components of classroom academic performance. *Journal of Educational Psychology, 82,* 33–40.

*Pintrich, P. R., & Garcia, T. (1994). Self-regulated learning in college students: Knowledge, strategies, and motivation. In P. R. Pintrich, D. R. Brown, & C. E. Weinstein (Eds.), *Student motivation, cognition, and learning: Essays in honor of Wilbert J. McKeachie* (pp. 113–134). Hillsdale, NJ: Lawrence Erlbaum Associates.

Pintrich, P. R., Smith, D. A. F., Garcia, T., & McKeachie, W. J. (1991). *A manual for the use of the motivated strategies for learning questionnaire (MSLQ).* Ann Arbor, MI: National Center for Research to Improve Postsecondary Teaching and Learning, University of Michigan.

Pokay, P., & Blumenfeld, P. C. (1990). Predicting achievement early and late in the semester: The role of motivation and use of learning strategies. *Journal of Educational Psychology, 82,* 41–50.

Pressley, M. (1986). The relevance of the good strategy user model to the teaching of mathematics. *Educational Psychologist, 21,* 139–161.

*Pressley, M., Ghatala, E. S., Woloshyn, V., & Pirie, J. (1990). Sometimes adults miss the main ideas in text and do not realize it: Confidence in responses to short-answer and multiple-choice comprehension questions. *Reading Research Quarterly, 25,* 232–249.

Pressley, M., Wood, E., Woloshyn, V. E., Martin, V., King, A., & Menke, D. (1992). Encouraging mindful use of prior knowledge: Attempting to construct explanatory answers facilitates learning. *Educational Psychologist, 27,* 91–109.

Pressley, M., & Harris, K. R. (1990). What we really know about strategy instruction. *Educational Leadership, 48,* 31–34.

*Pressley, M., Snyder, B. L., Levin, J. R., Murray, H. G., & Ghatala, E. S. (1987). Perceived readiness for examination performance (PREP) produced by initial reading of text and text containing adjunct questions. *Reading Research Quarterly, 22,* 219–236.

Pressley, M., Symons, S., Snyder, B. L., & Cariglia-Bull, T. (1989). Strategy instruction research comes of age. *Learning Disability Quarterly, 12,* 16–30.

Readence, J. E., Bean, T. W., & Baldwin, R. S. (1985). *Content area reading: An integrated approach* (2nd ed.). Dubuque, IA: Kendall/Hunt.

Rickards, J. P., & August, G. J. (1975). Generative underlining strategies in prose recall. *Journal of Educational Psychology, 67,* 860–865.

Risko, V., & Alvarez, M. C. (1986). An investigation of poor readers' use of a thematic strategy to comprehend text. *Reading Research Quarterly, 21,* 298–316.

Rosenshine, B. V. (1979). Content, time, and direct instruction. In P. L. Peterson & H. J. Walberg (Eds.), *Research on teaching: Concepts, findings, and implications.* Berkeley, CA: McCutchan.

Sanford, A. J., & Garrod, S. C. (1981). *Understanding written language: Explorations in comprehension beyond the sentence.* New York: Wiley.

*Schiefele, U. (1991). Interest, learning, and motivation. *Educational Psychologist, 26,* 299–323.

Schoenfeld, A. H. (1985). *Mathematical problem solving.* Orlando, FL: Academic Press.

Schoenfeld, A. H. (1988). When good teaching leads to bad results: The disasters of "well-taught" mathematics courses. *Educational Psychologist, 23,* 145–166.

*Schommer, M. (1990). Effects of beliefs about the nature of knowledge on comprehension. *Journal of Educational Psychology, 82,* 498–504.

*Schommer, M. (1994a). An emerging conceptualization of epistemological beliefs and their role in learning. In R. Garner & P. A. Alexander (Eds.), *Beliefs about text and instruction with text* (pp. 25–40). Hillsdale, NJ: Lawrence Erlbaum Associates.

*Schommer, M. (1994b). Synthesizing epistemological belief research: Tentative understandings and provocative confusions. *Educational Psychology Review, 6,* 293–319.

Schommer, M., Calvert, C., Gariglietti, G., & Bajaj, A. (1997). The development of epistemological beliefs among secondary students: A longitudinal study. *Journal of Educational Psychology, 89,* 37–40.

Schommer, M., & Hutter, R. (1995, April). *Epistemological beliefs and thinking about everyday controversial issues.* Paper presented at the meeting of the American Educational Research Association, San Francisco.

*Schommer, M., & Surber, J. R. (1986). Comprehension-monitoring failure in skilled adult readers. *Journal of Educational Psychology, 78,* 353–357.

*Schommer, M., & Walker, K. (1995). Are epistemological beliefs similar across domains? *Journal of Educational Psychology, 87,* 424–432.

*Schunk, D. H. (1991). Self-efficacy and academic motivation. *Educational Psychologist, 26,* 207–232.

*Simpson, M. L. (1994). Talk throughs: A strategy for encouraging active learning across the content areas. *Journal of Reading, 38,* 296–304.

*Simpson, M. L., & Nist, S. L. (1990). Textbook annotation: An effective and efficient study strategy for college students. *Journal of Reading, 34,* 122–129.

*Simpson, M. L. & Nist, S. L. (1997). Perspectives on learning history: A case study. *Journal of Literacy Research, 29,* 363–395.

*Simpson, M. L., Olejnik, S., Tam, A. Y., & Supattathum, S. (1994). Elaborative verbal rehearsals and college students' cognitive performance. *Journal of Educational Psychology, 86,* 267–278.

Spilich, G. J., Vesonder, G. T., Chiesi, H. L., & Voss, J. F. (1979). Text processing of domain-related information for individuals with high and low domain knowledge. *Journal of Verbal Learning and Verbal Behavior, 18,* 275–290.

Steffensen, M. S., Joag-dev, C., & Anderson, R. C. (1979). A cross-cultural perspective on reading comprehension. *Reading Research Quarterly, 15,* 10–29.

Stordahl, K. E., & Christensen, C. M. (1956). The effect of study techniques on comprehension and retention. *Journal of Educational Research, 49,* 561–570.

Strode, S. L. (1991). Teaching annotation writing to college students. *Forum for Reading,* *23,* 33–44.

Svinicki, M. D. (1994). Research on college student learning and motivation: Will it affect college instruction? In P. R. Pintrich, D. R. Brown, & C. E. Weinstein (Eds.), *Student motivation, cognition, and learning: Essays in honor of Wilbert J. McKeachie* (pp. 331–342). Hillsdale, NJ: Lawrence Erlbaum Associates.

Thiede, K. W., & Dunlosky, J. (1994). Delaying students' metacognitive monitoring improves their accuracy in predicting their recognition performance. *Journal of Educational Psychology, 86,* 290–302.

*Thomas, J. W., & Rohwer, W. D. (1986). Academic studying: The role of learning strategies. *Educational Psychologist, 21,* 19–41.

Thomas, S., & Oldfather, P. (1997). Intrinsic motivations, literacy, and assessment practices: "That's my grade. That's me." *Educational Psychologist, 32,* 107–123.

Thorndike, E. L. (1917). Reading as reasoning: A study of mistakes in paragraph reading. *Journal of Educational Psychology, 8,* 323–332.

Tierney, R. J., & Cunningham, J. W. (1984). Research on teaching reading comprehension. In P. D. Pearson (Ed.), *Handbook of reading research* (pp. 609–656). New York: Longman.

Vesonder, G. T., & Voss, J. F. (1985). On the ability to predict one's own responses while learning. *Journal of Memory and Language, 24,* 363–376.

*Voss, J. F., & Silfries, L. N. (1996). Learning from history text: The interaction of knowledge and comprehension skill with text structure. *Cognition and Instruction, 14,* 45–68.

*Wade, S. E., & Trathen, W. (1989). Effect of self-selected study methods on learning. *Journal of Educational Psychology, 81,* 40–47.

Weinstein, C. E. (1994). A look to the future: What we might learn from research on beliefs. In R. Garner & P. A. Alexander (Eds.), *Beliefs about text and instruction with text* (pp. 294–302). Hillsdale, NJ: Lawrence Erlbaum Associates.

Weinstein, C. E. (1997, March). *A course in strategic learning: A description and research data.* Paper presented at the annual meeting of the American Educational Research Association, Chicago.

*Weinstein, C. E., Meyer, D. K., & Van Mater Stone, G. (1994). Teaching students how to learn. In W. J. McKeachie (Ed.), *Teaching tips* (pp. 359–367). Lexington, MA: Heath.

Williams, J. P. (1994). The importance of examining beliefs about text. In R. Garner & P. A. Alexander (Eds.), *Beliefs about text and instruction with text* (pp. xi–xv). Hillsdale, NJ: Lawrence Erlbaum Associates.

*Willoughby, T., Wood, E., & Khan, M. (1994). Isolating variables that impact on or detract from the effectiveness of elaboration strategies. *Journal of Educational Psychology, 86,* 279–289.

Wilson, P. T., & Anderson, R. C. (1986). What they don't know will hurt them: The role of prior knowledge in comprehension. In J. Orasanu (Ed.), *Reading comprehension: From research to practice* (pp. 31–48). Hillsdale, NJ: Lawrence Erlbaum Associates.

*Wineburg, S. S. (1991). On the reading of historical texts: Notes on the breach between school and academy. *American Educational Research Journal, 28,* 495–519.

*Winne, P. H. (1995). Inherent details in self-regulated learning. *Educational Psychologist, 30,* 173–188.

*Wittrock, M. C. (1986). Students' thought processes. In M. C. Wittrock (Ed.), *Handbook of research on teaching* (pp. 297–314). New York: Macmillian.

*Wittrock, M. C. (1990). Generative processes of comprehension. *Educational Psychologist, 24,* 345–376.

*Wittrock, M. C. (1992). Generative learning processes of the brain. *Educational Psychologist, 27,* 531–541.

*Zimmerman, B. J., Bandura, A., & Martinez-Pons, M. (1992). Self-motivation for academic attainment: The role of self-efficacy beliefs and personal goal setting. *American Educational Research Journal, 29,* 663–676.

5

Textbook Study Reading

David C. Caverly
Southwest Texas State University

Vincent P. Orlando
Metropolitan State College of Denver

Jo-Ann Lynn Mullen
University of Northern Colorado

S tudents often come to developmental reading courses or learning centers at the college level to seek help. In these programs, the focus of instruction may range from basic literacy development to the critical reading necessary for upper division and graduate-level material. Usually, at some point in the instructional process, students are taught strategies that can help them learn while reading; that is, they learn how to "study read." This chapter reviews the literature on teaching students strategies for study reading college level material.

At the outset, we define *textbook study reading* as a strategic approach to reading in which students adjust their comprehending behavior before, during, and after reading with the purpose of satisfying a specific task. In study-reading ability, comprehending is strategically directed toward a specific task demand, such as gaining knowledge for a future career or for passing a course test (cf. Anderson & Armbruster, 1984; McKeachie, 1988; Thomas & Rohwer, 1986; Wade & Reynolds, 1989).

Previous reviews of study-reading strategies conclude that most are successful given certain variables. First, a given study-reading strategy's success varies with what the *student* brings to reading: reading ability, prior knowledge, and motivation (Anderson, 1978; Cook & Mayer, 1983). Second, a given study reading strategy's success varies in effectiveness depending on the content, difficulty, and organization of the *material*

(Baker & Brown, 1984; Jonassen, 1985; McConkie, 1977). Third, it is necessary to *instruct* students in how to apply a study-reading strategy (Dansereau, Actkinson, Long, & McDonald, 1974; Goetz, 1984; Mayer, 1988a, 1988b; Orlando, 1978). Fourth, study reading strategies are dependent on the type and time of *task demand* presented to the student (Baker & Brown, 1984; Cook & Mayer, 1983; Gibbs, Morgan, & Taylor, 1982; Levin, 1986; Marton & Saljo, 1976a, 1976b). A more recent review suggests that a combination of these four variables best explains the effectiveness of any given study-reading strategy (Caverly & Orlando, 1991). Specifically, understanding the unique and combined effects of each of the four variables (i.e., student, material, instruction, and task demand) is crucial for understanding the effectiveness of any given study-reading strategy. The question, therefore, is not whether study-reading strategies are successful. Rather, it is where, when, and under what conditions a strategy is successful. This chapter updates our previous review (Caverly & Orlando, 1991), provides recommendations for what should be taught to students about selecting a strategy for textbook study reading, and proposes what research still needs to be completed.

A THEORETICAL FOUNDATION

Most theorists consider strategic reading as the most successful approach when study reading (Caverly & Orlando, 1991; Paris, Lipson, & Wixson, 1983; Wade, Trathen, & Schraw, 1990). This perspective provides instruction to students to select a study-reading strategy on the basis of their abilities, the type of material they are reading, and the purpose for which they are reading. The interaction of these four factors (instruction, student, material, and task demands) was first proposed by Jenkins (1979) as a tetrahedral model for research in cognitive psychology. Later, Brown (1980) used this same model to illustrate reading research in general. Then, Brown, Campione, and Day (1981); McKeachie (1988); and Nist (1985) adapted the model to illustrate the interactions present in college reading and study-reading strategies.

Each of the four vertices of Fig. 5.1 represents a variable that affects the success of any given study-reading strategy. Often only one edge of this model is taught thus representing a two-way interaction between variables. Here, a novice developmental reading instructor teaches students mapping, for example, as a generic study-reading strategy applicable in all study-reading tasks. Other times, one plane of this model is taught thus representing a three-way interaction among variables. Here, a more knowledgeable developmental reading instructor might teach students to use mapping for history textbooks, but to adapt it when studying math or literature. Still other times, a wise developmental reading instructor teaches students to be aware of the interaction among all four edges and all four planes of this model, thus a four-way interaction. Here, students learn that mapping is appropriate under certain task demand conditions given certain material and student abilities, but other study-reading strategies are more effective or more efficient under other conditions.

This wise developmental reading instructor then moves on and teaches students to be metacognitively aware of their progress while reading (Wade & Reynolds, 1989). Here, successful students become independent as they are metacognitively aware of *self* (their own strengths and weaknesses), *strategy* (what strategies they might choose to

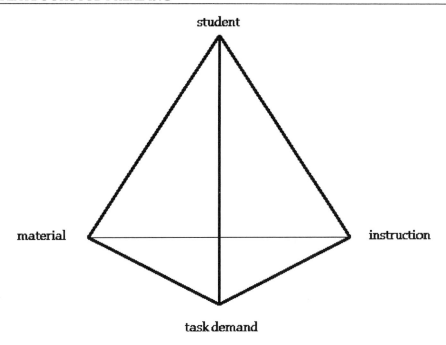

FIG. 5.1. A tetrahedral model of the factors involved in study reading.

study a textbook or a novel), *task* (how they have to recognize the text structure to pre-pare for a midterm essay), and *performance* (how they monitor the success of their study-reading strategy choice). This wise developmental reading instructor shifts the fo-cus from the teacher-centered, tetrahedral instructional model to a student-centered, strategic reading, process model proposed by Wade and Reynolds (1989. For a further discussion, see Nist & Holschuh, chap. 4, this volume.)

FRAMEWORK FOR DISCUSSION

The four planes of Fig. 5.1 are used as a framework for reviewing the research literature surrounding study-reading strategies. We begin the review of each study-reading strategy with how the student variables were manipulated or controlled in the research. That is, what skills and abilities did students bring with them to the experimental study situation, and how did these variables affect what they learned? Although students often bring a variety of attributes to any study situation, two variables have been singled out in the lit-erature as important to study reading: the students' *reading ability* and whether the stu-dents' *background knowledge* was taken into account.

A second set of variables involve how the reading material was manipulated or controlled in the research. Is a given study-reading strategy equally effective in all types of material students must study? Four material variables have been examined in the liter-ature: the *content* or subject matter of the text; the readability or *difficulty* of the text; the *length* of the material; and the explicitness of the *text structure*.

A third set of variables is the extent to which the instruction was manipulated or controlled. That is, what is the effect of how the strategy was taught on how students performed? Three variables have been examined: whether students received any *instruction* in the use of the study-reading strategy, whether students had *knowledge of the task demand* before they studied, and whether students were *taught to review* the material after study but before being tested.

A fourth set of variables considered how the task demand was manipulated or controlled. That is, how has student performance been measured after applying a given study-reading strategy? Two variables that have been examined in the literature: the *test type*, or whether the test measured recognition, recall, or both; and the *test administration delay*, or the amount of time that elapsed between use of the study-reading strategy and administration of the test.

It is our premise that the tetrahedral model, with four clusters of 11 variables, provides a useful set of criteria for reviewing the research literature, drawing conclusions about sound instruction, and determining implications for additional research. In order to bring some semblance of order to this process, an integrative review (cf. Jackson, 1980) using the tetrahedral model was completed. Our primary research question for this integrative review was how effective and efficient are specific study-reading strategies in light of individual and interactive effects of the four sets of variables.

STUDY READING RESEARCH

Students can use many learning strategies when studying. Weinstein and Mayer (1985) provided a useful classification of these strategies outlining eight major categories shown in Table 5.1.

TABLE 5.1
Study-Reading Strategies Theoretical Framework

	Basic	*Complex*
Rehearsal	Techniques for repeating a list if items, such as common memorizing or rereading the text	Techniques for marking material to be learned, such as underlining
Elaboration	Techniques for generating mental images to remember, such as imaging	Techniques for describing how new information fits into old knowledge, such as generative notetaking
Organizational	Techniques for grouping lists of items, such as mnemonics	Techniques for recognizing and recalling the structure of the information, such as outlining or mapping
Monitoring	Techniques for establishing a learning goal and monitoring one's progress toward that goal, such as SQ3R	
Affective and Motivational Strategies	Techniques for controlling volitional strategies, such as attention, concentration, anxiety, and time management	

Surveys of materials and student usage at the college level confirm that these eight categories of study reading strategies are indeed the most commonly used (Annis & Annis, 1982; Fairbanks, 1973; Starks-Martin, 1996). To focus this review on study-reading strategies, we use the tetrahedral model and an integrative review procedure to examine five of the most common, complex study-reading strategies: *underlining* as indicative of complex rehearsal strategies, generative *notetaking* as indicative of complex elaboration strategies, *outlining* and *mapping* as indicative of complex organizational strategies, and *Survey, Question, Read, Recite, Review (SQ3R)* as indicative of comprehension monitoring strategies. Other student-oriented comprehension strategies are reviewed in Anderson and Armbruster (1984) and Nist and Holschuh (chap. 4, this volume). A review of the affective and motivational strategies connected with study reading, while certainly relevant is beyond the scope of this chapter and is provided in Algood, Risko, Alvarez, and Fairbanks (chap. 8, this volume).

Complex Rehearsal Strategy: Underlining

Underlining or highlighting (hereafter called simply underlining) is representative of what Weinstein and Mayer (1985) called a *complex rehearsal strategy*. This study-reading strategy involves selecting important ideas and marking them for subsequent review. Theoretically, if important ideas are found, marked, and reviewed, performance on subsequent tests is enhanced.

Underlining is by far the most common study-reading strategy in postsecondary education with surveys finding ranging from 50% to 97 % of students using this strategy on a regular basis (Adams, 1969; Annis & Annis, 1982; Charters, 1925; Fowler & Barker, 1974; Marxen, 1996). Many researchers report that students feel a sense of security while underlining as they believe they are selecting the important ideas, monitoring their understanding while reading, and preparing the text for later review. Such a proliferation in the use of underlining runs counter to the arguments made against this strategy both by study-reading theorists (Berg & Rentle, 1966; Crawford, 1938; Stahl, Simpson, & Hayes, 1992) and study-reading authors (Bryant & Lindeman, 1995; Laycock & Russell, 1941).

Several studies on underlining also involve students being given experimenter-generated underlined text to explore the von Restorrf effect (Wallace, 1965), where items recognized as being differentiated from their background are more likely to be recalled than items blending into the background. While exploring the effect of underlining on recognition and recall tasks in general, these studies have little relationship to what we as college developmental reading teachers might teach students to do for themselves. Furthermore, student-generated underlining has consistently proven to be as effective, if not more so, when compared to experimenter-generated underlining (Nist & Hogrebe, 1987; Rickards & August, 1975). Therefore, we chose to look only at those experiments in which students marked the material themselves.

Student Variable.   Although several student variables were addressed in the underlining literature, we focus on the two most explored variables: reading ability and background knowledge. One clear conclusion from the literature is that teaching the use of underlining to students below or above a certain level of reading ability is not appropriate as there is a consistent finding that reading ability correlates highly with underlining (Arnold, 1942; Blanchard & Mikkelson, 1987; Crewe, 1968; Snyder, 1984; Stordahl & Christensen, 1956; Todd & Kessler, 1971; Zanias, 1996). If students are novice readers, still struggling with word recognition and literal comprehension strategies, they are often unable to recognize important concepts and thus underline randomly. Teaching these students to underline without teaching them how to recognize main ideas, for example, is fruitless.

Using students' academic aptitude (as measured by college entrance tests) as an ability variable supports this conclusion. Students who scored higher on academic aptitude tests tended to perform better on reading tests regardless of the study-reading strategy they were asked to use (Hakstain, 1971; Klare, Mabry, & Gustfason, 1955; Stordahl & Christensen, 1956). In one study, where students were better than average readers and were required to use underlining unnaturally in an experimental study, it was found that underlining tended to interfere with their existing study-reading strategies and reading performance was actually hindered (Marxen, 1996).

Student background knowledge also seems to have a positive effect on underlining. Five studies chose to control for background knowledge by using it as a covariate (Arnold, 1942; Brady & Rickards, 1979; Crewe, 1968; Fass & Schumacher, 1978; Stordahl & Christensen, 1956). This technique served to factor out the consistent positive effect of background knowledge on comprehension (Anderson & Pearson, 1984) and consequently reduced the chances that students using underlining would show any increase in performance scores. Thus, the weak performance found in these studies could be due to weak background knowledge rather than the limited effect of underlining.

Three other experiments (Davis & Annis, 1976; Nist & Hogrebe, 1987; Snyder, 1984) explored the effect of background knowledge and found strong background knowledge can facilitate underlining, lack of background knowledge cannot be overcome by underlining, and inducing students to engage their background knowledge did not necessarily foster recall. These seemingly contradictory results might be explained by the general lack of adequate instructional strategies for teaching students to engage background knowledge (Caverly, 1982; Paris, 1988; Schumacher, 1987). Theoretically, if there is appropriate background knowledge available and it is engaged effectively, background knowledge should serve to reduce the amount of text underlined as students focus only on marking the most important concepts. However, the research with college age students has not found this to be case. Other research with middle school readers confirms this conclusion (Karpinus & Haynes, 1983).

In summary, we draw these conclusions about the effect of student variables on underlining:

- Teaching the use of underlining to students who have a low level of reading ability is not appropriate. Student must first learn how to find main ideas before they learn how to underline them.
- The relationship between reading ability and underlining is curvilinear. Good readers seem to have study-reading strategies that are effective and tend to be hindered by imposing underlining on them. Underlining also give false hope to poorer readers as they randomly underline ideas.

- Underlining cannot overcome weak background knowledge or lack of strategies for engaging background knowledge.

Material Variable.   In the studies we reviewed, nine different content areas were used, with the large majority covering social science topics. Researchers' emphasis on social science topics is appropriate given that the largest quantity of reading required by students at the college level is within the social sciences (Caverly & Orlando, 1985). Still, the research reviewed presents no evidence that the underlining strategy is more effective with any particular type of content area. Those studies that did manipulate the material variable (Harris, 1990; Idstein & Jenkins, 1972; Stordahl & Christensen, 1956) found no consistent effect for content on students' performance with underlining.

It has been hypothesized (Rohwer, 1984; Schumacher, 1987) that the difficulty of the material (i.e., readability level, length of the passage, explicitness of the structure, and relevance for the student) should determine the effectiveness of underlining, particularly because reading ability seems to be a factor in the effectiveness of underlining. It was reasoned that if the demands of the material are great, underlining should allow external storage of the ideas gathered, thus facilitating later review and reducing the processing demands (e.g., Rickards, 1980). Therefore, it would be prudent to manipulate the interaction between the subject and the material variables when attempting to determine the effectiveness of the underlining strategy.

Few studies we reviewed described the difficulty of the material used. In those studies, most of passages were below the reading level of the students so material difficulty was not necessarily a factor. Fass and Schumacher's (1978) study was the only one that actually manipulated the difficulty of the material, finding that underlining was more helpful with material the students deemed harder than with material they deemed easy. This difference may be due more to the interaction among the ability of the student, interest, or the explicit structure of the material than with the success of the study-reading strategy. With a paucity of research exploring this subject/material interaction, no definitive conclusions can be drawn.

In terms of the length of the material, the passages in the studies reviewed ranged from 44 words (Todd & Kessler, 1971) to more than 10,000 words (Peterson, 1992). Our review indicates that when the material is longer, the effectiveness of underlining diminishes. Todd and Kessler (1971) as well as Brown and Smiley (1977) reported underlining to be more effective in shorter material, whereas Idstein and Jenkins (1972) and Marxen (1996) demonstrated underlining to be less effective in longer passages. Still, questions must be raised regarding the generalizability of research in which shorter passages of fewer than 500 words were used when it is unlikely that students will have to study material that short.

Only a few studies considered the explicitness of the material's structure. Of these, only Rickards and August (1975) found that explicit structure interfered with the effectiveness of underlining. Presumably what the students thought was important ran counter to what the structure was suggesting to be important thus their performance was hindered. Several other studies (Brady & Rickards, 1979; Brown & Smiley, 1977; Earp, 1959; Weatherly, 1978) found no effect of text structure on the effectiveness of underlining. This inconsistency might be explained by exploring the student–material–instructional interactions of the tetrahedral model. None of these studies spent more than 1 hour teaching students how to use text structure to decide what to underline; that is, how to select the major concepts as identified by the explicit or implicit text structure and then to mark them. Having learned to recognize and use text structure could result in students' marking the text more effectively. Still, two studies (Nist & Hogrebe, 1987; Peterson, 1992) demonstrated that underlining does not necessarily foster the deeper processing (Craik & Tulving, 1975) that is required to recognize text structure. Thus it is not surprising that underlining did not improve performance when text structure was not explicit.

In summary, four conclusions can be drawn about the effect of material variables on underlining:

- Because most studies used social science material, and only two studies manipulated content area finding no difference, the effect of underlining on the different content areas is unknown.
- Underlining may be more effective with harder passages if performed well and if major points are identified; however, only one study manipulated this variable, so it is difficult to draw any conclusions.
- Underlining seems to be less effective in longer material (more than 500 words) due to the concept load.
- Contradictory results with the effect of text structure on underlining may be due more to researchers' failure to provide sufficient instruction in recognizing important concepts from the text structure.

Instruction Variable.   An analysis of the instructional variables verifies that instruction has a distinct effect on underlining. For example, strong evidence supports the notion that unless students are taught to review material either after reading or before the test underlining has no effect (Annis & Davis, 1978; Brown & Smiley, 1977; Crewe, 1968; Harris, 1990; Hartley, Bartlett, & Branthwaite, 1980; Idstein & Jenkins, 1972). In those studies that actually manipulated the review factor (Brown & Smiley, 1977; Crewe, 1968; Idstein & Jenkins, 1972), the longer and more thorough the review, the better the performance. A shallow, simple review does not seem adequate even with older students as illustrated in the Brown and Smiley study.

If underlining is to be an effective study-reading strategy, students must be taught how to recognize important main ideas to mark (especially poor readers) and to review those ideas before the test (Brady & Rickards, 1979; Hartley et al., 1980; Johnson, 1988; Marxen, 1996; Todd & Kessler, 1971; Weatherly, 1978). Even when important ideas are marked and reviewed, underlining does not always guarantee improved performance on tests that measure ideas not marked, as we see later.

As part of this strategic approach, underlining seems to be more effective when combined with other study reading strategies. When underlining is combined with notetaking (Stone & Miller, 1991; Wade et al., 1990; Zanias, 1996), it seems to be more effective for reading improvement than underlining alone. Here, students were taught to mark important ideas by underlining them and then convert what they marked into a marginal note, thus providing an opportunity for deeper processing.

In summary, we can draw three conclusions about the effect of instructional variables on underlining:

- Teaching students to review what they have underlined before giving them a test markedly improves their performance, if the test happens to measures what they underlined.
- Providing students with even a limited amount of instruction in how to underline important main ideas and the need to review those ideas is important for enhanced performance.
- Underlining is more effective if used as a strategy for marking where important ideas lie in the text and if those ideas are subsequently converted into a marginal note.

Task Demand Variable.   Underlining and review fosters intentional recall; that is, underlining and subsequent review helps if the task demand measures what happened to be underlined (Amer, 1994; Bausell & Jenkins, 1977; Marxen, 1996; Nist & Hogrebe, 1987; Smart & Bruning, 1973). Underlining also hinders incidental recall (i.e., that which was not underlined and subsequently not reviewed) in some studies (Kulhavy, Dyer, & Silver, 1975; Nist & Hogrebe, 1987; Peterson, 1992; Rickards & August, 1975), while helping in other studies (Brady & Rickards, 1979; Hartley et al., 1980; Johnson, 1988). In the latter three studies where incidental recall was fostered, extensive instruction was provided for how to underline important superordinate ideas, how those ideas are supported by subordinate ideas that do not need to be underlined, and how those ideas that are underlined must be reviewed before the test. This was not the case in the former four studies where instruction was minimal. A meta-analysis (Caverly, 1985) also suggests that underlining seems to be more effective for intentional recall tasks than for incidental recall; the effect scores were + 0.25 and + 0.05, respectively. Here, again, we see a potential interaction between instructional and task demand variables.

Moreover, more recent research suggests that underlining even with subsequent review does not help inferential recall (Bartel, 1993–1994; Harris, 1990; Peterson, 1992). This is not surprising as there is little in an underlining study-reading strategy that would allow for any inference being made from the text while reading between the lines.

In terms of the time lag between study reading and test administration, most of the tests were delayed, with the gap ranging from 5 minutes (Brown & Smiley, 1977) to 47 days (Crewe, 1968). No clear pattern emerged from these studies. However, a meta-analysis of the data (Caverly, 1985) suggests a slight increase in positive effect for underlining when compared with no underlining as the delay in testing becomes longer.

In summary, we can draw these conclusions about the effect of task demand variables on underlining:

- Underlining seems to be more effective for intentional recall than incidental recall unless extensive instruction is provided.
- No clear pattern emerged for the effect of underlining on test delay.

Summary of Research on Underlining.   Based on this review, underlining should not be taught to students who are not developmentally ready to use it (e.g.,
those who are unable to recognize main ideas); underlining cannot overcome poor reading ability. Underlining may not help in longer, harder material but the research is scanty.
Underlining seems to help only if what the student underlined was on the test. If the test
measures concepts not underlined or inferred from the text, underlining does not seem
to help. Underlining is not effective unless the student is taught to regularly review what
they have underlined.

In the end, underlining is a complex rehearsal strategy necessary but not sufficient
for the complex study demands of college (cf. Spiro, Coulson, Feltovich, & Anderson,
1994). Although it is a common strategy, students should be encouraged to use more sophisticated study-reading strategies (Stahl et al., 1992).

Complex Elaboration Strategy: Notetaking

Another major group of study-reading strategies are what Weinstein and Mayer (1985)
called *complex elaboration strategies*. This type of strategy directs students to monitor their
understanding during and after reading by fostering recognition and subsequent elaboration of the material. Several study-reading strategies are available to college-level students, but perhaps the most commonly used is *notetaking/annotating* (hereafter
notetaking). Here, students rewrite what they have learned from reading either in the
margin of the textbook or on separate sheets of paper. These notes can take several forms
ranging from verbatim accounts, to notations that represent the structure of the information, to critical evaluations of what was read (Eanet & Manzo, 1976).

Analyses of notetaking (Carrier & Titus, 1979; Hartley & Davies, 1978) have
drawn conclusions from research that has examined both notetaking from lectures and
notetaking from textbooks; that is, notetaking while listening and notetaking while
reading. We believe that although listening and reading are reciprocal processes, they are
not identical. Conclusions drawn from a transitory process such as listening are not necessarily adaptable to a protracted process such as reading. For example, with listening it is
difficult (if not impossible) to stop the input in order to consider what is being learned.
With reading, the input can be halted at any point to review the message and think about
what is being learned. Therefore, the process and the intent of notetaking while listening
to a lecture are different from those of notetaking while reading a text. The analysis presented here examines only research dealing with notetaking from text. For a discussion
of notetaking from lectures, see Armbruster (chap. 7, this volume).

Student Variables.   Many student variables are evident in this literature,
but two are specifically analyzed here: reading ability and prior knowledge. Our analysis
shows that teaching notetaking to students below a certain level of reading ability is not
recommended. This conclusion was evident in the research that identified differences in
performance due to students' reading ability (Balajthy & Weisberg, 1990; Fox & Siedow,
1985; Pena-Paez & Surber, 1990; Santa, Abrams, & Santa, 1979; Shimmerlik & Nolan,
1976). It seems that students must be able to recognize important information in the material before notetaking can help. Otherwise, they tend to take verbatim notes of irrele-

vant concepts. As with underlining, notetaking cannot overcome lack of ability to find the main idea.

No definite conclusions can be drawn, however, regarding the role of students' background knowledge in their use of notetaking as a study-reading strategy. In only a few of the studies (Arnold, 1942; Bretzing & Kulhavy, 1979, 1981; Caverly, 1982; Davis & Annis, 1976; Dyer, Riley, & Yenkovich, 1979; Okey, 1962; Orlando, 1980) was any consideration of students' background knowledge even reported. In five of these studies, background knowledge was controlled by pretesting for it and then either using it as a covariate, removing students who possessed it from the study, or selecting material on which the students were not likely to have background knowledge.

Initial evidence from the three studies that did manipulate background knowledge (Bretzing & Kulhavy, 1981; Caverly, 1982; Davis & Annis, 1976) suggests that if students engage their background knowledge, they are better able to recognize any implicit structure present in the material and use that structure to organize their notes. But, if the structure is explicit in the material, students tend to use a shallower level of processing, causing a concomitant reduction in performance. Students are less likely to impose their own structure from their background knowledge when taking notes and use the author's structure instead. This result seems to indicate an interaction among the student, material, instruction, and task variables. Students need to learn how to recognize the structure present in the material and determine whether their background knowledge imposes a structure that helps them perform well given specific task demands.

In summary, two conclusions can be drawn about the effect of subject variables on notetaking:

- Teaching notetaking to students who are unable to recognize main ideas is inappropriate. Notetaking should not be taught until a basic level of literal comprehension is reached.
- The effect of engaging background knowledge is unclear because of the small number of studies that have addressed this issue. If background knowledge is engaged before or during reading, notetaking may facilitate recall, either by directing students' attention to the structure of the material if their knowledge is weak or by causing students to impose their own structure onto the material in lieu of the author's.

Material Variables.   Several studies that were reviewed manipulated content, readability, length, and explicit structure material variables. Researchers have used six different content areas with a greatest majority in the social sciences. This choice of material by experimenters seems well founded. As noted earlier, social sciences seem to make up the bulk of the reading load in college (Caverly & Orlando, 1985).

A second material variable is readability level. Schumacher (1987) hypothesized that the material's level of difficulty can affect notetaking by affecting students' ability to identify the main idea for subsequent encoding. If the material is exceptionally difficult, students with weak reading skills might have trouble recognizing the ideas important enough for notetaking. In the literature reviewed, only half of the studies reported the material's level of difficulty. Of those studies, only three (Caverly, 1982; Mathews, 1983; McKune, 1958) used college-level material; the other studies used material that was deemed "easy." Results from these latter group of studies do not allow us to draw conclusions about the effectiveness of notetaking in authentic study-reading situations in which the processing demands are often great.

A third variable explored was length of material. Schumacher (1987) again hypothesized that if the material is longer, notetaking should help reduce the number of ideas needing retrieval during recall. Research seems to support this view. In 13 studies in our analysis, the material used was short (fewer than 1,000 words). Another 17 studies used much longer material. Our analysis found that the 13 studies using shorter material had equivocal results when comparing performance after taking notes with performance using other study-reading strategies. On the other hand, in all but 1 of the 17 studies using longer material, performance improved after notetaking. So, it seems notetaking seems to improve performance in longer material.

This conclusion must be qualified, however, because in many of these studies, the effect of length of material on subsequent test performance was obscured by other variables—for instance, the use of easy material. It seems that notetaking may not be a beneficial study-reading strategy to recommend when students are faced with short, easy material. The effort required by notetaking may not be warranted with this material, given its light processing demands. When faced with longer material, however, students might select notetaking as a viable strategy.

A final material variable that may influence the effectiveness of notetaking is the explicit structure of the text. Several theorists (Baker & Brown, 1984; Breuke, 1984; Jonassen, 1985; McConkie, 1977) hypothesized that if the structure of the passage is explicit, students use that structure to identify main ideas and to create verbatim notes at a shallow level of process. If the structure is implicit, however, students are forced to parse out the structure, processing the material at a deeper level, and presumably enhance performance. Our analysis identified only six studies that reported the structure of the material, and only two of these studies actually manipulated structure (Schultz & DiVesta, 1972; Shimmerlik & Nolan, 1976). The results of these two studies demonstrated that when the text material did not have an explicit structure, better students imposed their own organization while study reading using notetaking. Imposed structure resulted in improved performance, particularly when the task demand required recognition or recall of high structural ideas.

In summary, we can draw the following conclusions about the effect of material variables on notetaking:

- Notetaking should improve performance in any content area, although it has been examined primarily in the social sciences.
- Notetaking is more useful for hard material, but not enough data are available to recommend it for college-level material (particularly for poor readers). They must first learn to recognize text structure to find the most important ideas before they learn to take notes on those ideas.
- Notetaking seems to be more productive with longer material. It is not pragmatic to use a processing intensive strategy like notetaking on shorter material.
- Notetaking tends to be verbatim when the material has an explicit structure; when the structure of the material is implicit, notetaking tends to help students (particularly better readers) impose a structure and thus improve their processing.

Instructional Variable. Several instructional variables have been identified in this review. A first variable is the apparent need to teach students how to take notes. Most students in these studies were told or induced to use notetaking without being taught how to take notes. In the few studies (Arnold, 1942; Hannah, 1946; Harris, 1990; Hynd, Simpson, & Chase, 1990; Okey, 1962; Zanias, 1996) where students were actually taught how to take notes, there was marked improvement in comprehension after notetaking. In other studies (Annis & Davis, 1978; Brown & Smiley, 1977; Davis & Annis, 1976; Wade & Trathen, 1989), students were allowed to use any study-reading strategy they preferred. Those students who spontaneously used notetaking showed better performance than those who opted for other study-reading strategies. If notetaking is taught properly, it might become the strategy of choice for students faced with a study-reading task.

Sometimes when notetaking was taught, it did not affect students' ability to remember information (Abuhmaidan & Brethower, 1990; Frazier, 1993). However, in the Abuhmaiden and Brethower study, instruction was limited to only 1 hour, so it is not surprising there was no improved recall. In the Frazier study, the sample size was only four students, so the results are questionable.

Next, if notetaking is to be effective in most situations, we must teach students to review their notes (Annis, 1979; Bretzing & Kulhavy, 1979; Dyer et al., 1979; Hynd et al., 1990; Kardash & Kroeker, 1989; Orlando, 1979). The encoding effect of notetaking seems to hold up for immediate recall whether students review or not. However, for delayed recall, review is necessary if students are to realize a benefit. In those studies that manipulated the review variable, significant improvement in delayed recall was found only if students reviewed their notes before the test. Indeed, some evidence in this literature suggests an instructional–task demand interaction, with students taking fewer notes when expecting an immediate test and more notes when expecting a delayed test.

Our review suggests that notetaking instruction needs to involve several features. Students need to be taught to take notes on the superordinate ideas rather than on the subordinate details and to make reference in these notes to the overall text structure for recall to be improved (Arnold, 1942; Hannah, 1946; Kulhavy et al., 1975; Orlando, 1980a; Rickards & Friedman, 1978; Santa et al., 1979). Most often, processing the superordinate ideas is the appropriate strategy for most study-reading task demands. Students need to be taught how notetaking can direct them to process the information on a deeper level, thus improving their recall (Stone & Miller, 1991). Students need to be taught that what matters is not the quantity but the quality of notes they take (Hakstain, 1971; Hynd et al., 1990; Orlando & Hayward, 1978), again helping them understand that noting the superordinate ideas is crucial.

In summary, these conclusions can be drawn about the effect of the instructional variables on notetaking:

- Instruction in notetaking is necessary for those who have not spontaneously developed the strategy (generally average and poor readers).
- Review is necessary for notetaking to be beneficial particularly in delayed recall tasks.
- Students need to be taught to take notes on the superordinate ideas and connect those ideas to the text structure for recall to be improved.

Task Demand Variable.   The role of the previous three variables on notetaking becomes particularly evident when we examine the task demand variable. A surface analysis suggests that notetaking is equally effective on recognition and recall types of tests. This test type variable was manipulated in only a few studies (Hakstain, 1971; Harris, 1990; Hynd et al., 1990; Kardash & Kroeker, 1989; Kulhavy et al., 1975). In the Hakstain studies, performance did not differ significantly between students who received a recognition test and those who received a recall test, although they were oriented toward expecting a certain type of test. On the other hand, in the remaining studies performance did differ depending on the type of test students expected to receive.

Several theorists (Anderson, 1980; Baker & Brown, 1984; Cook & Mayer, 1983; Gibbs et al., 1982; Levin, 1986; Weinstein & Mayer, 1985) predicted that knowledge of task demand is an important factor in the success of notetaking as a study-reading strategy. Researchers in only half the studies, however, told students that they were going to be tested after study reading or gave them an idea of what the test would cover. In other studies (Hakstain; 1971; Kardash & Kroeker, 1989; Hynd et al., 1990; Kulhavy et al., 1975) knowledge of the type of test was manipulated. In these studies, specific knowledge of the test content did not significantly benefit students. However, it is difficult to determine whether students adjusted their processing to fit their knowledge of what the test would cover or whether they adjusted their processing because they knew they were going to have a test (Anderson & Armbruster, 1982). Therefore, it is difficult to tell whether knowledge of test type affects performance.

On the surface, our analysis seems to suggest that task demand knowledge is not a cogent factor in the effectiveness of notetaking, contrary to the predictions by theorists. However, if the student–instructional–task demand interaction is explored, support for the transfer appropriate processing principle (Morris, Bransford, & Franks, 1977) is found. Presumably, in any empirical environment, most college students would expect to be tested whether or not the researcher told them they would be. Some of these students would choose to adjust their processing accordingly. When asked only to read or reread material, they might still mentally rehearse the information, counter to the instructional instructions given before reading. These students would be intentionally processing information to match what they perceive the task demand to be; therefore, the transfer appropriate processing principle would be activated whether or not it was part of the directions. Other students would follow the instructional directions religiously to satisfy their perception of the task demand. In either situation, if the actual task demand reflects either the students' perceptions of the task demand or the specific instruction requested of the students, notetaking likely improves performance. When the task demand measures knowledge other than what was encoded, performance likely will drop.

A question arises as to whether performance is linked to task demand knowledge and the consequent adjustment in processing, or whether it results from the task demand fortuitously matching the information that was encoded. This may be a "chicken or egg" type of argument. Both correct knowledge of the task demand and appropriate processing strategies are necessary for successful performance following notetaking (Kardash & Kroeker, 1989; Kulhavy et al., 1975). Therefore, the theorists were correct when the importance of the transfer appropriate processing principle was predicted.

This seemingly contradictory result might be explained by the encoding specificity principle (Tulving & Thompson, 1973), as well as by the fact that the test happened to match students' encoding behavior. Knowledge that a test will be given and knowledge of the type of test are not the important variables. What seems to be important in teaching students about the effectiveness of notetaking is the combined effect of these two variables and the students' ability to adjust processing at the time of encoding and retrieval.

Similarly, whether the test was administered immediately or after a delay is not an important variable on its own. What seems to influence the effectiveness of notetaking is the interactive effect of the time of the test with either a conscious choice or an induced decision to review. Notetaking seems to improve immediate recall with or without review. However, delayed recall was generally not enhanced unless students reviewed their notes before the test (Harris, 1990; Kardash & Kroeker, 1989). In two studies in which performance improved on the delayed test without review (Dyer et al., 1979; Fox & Siedow, 1985), other variables may have intervened. For example, in the Fox and Siedow study, the material was shorter than 200 words. In the Dyer et al. study, the material was deemed very easy. There may not have been a need to review such short or simple information.

In summary, these conclusions can be drawn about the effect of the task demand variables on notetaking:

- Students should be taught to identify the type of test they will be required to take and then adjust their notetaking accordingly.
- If the test is to be delayed beyond immediate recall, review is necessary.

Summary of Research on Notetaking.   We can conclude from this research that notetaking while study reading a textbook helps students improve subsequent task performance. Given an appropriate instruction, students can produce a set of notes after engaging in deeper encoding processes that is useful to prepare for any type of test. Then, if a delayed task demand requires recall, they can review those notes to help them boost performance.

Complex Organizational Strategies: Outlining and Mapping

A third major group of study-reading strategies categorized by Weinstein and Mayer (1985) are *complex organizational strategies*. Here, students are directed to recognize and summarize the organization of the material in a structured way in order to facilitate comprehension and recall. Perhaps the most common of these study-reading strategies is outlining in which students reconstruct the explicit or implicit structure of concepts presented by the author in a linear, hierarchical list.

More recently, a type of outlining strategy known as *mapping* (and its many variations that include knowledge maps, concept maps, semantic maps, ConStruct procedure, networking, Node Acquisition Integration Technique, and schematizing) has been promoted as a replacement for the older style of outlining. This group of study-reading strategies directs students to construct a diagram, or spatial image, of the text's structure using nodes to represent the main ideas or supporting details and links to represent the relationships between these nodes. In the mapping type of study-reading strategy, students are often taught to label the connections using common rhetorical structures such as categorization, problem–solution, comparison–contrast, cause–effect, and time–order (Armbruster, 1979; Meyer, 1977).

Outlining emerged from a product theoretical perspective of the study-reading process while mapping is based more on a process and intent perspectives (Caverly & Orlando, 1991). Mapping differs from outlining in that it encourages students to match their background knowledge to the text and to generate spatial images representing this interaction. To improve our integrative analysis of this group of study-reading strategies, we combined the literature on outlining and mapping as we reviewed the variables of the tetrahedral model.

Student Variables.   From our review of the literature, we found a clear interaction between the student–instruction variables. When taught to students, outlining or mapping study-reading strategies improve performance among low reading ability students (Amer, 1994; Draheim, 1986; Iovino, 1993; Lipsky, 1989; Lipson, 1995) as well as average reading ability students (Boyle & Peregoy, 1991; Hall, Dansereau, & Blair, 1990; Holley, Dansereau, McDonald, Garland, & Collins, 1979; Salisbury, 1935; Spiegel & Barufaldi, 1994; Vaughn, Stillman, & Sabers, 1978). However, when high-reading ability students are taught to use outlining, it tends to interfere with their spontaneous choice of study-reading strategies (Balajthy & Weisberg, 1990; Thornton, Bohlmeyer, Dickson, & Kulhavy, 1990). If outlining or mapping are not taught, only high-ability students showed improved performance (Arkes, Schumacher, & Gardner, 1976; Castaneda, Lopez, & Romero, 1987; Good, 1926). So, it seems that simply advising students to use outlining or mapping is not warranted.

Another finding was that background knowledge may affect performance. Most studies who considered background knowledge removed its effect from the experiment by controlling it or matching students in the design (Castaneda et al., 1987; Dansereau, Brooks, Holley, & Collins, 1983; Diekhoff, Brown, & Dansereau, 1982; Stordahl & Christensen, 1956; Vaughn et al., 1978; Willmore, 1966). This research technique served to factor out the consistent positive effect of background knowledge on comprehension (Anderson & Pearson, 1984) and consequently reduced the chances that students using outlining or mapping would show any increase in performance scores.

Only three studies actually manipulated background knowledge (Arnold, 1942; Lipson, 1995; Pugh-Smith, 1985). Arnold found no consistent effect for students with superior background knowledge, although students who used an outlining study-reading strategy tended to have the poorest performance when compared to other study-reading strategies. No attempt was made by Arnold to teach students to engage their background knowledge while reading thus reducing its effect. Lipson found that mapping was superior to other study-reading strategies, but did not see a gain in "scriptally implicit questions" on her test. This may be due more to lack of background knowledge of the content area tested than due to lack of interaction of background knowledge to strategy success. Level of background knowledge needs to be manipulated in future research efforts to identify its effect on mapping.

Pugh-Smith (1985), on the other hand, argued that students with weak background knowledge are often forced to depend on what she calls "bootstrapping" techniques. Students spontaneously select a study-reading strategy like outlining or mapping that on the surface would seem to improve their understanding, but implicitly limits them to use the textbook as the only source of information. This usually results in poor performance. Rather, if students select several supplementary sources to build background knowledge as they are attempting to understand the textbook, a process she calls "scaffolding," comprehension might be improved. Caverly (1998) and Peterson, Caverly, and Nicholson (1998) explored scaffolding through teaching students a mapping strategy called Gathering, Arranging, and Presenting (GAP). Initial evidence suggests improves performance is found when students gather background knowledge, arrange that newfound knowledge by assimilating and accommodating it into old knowledge represented by maps created for a difficult text, and then present that newfound knowledge to peers to confirm one's understanding. Further research on the impact of background knowledge is needed.

In summary, these conclusions can be drawn about the effect of the student variables on outlining and mapping:

- Students need instruction to use outlining or mapping effectively.
- Outlining or mapping can significantly improve reading performance among students with lower levels of ability.
- Initial evidence suggests that outlining or mapping cannot make up for lack of background knowledge. However, newer stategies are being developed that help students engage their background knowledge.

Material Variable.   The majority of content areas where students were taught to outline or map was in the social sciences. However, a substantial number of studies explored study reading in the sciences (Amer, 1994; Balajthy & Weisberg, 1990; Hall et al., 1990; McCagg & Dansereau, 1991; Naidu & Bernard, 1992; Spiegel & Barufaldi, 1994). Two studies even looked at the effect of outlining and mapping on narrative material (Idol, 1987; Thornton et al., 1990). Still, no experiment manipulated the content variable to measure its effect on outlining or mapping. So, it is difficult to see a beneficial effect for outlining and mapping in one content area over another.

For those studies that reported the difficulty of the material, all but four (Boyle & Peregoy, 1991; Castaneda et al., 1987; Lipsky, 1989; McCagg & Dansereau, 1991) selected material deemed at or above reading level of the students. Implicit in this research is a student–material interaction. Unlike underlining or notetaking, it is assumed that outlining and mapping are strategies intended for use with material deemed more difficult for students.

In terms of the length of the material, there seems to be a material–instruction interaction. When shorter material (fewer than 1,000 words) was used, instruction did not seem as necessary; the effectiveness of outlining and mapping is equivocal. Two studies (Long & Aldersley, 1982; Smith & Standal, 1981) found a significant improvement with shorter material following instruction in and use of outlining or mapping whereas three studies (Arkes et al., 1976; Castaneda et al., 1987; Good, 1926) demonstrated improvement when using shorter material without instruction. When using longer material, however, eleven studies demonstrated improvement following instruction in outlining or mapping (Boyle & Peregoy, 1991; Dansereau, Collins, et al., 1979; Dansereau et al., 1983; Diekhoff et al., 1982; Holley et al., 1979; Iovino, 1993; Lipsky, 1989; McCagg & Dansereau, 1991; Ruddell & Boyle, 1984, 1989; Snyder, 1984; Vaughn et al., 1978), while only two demonstrated improvement without instruction (Mathews, 1938; Pugh-Smith, 1985).

The structure of the text material seems to be at the foundation of the effectiveness of outlining and mapping study-reading strategies. Most outlining and mapping instructional strategies emphasize identifying the text structure, and its reproduction is often the task demand. Our review found experiments that reported identifying or manipulating the structure of the material. In three of these studies, the structure of the material was manipulated ranging from explicit to implicit (Castaneda et al., 1987; Good, 1926; McClusky & Dolch, 1924). McClusky and Dolch provided one passage and varied the explicitness of the structure from using no signal words (implicit structure), to providing transitions (vague structure), to numbering the sentences (explicit structure). Good used the same passage that McClusky and Dolch used but manipulated the complexity of the structure by obscuring or not obscuring the main idea with explanatory supporting ideas. Castaneda et al. made the structure more implicit by selecting three passages of increasing length as well as increasing lexical and syntactic difficulty. Although the sample of research is fairly small, these studies confirm the student–material–instructional interaction. Students with low reading ability were not able to recognize implicit or embedded structure without instruction.

Two other research studies (Boyle & Peregoy, 1991; Ruddell & Boyle, 1989) explored whether outlining or mapping was more effective in certain types of text structure patterns: informational, thesis–proof, problem–solution, or comparison–contrast. Ruddell and Boyle (1989) taught two groups mapping, compared them to a control group not taught, then had students read sociology passages with these different organizational patterns. Mapping groups performed better on essays in terms of holistic grading, more cohesive ties, and longer essays. No significant difference in ability to recognize main ideas and supporting details was reported, although those students who mapped recalled more details than the control group. Moreover, mapping seemed to help students recall better from the more complex text structure (problem–solution) than from the simpler text structure (informational). Replicating this study with a psychology text, Boyle and Peregoy found similar performance on the essay task, recall task, and better recall from the more complex thesis–proof text structure compared to a comparison–contrast text structure.

In summary, we can draw the following conclusions about the effect of material variables on outlining and mapping:

- Because none of the research manipulated content, the influence of this variable on the effectiveness of outlining and mapping cannot be said to be more effective in one content area versus another. However, mapping has a robust effect of being effective in both social science and science material.
- Outlining and mapping were generally more successful with material that was deemed at or above the reading level of the student.
- The effectiveness of outlining and mapping is more dependent on instruction with longer material than it is with shorter material.
- With implicitly structured material, outlining and mapping are effective study-reading strategies for students with low reading ability only if they receive instruction.

- Initial evidence suggests mapping is more effective with more complex text structures than simpler text structures.

Instruction Variable. An instructional variable is a major factor in outlining and mapping research. In studies where outlining or mapping was taught to students, developmental college students' reading performance consistently improved (cf. Amer, 1994; Balajthy & Weisberg, 1990; Dansereau et al., 1983; Diekhoff et al., 1982; Iovino, 1993; Lipson, 1995; Long & Aldersley, 1982; Salisbury, 1935; Spiegel & Barufaldi, 1994).

Another factor was the length of instruction. Several studies found greater success when extensive instruction (from 5 to 32 hours) was provided in underlining or mapping than when little instruction was provided (less than 2 hours; Rauch & Fillenworth, 1980; Thornton et al., 1990). Because outlining and mapping are complex study-reading strategies if performed adequately, the need for extensive instruction is not surprising.

We found that reviewing an outline or map prior to the test made a difference, particularly in studies that used longer material and that required students to produce verbatim recall. This conclusion must be tempered, however, as only three studies reported allowing for review before the task demand (Castaneda et al., 1987; Pugh-Smith, 1985; Willmore, 1966). In the Castaneda et al. study in which review was manipulated, the researchers found that verbatim recall of shorter material was significantly hindered following the use of mapping without review.

The effect of adjusting one's processing to fit the task demand is less obvious in this literature. In 12 of the studies, task demand knowledge was directly or indirectly manipulated. In some studies, the students were told what to expect on the test (two experiments in Arkes et al., 1976); in some studies, they performed the study-reading strategy while completing the test (Good, 1926; McClusky & Dolch, 1924; Pugh-Smith, 1985); and in others studies, they took several practice tests similar to the criterion test before the experiment (Arnold, 1942; Dansereau et al., 1983, Holley et al., 1979; Long, 1977; Stordahl & Christensen, 1956; Willmore, 1966).

In some studies, knowledge of test demands did not help improve performance following outlining or mapping. A closer examination of these studies reveals that this lack of improved performance might have been caused by the students' inability to review prior to the task demand (Arnold, 1942; Long, 1976; McClusky & Dolch, 1924; Stordahl & Christensen, 1956), or by low reading ability among the students (Arnold, 1942; Long, 1976; Stordahl & Christensen, 1956; Willmore, 1966). Conversely, the improved performance demonstrated in the other studies may be attributed to variation in the ability of the students (Arkes et al., 1976; Good, 1926; Holley et al., 1979; Pugh-Smith, 1985) or to the amount of instruction they received (Dansereau et al., 1983; Holley et al., 1979; Thornton et al., 1990). Within our review, a student–instructional interaction seems to be masking the variable of task demand knowledge.

Other studies point to the significance of adequate instruction if mapping is to have a positive effect on students' studying. Spiegel and Barufaldi (1994) compared underlining, mapping, rereading, and highlighting; provided 14 hours of instruction; and found mapping more effective than underlining, rereading or highlighting. Rauch and Fillenworth (1980) compared mapping to self-selected strategies, teaching mapping and the other strategies in two 50-minute sessions. Results indicated no significant difference among strategies although mapping groups improved the most.

Still other studies (Balajthy & Weisberg, 1990; Boyle & Peregoy, 1991; Ruddell & Boyle, 1989) specifically examined whether reading performance would be improved among poor readers who were taught to recognize and use the text structure to create a map and then to summarize from that map. After four training sessions, students who were poor readers produced better maps than better readers without instruction, but their ability to perform on a comprehension test or produce a summary was not improved. Had these researchers added future instruction particularly on the need to review the map, performance might have been improved. Caverly, Sundin, Nicholson, and Oelke (1990), on the other hand, taught students to recognize text structure through a text mapping computer program. During the 8-week study, students learned how to recognize superordinate, coordinate, and subordinate relationships between ideas in text as well as text structure patterns (cf. Meyer, 1977). Research demonstrated improved standardized test performance and subsequent improvement in grade point average.

In summary, we can draw three conclusions about the effect of instructional variables on outlining and mapping:

- The effectiveness of outlining and mapping is dependent on instruction, particularly for poorer readers.
- Review before a verbatim recall task demand tends to be necessary for successful performance.
- Task demand knowledge seems to be embedded in a student–instructional interaction in which students' ability and opportunity for review must also be considered.

Task Demand Variable.   Test type had a distinct influence on the effectiveness of outlining and mapping. Three studies used either standardized tests that did not allow outlining or mapping to be used (Salisbury, 1935; Smith & Standal, 1981), or ethnographic measures that observed spontaneous use of outlining or mapping (Pugh-Smith, 1985). Most studies, however, used experimenter-designed recognition and/or recall tests after students studied a text passage. Improved performance was not found on a great majority of these studies where recognition-type tests followed outlining or mapping (Arnold, 1942; Boyle & Peregoy, 1991; Iovino, 1993; Lipsky, 1989; Long, 1976; Mathews, 1938; McKune, 1958; Rauch & Fillenworth, 1980; Ruddell & Boyle, 1989; Snyder, 1984; Stordahl & Christensen, 1956; Thornton et al., 1990; Willmore, 1966). Improved performance was found, however, in studies that used recall measures after instruction (Amer, 1994; Arkes et al., 1976; Boyle & Peregoy, 1991; Balajthy & Weisberg, 1990; Castaneda et al., 1987; Dansereau & Collins, et al., 1979; Dansereau et al., 1983; Hall et al., 1990; Holley et al., 1979; Iovino, 1993; Lipson, 1995; Long & Aldersley, 1984; McCagg & Dansereau, 1991; Naidu & Bernard, 1992; Snyder, 1984; Spiegel & Barufaldi, 1994). It seems that recognition task demands were not sensitive enough to measure the benefits of outlining and mapping. This may be due to the nature of the outlining and mapping task that directs students to attend to main ideas and the relationships among them, while deemphasizing details. It is difficult to tell what ratio of main ideas to details was present on these recognition tests. Students using an outlining or mapping strategy are less likely to demonstrate improved performance on a task demand that focuses on detail than on a task demand that focuses on main ideas. This conclusion is consistent with those of previous reviews (Anderson, 1978; Holley & Dansereau, 1984; McKeachie, 1988).

When considering the delay between using outlining or mapping and taking the test, no clear pattern emerged. But when the instructional–task demand interaction is examined, a possible effect emerges. In those studies in which students showed no improvement on an immediate test, review was not allowed before the test. In those studies in which students showed no improvement on a delayed test, again review was not allowed before the test. It seems that review is a potential variable in the success of outlining or mapping over both the short and the long run. In the study-reading strategies discussed earlier, teaching students to review before the test was an important factor in eventual success on the task demand. Unfortunately, only one study (Hall et al., 1990) reported teaching students how to review their outlines or their maps.

In summary, these conclusions about the effect of the task demand variables on outlining or mapping can be drawn:

- Outlining and mapping seem to improve students' performance when the task demand focuses more on main ideas than on details; thus, outlining and mapping seem to favor the encoding and recall of main ideas over the encoding and recall of details.
- Review seems to be a potential factor for outlining and mapping to improve performance on either immediate or delayed tests as it has been in other study-reading strategies.

Summary of Research on Outlining and Mapping. Based on this review, we conclude that students must be taught how to use the outlining and mapping study-reading strategies. This is particularly true for students with low reading ability and students working with longer material (more than 1,000 words). There is some evidence that students must be taught not only how to use these study-reading strategies but also how to assess the interaction between their purpose for reading (i.e., their knowledge of the task demand) and how well their background knowledge matches the material. Moreover, there are some indications that review might be necessary for students to perform before any test. If students can assess their abilities, the text, and the context, and also adjust their processing accordingly, outlining and mapping seem to be effective strategies for improving the recall of main ideas, although not necessarily of details.

Comprehension Monitoring Strategy: SQ3R

A fourth group of study-reading strategies posited by Weinstein and Mayer (1985) are *comprehension monitoring strategies*. Study-reading strategies within this group are often labeled *metacognitive strategies*. They direct students to establish goals for the study situation, to assess progress toward these goals, and to modify processing if progress is unsatisfactory. A theoretical foundation for metacognitive strategies is discussed in Nist and Holschuh (chap. 4, this volume).

One common study-reading strategy that is taught to lead students to monitor their comprehension is SQ3R developed by Robinson (1946, 1961, 1970). This strategy directs the students to complete activities before reading (Survey the material by skimming it for organizing information and formulate Questions or goals by converting the subheadings into questions), during reading (Read to answer the questions, monitor progress in answering the questions, and modify processing if progress is unsatisfactory), and after reading (Recite the answers to the questions and Review the answers). Of all the independent reading strategies available for the college developmental reading student, SQ3R and its many variations are the most often taught (Stahl, 1983). Nevertheless, anyone with a passing exposure to the literature realizes that it too is often the most maligned study-reading strategy (Adams, Carnine, & Gersten, 1982; Stahl, 1983).

Several researchers have reviewed the theoretical and empirical foundations used to support the use of SQ3R for college developmental readers (Anderson & Armbruster, 1982; Bahe, 1969; Basile, 1978; Caverly, 1985; Caverly & Orlando, 1991; Crewe & Hultgren, 1969; Graham, 1982; Gustafson & Pederson, 1984, 1985; Jacobowitz, 1988; Johns & McNamara, 1980; Kopfstein, 1982; Kremer, Aeschleman, & Peterson, 1983; Orlando, 1978, 1984; Palmatier, 1971; Scappaticci, 1977; Snyder, 1984; Stahl, 1983; Tadlock, 1978; Walker, 1982; Wark, 1965). These reviewers conclude that although some of the individual steps may have merit, little evidence validates the use of the entire system as designed by Robinson (1946). Further, their analyses found little empirical evidence to suggest that SQ3R is more effective than reading or rereading. Nevertheless, it is still one of the most prevalent study-reading strategies.

Student Variables   Virtually every study we reviewed taught SQ3R, which is not surprising due to the complexity of the strategy. Thus the research conclusions we draw may reflect more the effect of instruction rather than the effect of the study-reading strategy itself. Nevertheless, teaching SQ3R does not seem to be sufficient to overcome a student's general lack of reading ability, although students at all levels seemed capable of learning how to use the strategy given enough instruction. SQ3R can provide a useful heuristic for successfully processing a text, but if students are struggling with word recognition or basic comprehension skills, SQ3R is insufficient to overcome these weaknesses.

Varying amounts of intensive and lengthy instruction seem to be needed for students with differing levels of reading ability if improved performance following the use of SQ3R is desired (Beneke & Harris, 1972; Briggs, Tosi, & Morley, 1971; Diggs, 1972; Foreman, 1982; Neal & Langer, 1992; Niles, 1963; Orlando, 1984; Trillin & Associates, 1980). Both a meta-analysis (Caverly, 1985) and empirical research (Orlando, 1980) suggest that at least 10 hours of instruction is necessary for SQ3R to be effective with low-ability students. For medium-ability students, 7 to 10 hours of instruction seems to be necessary; whereas for high-ability students, success has been demonstrated with less than 7 hours of instruction (Butler, 1983; Galloway, 1983; Gurrola, 1974; Martin, 1983). Three studies (Galloway, 1983; Gurrola, 1974; Snyder, 1984) found no improvement among low-ability students even after instruction. However, a closer examination of these three studies reveals that students received less than 6 hours of instruction in SQ3R. It was simply not enough to predict any gain following the use of SQ3R.

Moreover, there seems to be strong evidence that students' attitudes toward the amount of effort needed to apply SQ3R on any textbook chapter affects both whether students use the strategy after instruction is over and their subsequent improvement when asked to perform the study-reading strategy during a research study (Briggs et al., 1971; Butler, 1983; Courtney, 1965; Doctor, Aponte, Bury, & Welch, 1970; Kremer et al., 1983; McReynolds & Church, 1973; Niple, 1968; Scappaticci, 1977; Wooster, 1953). Not only must students be taught cognitively how to perform the study-reading strategy, but they must be convinced affectively of the value of using the strategy.

Little is known regarding the effect of background knowledge on SQ3R. Only a few studies manipulated this variable (Butler, 1983; Willmore, 1966), but the act of controlling it removes any effect rather than taking it into account. This procedure factors out the consistently positive effect of background knowledge on reading comprehension (Anderson & Pearson, 1984) and thus reduces the chance of any positive performance effects for SQ3R.

In a recent adaptation to SQ3R, however, Caverly, Mandeville, and Nicholson (1995) developed a strategy called PLAN (i.e., Preview, Locate, Add, and Note), which specifically directs students to utilize their background knowledge during the preview step. In later research, Caverly and Peterson (1996) demonstrated PLAN as effective for improving college developmental reading students performance on pre- and posttest measures, standardized reading tests, as well as future semester grade point averages. With these low-level readers, however, upwards of 45 hours of instruction was provided to promote such performance.

In summary, these conclusions can be drawn about the effect of the student variables on SQ3R:

- Students must be taught how to use SQ3R.
- Students with low reading ability must be taught for a longer period of time than those with medium ability, who, in turn, must be taught longer than those with high ability. However, SQ3R is not helpful for readers struggling with basic word recognition or comprehending skills.
- Instruction for developmental reading students must incorporate the value of SQ3R along with the procedures on to use it.
- The effect of students' background knowledge on SQ3R cannot be determined because it was not considered in any of the research. However, adaptations to SQ3R (e.g., PLAN) incorporating engagement of background knowledge have suggested improved reading performance.

Material Variable.   The great majority of content areas that were used in the research examining SQ3R was from the social sciences. Little is known about the effect of SQ3R in other content areas.

Few conclusions can be drawn about the difficulty of the material used by these researchers, because only a few report the level of the material used. Those reported were college level or higher (Chastain & Thurber, 1989; Holmes, 1972; Martin, 1983; Snyder, 1984; Wooster, 1953). Unlike the previous study-reading strategies we have reviewed, however, most of these studies used textbooks from college students' current classes in an attempt to teach them how to transfer the SQ3R study-reading strategy to their required reading material (Beneke & Harris, 1972; Briggs et al., 1971; Chastain & Thurber, 1989; Doctor et al., 1970; Harris & Ream, 1972; Kremer et al., 1983; McReynolds & Church,

1973; Robinson, 1961). The subsequent success found when students used SQ3R in this more challenging material is encouraging.

Not unexpectedly, the material used in the studies examining SQ3R was considerably longer than the material typically found in the research on underlining or notetaking study-reading strategies. This is primarily due of the nature of SQ3R, which requires material with an introduction, several subtitled sections, and a summary. The length of the material did not seem to affect performance.

We can draw few conclusions based on the structure of the material because virtually no experiment manipulated the effect of text structure on the use of SQ3R. This was a rather surprising finding considering the extent of the literature on the effect of explicit structure on comprehension (Stahl et al., 1992; Swafford, 1990). Perhaps one explanation for this gap in the research is that the experimenters assumed the five organizational components (introduction, subheading, highlighted words, graphics, and summary) that students are induced to use during the survey step imposes an explicit structure. Given the product perspective (cf. Caverly & Orlando, 1991) that we believe is inherent in Robinson's (1970) directions, this assumption is not unexpected. Much of the inconsistent results of the research on SQ3R might be explained by the uncritical acceptance of this assumption by students and instructors. If instruction in SQ3R encouraged students to recognize the explicit and implicit organizational structure of the material, performance might be improved.

In summary, we can draw the following conclusions about material variables on SQ3R:

- Little can be said about the effect of SQ3R on various content areas because social science material was the primary material used.
- The material used in the research analyzed was generally at or above the college readability level, but no studies manipulated effects due to the material.
- The material was generally longer than that used in research on other study-reading strategies; this difference was probably due to the inherent nature of the SQ3R study-reading task requiring an entire chapter.
- No conclusion can be drawn regarding the effect of the structure of the material on the SQ3R study-reading strategy although we would predict it would make a difference.

Instruction Variable.   One distinct instructional variable is the importance of teaching students the SQ3R study-reading strategy. Virtually every study taught this strategy with the length of instruction ranging from 1 hour to 15 weeks. Still, previous reviews have questioned the quality of this instruction (Anderson & Armbruster, 1982; Bahe, 1969; Basile, 1978; Entwistle, 1960, 1978, 1994; Fox, 1962; Orlando, 1978; Palmatier, 1971; Pask, 1976a, 1976b). For example, often students are taught that the subheadings reflect the most important information in the material used and should automatically be converted into questions irrespective of the task demand. A review of textbooks (Armbruster & Anderson, 1984) found that most had inadequate subheadings that failed to communicate either the important information or how that information was organized. Blindly converting these to questions for reading may not satisfy the task demands of the study reading.

A second important instructional variable is review, given its effect on underlining and notetaking, and given that it is presumably inherent in the last two steps of the SQ3R strategy (i.e., Recite and Review). Nevertheless, only a few studies (Butler, 1983; Chastain & Thurber, 1989; Holmes, 1972; Willmore, 1966; Wooster, 1953) provided an opportunity for students to review before the task demand, and the results were equivocal. With longer passages more likely to require the use of SQ3R, this failure to provide a review opportunity seems counterintuitive to the intention of the recite and review steps. This instructional interaction might have much to do with the failure of the research to demonstrate consistent improved performance when students use SQ3R.

In summary, these conclusions about the effect of the instructional variables on SQ3R can be drawn

- The amount of instruction needed for SQ3R to be effective is directly related to the student's level of reading ability. Longer amounts of instruction for less able students and shorter amounts for more able.
- Lack of research makes it impossible to draw conclusions about the effect of reviewing before the task demand.

Task Demand Variable.   The task demand variables seem to have a distinct but inconsistent effect on SQ3R. In only 3 of the 13 experiments that used a recognition test as the task demand was SQ3R found to be effective (Butler, 1983; Chastain & Thurber, 1989; Martin, 1983). Similarly, in studies that used recall tasks (Gurrola, 1974; Stoodt & Balbo, 1979), the use of SQ3R had equivocal results. SQ3R was found to be effective, however, in four experiments that used the students' grade point average (GPA) as the criterion (Beneke & Harris, 1972; Briggs et al., 1971; Driskell & Kelly, 1980; Heerman, 1972). This finding suggests that recognition and recall tasks are not sensitive enough to identify performance differences with SQ3R. However, conclusions based on GPA must be made carefully because so many other factors can influence grades.

If we examine the interaction between the instructional and the task demand, we can see a reason for these inconsistent performance findings. For example, the amount of instruction given to low-ability students was often insufficient. In the experiments in which students demonstrated no improvement on recognition or recall types of task demands, less than 8 hours of instruction was provided with only one exception (Holmes, 1972). Therefore, it is difficult to draw conclusions about the effect of SQ3R on reading performance using these task demand variables. One interpretation is that SQ3R does not affect reading comprehension and retention directly, but affects it indirectly through improving students' attitudes toward study. This improvement in students' attitudes about the amount of effort necessary to study read college-level material would then be manifested in improvement in long-term criterion measures such as GPA. Future research is needed to verify this hypothesis.

Another explanation for why SQ3R affects performance on GPA but not on recognition or recall tests is that the longer term measure allows more trial applications for learning this study-reading strategy. That is, success on GPA measures could be related to our second task demand variable, test administration delay. A recognition or recall task demand tends to measure application of the study-reading strategy after a single application. In most empirical studies, students apply SQ3R to a passage and then take a recognition or recall test either immediately or several days later. If the task demand is semester GPA, however, students have the opportunity to apply SQ3R several times in a variety of study situations before their performance is measured. It may be that a positive performance effect for SQ3R shows up only after students have had a chance to apply the study-reading strategy several times.

A test of this hypothesis is implicit in several experiments in which students who learned SQ3R demonstrated improved performance (as measured by GPA) after one semester (Briggs et al., 1971; Driskell & Kelly, 1980; Stoodt & Balbo, 1979; Wooster, 1953), after two semesters (Heerman, 1972), and after three semesters (Beneke & Harris, 1972). As stated earlier, however, caution is advised in drawing global conclusions from these data because many other unmeasured intervening variables may have affected this improvement in GPA.

In summary, we can draw two conclusions about the effect of task demand variables on SQ3R:

- Successful performance following the use of SQ3R may require several applications of the strategy.
- Long-term performance gain may be a factor of the criterion measure.

Summary of Research on SQ3R.   A strong student–instruction–task demand interaction seems to be present in the use of SQ3R. Substantial, effective instruction is necessary for students with low or medium reading ability to succeed with this strategy. This instruction should include an attempt to build students' awareness of the effort required in using this strategy. Success is apparent only in long-term measures such as GPA. On the other hand, we know very little about the effect of students' background knowledge, or of the effect of material variables, on SQ3R as a study-reading strategy.

IMPLICATIONS FOR INSTRUCTION

Based on this integrative review, we can conclude that under certain conditions, all five of these strategies help improve students' ability to study textbooks. These study-reading strategies have the potential to improve students' acquisition of important material, develop deeper encoding of this information, encourage a more thorough integration of information into prior knowledge, develop cues for retention, and provide a permanent storage device for later review. Such strategies can direct students to understand and remember more of what they read. For this potential to be realized, however, students must be taught how to select a study-reading strategy on the basis of their knowledge of these conditions. This finding directly supports the intent perspective of study reading (Caverly & Orlando, 1991).

We suggest that the individual and combined effects of 10 of the 11 variables we used to examine the literature must be considered when teaching students to use these study-reading strategies. The variable that we cannot conclude has an effect on these study-reading strategies is the content area of the material to which the strategies is applied. The great majority of studies we reviewed did not manipulate this variable. Because of the predominate use of social science materials, our research review does not allow us to draw conclusions about the effects of these study-reading strategies on other content areas.

We conclude that these study-reading strategies should not be taught to students who are developmentally struggling with word recognition and basic comprehension skills. Our review suggests that students with low reading ability will not profit from underlining or notetaking if the material is considered hard because of readability, length, or implicit structure; nor will students benefit if they are not allowed to review before the task demand. This interaction seems to be the result of students' inability to recognize what is important in the text (i.e., the main idea or high structural idea). There is some evidence, however, that once students with low reading ability have been taught how to find these main ideas and how to review what has been underlined or noted, they can learn to use underlining or notetaking effectively. Such instruction must center around a strategic approach to reading (Baker & Brown, 1984).

Students must be taught to recognize and take note of the explicit structure provided by the author to help in encoding and subsequent recall. If the structure is implicit, on the other hand, students must be taught how to engage their background knowledge to construct a personal structure to help in encoding and recall. Furthermore, students must be taught how to monitor their processing when underlining or notetaking in relationship to the demands of the task demand. This strategic approach requires a time commitment on the part of the students, as well as task demand knowledge, or knowledge of what the author and the instructor want them to understand. Given this commitment, both underlining and notetaking strategies can be more effective (producing better performance on a task demand) than reading or rereading, but they cannot necessarily be considered more efficient (i.e., less time consuming). Students must come to understand the trade-off between strategies that may produce better results and those that take less time to complete.

Outlining, mapping, and SQ3R tend to be more effective for students with low and medium reading ability (after they have learned how to use these strategies) when the material is more difficult and when the opportunity for review is provided. Knowledge of the task demand and whether the task demand measures main ideas more than details also influences effectiveness. Readers of all ability levels, however, need to be taught how to use these three study-reading strategies. They also need instruction in how to integrate these study-reading strategies into their existing repertoire of strategies. All students must be taught to create their outlines, maps, or SQ3R questions on the basis of their perceptions of the task demand. They must also be taught to review their outlines, maps, or answers to their questions before the test.

Finally, students must be taught to believe in and complete the extensive steps inherent in these study-reading strategies—that is, the support strategies described by Dansereau (1985). Evidence suggests that unless students change their attitudes about these strategies, they will not continue the effort necessary for applying them outside of the empirical setting or developmental classroom. This is particularly true for SQ3R, which requires several applications with guided feedback to demonstrate improved performance. Therefore, students need to learn about the cost effectiveness (more time but better performance) of study-reading strategies like outlining, mapping, or SQ3R and be apprised of the metacognitive criteria they can use to evaluate their effective and efficient use of these strategies.

Effective (Heavy teacher/material demands)		Efficient (Light teacher/materials demands)
Outlining	Notetaking	Reading only
Mapping	Summarizing	Rereading
SQ3R/PLAN		Underlining/Highlighting

FIG. 5.2. Demand model for choosing study-reading strategies.

College reading instructors need to explore pedagogical techniques for teaching students how to perceive these contextual constraints, how to choose a study-reading strategy to match those constraints, how to monitor the application of a given study-reading strategy within a given context, and how to adjust the strategy or change to a new one when the choice was inappropriate (Pressley, Borkowski, & O'Sullivan, 1984). In other words, college reading instructors need to teach their students metacognitive control of study-reading strategies. Campione and Armbruster (1985) discussed initial attempts at this instruction. Wade and Reynolds (1989) and Simpson, Stahl, and Hayes (1989) presented other instructional strategies applicable to college-age students. Nist and Holshuch (chap. 4, this volume) review two new attempts. Another avenue we have explored is using a decision-making model to teach students how to perceive contextual constraints and choose a strategy based on these constraints (see Fig. 5.2).

We use this model to teach our students that certain study-reading strategies are more efficient (i.e., less time consuming) than other strategies, but not as effective in terms of improved performance. For example, underlining and rereading strategies take less time but also do less to increase performance on tests than a notetaking strategy, which in turn takes less time but does less to improve test performance than outlining, mapping, or SQ3R. Presenting study-reading strategies along this continuum seems to help students understand that different strategies have different strengths in different contexts. This latest review continues to support the effectiveness dimension of this model; the efficiency dimension must be left to future empirical research or integrative and meta-analytic reviews.

After presenting the model to students, we teach them how to identify a particular strategy for each particular study situation. To help in this metacognitive decision, two criteria are taught to students. First, a given strategy might be chosen on the basis of the teacher's demands (e.g., the role of the reading material in tests, lectures, or classroom discussions). Second, a strategy might be chosen on the basis of material demands (e.g., readability, length, background knowledge needed, ability level required). If the demands of the teacher and the material are heavy, a strategy that is more effective (such as SQ3R or mapping) is appropriate. If the demands are light, a strategy that is less effective but more efficient (such as underlining) makes sense. If the demands are contrasting, a compromise strategy (such as notetaking) is appropriate. Students are taught how to identify such demands and how to use these criteria for selecting a demand-appropriate, study-reading strategy. Preliminary evidence based on student feedback is encouraging. Further research needs to be completed regarding the placement of each strategy along the dual continuum of effectiveness and efficiency.

FUTURE RESEARCH AND INSTRUCTIONAL AVENUES

This review makes evident several specific research and instructional avenues. In particular, we recommend that the student–instructional interaction present in these study-reading strategies be explored further to verify the role of background knowledge in their successful use. Following the research of Lipson (1995), Nist and Hogrebe (1987) , Smith (1982), and Pugh-Smith (1985), background knowledge should be manipulated within the research paradigm to see its effect on performance following the use of these study-reading strategies.

In terms of research, other specific metacognitive strategies that monitor the progress of processing toward satisfying the intent for reading need to be developed and tested. Particularly promising is the recent work of Wade and Reynolds (1989), Simpson et al. (1989), and Caverly et al. (1995). Also, it would seem warranted to continue this integrative review with the study-reading strategies that are not directly addressed here. For example, a thorough exploration of rereading and summarizing is needed. Such an analysis has already begun, using a meta-analysis technique (Caverly, 1985) and other integrative reviews (Cook & Mayer, 1983; Thomas & Rohwer, 1986; Weinstein & Mayer, 1985).

In addition, other variables should be explored to determine their individual and combined effects on these study-reading strategies. Additional student variables that might be considered include age, attitude, and academic aptitude. Another material variable that influences the effectiveness of study-reading strategies is the relevance of the material for the students. Other potentially important instructional variables are metacognitive knowledge and length of instruction. Finally, task demand variables that should be examined include intentional versus incidental types of recall, as well as the significance of performance on criterion measures. Many of the studies in this review demonstrated statistically significant improvement with a 50% to 60% level of performance. This may satisfy an empirical paradigm, but it will not help a student pass a course. These integrative analyses should be continued in order to come to some consensus on the validity of each study-reading strategy within the contextual constraints of the study situation.

A general conclusion that seems evident from this review of research is that most study-reading strategies are effective, but no one study-reading strategy is appropriate for all students in all study situations. This theoretical position has been argued elsewhere (Anderson & Armbruster, 1984; Elshout-Mohr, 1983; Ford, 1981; Laurillard, 1979; McKeachie, 1988; Schumacher, 1987) and has been verified here. To help their students deal with the variety of demands they face in higher education, college reading instructors should teach students to expand their repertoire of study-reading strategies.

REFERENCES AND SUGGESTED READINGS

Abuhmaidan, Y. A., & Brethower, D. M. (1990). Use of study aids to improve comprehension of technical material. *Journal of College and Adult Reading and Learning, 22*(1), 1–18.

Adams, A., Carnine, D., & Gersten, R. (1982). Instructional strategies for study reading content area texts in the intermediate grades. *Reading Research Quarterly, 17,* 27–55.

Adams, E. K. (1969). The graphical aid to comprehension. In G. B. Schick & M. M. May (Eds.), *Reading: Process and pedagogy* (pp. 12–22). Milwaukee, Wl: National Reading Conference.

Amer, A. A. (1994). The effect of knowledge-map and underlining training on the reading comprehension of scientific texts. *English for Specific Purposes, 13*(1), 35–45.

Anderson, R. C., & Pearson, P. D. (1984). A schema-theoretic view of basic processes in reading. In P. D. Pearson (Ed.), *Handbook of reading research* (pp. 255–292). New York: Longman.

Anderson, T. H. (1978). *Study skills and learning strategies. Tech Report Number 104.* Champaign-Urbana, IL: University of Illinois, Center for the Study of Reading.

Anderson, T. H. (1980). Study strategies and adjunct aids. In R. J. Spiro, B. C. Bruce, & W. E. Brewer (Eds.), *Theoretical issues in reading comprehension* (pp. 483–502). Hillsdale, NJ: Lawrence Erlbaum Associates.

Anderson, T. H., & Armbruster, B. B. (1982). Reader and text: Study strategies. In W. Otto & S. White (Eds.), *Reading expository material* (pp. 219–242). San Diego, CA: Academic Press.

*Anderson, T. H., & Armbruster, B. B. (1984). Studying. In P. D. Pearson (Eds.), *Handbook of reading research* (pp. 657–680). New York: Longman.

Annis, L. E. (1979). Effect of cognitive style and learning passage organization on study technique effectiveness. *Journal of Educational Psychology, 71,* 620–626.

Annis, L. E., & Davis, J. K. (1978). Study techniques and cognitive style: Their effect on recall and recognition. *Journal of Educational Research, 71,* 175–178.

Annis, L. F., & Annis, D. B. (1982). A normative study of students' reported preferred study techniques. *Reading World, 21*(3), 201–207.

Arkes, N. R., Schumacher, G. M., & Gardner, E. T. (1976). Effects of instructional on the retention of prose material. *Journal of Educational Psychology, 68,* 536–545.

Armbruster, B. B. (1979). *An investigation of the effectiveness of "mapping" texts as a studing strategy for middle school students.* Unpublished doctoral dissertation, University of Illinois, Champaign-Urbana.

Arnold, H. F. (1942). The comparative effectiveness of certain study techniques in the field of history. *Journal of Educational Psychology, 32,* 449–457.

Bahe, V. R. (1969). Reading study instruction and college achievement. *Reading Improvement, 6,* 57–61.

*Baker, L., & Brown, A. L. (1984). Metacognitive skills and reading. In P. D. Pearson (Eds.), *Handbook of reading research* (pp. 353–394). New York: Longman.

*Balajthy, E., & Weisberg, R. (1990). *Effects of reading ability, prior knowledge, topic interest, and locus of control on at-risk college students' use of graphic organizers and summarizing.* (ERIC Document Reproduction Service No. ED 325 838)

Barnett, J. (1997). *Self-regulation of reading college textbooks.* (ERIC Document Reproduction Service No. ED 406 654).

Bartel, B. (1993–1994). What research has to say about instruction in text-marking strategies. *Forum for Reading, 24,* 11–19.

Basile, D. D. (1978). Helping college students understand their textbooks. *Reading World, 17*(4) 289–294.

Bausell, R. B., & Jenkins, J. R. (1977). Effects on prose learning of frequency of adjunct cues and the difficulty of the material cued. *Journal of Reading Behavior, 9*(3), 227–232.

Beneke, W. M., & Harris, M. B. (1972). Teaching self-control of study behavior. *Behavior Research and Therapy, 10,* 35–41.

Berg, P., & Rentle, V. (1966). Improving study skills. *Journal of Reading, 9,* 343–348.

Blanchard, J., & Mikkelson, V. (1987). Underlining performance outcomes in expository text. *Journal of Educational Research, 80*(4), 197–201.

Boyle, O., & Peregoy, S. F. (1991). The effects of cognitive mapping on students' learning from college text. *Journal of College Reading and Learning, 23*(2), 14–22.

Brady, P. J., & Rickards, J. P. (1979). How personal evaluation affects the underlining and recall of prose material. *Journal of Reading Behavior, 11*(1), 61–68.

Bretzing, B. H., & Kulhavy, R. W. (1979). Notetaking and depth of processing. *Contemporary Educational Psychology, 4,* 145–154.

Bretzing, B. H., & Kulhavy, R. W. (1981). Notetaking and passage style. *Journal of Educational Psychology, 73,* 242–250.

*Breuke, J. A. (1984). A theoretical framework for spatial learning strategies. In C. D. Holley & D. E. Dansereau (Eds.), *Spatial learning strategies: Techniques, applications, and related issues* (pp. 21–43). San Diego, CA: Academic Press.

Briggs, R. D., Tosi, D. J., & Morley, R. M. (1971). Study habit modification and its effects on academic performance: A behavioral approach. *Journal of Educational Research, 64,* 347–350.

*Brown, A. L. (1980). Metacognitive development in Reading. In R. J. Spiro, B. C. Bruce, & W. E. Brewer (Eds.), *Theoretical issues in reading comprehension* (pp. 453–482). Hillsdale, NJ: Lawrence Erlbaum Associates.

*Brown, A. L., Campione, J. C., & Day, J. D. (1981). Learning to learn: On training students to learn from texts. *Educational Researcher, 10,* 14–21.

*Brown, A. L., & Smiley, S. S. (1977). *The Development of strategies for studying prose passages* (Tech. Rep. No. 66). Champaign-Urbana, IL: University of Illinois, Center for the Study of Reading.

Bryant, D., & Lindeman, T. (1995). *College study skill text analysis based on validated research recommendations.* (ERIC Document Reproduction Service No. ED 385 829)

Butler, T. H. (1983). *Effect of subject and training variables on the SQ3R study method.* Unpublished doctoral dissertation, Arizona State University, Tempe, AZ.

Campione, J. C., & Armbruster, B. B. (1985). Acquiring information from texts: An analysis of four approaches. In J. W. Segal, S. E. Chapman, & R. Glaser (Eds.), *Thinking and learning skills: Vol. 1. Relating instruction to research* (pp. 317–359). Hillsdale, NJ: Lawrence Erlbaum Associates.

Carrier, C. A., & Titus, A. (1979). The effects of notetaking: A review of studies. *Contemporary Educational Psychology, 4,* 299–314.

Castaneda, S., Lopez, M., & Romero, M. (1987). The role of five induced learning strategies in scientific text comprehension. *Journal of Experimental Education, 55*(3), 125–130.

Caverly, D. C. (1982). *The effect of three studying strategies upon comprehension and recall.* Unpublished doctoral dissertation, Indiana Unversity, Bloomington, IN.

Caverly, D. C. (1985, December). *Textbook study strategies: A meta-analysis.* Paper presented at the National Reading Conference, San Diego, CA.

Caverly, D. C. (1998). Techtalk: GAP, a reading strategy for multiple sources. *Journal of Developmental Education, 22*(2), 38–39.

Caverly, D. C., Mandeville, T. P., & Nicholson, S. A. (1995). PLAN: A study-reading strategy for informational text. *Journal of Adolescent & Adult Literacy, 39*(3), 190–99.

Caverly, D. C., & Orlando, V. P. (1985). *How much do college students read their texts?* Paper presented at the Western College Reading Learning Association Colorado State Conference, Colorado Springs, CO.

*Caverly, D. C., & Orlando, V. P. (1991). Textbook study strategies. In R. F. Flippo & D. C. Caverly (Eds.), *Teaching reading & study strategies at the college level* (pp. 86–165). Newark, DE: International Reading Association.

Caverly, D. C., & Peterson, C. L. (1996, October). *Long term effects of a whole language college reading program.* Paper presented at the National Research Conference on Developmental Education, Charlotte, NC.

Caverly, D. C., Sundin, S., Nicholson, S., & Oelke, E. (1990, October). *Empowering T.A.S.P. developmental readers through computers.* Paper presented at the Conference on Academic Support Programs, San Antonio, TX.

Charters, J. A. (1925). Methods of study used by college women. *Journal of Educational Research, 10,* 344–345.

*Chastain, G., & Thurber, S. (1989). The SQ3R study technique enhances comprehension of an introductory Psychology textbook. *Reading Improvement, 26*(1), 94–96.

Cook, L. K., & Mayer, R. E. (1983). Reading strategies training for meaningful learning from prose. In M. Pressey & J. Levin (Eds.), *Cognitive strategies research: Educational applications* (pp. 87–131). New York: Springer-Verlag.

Courtney, L. (1965). Organization produced. In H. L. Herber (Eds.), *Developing study skills in secondary schools* (pp. 77–97). Newark, DE: International Reading Association.

Craik, E. M., & Tulving, E. (1975). Depth of processing and the retention of words in episodic memory. *Journal of Experimental Psychology: General, 104,* 268–294.

Crawford, R. C. (1938). *How to teach.* Los Angeles, CA: School Book Press.

Crewe, J. C. (1968). *The effect of study strategies on the retention of college text material.* Unpublished doctoral dissertation, University of Minnesota, Minneapolis, MN.

Crewe, J. C., & Hultgren, D. (1969). What does research really say about study skills? In G. B. Schick & M. M. May (Eds.), *The psychology of reading behavior* (pp. 75–79). Milwaukee, WI: National Reading Conference.

Dansereau, D. E., Actkinson, T. R., Long, G. L., & McDonald, B. (1974). *Learning strategies: A review and synthesis of the current literature.* (ERIC Document Reproduction Service No. ED 103 403).

Dansereau, D. E., Brooks, L. W., Holley, C. D., & Collins, K. W. (1983). Learning strategy training: Effects of sequencing. *Journal of Experimental Education, 51*(3), 102–108.

*Dansereau, D. E., Collins, K. W., McDonald, B. A., Garland, J., Holley, C. D., Deikhoff, G., & Evans, S. H. (1979). Development and evaluation of a learning strategy training program. *Journal of Educational Psychology, 71*(1), 64–73.

Dansereau, D. E., McDonald, B. A., Collins, K. W., Garland, J., Holley, C. D., Deikhoff, G., & Evans, S. H. (1979). Development and evaluation of a learning strategy program. In H. F. O'Neil & C. D. Speilberger (Eds.), *Cognitive and affective learning strategies* (pp. 3–43). San Diego, CA: Academic Press.

Dansereau, D. F. (1980). *Learning strategy research.* Paper presented at the NIE-LRDC Conference on Thinking and Learning Skills, Pittsburgh, PA.

*Dansereau, D. F. (1985). Learning strategy research. In J. W. Segal, S. F. Chapman, & R. Glaser (Eds.), *Thinking and learning skills: Relating instruction to research* (pp. 209–239). Hillsdale, NJ: Lawrence Erlbaum Associates.

Davis, J. K., & Annis, L. (1976). The effects of study techniques, study preference, and familiarity on later recall. *Journal of Experimental Education, 18*, 92–96.

Diekhoff, G. M., Brown, P. J., & Dansereau, D. E. (1982). A prose learning strategy training program based upon network and depth of processing model. *Journal of Experimental Education, 50*, 180–184.

Diggs, V. M. (1972). *The relative effectiveness of the SQ3R method, a mechanized approach, and a combination method for teaching remedial reading to college freshmen.* Unpublished doctoral dissertation, West Virginia University, Morgantown, WV.

Doctor, R. M., Aponte, J., Bury, A., & Welch, R. (1970). Group counseling vs. behavior therapy in the treatment of college underachievers. *Behavior Research and Therapy, 8*, 89–98.

Draheim, M. E. (1986). *Directed reading-thinking activity, conceptual mapping, and underlining: Their effects on expository text recall in a writing task.* (ERIC Document Reproduction Service No. ED 285 137)

Driskell, J. L., & Kelly, E. L. (1980). A guided notetaking and study skill system for use with university freshmen predicted to fail. *Journal of Reading, 23*, 323–331.

Dyer, J. W., Riley, J., & Yenkovich, E. R. (1979). An analysis of three study skills. *Journal of Educational Research, 73*, 3–7.

Eanet, M. G., & Manzo, A. V. (1976). REAP - A strategy for improving reading/writing/study skills. *Journal of Reading, 19*, 647–652.

Earp, N. W. (1959). *The effect of certain study conditions on the achievement of college freshmen.* Unpublished doctoral dissertation, University of Northern Colorado, Greeley, CO.

Elshout-Mohr, M. (1983). The research perspective of the study skill group of the COWO University of Amsterdam. *Higher Education, 12*, 49–60.

Entwistle, N. J. (1960). Evaluation of study skills courses: A review. *Journal of Educational Research, 53*, 243–251.

Entwistle, N. J. (1978). Knowledge structures and styles of learning: A summary of Pask's recent research. *British Journal of Educational Psychology, 48*, 255–265.

*Entwistle, N. J. (1994). *Experiences of understanding and strategic studying.* (ERIC Document Reproduction Service No. ED 374 704)

Fairbanks, M. M. (1973). *An analytical study of the relationship of specified features of reported college reading improvement programs to program effect on academic achievement.* Unpublished doctoral dissertation, West Virginia University, Morgantown, WV.

Fass, W., & Schumacher, G. (1978). Effect of motivation, subject activity, and readability on the retention of prose material. *Journal of Educational Psychology, 70,* 803–807.

*Feeley, J. T., & Wepner, S. B. (1985). *Does prior knowledge affect college students' performance on a state developed reading competency test?* (ERIC Document Reproduction Service No. ED 262 384)

Ford, N. (1981). Recent approaches to the study and teaching of "effective learning" in higher education. *Review of Educational Research, 51,* 345–377.

Foreman, S. (1982). *Reading-study systems and study management training in college academic skills.* Unpublished doctoral dissertation, University of Pittsburg, Pittsburg, PA.

Fowler, R. L., & Barker, A. S. (1974). Effectiveness of highlighting for retention of textual material. *Journal of Applied Psychology, 59,* 358–384.

Fox, B. J., & Siedow, M. D. (1985). An investigation of the effects of notetaking on college students' recall of signalled and unsignalled text. *Journal of Research and Development in Education, 18,* 29–36.

Fox, L. (1962). Effecting the use of efficient study habits. *Journal of Mathematics, 1,* 75–86.

*Frazier, D. W. (1993). Transfer of college developmental reading students' textmarking strategies. *Journal of Reading Behavior, 25*(1), 17–41.

Galloway, J. S. (1983). *A comparison of the effectiveness of two studying techniques: The SQ3R and the HM Study Skills Program Level I Mapping Technique.* Unpublished doctoral dissertation, University of South Carolina, Columbia, SC.

*Gibbs, G., Morgan, A., & Taylor, E. (1982). A review of the research of Ference Marton and the Goteborg group: A phenomenological research perspective on learning. *Higher Education, 11,* 123–145.

Glynn, S. M. (1978). Capturing readers' attention by means of typographical cueing strategies. *Educational Technology, 18,* 7–12.

Goetz, E. (1984). The role of spatial strategies in processing and remembering text: An information processing approach. In C. D. Holley & D. E. Dansereau (Eds.), *Spatial learning strategies: Techniques, applications, and related issues* (pp. 47–71). San Diego, CA: Academic Press.

Good, C. V. (1926). Proficiency in outlining. *English Journal, 15,* 737–742.

Graham, S. (1982). Comparing the SQ3R method with other study techniques for reading improvement. *Reading Improvement, 19*(1), 45–47.

Gurrola, S. (1974). *Determination of the relative effectiveness and efficiency of selected combinations of the SQ3R study method.* Unpublished doctoral dissertation, New Mexico State University, Las Cruces, NM.

Gustafson, D. J., & Pederson, J. E. (1984). *SQ3R—Myth or sound procedure?* (ERIC Document Reproduction Service No. ED 259 322).

*Gustafson, D. J., & Pederson, J. E. (1985). *SQ3R: Surveying and questioning the relevant, recent (and not so recent) research.* (ERIC Document Reproduction Service No. ED 269 736).

Hakstain, A. R. (1971). The effects of type of examination anticipated on test preparation and performance. *Journal of Educational Research, 64,* 319–324.

Hall, R., Dansereau, D. F., & Blair, R. (1990). *Student-versus expert-generated knowledge maps: Postorganization, initial acquisition, and transfer.* (ERIC Document Reproduction Service No. ED 317 599)

Hannah, D. C. (1946). *An analysis of students' work habits.* Unpublished master's thesis, Ohio State University, Columbus, OH.

*Harris, J. (1990). *Text annotation and underlining as metacognitive strategies to improve comprehension and retention of expository text.* (ERIC Document Reproduction Service No. ED 335 669)

Harris, M. B., & Ream, E. (1972). A program to improve study habits of high school students. *Psychology in the Schools, 9,* 325–330.

Hartley, J., Bartlett, S., & Branthwaite, A. (1980). Underlining can make a difference—sometimes. *Journal of Educational Research, 73*(4), 218–224.

*Hartley, J., & Davies, I. K. (1978). Notetaking: A critical review. *Programmed Learning and Educational Technology, 15,* 207–224.

Heerman, J. E. (1972). *The effect of a reading improvement program upon academic achievement in college.* Unpublished doctoral dissertation, University of Connecticut, Storrs, CT.

*Holley, C. D., & Dansereau, D. F. (1984). Networking: The techniques and the empirical evidence. In C. D. Holley & D. F. Dansereau (Eds.), *Spatial learning strategies: Techniques, applications, and related issues* (pp. 81–106). San Diego, CA: Academic Press.

Holley, C. D., Dansereau, D. F., McDonald, B. A., Garland, J. C., & Collins, K. W. (1979). Evaluation of a hierarchical mapping technique as an aid to prose processing. *Contemporary Educational Psychology, 4*(3), 227–237.

Holmes, J. T. (1972). *A comparison of two study-reading methods for college students.* Unpublished doctoral dissertation, University of Northern Colorado, Greeley, CO.

Hynd, C. R., Simpson, M. L., & Chase, N. D. (1990). Studying narrative text: The effects of annotating vs. journal writing on test performance. *Reading Research and Instruction, 29*(2), 44–54.

Idol, L. (1987). Group story mapping: A comprehension skill for both skilled and unskilled readers. *Journal of Learning Disabilities, 20,* 196–205.

Idstein, P., & Jenkins, J. R. (1972). Underlining vs. repetitive reading. *Journal of Educational Research, 65,* 321–323.

*Iovino, S. F. (1989). *The effect of dominant hemispheric processing modes and notetaking strategy on the comprehension and retention of academically underprepared college readers.* (ERIC Document Reproduction Service No. ED 333 337)

*Iovino, S. F. (1993). A study of the effects of outlining and networking on college student comprehension and retention of expository text. *Research and Teaching in Developmental Education, 10*(1), 43–64.

Jackson, G. B. (1980). Methods for integrative review. *Review of Educational Research, 50,* 438–460.

Jacobowitz, T. (1988). Using theory to modify practice: An illustration with SQ3R. *Journal of Reading, 32*(2), 126–131.

*Jenkins, J. J. (1979). Four points to remember: A tetrahedral model and memory experiments. In L. S. Cermak & F. I. M. Craik (Eds.), *Levels of processing in human memory* (pp. 21–33). Hillsdale, NJ: Lawrence Erlbaum Associates.

Johns, J. L., & McNamara, L. P. (1980). The SQ3R study technique: A forgotten research target. *Journal of Reading, 23*(8), 704–708.

Johnson, L. L. (1988). Effects of underlining textbook sentences on passage and sentence retention. *Reading Research and Instruction, 28*(1), 18–32.

Jonassen, D. H. (1985). The electronic notebook: Integrating learning strategies in coursework to raise the levels of processing. In B. S. Alloway & G. M. Mills (Eds.), *Aspects of educational technology* (pp. 42-54). London: Kegan Paul.

*Kardash, C. M., & Kroeker, T. L. (1989). Effects of time of review and test expectancy on learning from text. *Contemporary Educational Psychology, 14*(4), 323–335.

Karpinus, B., & Haynes, J. A. (1983). *Effects of prior knowledge, text-order and underlining on recall of information from text.* (ERIC Document Reproduction Service No. ED 237 968)

Klare, G. R., Mabry, J. E., & Gustafson, L. M. (1955). The relationship of patterning (underlining) to immediate retention and to acceptablitiy of technical material. *Journal of Applied Psychology, 39*(1), 41–42.

Kopfstein, R. W. (1982). *SQ3R doesn't work—or does it?* (ERIC Document Reproduction Service No. ED 216 327)

Kremer, J. E., Aeschleman, S. R., & Petersen, T. P. (1983). Enhancing compliance with study skill strategies: Techniques to improve self-monitoring. *Journal of College Student Personnel, 24*(5), 18–24.

Kulhavy, R. W., Dyer, J. W., & Silver, L. (1975). The effects of notetaking and test expectancy on the learning of text material. *Journal of Educational Research, 68,* 363–365.

*Lambiotte, J. G., & Dansereau, D. F. (1992). Effects of knowledge maps and prior knowledge on recall of science lecture content. *Journal of Experimental Education, 60*(3), 189–201.

Laurillard, D. M. (1979). The processes of student learning. *Higher Education, 8,* 395–409.

Laycock, S. R., & Russell, D. H. (1941). An analysis of thirty-eight how to study manuals. *School Review, 49,* 370–379.

*Levin, J. R. (1986). Four cognitive principles of learning-strategy instruction. *Educational Psychologist, 21,* 3–17.

*Lipsky, S. A. (1989). *Effect of field independence/dependence on two textbook notetaking techniques.* (ERIC Document Reproduction Service No. ED 311 983)

*Lipson, M. (1995). The effect of semantic mapping instruction on prose comprehension of below-level college readers. *Reading Research and Instruction, 34*(4), 367–378.

Long, G. (1976). *The development and assessment of a cognitive process based learning strategy training program enhancing prose comprehension and retention.* Unpublished doctoral dissertation, Texas Christian University, Fort Worth, TX.

Long, G. L., & Aldersley, S. (1982). Evaluation of a technique to enhance reading comprehension. *American Annals of the Deaf, 12*(7), 816–820.

Long, G. L., & Aldersley, S. (1984). Networking: Applications with hearing impaired students. In C. D. Holley & D. F. Dansereau (Eds.), *Spatial learning strategies: Tech-*

niques, applications, and related issues (pp. 109–125). San Diego, CA: Academic Press.

Martin, J. A. (1983). *An investigation into self-questioning as a study technique for college developmental students.* Unpublished doctoral dissertation, University of Georgia, Athens, GA.

*Marton, E., & Saljo, R. (1976a). On qualitative differences in learning 1: Outcomes and process. *British Journal of Educational Psychology, 46,* 4–11.

*Marton, E., & Saljo, R. (1976b). On qualitative differences in learning 2: Outcome as a function of the learner's conception of task. *British Journal of Educational Psychology, 46,* 115–127.

*Marxen, D. E. (1996). Why reading and underlining a passage is a less effective study strategy than simply rereading the passage. *Reading Improvement, 33*(2), 88–96.

Mathews, C. O. (1938). Comparison of methods for immediate and delayed recall. *Journal of Educational Psychology, 44,* 101–106.

*Mayer, R. E. (1988a). Instructional variables that influence cognitive processes during reading. In B. K. Britton & S. M. Glynn (Eds.), *Executive control processes in reading* (pp. 201–216). Hillsdale, NJ: Lawrence Erlbaum Associates.

*Mayer, R. E. (1988b). Learning strategies: An overview. In C. E. Weinstein, E. T. Goetz, & P. A. Alexander (Eds.), *Learning and study strategies: Issues in assessment, instruction, and evaluation* (pp. 11–24). San Diego, CA: Academic Press.

*McCagg, E. C., & Dansereau, D. F. (1991). A convergent paradigm for examining knowledge mapping as a learning strategy. *Journal of Educational Research, 84*(6), 317–324.

McClusky, E. D., & Dolch, E. W. (1924). A study outline test. *School Review, 32,* 757–772.

McConkie, G. W. (1977). Learning from text. In L. Schulman (Eds.), *Review of research in education* (pp. 3–48). Itasca, IL: Peacock.

*McCormick, S., & Cooper, J. O. (1991). Can SQ3R facilitate secondary learning disabled students' literal comprehension of expository text? Three experiments. *Reading Psychology, 12*(3), 239–271.

McKeachie, W. J. (1984). Spatial strategies: Critique and educational implications. In C. D. Holley & D. E. Dansereau (Eds.), *Spatial learning strategies: Techniques, applications, and related issues* (pp. 301–312). San Diego, CA: Academic Press.

*McKeachie, W. J. (1988). The need for study strategy training. In C. E. Weinstein, E. T. Goetz, & P. A. Alexander (Eds.), *Learning and study strategies: Issues in assessment, instruction, and evaluation* (pp. 3–9). San Diego, CA: Academic Press.

McKune, E. J. (1958). *An investigation of the study procedures of college freshmen.* Unpublished doctoral dissertation, Colorado State College, Greeley, CO.

McReynolds, W. T., & Church, A. (1973). Self-control, study skills development, and counseling approaches to the improvement of study behavior. *Behavior Research Therapy, 11,* 233–235.

*Meyer, M. J. E. (1977). The structure of prose: Effects on learning and memory and implications for educational practice. In R. C. Anderson, R. J. Spiro, & W. E. Montague (Eds.), *Schooling and the acquisition of knowledge* (pp. 179–200). Hillsdale, NJ: Lawrence Erlbaum Associates.

*Morris, C. D., Bransford, J. D., & Franks, J. J. (1977). Levels of processing versus transfer appropriate processing. *Journal of Verbal Learning and Verbal Behavior, 16*, 519–533.

Naidu, S., & Bernard, R. M. (1992). Enhancing academic performance in distance education with concept mapping and inserted questions. *Distance Education, 13*(2), 218–233.

Neal, J. C., & Langer, M. A. (1992). A framework for teaching options for content area instruction: Mediated instruction of text. *Journal of Reading, 36*(3), 227–230.

Niles, O. S. (1963). Comprehension skills. *The Reading Teacher, 17,* 2–7.

Niple, M. (1968). *The relationship of different study methods to immediate and delayed comprehension.* Unpublished doctoral dissertation, Ohio State University, Columbus, OH.

*Nist, S. L. (1985). Tetrahedral models of learning. *Journal of College Reading and Learning, 18,* 12–19.

*Nist, S. L., & Hogrebe, M. C. (1987). The role of underlining and annotating in remembering textual information. *Reading Research and Instruction, 27*(1), 12–25.

*Nist, S. L., & Simpson, M. L. (1988). The effectiveness and efficiency of training college students to annotate and underline text. *National Reading Conference Yearbook, 37,* 251–257.

*O'Shea, L. J., & O'Shea, D. J. (1994). A component analysis of metacognition in reading comprehension: The contributions of awareness and self-regulation. *International Journal of Disability: Development and Education, 41*(1), 15–32.

Okey, J. J. (1962). *Achievement with two college textbook reading methods with considerations for locus of control influence.* Unpublished doctoral dissertation, West Virginia University, Morgantown, WV.

Orlando, V. P. (1978). *The relative effectiveness of a modified version of SQ3R on university students' study behavior.* Unpublished doctoral dissertation, Pennsylvania State University, University Park, PA.

*Orlando, V. P. (1979). Notetaking vs. notehaving: A comparison while studying from text. In M. L. Kamil & A. J. Moe (Eds.), *Reading research: Studies and application* (pp. 177–182). Clemson, SC: National Reading Conference.

Orlando, V. P. (1980a). A comparison of notetaking strategies while studying from text. In M. L. Kamil & A. J. Moe (Eds.), *Perspectives on reading: Research and instruction* (pp. 219–222). Clemson, SC: National Reading Conference.

*Orlando, V. P. (1980b). Training students to use a modified version of SQ3R: An instructional strategy. *Reading World, 20,* 65–70.

Orlando, V. P. (1984, March). *Reflective judgement: Implications for teaching developmental students.* Paper presented at the Western College Reading Association, San Jose, CA.

Orlando, V. P., & Hayward, K. G. (1978). A comparison of three study techniques for college students. In P. D. Pearson & J. Hansen (Eds.), *Reading: Disciplines inquiry in process and practice* (pp. 242–245). Clemson, SC: National Reading Association.

Palmatier, R. A. (1971). The last 2 R's: A research view. In D. M. Wark (Eds.), *College and adult reading* (pp. 120–130). Minneapolis, MN: North Central Reading Association.

Paris, S. (1988). Models and metaphores of learning strategies. In C. E. Weinstein, E. T. Goetz, & R. A. Alexander (Eds.), *Learning and study strategies: Issues in assessment, instruction, and evaluation* (pp. 299–321). San Diego, CA: Academic Press.

*Paris, S., Lipson, M. Y., & Wixson, K. (1983). Becoming a strategic reader. *Contemporary Education Psychology, 8,* 293–316.

Pask, G. (1976a). Conversational techniques in the study and practice of education. *British Journal of Education, 46,* 12–25.

*Pask, G. (1976b). Styles and strategies of learning. *British Journal of Educational Psychology, 46,* 216–248.

Pena-Paez, A., & Surber, J. R. (1990). Effect of study strategy skill level on test performance. *English Quarterly, 23*(1–2), 31–39.

Peterson, C. L., Caverly, D. C., & Nicholson, S. (1998, November). *Technology for organizing knowledge: A new support for developmental students.* Paper presented at the College Reading Learning Association, Salt Lake City, UT.

*Peterson, S. E. (1992). The cognitive functions of underlining as a study technique. *Reading Research and Instruction, 31*(2), 49–56.

*Pichert, J. W., & Anderson, R. C. (1977). Taking different perspectives on a story. *Journal of Educational Psychology, 69*(4), 309–315.

*Porter, N. (1876). *Books and reading.* New York: Scribner and Armstrong.

Pressley, M., Borkowski, J. G., & O'Sullivan, J. T. (1984). Memory strategy instruction is made of this: Metamemory and durable strategy use. *Educational Psychologist, 19,* 94–107.

*Pruisner, P. A. P. (1995). *Graphic learning strategies for at-risk college students.* (ERIC Document Reproduction Service No. ED 391 483)

*Pugh-Smith, S. (1985). Comprehension and comprehension monitoring of experienced readers. *Journal of Reading, 28*(4), 292–300.

Rauch, M., & Fillenworth, C. (1980). *Cognitive mapping: Understanding, organizing, and remembering written discourse.* (ERIC Document Reproduction Service No. ED 197 327)

Rickards, J. P. (1980). Notetaking, underlining, inserted questions, and organizers in text: Research conclusions and educational implications. *Educational Technology, 20*(6), 5–11.

Rickards, J. P., & August, G. J. (1975). Generative underlining in prose recall. *Journal of Educational Psychology, 6,* 860–865.

Rickards, J. P., & Friedman, E. (1978). The encoding versus the external storage hypothesis in notetaking. *Contemporary Educational Psychology, 3,* 136–143.

Rigney, J. W. (1978). Learning strategies: A theoretical perspective. In H. E. O'Neil (Eds.), *Learning strategies* (pp. 165–205). San Diego, CA: Academic Press.

Robinson, F. P. (1946). *Effective study* (2nd ed). New York: Harper & Row.

Robinson, F. P. (1961). *Effective study* (3rd ed). New York: Harper & Row.

*Robinson, F. P. (1970). *Effective study* (4th ed). New York: Harper & Row.

*Rohwer, W. D. (1984). An invitation to an educational psychology of studying. *American Psychologist, 19,* 1–14.

*Rosenblatt, L. (1978). *The reader, the text, and the poem.* Carbondale, IL: Southern Illinois University Press.

Ruddell, R., & Boyle, O. (1984). *A study of the effects of cognitive mapping on reading comprehension and written protocols. Technical Report No. 7.* (ERIC Document Reproduction Service No. ED 252 811)

*Ruddell, R., & Boyle, O. (1989). A study of cognitive mapping as a means to improve summarization and comprehension of expository text. *Reading Research and Instruction, 29*(1), 12–22.

Ryan, J. A. (1969). *Text book underlining as an index of student identification of relevant instructional content. Final report. WSU-CORD.* (ERIC Document Reproduction Service No. ED 053 431)

Salisbury, R. (1935). Some effects of training in outlining. *English Journal, 24,* 111–116.

Sanders, V. (1979). *A meta-analysis: The relationship of program content and operation factors to measured effectiveness of college reading-study programs.* Unpublished doctoral dissertation, University of the Pacific, Forest Grove, CA.

Santa, C. M., Abrams, L., & Santa, J. L. (1979). Effects of notetaking and studying on the retention of prose. *Journal of Reading Behavior, 11,* 247–260.

Scappaticci, E. T. (1977). *A study of SQ3R and select and recite reading and study skills methods in college classes.* Unpublished doctoral dissertation, Lehigh University, Bethlehem, PA.

Schnell, T. R., & Rocchio, D. J. (1978). A comparison of underlining strategies for improving reading comprehension and retention. *Reading Horizons, 18,* 106–109.

Schultz, C. B., & DiVesta, F. J. (1972). Effects of passage organization and notetaking on the selection of clustering strategies and on recall of textual material. *Journal of Educational Psychology, 63,* 244–252.

Schumacher, G. M. (1987). Executive control in studying. In B. K. Britton & S. M. Glynn (Eds.), *Executive control processes in reading* (pp. 107–144). Hillsdale, NJ: Lawrence Erlbaum Associates.

*Schumm, J. S. (1991). Considerate and inconsiderate text instruction in postsecondary developmental reading textbooks: A content analysis. *Reading Research and Instruction, 30*(4), 42–51.

Shimmerlik, S. M., & Nolan, J. D. (1976). Reorganization and the recall of prose. *Journal of Educational Psychology, 68,* 779–786.

Simpson, M. L. (1984). The status of study strategy instruction: Implications for classroom teachers. *Journal of Reading, 28,* 136–142.

*Simpson, M. L. (1986). PORPE: A writing strategy for studying and learning in the content areas. *Journal of Reading, 29,* 407–414.

*Simpson, M. L. (1996). Conducting reality checks to improves students' strategic learning. *Journal of Adolescent and Adult Literacy, 40*(2), 102–109.

Simpson, M. L., & Nist, S. L. (1992). A case study of academic literacy tasks and their negotiation in a university history class. In C. K. Kinzer & D. J. Leu (Eds.), *Literacy research, theory, and practice: Views for many perspectives. 41st yearbook of the National Reading Conference* (pp. 253–260). Chicago: National Reading Conference.

*Simpson, M. L., & Stahl, N. A. (1987). PORPE: A comprehensive study strategy utilizing self-assigned writing. *Journal of College Reading and Learning, 20,* 51–57.

Simpson, M. L., Stahl, N. A., & Hayes, C. G. (1989). PORPE: A research validation. *Journal of Reading, 33,* 22–28.

Smart, K. L., & Bruning, J. L. (1973). *An examination of the practical impact of the Von Restorrf effect.* (ERIC Document Reproduction Service No. ED 102 502)

Smith, E. R., & Standal, T. C. (1981). Learning styles and study techniques. *Journal of Reading, 24*(7), 599–602.

*Smith, S. L. (1982). Learning strategies of mature college learners. *Journal of Reading, 26,* 5–12.

Snyder, V. (1984). *Effects of study techniques on developmental college students' retention of textbook chapters.* (ERIC Document Reproduction Service No. ED 243 363)

*Spiegel, G. F., Jr., & Barufaldi, J. P. (1994). The effects of a contribution of text structure awareness and graphic postorganizers on recall and retention of science knowledge. *Journal of Research in Science Teaching, 31*(9), 913–932.

*Spiro, R. J., Coulson, R. L., Feltovich, P. J., & Anderson, D. K. (1994). Cognitive flexibility theory: Complex knowledge acquisition in ill-structured domains. In R. B. Ruddell, M. R. Ruddell., & H. Singer (Eds.), *Theoretical models and processes of reading* (4th ed., pp. 602–615). Newark, DE: International Reading Association.

Stahl, N. A. (1983). *A historical analysis of textbook study systems.* Unpublished doctoral dissertation, University of Pittsburg, Pittsburg, PA.

*Stahl, N. A., Simpson, M. L., & Hayes, C. G. (1992). Ten recommendations from research for teaching high-risk college students. *Journal of Developmental Evolution, 16*(1), 2–10.

*Stallworth-Clark, R., Scott, J. S., & Nist, S. L. (1996). *The teaching-learning process and postsecondary at-risk reading students: cognitive, metacognitive, affective, and instructional variables explaining academic performance.* (ERIC Document Reproduction Service No. ED 394 419)

*Starks-Martin, G. (1996). *Using "think-alouds," journals, and portfolios to assess Hmong students' perceptions of their study/learning strategies.* (ERIC Document Reproduction Service No. ED 399 803)

Stone, N., & Miller, K. (1991). *Developmental college reading: Secrets of our success.* (ERIC Document Reproduction Service No. ED 329 317)

Stoodt, B. D., & Balbo, E. (1979). Integrating study skills instruction with content in a secondary classroom. *Reading World, 18,* 242–252.

Stordahl, J. B., & Christensen, C. M. (1956). The effect of study techniques on comprehension and retention. *Journal of Educational Research, 49,* 561–570.

*Swafford, J. (1990). Comprehension strategies research and college developmental studies students. *Forum for Reading, 22*(1), 6–14.

Tadlock, D. F. (1978). SQ3R: Why it works, based on an information processing theory of learning. *Journal of Reading, 22,* 110–112.

*Thomas, J. W., & Rohwer, W. D. (1986). Academic studying: The role of learning strategies. *Educational Psychologist, 21,* 19–41.

*Thornton, N. E., Bohlmeyer, E. M., Dickson, L. A., & Kulhavy, R. W. (1990). Spontaneous and imposed study tactics in learning prose. *Journal of Experimental Education, 58*(2), 111–124.

*Todd, J. (1854). *The student's manual.* New York: Baker and Taylor.

Todd, W. B., & Kessler, C. C. (1971). The impact of level of difficulty on four measures of recall of meaningful written material. *Journal of Educational Psychology, 62,* 229–234.

*Trillian, A. S., & Associates (1980). *Teaching basic skills in college.* San Francisco, CA: Jossey-Bass.

*Tulving, E. (1972). Episodic and semantic memory. In E. Tulving & W. Donaldson (Eds.), *Organization in memory* (pp. 381–403). San Diego, CA: Academic Press.

Tulving, E., & Thompson, D. M. (1973). Encoding specificity and retrieval processes in episodic memory. *Psychological Review, 80,* 352–373.

Vaughn, J., Stillman, P. L., & Sabers, D. L. (1978). *Construction of idealtional scaffolding during reading.* (ERIC Document Reproduction Service No. ED 165 109)

*Wade, S. E., & Reynolds, R. E. (1989). Developing metacognitive awareness. *Journal of Reading, 33*(1), 6–15.

*Wade, S. E., & Trathen, W. (1989). Effect of self-selected study methods of learning. *Journal of Educational Psychology, 81*(1), 40–47.

*Wade, S. E., Trathen, W., & Schraw, G. (1990). An analysis of spontaneous study strategies. *Reading Research Quarterly, 25*(2), 147–166.

Walker, J. E. (1982, April). *Study strategies: Too many, too few ... or just right.* Paper presented at the annual meeting of the Western College Reading Learning Association, Long Beach, CA.

Wallace, W. P. (1965). Review of the historical, empirical, and theoretical status of the von Restorrf phenomenon. *Psychological Bulletin, 63,* 410–424.

Wark, D. M. (1965). Survey Q3R: System or superstition. In D. M. Wark (Eds.), *College and adult reading* (pp. 161–168). Minneapolis, MN: North Central Reading Association.

*Watts, I. (1741). *The improvement of the mind, or a supplement to the art of logic.* Baltimore, MD: Baly & Burns.

Weatherly, J. J. (1978). *The effect of underlining and study time on the recall of written materials.* Unpublished docotoral dissertation, Georgia State University, Atlanta, GA.

*Weinstein, C. E. (1977). Elaboration skills as a learning strategy. In H. E. O'Neil & C. D. Spielberger (Eds.), *Cognitive and affective learning strategies* (pp. 31–55). San Diego, CA: Academic Press.

*Weinstein, C. E., & Mayer, R. E. (1985). The teaching of learning strategies. In M. C. Wittrock (Eds.), *Handbook of research on teaching* (pp. 315–327). New York: Macmillian.

Weinstein, C. E., & Underwood, V. L. (1985). Learning strategies: The how of learning. In J. W. Segal, S. E. Chapman, & R. Glaser (Eds.), *Thinking and leaning skills: Vol. 1. Relating instruction to research* (pp. 241–258). Hillsdale, NJ: Lawrence Erlbaum Associates.

Weist, R. M. (1972). The role of rehearsal: Recopy or reconstruct. *Journal of Verbal Learning and Verbal Behavior, 11,* 440–450.

Wickelgren, W. A. (1973). The long and short of memory. *Psychological Bulletin, 80,* 425–438.

Willmore, D. J. (1966). *A comparison of four methods of studying a college textbook.* Unpublished doctoral dissertation, University of Minnesota, Minneapolis.

*Wittrock, M. C. (1988). A constructive review of learning strategies. In C. E. Weinstein, E. T. Goetz, & P. A. Alexander (Eds.), *Learning and study strategies: Issues in assessment, instruction, and evaluation* (pp. 287–298). San Diego, CA: Academic Press.

*Wittrock, M. C., Marks, C. B., & Doctorow, M. (1975). Reading as a generative process. *Journal of Educational Psychology, 67,* 484–489.

Wooster, G. E. (1953). *Teaching the SQ3R method of study: An investigation of the instructional approach.* Unpublished doctoral dissertation, Ohio State University, Columbus, OH.

*Zanias, G. S. (1996). *The effect of supplementary entries on reading comprehension tests in college level, developmental reading classes.* (ERIC Document Reproduction Service No. ED 393 080).

6

Reading, Writing, and the College Developmental Student

⇜⟨§§⟩⇝

Maria Valeri-Gold
Mary P. Deming
Georgia State University

Reading and writing are integral components of language arts programs from elementary school through postsecondary grade levels. Most college developmental programs include reading and writing courses, some of which combine both disciplines into one course. This practice is not accepted universally as college developmental educators continue to debate whether or not reading and writing should be taught as separate disciplines or as integrated, related fields of study. Discussions also continue on how best to integrate reading and writing into the college curriculum and what methods and materials are appropriate for instructing and assessing students in these areas (Hayes, 1990; Tierney & Shanahan, 1991). In the past, college educators were concerned primarily about analyzing the products (written samples) of their students' reading and writing, rather than looking at the students' processes. Currently, many reading and writing educators now evaluate students' reading products and processes.

Historically, reading and writing have been viewed as two separate processes with little in common (Kucer & Harste, 1991). However, research during the last 20 years has examined the relationship between reading and writing (Linnehan, 1994; Rubin & Hansen, 1984; Shanahan, 1997). Much of the current research is guided by the theory that both reading and writing involve the making of meaning.

Tierney and Pearson (1983) stated that

> meaning is created as a reader uses his background of experience together with the author's cues to come to grips both with what the writer is getting him to do or think and what the reader decides and creates for himself. As a writer writes, she uses her own background of experience to generate ideas and, in order to produce a text which is considerate to her idealized reader, filters these drafts through her judgments of what her reader's background of experience will be, what she wants to say, and what she wants the reader to get to think and do. (p. 568)

This meaning-making process involves many similar and overlapping cognitive processes, specifically, planning, drafting, aligning, and revising (Tierney & Shanahan, 1991) with the nature of this meaning-making process depending on the cognitive development of the learner. Research has also investigated how reading and writing affect learning and thinking outcomes (Tierney & Shanahan, 1991).

Furthermore, research and experience attest to the value of teaching reading and writing to college developmental students. Many college students lack the cognitive development to perform college-level reading and writing tasks. Likewise, many college developmental learners are not aware of how they read and write; nevertheless, they use reading and writing strategies that help them comprehend information found in the text.

THEORY

Because any reading or writing research project or teaching method rests on epistemological assumptions and models of reading and writing processes, a coherent theoretical approach to the interrelationships of reading–writing processes is needed (Rosenblatt, 1988). Various theories have evolved from psycholinguistics, cognitive psychology, and reading and writing research studies (Huot, 1988). Based on the composing model of reading, reading and writing are viewed as constructive processes in which readers and writers are composing meaning by interacting with the text (Tierney & Pearson, 1983). According to Iser (1978), "reading is not simply a text-based activity, but an interactive (transactive process) in which reader and the text both contribute to the meaning that evolves" (p. 588). In Shanklin's (1982) reading theory-based model of the writing process, reading and writing are integrated in that both reading and writing are constructive and developmental processes; both require learners to use prior knowledge and interpretive skills to grasp the author's meaning, utilize self-directed feedback, and employ the reciprocal transactive process.

As students read and write, they compose meaning from their background knowledge of personal experiences, memories, and associations to create an understandable text (Butler & Turbill, 1987; Collins, 1990; McGinley & Kamberelis, 1996). According to Wittrock (1984), "readers and writers develop meaning by constructing relationships between the text and what they know, believe, and experience" (p. 77). When writers compose, they use text to convey information. Writers produce texts with structure; readers use structure when they construct meaning.

Reading–writing processes are comprised of interactive subprocesses through which meaning is derived by making and relating connections between the text and prior knowledge and using a variety of learning strategies to promote understanding (Peregoy & Boyle, 1993). This knowledge depends on real-life experiences and events (Holladay, 1988). According to Tierney and Shanahan (1991), "meaning-making is related to what and how readers and writers negotiate with their inner selves and with others" (p. 255).

When readers and writers practice reading and writing within academic contexts, for example, they recognize the need to make and create meaning by developing their own understandings of texts. They participate as engaged readers and writers within the academic community. They interact with their peers and instructors. Making and creating meaning involve a reciprocal transaction between the reader and the writer. This transaction involves an awareness of the writer's meaning, purpose, and understanding (Nystrand, 1986). The transaction can be illustrated, for example, in a collaborative classroom activity in which students can discuss the author's purpose in a text and explain their interpretations until they can formulate a response that satisfies their peers and their instructor. Salvatori (1983) noted that students approach text with their own purposes and meaning making that go beyond the text. During this reciprocal process, readers and writers can also examine and rearrange experiences, separate themselves from their experiences instead of just identifying with them, stand apart from the object, and reconsider, analyze, and evaluate their thoughts (Bartholomae & Petrosky, 1986; McCarthy, 1987). Thus, readers extract and sequentially reorder events from text to build meaning and to interact with the text (Salvatori, 1986).

Tierney and Pearson (1983) explained the interactive nature of reading and writing. Their composing-reading model contends that reading and writing involve similar, shared, linguistic, and cognitive elements. As readers read and writers compose, both plan, draft, align, revise, and monitor as they read and write. Spivey and King (1989) described these processes in similar terms: selecting, organizing, and connecting.

According to Tierney and Pearson (1983), readers and writers compose meaning when planning their reading and writing. *Planning* involves two processes: (a) setting goals and (b) using prior knowledge based on their background of personal experiences. During the planning process, readers develop goals when they establish their purposes for reading and use learning strategies such as developing questions (who, when, where, what, why, or how), taking notes, forming outlines, or utilizing their background knowledge to make a connection between what they read and what they already know. Planning includes questioning, reflecting, and redefining goals in order to understand the topic.

Writers also plan while they write. They develop goals that are procedural (How will I develop this topic?), substantive (What do I want to say about this topic?), and intentional (How can I get my point across to my audience?; Flower & Hayes, 1980). Likewise, readers construct procedural goals (How can I comprehend this topic?), substantive goals (How can I make connections between what I know and what I still need to learn?), and intentional goals (How can I understand the author's main idea?). "These goals can be embedded in on another or addressed concurrently; they may be conflicting or complimentary. As a reader reads (just as when a writer writes), goals may emerge, be discovered or change" (Tierney & Pearson, 1983, p. 569).

Drafting may be defined as "the refinement of meaning which occurs as readers and writers deal directly with print on the page" (p. 571). During the drafting process, getting started is just as important for the reader as it is for the writer. Both readers and writers need to create a first draft. Readers look for clues to help them discover the upcoming meaning of the text. From these clues, they hypothesize what is to follow. Descriptions of the drafting process suggest that

> what drives reading and writing is this desire to make sense of what is happening—to make things cohere. A writer achieves that fit by deciding what information to include and what to withhold. The reader accomplishes that by filling in the gaps ... or making unsaid connections. (p. 572)

The next step of the composing model of reading, *aligning*, is comprised of "two facets: stances a reader or writer assumes in collaboration with their author or audience, and roles within which the reader or writer immerse themselves as they proceed with the topic" (p. 572). During the aligning process, a reader selects the author's viewpoint or position while reading the text. The reader and the author are involved or immersed in a collaborative relationship. The reader is negotiating meaning with the text by directly observing, participating, or assuming the role of a character or inanimate object. While exchanging roles, the reader pictures or visualizes the information presented in the text and negotiates meaning. The reader and the writer focus on the topic with a specific point or view or attitude in order to comprehend the author's meaning. Alignment requires that readers and writers reread, rethink, reexamine, and review the author's stance in order to interpret the text. According to Tierney and Pearson (1983), "adopting an alignment is akin to achieving a foothold from which meaning can be more readily available" (p. 573).

Revising is important to the reading and writing process. Revising helps readers develop an understanding of the author's stance and text by pausing and reflecting on what they have read (Tierney & Pearson, 1983).

> In fact, to suggest that a reader should approach text as a writer who crafts an understanding across several drafts—who pauses, rethinks, and revises—is almost contrary to some well-established goals readers proclaim for themselves (e.g. that efficient reading is equivalent to maximum recall based upon a single fast reading). (p. 577)

During the revision process, readers should reexamine the text. Similarly, the writers reread, reexamine, revise, and reflect on the text by carefully selecting words that convey their meaning. They write multiple drafts in order to represent their thoughts and ideas in a cohesive format for a particular audience.

Monitoring requires readers and writers to evaluate what they read and wrote about while composing meaning. During the monitoring process, readers are engaged in a conversation or dialogue with an inner reader or the other self (Murray, 1982). This inner reader recalls, retrieves, and connects the information that

> the writer has written, is writing, or will write to what the reader has read, is reading, or will read.... This other self oversees what the reader and writer is trying to do, defines the nature of collaboration between reader and author, and decides how well the reader as writer or writer as reader is achieving his or her goals. (pp. 577–578)

Based on this composing model of reading, studies indicate that adult writers use planning (Flower & Hayes, 1981) and revision (Faigley & Witte, 1981); however, high school students and college students do little planning and revising (Butler-Nalin, 1984). Schallert and Tierney (1982) noted similar findings and stated that revision is not a common practice among readers. Most readers read a page of text quickly and do not stop to develop or reexamine their interpretations about the text.

Reading and writing are also connected with changes in students' cognitive development (Chall, 1983; Shanahan, 1984, 1988, 1997; Shanahan & Lomax, 1986, 1988), with younger readers more concerned with words than older readers. As readers become more proficient, their attention turns to interpretation and communication (Shanahan, 1997).

Other theorists have examined the relationship between reading and writing by studying students' reasoning, problem solving, and information-processing strategies and activities. Shanahan and Tierney (1990) noted the work of researchers (Birnbaum, 1982; Langer, 1986; S. Martin, 1987; Ryan, 1985) who used various techniques to identify "relations across reading and writing between entities such as idea generation, metacognition, structuring, evaluating, revising, monitoring, questioning, and hypothesizing" (p. 15). (For a discussion of teaching reading–writing to ESL students, see Pintozzi & Valeri-Gold, chap. 10, this volume.)

RESEARCH

Shanahan and Tierney (1990) also referred to the recent numerous summaries of research studies and theoretical analyses dealing with the reading–writing processes. They wrote a review of the literature in which they compared the literature written from three different theoretical perspectives: the shared knowledge–shared process point of view; the communications point of view; and, the collaborative uses of reading and writing point of view. In addition, Irvin (1992) conducted a survey to identify all the studies dealing with reading and writing connections written between 1900 and 1984. Two-hundred and seventy studies, mostly dissertations, were analyzed. Results from the survey indicated that the number of studies in the area of reading and writing connections increased in the 1980s, and these studies appeared in various journal types, in particular, those in education and psychology. Studies conducted from 1929 to 1971 were conducted primarily by educators, studies performed from 1972 to 1981 were conducted by psychologists, and recent studies from 1982 to 1984 were completed by researchers from a variety of disciplines. Irwin's review ends with an annotated bibliography of what reviewers considered the best studies conducted during the time frame examined.

Stotsky (1983) provided a commonly quoted review of the literature related to the research on the reading–writing relationship up to 1983. She divides her review into type of research study: correlational or experimental. According to Stotsky, most correlational studies fall into three categories: those correlating measures of reading achievement with measures of writing ability; those correlating measures of reading experience with measures of writing ability; and those correlating measures of reading ability with measures of syntactic complexity in students' composition.

Studies examining the influence of writing on reading may be subdivided into two groups: "those attempting to improve writing through writing instruction, with effects on reading; and those attempting to improve reading through the use of writing" (p. 631). Most research studies examining writing instruction were experimental. In addition, studies examining the influence of reading on writing could also be subdivided into two groups: "those attempting to improve reading, with effects on writing; and those attempting to improve writing though reading instruction, the use of literary models, or additional reading experiences" (p. 634).

READING, WRITING, AND PRODUCT
OR PERFORMANCE CORRELATIONAL STUDIES

Of particular interest were the correlational studies that explained the nature of the reading–writing relationship (Braun, 1984; McCarthy, 1987; Shanahan, 1984; Shanahan & Lomax, 1986, 1988; Tierney, 1988, Tierney & Shanahan, 1991). Correlational studies were conducted to examine the students' reading and writing products or performance and were based on the theory that reading and writing share knowledge and teaching them together has instructional implications.

It should be noted, however, that the majority of the correlational studies were conducted with elementary, junior high, and high school students; investigations that focused on college students, in particular, developmental learners, were not extensive. Using Stotsky's (1983) categories, we highlight some of the major studies, examining the relationship between reading and writing.

Stotsky (1983) began her review investigating the relationship between reading achievement and writing ability with Loban's (1964) landmark correlational study. Loban examined the reading and writing abilities of 220 students across 12 grade levels. The Stanford Achievement Test was used to measure student performance, and one holistically scored writing sample was used to assess students' writing in response to a picture prompt. A positive relationship existed between reading and writing with those students who performed at either high or low levels of ability. Students who read at a higher reading level wrote at a superior level; students who wrote below grade level read below their reading age.

Similar studies have been conducted to determine how reading and writing are related, but findings from these investigations revealed that these interactive relationships vary according to grade levels and proficiency (Juel, Griffith, & Gough, 1986; P. Martin, 1977; Schewe & Froese, 1987; Shanahan & Lomax, 1988; Shanahan, 1997; Tierney, 1983).

Additional correlational studies were conducted to measure reading achievement and writing ability in elementary through postsecondary grade levels (Calhoun, 1971; Campbell, 1976; D'Angelo, 1977; Fishco, 1966; Grimmer, 1970; Grobe & Grobe, 1977; Maloney, 1967; Piexotto, 1946; Schonell, 1942; H. Taylor, 1981; Thomas, 1976; Woodfin, 1968). Results from these studies indicate a positive relationship between reading achievement with measures of writing ability.

Studies correlating reading achievement with writing ability, focusing specifically on college freshman were conducted by Calhoun (1971), Grobe and Grobe (1977), Piexotto (1946), and H. Taylor (1981). Piexotto (1946) reported low but significant correlations between scores on the English Essay Test, a reading test, and the verbal section of the Scholastic Aptitude Test (SAT) with college freshmen. A significant relationship between reading comprehension and writing achievement in college freshmen was reported by Calhoun (1971) and Thomas (1976). In Grobe and Grobe's (1977) study, significantly higher reading scores were reported for college freshman who were good writers than for average writers. The researchers suggest that the significant relationship between writing and reading ability could be influenced by many factors. Exposure to print materials helps facilitate the learning of writing skills. Students who are trained in the organization of a text might produce more effective writing of their own, and finally, the organization in writing might be learned through reading instruction.

In a study with community college composition students, H. Taylor (1981) found a positive relationship between listening comprehension and reading comprehension with final course grades for college freshmen. No relationship existed between listening comprehension and course grade, but a significant relationship was found between reading comprehension as measured by a standardized reading test and final course grades.

As noted in Stotsky (1983), results from several correlational studies indicated positive relationships exist between writing quality and reading experiences (Barbig, 1968; Felland, 1981; Woodward & Phillips, 1967). Again, it should be noted that investigations examining the relationship between writing ability and the time spent reading with college learners was limited because the majority of studies were performed with middle, junior high, and high school students. Woodward and Phillips (1967) found that first semester college freshman writers had less reading experience in high school than did good writers.

Thomas (1976) reported that a significant relationship existed between writing achievement and the amount and variety of reading experiences. Felland (1981) in his research with 12th-grade superior writers and 12th-grade average writers concluded that superior writers were more likely to (a) be encouraged to read by their parents, (b) be expected to attend college, (c) have a father employed in a profession, (d) be highly confident in their writing ability, (e) have more books in the home, (f) enjoy the content areas, and (g) be in the top 25% of their graduating class than were average writers.

Further investigations have measured the relationship between reading ability and syntactic structure (Stotsky, 1983) while composing and its positive effect on comprehension (Johnson, 1981; Perron, 1977; Straw & Schreiner, 1982). Studies focusing with college learners were conducted by Fuller (1974), Thomas (1976), and Heller (1980). Fuller's (1974) research investigated the relationship between reading achievement and oral and written language of students enrolled in community college remedial reading and writing classes. Her results revealed that for these students "disparity in reading achievement bore little or no relationship to oral and/or written syntactic complexity" (p. 70). Furthermore, students in the study used a more complex syntactic level when writing than when speaking. Thomas (1976) noted that a positive correlation existed between reading achievement and sentence maturity with college-level students. Heller's study (1980), examined syntactic elements in the expository writing of college freshmen at two reading levels. Higher level readers exhibited longer t-units through such nonclausal structures as prepositional phrases, intra t-unit coordination of details, and passive verb phrases; while lower readers produced shorter t-units. A t-unit may be defined as a "single main clause plus whatever other subordinate clauses or nonclauses are attached to, or embedded within, that main clause" (Hunt, 1977, pp. 92–93).

Stotsky (1983) also included studies examining reading–writing behaviors during reading–writing processes. Many of these studies suggest that proficient writers plan and reread during writing than less-proficient writers; proficient readers and writers view themselves as active readers and writers engaged in their own reading and writing (Birnbaum, 1982). One significant study done with college developmental learners was conducted by Atwell (1981). Atwell viewed the writing compositions of 10 students of above-average writing ability and 10 developmental learners in order to investigate the role of reading in the writing process. Both groups wrote personal essays and these sessions were videotaped. For the first half of the writing session, students engaged, planned, organized, and wrote as they normally did. During the second half of the session, students wrote with invisible ink pens so that they could not reread what they had written. After the sessions, students read their completed written products and discussed the strategies they used while composing. Analysis of the data revealed that there was no difference between the makeup of the writings between those who were and were not able to reread their text. All writers did indicate, however, that they reread what they wrote, suggesting that reading and writing are related.

Another correlational study focused on the relationships among performance, skills, and attitudes of college freshmen. Brown (1986) measured the effects of reading and writing apprehension on college basic writers. Results were analyzed from three survey measures and expository paragraphs and essays written by 59 college freshmen enrolled in a basic writing course. The instruments used were the (a) the Reading Apprehension Measure; (b) Vocabulary and Comprehension on the Nelson–Denny Test, Form D; and (c) the Miller–Daly Writing Apprehension Test. Results suggested that the course, designed to equip students with strategies for composing, helped students gain the confidence necessary to increase writing skill. Results also indicated that students' writing skills were enhanced when they understood the connection between reading and writing and that requiring students to read carefully and critically could be a detriment to student confidence. The significant positive relationship between grades and reading performance measures indicate that students' roles as readers and writers cannot be separated easily. In addition, the positive correlation found between course grade and the placement essay score suggested that the placement essay provided more finely scaled information than expected. Finally, results suggested that the course's critical reading demands may have driven students' perceptions of apprehension to extremes.

A recent study was conducted by Hamer (1997) who compared the performance of 29 developmental learners enrolled in a community college who completed reading-related writing exercises to those who did not. Both groups read and wrote about their assigned readings (reading–writing focused) and those who read (reading-focused) to meet the course requirements. Results of the study indicated that "reading–writing focused students wrote more extensively in response to what was read, while the primarily reading students wrote to respond to questions requiring generally brief answers" (p. 25).

Reading, Writing, and Experimental Studies

Experimental studies have been conducted to demonstrate how specific reading and writing techniques and strategies can enhance comprehension and retention of information in content area classes. Such studies include those investigating summary writing, outlining, and notetaking. Results from these studies suggest that providing students with opportunities to write summaries improves comprehension and recall (Garner, 1985; Hill, 1991; Newlun, 1930). Glover, Plake, Roberts, Zimmer, and Palmer (1981), Jencke (1935), and K. Taylor (1978), performed studies specifically with college students. Jencke (1935) found that precis' writing increased the comprehension and the vocabulary knowledge of students at both the high school and college levels as measured by a vocabulary and untimed reading exam. K. Taylor (1978) noted that summary writing improved when college-level students practiced paraphrasing and writing summaries for a passage during a 3-week training program. Glover et al.'s study (1981) revealed that students who were taught how to paraphrase an essay were able to recollect more relevant ideas from the essay than students who were taught to write only important words while reading the essay.

Writing summaries can also enhance students' understanding of both narrative and expository text structure (Bean & Steenwyck, 1984; Gordon & Braun, 1982; B. M. Taylor & Beach, 1984). Students who were taught notetaking and underlining increased their understanding of the written materials (Barton, 1930; Kulhavy, Dyer, & Silver, 1975). These studies were conducted with elementary through high school grade-level students. Experimental research with college learners, and specifically, developmental students is needed in these areas.

Studies examining how reading can affect writing revealed that students who read more improved their writing skills especially in grammar and usage (Clark, 1935; Elley, Barham, Lamb, & Wyllie, 1976; Strom, 1960). DeVries (1970) and Heys (1962) found that with middle and high school students that assigned readings affect students' writing more than extra writing practice. Christiansen (1965) found that both experimental and control groups improved their writing when extra reading and writing assignments were given to college freshmen enrolled in a 15-week semester course.

Other mentionable studies that examined how improving writing affects reading with college freshmen were conducted by Walker-Lewis (1981) and Wolfe (1975). According to Walker-Lewis (1981), developmental students in a college-level reading course who wrote in expressive and receptive modes and received training in reading had better reading comprehension than that of the control group.

Wolfe (1975) examined the effects of teaching reading vocabulary on the writing vocabulary of college freshmen enrolled in a remedial reading course. Findings from this study revealed that students who used the new vocabulary words in a sentence enhanced their retention of the more challenging words than did students just reading new words in a sentence.

Still other investigations showed that writing improves reading comprehension because both reading and writing are interactive processes that involve meaning making (Applebee, 1984; Gebbard, 1983; Shanahan, 1980). A limited group of investigations (as cited in Stotsky, 1983), however, focused on the improvement of writing skills through reading instruction with college-level students (Calhoun, 1971; Campbell, 1976; Eurich, 1931; Mathews, Larsen, & Butler 1945; Schneider, 1971). In these studies, no significant differences were found between experimental and control groups in either writing or reading ability. However, Bossone and Quitman (1976) reported significant improvements on both reading and writing with more than 200 high school and remedial college students enrolled in 15-week semester English courses. In particular, researchers examined the effects on students' expository writing in highly structured English courses that correlated reading instruction and writing instruction. Findings revealed that 80% of the students in the experimental group improved their essays as compared to 45% of the students in the control group. Both high school and college students in the experimental groups showed significant gains in reading as measured by a standardized reading test as compared to the control groups. Both the experimental and control groups significantly improved in reading on a curriculum-based reading assessment test.

Reading, Writing, and Cognitive Processes

Reading and writing are based on cumulative abstract processes, and the cognitive restructurings caused by reading and writing develop the higher reasoning processes involved in extended abstract thinking (Havelock, 1963; Squire, 1983). Good readers and writers develop higher order thinking processes that involve reasoning, recognizing patterns of organization, and synthesizing the author's ideas. Reading–writing processes include exploration and comparison of what readers and writers state and what they mean and what others say and mean (Carothers, 1959). Thus, an analysis of the cognitive processes becomes essential for understanding how reading and writing are related (Ong, 1972).

Research on the reading–writing connection suggest that readers and writers share many of the same cognitive processes as they strive to make meaning (Loban, 1964; Martin, 1977; Rosenblatt, 1994; Shanahan, 1988; Shanahan & Lomax, 1988, Tierney & Pearson, 1983; Tierney & Shanahan, 1991). Data collection does not include merely the examination of students' reading and writing products, but also an analysis from qualitative descriptive information such as observations, interviews, and think-aloud strategies.

Qian (1990) in a review of the tenets of the reading and writing interactive model notes that research supports the belief that reading–writing processes share a common knowledge and similar mental processes. Reading and writing are interactive processes in which participants go through the same activities such as planning, drafting, aligning, revising, monitoring, and checking outcomes. Readers and writers also share similar mental operations by engaging in reflective thinking after finishing a text. Finally, the interactive model suggests that students should be encouraged to write as soon as they start reading. Raphael and Englert (1988) noted that reading and writing are complex cognitive processes that involve three similar strategies—planning (prewriting or prereading), drafting (writing or guided reading), and revising (modifying and extending, or postreading). Ryan (1985) identified six thinking strategies students use as they read and write when examining the verbal protocols of eight above-average fifth-grade readers as they read and wrote in the narrative and expository genres: (a) reporting (reproducing and paraphrasing a message, (b) conjecturing (hypothesizing, predicting outcomes, and inferencing), (c) contextualizing (relating concepts and events through imagining and creating scenarios, (d) structuring, (e) monitoring, and (f) revising (fix-up strategies).

Martin (1987) found similar results, and noted that readers and writers use the same cognitive processes, but vary in the number of times they used reading and writing strategies. Martin developed eight categories of meaning-making strategies: (a) monitoring, (b) phrasing content, (c) using content prior knowledge, (d) using text from knowledge, (e) rereading, (f) questioning, (g) inferencing, and (h) making connections to author/audience. During writing, students were concerned about content knowledge; during reading, they were concerned with paraphrasing content.

Kirby (1986) in research with five at-risk college basic readers, videotaped four sessions of their reading and writing behaviors and concluded introspective interviews about the students' backgrounds and attitudes concerning their reading–writing processes. Retrospective interviews were conducted as well, asking students to recall certain reading–writing behaviors. The college freshmen in the study read narrative and expository text and wrote and revised expressive and transactive text on topics similar to those in their reading selections. Kirby found that students used similar but limited reading–writing strategies despite the differences in types of text and their success in using these strategies to construct meaning. While writing, college developmental students planned different types of writing in similar ways and used rereading, writing nonstop, revising, pausing, and discovering ideas while composing. In addition, students relied on their background of experiences to complete their reading and writing tasks.

Tierney and Pearson (1983) constructed a composing-reading model in which they suggest that reading and writing share similar cognitive processes: (a) goal setting, (b) knowledge mobilization, (c) projection, (d) perspective-taking, (e) refinement, (f) review, (g) self-correction, and (h) self-assessment.

Langer's research (1986) indicated that although reading and writing appear to share many of the same cognitive processes, differences are evident. She stated that both readers and writers used meaning to create and refine ideas, but readers generated more ideas when they read and formulated more ideas when they wrote. Readers focused on ideas as they read; writers used strategies to create meaning. The strategies included: (a) generating ideas, (b) creating meaning, (c) evaluating, and (d) revising; while reasoning operations were: (e) hypothesizing, (f) noting evidence, (g) validating, and (h) questioning using schemata.

Holladay (1988) recognized seven cognitive skills readers use similar to Langer's processes:

> 1) clarifying the purpose of a text, 2) generating ideas, 3) identifying important aspects of the text, 4) focusing attention first on major aspects of the text, 5) perceiving and revealing structure, connections, and relationships, and 6) monitoring reading and writing by selecting, choosing, and questioning to determine if goals are being met, and 7) taking corrective action if necessary. (p. 189)

Reading, Writing, and Critical Thinking

Readers and writers also appear to share similar mental operations while engaging in reflexive thinking after they have finished their respective texts. Research from the interactive perspective shows that writing affects students' reading comprehension and critical thinking, and that combining reading and writing contributes to a wider range in the quantity and quality of revisions to writing.

In a study with 137 undergraduate students, Tierney, Soter, O'Flahavan, and McGinley (1989) questioned whether writing in combination with reading prompts more critical thinking than reading by itself, or whether writing singularly, or either reading or writing combined with questions or with a knowledge activation activity prompts critical thinking. Results indicated significant difference between students who both read and write and students who performed other activities. In particular, students who read and wrote produced more revisions in their writing, indicating thinking critically allows for stronger revisions. As a result, the researchers contend that reading and writing together prompts more critical thinking than when reading and writing are taught separately or when reading is combined with knowledge-activation activities or questioning activities.

Other studies suggest that writing and reading together can enhance thinking and reasoning operations depending on the purpose of the assignment, topic or problem, type of exercise, and the learning style of the learner (Ackerman, 1990; Applebee, 1984; Colvin-Murphy, 1986; Greene, 1989; Kennedy, 1985; McGinley & Tierney, 1989; Nelson & Hayes, 1988; Spivey & King, 1989). A limited number of studies suggest that critical thinking improved when readers were able to interpret and understand the author's purpose as they analyzed difficult text (Crismore, 1985; Tierney, LaZansky, Raphael, & Cohen, 1987).

Kennedy (1985) and Nelson and Hayes (1988) examined critical thinking with college learners. Kennedy (1985) observed the reading and writing processes of three proficient and three less-proficient college readers. After reading three articles on the subject of communication, students were asked to write an objective essay. The purpose of the study was to examine how students differed in their use of outside reading sources to learn about their subjects and to compose an essay. Kennedy observed that both groups of students used various reading sources as they prepared to write an essay, but found that students differed in their ability to use these sources. More proficient readers used a variety of reading and writing strategies to help them write their essays such as reading and writing for specific purposes, taking notes, quoting sources to support the thesis of their essays, and rereading and revising their essays to integrate outside sources with their own ideas and beliefs. The less-proficient readers, however, did not employ a wide variety of reading and writing study strategies. Instead, they relied heavily on outside sources, rereading them and quoting material from these outside sources frequently in their essays.

Nelson and Hayes (1988) examined how college students searched for information while writing research papers and examined students' decision-making processes and their completion of research related tasks. In the first study, eight freshmen and eight advanced writers (upperclassmen and graduate students) were asked to research and to write about the relationship between the United States and a particular Latin American country. Findings from this study indicated that each group of writers used different goals and strategies as revealed in their written records of their processes (process logs) and their think-aloud protocols. Further analysis revealed that students' strategies for designing their search, locating sources, and accepting or rejecting their sources were based on their conceptions of the research task, namely that of searching for facts (content-driven) or for finding a particular situation (issue-driven). Freshman writers defined tasks as a "fact-finding mission" (as cited in McGinley & Tierney, 1989, p. 260) and consequently skimmed material for factual information that easily fit their essays. On the other hand, when writing more issue-based papers, students searched for content based on the reliability and importance of the information as it related to their pertinent goals of their papers.

In their second study, Nelson and Hayes (1988, as cited in McGinley & Tierney, 1989), studied the processes and strategies of eight college undergraduates enrolled in a variety of content area courses including those from the arts, sciences, and the humanities as they prepared research papers. Results from the students' process logs revealed that students "tended to apply either very efficient 'low-investment' strategies requiring little engagement, or more time consuming 'high investment' strategies" (p. 260).

In a recent study, Ackerman (1990) explored how writers with extensive experience and learning in an academic discipline used typical and rhetorical knowledge to construct synthesis essays. Twenty psychology graduate students and 20 business graduate students wrote synthesis essays on either the topics of supply-side economics or rehearsal in memory. Half of the subjects completed think-aloud protocols, and their composing processes were analyzed for difference qualities and frequencies of elaborations and rhetorical awareness and for task representation. An ANOVA indicated that high knowledge writers demonstrated unique elaborative and rhetorically sensitive performance, high knowledge writers included more new information in their essays in the top levels of essay organization, and low knowledge writers elaborated less but relied on structural and content-based awareness to compose. Findings confirmed the interrelatedness of comprehension processes and composing processes and illustrated how writers, with varying levels of topic familiarity, use their knowledge of disciplinary topics and their experience as readers and writers to compose synthesis essays.

RECOMMENDATIONS FOR FUTURE RESEARCH

According to Shanahan (1997), "surprisingly, given the long history and nearly universal acceptance of the idea of integration at all of levels of education, there have been few investigations of its effects" (p. 15). In addition, based on the review of the literature regarding the relationships between reading and writing, it becomes evident that qualitative and quantitative research studies with college developmental populations are lacking. More comprehensive correlational studies with college developmental learners based on well-developed theoretical frameworks need to be conducted using a multitude of variables such as "the role of content knowledge, expository text structure, use and interpretation of rhetorical devices and structures" (Tierney & Shanahan, 1991, p. 250).

Experimental studies that further demonstrate the cause–effect relationship between reading and writing are also needed in order to explore the effect of college developmental students' processes and products on instruction. Additional studies might be designed to examine the effect of author awareness and its impact on reading and writing (Tierney & Shanahan, 1991). Still other studies need to be designed that demonstrate the effect of planning, aligning, drafting, revising, and monitoring on college students' reading and writing. The role of individual learning styles and preferences and their impact on integrating reading and writing needs to be explored in depth. Reading–writing developmental educators need to conduct more action research in their classrooms to determine the effects, if any, of integrating reading and writing have on the literacy learning of their students.

POSTSECONDARY PROGRAMS, COURSES, AND PRACTICES INCORPORATING THE READING–WRITING CONNECTIONS

Although some colleges and universities have programs that combine reading and writing as shared processes, more programs and practices are needed. Included here is a limited review of some of these programs and practices.

Perhaps the most well-known program combining reading and writing on the college level for underprepared students was founded at the University of Pittsburgh by David Bartholomae and Anthony Petrosky in the late 1970s and described in their landmark book *Facts, Artifacts, and Counterfacts* (1986). The basic reading–writing course described in this book is taught like a college seminar and is worth six semester credit hours. Most courses are team-taught and meet three times a week for 2-hour sessions. The course is arranged around a single problem such as "Work," or "Growth and Change in Adolescence" (p. 30). Two strands with linked, sequential assignments (12 sets of assignments) guide the course. By the end of the term, students have read approximately 12 books and have written on average 25 assignments with revisions. Student papers are copied and are used as an additional text for the course with class discussion focusing on these writings. Students produce a collective autobiography.

> There are no lectures or general discussions. We don't discuss "the family," in other words, but what X has said about families, and the seminar meetings as a result become workshops or proving grounds, where students learn to read and write in an academic setting. (p. 30)

Student papers are also used for case studies within the course. For example, when studying the theme of growth and change in adolescence, the class uses these papers to study adolescent development while at the same time learning what it is like to be a college reader and writer. From each others' experiences, students are able to develop a theory of adolescence. Next, students read and analyze texts from professional writers related to the theme that they are studying and place their work side by side with the professional's opinions of the subject.

Developmental students at Quinipiac College in Connecticut enroll in a regular college-level English 101 composition course that meets for additional class time in specially designed "intensive" sections of the course. These sections meet for 5 hours of instructional time, and students receive regular college credit for the course. One of the purposes of this course is to provide assignments that integrate reading and writing. In particular, the faculty wanted their students to be able to "synthesize, analyze, and criticize course readings and to position themselves and the readings in relation to the discipline" (Segall, 1995, p. 40). Developmental students read the same texts and respond and complete the same assignments as regular college composition students. Courses are arranged thematically including topics related to "power and control, censorship, campus issues, or self esteem" (p. 43). The only difference between the intensive sections and other college composition courses is that intensive classes meet for an additional 2 hours a week in which instructors can schedule workshops, individual conferences or group work; the other college composition courses met for only 3 hours a week.

The developmental writing program at Michigan State University offers a course to college developmental learners based on the theory that reading and writing should be taught together. The primary goal of this program is to empower students so that they can express themselves in writing for the academic community. A secondary goal is to help students gain the confidence in themselves in order to graduate from college. Faculty loads and class size are small; therefore, students are given individual attention to meet their needs (Korth, 1991).

Reading students at the Community College of Allegheny Campus–North Campus engage in reading-related writing exercises. Classes meet twice a week for 1 hour and 40 minutes during a semester-long course. The semester is divided into four units in which students read narratives in the first unit, short stories in the second unit, essays in the third unit, and essays on a particular topic in the fourth unit. Students are asked to read, discuss, and answer questions about their reading assignments. They are also asked to make connections between the assigned readings.

Students complete 15 in-class writing assignments and 2 out-of-class assignments for a total of 17 assignments. The reading-related writing assignments are developed to allow students to interact with the text as they read. These assignments include those designed to help students increase metacognitive awareness, extend text, organize the information in the text, and use background knowledge and experiences to relate to the readings. Activities include organizing, analyzing, and synthesizing events that occur in the reading selections (Hamer, 1997).

Since 1991, we (Valeri-Gold & Deming, 1994) have team-taught a combined reading–writing class at Georgia State University with college developmental learners. This combined team-taught course was designed to present the study of reading and writing as related processes instead of as separate disciplines. This philosophy is supported by our belief readers and writers share the same processes as they strive to make meaning. The reading–writing processes involve gathering of ideas, questioning, and hypothesizing (Tierney & Shanahan, 1991).

In the team-taught combined reading–writing course, students use a text that includes diverse literary selections based on a variety of themes ranging from personal concerns to more abstract issues. These thematically arranged literary selections were chosen to represent a diversity of cultures and include essays, magazine articles, short stories, and poems.

Students are introduced to a discussion of the reading–writing processes, an explanation of individual reading–writing preferences, and suggestions for strategies that students can use before, during, and after their reading–writing processes. Students are also presented with a variety of ways to respond to what they are reading and writing through the use of journal writing, portfolios, and collaborative projects.

In addition to the programs that combine reading and writing as interrelated disciplines with college students, other college developmental educators engage in specific classroom activities that integrate reading and writing. For example, Mink (1988) uses journal writing and small group discussions with composition and literature classes to integrate reading, writing, and discussion. Students are actively involved as engaged readers and writers through their independent reading, writing, and thinking activities, the sharing of ideas in collaborative groups, writing reflections in their journals, and relating ideas formulated from large and group discussions in formal writing assignments and projects.

Reading and writing are integrated into one course at San Jose State University in California. This course consists of two levels: Academic English 1 and Academic English 2, both 5-hour semester courses. Students spend 3 hours in class and 2 hours in the Language Development Center. While in the center, students spend 30 minutes working with a peer tutor on a class writing assignment. Additional time is spent working with peer groups and composing assignments on the computer. Class and lab assignments are designed to combine and foster reading–writing growth. For example, students respond to what they read, and practice reading and writing strategies such as determining the main idea with forming theses and using thesis statements to plan essays. Other assignments include assuming the role of both the reader and the writer and understanding the author's purpose for writing for a specific audience (L. Smith, personal communication, October 27, 1997).

Basic writers enrolled at San Francisco State University take a reading course concurrent with their writing class. All writing assignments in the composition course are based on readings. Students are required to write summaries for the first month of class, first writing summaries of paragraphs and then summaries of short essays. While composing summaries, they are taught how to find the general point, how to find the main points of each paragraph, and how to identify conclusions. In addition, students write six essays based on their readings over the rest of the semester. Writing assignments are based entirely on the reading. For example, students are required to read seven articles on a particular topic such as covering problems with U.S. education and the nature of Asian educational methods. Students are then assigned to summarize the problems and to examine the Asian methods to see which, if any, of them might be incorporated to improve U.S. education. In other assignments, students are asked to read arguments for and against the censorship of high school newspapers and to evaluate these arguments and come to their own conclusions (W. Robinson, personal communication, September 25, 1997).

High-risk freshmen at Rider University in New Jersey are enrolled in paired courses with content-level classes such as psychology, history, and sociology. Students register for these paired courses during a 2-day orientation during the summer. Groups of 100 to 200 students are tested on a Sunday and on a Monday they meet with an advisor for a short time and then register for the open sections (J. Simon, personal communication, 1997).

Developmental learners in the Gateway Program at Community College at Philadelphia enroll in paired reading–writing classes with content-specific courses as well. For example, students might enroll in a history course with a reading–writing teacher committed to the context of the discipline (T. Ott, personal communication, October 29, 1997).

At Foothill Community College in California, students enroll in two five-unit courses, a class in writing taught in tandem with the reading class which is scheduled first. These team-taught classes focus on one issue each term, such as African American issues. In one class, students discuss the readings and how to write about them, while in the other class, students discuss writing and how to use the readings as a source of information (L. Lane, personal communication, October 22, 1997).

El-Hindi (1997) used metacognitive strategies for reading and writing with college students from underrepresented populations at precollege summer intensive programs.

Students use reflective journals also known as *reading logs* to self-monitor their thought processes as they engage in various reading–writing assignments. In particular, students are taught to "evaluate their successes as writers, react to their written texts as readers, and examine their texts holistically to see connections among different parts of their texts" (p. 11). Students read weekly chapters from *Writing With Power* (Elbow, 1998) and articles by other modern writers.

Blanton (1997) used the newspaper to strengthen the reading, writing, and thinking skills of developmental reading students at Long Beach City College in California. Students select topics of interest, read articles related to their topics, and then write summaries of the articles. Students also participate in literature circles and write responses in journals to books they are studying (J. Blanton, personal communication, October 22, 1997).

Johnson (1997) used essays and articles related to themes of reading and writing, such as William Saroyan's "Why I Write." Students complete the reading of the book during the academic term and write guided response entries in their journals. They choose to read an additional five articles on a particular theme and summarize these articles. Next, they are asked to synthesize their ideas by writing a paper using the five articles and creating their own point of view. Students also write responses to passages from Stephen Covey's books using the computer program "Write On" (K. Johnson, personal communication, November 6, 1997).

Developmental students at Upsala College in New Jersey were enrolled in courses that integrated reading, writing, and mathematics. For example, in a statistics class students were asked to read problems, to understand a practical situation, and to apply their math skills to a situation in a way that was useful and clarifying (A. Gourgey, personal communication, November 6, 1997).

McGee and Richgels (1990), in their belief that reading and writing share a symbiotic relationship, offered strategies that foster critical-thinking skills that are applicable at the college level. In order to encourage students to strengthen critical understanding of texts, they recommend using letters to the editor, extended writing about literature, and extended writing about content. They also recommend exercises that call on students' prior knowledge including exercises such as guided writing procedures, and K-W-L exercises in which students write what they already know about the topic, what they want to learn, and what they still need to learn (Ogle, 1986). To foster student involvement, they recommend the use of trade books, character identification exercises, and writing from different perspectives.

CONCLUSIONS

According to Smith (1982), reading and writing must complement each other in order for students to achieve the creative and communicative power that language offers.

Morrow (1997) wrote that "reading and writing are, quite simply, different, albeit complementary, ways of knowing the world" (p. 466). She asks college instructors to explore "how" they ask students to read texts and instead suggests that we consider "reading to build an intellectual repertoire.... Reading for ambiguity.... Reading for the unexpected.... Reading for the play of language.... Reading for strategies of persuasion.... Reading for genre conventions" (pp. 467–469).

Understanding the relationships between reading and writing can help educators design effective programs and teach courses that help students improve their reading and writing (Squire, 1983). Integrating both disciplines creates a community of learners, challenges students intellectually, changes students' attitudes toward learning, and strengthens or changes the current curriculum (Bain, 1993). Farrell (1977) stated that "reading and writing affect how people communicate, what they think is involved in communicating, and what they think is involved in thinking" (p. 448). Thus, teaching reading and writing as integrated forms of communication is essential for today's college developmental programs.

REFERENCES AND SUGGESTED READINGS

Ackerman, J. M. (1990). *Reading, writing, and knowing. The role of disciplinary knowledge in comprehension and composing* (Tech. Rep. No. 40). Berkeley, CA: University of California, Center for the Study of Writing.

Applebee, A. (1984). *Contexts for learning to write: Studies of secondary school instruction.* Norwood, NJ: Ablex.

Atwell, M. (1981, November). *The evolution of text: Interrelationship of reading and writing in the composing process.* Paper presented at the annual conference of the National Council of Teachers of English, Boston.

Bain, D. L. (1993). Cabbages and kings: Research directions in integrated/interdisciplinary curriculum. *The Journal of Educational Thought, 27*(3), 312–331.

Barbig, E. V. (1968). An exploration of growth in written composition to determine the relationship between selected variables to poor writing in grades 9 and 12 (Doctoral dissertation, University of Tennessee, 1968). *Dissertation Abstracts International, 29,* 2140A.

*Bartholomae, D., & Petrosky, A. (1986). *Facts, artifacts and counterfacts: Theory and method for a reading and writing course.* Upper Montclair, NJ: Boyton.

Barton, W. (1930). *Outlining as a study procedure.* (Contributions to Education No. 411). New York: Columbia University, Teachers College, Bureau of Publications.

Bean, T. W., & Steenwyck, F. L. (1984). The effect of three forms of summarization instruction on sixth graders' summary writing and comprehension. *Journal of Reading Behavior, 16,* 297–306.

Birnbaum, J. C. (1982). The reading and composing behavior of selected fourth- and seventh-grade students. *Research in the Teaching of English, 16*(3), 241–260.

Bossone, R., & Quitman, L. A. (1976). *A strategy for coping with high school and college remedial English students.* Bloomington, IN: ERIC Clearinghouse. (ERIC Document Reproduction Service No. ERIC 130 268)

*Braun, C. (1984, June). *Reading–writing connections: A case analysis.* Paper presented at the Colloquium on Research in Reading and Language Arts in Canada, Lethbridge, Alberta, Canada.

*Brown, S. (1986, March). *Reading-writing connections: College freshman basic writers' apprehension achievement.* Paper presented at the annual meeting of the Conference on College Composition and Communication, New Orleans.

Butler, A., & Turbill, J. (1987). *Towards a reading-writing classroom.* Portsmouth, NH: Heinemann.

Butler-Nalin, K. (1984). Revising patterns in student writing. In A. N. Applebee (Ed.), *Contexts for learning to write: Studies of secondary school instruction* (pp. 121–133). Norwood, NJ: Ablex.

*Calhoun, J. (1971). The effects of analysis of essays in college composition classes on reading and writing skills. (Doctoral dissertation, Boston University, 1971). *Dissertation Abstracts International, 32,* 1971A.

*Campbell, M. L. (1976). An investigation of the relationship between secondary generative and receptive communication skills at the college freshman level (Doctoral dissertation, University of Southern Mississippi, 1976). *Dissertation Abstracts International, 37,* 5655A.

*Carothers, J. C. (1959). Culture, psychiatry, and the written word. *Psychiatry, 22,* 309–320.

Chall, J. S. (1983). *The stages of reading development.* New York: McGraw-Hill.

Christiansen, M. (1965). Tripling writing and omitting readings in freshman English: An experiment. *College Composition and Communication, 16,* 122–124.

Clark, J. D. (1935). A four-year study of freshman English. *English Journal, 24,* 404–410.

*Collins, N. C. (1990). *The reading and writing relationship: A case for confluent instruction.* Bloomington, IN: ERIC Clearinghouse. (ERIC Document Reproduction Service No. ED 313 660)

Colvin-Murphy, C. (1986, December). *Enhancing critical comprehension of literacy texts through writing.* Paper presented at the annual meeting of the National Reading Conference, Austin, TX.

Crismore, A. (1985). *Metadiscourse as rhetorical act in social studies text: Its effect on student performance and attitude.* Unpublished doctoral dissertation, University of Illinois, Chicago.

D'Angelo, J. L. (1977). Predicting reading achievement in a senior high school from intelligence, listening, and informative writing (Doctoral dissertation, University of Pittsburgh, 1977). *Dissertation Abstracts International, 38,* 2027A.

DeVries, T. (1970). Reading, writing, frequency, and expository writing. *Reading Improvement, 7,* 14–15, 19.

Elbow, P. (1998). *Writing with power* (2nd ed.). New York: University of Oxford Press.

*El-Hindi, A. E. (1997). Connecting reading and writing: College learners' metacognitive awareness. *Journal of Developmental Education, 21*(2), 10–18.

Elley, W., Barham, J. H., Lamb, H., & Wyllie, M. (1976). The role of grammar in a secondary school English curriculum. *Research in the Teaching of English, 10,* 5–21.

Eurich, A. C. (1931). *The reading abilities of college students: An experimental study.* Minneapolis: University of Minnesota Press.

Faigley, L., & Witte, S. (1981). Analyzing revision. *College Composition and Communication, 32,* 400–414.

Farrell, T. J. (1977). Literacy, the basics, and all that jazz. *College English, 38,* 443–460.

Felland, N. (1981). A national study of the level of composition achievement (superior/average) of twelfth grade composition students in selected personal characteristics/environmental factors (Doctoral dissertation, Northern Illinois University, 1980). *Dissertation Abstracts International, 41,* 3037A.

Fishco, D. T. (1966). A study of the relationship between creativity in writing and comprehension in reading in selected seventh grade students (Doctoral dissertation, Lehigh University, 1966). *Dissertation Abstracts International, 27,* 3220A.

*Flower, L., & Hayes, J. (1980). The dynamics of composing: Making plans and juggling constraints. In L. Gregg & E. R. Steinberg (Eds.), *Cognitive processes in writing* (pp. 31–50). Hillsdale, NJ: Lawrence Erlbaum Associates.

*Flower, L., & Hayes, J. (1981). A cognitive process of theory of writing. *College Composition and Communication, 32,* 365–387.

Fuller, K. M. (1974). An investigation of the relationship of reading achievement and oral and written language of students enrolled in reading and English classes at Gainesville Junior College (Doctoral dissertation, University of Georgia, 1974). *Dissertation Abstracts International, 35,* 6692A.

Garner, R. (1985). Test summarization deficiencies among older students. *American Educational Research Journal, 22*(4), 549–650.

Gebbard, A. (1983). Teaching writing in reading and the content areas. *Journal of Reading, 27,* 207–211.

Glover, J., Plake, B., Roberts, B., Zimmer, T., & Palmer, J. (1981). Distinctiveness of encoding: The effects of paraphrasing and drawing inferences on memory from prose. *Journal of Educational Psychology, 73,* 736–744.

Gordon, C. J., & Braun, C. (1982). Story schemata: Metatextual aid to reading and writing. In J. A. Niles & L. A. Harris (Eds.), *New inquiries in reading research and instruction* (pp. 262–268). Rochester, NY: National Reading Conference.

Greene, G. M. (1989, November). *Intertextuality and moves to authority in writing from sources.* Paper presented at the annual meeting of the National Reading Conference, Austin, TX.

Grimmer, F. (1970). The effects of an experimental program in written composition on the writing of second-grade children (Doctoral dissertation, University of Georgia, 1970). *Dissertation Abstracts International, 31,* 5666A.

Grobe, S. F., & Grobe, C. H. (1977). Reading skills as a correlate of writing ability in college freshmen. *Reading World, 17,* 50-54.

*Hamer, Arden A. B. (1997). Adding in-class writing to the college reading curriculum: Problems and pluses. *Forum for Reading, 27,* 25–34.

Havelock, E. A. (1963). *Preface to Plato.* Cambridge, MA: Harvard University Press.

*Hayes, C. G. (1990). *Using writing to promote reading to learn in college.* Bloomington, IN: ERIC Clearinghouse. (ERIC Document Reproduction Service No. ED 322 499)

*Heller, M. (1980). The reading-writing connection: An analysis of the written language of university freshmen at two reading levels (Doctoral dissertation, Oklahoma State University, 1979). *Dissertation International Abstracts, 40,* 4452A.

Heys, F. (1962). The theme-a-week-assumption: A report of an experiment. *English Journal, 51,* 320–322.

Hill, M. (1991). Writing summaries promotes thinking and learning across the curriculum—But why are they so difficult to write? *Journal of Reading, 34,* 536–539.

*Holladay, S. (1988). Integrating reading and writing. *Teaching English in the Two-Year College, 15*(3), 187–194.

Hunt, K. W. (1977). Early blooming and late blooming syntactic structures. In C. R. Cooper & L. Odell (Eds.), *Evaluating writing: Describing, measuring, judging* (pp. 91–104). Urbana, IL: National Council of Teachers of English.

*Huot, B. (1988). Reading/writing connections on the college level. *Teaching English in the Two-Year College, 15*(2), 90–98.

*Irvin, J. W. (1992). Reading/writing research: 1900 to 1984. In J. W. Irwin & M. A. Doyle (Eds.), *Reading/writing connections: Learning from research* (pp. 262-284). Newark, DE: International Reading Association.

Iser, W. (1978). *The act of reading: A theory of aesthetic response.* Baltimore: The John Hopkins Press.

Jencke, G. (1935). *A study of precis writing as a composition technique.* (Contributions to Education, No. 644). New York: Columbia University, Teachers College, Bureau of Publications.

Johnson, N. (1981). A comparison of syntactic writing maturity with reading achievement (Doctoral dissertation, East Texas State University, 1980). *Dissertation Abstracts International, 41,* 4346A.

Juel, C., Griffith, P., & Gough, P. (1986). A longitudinal study of the changing relationships of word recognition, spelling, reading comprehension, and writing from first to second grade. *Journal of Educational Psychology, 78,* 243–255.

Kennedy, M. L. (1985). The composing processes of college students' writing from sources. *Written Communication, 2,* 434–456.

*Kirby, K. (1986). *Reading and writing processes of selected high-risk freshmen.* Unpublished doctoral dissertation, University of Georgia, Athens.

Korth, P. A. (1991, March). *The developmental level writing program at Michigan State University.* Paper presented at the annual meeting of the Conference on College Composition and Communication, Boston.

*Kucer, S. B., & Harste, J. C. (1991). The reading and writing connection: Counterpart strategy lessons. In B. L. Hayes (Ed.), *Effective strategies for teaching reading* (pp. 123–152). Needham Heights, MA: Allyn & Bacon.

Kulhavy, R., Dyer, J., & Silver, L. (1975). The effects of notetaking and test expectancy on the learning of text material. *Journal of Educational Research, 68,* 363–365.

Langer, J. A. (1986). *Children reading and writing: Structures and strategies.* Norwood, NJ: Ablex.

*Linnehan, P. J. (1994). Exploiting the reading writing connection in a basic writing course. *English in Texas, 26*(2), 54–59.

Loban, W. (1964). *Language ability: Grades seven, eight, and nine.* Berkeley, CA: University of California. (ERIC Document Reproduction Service No. ED 001 275)

Maloney, H. G. (1967). An identification of excellence in expository composition performance in a selected 9A population with an analysis of reasons for superior performance (Doctoral dissertation, Columbia University, 1967). *Dissertation Abstracts International, (28),* 3564.

Martin, P. (1977). A comparative analysis of reading and writing skills: Six case studies. *English in Australia, 40,* 51–53.

Martin, S. (1987, December). *The meaning-making strategies reported by proficient readers and writers.* Paper presented at the meeting of the National Reading Conference, St. Petersburg, FL.

Mathews, E., Larsen, R., & Butler, G. (1945). Experimental investigation of the relation between reading training and achievement in college composition classes. *Journal of Educational Research, 38,* 499–505.

McCarthy, L. P. (1987). A stranger in strange lands: A college student writing across the curriculum. *Research in the Teaching of English, 21*(3), 233–265.

*McGee, L. M., & Richgels, O. (1990). Learning from text using reading in writing. In T. Shanahan (Ed.), *Reading and writing together: New perspectives for the classroom* (pp. 145–160). Norwood, MA: Christopher-Gordon Publishers.

McGinley, W., & Kamberelis, G. (1996). Maniac magee and ragtime tumpie: Children negotiating self and world through reading and writing. *Teaching of English, 30*(1),75–113.

McGinley, W., & Tierney, R. J. (1989). Traversing the topical landscape. *Written Communication, 6,* 243–269.

*Mink, J. S. (1988, March). *Integrating reading, writing, and learning theory: A method to our madness.* Paper presented at the annual meeting of the Conference on College Composition and Communication, St. Louis, MO.

Morrow, N. (1997). The role of reading in the composition classroom. *Journal of Advanced Composition, 17,* 453–472.

Murray, D. (1982). Teaching the other self: The writer's first reader. *College Composition and Communication, 33,* 140–147.

Nelson, J., & Hayes, J. P. (1988). *How the writing context shapes college students' strategies for writing from sources.* (Tech. Rep. No. 101). Pittsburgh, PA: University of Pittsburgh, Center for the Study of Reading.

Newlun, C. (1930). *Teaching children to summarize in fifth grade history.* (Contributions to Education No. 404). New York: Columbia University, Teachers College, Bureau of Publications.

Nystrand, M. (1986). *The structure of written communication.* New York: Academic Press.

Ogle, D. M. (1986). K-W-L: A teaching model that develops active reading of expository text. *The Reading Teacher, 39*(6), 564–570.

Ong, W. J. (1972). Media transformation: The talked book. *College English, 34,* 405–410.

Peregoy, S., & Boyle, O. (1993). *Reading, writing, and learning in ESL: A resource book for teachers.* White Plains, NY: Longman.

Perron, J. (1977). *The impact of mode on written syntactic complexity: Part IV-across-the grades' differences and general summary.* (Studies in Language Education No. 30). Athens: University of Georgia, Department of Language Education.

Piexotto, H. (1946). The relationship of college board examination scores and reading scores for college freshmen. *Journal of Applied Psychology, 30,* 406–411.

Qian, G.(1990, November). *Review of the interactive model: Reconsideration of reading and writing relationship.* Paper presented at the annual meeting of the College Reading Association, Nashville.

*Raphael, T. E., & Englert, C. S. (1988). *Integrating writing and reading instruction.* (Occasional Paper No. 118). East Lansing, MI: Michigan State University, East Lansing Institute for Research on Teaching.

*Rosenblatt, L. M. (1988). *Writing and reading: The transactional theory.* (Tech. Rep. No. 416). Cambridge, MA: Bolt, Beranek and Newman.

*Rosenblatt, L. M. (1994). The transactional theory of reading and writing. In R. B. Ruddell, M. R. Ruddell, & H. Singer (Eds.), *Theoretical models and processes of reading* (pp. 1057–1092). Newark, DE: International Reading Association.

Rubin, A., & Hansen, J. (1984). *Reading and writing: How are the first two "rs" related?* (Reading Education Rep. No. 51). Cambridge, MA: Bolt, Beranek and Newman.

Ryan, S. M. (1985). An examination of reading and writing strategies of selected fifth grade students. In J. Niles & R. Lalik (Eds.), *Issues in literacy: A research perspective* (pp. 386–390). Rochester, NY: National Reading Conference.

*Salvatori, M. (1983). Reading and writing a text: Correlations between reading and writing patterns. *College English, 45,* 657–666.

*Salvatori, M. (1986). The dialogical nature of basic readers and writer. In D. Bartholomae & A. Petrosky, (Eds.), *Facts, artifacts, and counterfacts* (pp. 137–166). Rochester, NY: Boyton.

Schallert, D., & Tierney, R. J. (1982). *Learning from expository text: The interaction of text structure with reader characteristics* (Final report). Washington, DC: U.S. Department of Education, National Institute of Education.

Schewe, A., & Froese, V. (1987). Relating reading and writing via comprehension, quality, and structure. In J. E. Readence & R. S. Baldwin (Eds.), *Research in literacy: Merging perspectives* (pp. 273–280). Rochester, NY: National Reading Conference.

Schonell, F. (1942). *Backwardness in the basic subjects.* Toronto: Clarke, Irwin.

Schneider, V. (1971). A study of the effectiveness of emphasizing the teaching of reading skills to improve composition skills in remedial English classes at Kansas Community Junior College (Doctoral dissertation, University of Kansas, 1971). *Dissertation Abstracts International, 31,* 6369A.

Segall, M. T. (1995). Embracing a porcupine: Redesigning a writing program. *Journal of Basic Writing, 14*(2), 38–47.

*Shanahan, T. (1980). The impact of writing instruction in learning to read. *Reading World, 19,* 357–368.

*Shanahan, T. (1984). Nature of the reading-writing relation: An exploratory multivariate analysis. *Journal of Educational Psychology, 76*(3), 466–477.

*Shanahan, T. (1988). The reading-writing relationship: Several instructional principles. *The Reading Teacher, 41,* 636–647.

*Shanahan, T. (1997). Reading–writing relationships, thematic units, inquiry learning … In pursuit of effective integrated literacy instruction. *The Reading Teacher, 51*(1), 12–19.

*Shanahan, T., & Lomax, R. G. (1986). An analysis and comparison of theoretical models of the reading–writing relationship. *Journal of Educational Psychology, 78*(2), 116–123.

*Shanahan, T., & Lomax, R. G. (1988). A developmental comparison of the three theoretical models of the reading-writing relationship, *Research in the Teaching of English, 22*(2), 196–212.

*Shanahan, T., & Tierney, R. J. (1990). Reading-writing connections: The relations among three perspectives. In J. Zutzell & S. McCormick (Eds.), *Literacy theory and research: Analysis from multiple paradigms* (pp. 13–34). Chicago: National Reading Conference.

Shanklin, N. (1982). *Relating reading and writing: Developing a transactional theory of the writing process.* Unpublished doctoral dissertation, Indiana University, Bloomington, IN.

Smith, F. (1982). *Writing and the writer.* New York: Holt, Rinehart, & Winston.

Spivey, N. N., & King, J. R. (1989). Readers as writers composing from sources. *Reading Research Quarterly, 24*(1), 7–26.

Squire, J. R. (1983). Composing and comprehending: Two sides of the same basic process. *Language Arts, 60*(5), 581–589.

*Stotsky, S.(1983). Research on reading/writing relationships: A synthesis and suggested directions. *Language Arts, 60,* 627–642.

Straw, S. B., & Schreiner, R. (1982). The effect of sentence manipulation on subsequent measures of reading and listening. *Reading Research Quarterly, 17,* 335–352.

Strom, I. (1960). Research in grammar and usage and its implications for teaching writing. Indianapolis, IN: *Bulletin of the School of Education of Indiana University, 36.*

Taylor, B. M., & Beach, R. W. (1984). The effects of text structure instruction on middle-grade students' comprehension and production of expository text. *Reading Research Quarterly, 19*(2), 134–146.

*Taylor, H. (1981). Listening comprehension and reading comprehension as predictors of achievement in college composition (Doctoral dissertation, University of Washington, 1981). *Dissertation Abstracts International, 42,* 66-A.

Taylor, K. (1978). *If not grammar, what?—Taking remedial writing instruction seriously.* Bloomington, IN: ERIC Clearinghouse. (ERIC Document Reproduction Service No. ED 159 668)

Thomas, F. (1976). The extent of the relationship between reading achievement and writing achievement among college freshmen (Doctoral dissertation, University of South Carolina, 1976). *Dissertation Abstracts International, 37,* 6320A.

*Tierney, R. J. (1983, December). *Analyzing composing behavior: Planning, aligning, revising.* Paper presented at the annual meeting of the National Reading Conference, Austin, TX.

*Tierney, R. J. (1988). *Writing and reading working together.* (Occasional Paper No. 5). Berkeley, CA: University of California, Center for the Study of Writing.

*Tierney, R. J., LaZansky, J., Raphael, T., & Cohen, P. (1987). Author's intentions and reader's interpretations. In R. Tarn, P. Andes, & P. Cohen (Eds.), *Understanding readers' understanding* (pp. 205–226). Hillsdale, NJ: Lawrence Erlbaum Associates.

*Tierney, R. J., & Pearson, P. D. (1983). Toward a composing model of reading. *Language Arts, 60,* 568–580.

*Tierney, R. J., & Shanahan, T. (1991). Research on the reading–writing relationship: Interactions, transactions, and outcomes. In R. Barr, M. L. Kamil, P. Mosenthal, & P. D. Pearson (Eds.), *Handbook of reading research* (Vol. 2, pp. 246–280). Hillsdale, NJ: Lawrence Erlbaum Associates.

*Tierney, R. J., Soter, A., O'Flahavan, J. F., & McGinley, W. (1989). The effects of reading and writing upon thinking critically. *Reading Research Quarterly, 24*(2), 134–173.

Valeri-Gold, M., & Deming, M. P. (1994). *Making connections through reading and writing.* Belmont, CA: Wadsworth.

Walker-Lewis, H. (1981). Using writing to improve the reading comprehension abilities of academically underprepared college students (Doctoral dissertation, Hofstra University, 1981). *Dissertation Abstracts International, 42,* 2053A.

Wittrock, M. C. (1984). Writing and the teaching of reading. In J. M. Jensen (Ed.), *Composing and comprehending* (pp. 77–83). Urbana, IL: National Council of Teachers of English.

Wolfe, R. (1975). An examination of the effects of teaching a reading vocabulary upon writing vocabulary in student composition (Doctoral dissertation, University of Maryland, 1975). *Dissertation Abstracts International.* (ED 114 818)

Woodfin, M. (1968). Correlations among certain factors and the written expression of third grade children. *Educational and Psychological Measurement, 28,* 1237–1242.

Woodward, J. C., & Phillips, A. (1967). Profile of the poor writer-The relationship of selected characteristics to poor writing in college. *Research in the Teaching of English, 1,* 41–53.

7

Taking Notes From Lectures

☙§§☙

Bonnie B. Armbruster
University of Illinois at Urbana–Champaign

Beyond elementary school, lecturing is a dominant form of transmitting instruction in U.S. classrooms. In a study by Putnam, Deshler, and Schumaker (1993) 60 Grade 7 and 60 Grade 10 teachers from eight school districts in three states were interviewed about their instructional practices. Results of the study included the finding that the teachers spend about 50% of their class periods lecturing, with slight increases in the amount of time spent lecturing from 7th to 10th grade. In college, lecturing becomes an even more pervasive instructional tool. As Carrier, Williams, and Dalgaard (1988) observed, "The lecture method remains a 'sacred cow' among most college and university instructors" (p. 223). Anderson and Armbruster (1986) reported that college students typically spend at least 10 hours per week attending lectures. Given that a normal course load for undergraduates is 15 credit hours, 10 hours per week amounts to 80% of class time spent listening to lectures.

Taking notes from a lecture is widely accepted as a useful strategy for learning lecture content. In a survey of U.S. and international university students by Dunkel and Davy (1989), 94% of U.S. students and 92% of international students reported that notetaking is a valued and important activity. As Carrier (1983) explained,

> perhaps no study strategy would be more staunchly defended by students and teachers alike than that of recording notes while listening to lectures. Asking students to surrender their notebooks and pens at the beginning of a lecture is likely to incite a minor uprising. Instructors too would be uncomfortable. Most have grown accustomed to viewing a roomful of students busily recording information as a sign that students are actively engaged in learning from the lecture. (p. 19)

As the use of lectures increases over a student's academic career, notetaking skills and strategies gain in importance. In recognition of this fact, many high schools and colleges offer study skills instruction, which typically includes considerable attention to notetaking. Notetaking is also featured in handbooks and manuals on studying skills.

What is known about the effect of notetaking on lecture learning? How can students improve learning from lectures? This chapter answers these questions by reviewing some of the vast research on college students' notetaking from lectures. The chapter begins with a brief overview of the theory regarding the value of taking notes from lectures, followed by a review of the research, focusing on research conducted within the past 15 years. A conclusion, including implications for practice and further research, rounds out the chapter.

OVERVIEW OF THE THEORY

Over the past 25 years, researchers in human learning have shifted their perspective from behavioral to cognitive psychology, with its focus on cognitive processes such as motivation, attention, knowledge acquisition, encoding, learning strategies, and metacognition. According to constructivist or generative (e.g., Wittrock, 1990) views of learning, learners are not passive recipients of information. Rather, learners actively construct, or generate, meaning by building relationships among the parts of the to-be-learned information and their existing knowledge, beliefs, and experiences. The building of relationships among parts of the to-be-learned information is referred to by Mayer (1984) as building *internal connections*, while the building of relationships among new information and other information, including existing knowledge, is called *external connections*.

Theoretically, then, the greatest learning occurs with the most generative notetaking activity. In other words, the greater quantity and quality of connections the learner can make among information in a lecture (internal connections) and between lecture information and prior knowledge (external connections), the greater the learning. For students taking notes from lectures, generative processing can occur at two stages—taking the notes while listening to the lecture and reviewing the notes prior to a course examination. Generative processing while taking notes is especially difficult because the task is so cognitively demanding. Students must listen to the lecture, select important ideas, hold and manipulate these ideas in working memory, interpret the information, decide what to record, and then write it down. Given sufficient time, generative processing during review should be easier because students do not have to engage in so many cognitive processes simultaneously.

We turn now to a review of research on notetaking from lectures. The review begins with research on the functions that notetaking serves in learning. Next, studies of "typical" notetaking—the type of notes students take when they are left to their own devices and how these notes affect learning—are discussed. Then, research on individual differences in learning and notetaking are reviewed. Finally, the review turns to research on efforts to improve notetaking and reviewing notes. Because most of the studies reviewed were conducted over the past 15 years, they were primarily cast within the predominant theoretical framework of constructivism and generative learning.

REVIEW OF THE RESEARCH

The Functions of Notetaking in Learning From Lectures

A study of notetaking from lectures conducted early in the cognitive research tradition was a seminal study by DiVesta and Gray (1972), which established two functions of taking notes from lectures: *encoding* and *external storage* (also known as the *process* and *product functions of notetaking*). The encoding, or process, function suggests that taking notes facilitates learning by affecting the nature of cognitive processing at the time the lecture is delivered and the notes taken. In other words, notetaking may be a generative activity because it encourages learners to build connections among lecture information and between lecture information and prior knowledge and experience. The external storage function suggests that notes are valuable as a product because they are a repository of information for later review and additional cognitive processing. The learner can review lecture notes to prevent forgetting, to relearn forgotten information, or as the basis for further generative activities.

The encoding and external storage functions of notetaking have been investigated in nearly 100 studies since DiVesta and Gray (1972). In these studies, the encoding function was measured by comparing the performance of students who listened to a lecture and took notes to those who listened to a lecture without taking notes, with neither group allowed to review prior to the criterion test. The external storage function was tested by comparing the performance of students who reviewed their notes with those who did not review their notes prior to the criterion test. These earlier studies of the encoding and external storage function have been reviewed extensively by Hartley (1983) and Kiewra (1985a, 1989). In general, the external storage function of notetaking has found support in the research literature, whereas findings regarding the encoding function are mixed. For studies comparing the two functions, the external storage function has proven more beneficial. In summary, as Hartley and Kiewra concluded in their reviews, both the encoding (process) and external storage (product) functions of notetaking contribute to learning from lectures; however, the external storage function appears to be more important.

Kiewra and colleagues (e.g., Kiewra, DuBois, Christensen, Kim, & Lindberg, 1989; Kiewra, DuBois, Christian, McShane, Meyerhoffer, & Roskelley, 1991) noted a methodological problem with the encoding versus external storage research paradigm. The traditional studies confounded the two functions because the subjects in external storage conditions had both recorded and reviewed their own notes, and had thus been involved in both encoding and external storage. Therefore, Kiewra et al. (1989) and Kiewra, DuBois, et al. (1991) proposed renaming the traditional storage function as an *encoding plus storage* function. They also proposed a new, independent storage function involving review of provided notes from a lecture the learner had not attended and therefore had not had the opportunity to encode. These variations produced three notetaking functions: the original encoding function (take notes/no review), the renamed encoding plus storage function (take notes/review), and the new external storage function (review-provided notes).

Kiewra and colleagues investigated these three newly defined functions of notetaking in two studies reported here. Kiewra et al. (1989) investigated the three functions of notetaking in conjunction with three notetaking techniques. Noting that in the traditional encoding versus external storage research, those in the external storage group had two opportunities to process the material (one while taking notes and one while reviewing) while the encoding group had only one opportunity for processing (while taking notes), Kiewra et al. equalized the processing opportunities among function groups in this study. Therefore, the function groups were redefined: encoding (takes notes on two occasions without review); encoding plus storage (takes notes one time and reviews notes the next); and external storage (reviews a set of borrowed notes on two occasions). (In addition to being assigned to one of the notetaking functions, students in the Kiewra et al., 1989, study were assigned to one of three notetaking techniques—conventional, skeletal, and matrix. These techniques, however, are not relevant to the present discussion; they are discussed later.)

In the first session of the study, students viewed a 19-minute videotaped lecture, according to directions appropriate to their assigned function and technique. One week later, they finished the second phase of the experiment and then completed four tests: free recall, factual recognition, synthesis (requiring forming a relationship that had not been explicitly stated in the lecture), and application (classifying new examples according to lecture concepts).

Results relevant to this discussion include the following: On the recall test, there was a main effect for notetaking function, with the encoding plus storage group outperforming both the encoding and external storage groups. The recognition test produced a marginally significant main effect for function, with follow-up tests indicating a significant advantage for the encoding plus storage group over the encoding group. There were no significant effects for the synthesis and application tests. Therefore, the opportunity to review notes appears to facilitate performance on lower level types of learning (recognition and recall), but not on higher levels of learning (synthesis and application).

In the Kiewra, DuBois, et al. (1991) study, the three notetaking functions and three notetaking techniques were again investigated. This time, however, processing opportunities for the function groups were not equated. The function groups were defined as: encoding (take notes/no review), encoding plus storage (take notes/review notes) and external storage (no lecture/review borrowed notes). University students viewed the same 19-minute videotaped lecture and then completed tests of cued recall and synthesis (requiring forming relationships not explicitly stated in the lecture).

Results relevant to this discussion included the following: (a) the encoding plus storage group outperformed the encoding group on both tests; (b) the encoding plus storage group outperformed the external storage group on the cued recall test; (c) on the synthesis test, the external storage group scored higher than the encoding only group; (d) there were no performance differences between students who took notes but did not review them and control students who neither took nor reviewed notes; and (e) there were no differences on either measure between the encoding group and a control group that simply viewed the lecture without taking notes or reviewing.

The results for notetaking function are consistent with results of earlier studies examining simply the encoding versus old, external storage functions: Students who review notes achieve more than students who do not review notes. The findings that the external storage function results in higher synthesis performance than the encoding function, and that there were no performance differences between students who took notes but did not review them and students who neither took nor reviewed notes indicates that notetaking alone does not serve an encoding function.

In summary, two studies (Kiewra et al., 1989; Kiewra, DuBois, et al., 1991) using reconceptualized functions of notetaking have replicated and extended previous findings. The bottom line is that the real value of taking notes is to have them available for review prior to performing the criterion task. The reason for this finding was stated previously: Because taking notes is such a cognitively demanding task, there is limited opportunity for generative processing at the time of encoding. Reviewing notes, however, offers a second opportunity for generative processing that is not as cognitively demanding as notetaking itself.

Research on the functions of notetaking reviewed so far have explored effects of notetaking on more traditional measures of learning from lectures, that is, various forms of recall and comprehension tests over lecture content. One study identified for this review, however, investigated the functions of notetaking with respect to a different measure of learning. Benton, Kiewra, Whitfill, and Dennison (1993) conducted a series of four experiments in which they studied the effects of various notetaking conditions on college students' ability to write a compare–contrast essay, a measure of learning often found on essay examinations in higher education. In the first two experiments, students either only listened or took notes on a 19-minute videotaped lecture using one of the three notetaking techniques used in previously reviewed studies by Kiewra et al. (1989, 1991) conventional notes, outline framework, or matrix framework. In Experiment 1, subjects listened to the lecture and then immediately composed a compare–contrast essay about lecture content either with or without notes present. Experiment 2 replicated Experiment 1 except that students wrote the essay 1 week after the lecture. The essays were analyzed for length (number of words and number of text units), as well as for two measures of organization—cohesion and coherence. In both experiments, students who wrote from their own notes (representing encoding plus external storage) composed longer and more organized essays than subjects writing without their notes (representing encoding only), thus lending further support to the encoding plus external storage function of notetaking for this measure of lecture learning. This encoding plus external storage effect was enhanced with the 1-week delay between lecture and writing. In other words, having one's own lecture notes available for reference enhances both the length and the organization of writing based on lecture content.

Because the first two experiments had not isolated the external storage effect of notetaking, Benton and colleagues (1993) conducted two more experiments. In Experiment 3, students viewed the same lecture as in the first two experiments without taking notes. Immediately after the lecture, they were asked to write the compare–contrast essay given either no notes or notes presented in one of the three notetaking formats. Experiment 4 replicated Experiment 3 except that there was a 1-week delay between the lecture and the essay writing. For the immediate writing task, no differences were found between the essays of those who had written with or without notes. For the delayed writing task of Experiment 4, however, students using provided notes wrote longer essays than students who did not write from notes. Therefore, the value of the external storage function of notetaking was demonstrated on a delayed task, but not on an immediate one. Apparently, the provision of notes compensated for loss of lecture information during the delay.

Having examined the general functions of notetaking in learning from lectures, we turn now to typical notetaking and how typical notetaking affects learning.

Typical Notetaking and Learning From Lectures

When left to their own devices, students, even college students, do not take very good notes. In particular, notes tend to be quite incomplete records of lecture content. According to Kiewra et al. (1989), earlier studies found that students often record fewer than 40% of lecture ideas. Several studies by Kiewra et al. have replicated this finding. In a study by Kiewra (1985c), students recorded only about 20% of a lecture's critical ideas. Kiewra, Benton, and Lewis (1987) found that students recorded 37% of total lecture ideas. In another study (Kiewra, DuBois, Christian, & McShane, 1988), students recorded 31% of lecture ideas. In a study by O'Donnell and Dansereau (1993), college students recorded only 25% of the total number of lecture idea units.

The quantity of notes taken appears to vary over time, as well. Scerbo, Warm, Dember, and Grasha (1992) found that students recorded increasingly less information in their notes over the course of a lecture. The fact that students record relatively few lecture ideas should not be surprising, given the cognitive complexity of the task. The decrease in quantity of notes over time probably reflects fatigue due to the demanding nature of the task of notetaking. With fatigue, one or more of the component cognitive processes may break down.

Researchers have investigated how the quantity of notes relates to learning. Kiewra (1985a) reviewed earlier research providing substantial evidence that students who take a greater quantity of notes tend to perform better on measures of learning from lectures. More recent studies have confirmed this finding. In a study by Kiewra and Fletcher (1984), the total number of words recorded in notes was significantly related to immediate and delayed test performance, particularly on items that asked students to summarize main ideas and relate main ideas to far transfer situations. Kiewra (1984) found that notes taken from a single lecture were significantly related to course achievement. Baker and Lombardi (1985) found significant positive correlations between the content of students' notes and performance on a multiple-choice test of lecture content administered 3 weeks after the lecture. The more information students included in their notes, the better they did on test items corresponding to that information. In a study by Kiewra, Benton, and Lewis (1987), although total number of words in notes was not related to learning on a lecture-specific test given 1 week after the lecture, note completeness was significantly related to performance on a subsequent course exam covering more than the specific lecture information. In a study by Kiewra and Benton (1988), the numbers of words, complex propositions, and main ideas in students' notes correlated significantly with their performance on a lecture-specific test as well as on a subsequent course exam over unrelated material. In a study by O'Donnell and Dansereau (1993), the number of words in students' notes correlated positively with free recall of both important ideas and details from a lecture. A study by Cohn, Cohn, and Bradley (1995) found a positive relationship between notetaking completeness and learning as measured by an immediate multiple-choice test covering lecture content. Finally, in the research of

Benton et al. (1993), length of lecture notes was significantly correlated with length and organization of compare–contrast essays students wrote about lecture content.

There is considerable evidence over several decades of research that note completeness is positively related to achievement. This result is consistent with research on the functions of notetaking. More complete notes may reflect greater generative processing during encoding. Alternatively, and probably more likely, the more complete students' notes, the more material students have available for review and the greater their opportunity for generative processing at the time of review.

In addition to examining the sheer quantity of notes, at least one study has also investigated how well notes represent the main ideas of the lecture. Kiewra, Benton, and Lewis (1987) found that although student notes were incomplete, they did capture the most important points of the lecture. The relative importance of the lecture information noted by students is also related to learning. In two studies (Einstein, Morris, & Smith, 1985; Kiewra & Fletcher, 1984), students who took notes capturing the most important lecture ideas recalled the most lecture content. However, the aforementioned study by Kiewra et al. (1987) found that, because students generally recorded the most important lecture points in their notes, it was the intermediate level ideas that correlated significantly with performance on both immediate and delayed tests of lecture content. In other words, the completeness of notes at intermediate levels of importance was the characteristic that most distinguished lower from higher achievers. Furthermore, the completeness, or elaborateness, of notes becomes more important over time, as shown by higher correlations between middle-level notes and achievement on a delayed test than on an immediate test. Again, this result supports the relative importance of the review function of notetaking: The more complete or elaborate the notes available for later review, the greater the potential for generative processing during review.

Individual Differences in Notetaking and Learning From Lectures

Although the previous section described research related to typical notetaking behaviors and their effect on learning, other research has shown that notetaking and learning from lectures is influenced by individual differences. Most of the individual differences investigated to date are differences in cognitive variables such as *working memory, cognitive style, and prior knowledge* (Kiewra, 1989).

Working memory, which is used to maintain, manipulate, and integrate information prior to storage in long-term memory, obviously plays an important role in taking notes from lectures. As noted previously, notetakers must focus on the lecture, select important information, and then hold and manipulate a representation of that information while taking notes. A few studies have found a relationship between working memory and notetaking. Kiewra (1989) reviewed earlier studies showing that students with greater working memory ability benefited from taking notes, while students with less memory ability did not benefit from notetaking. Presumably, for students with less working memory ability, notetaking actually interferes with their ability to encode information from the lecture.

Kiewra et al. (Kiewra & Benton, 1988; Kiewra, Benton, & Lewis, 1987) extended this earlier work by examining the relationship between working memory ability and notetaking behaviors. Furthermore, they measured working memory not as capacity only, but as a measure of ability to both hold and manipulate verbal information in working memory. Kiewra and colleagues found that the ability to manipulate information in working memory was directly related to notetaking behavior. Specifically, students who are less able to hold and manipulate information in working memory recorded fewer words and total ideas (Kiewra & Benton, 1988; Kiewra et al., 1987), as well as fewer subordinate ideas (Kiewra et al., 1987). Thus, the result using a more sensitive measure of working memory confirmed the results of other research in showing less effective notetaking among students with poorer working memories. On the other hand, a study by Cohn, Cohn, and Bradley (1995) failed to find a relationship between working memory and the number of words recorded in notes, although working memory did have an important effect on lecture-specific learning.

Another cognitive variable related to notetaking is the cognitive style of field independence and field dependence. Field-independent learners have an active, flexible, hypothesis-testing approach to learning; they abstract and restructure incoming information. Field-dependent learners, on the other hand, have a more passive and rigid approach to learning; they tend to process the information in its given structure. Frank (1984) investigated the effect of field independence and field dependence and four different notetaking techniques (no notes, student's notes, outline framework of lecture content on which students were to take notes, and complete outline plus any additional notes the student wished to add) on immediate learning from a lecture as measured by comprehension-level items. Results included the finding that field-independent students outperformed field-dependent students in the students' notes condition; however, there were no differences in performance between the two types of learners for the other three notetaking techniques. Also, field-dependent students performed significantly worse when they took their own notes than when they were provided with a complete outline on which to take notes. Frank also analyzed the notes of field dependent and field independent students. Compared to the notes of field-dependent students, the notes of field-independent students were more efficient (calculated as the ratio of information units recorded to number of words recorded) and tended to be in an outline format. Apparently the more active learning style of field-independent students enabled them to benefit more from the encoding function of notetaking. The field-dependent students, on the other hand, had difficulty abstracting and organizing information from the lecture. External structural support in the form of a complete outline helped these learners, perhaps by aiding either their encoding or their review.

Kiewra and Frank (1988), pointing out that the previous Frank (1984) study failed to differentiate between the encoding and external storage effectiveness of instructional supports for field-dependent learners, undertook a study to correct this shortcoming. In Kiewra and Frank, field-dependent and field-independent students used one of three notetaking techniques (personal notes, skeletal notes consisting of headings and subheadings of critical lecture points, or detailed instructor's notes containing all critical lecture points organized into an outline form) to record notes from a 20-minute videotape. Following the lecture, students completed an immediate multiple-choice test consisting of 50% factual items and 50% higher order knowledge items (application, analysis, synthesis, and problem solving). Five days after the lecture, students had an opportunity to review their notes prior to completing the same test. Results included the finding that field-independent learners outperformed field-dependent learners on both factual and higher order items. Furthermore, the cognitive style differences were more pronounced on the immediate factual test than on the delayed factual test, when time was allowed for review and additional encoding. The authors concluded that field-dependent learners benefit more from the external storage function of notetaking than from the initial encoding function.

Another cognitive variable that has received little attention to date in notetaking research is prior knowledge. Peper and Mayer (1986) examined the interaction of prior knowledge of lecture topic and notetaking behavior on near and far transfer tasks. Subjects with low prior knowledge who took notes performed better on far transfer tasks that those who did not take notes; nonnotetakers with low prior knowledge, however, performed better on near transfer tasks. On the other hand, for subjects with higher prior knowledge of the lecture topic, notetakers did not outperform nonnotetakers on the far transfer task. Peper and Mayer speculated that subjects with adequate background knowledge automatically generate external connections, or connections between lecture content and what they already know, whereas those without adequate background knowledge benefit from potentially generative activities like taking notes to help them make connections between lecture content and prior knowledge.

Besides prior knowledge of lecture content, another form of prior knowledge is knowledge of the language in which the lecturer is speaking. Dunkel, Mishra, and Berliner (1989) examined the effect of language proficiency on learning from lectures. Native and nonnative speakers of English either listened only or listened and took notes on a 22-minute videotaped lecture. Immediately following the lecture, the students completed a multiple-choice test over lecture concepts and details. The relevant result here is that native speakers recalled significantly more of the concept and detail information presented in the lecture than did the nonnative speakers. However, there was no significant interaction between notetaking and language proficiency. The authors speculated that cognitive competition among the international students' first and second languages interferes with encoding of lectures delivered in the second language, a result which theoretically should be compounded by notetaking. Further research is obviously needed to shed light on the relationship between notetaking functions and language proficiency.

A final cognitive difference that has been studied to some extent is the difference between learning disabled and nonlearning disabled college students. Hughes and Suritsky (1993) reported on an earlier study by Suritsky, in which she interviewed college students with learning disabilities about the difficulties they had with notetaking, the reasons for those difficulties, and the strategies they used to take notes. These students believed they had significant problems with taking notes during lectures and did not report using systematic and efficient strategies to help themselves. Hughes and Suritsky (1993) followed up on this study by comparing the lecture notes of 30 learning disabled (LD) and 30 nondisabled (ND) college students. Signficant differences were found on the number of information units recorded, with ND students recording an astounding 60% to 70% more lecture information than LD students. One factor accounting for the relatively low amount of lecture information recorded by LD students may be that they did not make nearly as much use of abbreviations in their notes as did ND students.

In summary, research has revealed several individual differences in notetaking and learning from lectures regarding the cognitive variables of (a) working memory, (b) cognitive style (field-dependence and field-independence), (c) prior knowledge of lecture content and language of lecture delivery, and (d) cognitive ability (learning disabled versus nonlearning disabled). First, students with greater working memory are more effective notetakers than students with less working memory ability. Second, field-independent students benefit more from the encoding function of notetaking, while field-dependent students benefit more from the external storage function. Third, compared to subjects with higher prior knowledge of lecture content, subjects with lower prior knowledge perform better on far transfer tasks, perhaps because notetaking helps them make connections between lecture content and their limited prior knowledge. Fourth, hearing a lecture in one's nonnative language may interfere with notetaking functions. Finally, learning disabled college students record significantly fewer notes than nonlearning disabled students.

Having examined the questions of what type of notes students take when left to their own devices and how individual differences in cognition affect notetaking and performance, we turn to the question of how to improve learning from lectures.

IMPROVING LEARNING FROM LECTURES

Based on the functions that notetaking can serve, two possibilities for improving learning from lectures are to enhance the initial encoding of lecture material by improving the generative processing that students engage in while taking notes, and the external storage function of notes by increasing the potential for generative processing during note review. Research on improving both notetaking and review is discussed in this section.

Improving Notetaking

Kiewra (1989) suggested three ways in which the quality of student notes might be improved in order to facilitate learning from lectures, based on generative theories of learning: (a) improve the completeness of notes (b) help students make relationships among lecture ideas and (c) help students make relationships between lecture ideas and prior knowledge. Kiewra et al. and other researchers have undertaken numerous studies to investigate techniques for improving notetaking. These techniques include giving simple verbal directions, providing lecture handouts of various kinds, and varying the lecture itself.

Verbal Directions. In an early study in this program of research, Kiewra and Fletcher (1984) tried to manipulate notetaking by directing students to take notes in different ways. Students were told to take notes in one of four different ways: writing their usual way, emphasizing factual details, focusing on conceptual main points, or discerning relationships within the material. Student notes were analyzed for factual, conceptual, and relational information. Results revealed that the differential directions had little effect on notetaking behavior: Students took about the same number of conceptual notes covering the main points of the lecture regardless of directions. The differential directions also had no significant effect on performance on immediate or delayed retention tests. Correlational analyses, however, disclosed that students who noted more main ideas outperformed more factual notetakers on factual, conceptual, and relational test items. The authors concluded that because simple verbal directions do not substantially change ingrained notetaking behaviors, more drastic manipulation is required, such as providing lecture handouts to guide notetaking.

Lecture Handouts.   A more effective way to improve notetaking is to provide students with some sort of lecture handout to guide their notetaking. In a review of earlier research, Kiewra (1985b) concluded that notetaking could be improved by providing students with partial outlines prior to the lecture. Research had shown that students who take notes on partial outlines generally learn more than students who take conventional, unassisted notes, because partial outlines organizing upcoming material focus attention on critical lecture ideas, guide notetaking, and provide effective cues for retrieval of lecture information.

Kiewra et al. then embarked on a series of experiments in which they attempted to manipulate notetaking behavior by providing different frameworks for notetaking. Studies by Kiewra et al. (1989) and Kiewra, DuBois, et al. (1991) were discussed earlier but are revisited here with respect to results that are relevant for improving notetaking using lecture handouts.

In the Kiewra et al. (1989) and Kiewra, DuBois, et al. (1991) studies, two types of notetaking frameworks were compared to conventional notetaking, or the student's own style of notetaking without a framework. An *outline framework* (also called a *linear* or *skeletal framework*) lists the main topics and subtopics in outline form, with space for taking notes within the outline. A matrix framework presents the main topics as column headings and the subtopics as row headings, with space in the matrix cells for taking notes.

Kiewra et al. (1989) articulated more completely in Kiewra, DuBois, et al. (1991), posited two theoretical benefits for outline and matrix notes. First, both frameworks should encourage students to take more complete notes, and, as previously discussed, note completeness is positively related to achievement. Both the outline and the matrix provide topics and subtopics, which help students attend to important information; the outline and matrix also provide spaces, which invite notetaking. A second theoretical benefit of outlines and matrices is fostering internal connections. Outlines emphasize superordinate–subordinate relationships within topics, while matrices show relationships both within and across topics. A matrix, more than an outline, allows students to synthesize ideas within and across topics.

In Kiewra et al. (1989), the type of notetaking framework influenced the type of notes students took. An analysis of notes taken revealed that skeletal notes contained significantly more idea units than conventional notes, with matrix notes falling in between. Also, notetakers were more efficient (i.e., they used fewer words to express an idea unit) when they used the skeletal and matrix frameworks than when they took conventional notes. However, Kiewra et al. (1989) failed to find an effect of notetaking framework on any of the four tests of learning outcomes: free recall, factual recognition, synthesis, and application.

Kiewra, DuBois, et al. (1991) found an effect for notetaking framework on type of notes taken as well as learning outcomes. In this study, matrix and linear (or outline) notetaking frameworks resulted in recording signficantly more lecture ideas than conventional notetaking. Specifically, matrix notes contained 47% of the lecture ideas, whereas conventional notes contained 32%. Also, matrix notetaking was the most effective of the three notetaking frameworks as measured by a cued recall test of lecture content, but not as measured by a test of synthesis of lecture concepts.

Kiewra, Benton, Kim, Risch, and Christensen (1995) conducted two experiments to investigate how notetaking frameworks influenced student notetaking and learning. In this experiment, students listened to a videotaped lecture and took notes conventionally or on outline or matrix frameworks. Among the relevant results of this experiment was that notetaking on an outline framework increased performance on tests of recall and relational learning, perhaps because outline notetakers took more notes than notetakers in the other two conditions.

The second experiment examined whether various notetaking formats influenced student notetaking. Students were assigned to one of seven notetaking conditions, which included conventional notes, two variations of the outline framework, and four variations of the matrix framework. Students recording notes in a flexible outline (in which subtopics were listed beneath topics in a changing order consistent with their presentation order in the lecture) recorded more notes than students using the other notetaking frameworks. The authors speculated that making the subtopic order of the outline consistent with information presentation in the lecture reduced the student's need to search for the appropriate space to take notes; the flexible outline also provided a cue about the upcoming subtopic. The various matrix formats also produced differences in quantity of notes recorded, with a full matrix producing somewhat greater notetaking than collapsed matrices with fewer subtopics to guide notetaking.

In another study on the effect of providing lecture handouts on learning from lectures, Morgan, Lilley, and Boreham (1988) investigated whether the detail in lecture handouts affected student notetaking as well as their performance on two cued recall tests. Students either took notes with no lecture handout or received one of three lecture handouts prior to the lecture: headings with full lecture text, headings with key points, or headings only. All lecture handouts provided space for students to take notes. The first cued recall test, which was unannounced, was given 2 days after the lecture, and the other announced test was given 2 weeks after the lecture. Regarding the effect of handouts on notetaking, the researchers found an inverse relationship between the amount of materials in the handout and the amount of notes that students recorded. In other words, the more information students were given, the fewer notes they took.

Regarding the effect of handouts on test performance, Morgan et al. found that students who had handouts with headings only performed the best on both tests. However, results for other conditions differed depending on time of testing. The authors concluded that handouts must facilitate both encoding and external storage functions of notetaking. The latter function, of course, depends on the amount of detail provided in the notes. Morgan et al. (1988) concluded, however, that more research was needed to tease out the complex relationship between nature of lecture handouts and cognitive processing.

The final study to be reviewed on lecture handouts is by Ruhl and Suritsky (1995). These researchers had college LD students view a 22-minute videotaped lecture in one of three conditions: pause procedure (three 2-minute pauses spaced at logical intervals during the lecture); lecture outline (received a lecturer-prepared outline of key points from the lecture), or both pause and lecture outline. Dependent measures included immediate free recall of the lecture, and two measures of note completeness—percentage of total correct information and percentage of partial correct information. Relevant results included the finding that the lecture outline was not as effective as the pause procedure for free recall. With regard to percentage of total correct notes, both the pause procedure and the outline plus the pause were equally effective and superior to the outline only. The authors speculated that for LD students, the outline may have distracted students during the lecture, a conclusion confirmed by several students who commented that it was difficult to keep up with the lecture and follow the outline concurrently. Ruhl and Suritsky suggested that LD college students may need direct instruction in how to effectively use outlines provided by instructors. Alternatively, the "flexible" outline used by Kiewra et al. (1995), in which outline topics follow the presentation order of the lecture, might be easier for LD students to use.

In summary, several studies in the past 15 years have examined the use of various types of lecture handouts, particularly outlines and matrices. It appears that outlines and matrices help students record more notes and facilitate some types of learning. However, as Morgan et al. (1988) suggested, the relationship between type of lecture handout and cognitive processing is extremely complex and warrants considerably more research.

Varying the Lecture. Another approach to improving notetaking is to vary the lecture. One way to vary a lecture presentation is to repeat it. Drawing on the previously reviewed research that showed a relationship between note completeness and learning, Kiewra et al. tried increasing the quantity and quality of notes by repeating a videotaped lecture presentation. Kiewra (1989) reported a study that he did (Kiewra, Mayer, Christian, Dyreson, & McShane, 1988), in which students took notes while watching a videotaped lecture one, two, or three times. Students were asked to record different notes each time. Results included the finding that students viewing the lecture three times noted significantly more lecture ideas in their final set of notes (41%) than did students who viewed the lecture only once (32%). Lecture idea units were also classified into three levels of importance. Although students viewing the lecture varying numbers of times did not differ significantly with respect to the most and least important ideas in their notes, students who viewed the lecture three times recorded a significantly greater number of idea units at the middle level of importance (41%) than did students who viewed the lecture only once (34%).

Later, Kiewra, Mayer, Christensen, Kim, and Risch (1991) conducted a similar study. In one experiment, students took cumulative notes on a lecture that was presented one, two, or three times and took a recall test without review. The second experiment replicated the first except that students were allowed to review their notes. In both experiments, students recorded the most important lecture information on the first viewing, with little representation of less important information. On subsequent viewings, students added less important information but did not add more important information. The authors concluded that students engage in a strategy of *successive differentiation*. First, they focus on the most important information. When they reach a ceiling on the most important information, they shift attention to less important information.

Another way to vary lectures is for the lecturer to provide cues to increase the salience of information. For example, the lecturer may cue information by writing it on the blackboard, or by saying something to the effect of "now, this is important." Baker and Lombardi (1985) examined the notes of students who listened to a lecture supplemented by two transparencies that acted as cues. The transparencies contained key words presented in a rough hierarchical structure, representing 35 propositions. The researchers found that virtually all students recorded all of the information from the transparencies, but recorded only 27% of additional information identified by the investigators as important. Also, as mentioned previously in the discussion of this study with regard to cuing lecture information, a significant positive relationship existed between notes taken and performance on test items related to the noted information.

Another study examining the effect of cuing was a study by Scerbo et al. (1992). Scerbo et al. compared the relative effectiveness of written and spoken cues, as well as investigating cuing schedules, or the timing of cues. Students viewed a 36-minute videotaped lecture in which certain statements were highlighted by either cues spoken by the lecturer or cues written on cue cards. Students were assigned to one of four types of cuing schedules: no cuing, cuing only in initial portion of lecture, cuing only in the final portion of lecture, or cuing throughout. The dependent measures included (a) the information recorded in notes for each lecture segment, (b) an immediate multiple-choice recogniton test, and (c) an immediate fill-in-the-blank recall test.

With regard to information recorded in notes, it was found that students in all conditions recorded fewer information units over the course of the lecture. The different cuing schedules did not affect recognition of lecture items, but it did affect recall of information. More written cues were recorded than spoken cues, but proportion of cued statements recorded decreased over time similarly for both spoken and written cues. More cued statements were retained than uncued statements, and retention was better for written than spoken cues. Finally, the different schedules of cuing had some subtle effects on notetaking and recall. For example, the group that received cues in the first segment only recorded the same number of ideas as the group that received cuing throughout in the second segment of the lecture, but by the third segment, the differences had disappeared. The authors concluded that providing cues, especially written cues, early in the lecture or throughout can facilitate immediate retention of lecture material.

Another method of varying the lecture that has been investigated to some extent is the *pause procedure*. This procedure entails pausing for brief periods of time during the lecture to permit student discussion and clarification of lecture content and updating of notes. Theoretically, such pauses could reduce the cognitive demands of the encoding function of notetaking, thereby enabling students to take more and better notes, as well as to engage in more generative processing of lecture content.

Among the researchers to explore the pause procedure in the past 15 years are Ruhl, Hughes, and Gajar, who have focused in particular on the effectiveness of the pause procedure for LD college students. Ruhl, Hughes, and Gajar (1990) presented videotaped lectures with and without pauses to both LD and ND college students. During lecture pauses LD and ND students worked in pairs to discuss lecture content, clarify concepts, or correct notes. Lectures were followed by immediate free recall tests; 1 week later, students completed a delayed free recall test and a multiple-choice test about lecture content. Students were instructed not to study for the delayed tests. Results indicated that the pause procedure significantly improved students' performance on the immediate free recall and objective tests, but not on the delayed free recall test. The authors concluded that the pause procedure may be effective for both LD and ND college students, at least for some kinds of learning measures.

Ruhl and Suritsky (1995) performed another study of the pause procedure, which has already been discussed in the section on lecture handouts. Recall that Ruhl and Suritsky (1995) had college LD students view a 22-minute videotaped lecture in one of three conditions: pause procedure (three 2-minute pauses spaced at logical intervals during the lecture); lecture outline (received a lecturer-prepared outline of key points from the lecture), or both pause and lecture outline. The students in the pause groups were briefly trained to use the pauses to update notes and to clarify and discuss the lecture content with randomly assigned, ND peers who had access to full lecture notes. Dependent measures included immediate free recall of the lecture, and two measures of note completeness—percentage of total correct information and percentage of partial correct information. Results included the finding that the pause procedure alone was the most effective for free recall. With regard to percentage of total correct notes, both the pause procedure and the outline plus the pause were equally effective and superior to the outline only. Therefore, this study also indicated that the pause procedure may be an effective way of improving notetaking by varying the lecture.

A final possibility for improving notetaking by varying the lecture is through computer-aided lecturing. In computer-aided lecturing, a computer and electronic presentation software are used to link topics found in various media sources (film, video, audio, text, animation, etc.). With the exploding development of multimedia software, college instructors are turning to computer technology to supplement their lectures in an attempt to facilitate comprehension and learning. Theoretically, computer-aided lecturing could help students make internal and external connections, thus improving their generative processing of lecture content.

Unfortunately, little research on computer-aided lecturing has been published to date. The only study identified for this review was a survey study of students in an introductory natural resource conservation course (Van Meter, 1994). According to the survey results, 94% of the 48 respondents believed that the computer-aided lecture helped them. Also, 79% of the students believed their notetaking would not have been as effective if the lecture material had been presented on a blackboard rather than by computer, whereas 62% of the students believed that their notetaking would have been less effective if the material had been presented by an overhead projector rather than by a computer.

So far this section has discussed research on improving the notes that students take. Among the possibilities for improving notetaking that have been researched are simple verbal directions, lecture handouts of various types, and varying the lecture through repetition, cuing of important information, pausing periodically, and enhancing the lecture with the use of computer software. Besides improving notetaking, another possibility for improving learning from lectures is to assist students (postlecture) in reviewing lecture content.

Reviewing Lecture Content

Two ways to enhance the review of lecture content have been explored in recent notetaking research—improving the content students have available for review and improving the method students use to review the content. Research on each of these methods is discussed next.

Improving Content for Review.   Because students do not take very complete or accurate notes, one possible way to improve learning from lectures is to provide students with some form of supplemental notes, such as a full transcript of the lecture provided by the instructor. Research on the relative effectiveness of personal lecture notes versus full instructor's notes was reviewed by Kiewra (1985b). Kiewra concluded that when lectures are followed by immediate review and testing, full lecture notes are not as effective as personal lecture notes, perhaps because the process of reviewing the instructor's notes may have interfered with the initial processing of lecture information. However, if there is a delay between lecture and review/testing, full instructor notes are beneficial for acquisition of factual knowledge, presumably because the instructor's notes were more complete and better organized.

On measures of higher order learning (application, analysis, synthesis, problem solving), however, Kiewra, citing three of his own studies, found no differences between reviewing own students' and instructor-provided notes. Kiewra speculated that the instructor's notes provided no advantage for higher order learning because students did not process them generatively during review. In other words, the instructors did not provide internal connections in the notes, and students did not spontaneously provide either internal or external connections.

In his review of previous research on reviewing notes, Kiewra (1985b) also concluded that reviewing both complete instructor notes *and* personal notes promotes higher achievement than reviewing only one of these. Reviewing both sets of notes combines the advantages of both completeness and accuracy of information as well as possibilities for generative learning. Finally, Kiewra (1985b) noted that, although researchers had explored the effect on notetaking and learning of providing students with partial outlines prior to the lecture, research had not yet compared the review benefits of skeletal notes compared to personal notes or full instructor notes.

Kiewra and his colleagues (1988) then set out to compare the benefits of various types of notes available for review. In Kiewra et al. (1988), college students viewed a 19-minute videotaped lecture without taking notes. One week later, students were given a 25-minute review period in which they either mentally reviewed (no notes) or reviewed one of three types of notes: (a) a complete transcript of the lecture; (b) notes in outline form, or (c) notes in matrix form (with outline and matrix defined as in the Kiewra et al. (1989) studies previously discussed). Following the review period, the students completed three types of tests—cued recall, recognition, and transfer (synthesis and application). One result was that reviewing any of the three forms of notes was better than mental review (review with no notes). This result, of course, is further confirmation of the value of the external storage function of notetaking. A second result was that both outline and matrix notes produced higher recall than the full transcript. The authors speculated that both outline and matrix notes helped the learner make internal connections among ideas, thus facilitating retrieval. A third result was that only the matrix notes produced significantly higher transfer performance. The researchers suggested that matrix notes allowed a more fully integrated understanding of the content (i.e., both internal and external connections), which facilitated performance on transfer tasks involving synthesis and application. Finally, the three note-reviewing groups performed similarly on the factual recognition test, apparently because these items involved the recognition of isolated facts, which is not likely to be influenced by forming internal connections.

In the previously discussed Benton et al. (1993) study, which used essay writing as the criterion task, two results are relevant to this discussion. Recall that in Experiment 4, students who had not taken notes were given either no notes or notes in one of three notetaking frameworks (conventional, outline, matrix) prior to writing a compare–contrast essay 1 week after the lecture. Among the results of that experiment was the finding that students who were given outline or matrix notes included more text units in their essays. Also, students provided with matrix notes wrote more coherent essays. These results suggest that, given a delay between the lecture and the time of writing, providing students with organized notes helps them write longer and more organized essays of lecture content.

In summary, research suggests that the type of notes students have available for review makes a difference in learning, especially as time lapses between the lecture and review/testing. Because students do not record very complete or accurate notes on their own, some form of supplemental notes can be helpful for review in preparation for taking a test or writing an essay. A complete transcript of the lecture may facilitate factual learning. For higher order learning and transfer, however, including essay writing, notes that invite generative processing, such as outline and matrix notes, are likely to be the most effective.

Improving Method of Review.   Another approach to improving learning from lectures is to address the method of review, or what students actually *do* during study sessions. Methods of reviewing lecture content have received little research attention. One researcher who has completed noteworthy research in the area, however, is King (1989, 1991, 1992). Although the first two studies reviewed here do not involve notetaking, they do involve learning from lectures and they are important background for the third study, which does include notetaking.

In her series of studies, King has adapted self-questioning research conducted in the area of reading to orally presented material. In King (1989), college students were assigned to one of four groups: (a) independent review, (b) independent self-questioning, (c) review in small, cooperative groups, and (d) self- and peer questioning in small cooperative groups. Students in the self-questioning groups received direct instruction in a self-questioning procedure involving the use of generic question starters to guide them in asking higher order comprehension questions. Examples of the generic question starters include, "explain why _____," "how does _____ affect _____?" and "what do you think would happen if _____?"

The study took place over a series of six lectures in a regular college course. After each lecture, students participated in 10- to 12-minute "study sessions" according to their treatment group, and then completed a comprehension test over the lecture content. The first lecture was followed by a pretest, and the last lecture by the posttest. All tests consisted of multiple-choice and open-ended questions eliciting higher order thinking (integration, elaboration, analysis, application). Results indicated that both self-questioning independently and in small cooperative groups significantly improved lecture learning over the course of the study. King (1989) attributed the success of the self-questioning strategy to the metacognitive effects of self-questioning—that is, the benefits of comprehension monitoring during learning. King further speculated that the self-questioning training may have improved students' initial encoding of the lecture.

King (1991) extended her investigation of the self-questioning technique to a younger population of ninth graders. (Despite the focus on college learners in this volume, this study with a younger population is included because it replicates King's findings with college students.) In the 1991 study, ninth graders were assigned to one of four groups: (a) self-questioning with reciprocal peer questioning, (b) self-questioning only, (c) discussion, and (d) independent review (control). Students in the two self-questioning conditions were provided with direct instruction in asking higher order questions, as described for the previous study. Students in the self-questioning with reciprocal peer questioning group were instructed to independently generate questions during the lecture, and then to spend their 12-minute study session posing their questions to the other members of their cooperative learning groups and discussing possible answers. The self-questioning only students used their study session time to write down the questions they had generated during the lecture and then answer them independently. Students in the discussion group listened to the lecture, followed by unguided discussion; students in the control group listened to the lecture and reviewed the material according to their preferred review strategy.

On postpractice and maintenance tests consisting of multiple-choice and open-ended questions eliciting higher order thinking (integration, elaboration, analysis, application), both self-questioning groups outperformed discussion review and independent review groups. Again, King attributed the results to the facilitation of metacognition in the self-questioning groups. With both ninth grade and college populations, King (1989, 1991) demonstated that a self-questioning strategy was not only effective in enhancing learning from lectures, but that it could also be readily taught and successfully maintained over time.

King (1992) directly compared self-questioning to other common lecture review strategies of college students. College students viewed a videotaped lecture, took notes in their usual fashion, and then engaged in one of three study strategies: (a) self-questioning, (b) summarizing, and (c) reviewing own notes (control). The self-questioning group was trained as described in the previous King studies (1989, 1991). The summarizing group was trained to generate a sentence, using their own words, about the main topic of the lecture, followed by other sentences connecting subtopics and main ideas.

There were several important results from the study. First, regarding learning from lectures, it was found that on an immediate recall test, summarizers recalled more than self-questioners, who in turn recalled more than those who reviewed their own notes. On a 1-week delayed recall test, the self-questioners somewhat outperformed (nonsignificantly) the summarizers; however, the self-questioners significantly outperformed the note reviewers. An analysis of lecture notes revealed that self-questioners and summarizers included more ideas from the lectures than students who took notes in their usual fashion, suggesting that the strategies affect initial encoding as well as review. In other words, given well-designed training, both guided self-questioning and summarizing are effective strategies for learning from lectures, more effective than simply taking notes and reviewing one's own notes. Self-questioning appears to be more effective than summarizing the longer the delay from lecture to testing.

King (1992) attributed these results to the generative nature of these strategies. Both summarizing and self-questioning require students to construct their own representations of lecture meaning, both during the lecture and when reviewing the lecture. According to King, the summarizing strategy helped students make internal connections among lecture ideas, whereas self-questioning promoted both internal and external connections, and was thus the more powerful of the two strategies.

Another study focusing on the review of lecture content was conducted by O'Donnell and Dansereau (1993). O'Donnell and Dansereau investigated individual versus cooperative review involving pairs of students. In cooperative review, one partner, the "recaller," attempts to recall from memory (without referring to notes) everything he or she call remember from the lecture, while a "listener," who has access to notes, listens carefully and reports errors or omissions in the recall of the recaller.

In the O'Donnell and Dansereau (1993) study, college students listened to a 25-minute audiotaped lecture in one of four treatments: (a) students who took notes and reviewed them individually immediately after the lecture, (b) pairs of students who took notes and were told to expect to cooperatively review the notes immediately after the lecture, (c) pairs of students, one who listened to the lecture without taking notes and subsequently summarized the information to a partner who took notes during the lecture, and (d) pairs of students who took notes during the lecture without expecting to review cooperatively, but who, in fact, did have an opportunity for cooperative review immediately following the lecture. Students were tested on their free recall of the lecture one week following the lecture, without a second period for review, and their recall protocols were scored for recall of central ideas and details.

Results included the finding of no significant differences for recall of central lecture ideas. However, for recall of details, students who expected to review individually but who actually reviewed with a partner recalled more than students who reviewed alone. Furthermore, partners who did not take notes but reviewed cooperatively recalled as much as their partner who did take notes. Partners who did not take notes but reviewed cooperatively also recalled as much as students who took notes and reviewed them on their own. These results suggested to the authors that the facilitative effects of cooperative review are primarily due to the review itself, rather than to differential encoding.

In summary, two possibilities for improving review have been investigated—improving the content students have to review and improving the method of review. Because students tend to be poor notetakers, supplementing the notes they have available for review is useful. The supplemental notes may be full transcripts of the lecture or other forms of notes such as outline notes or matrix notes. Full-instructor notes can facilitate factual learning, while outline or matrix notes may be more beneficial for higher order learning. Regarding method of review, researchers have found positive results with variations of cooperative review, in which students work together to review lecture content.

CONCLUSIONS

Guided by constructivist and generative views of learning, research on taking notes from lectures has moved forward significantly in the past 15 years, thanks primarily to the work of Kiewra et al. Kiewra reconceptualized and clarified the functions of notetaking, adding the function of encoding *plus* external storage to the original encoding and external storage functions proposed by DiVesta and Gray (1972). The research of Kiewra and others has confirmed that the real value of taking notes lies in having them available for review, especially with increased time between the lecture and the criterion task. Researchers have discovered more about the types of notes students take when left to their own devices, as well as how individual differences, particularly in cognition, affect notetaking behavior. Finally, researchers have explored several ways to facilitate notetaking and review in order to improve learning from lectures. The research reviewed in this chapter has important implications for practice as well as suggesting several areas where further research is needed.

Implications for Practice

Research has confirmed that the quantity and quality of the notes that students take is related to their achievement. Unfortunately, because taking notes during lectures is such a cognitively demanding task, students do not take very effective notes. Research has suggested some ways to improve both the taking of notes and the reviewing of notes.

One way to improve notetaking is to provide lecture handouts. Two main types of lecture handouts investigated in recent years are outlines and matrices. Theoretically, both outlines and matrices serve as advance organizers, focus student attention, provide guides for notetaking, and give retrieval cues. Outlines and matrices can also encourage generative processing during both notetaking and review by helping students make internal and external connections. Several studies have found that outlines (especially outlines that follow the order of lecture presentation) and matrices can help students take more complete notes and can facilitate some types of learning. These lecture handouts may be especially helpful for certain types of students, such as field-dependent learners. However, it is not possible to make more precise recommendations until further research has teased out the complex relationships between notetaking format and cognitive processing.

Another way to improve notetaking is to make changes in the lecture. The easiest alteration is simply to videotape the lecture and make it available for repeated viewings. As students view the lecture repeatedly, they are able to record more information, particularly information at lower levels of importance. Theoretically, students also have more opportunity for generative processing at encoding. This way of improving notetaking is probably not very practical, however. For many reasons, instructors may prefer not to be videotaped as they lecture. Also, most students probably do not have the time or the motivation to view a videotaped lecture more than once.

Other ways of varying the lecture that have been explored include the pause procedure, providing written or oral cues, and computer-aided lecturing. Although these methods seem promising, perhaps especially for certain populations of college students, recent research on each of these methods is too sparse to warrant specific recommendations for practice.

Besides improving notetaking, learning from lectures can also be enhanced by improving how the lecture content is later reviewed. One way to strengthen review is to improve the content students have to review, especially as time lapses between the lecture and the time of review and testing. Interestingly, more is not necessarily better. That is, providing a complete transcript of the lecture may only be effective for improving factual learning. For higher order learning and transfer, including essay writing, providing outline and matrix notes is likely to be more helpful, perhaps because these forms of notes encourage more generative processing.

Another way to improve review is to improve the method students use to review. The methods that have yielded positive results to date involve some form of cooperative review. Training students to work together to ask and answer higher order, open-ended questions or to generate summaries based on the lecture appear to be promising strategies. Once again, however, more research is needed, which brings us to the final section of this chapter.

Implications for Further Research

With any luck, Kiewra has laid to rest the debate about the functions of notetaking. It seems clear that both the encoding and external storage functions of notetaking are important for learning. Furthermore, taking and reviewing notes is simply a practical reality. Unless and until lectures are replaced with more effective pedagogical tools, college students are likely to continue to both take notes and review them prior to course examinations. Therefore, it seems important for research to focus more on how to improve the encoding and external storage functions with respect to various types of learners and learning outcomes.

Regarding ways to improve notetaking, lecture handouts seem relatively practical and promising. As noted, however, the relationship between type of lecture handout and cognitive processing is very complex, and much research remains to be done. Kiewra et al.'s work exploring the effect of different types of outlines and matrices needs to be extended. It is also important to explore other ways of representing lecture content. Matrices, for example, are useful for, but restricted to, portraying multiple attributes of multiple concepts. Lecture content that is organized in different ways might be represented by different types of graphic organizers, such as hierarchical trees or flow charts.

Other research on notetaking might investigate ways to train students to become more strategic notetakers. Although courses and manuals on study skills address notetaking, little if any research on the effectiveness of such instruction exists. It seems likely that the kind of systematic, direct instruction and "informed strategy training" (e.g., Palincsar & Brown, 1984; Paris, Cross, & Lipson, 1984) that has been successfully used to teach various cognitive strategies, such as King's self-questioning during review (King, 1989, 1991, 1992), should be applied to teaching notetaking strategies as well.

Reviewing notes is an area that seems particularly ripe for research. Existing research seems silent on what students do when they review their notes prior to an examination. Therefore, naturalistic research on students' actual process of reviewing would be helpful. Research is also needed on the placement and length of review activities. For example, when should review occur with respect to the lecture? The exam? How many times should notes be reviewed, and for how long?

There is also a great deal of research to be done on ways to improve review. More research on the cooperative review methods discussed previously would be welcome. But researchers also need to address methods that individuals can pursue in reviewing lecture content. For example, elaborating or transforming notes in some way might be a useful generative review activity. Writing an essay is an example of an activity that could be done not only as a criterion task but also as a way of reviewing notes.

In future research on improving notetaking and review, researchers need to pay heed to the criterion tasks they use as measures of learning. Kiewra et al. and King, for example, are to be commended for including multiple measures of learning, from factual learning to higher order learning such as synthesis, application, and problem solving. Nevertheless, these are still paper-and-pencil measures, as typically found on college course examinations. Future research needs to include other kinds of learning outcomes. Because lectures are often used in the workplace as well, it is increasingly important to use workplace-like criterion tasks, perhaps including performance-based tasks such as writing a report or implementing a procedure.

The role of computer technology in lecturing, notetaking, and reviewing is an obvious candidate for more research. For example, in computer-aided lecturing, does linking topics from various media sources facilitate forming internal and external connections, or does it result in information and cognitive overload, thus rendering notetaking even more difficult? Another question concerns the use of computers as notetaking aids. With the increasing accessibility of laptop computers, more college students are using computers to take lecture notes. Does computer notetaking improve the quantity and quality of the notes students take? Does it make it easier for students to manipulate or elaborate notes during review, and if so, to what effect? Finally, what effect might computers have on reviewing lecture content? For example, what role could e-mail, chat rooms, listservs, or other online discussion groups play in helping students review?

Finally, research on individual differences in notetaking and review seems critically important. Researchers have investigated the effect of several cognitive variables on notetaking from lectures, but much research remains to be done. For example, researchers at Penn State (e.g., Ruhl et al., 1990; Suritsky & Hughes, 1991; Hughes & Suritsky, 1993; Ruhl & Suritsky, 1995) made a compelling case for more research addressing the needs of increasing numbers of LD college students who experience significant difficulties taking notes from lectures. In addition, with the increasing linguistic diversity of the U.S. population and the large numbers of international students enrolled in U.S. colleges and universities, it seems essential for researchers to address the needs of nonnative speakers of English as they take notes. Conversely, it might be interesting to study notetaking of native speakers of English as they attempt to take notes from international professors and teaching assistants.

In closing, research has revealed much about the functions of notetaking and how to improve notetaking, but there is still much to be learned about notetaking as a tool for learning from college lectures.

REFERENCES AND SUGGESTED READINGS

Anderson, T. H., & Armbruster, B. B. (1986). *The value of taking notes* (Reading Education Report No. 374). Champaign: University of Illinois at Urbana–Champaign, Center for the Study of Reading.

Baker, L., & Lombardi, B. R. (1985). Students' lecture notes and their relation to test performance. *Teaching of Psychology, 12,* 28–32.

Benton, S. L., Kiewra, K. A., Whitfill, J. M., & Dennison, R. (1993). Encoding and external-storage effects on writing processes. *Journal of Educational Psychology, 85,* 267–280.

Carrier, C. A. (1983). Notetaking research: Implications for the classroom. *Journal of Instructional Development, 6,* 19–26.

Carrier, C. A., Williams, M. D., & Dalgaard, B. R. (1988). College students' perceptions of notetaking and their relationship to selected learner characteristics and course achievement. *Research in Higher Education, 28,* 223–239.

Cohn, E., Cohn, S., & Bradley, J. (1995). Notetaking, working memory, and learning principles of economics. *Journal of Economics Education, 26,* 291–307.

DiVesta, F. J., & Gray, G. S. (1972). Listening and note taking. *Journal of Educational Psychology, 64,* 321–325.

Dunkel, P., & Davy, S. (1989). The heuristic of lecture notetaking: Perceptions of American & international students regarding the value & practice of notetaking. *English for Specific Purposes, 8,* 33–50.

Dunkel, P., Mishra, S., & Berliner, D. (1989). Effects of note taking, memory, and language proficiency on lecture learning for native and nonnative speakers of English. *TESOL Quarterly, 23,* 543–549.

Einstein, G. O., Morris, J., & Smith, S. (1985). Note-taking, individual differences, and memory for lecture information. *Journal of Educational Psychology, 77,* 522–532.

Frank, B. M. (1984). Effect of field independence-dependence and study technique on learning from a lecture. *American Educational Research Journal, 21,* 669–678.

Hartley, J. (1983). Notetaking research: Resetting the scoreboard. *Bulletin of the British Psychological Society, 36,* 13–14.

Hughes, C. A., & Suritsky, S. K. (1993). Notetaking skills and strategies for students with learning disabilities. *Preventing School Failure, 38,* 7–11.

Kiewra, K. A. (1984). The relationship between notetaking over an extended period and actual course-related achievement. *College Student Journal, 17,* 381–385.

*Kiewra, K. A. (1985a). Investigating notetaking and review: A depth of processing alternative. *Educational Psychologist, 20,* 23–32.

Kiewra, K. A. (1985b). Providing instructor's notes: An effective addition to student notetaking. *Educational Psychologist, 20,* 33–39.

Kiewra, K. A. (1985c). Students' note-taking behaviors and the efficacy of providing the instructor's notes for review. *Contemporary Educational Psychology, 10,* 378–386.

*Kiewra, K. A. (1989). A review of note-taking: The encoding-storage paradigm and beyond. *Educational Psychology Review, 1,* 147–172.

Kiewra, K. A., & Benton, S. L. (1988). The relationship between information-processing ability and notetaking. *Contemporary Educational Psychology, 13,* 33–44.

Kiewra, K. A., Benton, S. L., Kim, S.-I., Risch, N., & Christensen, M. (1995). Effects of note-taking format and study technique on recall and relational performance. *Contemporary Educational Psychology, 20,* 172–187.

Kiewra, K. A., Benton, S. L., & Lewis, L. B. (1987). Qualitative aspects of notetaking and their relationship with information-processing ability and academic achievement. *Journal of Instructional Psychology, 14,* 110–117.

Kiewra, K. A., & Fletcher, J. J. (1984). The relationship between levels of notetaking and achievement. *Human Learning, 3,* 273–280.

Kiewra, K. A., DuBois, N. F., Christian, D., & McShane, A. (1988). Providing study notes: Comparison of three types of notes for review. *Journal of Educational Psychology, 80,* 595–597.

*Kiewra, K. A., DuBois, N. F., Christian, D., McShane, A., Meyerhoffer, M., & Roskelley, D. (1991). Note-taking functions and techniques. *Journal of Educational Psychology, 83,* 240–245.

Kiewra, K. A., DuBois, N. F., Christensen, M., Kim, S-I., & Lindberg, N. (1989). A more equitable account of the note-taking functions in learning from lecture and from text. *Instructional Sciences, 18,* 217–232.

Kiewra, K. A., & Frank, B. M. (1986). Cognitive style: Effects of structure at acquisition and testing. *Contemporary Educational Psychology, 11,* 253–263.

Kiewra, K. A., & Frank, B. M. (1988). Encoding and external-storage effects of personal lecture notes, skeletal notes, and detailed notes for field-independent and field-dependent learners. *Journal of Educational Research, 81,* 143–148.

Kiewra, K. A., Mayer, R. E., Christian, D., Dyreson, M., & McShane, A. (1988, April). *Quantitative and qualitative effects of repetition and note-taking on learning from video-taped instruction.* Paper presented at the annual meeting of the American Educational Research Association, New Orleans, LA.

Kiewra, K. A., Mayer, R. E., Christensen, M., Kim, S.I., & Risch, N. (1991). Effects of repetition on recall and notetaking: Strategies for learning from lectures. *Journal of Educational Psychology, 83,* 120–123.

King, A. (1989). Effects of self-questioning training on college students' comprehension of lectures. *Contemporary Educational Psychology, 14,* 366–381.

King, A. (1991). Improving lecture comprehension: Effects of a metacognitive strategy. *Applied Cognitive Psychology, 5,* 331–346.

King, A. (1992). Comparison of self-questioning, summarizing, and notetaking-review as strategies for learning from lectures. *American Educational Research Journal, 29,* 303–323.

Mayer, R. E. (1984). Aids to text comprehension. *Educational Psychologist, 19,* 30–42.

Morgan, C. H., Lilley, J. D., & Boreham, N. C. (1988). Learning from lectures: The effect of varying the detail in lecture handouts on note-taking and recall. *Applied Cognitive Psychology, 2,* 115–122.

O'Donnell, A., & Dansereau, D. F. (1993). Learning from lectures: Effects of cooperative review. *Journal of Experimental Education, 61,* 116-125.

Palincsar, A. S., & Brown, A. L. (1984). Reciprocal teaching of comprehension-fostering and monitoring activities. *Cognition and Instruction, 1,* 117–175.

Paris, S., Cross, D., & Lipson, M. (1984). Informed strategies for learning: a program to improve children's reading awareness and comprehension. *Journal of Educational Psychology, 76,* 1239–1252.

Peper, R. J., & Mayer, R. E. (1986). Generative effects of note-taking during science lectures. *Journal of Educational Psychology, 78,* 34–38.

Putnam, M. L., Deshler, D. D., & Schumaker, J. B. (1993). The investigation of setting demands: A missing link in learning strategy instruction. In L. S. Meltzer (Ed.),

Strategy assessment and instruction for students with learning disabilities (pp. 325–354). Austin, TX: PRO-ED.

Ruhl, K. L., Hughes, C. A., & Gajar, A. H. (1990). Efficacy of the pause procedure for enhancing learning disabled and nondisabled college students' long- and short-term recall of facts presented through lecture. *Learning Disability Quarterly, 13*, 55–64.

Ruhl, K. L., & Suritsky, S. (1995). The pause procedure and/or an outline: Effect on immediate free recall and lecture notes taken by college students with learning disabilities. *Learning Disability Quarterly, 18*, 2–11.

Scerbo, M. W., Warm, J. S., Dember, W. N., & Grasha, A. F. (1992). The role of time and cuing in a college lecture. *Contemporary Educational Psychology, 17*, 312–328.

Suritsky, S. K., & Hughes, C. A. (1991). Benefits of notetaking: Implications for secondary and postsecondary students with learning disabilities. *Learning Disability Quaterly, 14*, 7–18.

Van Meter, D. E. (1994). Computer-aided lecturing. *Journal of Natural Resources and Life Sciences Education, 23*, 62–64.

Wittrock, M. C. (1990). Generative processes of comprehension. *Educational Psychologist, 24*, 345–376.

8

Factors That Influence Study

❧ § § ❧

Whitney Pitts Allgood
Victoria J. Risko
Vanderbilt University

Marino C. Alvarez
Tennessee State University

Marilyn M. Fairbanks
Emeritus, West Virginia University

We have known for some time that certain factors separate students who succeed in college from those who have difficulty. This chapter identifies and discusses three factors that affect students' ability to achieve in college—the ability to "navigate" and understand course expectations, motivation, and self-efficacy. An examination of these three areas is useful for understanding how external factors, such as the demands and discourse of college classes, and internal factors, such as feelings of motivation and self-efficacy, affect students' performance. We begin our discussion of these factors by identifying study habits that either facilitate or inhibit students' development in these three areas.

WHAT SUCCESSFUL STUDENTS DO ...
AND OTHERS DON'T DO

Numerous studies focusing on characteristics of students who succeed in college and those who experience difficulties point to variables such as students' ability to adopt and use strategies appropriate for course requirements (e.g., Elkeland & Manger, 1992; Entwistle, 1990), students' perception of the college curriculum and belief in their ability to succeed (e.g., Glover, 1996; Senecal, Koestner, & Vallerand, 1995), and the students' ability to self-regulate studying and learning (e.g., Drozd, 1994; Peniston, 1994).

Students who succeed in college are more likely to be aware of cognitive rules and more likely to use metacognitve knowledge to justify, plan, and evaluate the cognitive processes they use. These students, described as self-regulated learners, know what skills they possess, what knowledge they have, and how they prefer to learn. They also analyze text and task characteristics and demands in order to select and use the processes and strategies most likely to result in learning (Nist, Simpson, Olejnik, & Mealey, 1991). Successful students have learned to monitor their study behaviors and learning progress, and adjust their behaviors to contextual demands (e.g., Elkeland & Manger, 1992). They understand the demands of academia and are able to monitor and evaluate their progress toward meeting those demands (e.g., Elkeland & Manger, 1992).

Students who are able to self-regulate and monitor their comprehension are described as *strategic readers* and these metacognitive acts (knowing *what* to do and *when* to do it to aid comprehension) have been linked to proficient reading and positive motivation (e.g., Paris, Wasik, & Turner, 1991). Borkowski, Carr, Rellinger, and Pressley (1990) suggested that the attributes of metacognition and positive self-esteem also relate to beliefs that one's own efforts can facilitate successful learning. Students who attribute success to effort tend to have higher self-efficacy, use of strategies, and expectations that they will succeed (Bruning, Schraw, & Ronning, 1995; El-Hindi & Childers, 1997; Pintrich & Schunk, 1996).

Unfortunately, many students are inadequately prepared for what is required of them to succeed in college. And many learners that fail believe their learning difficulties are caused by factors they cannot control. For example, they may believe that they have limited ability, assignments are too difficult, teaching is poor, materials are uninteresting, and that they are the victims of poor luck (El-Hindi & Childers, 1997).

Specific problems that college students experience have been documented for several decades by college instructors and researchers. Shaughnessy (1977), for example, discusses her observations of students enrolled at City University of New York (CUNY) when open admissions became popular in the early 1970s. She describes students enrolled in her college reading and writing courses as being "left so far behind others in their formal education that they appeared to have little chance of catching up" (p. 3). Many of these students seemed to have difficulty "reconciling the worlds of home and school, a fact which by now had worked its way deep into their feelings about school and about themselves as students" (p. 3). These students came to college because they wanted a better life than their parents had and they wanted to offer their children a better life than their own. How they were going to accomplish this was "not at all clear" to them (p. 3). Shaughnessy concluded that many of her students would fail unless pedagogies were designed and adjusted to help them succeed.

Rose's (1989) analysis of college students' difficulties expands on the position put forward a decade earlier by Shaughnessy. Rose suggests that problems experienced by college students are cognitive and social. Rose described several reasons why students fail, including insufficient or varying orientations toward inquiry, a view of knowledge as something that involves memorizing facts and formulas (which he argues is shaped in large part by the typical secondary school experience), and "conceptualizations of disciplines which are out of sync with reality" (Rose, 1989, p. 191).

As Rose (1989) lamented, the lack of preparation many students receive at the secondary school level can constrain students' success in higher education. Many "feel estranged because once familiar cognitive landscapes have shifted, because once effective strategies have been rendered obsolete; and still others ... know more than their tests reveal but haven't been taught how to weave that knowledge into coherent patterns" (p. 8).

First generation college students seem to experience a variety of problems similar to those documented by Shaughnessy (1977). These include a difficulty in adjusting to college life due to fears that they will be unsuccessful because of their inadequate preparation and limited knowledge of strategies (e.g., how to manage study time and assignments) necessary to navigate the college curriculum. Students view college instructors as impersonal and college in general as an impenetrable bureaucratic system comprised of difficult and intimidating requirements (Zwerling & London, 1992).

Fairbanks, coauthor of this chapter, taught reading, writing, and study skills classes within community college and university reading programs for more than 20 years. During that time, she came to a greater understanding of the various reasons some students failed while others succeeded. She contends that college students enrolled in literacy support classes require a pedagogy that is responsive simultaneously to their academic needs, feelings of insecurity, and life circumstances—circumstances that involve conflicts and contradictory actions. For example, many of her community and junior college students went to school full time while also working full time. As one student told her, "I am working to have enough money to go to school and failing my classes because of my work requirements."

Being distracted by job requirements was often complicated by students' doubts about their ability to succeed in college. And these doubts were fueled, in some instances, by their beliefs that the literacy and study skills courses offered in college would do little to help them achieve their goals. Often, these students had a long history of literacy problems and years of instruction that failed, in their estimation, to enhance their literacy development and preparedness for college success. Because they continued to experience literacy difficulties, they thought that special study skills classes in college could not help them. Furthermore, enrollment in these reading skills courses added additional burdens. These courses, usually taken as electives, often provided no credit although assignments were required. Consequently, motivation and persistence were often negatively affected.

Similar observations are reported by Kangas, Budros, and Ferraro (1991) who investigated reasons for students' withdrawal from San Jose Community College. Academic difficulties, lack of money, and full-time work impeded these students' ability to persist in school. Almost half of the students (48%) revealed a general lack of belief that college could benefit their lives. Seventy-one percent of these students considered dropping out of college within the first 4 weeks and 85% did not talk to an instructor before doing so. Interviews with these students revealed that their low self-confidence was exacerbated by a lack of emotional support in their private lives.

Students' ability to understand what is expected of them and monitor their learning in ways that enhance their motivation to succeed and develop self-efficacy are influenced by many individual and situational factors. Instructors such as Shaughnessey, Rose, Fairbanks, and others suggest that such complex problems require instruction that is multifaceted, accommodates several issues simultaneously, and responds to individual needs of students. This instruction also must be sensitive to the "cultural contexts" impacting on each students' academic effort and development (Purcell-Gates, 1995).

INTERNAL AND EXTERNAL FACTORS RELEVANT TO EFFECTIVE STUDY PREVIOUSLY REVIEWED

Earlier examinations of internal and external study factors (Risko, Alvarez, & Fairbanks, 1991; Risko, Fairbanks, & Alvarez, 1991) focused on five areas that influenced students' study habits and academic achievement in college. Here we revisit the conclusions and implications of these earlier examinations in order to discuss possible relationships among those five factors (i.e., time management, study environment management, library use, motivation, and memory and attention) and the three we chose to consider in this current chapter.

Our earlier analysis of related literature on time management led us to conclude that there is no single time management plan that works for all students in all learning situations. "How a student manages time is personal and idiosyncratic [therefore] use of time must be flexible and responsive to students' learning needs" (Risko, Alvarez, & Fairbanks, 1991, pp. 201, 203). It is important to note that students who achieve have adopted strategies to monitor and manage their time for studying and success in course work reinforces continued use of these strategies.

Our analysis of literature related to study environment management suggested that the term "study environment" encompasses several variables such as "time management, memory and concentration, knowledge of learning strategies, and motivation and interest" (Risko, Alvarez, & Fairbanks, 1991, p. 221). We noted that some students' study is enhanced when they play music while they study, when they study with peers, and when they are selective about place of study. For other students, these factors seem less influential. Once again, students' selective use of these variables requires students to be aware of what works best for them and to know how to adjust and discontinue habits that are less than helpful.

For the analysis of library use, we made a distinction between *library skills* and *research skills*. Library skills are those needed to search for information, and research skills are those needed to search for knowledge. Our survey of literature and research in this area also pointed to the fact that technology has a significant impact on how library information is accessed. In regard to research skills, the findings pointed to the need for undergraduates to understand research skills as "encompassing in-depth knowledge about a specific subject area, knowledge of research methods associated with the discipline, the ability to gather and test primary data … and the ability to think in a particular subject area" (Stoan, 1984, cited in Risko, Alvarez, & Fairbanks, 1991, p. 224). In regard to technology, students need to build, and continue to build, understandings of how information technology can aid their efforts to access multiple resources and how it has changed the organization and networking of these materials within college and university libraries. Specific recommendations for engaging students' learning with technology are provided later.

Our analysis of motivational factors provided information about four interrelated categories: (a) assuming responsibility for academic achievement or improvement, (b) developing positive attitudes toward self and surroundings, (c) setting goals, and (d) managing stress and anxiety. Within these categories, locus of control, attributions, academic job involvement, self-monitoring, self-reinforcement, problem solving, extrinsic rewards and contingency contracting were examined. Three areas were identified as important for successful study. These include problem solving, self-monitoring, and goal setting. All of these areas were found to be in need of further research and, as it turns out, motivation is still a very active research area that continues to inform and influence multiple individual disciplines and pedagogy as a whole. We elaborate on this concept.

The review of memory and attention suggested a strong link between factors associated with motivation and habits or strategies that tend to increase attention and memory skills (Risko, Alvarez, & Fairbanks, 1991). We concluded that college students need to be taught to control their own study efforts. This includes establishing self-reinforcing schedules, generating questions about the materials being studied, being self-disciplined, making decisions about what is important for them to learn and remember, and becoming aware of the processes of learning applicable to different learning contexts. Specific suggestions for enhancing students' strategic learning are provided later. (Also, see Flippo, Becker, & Wark, chap. 9, this volume, for related information.)

Our previous and current reviews of factors related to study habits help us identify personal, social, and contextual variables that affect achievement. Students' unique experiences prior to and during college, and unique abilities and beliefs affect their preparation for and approach to college study requirements. And, in turn, these factors are influenced by particular characteristics of the college environment and curriculum, course and instructor differences, and life circumstances. These variables are discussed in more depth later. Specifically, we discuss why it is important to consider how students interpret the college context, an area we refer to as "ability to navigate academia," and attributes commonly associated with student motivation and feelings of self-efficacy. We explain how course characteristics, study activities, and student beliefs about outcomes can be developed in ways that are most likely to facilitate academic achievement for all students (Warkentin, Griffin, & Bates, 1994).

NAVIGATING ACADEMIA

It hits you forcefully … the affluence of the place, the attention to dress and carriage, but the size, too—vast and impersonal, a labyrinth of corridors and classrooms and libraries; you're also struck by the wild intersection of cultures, spectacular diversity, compressed by a thousand social forces. (Rose, 1989, p. 3)

For many students, the first few days on a college campus can be shocking and disconcerting. Being away from home for the first time, living in a dorm with strangers with whom they may have little in common, commuting to the campus, learning how to self-manage time and money, and finding their way from building to building and classroom to classroom can be trying experiences for 18- or 19-year-old students. Returning to college later in life also poses unique problems and situations for nontraditional students. These students are coping with academic rigors that may not be in accordance with their high school experiences. Regardless of their background, some students may be anxious, others apprehensive, still others somewhat bewildered. All these experiences can be stimulating, confusing, and sometimes even depressing. The social dimensions of college life interact with the cognitive and affective dimensions in very important ways. One such interactive dimension specific to studying and learning outcomes is described by Gee (1992) as "discourse communities."

Discourse communities, specific to college, are social and academic situations (e.g., family, dorm, cafeteria, student union, clubs, organizations, college classes, etc.) where the ability to fit in or even understand what is happening, why it is happening, and one's role in the situation is dependent on expected behavioral norms specific to, defined by, and in turn defining of the situation or discourse community. Each situation demands a somewhat different discourse community that is determined by the social, cultural, and academic setting in which it occurs. When students become engaged within a particular discourse community for which they have little prior knowledge or experience, such as a class in computer applications, they often need to rely on other students or the teacher to provide the grounding necessary to help them understand these new experiences. Students who are unfamiliar with the particular discourse can be coached to become active participants when they are encouraged to become "apprentices" to the instructors and peers who are more familiar with the situational requirements (Gee, 1992).

Gee's concept of apprenticeship, similar to Vygotsky's (1978) notion of mediated learning and Rogoff's (1991) description of teaching and guided participation, provides a framework for developing scaffolds to support students' participation in new discourse communities. Instructors who involve students in classroom discussions can learn what students already know about the subject and help them apply this information to the content under study. Knowing what students know and need to know, instructors help students move from guided to independent learning as the students are introduced to new concepts and learn to make applications of these within the domains under study. Gee encouraged developmental evaluation, or working closely with a student to see what can be learned when support is provided. Explicit teaching does have a place in instruction, but it is only effectively "directed at minds already prepared through having begun and been supported in apprenticeships with the requisite discourse" (Gee, 1992, p. 136). Many procedures can be adopted by college instructors. These include providing models of appropriate responses to given situations and inviting evaluations and reflection (Collins, Hawkins, & Carver, 1991), modeling procedures for summarizing text ideas (Wong, 1985), coaching students to generate graphic organizers to make connections across multiples concepts and multiple texts (Hartman & Alison, 1996), and helping students regulate the difficulty of material by studying small chunks at a time (Collins et. al., 1991). Lee (1998) suggested that helping students reflect on their personal experiences "through the lenses of their disciplines during classroom and study time" and then relate them to the topics they are studying is a vital component of liberal education, which should become a routine for college students. The role of schema activation and schema construction are vital processes in the acquisition and learning of new information and self-directed strategies.

Schema Activation and Schema Construction

In order for students to successfully navigate their courses, it is important that they relate their world knowledge and experience to what they know about any given topic they are studying. There is evidence to suggest that both good and less able readers do not use schemata appropriately or are unaware of whether the information they are reading is consistent with their existing knowledge (Bartlett, 1932; Bransford, 1985). Too often students are subjected to lectures or given course-specific handouts that contain facts and ideas about which they have little understanding. These students may be encouraged by their instructors to take this material and make sense of it, but if this new information cannot be related to their prior knowledge or experience, their efforts may be directed at memorizing information that holds little meaning to them.

Schema theory explains how prior knowledge can be activated; however, it does not account for how schema is constructed. Bransford (1985) pointed out that schema activation and schema construction are two different processes. It is possible for a learner to activate existing schemata of a given topic; however, it does not necessarily follow that a learner can use this activated knowledge to facilitate acquisition of new knowledge and skills. Critical thinking theory provides an explanation for activating existing schemata and for constructing new ones (Norris & Phillips, 1987). Situating lessons and assignments that require meaningful learning outcomes based on the processes of critical thinking enables students to use strategies for achieving understanding. In academic environments such as these, students can contrast ideas and engage in reflective thinking (Dewey, 1933). A learner can either weigh alternative interpretations, dismiss others, make a decision to evaluate multiple possibilities, or accept information as being reasonable, authentic, and accurate. This process of thinking critically when confronted with problems and tasks helps students to modify or extend their understanding of a given topic.

Instruction supported by schema theory and critical thinking theory situates the introduction of new information within contexts that are relevant to students' background experiences and prior knowledge. Within such frameworks, learning is maximized when materials and assignments are related to what students know and when students understand the importance for acquiring new information. Likewise, students can become actively involved in the learning process when they are asked to make connections between what they are learning and what they already know, and when they are enabled to select from an array of strategies that help them apply personal meaning to newly acquired facts and ideas. Instructors can help students achieve personal meanings through dialogic conversations in the classroom in which both students and the instructor display their understandings and interpretations of information.

Learning With Technology

Navigating academia in college classrooms also requires multiple uses of technology. Technology is one discourse community that changes the way we view education and the workplace and continues to impact these domains at a rapid pace. Some students come to college with much more experience with computer applications to manage their academic studies than others. Instructors are demanding that their students use and learn with technology by asking them to communicate via e-mail through personal directives with them or other students in class or on listservs. Students are asked to access the World Wide Web (WWW) for locational and reference materials, and develop their own programs for interactive learning. Providing students with lessons and assignments that require them to think with technology can help them construct meaning of target concepts (Alvarez, 1997). For example, students in Alvarez's class are involved in an electronic listserv consortium with students at other universities throughout the country enrolled in a similar course. The shared learning that occurs is useful for helping students explain and elaborate on their developing knowledge. Students share ideas using the Internet. In another of his classes, students use an Interactive Vee Diagram developed by Alvarez that appears on a website to send and receive feedback concerning their research assignments. Collaborations afforded by these uses of technology facilitate concept development, critical and imaginative thinking, and applications of information to resolve issues and problems.

The literacy skills described demand more attention to the kinds of visual aids contained within electronic environments (see Reinking & ChanLin, 1994), and a more sophisticated degree of receptive and expressive reasoning abilities then what is required for reading narrative and expository prose. Students are interacting with a variety of information sources on the Internet (Gilster, 1997). Conventional reading tasks embedded within linear and sequential formats are changed to those that are embedded within the analysis of electronic word and visual graphic displays. These displays take the viewer from one place to another through a series of choices (Alvarez, 1997). Essential within this changing model of reading requirements is that teachers and students are prepared to take on this new form of literacy. Students are required to "read" information presented in text, graphics, and video formats. Interactive engagements with electronic text are necessary functions rather than options as students search for information that adds to their knowledge base.

Additionally, goals for technology-based instruction include those that invite students' in-depth learning of course content. Meeks-Hager and Eanet (1996), for example, described how asynchronous learning networks within their distance learning programs invite students to participate in online discussions about course content. These activities engage students in meaningful, course-related discussions and facilitate involvement of students who may not typically take an active role in class discussions. Other researchers report similar findings. Andriotle, Lytle, and Monsanto (1995) reported on students' favorable response to online discussions provided within an engineering course offered at Drexel University. Students cited more access to the instructor than in conventional course deliveries and more communication with fellow students to support their positive feedback. Fyock and Sutphin (1995) observed students naturally engaged in cooperative activities, and these students reported that they took more responsibility for their own learning and acquired more acquaintances and friends. Barson, Frommer, and Schwartz (1993) found students felt they had more access and individual attention from the instructor and worked more collaboratively than in traditional classrooms. (For further discussion, see Caverly & Peterson, chap. 11, this volume.)

MOTIVATION

> We live in America with so many platitudes about motivation and self-reliance and individu-alism … that we find it hard to accept the fact that they are serious nonsense. To journey up through the top levels of the American educational system will call for support and guidance at many, many points along the way. You'll need people to guide you into foreign conversa-tions that seem … threatening. You'll need models to show you how to get at what you don't know. You'll need people to watch out for you. (Rose, 1989, p. 47)

In a previous review (see Risko, Fairbanks, & Alvarez, 1991), we cited several motiva-tional factors that influence learning among college students who have a history of expe-riencing academic problems during their high school years. We noted that students who experience academic difficulties lack a positive self-concept for learning unfamiliar facts and concepts, and attribute their misfortune to bad luck rather than focusing on their own abilities to self-monitor and use appropriate study strategies. We concluded that the introduction of survival skills early in their program combined with encouragement of success, even on a limited scale, motivates college students intrinsically to achieve aca-demic success for themselves. In other words, although it is always the hope to have stu-dents who are intrinsically motivated, students often need some external help. Very often well-intentioned mentors, parents, and peers verbally encourage struggling stu-dents; as "nice" as this encouragement to get motivated is it often is not enough. Strug-gling students need active support, effective learning tools, and real opportunities for success if they are to become intrinsically motivated.

A complex relationship exists between motivational variables and study behav-iors. We attribute many adverse reactions to study requirements to students' inability to use effective learning strategies. Whether students even use the learning strategies they have acquired is dependent on the extent of their motivation (Tuckman, 1996). We fur-ther believe that the path for easing students past failure and a low self-concept is to teach them through demonstration and modeling how to learn despite their age, circum-stance, or placement in an academic environment. Effective instruction occurs by changing the *meaning* of experience for the learner, not changing behavior. The instruc-tor needs to be aware of cognitive and emotional characteristics exhibited by students that may discourage motivation for academic learning and take steps to remedy negative signs as they surface. This section elaborates on the role that negative factors play in hin-dering student academic success and offers positive resolutions.

Disparaging Motivational Factors

A number of reasons can account for students' negative motivation. Social values in-stilled in students during their formative years can affect their motivation to learn one thing rather than another; if parents and peers do not value academic achievement, or do value it but do not know how to communicate that value, then it is likely that these students will not be motivated enough to learn and use effective study and learning strat-egies in college. There is considerable evidence supporting claims that students develop negative orientations to studying and learning as a result of difficulties they have in school (e.g., Johnston & Winograd, 1985). This is particularly true with students who experience successive failure; they "become progressively less motivated as a function of years of experience in school" (den Heyer, 1981, p. 59).

Attribution theory helps to explain the relentlessness of this downward spiral. "Attribution of frequently experienced failure in ability, a stable internal cause, will increasingly lower the [student's] expectancy of success and self-esteem. At the same time, the belief that success, when it is experienced, is due to external causes such as luck or ease of task does little to increase success expectancy or enhance self-esteem" (den Heyer, 1981, pp. 59–60).

Students suffering from extreme passive failure have deficits in the cognitive, affective, and motivational domains. In the cognitive domain, these students lack the ability to see relationships between elements in a task. They lack motivation because they see their ability as something that is stable, fixed, beyond their personal control but controlling everything they do. All of their failures are attributed to their perceived lack of ability, and when they do succeed they consider it a fluke, a mistake, or assume the task was just too easy (e.g., Johnston & Winograd, 1985).

Motivational Factors

To change the meaning of experience for students so that they can become motivated to learn new information in meaningful ways, we need to acknowledge that students come to school with different abilities, skills, and aptitudes. Students who are less motivated because of academic deficiencies need to be stimulated to accede to a level that they have seldom experienced during their previous school years. They need to be shown by words and deeds, sometimes within out-of-class meetings and conferences (Jaasma & Koper, 1999) that the instructor wants them to achieve academic success. These students want classes that involve them in the learning process in ways that are interesting, have practical merit, and relate to their known experiences and knowledge. Challenging class activities accompanied with clear, obtainable, and meaningful outcomes are favored by these students as opposed to those that signify endurance as the mainstay for completion (i.e., those college courses known as "weed-out" courses).

Providing opportunities to let students "show what they can do" prompts interest and creativity and spurs motivation. Chances for success are enhanced when class lessons and assignments are crafted in ways that stimulate students to achieve. It is important for students to internalize what they are learning by imposing their own personal meaning on newly acquired information. Being told what they need to know is not the same as being able to envision how this new information is important. Students need to assimilate and accommodate new information in ways that meet their individual life experiences and goals.

In order to ensure cognitive and affective motivational stability for students it is necessary to change the meaning of their experience by providing a stimulating and challenging academic learning environment. Some ways to accomplish this objective include: (a) encouraging students to make use of their emotional intellect when confronted with new learning situations; (b) helping them become aware of their own experiences and world knowledge when reading, viewing, and listening to information being delivered; and, (c) instilling within them a sense of having knowledge and self-worth. Too often these students have been made to feel that they have little to contribute to academic discussions and therefore rely on others to provide information. Providing reinforcement in ways that encourage understanding, together with clear reasons and explanations of progress, and placing value on students' learning instead of their grades or test performances (Archer & Schevak, 1998) enable students to better understand the educational process and the relevance for learning new material.

Motivational Strategies

Students need to be presented with a change from what they have been accustomed to in past schooling environments. It stands to reason that if students had difficulty in the past, using similar teaching methods such as lecture and assignments that lack specifications for clear and concrete outcomes, they will continue to do poorly. It is important for the instructor to present materials that are organized and relevant to students' world knowledge and experience. Anticipated outcomes should be explained in detail with examples of the kinds of products that are expected.

The processes necessary for completing these product outcomes must also be demonstrated. It is during this stage when students need to synthesize information (e.g., joining, selecting, discarding, implying, and entailing). It is also during this stage when students encounter obstacles and begin to become discouraged. The instructor can aid by taking time to teach processing strategies. For example, using concept maps to demonstrate the conceptual organization of course content helps students discern relationships across ideas and concepts that are being developed. They are also able to internalize the mapping process as they map their textbooks, plan the organization of papers, or prepare to give oral presentations (Novak, 1998; Novak & Gowin, 1984; Pauk, 1989). Taking time to teach students effective notetaking procedures that enable them to combine and manipulate the reading and lecture information in multiple ways (e.g., incorporating strategies such as SQ5R[1]) when studying enables students to reinforce sound self-monitoring learning strategies (Pauk, 1993). It is equally important that instructors provide opportunities for their students' to set goals for themselves and provide timely and pertinent feedback about students' progress.

One way for the instructor to monitor student progress is to have students keep a reaction journal of class activities, assignments, and readings. The instructor is then able to keep abreast of students' beliefs, feelings, and thoughts as they develop and change throughout the semester. Reading and responding to their writings both orally and in their journals can enable students to better identify their own progress and understanding of the course content. Conferencing with students bimonthly on an individual basis is another way for assessing student understanding and progress. Feedback and acknowledgment of students' goals and accomplishments provide a way to "honor" students voices and to illustrate the concern and responsiveness of the instructor (Oldfather, 1995). A rapport is developed between students and the instructor, thereby increasing

---

[1]We adapted Francis P. Robinson's Survey, Question, Read, Recite, Review (SQ3R) cited in *Effective Reading*, Harper & Row, New York, 1962, to Survey, Question, Read, Record, Recite, Reflect, and Review (SQ5R).

positive motivation for future learning and establishing a mechanism for deliberations when facts and ideas need to be clarified.

SELF-EFFICACY

> Faculty would announce office hours. If I had the sense, I would have gone, but they struck me as aloof and somber men, and I felt stupid telling them I was ... well—stupid.... So I went to school and sat in class and memorized more than understood and whistled past the academic graveyard. I vacillated between the false potency of scorn and feelings of ineptitude. I was out of my league. (Rose, 1989, pp. 43, 45)

Self-efficacy is an internal set of belief systems that enables individuals to monitor their thoughts, feelings, and actions (Bandura, 1977, 1986). Corresponding to their beliefs about their capabilities, students learn to change and regulate their actions and alter their academic experiences. Being able to derive meaning from their experiences comes from learning from others, reflecting on what has been experienced in the past, and being able to monitoring one's own behavior in the process. Within an academic setting, self-efficacy influences how well and to what extent a student believes in his or her capacity to achieve in a given course. Learners with high self-efficacy beliefs have a tendency to persevere and expend more effort when facing difficult learning situations. Conversely, those learners who have low self-efficacy beliefs tend to become discouraged and feel that they cannot cope with a difficult situation. Although they believe that there are strategies for responding to difficult situations, they believe that they are incapable of producing such responses (Maimon, 1995; Mayo, 1996). Self-efficacy may influence which activities a student seeks to engage in, how much effort a student spends on a given activity, how long a student persists at an activity when challenged by it, and overall achievement (Schunk, 1996).

Although general ability is a significant predictor of achievement, it does not influence strategy use the way self-efficacy does (Horn, Bruning, Schraw, Curry, & Katkanant, 1993; Pajares, 1996; Warkentin et al., 1994). In order for students to develop positive self-efficacy beliefs they need to acquire competence and skills in coping with difficult lessons and assignments. They also need to feel optimistic about their ability to control factors contributing to the difficulty of specific tasks. Unfortunately, performance spirals downward when students perceive that they are failures and these negative feelings have an adverse affect on efforts and use of strategies that can help them achieve in difficult situations (Mayo, 1996).

The challenge for instructors is to provide learning environments that offer students interesting and challenging lessons while at the same time providing strategies that can develop independent critical and imaginative thinking. In addition, because of the positive relationship between high selfefficacy and the use of higher order cognitive strategies, it is imperative that instructors explicitly teach and model those strategies most necessary for achievement in their course. Students who have a broader range of effective learning strategies at their command are more confident about their ability to succeed at a task, and students who are more confident about their ability to succeed at a task use more effective strategies.

There are a number of instructional methods teachers can use to expose students to effective learning strategies and foster increased self-efficacy in their students. We mention a few here to serve as examples and indicators of the direction instructors need to take in their teaching to ensure that students can succeed in their courses. Instructors can incorporate text adjuncts and lectures and discussions by using strategies that aid text comprehension. In this way, the instructor is mediating the students' learning and study behaviors while demonstrating strategies that can facilitate achievement in particular courses (Wilhite, 1992).

Reading and study guides (e.g., organized to provide guiding questions to activate prior knowledge and facilitate interpretations) can be developed by the instructor and given to students to accompany their reading of the text. Instructors can aid their students by teaching and modeling strategies that students (e.g., self-questioning and summary strategies) can implement for themselves. Concept mapping, discussed previously, can be used to introduce concepts within a text and provides another example of strategy learning; so too, can students be taught to take notes that can be manipulated by them to aid their understanding of new information. For example, the Cornell Note Taking System (Pauk, 1993) provides students with a strategy that enables them to record information, write pertinent associated statements and questions, reflect on these combined writings, summarize information according to relevant categories, and serve as a review for an examination. Instructors can provide a skeletal page using a notetaking strategy such as the Cornell Note Taking System and have students take notes on a well-prepared and organized lecture to aid them in the process.

Strategies such as these can influence student achievement by enabling them to become more confident when confronted with new information and encourage students to believe that they can control new learning situations by choosing and implementing "tools" they have learned for solving problems. We believe that students' academic achievement is enhanced when students' learn to control their own study efforts. Williams (1996), for example, indicated that high school students reporting strong self-efficacy in self-regulated learning strategies demonstrated increased student achievement in core content areas of math, social studies, science, and reading. Feelings of self-efficacy can increase motivation toward specific tasks and accomplishments, and increase levels of performance (Schunk, 1996).

CONCLUSION AND IMPLICATIONS

We began this chapter with an overview of why some students succeed and others fail to achieve in college. This overview led us into a look back at our earlier review of several factors related to successful study (Risko, Alvarez, & Fairbanks, 1991; Risko, Fairbanks, & Alvarez, 1991). We then focused our discussion on information related to students' ability to understand the contexts of higher education, student motivation, and self-efficacy. As others have noted (e.g., Nist et al., 1991), the most comprehensive, accurate, and informative picture of studying is one that includes the students' perception of their college environment and the affective domain.

Our earlier reviews (Risko, Alvarez, & Fairbanks, 1991; Risko, Fairbanks, & Alvarez, 1991) and current examination of study factors indicate that the most successful efforts to help college students succeed have been those that acknowledge the "inter-action among text, task and learner [characteristics] that make for optimum learning" (Nist et al., 1991, p. 871). We agree with Nist et al. (1991) and others (e.g., Archmabeault, 1992; Boll, Connell, & Nunnery, 1995; Hadwin & Winne, 1996; Meyer, 1991; Meyer, Cliff, & Dunne, 1994; Peelo, 1994; Rose, 1989) who argued that no one study strategy will be effective for all students, or even the same student, all of the time. Researchers who have examined study factors among college students have demon-strated that there are qualitative differences in the way students approach and engage in learning tasks, that there are contextual influences on engagement, and that different students have different conceptions of learning (Meyer, 1991). Students who approach studying and learning differently also have varying conceptions of effective teaching. Not surprisingly, these conceptions are directly related to their personal approaches to learning. Furthermore, variation in approaches to learning do not only appear in groups of individuals, but within individuals (Meyer et al., 1994).

As we conclude this chapter, we identify one instructional strategy as an illustra-tive example of how instructors can support students' learning and account for the fac-tors discussed in this chapter. This strategy, referred to as the PLAE procedure by Simpson and Nist (1984), leads students through the following steps:

1. Preplanning where tasks and goals are identified;
2. Listing the most appropriate strategies for the text and task in a specific and se-quential outline;
3. Activating the outlined plan and monitoring it so that as soon as it becomes in-effective new strategies can be selected and implemented;
4. Evaluating the success of the plan based on learning outcomes or test perfor-mance.

The PLAE procedure illustrates how students can be encouraged to reflect on their strengths and weaknesses relative to tasks and goals, so that they are able to devise and carry out the most effective and efficient plan. This reflection includes, for example, the following self-questions: *Is this something I'm interested in or motivated by? Am I confi-dent about my ability to complete this task? Do I find this task worthwhile? What do I already know about this topic? What skills and strategies do I possess that will be most helpful to me in completing this task? Am I going to need help from my instructor or peers in completing this task?* Students' answers to these questions might not be positive (i.e., "*I am not interested in this topic*"; "*I'm not confident about my ability to complete it*"; "*I don't find it worthwhile*"; "*I don't know anything about this*"); instructors need to let students know that it is okay. What is important is that students are aware of their position relative to the task so that they can devise a plan that calls on the strategies and support that will most likely earn them their desired outcome.

Study skills needed for helping students operationalize their plans for study are most successfully taught and learned when metalearning, self-regulation, or executive control strategies are also taught. Meyer's (1991) conception of metalearning requires facilitating the student's ability to recognize the congruency between appropriate mo-tives for a learning situation and matching strategies. Once this has been accomplished, the student is better prepared to control these factors. This, of course, is easier for some students than for others. But when a learning dialogue is established between instructors and students in each course and the interactions are natural and directed toward careful monitoring of students' learning, there is a greater likelihood of students successfully internalizing the metalearning concept and its corresponding strategies (Meyer et al., 1994). Archambeault (1992) supported classroom instruction that enhances students' awareness of the components of their own study style and increases their ability to select strategies that are appropriate to the task.

Students encounter different problems at various stages of the college experience (Elkeland & Manger, 1982). Not only do students change and grow personally over time (goals, priorities, interests, emotional state, knowledge base, and so on are all unstable and unpredictable factors that influence how students approach their education), the courses they encounter have varying characteristics. A student's motivation to achieve in one course at one time (or in the same course at two different times) might be totally different from his or her motivation for another course at the same time; therefore, the approach in terms of studying taken by the student varies as will, most probably, the level of achievement attained.

The most effective approach to teaching study skills seems to be one that is embedded in course content. That is, the content instructor might teach strategies for succeeding in the courses they teach and college study skills instructors can "piggy-back" their instruction so that students can apply what they are learning in the study skills lab to their content courses. (For information on supplemental instruction [SI] see Johnson & Carpenter, chap. 12, this volume.) For example, Fairbanks (1985) interacted with content instructors and attended their classes to inform their own instruction. They then taught study strategies that would support the students' learning within these specific classes. We support this instructional approach because it is our belief that students are more likely to value, learn, and continue using strategies that are taught when they need them (Gillis & Olson, 1989). A further potential benefit to teaching study strategies within the context of a particular course and its characteristics is that it has been shown to improve mastery of course content: "Educators can simultaneously increase student mastery of course content and improve study habits" (Gillis & Olson, 1989, p. 10).

Unfortunately, it is not always feasible to teach study approaches and behaviors within course content. Therefore, we recommend that students be taught early on how to self-monitor (i.e., How am I doing? Do I understand what I am reading/what the teacher is saying? Am I progressing toward my learning/achievement goals at a reasonable pace or do I need some support?) and self-regulate. Students also need to understand the various discourse communities that can be found in higher education, and they need someone who will actively mentor and guide them so that they are never afraid to approach a professor for help because they feel inadequate, they don't know how to ask their question, or they are afraid it is not a valid question. The students in Rose's book, including himself, had the advantage of having an involved mentor who knew their circumstances and who actively guided them through the maze of academia. Finally, for students who are apparently struggling with the college experience, interventions need to come early and need to be relevant to the context of their whole lives as well as the academic context.

In those cases where students seek guidance from counselors or advisors on study techniques, we found Peelo's (1994) advice to "retain a nondirective philosophy as a basis for helping [them] develop their own strategies and styles in negotiating learning challenges" (p. 151) to be sound and in accordance with the majority of research in this area. The teaching of specific study strategies should be secondary to the development of students as "active participants" in their own learning (Nist et al., 1991, p. 850) who "recognize the functional relationships between their patterns of thought and action ... and social and environmental outcomes" (Nist et al., 1991, p. 850).

Based on our review of the literature and research on study factors, we suggest the following avenues of further research:

- How do course characteristics influence students' affective orientations for achieving?
- How can/are college and university teachers weave[ing] the explicit teaching of study approaches and learning theory for their particular discourses into their course content?
- What are higher education institutions doing (or what can they do) to encourage, develop, monitor, and evaluate the explicit teaching of study approaches and learning theory for discourses specific to and embedded within course content?
- How can secondary education better prepare students for the rigors of higher education (e.g., promoting deep processing over surface processing) and begin fostering in students self-regulatory practices and behaviors?

REFERENCES AND SUGGESTED READINGS

Alvarez, M. C. (1997). Thinking and learning with technology: Helping students construct meaning. NASSP Bulletin, 81(592), 66–72.

Andriotle, S. J., Lytle, R. H., & Monsanto, C. A. (1995). Asynchronous learning networks: Drexel's experience. Technological Horizons in Education Journal, 23(3), 97–101.

Archambeault, B. (1992). Personalizing study skills in secondary students. Journal of Reading, 35(6), 468–472.

Archer, J., & Schevak, J. J. (1998). Enhancing students' motivation to learn: Achievement goals in university. Educational Psychology, 18(2), 205–223.

Bandura, A. (1977). Self-efficacy: Toward a unifying theory of behavioral change. Psychological Review, 84, 191–215.

Bandura, A. (1986). Social foundations of thought and action: A social cognitive theory. Englewood Cliffs, NJ: Prentice-Hall.

Barson, J., Frommer, J., & Schwartz, J. (1993). Foreign language using e-mail in a task oriented perspective: Interuniversity experiments in communication and collaboration. Journal of Science and Technology, 2(4), 565–584.

Bartlett, F. C. (1932). Remembering: A study in experimental and social psychology. London: Cambridge University Press.

Boll, L., Connell, A. A., & Nunnery, J. A. (1995). An exploratory study of college students' study activities and their relationship to study context, reference course and achievement.

Paper presented at the annual meeting of the American Educational Research Association, San Francisco, CA.

*Borkowski, J. G., Carr, M., Rellinger, E., & Pressley, M. (1990). Self-regulated cognition: interdependence of metacognition, attributions, and self-esteem. In B. F. Jones & L. Idol (Eds.), *Dimensions of thinking and cognitive instruction* (pp. 53–92). Hillsdale, NJ: Lawrence Erlbaum Associates.

Bransford, J. D. (1985). Schema activation and schema acquisition. In H. Singer & R. B. Ruddell (Eds.), *Theoretical models and processes of reading* (pp. 385–397). Newark, DE: International Reading Association.

*Bruning, R. H., Schraw, G. J., & Ronning, R. R. (1995). *Cognitive psychology and instruction.* Englewood Cliffs, NJ: Prentice-Hall.

Collins, A., Hawkins, J., & Carver, S. M. (1991). *A cognitive apprenticeship for disadvantaged students.* Washington, DC: U.S. Department of Education, OERI, Educational Resources Information Center.

den Heyer, K. (1981). Reading and motivation. In J. R. Edwards (Ed.), *The social psychology of reading: An interdisciplinary monograph series for language professionals* (Vol. 1, pp. 51–60). Silver Spings, MD: Institute of Modern Languages.

Dewey, J. (1933). *How we think.* Boston: D.C. Heath.

Drozd, G. P. (1994, November). *Is depression related to study habits?* Paper presented at the annual meeting of the Mid-South Research Association, Nashville, TN.

El-Hindi, A., & Childers, K. D. (1997). Metacognitive awareness, attributional beliefs and learning strategies of at-risk college readers. In C. K. Kinzer, K. A. Hinchman, & D. J. Leu (Eds.), *Inquiries in literacy theory and practice* (pp. 127–135). Chicago: National Reading Conference.

Elkeland, O., & Manger, T. (1992). Why students fail during their first university semesters. *International Review of Education, 38*(6), 489–504.

Entwistle, N. J. (1991). Approaches to learning and perceptions of the learning environment: Introduction to the special issue. *Higher Education, 22*(3), 201–204.

Fyock, J., & Sutphin, D. (1995). Adult supervision in the distance learning classroom: Is it necessary? *Technological Horizons in Education Journal, 23*(4), 89–91.

*Gee, J. P. (1992). *The social mind.* New York: Bergin & Garvey.

Gillis, M. K., & Olson, M. W. (1989). Effects of teaching learning strategies with course content. ED 339259.

Gilster, P. (1997). *Digital literacy.* New York: Wiley.

Glover, J. W. (1996, October 31–November 3). *Campus environment and student involvement as predictors of outcomes of the community college experience.* Paper presented at the annual meeting of the Association for the Study of Higher Education, Memphis, TN.

Hadwin, A. F., & Winne, P. H. (1996). Study strategies have meager support: A review for recommendations for implementation. *Journal of Higher Education, 67*(6), 692–715.

Hartman, D. K., & Allison, J. (1996). Promoting inquiry-oriented discussions using multiple texts. In L. B. Gambrell & J. F. Almasi (Eds.), *Lively discussions! Fostering engaged reading* (pp. 106–133). Newark, DE: International Reading Association.

Horn, C., Bruning, R., Schraw, G., Curry, E., & Katkanant, C. (1993). Paths to success in the college classroom. *Contemporary Educational Psychology, 18,* 464–478.

Jaasma, M. A., & Koper, R. J. (1999). The relationship of student–faculty out-of-class communication to instructor immediacy and trust and to student motivation. *Communication Education, 48*(1), 41.

Johnston, P. H., & Winograd, P. N. (1985). Passive failure in reading. *Journal of Reading Behavior, 17*(4), 279–301.

Kangas, J. A., Budros, K., & Ferraro, P. (1991). *San Jose City College withdrawing students study* (Research Rep. No. 119). (ERIC Document Reproduction Service No. ED348 097).

Lee, V. S. (1998). Relating student experience to courses and the curriculum. *The Class Act.* A Publication of the Center for Teaching, Nashville, TN: Vanderbilt University.

Maimon, L. (1995). The effects of perceptions of failure and test instructions on test performance of community college students. In W. M. Linek & E. G. Sturtevant (Eds.), *Generations of literacy* (pp. 145–160). Harrisonburg, VA: The College Reading Association.

*Mayo, K. E. (1996). A case study of reading using holistic intervention with an undergraduate university student. In E. G. Sturtevant & W. M. Linek (Eds.), *Growing literacy* (pp. 211–226). Harrisonburg, VA: The College Reading Association.

Meeks-Hager, J., & Eanet, M. (1996). Learning from a distance: Triumphs and challenges. In K. Camperell, B. L. Hayes, & T. Telfer (Eds.), *Literacy: The information superhighway to success* (pp. 79–84). Logan: Utah State University.

Meyer, J. H. F. (1991). Study orchestration: the manifestation, interpretation and consequences of contextualized approaches to studying. *Higher Education, 22,* 297–316.

*Meyer, J. H. F., Cliff, A. F., Dunne, T. T. (1994). Impressions of disadvantage: Monitoring and assisting the student-at-risk. *Higher Education, 27,* 95–117.

*Nist, S. L., & Simpson, M. L. (1989). PLAE, A validated study strategy. *Journal of Reading, 33*(3), 182–186.

*Nist, S. L., Simpson, M. L., Olejnik, S., & Mealey, D. L. (1991). The relation between self-selected study processes and test performance. *American Educational Research Journal, 28*(4), 849–874.

*Norris, S. P., & Phillips, L. M. (1987). Explanations of reading comprehension: Schema theory and critical thinking theory. *Teachers College Record, 89,* 281–306.

*Novak, J. D. (1998). *Learning, creating, and using knowledge.* Mahwah, NJ: Lawrence Erlbaum Associates.

*Novak, J. D., & Gowin, D. B. (1984). *Learning how to learn.* New York: Cambridge University Press.

Oldfather, P. (1995). Commentary: What's needed to maintain and extend motivation for literacy in the middle grades. *Journal of Reading, 38,* 420–422.

Pajares, F. (1996). Self-efficacy beliefs in academic settings. *Review of Educational Research, 66*(4), 543–578.

Paris, S. G., Wasik, B. A., & Turner, J. C. (1991). The development of strategic readers. In D. Pearson, R. Barr, M. Kamil, & P. Mosenthal (Eds.), *Handbook of reading research* (pp. 609–640). New York: Longman.

Pauk, W. (1989). *How to study in college* (4th ed.). Boston: Houghton Mifflin.

*Pauk, W. (1993). *How to study in college* (5th ed.). Boston: Houghton Mifflin.

Peelo, M. (1994). The experience of study counseling. *Adults Learning, 5*(6), 151–152.

Peniston, L. C. (1994). *Strategies on time management for college students with learning disabilities*. Paper presented at the annual meeting of the Center for Academic Support Programs, Lubbock, TX.

*Pintrich, P., & Schunk, D. H. (1996). *Motivation in education: Theory, research, and applications*. Englewood Cliffs, NJ: Prentice-Hall.

Purcell-Gates, V. (1995). *Other people's words: The cycle of low literacy*. Cambridge, MA: Harvard University Press.

Reinking, D., & ChanLin, L.J. (1994). Graphic aids in electronic texts. *Reading Research and Instruction, 33*(3), 207–232.

*Risko, V. J., Alvarez, M. C., & Fairbanks, M. M. (1991). External factors that influence study. In R. F. Flippo & D. C. Caverly (Eds.), *Teaching reading & study strategies at the college level* (pp. 195–236). Newark, DE: International Reading Association.

*Risko, V. J., Fairbanks, M. M., & Alvarez, M. C. (1991). Internal factors that influence study. In R. F. Flippo & D. C. Caverly (Eds.), *Teaching reading & study strategies at the college level* (pp. 237–293). Newark, DE: International Reading Association.

Rogoff, B. (1990). *Apprenticeship in thinking*. New York: Oxford University Press.

*Rose, M. (1989). *Lives on the boundary*. New York: Penguin Books.

Schunk, D. H., (1996). Attributions and the development of self-regulatory competence. Paper presented at the Annual Conference of the American Education Research Association. (ERIC Document Reproduction Service No. ED 394 662)

Senecal, C., Koestner, R., & Vallerand, R. J. (1995). Self-regulation and academic procrastination. *The Journal of Social Psychology, 135*(5), 607–619.

*Shaughnessy, M. P. (1977). *Errors and expectations: A guide for the teacher of basic writing*. New York: Oxford University Press.

Tuckman, B. W. (1996). The relative effectiveness of incentive motivation and prescribed learning strategy in improving college students' course performance. *Journal of Experimental Education, 64*(3), 197–210.

Vygotsky, L. S. (1978). *Mind in society*. Cambridge, MA: Harvard University Press.

Warkentin, R. W., Griffin, B., & Bates, J. A. (1994). *The relationship between college students' study activities, content knowledge structure, academic self-efficacy and classroom achievement*. Paper presented at the annual conference of the American Educational Research Association, New Orleans, LA.

Wilhite, S. C. (1992). *Self-concept of academic ability, self-assessment of memory ability, academic aptitude, and study activities as predictors of college course achievement*. ED 350308.

Williams, J. E. (1996). *Promoting rural students' academic achievements: An examination of self-regulated learning strategies*. Paper presented at the annual meeting of the American Educational Research Association. New York, NY.

Wong, B. Y. L. (1985). Self-questioning instructional research: A review. *Review of Educational Research, 55*, 227–268.

Zwerling, L. S., & London, H. (Eds.). (1992). First generation students: Confronting the cultural issues. *New Directions for Community Colleges(80)*.

9

Preparing for
and Taking Tests

$\backsim\!\!\$\$\!\!\backsim$

Rona F. Flippo
Fitchburg State College

Marilyn J. Becker
David M. Wark
University of Minnesota

This chapter examines test taking at the college level. A review of the literature on test wiseness and test-taking skills, coaching for tests, and theories of and treatment for test anxiety is provided. A section on implications for practice contains suggestions on how instructors can integrate strategies of preparing for and taking tests into curriculum and how students can apply them. Finally, we include a brief summary of implications for future research.

TEST PREPARATION AND TEST PERFORMANCE

Achievement on tests is a critical component for attaining access to and successfully negotiating in advanced educational and occupational opportunities. Students must perform acceptably on tests to pass their courses and receive credit. Students expecting to receive financial aid must have appropriate grades and test scores to qualify. Admission to graduate school depends largely on test grades. Some occupations require tests to advance, or simply to remain employed in a current position. Many professionals must pass tests to qualify for certification or licensure in their fields. Considering all the ways test scores can affect lives, knowing the techniques of preparing for and taking tests can be very useful. That information, along with methods of teaching it, should be part of every reading and learning skills instructor's professional toolkit, and embedded into instructional activities across academic curriculums.

The research literature supports the idea that special instruction in preparing for and taking a test can improve performance and result in higher test scores within the college curriculum. Studies show positive effects among various populations for a variety of approaches. Marshall (1981) cited reports from 20 institutions of higher education. In this sample, 41% of the students were found to leave before the start of their second year, and 50% before completing graduation requirements. Some of these dropouts and transfers are, of course, due to financial, social, personal, and developmental concerns. However, the author cites studies showing that retention is improved when supportive services like instruction in learning and academic performance skills are made available to students. Other researchers have found similar results. Arroya (1981) showed that Chicano college students' test and class performance, as well as their study skills, improved when they were taught to use better study and test taking procedures through a self-monitoring and modeling approach. Evans (1977) produced the same type of positive results working with African American students using a combination of anxiety reduction and basic problem-solving methods. An intervention that included a combination of instruction in test-taking skills and participation in cooperative learning activities for nursing students (Frierson, 1991) improved students' classroom performance and standardized test performance.

Furthermore, the literature shows clearly that even major tests appear amenable to test practice and training. To name only a few, scores on the Scholastic Aptitude Test (SAT; Powers, 1993; Slack & Porter, 1980), the Graduate Record Examination (GRE; Evans, 1977; Swinton & Powers, 1983), and the National Board of Medical Examiners (NBME; Frierson, 1991; Scott, Palmisano, Cunningham, Cannon, & Brown, 1980) increased after use of a variety training approaches.

The literature covers many distinct topics under the broad categories of test preparation and test taking, including philosophical orientations, specific drills for coaching students to take certain tests, special skills such as reducing test anxiety, and test-wiseness strategies. This chapter reviews the research and application literature relevant to these areas for the postsecondary and college student. Some of the studies reviewed were conducted with younger student populations. We include those when findings or implications are useful to postsecondary and college students or to reading and learning skills specialists working with that population.

Instruction in test preparation and test taking can make a difference in some students' scores. The literature shows that students from different populations, preparing for tests that differentiate at both high and low levels of competence, may improve their scores using a number of training programs. This chapter explains and extends these results.

TEST WISENESS AND TEST-TAKING SKILLS

Test wiseness is a meaningful but often misunderstood concept of psychological measurement. In fact, the notion of test wiseness is often used as ammunition in the battle over the value of objective testing. The varied and vocal opponents of objective testing have claimed that high-scoring students may be second rate and superficial, performing well because they are merely clever or cynically test wise (Hoffman, 1962).

Other, more temperate scholars, analyzing the problems of test preparation and test taking, have suggested that lack of test wiseness simply may be a source of measurement error. Millman, Bishop, and Ebel (1965), who did early extensive work in the field, said that

> test wiseness is defined as a subject's capacity to utilize the characteristics and formats of the test and/or the test taking situation to receive a high score. Test wiseness is logically independent of the examinee's knowledge of the subject matter for which the items are supposedly measures. (p. 707)

Millman et al. and Sarnacki (1979) presented reviews of the concept and the taxonomy of test wiseness.

The concept of test wiseness was first put forth by Thorndike (1951) in regards to the effect that persistent and general characteristics of individuals may contribute to test scores and affect test reliability. Specifically, Thorndike (1951) claimed the following:

> performance on many tests is likely to be in some measure a function of the individual's ability to understand what he is supposed to do on the test. Particularly as the test situation is novel or the instructions complex, this factor is likely to enter in. At the same time, test score is likely to be in some measure a function of the extent to which the individual is at home with tests and has a certain amount of sagacity with regards to tricks of taking them. (p. 569)

In their discussion of the construct of test wiseness, Green and Stewart (1984) described test wiseness as a combination of learned and inherent abilities. They suggest that one's performance on a test is influenced by level of intellectual or cognitive abilities, as well as comprehending and responding to the tasks required by the test (i.e., test-taking skills). That students may differ in the dimension of test-taking skills appears supported by the following studies.

Case (1992) conducted a study on the relationship between scores on Part I and Part II examinations of the NBME given to measure skills and knowledge in the undergraduate medical education curriculum, and the American Board of Orthopaedic Surgery (ABOS) certification exam given at the end of residency. Results revealed statistically significant relationships between the Part I and Part II exams and the ABOS, despite the fact that the content of Part I is not directly linked to the knowledge and skills required in residency. The author interpreted these findings as suggesting that those who have done well on exams tend to continue to do well on similarly formatted exams, and that this is possibly due to good test-taking skills.

Consistency of performance on a specific type of test was also observed in a study by Bridgeman and Morgan (1996). They studied the relationship between scores on the essay and multiple-choice portions of advanced placement (AP) tests and compared student performance with scores obtained on similarly formatted exams. Results indicated that students in the high multiple-choice score/low essay test score group performed much better on other multiple-choice tests than the low multiple-choice score/high essay test score group and vice versa. Bridgeman and Morgan concluded that the different test formats were measuring different constructs. In both studies, the consistency in level of performance across testing experiences is notable. The high ability level of the subjects in these studies (e.g., residents in a competitive medical specialty and high achieving high school students) would appear to substantiate the existence of test-taking skills independent of general cognitive and intellectual abilities.

Contemporary formulations view test wiseness as a broad collection of skills and possibly traits that in combination with content knowledge promote optimal test performance. Test wiseness therein refers to the factors of cognitive skills, general test-taking skills and other personal attributes that contribute to exam scores independent of students' knowledge of the information being tested. How can that happen? Test-wise students develop test-taking strategies that they apply across tests. They know how to take advantage of clues left in questions by some test writers. They know that if they change their answers after some reflection, they generally improve their scores. They never leave questions blank when there is no penalty for guessing. They maintain good timing on exams so as to correctly answer the greatest number of questions in the allotted time. They plan learning and study activities that match the way in which they are asked to apply information on the test. They utilize reasoning and problem-solving skills in the context of the testing situation. They attend to all factors that influence test performance.

Some readers may question the necessity or propriety of teaching test wiseness. Should professionals committed to strengthening the skills of learning engage in such an endeavor? If, as Millman et al. (1965) suggested, lack of test wiseness is a source of measurement error, the answer seems to be yes. In fact, teaching all students to be test wise should increase test validity. If, as suggested by Green and Stewart (1984), test wiseness includes a combination of learned and inherent abilities, then it would be the obligation of educational institutions to provide instruction in test-taking skills. Scores would better reflect the underlying knowledge or skill being tested rather than sensitivity to irrelevant aspects of the test, or the incomplete or misapplication of knowledge. Should reading and learning skills professionals teach their colleagues how to write items that cannot be answered solely by test wiseness? Again, yes (see Haladyna & Downing, 1989 for guidelines on multiple-choice item writing). To the extent that items are focused, and all the alternatives are plausible, test validity will be increased. Therefore, it seems to be a good idea to teach students and instructors to be test wise.

Strategies of High-Scoring Students

Some researchers have attempted to determine the various strategies used by high-scoring test takers. Although Paul and Rosenkoetter (1980) found no significant relationship between completion time and test scores, they did find that better students generally finish examinations faster. There were exceptions, however. Some poorer students finished early, and some high scorers took extra time to contemplate answers. More recent studies have further supported the lack of a relationship between speed and performance on exams. Lester (1991) looked at student performance on undergraduate abnormal psychology multiple-choice exams and found no association between time spent on the exams and the scores obtained. Results of data analysis have also found no relationship between level of performance and time taken to complete statistics exams in a graduate level course (Onwuegbuzie, 1994). Higher scorers seemingly have two strategies: know the material well enough to go through the test very quickly; or go through the test slowly, checking, changing, and verifying each answer. Either strategy seems to be an effective approach.

In an effort to determine what test-taking strategies are used by A students compared with those used by C and F students, McClain (1983) asked volunteers taking a multiple-choice exam in an introductory psychology course to verbalize their test-taking procedures while taking the exam. She found that, unlike the C or F students, the A students consistently looked at all alternative answers and read the answers in the order in which they were presented in the test. They also anticipated answers to more questions than did the lower scoring students. In addition, they were more likely to analyze and eliminate incorrect alternatives to help determine the correct answer. The A students also skipped more questions they were unsure of (coming back to them later) than did the C and F students. On a later exam, some of the C and F students who reported using the strategies characteristic of the A students reported an improvement in their exam scores.

Kim and Goetz (1993) sought to determine effective exam-taking strategies by examining the types of marks made on the test sheets by students on multiple-choice exams in an undergraduate educational psychology course. Among the different categories identified in the study, the use of answer option elimination marks was found to be significantly related to students' test scores with increased test scores associated with greater frequency of marking of eliminated options. It was also noted that test markings increased as the question difficulty increased. The authors proposed that the markings on tests could serve to aid in facilitating retrieval of information from long-term memory, assist students in focusing on important information, and decrease information load; and they further concluded that training in the use of marking strategies might improve test scores.

Huck (1978) was interested in what effect the knowledge of an item's difficulty would have on students' strategy. His hypothesis was that students might read certain items more carefully if they were aware of how difficult those items had been for previous test takers. The study revealed that knowing the difficulty of an item had a significant and positive effect on test scores. It is not clear, however, how the students used that information to improve their scores.

Anticipated test difficulty in association with anticipated test format has also been studied in relation to performance on tests. Thiede (1996) researched the effect of anticipating recall versus recognition test items on level of exam performance. Results indicated that superior performance was associated with anticipating recall test items regardless of the actual item type used on the test. It was proposed that this might be related to increased encoding of associations and increased effort in preparing for a recall versus recognition test, in relation to perceptions that a recall test is more difficult than a recognition test.

A fascinating use of prior knowledge has come to light with reading tests. Chang (1979) found that a significant number of the undergraduate students he tested were able to correctly answer questions about passages on a standardized reading comprehension test without seeing the text. Some authors would say that the questions could be answered independently of the passages. Chang, on the other hand, attributed the students' success to test wiseness. Blanton and Wood (1984) designed a specific four-stage model to teach students what to look for when taking reading comprehension tests, making the assumption that students could be taught to use effective test-wiseness strategies for reading comprehension tests.

A similar investigation was undertaken by Powers and Leung (1995). They conducted a study to determine the extent to which verbal skills versus test wiseness or other such skills were being utilized to answer reading comprehension questions on the new SAT. Test takers were asked to answer sets of reading questions without the reading passages. Results indicated that students were able to attain a level of performance that exceeded chance level on the SAT reading questions. However, it was noted that the strategies for answering questions without the reading passages reflected use of verbal reasoning rather than test-wiseness skills. Specifically, students were observed to attend to consistencies within the question sets and to use this information to reconstruct the theme of the missing passage.

It appears that at least some test-taking strategies develop with age. Slakter, Koehler, and Hampton (1970) reported that fifth graders were able to recognize and ignore absurd options in test items. This is a fundamental strategy, one whose appearance demonstrates a developing sense of test wiseness. In the same study they looked at another basic strategy, eliminating two options that mean the same thing. Being able to recognize a similarity is developmentally and conceptually more advanced than recognizing an absurdity. Not surprisingly, these authors found that the similar option strategy did not appear until the eighth grade. In a study of strategies for taking essay tests, Cirino-Grena (1981) distributed a questionnaire. Higher scoring students reported using the following strategies: quoting books and articles, rephrasing arguments several times, rephrasing the questions, and including some irrelevant material in the answer. The most common strategy used by all students, however, was that of expressing opinions similar to those of the teacher. In relation to the use of marking on tests as a means of facilitating retrieval from long-term memory, metacognitive research has suggested that younger students would be less strategic in their use of test marking in comparison with older students (Flavell, 1985).

Recognizing Cues

Another proposed test-wiseness skill is the ability to make use of cues in the stems or the alternative answers by test writers (Millman et al., 1965). Some test constructors may, for example, write a stem and the correct answer, and generate two good foils. Stumped for a good third foil, such a teacher may take the easy way out by restating one of the false foils. But a test wise student spots the ruse and rejects both similar alternatives. Or perhaps the correct answer is the most complete, and hence the longest. These and other cues can take a variety of forms, and can be found in a variety of test types, including multiple-choice, true–false, matching, and fill-in-the-blank.

There is an interesting body of literature investigating the effects of using cues to select correct answers. An illustrative example is the work of Huntley and Plake (1981), who investigated cues provided by grammatical consistency or inconsistency between the stem and the set of alternatives. They focused on singular/plural agreement and vowel/consonant clues. A stem might contain a plural noun that could give a clue to the correct answer if any of the alternatives did not have agreement in number. A stem ending in "a" or "an" might also provide a clue to the correct choice depending on whether the alternatives began with vowels or consonants. The authors found that there was some cuing with these patterns and recommended that test makers write multiple-choice items to avoid grammatical aids.

Other cues have to do with the position or length of the correct answer. Inexperienced test writers have a tendency to hide the correct alternative in the B or C position of a multiple-choice alternative set, perhaps thinking that the correct choice will stand out in the A or D position and be too obvious. Jones and Kaufman (1975) looked at the position and length of alternatives on objective tests to determine their effects on responses. They found that the students involved in their research project were more likely to pick out a correct response because of its B or C position than because of its length in relation to the other choices. Both cues had an effect, however; apparently some students are alert for the possibility of such cues.

A study by Flynn and Anderson (1977) investigated four types of cues and their effects on students' scores on tests measuring mental ability and achievement. The four cues were (a) options that were opposites, so that if one were correct, the other would be incorrect (e.g., "the war started in 1812" versus "the war ended in 1812"), (b) longer correct options; (c) use of specific determiners; and (d) resemblance between the correct option and an aspect of the stem. The undergraduate subjects were given a pretest of test wiseness and classified as either test-wise or test-naive. The instruction was given for recognizing the four cues. The students showed no gains on the ability and achievement tests, although the students who were classified as test-wise did score higher than those classified as test-naive. Perhaps those students who were originally labeled test-wise used test-taking strategies other than the ones measured, or were brighter or better guessers. It is also possible that the target cues were not present in the ability and achievement tests. In any case, it seems that the more test-wise students were more effective in applying some strategies to various testing situations.

Two studies focused on technical wording as a cue. In one, Strang (1977) used familiar and unfamiliar choices that were either technically or nontechnically worded. He asked students, in a somewhat artificial situation, to guess on each item. He found that nontechnically worded options were chosen more often than technically worded items regardless of familiarity. In the second study, Strang (1980) used questions that required students either to recall or to interpret familiar content from their child growth and development course. The items contained different combinations of technically and nontechnically worded options. The students had more difficulty with recall items in which the incorrect option was technically worded. Strang suggested that this difficulty might spring from students' tendency to memorize technical terms when studying for multiple-choice tests. They would thus use technical words as cues to a correct choice.

Smith (1982) made a subtle contribution to the test wiseness cues research with the notion of convergence. He points out one of the principles of objective item construction; every distracter must be plausible. If it is not, it contributes nothing to the value of the item as measurement. Smith offers the following example of implausibility:

Who was the 17th president of the United States?

a. Andrew Johnson
b. 6 3/8
c. 1812
d. A Crazy Day for Sally

Clearly, foils need to be plausible if the item is to discriminate between students who know the content of the test domain and those who do not. However, the requirement that foils be plausibly related to the stem creates a problem. Many test writers generate a stem first, and then the correct answer. To build a set of plausible foils, they consider how the correct answer relates to the stem. To use Smith (1982) again, suppose Abraham Lincoln is the correct answer to a history question. Most likely, the question has something to do with either U.S. presidents or personalities from the Civil War era. So a plausible set of alternatives might include those two dimensions. Alternatively, it could include people from Illinois or men with beards. Using the first possibility, a set of alternatives might be:

a. Abraham Lincoln
b. Stephen Douglas
c. Robert E. Lee
d. James Monroe

Smith suggests that test-wise students look for the dimensions that underlie the alternatives. In this case, the dimensions are shown in Fig. 9.1.

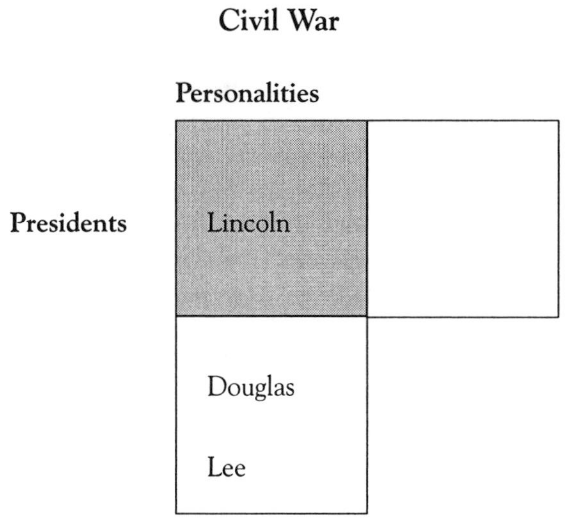

Civil War

FIG. 9.1. Dimensions that underlie alternatives for multiple-choice questions.

Lincoln is the only alternative on which the two dimensions converge.

Smith (1982) reported a number of experimental studies to test the use of the convergence cue. Leary and Smith (1981) gave graduate students in education some instruction in recognizing dimensions and selecting the convergence point. Then they gave students items from the abstract reasoning section of the Differential Aptitude Test, the verbal section of the SAT, and the Otis Quick Score Mental Ability Test. They asked the students to find correct answers without seeing the stems. Subjects scored significantly better than chance on all three tests. It appears that convergence can be a usable cue.

Next, Smith (1982) randomly divided a group of high school students and gave the experimental group 2 hours of instruction in finding the convergence point. The control group had 2 hours of general test-taking instruction. Both groups had previously taken the Preliminary Scholastic Aptitude Test (PSAT) and took the SAT after the experiment. The mean for the experiment group, adjusted for the PSAT covariate, was 39 points higher on the verbal subscale. Smith believes that convergence training is the explanation of the findings.

Test wiseness does seem to be due, in part, to sensitivity to certain cues in the items. Some of the cues are obvious to those who are familiar with the grammatical conventions of the language. The cue effect of familiar technical words is another example. Other cues, like position and length of the correct answer, seem to be the result of repeated exposure to the various forms of objective test items. The cues based on the logical relationships between alternatives are probably of a different sort, and may depend on the test takers' general intellectual ability or other characteristics. With that possibility in mind, it is interesting that studies have achieved positive results in teaching sophisticated cue use. Although it is hard to cleanly separate cues from strategy, it does seem that the cue approach to teaching test wiseness is more effective.

Changing Answers

There is a false but persistent notion in the test taking field that a student's first answer is likely to be correct. The implication is that one should stay with the first choice, because changing answers is likely to lead to a lower score. Contrary to this belief, research indicates that changing answers produces higher test scores (Edwards & Marshall, 1977; Geiger, 1990; Geiger, 1991; Lynch & Smith, 1975; McMorris & Leonard, 1976; Mueller & Schwedel, 1975; Schwarz, McMorris, & DeMers,1991; Smith, Coop, & Kinnard, 1979). These studies confirm earlier research findings that changing answers is, in fact, a mark of test wiseness. The research on this point is remarkably consistent.

To begin, it should be clear that answer changing is not a random event. Lynch and Smith (1975) found a significant correlation between the difficulty of an item and the number of students who changed the answer to that item. They suggested that other items on the test may have helped the students reconsider their answers for the more difficult items. It seems possible that changes produce higher scores because later items help students recall information they did not remember the first time through. Three studies have looked into the answer-changing patterns of males and females (Geiger, 1990; Mueller & Schwedel, 1975; Penfield & Mercer, 1980). None of the studies found a significant difference in score gains as a function of the gender of the test taker. For the most part, higher scoring students gained more points by changing answers than did their lower scoring colleagues (Geiger; Mueller & Schwedel; Penfield & Mercer). Only one study (Smith et al., 1979) found that the lower scoring group benefited more from their answer changes. In general, the higher scoring students made more changes (Lynch & Smith; Mueller & Schwedel; Penfield & Mercer).

McMorris and Leonard (1976) looked into the effect of anxiety on answer-changing behavior and found that low-anxiety students tended to change more answers, and to gain more from those changes, than did high-anxiety students. However, both groups did gain.

In writing about the answer-changing research, Wilson (1979) cited many of the same findings already discussed. She reiterated the main concern of most of those researchers; that students should know the true effects of answer changes (Edwards & Marshall, 1977; Lynch & Smith, 1975; Mueller & Schwedel, 1975; Smith et al., 1979). It seems that changing answers is a good test strategy when, after some reflection or a review of previous responses, the student thinks changing is a wise idea. In general, the low-anxiety, high-scoring students both make more changes and benefit more, in spite of contrary belief.

When looking specifically at accuracy of student perceptions of changing test answers, Geiger (1991) found that students had negative perceptions of answer changing and that they underestimated the benefits to their exam scores. In this study, students' introductory accounting tests were examined under high illumination for erasure marks associated with answer changing. Findings indicated that on average for every point lost due to changing answers on the multiple-choice exams, three points were gained. Furthermore, it was found that the majority of students (65%) underestimated the benefit of this strategy, whereas 26% correctly perceived the outcome of their behavior and 9% overestimated the outcome. Gender differences were noted, with men being more apt to perceive answer changing as beneficial. The author concluded that students should be made aware of the utility of this test-wise strategy, especially if answer alternatives not originally selected appear to be plausible.

As a means of gaining insight as to the reasons behind changing answers, Schwarz et al. (1991) conducted personal interviews with students in graduate level college courses. Six reasons for changing answers were identified. These included the following in order of frequency: rethought and conceptualized a better answer (26%), reread and understood the question better (19%), learned from a later item (8%), made clerical corrections (8%), remembered more information (7%), and used clues (6%). Although the majority of changes for each of the reasons was from wrong to right answer, the "remembered" was most beneficial, followed by "reread" and "clerical."

Retesting

A final area of research delves into the effects of simply repeating a test in the original or parallel form. The second score reflects a number of effects: regression to the mean, measurement error, and the increased information gained by study between tests. But part of the difference is due to a type of test wiseness. An instructor may give several tests during a course, and students may begin to see a pattern in the types of questions asked. Besides giving students some direction for future test preparation, this may help them develop a certain amount of test wiseness. Can the effects be generalized? The research on retesting starts with the premise that the actual taking of the test helps students develop certain strategies for taking similar tests at a later time. Some of the retesting research involves typical classroom exams. Other studies cover the effects of repeated testing on standardized measures of intelligence, personality, or job admission.

Studying classroom tests, Cates (1982) investigated whether retesting would improve mastery and retention in undergraduate courses. The study sample included 142 students from five different sections of educational psychology taught over a 3-year period. Of the 202 retests taken to improve an original score, 139 (or 68.8%) showed improved performance. The mean gains in tested performance ranged from 1.2% to 6.3%. The author notes that the students frequently took retests 2 to 4 weeks after the original test date, suggesting that distributing test practice may be an effective strategy in increasing knowledge of the subject material. However, the gains are rather modest.

Allowing that retesting can produce some gains, are the gains specific to the content of the retested items, or do they constitute a type of general test wiseness? Bondy (1978) found that reviewing specific questions from a multiple-choice test improved students' performance on a retest involving those specific items. However, the students who had reviewed those questions scored no better on reworded items than did students who had not reviewed the questions and answers. Similarly, simple retesting does not seem to be very effective if the item wording is changed.

A study done by Tips, Jongsma, and Pound (1978) indicates that retesting may improve test scores. The study was done with 55 college students who were enrolled in a noncredit reading improvement course. The purpose of the study was to record the effects of an instructional unit on taking an analogy test. The results showed that college students can improve analogy test performance with instruction on a test preparation strategy. However, the instruction may be no more effective than the practice effects of retesting.

For classroom testing, it seems, the results on simple testing and retesting are not very exciting. However, a study investigating the effects of repeated testing over the course of term has yielded more positive effects on performance outcomes. Zimmer and Hocevar (1994) examined the effects of distributed testing on achievement. Undergraduate students in a basic learning course for teachers were assigned to experimental and control groups. Ten-point achievement tests were given to the experimental group for 10 weeks. A large and statistically significant performance difference was noted on the 100-point cumulative final exam (which contained items parallel to those of the 10-point tests) when comparing the scores of the experimental (M_{exp} = 75.03) and control (M_{con} = 54.77) groups. The authors concluded that the use of paced tests has a positive effect on classroom performance. Although noting the differences in achievement, the precise factors underlying such differences were not determined, but may have included increased focus on distributed learning of course material (prompted by paced evaluations) and improved test wiseness.

What about the effect of simple retesting on more standardized tests? Various types of tests have been studied in the research. Catron and Thompson (1979) looked into gains on the Weschler Adult Intelligence Scale (WAIS). Using four test–retest intervals, they found that regardless of the time between the original test and the retest, the gains on the performance IQ section were greater than the gain on the verbal IQ section. The researchers believe that the experience of taking a test alters the results of any similar test taken afterward. One would not expect retesting to alter basic traits. Hess and Neville (1977)

studied retest effects on personality tests using the Personality Research Form. Their results led to the conclusion that what subjects learn or think about after seeing their test
results affects future scores on a personality test. Thus the intervening event, not the retesting, is what is powerful. Finally, Burke (1997) looked at the retest effects for scores on
aptitude tests administered to Royal Air Force applicants. Results showed that simply retesting produced statistically significant gains in test scores. Burke also found that the
size of the retest effect varied by the type of test, but that the retest gains were consistent
irrespective of amount of time between the initial and retest administrations.

But still the question remains: Can retesting affect scores on basic characteristics?
Wing (1980) did a study using a multiple abilities test battery in use nationwide since
1974 as an entrance criterion for federal professional and administrative occupations.
The major concern of the study was to see whether practice would aid test repeaters.
During the first 3 years, alternate forms of the test battery were administered on 17 occasions to 600,000 subjects, with a little less than 3% of these subjects taking the test battery two or more times. The findings are that score gains depended on age, gender, and
the number of previous testings. Older test takers averaged lower gains than younger test
takers. Wing also found a difference in subtest gains by gender. Compared with scores for
males, the average gains for females were higher in inductive reasoning, the same in verbal ability and deductive reasoning, and lower in judgment and numerical items. Applicants with lower initial scores repeated the test more often. Higher final scores were
recorded by those who repeated the battery the most times. It seems unlikely that scores
on these tests could be improved by study of the content. The improvement is probably
at least partly due to test wiseness gained from simple retesting.

In summary, it seems that retesting, without any explicit content tutoring, can
have positive effects on certain scores. However, the studies that show effects allow for
repeated retesting. Perhaps the gain is due in part to regression upward toward the mean,
and in part to a test-specific type of test wiseness.

Test Wiseness and Test-Taking Skills Instruction

There are some empirical findings on attempts to teach test-wiseness strategies. Flippo
and Borthwick (1982) taught test-wiseness strategies to their undergraduate education
students as part of a teacher training program. Each of their trainees later taught test
wiseness as part of their student teaching. At the completion of the treatment activities,
they gave each class of children a unit test they had developed. The results showed no
significant difference between experimental and control groups' performance.

Focusing on an older population, Bergman (1980) instructed junior college students in test wiseness. His treatment group of nonproficient readers was enrolled in a
reading and study skills improvement class. The control groups either practiced taking
tests or received no extra instruction or practice. Bergman found no significant difference in scores on multiple-choice and open-ended questions for those receiving instruction. It may be that the time devoted to test-wiseness instruction in each of these studies
was too short. Perhaps coaching over a longer period of time would have proved more
successful. Moreover, strategy effects may be too small to be measurable by tests with the
reliability typical of student teacher exams such as were used in the Flippo and
Borthwick (1982) study.

Wasson (1990) conducted a study to compare the effectiveness of a specialized workshop on test-taking and test-taking instruction embedded within a college survival skills course. Basing workshop content on the model of Hughes, Schumaker, Deschler, and Mercer (1988), results indicated that there was a significant difference in the scores of the Comparative Guidance and Placement Program (CGP) English placement exam workshop students when compared to the students receiving in class test-taking instruction. Results support the use of more intensive and specialized focus programming for test-taking skills for low-achieving college students.

Similar progress in academic achievement was observed in a study by Frierson (1991) that investigated the effects of test taking and learning team interventions on classroom performance of nursing students. The treatment conditions included a group with combined test-taking skills and learning team activities, a test-taking skills group and a comparison group. Learning team activities included regular cooperative review of course materials; test-taking skills activities consisted of instruction in general test taking and utilization of trial tests for practice and to provide for self-assessment. Results reflected significant differences in grade point average (GPA) at the end of the semester between the combined intervention group and the other groups, and between the test-taking and comparison groups. In addition, determination of effect sizes revealed that 89% of the participants in the test-taking and learning team group had GPAs that were higher than the comparison group mean GPA, and that 67% of the test-taking group participants had GPAs higher than the comparison group mean.

Many studies of other instruments support the idea that test preparation has a positive effect on the academic retention of various populations of postsecondary students. Arroyo (1981) stated that Chicano college students have a higher dropout rate than do Anglo-Americans at all levels and notes that one factor contributing to this rate is poor academic performance due to lack of learned skills or educational preparation. Arroyo tried to improve the test performance and increase the class participation of Chicano college students by teaching them productive studying skills in preparation for testing. Arroyo's coaching procedures were based on self-monitoring and self-reinforcement, along with shaping instructions and reinforcement from a Chicano program director. The results were impressive: students increased the time spent studying and improved in both test results and class performance.

In summary, the identification of test-taking strategies and methods to teach them continue to be areas needing further development. Good test takers possess a variety of strategies, at least some of which require a certain level of cognitive development. Although the idea of teaching improved test-taking strategies is intuitively acceptable, few researchers have reported success. Perhaps the techniques take a long time to learn or require more intensive instruction or learning. It is also possible that individual differences such as personality, anxiety level, and intelligence affect the application of test-wiseness skills in actual testing situations.

Conclusions

The literature on test wiseness and test-taking skills supports several conclusions. Some strategies have been identified for helping on essay and multiple-choice tests. Avoiding absurd options and rejecting options that mean the same thing are common strategies.

Probably one part of any strategy is recognizing the presence of certain cues in the test items, such as grammatical agreement, length, convergence, and technical wording. Students who are test-wise can recognize these cues and may implicitly use them when the situation allows it. Almost all students, regardless of level of anxiety and test wiseness, can improve their scores by changing answers as they work. And simple retesting, even without any formal review of content, has a small but positive impact on scores. Furthermore, instruction in test-taking skills is an educational imperative.

COACHING

Coaching is a controversial area in test preparation, partly because the term is poorly defined. Both Anastasi (1981) and Messick (1981) acknowledged that the word has no agreed on meaning in the measurement field and as suggested by Messick (1982), controversy over coaching has been fueled by the variety of definitions for this term. A coaching program can include any combination of interventions related to general test taking, test familiarization, drill and practice on sample test items, motivational encouragement, subject matter review, or cognitive skill development that are focused on optimizing test performance on a specified standardized exam. Special modules such as test anxiety reduction may also be included. The duration of a coaching program may be from 1 hour to 9 hours or more (Samson, 1985).

Because the operational definition of coaching is varied, it evokes a range of reactions and raises a variety of issues. This chapter uses a widely permissive definition and includes studies that involve any test preparation or test-taking technique in addition to formal instruction in the knowledge content of a test.

One of the issues raised by coaching is actually a problem of social policy. The argument is that students from economically disadvantaged schools or families cannot afford expensive coaching courses (Nairn, 1980). If effective methods of test preparation are not available to all, certain test takers would have an unfair advantage over others (Powers, 1993). Consequently, decisions based on the results of tests when some students have had coaching and some have not are inherently inequitable. The same argument is offered when the examinees are not uniformly told of the kinds of special preparation they should undertake (Messick, 1982). Anastasi (1988) stated that individuals who have deficient educational backgrounds are more likely to reap benefits from special coaching than those who have had "superior educational opportunities" and who are already prepared to do well on tests.

Another more technical debate focuses on the problem of *transfer*. What is transferred from the coaching to the test taking, and ultimately to the performance being assessed or predicted? Anastasi (1988) believed that the closer the resemblance between the test content and the coaching material is, the greater the improvement in test scores is. However, the more restricted the instruction is to specific test content, the less valid the score is in extending to criterion performance. Similarly, if skill development in test-taking "tricks" effects score improvement, then a question arises as to what degree test scores are indicative of academic abilities versus the ability to take tests (Powers, 1993). In essence, the argument is that coaching reduces the validity of the test.

A third issue is that of maximal student development. One thing to be considered is the cost associated with coaching programs in terms of the types of academic opportunities that are not being accessed as time, energy, and financial resources are committed to test-coaching courses (Powers, 1993). Another concern is associated with the value of the types of skills promoted by coaching. Green (1981) suggested that certain types of coaching should, in fact, become long-term teaching strategies. The notion is that comprehension and reasoning skills should be taught at the elementary and secondary levels and that school programs should integrate the development of thought with the development of knowledge. Schools also should prepare students in managing anxiety around test taking and other evaluative situations, and not simply familiarize them with test format and test-taking skills.

Note that the social policy, transfer of training, and student development arguments make a common assumption: coaching does have a real, observable effect. If not, there would be no reason to fear that many underprivileged students are disadvantaged by their inability to afford coaching classes. Similarly, if coaching were not associated with gains in certain important test scores, there would be no need to debate whether the gain signified an increase in some basic underlying aptitude or whether the schools should take the responsibility of coaching scholarship. These arguments do not settle the debate. In fact, they raise a basic question: How effective is coaching?

The Effects of Coaching

Consider the SAT. Anastasi (1988) reported that the College Board, concerned about ill-advised commercial coaching, has conducted well-controlled experiments and has also reviewed the results of others studies in this area. The samples included White and minority students from urban and rural areas and from public and private schools. The general conclusion was that intensive drill on test items similar to those on the SAT do not produce greater gains in test scores than those earned by students who retake the SAT after an additional year of regular high school instruction. However, some scholars conclude that coaching was effective if an intensive short program produced the same gain as a year's regular study.

Anastasi (1988) also noted that new item types are investigated for their susceptibility to coaching by major testing organizations (e.g., College Board, GRE Board). When test performance levels can be significantly raised by short-term instruction or drill on certain item types, these item types are not retained in the operational forms of the test. This would appear to thus circumvent attempts to effect score improvement solely through coaching on test-taking strategies for discrete item types.

In a comprehensive review and meta-analysis of 48 studies on the effectiveness of coaching for the SAT, Becker (1990) investigated the effect of coaching for studies that employed pre- and posttest comparisons, regardless of whether or not the studies incorporated the use of a comparison group. Becker also looked at whether or not coaching effects differed between the math and verbal sections of the SAT. It was found that longer coaching programs result in greater score increases than shorter programs, that the effects of coaching for the math section of the SAT (SAT–M) were greater than for the verbal section (SAT–V), and that coaching effects for more scientifically rigorous studies (e.g., those that control for factors such as regression, self-selection, motivational differences) are reduced in comparison to studies in which such factors are not controlled for (e.g., studies that merely compare score gains of coached students with national norms). After investigating studies that solely employed comparison groups, studies that could be ascertained to provide the most rigorous evaluations of coaching effects, Becker (1990) determined that "we must expect only modest gains from any coaching intervention" (p. 405), average gains of approximately 9 points for the SAT–V and 19 points for the SAT–M.

In reviewing more recent studies on the effects of SAT coaching, Powers (1993) concluded that coaching programs tend to have a small effect on SAT–V scores and a modest effect on SAT–M scores. Among these studies that controlled for growth, practice, and other factors common to coached and uncoached students, the median SAT–V and SAT–M score gains were found to be 3 points and 17 points, respectively.

Coffman (1980), writing from a perspective of 17 years of experience at the Educational Testing Service, recalled thousands of studies on the SAT and concludes that although it is difficult to differentiate teaching from coaching, "there is some evidence … that systematic instruction in problem-solving skills of the sorts represented by SAT items may improve not only test performance but also the underlying skills the test is designed to assess" (p. 11).

Swinton and Powers (1983) studied university students to see the effects of special preparation on GRE analytical scores and item types. They coached students by offering familiarization with the test. Their results showed that scores may improve with practice on items similar to those found on the test. The authors contend that if the techniques learned in coaching are retained, students may improve performance on the GRE and in graduate school.

Evans (1977) conducted another study dealing with the GRE, using a special course designed to aid Black and Chicano volunteer subjects in preparing for the exam. Students received four sessions focusing specifically on instruction in the basic mathematics required for the test, including strategies for dealing with the various types of questions found on the GRE. In addition, the course included a one-session discussion of the GRE and its uses that was designed to reduce anxiety. Students in the program showed a small but consistent increase in GRE Quantitative scores. The increase was found early in the program, and there was no evidence that the program's effectiveness varied by gender or by ethnic group.

Other studies that indicate positive results from coaching involve the NBME. The NBME is a standardized test of considerable importance. A passing grade on Part 1 is required for graduation from a majority of the medical schools in the United States. Weber and Hamer (1982) found that students in medical schools that offered or recommended a review course for Part 1 earned higher scores than students from schools that did not. The difference was slight but statistically significant. Scott et al. (1980), over a 3-year period, followed 55 second-year medical students who purchased a commercial test-coaching service. The students scored significantly higher on the exam than students who had not received coaching but who had comparable basic science GPAs. Although the participants did not think the commercial course offered a shortcut to passing the test, they saw the coaching as a well-organized, condensed review program that helped them focus on the most important concepts.

Another study related to NBME performance was conducted with ethnic minority medical students. It has been observed that the fail rate for first time minority student test takers on the NBME has been several times the percentage of nonminority students (Frierson, 1991). Frierson (1984) investigated the effectiveness of an intervention program for minority students that included instruction on effective test-taking strategies, practice trial exams, self-assessment based on trial exams and cooperative participation in learning teams on improving scores and pass rates. Analysis of the results revealed that mean exam scores and pass rate differences between minority students and nonminority students were not statistically significant. Also, the difference in pass rates between minority students from this and the previous year (without the intervention program) were statistically significant.

Similar to the NBME medical exam, the State Board Examination (SBE) for nurses has presented as a formidable challenge for ethnic minority students (Frierson, 1991). Two groups of senior nursing students at a predominantly Black college were provided learning teams intervention and instruction in test-taking skills (Frierson 1986, 1987). The difference between predicted and actual mean scores on the SBE were statistically significant for both intervention groups, and it was also found that significant differences occurred in mean GPAs for the study participants across the three groups (test-taking skills group, test-taking skills plus learning team group, and comparison group). There was a statistically significant difference in level of performance between the test-taking and learning team group and the other two groups, as well as between the test-taking and comparison groups.

Naugle and McGuire (1978) documented that Georgia Institute of Technology students who attended a workshop to prepare for the Georgia Regents' Competency Test achieved a 10% greater passing rate than a sample of students who did not attend the workshop. The workshop had a dual purpose: to increase motivation by pointing out that those who failed the test once and made no special preparation for the second time generally failed again and would be refused a diploma, and to teach the students how to apply writings skills on the exam. The coaching was designed, in part, to produce effects by appealing to individual pride and self-interest.

Two meta-analyses looked at the effect of coaching on achievement tests and on a variety of aptitude tests. Samson (1985) summarized 24 studies involving achievement test performance of elementary and secondary students. Bangert-Drowns, Kulik, and Kulik (1983) reviewed 25 studies, mostly of secondary and college students that looked at the effects of coaching for aptitude tests other than the SAT. Thirteen studies were common to the two papers. Both reports came to similar conclusions.

Samson (1985) found that across all types of treatments the average effect size of coaching was .33 (in other words, among all students involved in any type of treatment the average gain was $SD = .33$). Thus, the average coached student moved from the 50th percentile to the 63rd. Bangert-Downs et al. (1983) found similar results. Across all variables, the average effect size was $SD = .25$, representing a gain from the 50th to the 60th percentile. Both analyses concurred in the main finding that coaching is associated with significant gains in test scores.

Both research studies also found the same secondary relationships. The first is that length of treatment made an important difference in the effectiveness of a coaching program. In the Samson (1985) study, coaching raised the average score from the 50th to the 57th percentile after 1 to 2 hours, to the 64th percentile after 3 to 9 hours, and back to the 62nd percentile after more than 9 hours. In the Bangert-Drowns et al. (1983) summary, the increases were to the 61st percentile after 1 to 2 hours, the 59th percentile after 3 to 6 hours, and the 64th percentile after 7 or 8 hours. Apparently, a program of between 6 to 9 hours is most effective. The general effect of coaching seems to be slightly greater for the younger students in the Samson study. That makes some sense, because the older students already have learned how to take tests. But the results of both studies agree that coaching can be effective.

The other secondary effect was type of treatment. For Samson (1985), general test-taking skills such as following directions, making good use of time, and using answer sheets correctly make up the effective program content. Those skills would be appropriate for younger students who did not have much practice with objective testing formats. In the Bangert-Drowns et al. (1983) study, the effective treatments focused not on simple test-taking mechanics but on "intensive, concentrated 'cramming' on sample test questions." The greatest gain was found in a single program that included 15.3 hours of instruction in recognizing and using the psycholinguistic cue system in the flow of language (McPhail, 1977).

These two reports also had some consistent negative findings. Both meta-analyses showed that reducing test anxiety and increasing motivation did not significantly increase scores in these samples. Perhaps the results would have been different if the authors had been able to group subjects by level of anxiety, motivation for school, risk taking, or some other individual differences.

Conclusions

Although level of effects vary, coaching does seem to work. Studies of commercial and other coaching courses have implications for test-preparation programming sponsored by educational institutions. The courses should be consistent with the school's curriculum and should provide a framework for review of the basic material taught and instruction in the underlying cognitive skills being tested (i.e., problem-solving and reasoning skills). This type of review would be a learning and thinking experience rather than simply a crash course or cramming strategy to pass an exam. In addition to the content review, coaching should include familiarization with the test format and cover specific processes for recalling and applying knowledge and skills as dictated by types of items to be encountered. Anxiety reduction or motivation enhancement should be part of the curriculum if appropriate.

TEST ANXIETY

One of the major problems students face in taking tests is test anxiety. Test-anxious students often earn lower scores on classroom tests than their ability would predict. The highly anxious student may have done a creditable job of preparation, using all the appropriate study techniques. Up to the moment of the exam, the student may be able to summarize and report content and demonstrate other necessary skills. But in the actual test situation, when it counts, this student fails to perform. Also, a student may experience interference with learning as anticipatory anxiety around a future test promotes avoidance behavior and impedes concentration and follow through on early learning tasks. Regardless of the precise way in which test anxiety is manifested in the individual student, there is well-documented evidence (Seipp, 1991; Tobias, 1985; Zeidner, 1990) of an inverse relationship between test anxiety and academic performance.

The typical test-anxious student may show distress in one or more of the following ways: physiologically (excessive perspiration, muscular tension, accelerated heartbeat), intellectually (forgetting, incorrect response fixation), or emotionally (worry, self-degradation). It is not unusual for college students to experience anxiety around test situations (Naveh-Benjamin, 1991), and Gaudry and Spielberger (1971) suggested that as many as 20% of a given college sample may suffer from severe and debilitating test anxiety.

Test anxiety, as a scientific concept, is approximately 50 years old (Mandler & Sarason, 1952). In their initial investigations, Mandler and Sarason asked students about their feelings and performance while being evaluated. Questions covered increases in heart rate, perspiration, feelings of uneasiness, and worry. From the responses, the authors computed a score of testing-produced anxiety. They found that students who had high levels of anxiety worked slower and showed more overt signs of anxiety on a block design test that was presented as a measure of academic aptitude. After completing six trials, the students were randomly told they scored either very high, about average, or very low. They were then asked to complete another six trials.

Specific findings from the second trial were linked to level of test anxiety. On the second series, the high-anxiety students showed depressed scores, regardless of their previous performance. It seems that these students collapsed under the pressure of further evaluation. For the low-anxiety students, however, further testing led to an improved performance. They were energized and worked faster. The effect was particularly strong for those low-anxiety students who were told they had done very poorly on the earlier test.

To account for those effects, Mandler and Sarason (1952) hypothesized two mechanisms that produced the anxiety-related deficit. In the psychological language of the day, they talked of two learned drives—one for task performance and the other for anxiety. In an evaluation situation, both drives operate. The learned task drive, in part, brought on the same effect. But the anxiety drive also elicited task-interfering feelings of inadequacy, memory blocking, helplessness, and excessive questioning. In the high-anxiety student, these two drives conflict and produce lower scores.

All of these feelings and thoughts, positive and negative, presumably were learned in the past, as the student was growing up and being evaluated by parents and teachers. Later, in a college testing situation, all the old learning came back when stimulated by evaluation. The net effect, which was predicted and then validated by research, is that as the test becomes more important and negative evaluation becomes more damaging, learned anxiety drive becomes stronger and has more destructive effects. Highly anxious students may flunk because of their anxiety, not because they do not know the material.

Since the classic work by Mandler and Sarason (1952), the investigation of test anxiety has blossomed. Reviews and updates on test anxiety by Allen (1971), Allen, Elias, and Zlotlow (1980), Hagtvet and Johnsen (1992), Jones and Petruzzi (1995), Schwarzer, van der Ploeg, and Spielberger (1989), Tryon (1980), and Wildemouth (1977) attested to the theoretical and empirical growth of the field. A meta-analysis by Hembree (1988) covered 562 high-quality studies. A volume edited by Sarason (1980) detailed work on a variety of special fields including the development of test anxiety in children, the physiological base of test anxiety, a variety of intervention models, and the impact of test anxiety on math and on computer-based learning environments. Much of the research has been aimed at understanding the dynamics of test-anxiety treatment, reducing subjective discomfort, and improving academic performance. This section focuses specifically on those treatment techniques that have been shown to improve grades among college students.

Measurement and Theories

As a prelude to a survey of treatment techniques, we present a brief overview of the measures and theories of test anxiety. The first instrument for measuring test anxiety, the Test Anxiety Questionnaire (Mandler & Sarason, 1952), contained 42 questions. Participants were asked to record their responses to each item by placing a mark on a horizontal line. The more discomfort they felt, the further to the right they made their mark. To score an item, the experimenter measured the number of centimeters from the left edge of the line to the check—a very unwieldy procedure. A more usable instrument was the Test Anxiety Scale (Sarason, 1978), a 37-item instrument covering most of the same experiences but in a much more convenient true–false scoring format. An earlier 16-item true-false Test Anxiety Scale (Sarason & Ganzer, 1962) is an excellent instrument for screening a large class. Wark and Bennett (1981) normed the scale for high-, medium-, and low-achievement students. The Test-Anxiety Inventory (Spielberger, 1980) and Sarason's "Reactions to Tests" (1984) are other instruments that have been used extensively in the study and treatment of test anxiety.

Several significant trends have arisen in the development of test-anxiety measures. One such development grew out of the work of Liebert and Morris (1967). They hypothesized that test anxiety had two components: (a) physiological and emotional arousal, such as increases in heart rate, perspiration, and muscular tension (the common overt symptoms of anxiety); and (b) worried thoughts about the negative consequences of failure, about doing poorly, and about lack of skills (conscious, internal talk that interfered with competent performance). When they did a factor analysis of the Test Anxiety Questionnaire, Liebert and Morris did indeed find these two factors, which they distilled into a short 10-item test called the Worry-Emotionality Questionnaire (Morris & Liebert, 1970). The two factors have very different effects on test taking.

Emotionality, or excessive physiological arousal, may or may not be detrimental to student performance. Some level of arousal is absolutely necessary for a student to learn, retain, and perform. The optimal level of arousal for any given task depends on a person's history, physiology, and state of health. If emotionality goes beyond that optimal level, performance may begin to deteriorate. But emotionality is not a universally negative variable; and, as posited by Pekrun (1992), other emotions may be no less important to learning and performance than is anxiety. For example, positive emotions (e.g., enjoyment, hope, pride) appear necessary for the developing of intrinsic and ongoing motivation. Also, there may be negative emotions other than extreme anxiety (e.g., boredom, hopelessness) that may be detrimental to learning and achievement through reducing task motivation. For purpose of this writing, however, we focus on the emotional component of anxiety and its relationship to academic performance.

Worry, the other factor, is seen as always being detrimental to test performance. The high-anxiety student has internal cognitive responses that interfere with optimal test performance. Hollandsworth, Galazeski, Kirkland, Jones, and Van Norman (1979) cleverly documented the kinds of internal statements made during a test by high- and low-anxiety students. Calm people recall themselves saying things like "I was thinking this was pretty easy," "I was just thinking about the questions mostly," or "I always love doing things like these little designs." Their comments contrast strongly with those recalled by anxious students: "I decided how dumb I was;" or "My mother would say ... don't set bad examples because I'm watching you." These internal statements may reduce performance by interfering with task-relevant thoughts, and may also increase emotionality.

Another important theory about cognitive variables affecting test anxiety was put forward by Wine (1971), who noted the importance of how students direct their attention. According to her analysis, calm students pay most attention to test items. Anxious students, on the other hand, attend to their internal states, their physiological arousal, and especially their negative self-talk. In essence, high-anxiety students are focusing their attention internally rather than externally to the examination, they are more distracted from cognitive tasks of tests, by "worry" than are low-anxiety students (Sarason, 1988; Wine, 1982). Wine was able to reduce test-anxiety effects by showing students how to attend to the test, and not to their internal states.

The attentional processes of high-anxiety students have also been studied in relation to general level of distractibility during tests (Alting & Markham, 1993). It was found that under evaluative test conditions, high test-anxiety students were significantly more distractible to nonthreatening stimuli present in the test environment than were low test-anxiety students. The authors suggested that cognitive interference from "worry" may need to be supplemented by considering the role of other types of distracting stimuli for high test-anxious students.

We have only touched on the trends in test-anxiety measurement here, summarizing the points that have implications for practice. The literature in this field is both extensive and quite technical. Interested readers should consult Gaudry and Spielberger (1971), Hagtvet (1985), Krohne and Laux (1982), or Sarason (1980).

In summary, there are three general approaches to test anxiety. The physiological or behavioral approach stresses the disruptive effects of arousal and emotionality. Treatment is geared toward helping students relax and desensitizing them to their presumed fear of tests and evaluations. The second approach flows from the worry or cognitive component of test taking. Students are taught how to change the way they think and talk about themselves in a test situation. The third approach involves teaching test-anxious students to focus on the exam, to use good test-taking skills, and to ignore distracting internal and external stimuli.

Reducing Emotionality

The most common technique for reducing emotionality and physiological arousal is relaxation and desensitization (Wolpe, 1969). In varying numbers of sessions, students are first taught how to use deep muscle relaxation (Jacobson, 1938). In that relaxed state, they are asked to imagine themselves in increasingly difficult situations. Students might be asked to imagine themselves studying a week before the exam, and to hold that scene in mind until they are comfortable with it. Then they would be asked to imagine studying the night before the exam, and to get comfortable with that idea. Succeeding mental images would involve the morning of the exam, walking to the exam, receiving the test, and taking the exam. Desensitization can be more effective than simple relaxation or no treatment at all (Aponte & Aponte, 1971). The desensitization may be done in massive doses rather than spread out over several days (Dawly & Wenrich, 1973). Or the students may be exposed only to the most feared items in the hierarchy; for instance, "Imagine that you have just received your test booklet and you cannot recall the answer to a single question." The technique of asking a relaxed student to imagine the most anxiety-provoking situation is called *implosion* (Cornish & Dilley, 1973).

In general, simple relaxation, systematic desensitization, and implosion techniques have not been shown to be strikingly effective test-anxiety treatment approaches. In her review, Tryon (1980) stated that systematic desensitization and implosion resulted in significant academic improvement for participants relative to no-treatment controls in only 7 of 17 studies. Another review (Allen et al., 1980) showed improvement in 22% of the reviewed studies. In general, it is fair to say that systematic desensitization worked in about 30% of the recorded studies, and those studies tended to be methodologically flawed in that they often did not contain a credible placebo procedure to control for nonspecific treatment effects.

One theoretically important refinement in the emotionality control research has demonstrated a high percentage of grade improvements. Instead of leaving control with the therapist, students are given more responsibility. Subjects are taught specific techniques to adjust their own level of relaxation. They might practice saying the word *calm* and pairing it with a relaxed state. Then, in a test situation when they say the word *calm* to themselves, the cue helps them relax and reduce the effects of anxiety (Russell & Sippich, 1974). Subjects also have been taught to control their own desensitization with good results (Denny & Rupert, 1977). Giving subjects control over relaxation seems desirable. Tryon (1980) reported that four of the five studies in which subjects had conscious control over relaxation led to significant grade improvements (Deffenbacher, Mathis, & Michaels, 1979; Delprato & DeKraker, 1976).

Reducing Worry

The generally higher effectiveness of client-controlled desensitization leads naturally to a discussion of the research on cognitive interventions. These procedures, flowing from interpretations by Wine (1971), deal with the worry component of test anxiety. Hollandsworth et al. (1979) documented the kinds of things high-anxiety students say to themselves during a test situation. Cognitive therapy techniques were developed to counter those negative, worrisome thoughts. Cognitive therapy techniques go beyond desensitization. Clients are taught to use coping imagery in which they imagine themselves reducing their tension, solving their problems, and being successful. Note the difference between emotion-oriented and worry-oriented therapy. With desensitization for emotionality, the clients relax and imagine themselves being comfortable in progressively more difficult situations. The therapist is generally in charge, and the focus is on emotionality or the physical component of test anxiety. In a cognitive therapy approach for worry, clients imagine themselves actively taking steps in the test situation to reduce the negative effects of anxiety. They might imagine themselves mentally relaxing and becoming calm, and giving themselves successful instructions and positive self-thoughts. In a cognitive approach to alleviate test panic, students would see themselves start to check the time, skim over the entire test, skip difficult items, and recall material from a chapter that contains the answer to a question. In essence, clients are taught to imagine themselves going through a therapeutically effective checklist of activities.

The results of the earliest studies of cognitive therapy on test anxiety were very encouraging. Miechenbaum (1972) taught test anxious students to be acutely aware of their negative self-verbalization and instruction. He also modified the standard desensitization procedures so that instead of just imagining themselves relaxing, students were taught to give themselves support statements and instruction in relaxation. The students in Miechenbaum's cognitive modification group made significant gains in grades. Holroyd (1976) found essentially the same result. His cognitive therapy group received training to be more aware of their negative internal self-talk and to prompt themselves to react well in stressful situations.

In her review, Tryon (1980) found that of four cognitive intervention studies monitoring academic performance, two showed significant grade improvement from cognitive therapy work. In review of later test-anxiety studies, Lent (1984) looked for grade change effects as a result of cognitive therapy. Of seven methodologically acceptable studies using some sort of cognitive intervention, he found only two that showed improvement in GPA. Both of those studies (Decker & Russell, 1981; Kirkland & Hollandsworth, 1980) used a treatment that involved study skills training as well as cognitive therapy. In fact, in the Decker and Russell study, cognitive restructuring and anxiety reduction were less effective than study skills counseling in improving grades. It would appear that cognitive restructuring to attack the worry component is not a great deal more effective than the desensitization techniques used to attack emotionality when grade change is the target of interest. That leads to another possible area, the use of study skills training as a technique for attacking test anxiety.

Improving Study Skills

The approach of reducing test anxiety by improving study skills is associated with a learning deficit model of test anxiety. This model purports that students who are inadequately prepared for an exam get highly anxious due to the perceived threat inherent in the test situation and that poor study and test-taking skills account for the lowered levels of academic performance (Tobias, 1985). However, some researchers have reported findings that would contradict the hypothesis that deficient study and test-taking skills cause high test-anxiety. Benjamin, McKeachie, Lin, and Holinger (1981), and Culler and Holahan (1980) found that students with high levels of study skills can also experience debilitating test anxiety.

Combined Approaches

The treatment of test anxiety would appear to not be an either–or approach. Rather, the literature illustrates the effectiveness of a combination of treatments. Allen (1971), working with a group of anxious, high-achieving college students (mean pretreatment GPA, 3.5) found that the most effective treatment involved systematic desensitization combined with study skills training. The skills content was based on the classic Survey, Question, Read, Recite, Review (SQ3R) text study strategy (Robinson, 1946). In addition, students were taught behavioral techniques for monitoring time, charting rate, and giving self-reinforcement. The students in the combination group improved their course examination percentile by 24%.

Similar results were reported by Mitchell and Ng (1972). They found the greatest impact from combining techniques. Each of the nine sessions they offered the mixed treatment group covered relaxation, desensitization, and skills work. Mitchell, Hall, and Piatkowska (1975) found that a combination of study skills instruction and systematic desensitization was more effective than either study skills plus relaxation training or intensive study skills instruction alone. On a 2-year follow-up, 73% of the students given desensitization plus study skills training were still in college, whereas only 25% of the relaxation group were still enrolled.

In a test-anxiety study with undergraduate college students, Dendato and Diener (1986) included four treatment conditions: relaxation/cognitive therapy, study skills training, a combination of relaxation/cognitive therapy and study skills training, and no treatment. Results indicated that the one treatment condition that was effective in both reducing test anxiety and increasing academic performance was the combined relaxation/cognitive and study skills training treatment.

A final study to be cited is that reported by Dogariu and Becker (1991). Treatment of test anxiety in medical students was studied by comparing the three treatment conditions of systematic desensitization plus study skills training, cognitive treatment plus study skills training, and no treatment. Systematic desensitization focused on the emotionality component of test anxiety, whereas cognitive therapy addressed the worry component. Findings indicated that when combined with study skills training, both the systematic desensitization and cognitive therapy groups experienced decreased test anxiety. However, only the cognitive therapy plus study skills training produced increased academic performance. There was no change in the no treatment group.

Research has further refined and clarified the general conclusion that a combination of techniques is effective in the treatment of test anxiety. Brown and Nelson (1983) studied a sample high-anxiety college students, all of whom scored above the 67th percentile on the Test Anxiety Survey (Sarason, 1978). Part of the group consisted of low achievers (GPA less than 2.7) and part consisted of high achievers (GPA greater than 3.3). The two subgroups differed in important ways. The high achievers knew more about good study skills. In addition, they were better able to stop their own negative self-descriptions during an examination. In a sense, they could handle their anxiety. The low achievers, on the other hand, lacked both information on study skills and the ability to counter their negative thinking.

Naveh-Benjamin, McKeachie, and Lin (1987) also found two categories of test-anxious students. Both types had trouble recalling material for an exam, but one type had good study skills and the ability to encode and organize materials in a way that matched the lecturer's structure, whereas the other type had trouble with encoding.

Covington and Omelich (1987) also studied types of highly anxious students and the ways they studied. The authors investigated the presence of anxiety blockage on both easy test items calling for recognition and difficult items measuring the ability to make generalizations or inferences. They found that high-anxiety students who used good study habits suffered some interference, but only on difficult items. Using a path analytic technique to partition the causal determinants of blockage, they estimated that the causal effects on test performance due to anxiety (7.34%) were greater than the effects due to study skills (1.05%). (The main determinant of test performance was intellectual ability, at 91.6%.)

Thus, Brown and Nelson (1983), Covington and Omelich (1987), and Naveh-Benjamin et al. (1987) agreed that there are subcategories of high test-anxious students. Benjamin et al. (1991) proposed two specific types of test-anxious students. First are those students who have effective learning skills and content knowledge, but fail to utilize these capabilities in the test situation due to cognitive interference that results in problems in retrieving and applying their knowledge. Second are those high test-anxiety students who possess inadequate learning skills and habits.

What can be said about the use of study skills counseling as a way to reduce test anxiety? Clearly, a behavioral approach to study skills improvement is an important variable in reducing test anxiety and raising grades (Hembree, 1988). Tryon (1980) concluded that packages that include study skills plus some other kind of intervention always show better results than no-treatment control groups. Deciding what type of student needs which type of treatment is a worthwhile subject of research. Until such can be determined, it would appear that treatment approaches that include elements to address the "worry" or the emotionality components of test anxiety in combination with study skills training would be most efficacious in affecting decreases in test anxiety with accompanying increases in academic performance.

Other Treatment Techniques

Several other methods for reducing test anxiety have been investigated. For the most part, they do not flow directly from the three previously discussed approaches. Rather, they appear to have evolved from other areas of psychological research.

Working from a general anxiety theory stance, Bushnell (1978) investigated a novel approach to reducing test anxiety. If, he speculated, high-anxiety students are sensitive to any stimulation that increases concern for evaluation, why not try reducing such stimulation? He had high-anxiety students take mid-quarter exams either in a large lecture hall where they saw other students or in a language lab where they were screened off from one another. He found that grades were significantly higher in the lab for both high- and low-anxiety students. For the high-anxiety students, the difference was marked. He also found that among mildly anxious students, those who sat next to highly anxious students earned lower scores than those who did not, regardless of test setting. Clearly, this research raises some interesting questions. Is the positive effect of the lab setting due to a reduction of visual distraction, or to the novelty of taking a test in a special place? The fact that the marginally anxious students were affected by the presence of anxious students, even in the lab, suggests that more than just visual separation is responsible for the test score effects. Although all the questions have not been answered, the data certainly do suggest interesting ways to reduce the effects of test anxiety.

In another facet of this field, there is fascinating and consistent literature on the impact of allowing students to express their feelings about a test. McKeachie, Pollie, and Speisman (1955) presented tests with a special answer sheet that had space to comment about any item. The students who received sheets with a comment section earned higher scores than the students who used conventional answer sheets. Smith and Rockett (1958) replicated the study but extended the effect. They used three groups of students, one given standard answer sheets, one given sheets that allowed for comments, and one that contained the message, "Please comment on anything unusual about each question." They found that the three types of answer sheets were associated with successively better test scores by high-anxiety students, and successively worse scores by low-anxiety students. Why does an invitation to comment about a test reduce anxiety effects for anxious students? Perhaps because the moment or two taken to write out any feelings about the item reduces some of the worry about the test. Students may feel that they have explained their answers, so they can stop worrying. Perhaps they feel that with the explanation, graders will give them the benefit of the doubt. Unfortunately, for the low-anxiety students, the invitation to comment seemed to lower motivation and drive.

The use of hypnosis in reducing test anxiety and improving academic performance has yielded positive results in a number of studies (i.e., Boutin & Tosi, 1983; Sapp, 1991; Sapp, 1992; Stanton, 1993). Hypnosis can be considered a cognitively based treatment. It combines the varying elements of relaxation, suggestion, and imagery to produce more effective behaviors. For the test-anxious student, focus would be on promoting the development of coping skills to better handle the threat of the test situation. The report by Boutin and Tosi (1983) is significant in that it demonstrated a positive and significant impact by their Rational Stage Directed Hypnotherapy on measures of irrational cognitions, anxiety, and GPA. In the context of a quarter-long learning skills course, Wark (1996) demonstrated that alert self-hypnosis training was associated with improved grades. Moreover, the more hypnotizable students actually continued to improve their grades in the quarter after learning to use alert, eyes-open hypnosis for reading, listening, and test taking. Although test anxiety reduction was only an incidental part of the course, the results show that hypnosis may be an important intervention, especially for certain students. This treatment for test anxiety is often available in counseling centers and clinics staffed by professionals skilled in the application of hypnotherapy techniques. Learning skills instructors with advanced degrees in psychology, education, or social work may by eligible for training in hypnosis by the American Society of Clinical Hypnosis or the Society of Clinical and Experimental Hypnosis. Both organizations offer training, but only to participants with documented professional education.

Observational learning from a model student is an example of a social learning theory approach to test anxiety reduction. Horne and Matson (1977) had a group of high-anxiety students listen to a series of tapes purporting to be group sessions of test-anxious patients. Over the course of a 10-week treatment, students heard three tapes, in which the model students expressed progressively less concern about test panic. During the sessions in which no tapes were played, counselors verbally reinforced the subjects' nonanxious self-reports. Students in other groups were treated by desensitization, flooding (asking students to imagine test failure), or study skills counseling. Horne and Matson found that modeling, desensitization, and study skills training were more effective than flooding in producing grade improvements and reducing anxiety. On the other hand, McCordick, Kaplan, Finn, and Smith (1979), comparing modeling with cognitive treatment and study skills, found that no treatment in their study was effective in improving grades. As these researchers admit, "the ideal treatment for test anxiety is still elusive" (p. 420).

Conclusions

What can we conclude about test anxiety? The most restrictive position, best exemplified by Kirkland and Hollandsworth (1980), is that educators would be better off scrapping the concept entirely. They believe that as far as test performance and grades are concerned, inadequate performance simply indicates ineffective test taking. Their conclusions are based on studies conducted with simple anagram tasks. Training in academic test-taking skills did seem to be more effective than either relaxation to reduce emotionality or meditation to reduce worry. Although anagram tasks are good research tools, they are not real work learning tasks.

What about more realistic measures? When performance is measured in GPA change, the Kirkland and Hollandsworth (1980) study showed that meditation was just as effective as study skills instruction, although relaxation was not as effective. These findings, along with those of Boutin and Tosi (1983), Wark (1996), and other studies cited in this chapter, fit with the more liberal conclusion in the general literature that a range of treatment approaches have been found effective in producing improvement in grades.

The field of test anxiety continues to evolve and expand as new discoveries are made in the areas of human learning and performance. The conclusions are expected to change in time. But for now, the problem of test anxiety would seem to be best addressed in the classroom through teaching students better ways to study and take tests, and improved methods for exerting active self-control over their own processes of preparing for and taking exams (Wark & Flippo, 1991). Of course, instructors can make some environmental changes to reduce test-anxiety effects. Bushnell (1978), McKeachie et al. (1955), and Smith and Rockett (1958) pointed the way to techniques that deserve more consideration. Teachers who do their best to reduce tension, project hope and kindness, and model efficiency rather than panic are also exercising good preventive counseling. In addition, it appears essential to promote positive academic self-concepts. The real challenge is to find and provide interventions that assist students in reducing debilitating anxiety and that promote optimal learning and performance.

IMPLICATIONS FOR PRACTICE

We have reviewed three aspects of the process of preparing for and taking examinations. The construct of test-wiseness presents a complex situation. High-scoring students report using some strategies to good effect. A presumed mechanism accounts for at least part of the test wiseness effect: a student's sensitivity to the various cues to the correct answer left by unpracticed item writers. Test-wise students apparently use cues to gain an advantage. To some extent, then, the strategies take advantage of certain errors in item construction and measurement. In addition, the test-wise student, when taking an exam, seeks to use a large body of accepted techniques of time use, skipping, and so on.

Test-wise students also seem to take risks and make guesses. In addition, test-wise students may be applying broader conceptual and reasoning skills in the test situation. Both the sensitivity to cues and the test taking techniques appear to be teachable. It is not yet clear whether a teacher can impart the judgment or wisdom to know which strategy to apply in a given instance, or the willingness to use it.

Although there is significant variability in the level of effectiveness observed in studies of coaching effectiveness, positive results consistently have been obtained. Students of a wide range of abilities have been shown to profit from certain kinds of coaching programs. The consensus from measurement experts is that the more disadvantaged and deficient a student's background, the greater the impact of test coaching. Yet the data also suggest that high-achieving medical students as well as students who are educationally impoverished show positive effects from coaching.

Finally, we reviewed the status of test anxiety as an aspect of test preparation and test taking. Test anxiety has been identified and studied for more than 50 years. In that period, research on the evaluation and treatment of the test-anxious student has continued to move ahead. It is now possible to teach students how to avoid the personal effects of anxiety, and to teach instructors how to arrange testing to reduce the likelihood that anxiety will adversely affect test scores.

How might reading and learning skills professionals use the information presented here? Perhaps by incorporating it into work with an individual student, by creating a test preparation unit in a class, or by developing a systematic program that is open to a wide audience. In any case, the actual form of the program will depend on the nature of the students, the needs of the institution, and the resources available. What follows is a set of suggested components for any program. Some of the suggestions are strongly supported by research evidence. Others are based on our own teaching and clinical experience.

Study Skills

Most test preparation programs assume that students know how to study and, in fact, have done so. If there is any reason to think otherwise, the program must have a study skills component. The literature on study skills instruction and on specific techniques for reading and studying textbook material is summarized elsewhere in this volume. Without reiterating here, we can say that specific study skills seem appropriate for the process of test preparation. Preparation for an exam should include instruction in the following areas:

Time scheduling
    Setting personal priorities
    Setting aside time for review and practice

Learning and review activities
    Active learning
    Massed sessions for reading and integration
    Spaced time for learning new material and maintaining previously
      learned material
    Self-testing

Memory
> Imagery and association techniques
> Mnemonic systems
> Methods for constructing and utilizing memorization aids

Effects of stressors on test performance
> Sleep deprivation
> Psychoactive substances
> Cumulative stress
> Test anxiety

Content Review

The review of successful test preparation programs is consistent on one point. Good programs are not simple content cram courses. They must be planned as an integrated package of experiences. In most cases, the presentation team is an interdisciplinary one. A reading and learning skills specialist presents the learning skills material and the test-wiseness strategies. Depending on staff make up, either the learning skills specialist or a psychologist helps students learn techniques to reduce test anxiety. But there must also be a subject matter expert (SME) on the team.

The SME must be knowledgeable both in the content area of the test and in the techniques of teaching the subject. He or she must know where students typically have trouble. If it is with the conceptual aspect, the SME must be prepared to offer important ideas at a more basic level. If the problem is computational, there must be drill and guidance to make the applications clear. If the problems are perceptual, the SME must teach the necessary discrimination that a competent student should demonstrate. The learning skills specialist may be the expert in memory techniques or in planning spaced versus massed reviews or group study sessions to go over facts, but the SME has to limit and define those concepts and facts.

Test Practice and Test Taking

The collection of suggestions for taking exams is vast. This chapter has reviewed the impact and value of many of them. Which techniques to teach in a particular situation is a decision for the reading and learning skills specialist. However, the following categories do seem to be generally valuable:

Use of time
> Read all directions thoroughly
> Review the entire test before starting
> Answer the easy questions first
> Skip difficult items and go back to them
> Plan time for review at the end
> Change any answer if it seems appropriate to do so

Guessing
  If there is no penalty for wrong answers, guess
  If there is a penalty, if one or more alternatives can be eliminated, guess

Beyond these general rules, instructors can find a body of more or less validated strategies that apply to specific item types. There is , for example, a set of strategies for the various objective items in general, for multiple-choice items, for matching items, and for analogies (Flippo, 1988). A similar body of suggestions exists for approaching and answering essay questions. Some of the suggestions are conventional: write neatly (Marshall & Powers, 1969; Raygor & Wark, 1980); and avoid spelling, grammar, and punctuation errors, which can result in lower scores (Scannell & Marshall, 1966). Note, however, that within certain limits, the lower the legibility of an answer, the higher the grade (Chase, 1983). Other suggestions are more complex and involve training students in patterns of precise thinking and organization. This discussion is not the place for those details. However, some excellent sources on this topic are available. They should be consulted for management procedures (Flippo, 1984) and specific examples to illustrate techniques. The works by Boyd (1988); Ellis (1996); Ferrett (1997); Flippo (1988, in press); Jalongo, Twiest, and Gerlach (1996); Majors (1997); Raygor and Wark (1980); and Sherman and Wildman (1982) are all appropriate for postsecondary and college students.

Test Anxiety

What can we conclude about the most effective ways to reduce test anxiety and increase grades for college students? The research literature has some clear suggestions (see especially Hembree, 1988). A good program will include as many as possible of the following specific components:

1. Self-controlled systematic desensitization. Teach deep muscle relaxation, using the script in Wolpe (1969) or any of various commercial audiotapes. While they are relaxed, have students imagine themselves going through the steps of study, and finally going into the exam. Have the students tell themselves to be calm while imagining being in the exam room. Have them direct themselves through the test wiseness steps they know. Relaxation and desentization are important, but the major benefit probably comes from calm students giving themselves instructions.

2. Cognitive self-instruction training. Teach students to be aware of any negative internal self-talk and to counter it with positive, supportive self-talk. Have students practice a self-instructional script that contains instructions to use test-wiseness strategies, to focus on exam items, and to give gentle self-support.

3. Behavior self-control techniques. Have students select a specific place for study and write precise goals for time and number of pages to read or problems to solve. Keep a chart of the number of hours spent in study and the goals met. Contract for rewards to be taken only when the goals are met. The payoff may be tangible or verbal self-reinforcement.

4. Learning skills instruction. This intervention is important for students who are anxious and who lack good study skills. Teach the student to do a prestudy Survey, ask

Questions about the content, Read for the answers to the questions, Recite the answers from memory, and Review all the previous questions and answers (SQ3R). This widely accepted plan was developed by Robinson (1946); however, there are many acceptable variations to SQ3R. Always be cautious in teaching the Questions step, no matter what it is called. Students will learn the answers to their questions, even if they are wrong (Wark, 1965).

5. Test-wiseness instruction. Anxious students should be taught a checklist of steps to recall during a test (e.g., plan time, eliminate similar options, look for associations, look for specific determiners). But note that the literature gives no support for test-wiseness training as an isolated treatment. Instruction in test wiseness seems to work only when combined with other interventions.

Some institutions may be planning a structured program to combat test anxiety. The suggestions discussed earlier should enable study skills teachers with some background in psychology to set up an effective anxiety management program. For those readers who want more details, two articles in the literature review (Mitchell et al., 1975; Mitchell & Ng, 1972) give complete descriptions of their treatment groups. Wark, Bennett, Emerson, and Ottenheimer (1981) gave details of an effective treatment program for students who are anxious when doing study-type reading and get low scores on their reading comprehension. Learning skills professionals with training in hypnosis can consult Boutin and Tosi (1983), Wark (1996), or Wark (1998) for useful information and models.

Some teachers may want to screen a class to pick out the students who are at risk for test anxiety. Those students identified by the screening can be referred for group or individual attention. For such screening purposes, an appropriate instrument is the Anxiety Scale developed by Sarason and Ganzer (1962). Wark and Bennett (1981) recommended using a cutoff score of 11 or above as a sign of test anxiety. Either article can be consulted for a copy of the items, which may be used without permission.

Evaluating an individual for test anxiety is essentially a clinical activity. Test anxiety and study skills tests are helpful in this evaluation. Each gives some additional information that can lead to a diagnosis. Part of the process should be obtaining a history of school experiences and conducting a assessment to determine recent anxiety experiences related to test taking.

IMPLICATIONS FOR FUTURE RESEARCH

Suggestions for further research in test preparation and test taking were implicit in many of the sources reviewed for this article. From an informal summary across the sources, two specific areas of concern seem to emerge. One is best characterized as a broad educational focus. Anastasi (1981) noted that current research is focusing on the development of widely applicable intellectual skills, work habits, and problem-solving strategies. The types of programs developed from this research would provide education rather than coaching or short-term cramming to pass certain test items (Flippo & Borthwick, 1982). Cheek, Flippo, and Lindsey (1997) suggested that test-wiseness training should begin in the elementary grades.

In the same tradition, Coffman (1980) said there is some evidence that instruction in item-oriented problem solving may improve the underlying skills that a test is designed to assess. Further research could develop systematic methods to improve not only test performance by also latent skills. This research should provide information about the detailed nature of these deeper abilities, along with the conditions under which they may be expected to improve. One result of this research thrust could be tailored to teach significant thinking skills that go beyond the strategies of test preparation and test taking.

If this broad type of suggested research can be called molecular, the second trend in the literature is more atomic. The assumption is that instruction can be given to help students simply become more test wise. Rickards and August (1975) suggested that research is needed on better ways to teach such pretest or early learning strategies such as underlining, organizing, and notetaking. But what is the psychological basis for using these techniques? Weinstein (1980) and others looked to research to refine our understanding of the covert processes involved in using cognitive strategies for learning and retention. Bondy (1978) suggests that further research be directed toward manipulating the variables within review sessions that are beneficial to students and efficient for instructors.

The results of the molecular and the atomic approach to test research is similar: the difference is in the hypotheses and methods used. If continued research can provide better strategies for test preparation, perhaps some of the negative aspects of testing can be reduced. More important, test-wiseness research may lead to new and important methods of teaching and learning. Tests will always be a fact of life for anyone moving up the educational ladder. But it is interesting to consider how learning might change if much of the negative aspect of testing were to be removed.

REFERENCES AND SUGGESTED READINGS

Allen, G. J. (1971). Effectiveness of study counseling and desensitization in alleviating test anxiety in college students. *Journal of Abnormal Psychology, 77*, 282–289.

Allen, G. J., Elias, M. J., & Zlotlow, S. F. (1980). Behavioral interventions for alleviating test anxiety: A methodological overview of current therapeutic practices. In I. G. Sarason (Ed.), *Test anxiety: Theory, research, and application* (pp. 155–186). Hillsdale, NJ: Lawrence Erlbaum Associates.

Alting, T., & Markham, R. (1993). Test anxiety and distractibility. *Journal of Research in Personality, 27*, 134–137.

Anastasi, A. (1981). Diverse effects of training on tests of academic intelligence. In W. B. Schrader (Ed.), *New directions for testing and measurement* (pp. 5–20). San Francisco: Jossey-Bass.

Anastasi, A. (1988). *Psychological testing.* New York: Macmillan.

Aponte, J. F., & Aponte, C. F. (1971). Group preprogrammed systematic desensitization without the simultaneous presentation of aversive scenes with relaxation training. *Behaviors Research and Therapy, 9*, 337–346.

Arroya, S. G. (1981). Effects of a multifaceted study skills program on class performance of Chicano college students. *Hispanic Journal of Behavior Science, 3*(2), 161–175.

Bangert-Drowns, R. L., Kulik, J. K., & Kulik, C. C. (1983). Effects of coaching programs on achievement test performance. *Review of Educational Research, 53,* 571–585.

Becker, B. J. (1990). Coaching for the Scholastic Aptitude Test: Further synthesis and appraisal. *Review of Educational Research, 60,* 373–417.

Benjamin, M., McKeachie, W. J., Lin, Y. G., & Holinger, D. P. (1981). Test anxiety: Deficits in information processing. *Journal of Educational Psychology, 73,* 816–824.

Bergman, I. (1980, January). *The effects of providing test-taking instruction for various types of examinations to a selected sample of junior college students.* (ED 180-566)

Blanton, W. E., & Wood, K. D. (1984). Direct instructions in reading comprehension test-taking skills. *Reading World, 24,* 10–19.

Bondy, A. S. (1978). Effects of reviewing multiple-choice tests on specific versus general learning. *Teaching of Psychology, 5*(3), 144–146.

Boutin, G. E., & Tosi, D. (1983). Modification of irrational ideas and test anxiety through Rational Stage Directed Hypnotherapy [RSDH]. *Journal of Clinical Psychology, 39*(3), 382–391.

*Boyd, R. T. C. (1988). *Improving your test-taking skills.* Washington, DC: American Institutes for Research.

Bridgeman, B., & Morgan R. (1996). Success in college for students with discrepancies between performance on multiple-choice and essay tests. *Journal of Educational Psychology, 88*(2), 333–340.

Brown, S., & Nelson, T. L. (1983). Beyond the uniformity myth: A comparison of academically successful and unsuccessful test-anxious students. *Journal of Counseling Psychology, 30*(3), 367–374.

Burke, E. F. (1997). A short note on the persistence of retest effects on aptitude scores. *Journal of Occupational and Organizational Psychology, 70,* 295–301.

Bushnell, D. D. (1978, March). *Altering test environments for reducing test anxiety and for improving academic performance.* (ED 161 946)

Case, S. (1992). *Validity of NBME Part I and Part II for the selection of residents: The case of orthopaedic surgery.* (ED344 894)

Cates, W. M. (1982). The efficacy of retesting in relation to improved test performance of college undergraduates. *Journal of Educational Research, 75*(4), 230–236.

Catron, D., & Thompson, C. (1979). Test–retest gains in WAIS after four retest intervals. *Journal of Clinical Psychology, 8*(3), 174–175.

Chang, T. (1979). Test wiseness and passage-dependency in standardized reading comprehension test items. *Dissertation Abstracts International, 39*(4–12), 7–8.

Chase, C. I. (1983). Essay test scores and reading difficulty. *Journal of Educational Measurement, 20*(3), 293–297.

Cheek, E. H., Flippo, R. F., & Lindsey, J. D. (1997). *Reading for success in elementary schools.* Boston: McGraw-Hill.

Cirino-Grena, G. (1981). Strategies in answering essay tests. *Teaching of Psychology, 8*(1), 53–54.

Coffman, W. E. (1980). The Scholastic Aptitude Test: A historical perspective. *College Board Review, 117,* A8–All.

Cornish, R. D., & Dilley, J. S. (1973). Comparison of three methods of reducing test anxiety: Systematic desensitization, implosive therapy, and study counseling. *Journal of Counseling Psychology, 20,* 499–503.

Covington, M. V., & Omelich, C. L. (1987). I knew it cold before the exam: A test of the anxiety-blockage hypothesis. *Journal of Educational Psychology, 79*(4), 393–400.

Culler, R. E., & Holahan, C. J. (1980). Test anxiety and academic performance: The effects of study-related behaviors. *Journal of Educational Psychology, 72,* 16–20.

Dawley, H. H., & Wenrich, W. W. (1973). Massed groups desensitization in reduction of test anxiety. *Psychological Reports, 33,* 359–363.

Decker, T. W., & Russell, R. K. (1981). Comparison of cue-controlled relaxation and cognitive restructuring versus study skills counseling in treatment of test-anxious college underachievers. *Psychological Reports, 49,* 459–469.

Deffenbacher, J. L., Mathis, J., & Michaels, A. C. (1979). Two self-control procedures in the reduction of targeted and nontargeted anxieties. *Journal of Counseling Psychology, 26,* 120–127.

Delprato, D. J., & DeKraker, T. (1976). Metronome-conditioned hypnotic-relaxation in the treatment of test anxiety. *Behavior Therapy, 7,* 379–381.

Dendato, K. M., & Diener, D. (1986). Effectiveness of cognitive/relaxation therapy and study-skills training in reducing self-reported anxiety and improving the academic performance of test-anxious students. *Journal of Counseling Psychology, 33*(2), 131–135.

Denny, D. R., & Rupert, P. A. (1977). Desensitization and self-control in the treatment of test anxiety. *Journal of Counseling Psychology, 45,* 272–280.

Dogariu, J. G., & Becker, M. J. (1991, November). *A comparison of two multicomponent treatment packages in the treatment of test anxiety.* Paper presented at the 102nd annual meeting of the Association of American Medical Colleges, Washington, DC.

Edwards, K. A., & Marshall, C. (1977). First impressions on tests: Some new findings. *Teaching of Psychology, 4*(4), 193–195.

*Ellis, D. B. (1996). *Becoming a master student* (8th ed.). Rapid City, SD: College Survival.

Evans, F. R. (1977, September). *The GRE-Q coaching/instruction study.* (ED 179 859)

*Ferrett, S. K. (1997). *Peak performance: Success in college & beyond.* New York: Glencoe.

Flavell, J. H. (1985). *Cognitive development.* Englewood Cliffs, NJ: Prentice-Hall.

Flippo, R. F. (1984). A test bank for your secondary/college reading lab. *Journal of Reading, 27*(8), 732–733.

*Flippo, R. F. (1988). *TestWise: Strategies for success in taking tests.* Torrance, CA: Fearon Teacher Aids/Frank Schaffer Publications.

*Flippo, R. F. (in press). *TestWise: Strategies for success in taking tests* (2nd ed.). Torrance, CA: Good Apple/Frank Schaffer Publications.

*Flippo, R. F., & Borthwick, P. (1982). Should testwiseness curriculum be a part of undergraduate teacher education? In G. H. McNinch (Ed.), *Reading in the disciplines* (pp. 117–120), Athens, GA: American Reading Forum.

Flynn, J., & Anderson, B. (1977, Summer). The effects of test item cue sensitivity on IQ and achievement test performance. *Educational Research Quarterly, 2*(2), 32–39.

Frierson, H. T. (1984). Impact of an intervention program in minority medical students' National Board Part I performance. *Journal of the National Medical Association, 76,* 1185–1190.

Frierson, H. T. (1986). Two intervention methods: Effects on groups of predominantly black nursing students' board scores. *Journal of Research and Development in Education, 19*(3), 18–23.

Frierson, H. T. (1987). Combining test-taking intervention with course remediation: Effects on National Board subtest performance. *Journal of the National Medical Association, 79*, 161–165.

Frierson, H. T. (1991). Intervention can make a difference: The impact on standardized tests and classroom performance. In W. R. Allen, E. G. Epps, & N. Z. Haniff (Eds.), *College in black and white: African American students in predominantly white and historically black public universities* (pp. 225–238). Albany: State University of New York Press.

*Gaudry, E., & Spielberger, C. D. (1971). *Anxiety and educational achievement.* Sidney, Australia: Wiley.

Geiger, M. A. (1990). Correlates of net gain from changing multiple-choice answers: Replication and extension. *Psychological Reports, 67*, 719–722.

Geiger, M. A. (1991). Changing multiple-choice answers: Do students accurately perceive their performance? *Journal of Experimental Education, 59*(3), 250–257.

Green, D. S., & Stewart, O. (1984). Test wiseness: The concept has no clothes. *College Student Journal, 18*(4), 416–424.

*Hagtvet, K. A. (1985). *The construct of test anxiety: Conceptual and methodological issues.* Bergen, Norway: University of Bergen.

Hagtvet, K. A., & Johnsen, T. B. (1992). *Advances in test anxiety research: Vol. 7.* Amsterdam/Lisse: Swets & Zeitlinger.

Haladyna, T. M., & Downing, S. M. (1989). A taxonomy of multiple-choice item-writing rules. *Applied Measurement in Education, 2*(1), 37–50.

*Hembree, R. (1988). Correlates, causes, effects, and treatment of test anxiety. *Review of Educational Research, 58*(1), 47–77.

Hess, A., & Neville, D. (1977). Test wiseness: Some evidence for the effect of personality testing on subsequent test results. *Journal of Personality Assessment, 41*(2), 170–177.

Hoffman, B. (1962). *The tyranny of testing.* New York: Collier.

Hollandsworth, J. G., Galazeski, R. C., Kirkland, K., Jones, G. E., & Van Norman, L. R. (1979). An analysis of the nature and effects of test anxiety: Cognitive, behavior, and physiological components. *Cognitive Therapy and Research, 3*(2), 165–180.

Holroyd, K. A. (1976). Cognition and desensitization in group treatment of test anxiety. *Journal of Consulting and Clinical Psychology, 44*, 991–1001.

Horne, A. M., & Matson, J. L. (1977). A comparison of modeling, desensitization, flooding, study skills, and control groups for reducing test anxiety. *Behavior Therapy, 8*, 1–8.

Huck, S. (1978). Test performance under the condition of known item difficulty. *Journal of Educational Measurement, 15*(1), 53–58.

Hughes, C. A., Schumaker, J. B., Deschler, D. D., & Mercer, C. D. (1988). *The test-taking strategy.* Lawrence, KS: Excellent Enterprises.

Huntley, R., & Plake, B. (1981, April). *An investigation of study sensitivity to cues in a grammatically consistent stem and set of alternatives.* (ED 218310)

Jacobson, E. (1938). *Progressive relaxation.* Chicago, IL: University of Chicago Press.

*Jalongo, M. R., Twiest, M. M., & Gerlach, G. J. (1996). *The college learner: How to survive and thrive in an academic environment.* Columbus, OH: Merrill.

Jones, L., & Petruzzi, D. C. (1995). Test anxiety: A review of theory and current treatment. *Journal of College Student Psychotherapy, 10*(1), 3–15.

Jones, P., & Kaufman, G. (1975). The differential formation of response sets by specific determiners. *Educational and Psychological Measurement, 35*(4), 821–833.

Kim, Y. H., & Goetz, E. T. (1993). Strategic processing of test questions: The test marking responses of college students. *Learning and Individual Differences, 5*(3), 211–218.

Kirkland, K., & Hollandsworth, J. G., Jr. (1980). Effective test taking: Skills-acquisition versus anxiety-reduction techniques. *Journal of Consulting and Clinical Psychology, 48,* 431–439.

*Krohne, H. W., & Laux, L. (1982). *Achievement, stress and anxiety.* London: McGraw-Hill.

Leary, L., & Smith, J. K. (1981, February). *The susceptibility of standardized tests to the convergence strategy of test-wiseness.* Paper presented at the annual meeting of the Eastern Educational Research Association, Philadelphia.

Lent, R. (1984). *The treatment of test anxiety: An updated review.* Unpublished research, University Counseling Services, Minneapolis, MN.

Lester, D. (1991). Speed and performance on college course examinations. *Perceptual and Motor Skills, 73,* 1090.

Liebert, R. M., & Morris, L. W. (1967). Cognitive and emotional components of test anxiety: A distinction and some initial data. *Psychological Reports, 20,* 975–978.

*Loulou, D. (1997). *How to study for and take college tests.* (Ed 404 378)

Lynch, D., & Smith, B. (1975). Item response changes: Effects on test scores. *Measurement and Evaluation in Guidance, 7*(4), 220–224.

*Majors, R. E. (1997). *Is this going to be on the test?* Upper Saddle River, NJ: Gorsuch Scarisbrick Publishers.

Mandler, G., & Sarason, S. B. (1952). A study of anxiety of learning. *Journal of Abnormal and Social Psychology, 47,* 166–173.

Marshall, J. C., & Powers, J. M. (1969). Writing neatness, composition errors, and essay grades. *Journal of Educational Measurement, 6,* 97–101.

Marshall, J. S. (1981, June). *A model for improving the retention and academic achievement of nontraditional students at Livingston College, Rutgers University.* (ED 203 831)

McClain, L. (1983). Behavior during examinations: A comparison of A, C, and F students. *Teaching of Psychology, 10*(2), 69–71.

McCordick, S. M., Kaplan, R. M., Finn, M. E., & Smith, S. H. (1979). Cognitive behavior modification and modeling for test anxiety. *Journal of Consulting and Clinical Psychology, 47*(2), 419–420.

McKeachie, W. J., Pollie, D., & Speisman, J. (1955). Relieving anxiety in classroom examination. *Journal of Abnormal and Social Psychology, 51,* 93–98.

McMorris, R., & Leonard, G. (1976, April). *Item response changes and cognitive style.* (ED 129 918)

McPhail, I. P. (1977). A psycholinguistic approach to training urban high school students in test taking strategies. *Dissertation Abstracts International, 37,* 5667A.

Messick, S. (1981). The controversy over coaching: Issues of effectiveness and equity. In W. B. Schrader (Ed.). *New directions for testing and measurement* (pp. 21–53). San Francisco: Jossey-Bass.

Messick, S. (1982). Issues of effectiveness and equity in coaching controversy: Implications for educational and testing practice. *Educational Psychologist, 17,* 67–91.

Miechenbaum, D. H. (1972). Cognitive modification of test-anxious college students. *Journal of Counseling and Clinical Psychology, 39,* 370–380.

Millman, J. C., Bishop, C. H., & Ebel, R. (1965). An analysis of test wiseness. *Educational and Psychological Measurement, 25,* 707–727.

*Mitchell, K. R., Hall, R. F., & Piatkowski, O. E. (1975). A program for the treatment of failing college students. *Behavior Therapy, 6,* 324–336.

*Mitchell, K. R., & Ng, K. T. (1972). Effects of group counseling and behavior therapy on the academic achievement of test-anxious students. *Journal of Counseling Psychology, 19,* 491–497.

Morris, L. W., & Liebert, R. M. (1970). Relationship of cognitive and emotional components of test anxiety to physiological arousal and academic performance. *Journal of Consulting and Clinical Psychology, 35,* 332–337.

Mueller, D., & Schwedel, A. (1975, Winter). Some correlates of net gain resulting from answer changing on objective achievement test items. *Journal of Educational Measurement, 12*(4), 251–254.

Nairn, A. (1980). *The reign of ETS: The corporation that makes up minds.* Washington, DC: Learning Research Project.

Naugle, H., & McGuire, P. (1978). *The preparatory workshop: A partial solution to an English compulsory exam failure rate.* (ED 163 489)

Naveh-Benjamin, M. (1991). A comparison of training programs intended for different types of test-anxious students: Further support for an information-processing model. *Journal of Educational Psychology, 83,* 134–139.

Naveh-Benjamin, M., McKeachie, W., & Lin, Y. (1987). Two types of test anxious students: Support for an information processing model. *Journal of Educational Psychology, 79*(2), 131–136.

Onwuegbuzie, A. J. (1994). Examination-taking strategies used by college students in statistics courses. *College Student Journal, 28*(2), 163–174.

Paul, C., & Rosenkoetter, J. (1980). Relationship between completion time and test score. *Southern Journal of Educational Research, 12*(2), 151–157.

Pekrun, R. (1992). The impact of emotions on learning and achievement: Towards a theory of cognitive/motivational mediators. *Applied Psychology: An International Review, 41*(4), 359–376.

Penfield, D., & Mercer, M. (1980). Answer changing and statistics. *Educational Research Quarterly, 5*(5), 50–57.

Powers, D. E. (1993). Coaching for the SAT: A summary of the summaries and an update. *Educational Measurement: Issues and Practice, 12*(2), 24–30, 39.

Powers, D. E., & Leung, S. W. (1995). Answering the new SAT reading comprehension questions without the passages. *Journal of Educational Measurement, 32*(2), 105–129.

*Raygor, A. L., & Wark, D. M. (1980). *Systems for study* (2nd ed.). New York: McGraw-Hill.

Rickards, J. P., & August, G. J. (1975). Generative underlining strategies in prose recall. *Journal of Educational Psychology, 76*(8), 860–865.

Robinson, F. P. (1946). *Effective study.* New York: Harper & Row.

Russell, R. K., & Sippich, J. F. (1974). Treatment of test anxiety by cue controlled relaxation. *Behavior Therapy, 5,* 673–676.

Samson, G. E. (1985). Effects of training in test-taking skills on achievement test performance. *Journal of Educational Research, 78,* 261–266.

Sapp, M. (1991). Hypnotherapy and test anxiety: Two cognitive-behavioral constructs. *The Australian Journal of Clinical Hypnotherapy and Hypnosis, 12*(1), 25–32.

Sapp, M. (1992). The effects of hypnosis in reducing test anxiety and improving academic achievement in college students. *The International Journal of Professional Hypnosis, 6*(1), 20–22.

Sarason, I. (1978). The test anxiety scale: Concept and research. In C. D. Spielberger & I. G. Sarason (Eds.), *Stress and anxiety* (Vol. 5, pp. 193–216), Washington, DC: Hemisphere.

*Sarason, I. (Ed.). (1980). *Test anxiety: Theory, research, and applications.* Hillsdale, NJ: Lawrence Erlbaum Associates.

Sarason, I. G. (1984). Stress, anxiety, and cognitive interference: Reactions to Tests. *Journal of Personality and Social Psychology, 46,* 929–938.

Sarason, I. G. (1988). Anxiety, self-preoccupation and attention. *Anxiety Research, 1,* 3–8.

*Sarason, I. G., & Ganzer, V. J. (1962). Anxiety, reinforcement, and experimental instruction in a free verbal situation. *Journal of Abnormal and Social Psychology, 65,* 300–307.

Sarnacki, R. (1979). An examination of test wiseness in the cognitive test domain. *Review of Educational Research, 49*(2), 252–279.

Scannell, D. P., & Marshall, J. C. (1966). The effect of selected composition errors on grades assigned to essay examinations. *American Educational Research Journal, 3,* 125–130.

Schwarz, S. P., McMorris, R. F., & DeMers, L. P. (1991), Reasons for changing answers: An evaluation using personal interviews. *Journal of Educational Measurement, 28*(2), 163–171.

Schwarzer, R., van der Ploeg, H. M., & Spielberger, C. D. (1989). *Advances in test anxiety research: Volume 6.* Berwyn, PA: Swets North America.

Scott, C., Palmisano, P., Cunningham, R., Cannon, N., & Brown, S. (1980). The effects of commercial coaching for the NBME Part 1 examination. *Journal of Medical Education, 55*(9), 733–742.

Seipp, B. (1991). Anxiety and academic performance: A meta-analysis of findings. *Anxiety Research, 4*(1), 27–41.

*Sherman, T. M., & Wildman, T. M. (1982). *Proven strategies for successful test taking.* Columbus, OH: Merrill.

Slack, W. V., & Porter, D. (1980). The Scholastic Aptitude Test: A critical appraisal. *Harvard Educational Review, 50,* 154–175.

Slakter, M. J., Koehler, R. A., & Hampton, S. H. (1970). Grade level, sex, and selected aspects of test wiseness. *Journal of Educational Measurement, 7,* 119–122.

Smith, J. (1982). Converging on correct answers: A peculiarity of multiple-choice items. *Journal of Educational Measurement, 19*(3), 211–220.

Smith, M., Coop, R., & Kinnard, P. W. (1979). The effect of item type on the consequences of changing answers on multiple-choice tests. *Journal of Educational Measurement, 16*(3), 203–208.

Smith, W. F., & Rockett, F. C. (1958). Test performance as a function of anxiety, instructor, and instructions. *Journal of Educational Research, 52*, 138–141.

Spielberger, C. D. (1980). *Preliminary manual for the Test Anxiety Inventory.* Palo Alto, CA: Mind Garden.

Stanton, H. E. (1993). Using hypnotherapy to overcome examination anxiety. *American Journal of Clinical Hypnosis, 35*(3), 198–204.

Strang, H. (1977). The effects of technical and unfamiliar options on guessing on multiple-choice test items. *Journal of Educational Measurement, 14*(3), 253–260.

Strang, H. (1980). The effects of technically worded options on multiple-choice test performance. *Journal of Educational Research, 73*(5), 262–265.

Swinton, S. S., & Powers, D. E. (1983). A study of the effects of special preparation of GRE analytical scores and item types. *Journal of Educational Psychology, 75*(1), 104–115.

Thiede, K. W. (1996). The relative importance of anticipated test format and anticipated test difficulty on performance. *The Quarterly Journal of Experimental Psychology, 49A*(4), 901–918.

Thorndike, R. L. (1951). Reliability. In E. F. Lindquist (Ed.), *Educational measurement* (pp. 560–620). Washington, DC: American Council on Education.

Tips, M., Jongsma, E. A., & Pound, P. E. (1978). *The effects of instruction in verbal reasoning strategies (analogies) in a college reading improvement course.* (ED 173 763)

Tobias, S. (1985). Test anxiety: Interference, defective skills and cognitive capacity. *Educational Psychologist, 3*, 135–142.

Tryon, G. S. (1980). The measurement and treatment of test anxiety. *Review of Educational Research, 2*, 343–372.

Wark, D. M. (1965). Survey Q3R: System or superstition? In D. Wark (Ed.), *College and adult reading* (pp. 3–4). Minneapolis, MN: North Central Reading Association.

Wark, D. M. (1996). Teaching college students better learning skills using self-hypnosis. *American Journal of Clinical Hypnosis, 38*(4), 277–287.

Wark, D. M. (1998). Alert hypnosis: History and application. In W. Matthews & J. Edgette (Eds.), *Current thinking and research in brief therapy* (Vol. 2, pp. 287–304). Philadelphia: Brunner/Mazel.

*Wark, D. M., & Bennett, J. M. (1981). The measurement of test anxiety in a reading center. *Reading World, 20*, 215–222.

Wark, D. M., Bennett, J. M., Emerson, N. M., & Ottenheimer, H. (1981). Reducing test anxiety effects on reading comprehension of college students. In G. H. McNinch (Ed.), *Comprehension: Process and product* (pp. 60–62). Athens, GA: American Reading Forum.

*Wark, D. M., & Flippo, R. F. (1991) Preparing for and taking tests. In R. F. Flippo & D. C. Caverly (Eds.), *Teaching reading & study strategies at the college level* (pp. 294–338). Newark, DE: International Reading Association.

Wasson, B. (1990). Teaching low-achieving college students a strategy for test taking. *College Student Journal, 24*(4), 356–360.

Weber, D. J., & Hamer, R. M. (1982). The effect of review course upon student performance on a standardized medical college examination. *Evaluation and the Health Professions, 5*(3), 35–43.

Weinstein, C. E. (1980, August). *The effects of selected instructional variables on the acquisition of cognitive learning strategies.* (ED 206 929)

Wildemouth, B. (1977). *Test anxiety: An extensive bibliography.* Princeton, NJ: Educational Testing Service.

Wilson, P. (1979). *Answer-changing behavior on objective tests: What is our responsibility?* (Ed 199 638)

Wine, J. (1971). Test anxiety and direction of attention. *Psychological Bulletin, 76,* 92–104.

Wine, J. (1982). Evaluation anxiety—a cognitive attentional construct. In H. W. Krohne & L. Laux (Eds.), *Achievement, stress and anxiety* (pp. 217–219). Washington, DC: Hemisphere.

Wing, H. (1980). Age, sex, and repetition effects with an abilities test battery. *Applied Psychological Measurement, 4*(2), 141–155.

*Wolpe, J. (1969). *Practice of behavior therapy.* New York: Plenum.

Zeidner, M. (1990). Statistics and mathematics anxiety in social science students—some interesting parallels. *British Journal of Educational Psychology, 61,* 319–328.

Zimmer, J. W., & Hocevar, D. J. (1994). Effects of massed versus distributed practice of test taking on achievement and test anxiety. *Psychological Reports, 74,* 915–919.

10

Teaching English as a Second Language (ESL) Students

இ§§௸

Frank J. Pintozzi
Kennesaw State University

Maria Valeri-Gold
Georgia State University

In his poignant autobiography, *Hunger of Memory,* Richard Rodriguez recalled his life as "a bilingual child, a certain kind—socially disadvantaged—the son of working class parents, both Mexican immigrants" (Rodriguez, 1982, p. 12). In this book, Rodriguez described the joys and struggles of learning the English language and the inevitable conflicts that developed between his own Hispanic traditions and the culture of the United States. What Rodriguez experienced in his schooling is more and more familiar to educators as the population of second-language students in postsecondary institutions increases rapidly.

Typically, these English as a second language (ESL) students are either immigrants like Rodriguez, or they are international students on *F–1 visas* (an identification card that permits an international student to study at a college or university in the United States for a designated time period) who are studying in our colleges and universities for undergraduate or graduate degrees. In 1990, 3.3 million immigrants in the United States were 21 years old or younger, and the numbers increase yearly (Gray, Vernez, & Rolph, 1996). Seventy-three percent of these immigrant students still in school planned to attend college versus 66% of native-born students (Gray et al., 1996). In addition, during the 1996–1997 academic year, a record 457,984 international students enrolled in colleges and universities in the United States. These students came from more than 61 foreign countries like Kenya, Peru, and Germany (Rubin, 1997).

However, the largest numbers of immigrants and international students pursuing higher education today come from East Asia (Japan, China, Republic of Korea, and Taiwan) and Latin America (Mexico, Brazil, and Venezuela).

As ESL students begin college, higher educators must address the learning needs of this culturally diverse population, particularly in the areas of reading and writing. In fact, along with acculturation, the greatest challenge for immigrant and international students in higher education is improving their English language skills (Celce-Murcia, 1991; Damen, 1987; Harmer, 1991; Hedge, 1988; Lightbown, 1993). Therefore, identifying the issues and developing effective reading and writing approaches for second-language learners in college must be a key consideration for the United States in the 21st century. With this premise in mind, this chapter (a) offers a theoretical foundation for understanding ESL students in higher education; (b) reviews the literature about teaching reading and writing to ESL students; (c) explains key cultural characteristics of East Asian and Hispanic college students (the two dominant cultural groups in higher education) as they relate to learning in the classroom; (d) identifies key issues and considerations affecting second-language students in the reading–writing classroom; (e) discusses effective reading and writing strategies that can be used with ESL students in college; (f) describes professional resources and organizations that would be helpful for those teaching reading and writing to ESL students in higher education; and (g) suggests implications for future research.

THEORETICAL FOUNDATION

Several elements can contribute to a theoretical foundation for teaching second language students in college reading and writing courses. For one, international and immigrant students in college reading and writing courses are different culturally and linguistically from native-born English speakers in the United States. They come from more diverse religious, ethnic, racial, geographic, social, and political backgrounds. Their linguistic heritage can also be very unlike that of students from the United States. Although some second-language students share the same Roman alphabet, a common cultural history, and various cognates, others do not. For example, students from many Middle Eastern, Asian, and African countries have a very different cultural history from the United States. In addition, the Russian, Arabic, Chinese, and Japanese alphabets are very unlike our Romanized version, and there are far fewer English cognates as well. Cognates are words in two or more languages that have similar pronunciations and meanings (e.g., in Spanish: mi cafe and telefono; in English: my coffee and telephone).

Second, educational researchers and practitioners use various acronyms to describe international and immigrant students. In the United States, the acronym most often used to describe non-English speaking students in higher education is ESL This acronym is also used to describe programs and approaches that are designed to help ESL students learn English (Chamot & O'Malley, 1994). Other terms sometimes used to identify or classify non-English speaking students in college are non-English proficient (NEP), limited English proficient (LEP), potentially English proficient (PEP), and English language learner (ELL; Wang, 1998). On the other hand, Teaching English as a Second Language (TESL) and Teaching English to Speakers of Other Languages (TESOL) refer to professional training and degree programs that prepare teachers wishing to instruct ESL students.

In addition to becoming familiar with acronyms, reading and writing teachers should be aware that second-language learners must develop proficiency in both BICS and CALP language skills (Celce-Murcia, 1991; Cummins, 1980). BICS stands for Basic Interpersonal Communication Skills, which are skills requiring oral fluency that are used in face-to-face situations. Sometimes these are referred to as *cultural survival skills* or *skills for everyday living*. Examples of BICS skills would be the ability to listen and carry on conversations with others in English; asking directions; ordering a meal; discussing information about family and country of origin; identifying numbers, dates, and times; and understanding the language used in the college classroom. CALP is an acronym for Cognitive Academic Language Proficiency, which consists of skills needed for students to succeed in such content areas as reading, writing, mathematics, social sciences, natural sciences, and business. Examples of such higher level cognitive skills would be comprehending, inferring, summarizing, interpreting, comparing and contrasting, and problem solving (Celce-Murcia, 1991).

Many second-language students enter colleges and universities with varying levels of proficiency in BICS and CALP skills. Consequently, college reading and writing instructors might be working with second language students who may be at the beginning, intermediate, or advanced levels of English language development. Beginning level Spanish-speaking students may engage in *codeswitching* (alternating back and forth between languages). Example: Mi cuento is about mi escuela in Venezuela. Translation: My story is about my school in Venezuela. Because adjectives often follow nouns in Spanish, Spanish speakers may sometimes write "house white" instead of "white house" because this phrase is a direct translation from the Spanish "casa blanca." The same noun–adjective reversal is true for Indochinese languages as well. Finally, because articles are rarely used in Japanese and Chinese, speakers of these languages have difficulty with common English articles such as *a, an,* and *the*. Example: "We went to store." instead of "We went to *the* store." Similarly, because nouns remain the same whether they are singular or plural, Chinese and Japanese students can have difficulty with subject–verb agreement. Example: "Tom visit Miami yesterday" instead of "Tom visited Miami yesterday."

Because these elements help to provide a theoretical foundation for instructing second-language learners, college reading and writing teachers should keep them in mind when planning lessons and activities for the classroom. Awareness of these elements promotes what Krashen (1995) called "comprehensible input," thus increasing opportunities for the teacher and the student to communicate more effectively with each other. (For a discussion of teaching reading and writing to all students, see Valeri-Gold & Deming, chap. 6, this volume.)

REVIEW OF THE LITERATURE

Integrating the Communicative Arts

For more than 10 years, research studies focusing on ESL learners have advocated moving away from the teaching of the communicative arts, specifically, reading, writing, speaking, and listening as isolated approaches to learning to instructional practices that emphasize the integration of these four language skills (Dubin, 1983; Hiebert, 1991; Russell, 1990; Ryan, 1995; Thonis, 1994). Integrating the communicative arts allows ESL students to interact with the text and to use language for different purposes in order to make meaning by using their prior knowledge and background of experiences (Chamot & O'Malley, 1994; Gantzer, 1996; Law & Ekes, 1990; Ryan, 1995). According to Smith (1983), providing ESL learners with classroom experiences of reading, writing, listening, and discussing texts written by experienced writers helps them strengthen their oral and written modes of communication.

Learning and Study Strategies

A number of ESL investigators also suggest integrating reading, writing, speaking, and listening across the curriculum that emphasizes learning and study strategies combined with a literature-based or content area curriculum or both (Benware, 1989; Bertrand & Stice, 1995; Bonilla & Goss, 1997; Chamot & O'Malley, 1994; Chamot & Stewner-Manzanares, 1985; Crandall, 1987; Early, 1990; Flores, 1991; Gaies, 1991; Gayle, 1992; Gillespie, 1994; Guadalupe, 1993; Halford, 1996; Heald, 1986; Jackson & Berkshire, 1996; Kim, 1988; Krashen, 1985b; Manzo & Manzo, 1990; Murphy, 1985; Pedersen, 1993; Peyton & Crandall, 1995; Snow, Met, & Genesee, 1989; Terdy, 1984; Yang, 1995). Such an integration of the communication arts with the teaching and modeling of study strategies in the content areas and literature allows students to construct meaning that promotes comprehension and critical thinking (Peregoy & Boyle, 1993).

We should note, however, that the majority of these investigations were conducted with elementary through high school ESL learners. Thus, more in-depth research studies need to be conducted with college level ESL learners in the area of reading. Bell (1995) asserted that a limited amount of research is available on ESL adult learners, who are assumed to have reached the necessary threshold level for literacy knowledge. According to Leki (1993),

> the separation of reading from writing may be the result of our natural inclination to divide language up ... and the fact that reading and writing processes can be isolated does not mean that teaching those isolated processes is the best way to help our students read and write with greater ease. (p. 25)

Despite the need for more reading research with college ESL learners in institutions of higher learning, of particular note, however, are several studies. First, Murphy (1985) studied the listening strategies of college students for whom English is a second language and analyzed their oral and written responses to listening selections. Analysis of the data resulted in 17 individual strategies classified in six broad categories. Murphy found that more proficient and less proficient listeners were distinguishable by the frequency of the strategies they used and the sequential patterns of strategies they followed. Findings suggest that listening is an interpretive language process in which a variety of strategies are interwoven and that textual and nontextual information combined with the strategies used determines the listener's interpretation of what he or she hears. Murphy's study implies that listening instruction should be integrated with reading, speaking, and writing activities. Jackson and Bershire (1996) concurred with Murphy's findings. They note that to learn any subject or interest area, students need to use listening strategies. O'Brien (1989) found that incorporating ESL reading and listening comprehension strategies into an ESL program using authentic materials about Canada improved students' reading and listening strategies by integrating geography, map skills, and culture.

In addition, Yang (1995) investigated how ESL students improved their use of learning strategies through awareness-raising in group interviews and informal training. Sixty-eight Taiwanese university students enrolled in two freshmen English classes participated in the study. Students were asked to respond to an English learning strategy questionnaire in the beginning and at the end of the semester. During the semester, students were interviewed in small groups, in which they examined and discussed details of their strategy use when learning vocabulary, listening, reading, writing, and speaking inside and outside the classroom. Statistical analysis of pre- and posttest results found significant increases in learning strategy use. Results from this study suggested that the group interview provided learners with an important opportunity to focus not only on language but also on the learning process. Yang also noted that learning strategy instruction should include: (a) discovering students' beliefs and strategies, (b) explaining and modeling strategies explicitly, (c) providing authentic context for strategy use, (d) making strategy training interactive, (e) dealing with students' motivation, and (f) implementing strategies and beliefs components within the language curriculum. Heald (1986), and Kim (1988), and Manzo and Manzo (1990) agreed with Yang's findings.

Additionally, Zhang (1994) administered a reading strategy inventory to 176 ESL graduate and undergraduate students who were from 36 countries in Europe, Africa, Asia, and South America. Findings from his study reveal that the subjects use of reading strategies as noted in the composite scores were a function of such variables as nationality, major, and English proficiency.

Whole-Language Perspective

Further analysis of the literature revealed that educators of college ESL learners advocate the teaching of reading and writing using a whole-language perspective. Blanton (1992) and MacGowan-Gilhooly (1991) found that a whole-language perspective to integrate language and content facilitates students' transition from ESL to college mainstream classes. Peyton and Crandall (1995) suggested utilizing a whole-language philosophy that emphasizes learner-centered strategies that revolve around the discussion of ESL students' personal, social, and academic concerns. In a whole-language classroom, writing assignments should stress a writing process approach in which learners brainstorm, write first drafts, form peer groups for feedback, and then continue to revise, edit, and write the final draft of their written products. Incorporating a whole-language philosophy into the college curriculum allows students to become engaging learners who search for meaning, monitor their own learning, and make educated guesses about the topic as they interact with the text (Oxford & Crookall, 1989). According to Carson (1993), reading and writing together allow students to develop critical literacy—the ability to transform information for their own purposes in reading and to synthesize their prior knowledge with another text in writing.

Integrating Literature

Additional analysis of research investigations conducted with college ESL learners stress the importance of integrating literature into the language curriculum in order to help nonnative speakers construct ideas and to develop cognitive, critical thinking, and problem-solving skills (Bertrand & Stice, 1995; Gayle, 1992; Heald, 1986; Pedersen, 1993; Vandrick, 1996). ESL learners should be introduced to a variety of literature genres such as essays, short stories, novels, and poems that represent a diversity of cultures, use written language for real and meaningful purposes, are geared to the age and interest level of the students, and support English acquisition (Garibaldi, 1994). Such an integration provides students with opportunities to read, write, react, and reflect on the characters, setting, plot, and the author's literary devices to help them develop their background knowledge about the literary piece, language, and culture with deeper levels of exploration and analysis (Gajdusek & vanDommelen, 1993).

Students should also be taught patterns of organization such as comparison–contrast, time–order, description, and cause–effect to help them see how ideas in a literary piece are developed and related to one another (Reid, 1993; Zhang, 1994). Other researchers note that educators need to help ESL readers interpret metaphorical expressions that they encounter in their literature because figurative language can be confusing (Garibaldi, 1994; Schifini, 1994). In addition to teaching organization structure and the interpretation of figurative expressions, researchers have found that teaching and modeling the study strategies of paraphrasing, summarizing, and mapping improve comprehension, background knowledge about the topic, critical thinking, vocabulary development, and most importantly, students' ability to read and write more effectively (Brock, 1990; Carson, 1993; Charry, 1988; Elliott, 1990; Gajdusek & vanDommelen, 1993; Hyland, 1992).

Integrating Content Area Subjects
With the Communicative Arts

ESL researchers advocate the combining of reading, writing, speaking, and listening with the formation of content learning-based programs and content study groups examining sociopolitical, linguistic, sociocultural, and sociocontextual issues with individualized and peer instruction that contribute to the cultural promotion of the language and language proficiency (Dolson, 1985; Hernandez-Chavez, 1984; Johnson, 1991). For example, Kasper (1996) found that using psychology texts in college ESL reading instruction increases ESL students' reading comprehension significantly, even if they are not psychology students. Using content area texts encourages students to construct schemata, increase metacognition of the reading process, and use efficient comprehension strategies. However, ESL readers need to be taught instructional strategies that help them understand expository text found in their content area subjects such as text structure, key ideas and concepts, and text features (graphs, timelines, typographical aids; Early, 1990; Mohan, 1986; Schifini, 1994). Many college reading and writing instructors would follow these same procedures for all learners.

Other ESL researchers advocate the use of theme-based courses, pre-courses, adjunct courses, or bridge courses where topics chosen from the three academic disciplines (humanities, social sciences, and natural sciences) link authentic academic course content material with academic study and learning skills (Adamson, 1990; Brinton, Snow, & Wesche, 1989; Gaies, 1991; Kasper, 1994; Krashen, 1985b; Raphan & Moser, 1994; Snow & Brinton, 1988). Schifini (1994) stated that additional research is needed to investigate how ESL learners construct meaning and gain new knowledge from academic content area texts.

Collaboration

Providing ESL learners with opportunities to collaborate or work together with peers in small discussion groups builds oral and written language skills (Díaz, 1988; Dupuy, 1996; Edelsky, Altwerger, & Flores, 1991; Ferris & Tagg, 1996; Thonis, 1994). Calderon (1989) noted that students working together in collaborative groups retain material better than students working on their own, and that cooperative learning encourages higher self-esteem and learning motivation. Calderon also stated that collaborative learning requires that (a) students understand and be prepared for collaborative groups, (b) teachers understand that their roles change from senders of knowledge to facilitators of the learning process, (c) students be assigned clearly defined roles in the group such as discussion leader, timekeeper, arbitrator, and recorder, (d) students receive feedback, and (e) assessments are clearly explained. Clarke (1994) suggested that native speakers collaborate with nonnative speakers or minority groups on written work, in-class assignments, projects, or readings. Thus, collaboration allows students to work and learn together thereby providing the social context in which students practice, manipulate, and master the language and ideas of the knowledge community.

Writing Processes

Although the number of studies in reading with college ESL students needs further exploration, additional analysis of the literature revealed that numerous studies were conducted from 1981 to 1998 that focused on the writing and writing processes of ESL college learners enrolled in 4-year institutions and 2-year colleges (Arani, 1993; Bardovi-Harlig, 1994; Best, 1987; Braine, 1994; Brenner, 1989). A more comprehensive listing of almost 3,500 works in the field of writing (bibliographies, monographs, textbooks, periodicals, dissertations, master's theses, conference papers, and Educational Resources Information Center, ERIC documents) in ESL/English as a foreign language (EFL), at all educational levels, from 1937 to 1993, was compiled by Tannacito (1995).

Noteworthy studies were conducted by Raimes (1987), Sheorey (1986), and Vriend (1988). Raimes (1987) examined the writing strategies of ESL writers at different levels of instruction. Findings indicate that native and nonnative writers had similar strategies, but ESL learners were less inhibited by attempts to correct their work. Little correlation was found among English proficiency, writing ability, and composing strategies. Sheorey (1986) analyzed the grammar errors of Indian native and nonnative students. He found that both groups considered verb tense and subject–verb agreement errors as serious grammatical errors. Vriend (1988) tested 107 college ESL students (with 14 native speakers as controls) with an open–cloze test for preposition use. Results indicated that Chinese speakers had only slightly greater difficulty on the test in comparison with a general ESL group. Vietnamese students scored considerably lower. The Chinese students outscored the group overall on questions involving scientific content despite lower overall test scores. The control group outscored all ESL groups but scored lower than expected.

Vocabulary

Word knowledge is essential for enhancing college ESL students' oral and written modes of communication and includes a range of skills and learning experiences provided through the integration of reading, writing, speaking, and listening (Nation, 1990; Stroller & Grabe, 1993; Templin, 1995; Zimmerman, 1997). Lay (1995) asserted that having college ESL students guess the meaning of unfamiliar words by using their eyes and minds to look inside the text enhances word knowledge. Johnson and Steele (1996) used numerous vocabulary building strategies with college ESL learners such as personal word lists, semantic mapping, imagery, and computer-assisted instruction to help them become independent learners of the tremendous amount of unfamiliar key terms and concepts they encounter in their content area classes. Zimmerman (1997) found that vocabulary instruction combined with self-selected reading assignments and course-related reading increased college ESL students' knowledge of words provided they were given: (a) multiple exposure to words; (b) exposures to words in meaningful contexts; (c) rich and varied information about each word; (d) establishment of ties among instructed words, student experience, and prior knowledge; and (e) active participation by students in the learning process. Despite the research investigations that have been conducted with college ESL students on vocabulary development, more research is needed in this area. According to Krashen (1989), however, the review of the literature suggests that vocabulary development is accomplished through word lists, drills, and skill-building activities, and that many of these assignments are not challenging. Thus, innovative and authentic methods and approaches for vocabulary development that integrate the communicative arts need to be developed. (For further discussion on vocabulary instruction, see Simpson & Randall, chap. 3, this volume.)

Test Anxiety and Performance

Other studies focus on the role of test anxiety and performance and how these two factors affect college ESL students' academic success (El-Banna, 1989; Madden & Murray, 1984). El-Banna (1989) administered a test anxiety inventory and English proficiencies tests for English language and syntax to 731 college ESL learners in Egypt. Results indicated that a significant interaction between gender differences and language anxiety exists. ESL learners with high language anxiety levels tended to do poorly on language tests, whereas ESL learners with low language anxiety levels seemed to perform successfully on the language tests used.

Madden and Murray (1984) conducted two empirical studies. In the first study, nine university students enrolled in two graduate courses in teaching ESL were given interviews following their midterm exam and after having been administered a standardized anxiety instrument. In the second study, 17 precollege ESL students from beginning to advanced language proficiency were interviewed following their placement exam and after the exam, they were administered the same anxiety measure. Findings revealed that time constraints, exam length, and unfamiliarity with the types of questions asked on the exam caused high levels of anxiety and stress in both groups. (See Flippo, Becker, & Wark, chap. 9, this volume, for further discussion.)

Authentic Assessment

The integration of the communicative arts that implements a whole-language philosophy emphasizes authentic methods for assessing ESL students. ESL learners tend to perform poorly on standardized tests compared to native speakers because they appear to lack the prior knowledge about the topic, find difficulty in choosing the correct responses, or are unable to read the selections (García, 1988, 1991, 1994). García (1991) found these findings to be true with Hispanic students. Researchers stress that reliance on standardized tests is not always reliable and viable with ESL students because these tests stress the mastery of basic reading skills rather than providing an assessment of the strategies and cognitive processes the learner uses (García, 1994; García & Pearson, 1991). García (1991) also noted that ESL students need more time to complete the tasks on the tests than native speakers, and they generally have better understanding of what they have read in their second language if they are allowed to use their first language to interpret word meaning (Lee, 1986).

Recent investigations emphasize the shift in formal methods of assessment to informal means of assessing ESL learners. Researchers advocate the use of portfolios (Hamp-Lyons, 1994; Harp, 1993; Mandel, Glazer, & Smullen Brown, 1993; Tierney, Carter, & Desai, 1991; Valencia, 1990; Valencia, Hiebert, & Afflerbach, 1994), interviews (Rhodes, 1993), and observations (Bird, 1989). For meaningful assessments to occur, investigators state that both the teacher and student should be involved in the assessment process (Altwerger & Ivener, 1994; Baca & Almanza, 1991). The assessment process should occur over an extended period of time and include a collection of formal and informal methods of evaluating ESL students in both their native language and in English (Stefanakis, 1998).

The aforementioned review of the literature pertaining to college ESL learners was a synopsis of the research investigations that have been conducted with ESL readers and writers. More research is needed to expand the educational, cultural, social, and political factors that affect the language skills of college ESL students enrolled in higher educational settings.

CULTURAL CHARACTERISTICS AND THEIR EFFECTS ON SECOND-LANGUAGE STUDENTS

Second-language speakers in the United States exhibit a vast array of languages and cultures. To discuss them all and their varied characteristics would not do justice to the rich diversity of cultures represented in the many countries of the Middle East, Asia, Latin America, or Africa. Consequently, our discussion of cultural characteristics and learning is limited to the two fastest growing segments of the second-language population, East Asians and Hispanics. The countries referred to here as East Asian are China, Japan, Korea, Taiwan, Vietnam, Cambodia, and Laos. Countries identified as Hispanic include Mexico, most countries in Central America and South America, and several Caribbean islands (Cuba, Puerto Rico, and the Dominican Republic). In addition, observations about specific cultures within these broad categories are made. These observations are generalizations based on research and experience (Pintozzi, 1995). However, there are also cultural variations and exceptions among East Asians and Hispanics, and this point should be kept in mind.

East Asian Students

Imagine an East Asian student enters your classroom. He or she sits down quietly and opens the textbook as you begin the day's lesson. The student seems to be listening attentively to your words, and when you ask if he or she understands the information, the student shakes his or her head and says "yes." When you give the students a quiz on the lesson, the student receives a failing grade. Only then you realize that this student did not understand the lesson at all.

The imaginative scene just described reveals several characteristics of East Asian cultures in the classroom. (Once again, these generalizations may apply in many cases, but there are always exceptions.) One is the honor accorded to someone who has a higher social status, such as a teacher. Respectful attitudes of behavior must be accorded to those in positions of honor within the family and society. Another is the value placed on harmony. An East Asian student rarely disagrees or says "no" because this action shows disrespect and might provoke conflict. Saying "yes" means the student hears you, but it does not necessarily mean that he or she *understands* what you are saying (Schilling, 1992).

A third typical cultural characteristic of the East Asian student is emotional restraint. Many educators comment on the difficulty of determining when an Asian student is happy, sad, or angry. Tong (1978) suggested that this trait is a legacy from Confucianism which was used by rulers to exert social controls over their kingdoms. Whether or not this conclusion is valid, it does help to explain such behavior, and with acculturation, East Asian students gradually reveal more of their feelings. Emotional restraint also explains why these students do not easily accept compliments. Humility is valued over vanity, and, although these students may appreciate compliments, they have been taught not to acknowledge them publicly.

A final cultural characteristic of East Asians that directly relates to learning is their preference for a field-independent learning style as opposed to a field-sensitive learning style (Ovando & Collier, 1985; Witkin, 1967). Students who are field-independent demonstrate such learning traits as analysis, task-centeredness, independent judgment and work patterns, a formal student–teacher relationship, and skill in spatial areas like math and science. On the other hand, students who are field-sensitive manifest such learning characteristics as synthesis, dependence on the social environment, sensitivity to others, a personal and informal student–teacher relationship, cooperative work patterns, and proficiency in verbal skills. In general, East Asians prefer a field independent learning style. In their home countries, they are used to a formal classroom environment where the teacher lectures and where rote memorization is the preferred means of learning. Student–teacher interaction is minimal, and students do not participate in a class discussion nor do they ask questions as they would do in a U.S. classroom (Ogbu, 1987).

Some cultural variations among East Asians are worth noting although there is some overlap among Southeast Asians, Chinese, Koreans, and Japanese. Koreans, for example, have a deep sense of national and community loyalty brought on by years of alternating oppression from the Chinese and Japanese. They also tend to be strongly ethnocentric and very supportive of members of their own group. Vietnamese display persistence and resourcefulness in achieving their goals. They may hold their eyes to one side when interacting with teachers, which may be misinterpreted as disrespect or defiance when, in reality, they are showing respect. Cambodians often possess well-developed survival skills due to oppression and genocide during the Pol Pot era. Therefore, they may be very tentative about committing themselves to a task. They are also very reflective and even introspective, which is the legacy of a strongly Buddhist culture.

Hispanic Students

The term *Hispanic* is confusing because it refers to so many countries and cultures in which Spanish or Portuguese is the dominant language. Persons of Spanish or Portuguese origin seldom refer to themselves as Hispanic just as few Americans describe themselves as Anglo. Some prefer calling themselves Latinos, Mexican American, Salvadorian, or Brazilian. Nevertheless, although differences exist between Mexican Americans, Central Americans, and South Americans, they share common ways of speaking, thinking, feeling, and acting that constitute what is known as a *Hispanic culture* (de Hainier & Lake, 1978). What, then, are some of the cultural characteristics of the Hispanic student and how do these traits affect learning? These questions are explored in the following discussion.

One of the major characteristics of the Hispanic student is the loyalty to the family (Vasquez, 1988). The motivation to succeed in college or on the job comes primarily from the idea that bearing the family name and supporting family members are very important responsibilities. These obligations can extend even to distant relatives in the belief that emotional, financial, and even educational well being come from sharing and helping each other.

A second cultural trait of the Hispanic student is a people orientation rather than a time orientation. Taking time with people is more important than being on time (Schilling, 1992). Native English speakers in the United States have a "live to work" attitude, whereas Hispanics favor a "work to live" or "work to enjoy life" attitude. Getting to know people gradually and casually is more important for the Hispanic than to finish the task as soon as possible. Another reason for this lack of time orientation is that in most Latin American schools, teachers rather than students move from class to class. In U.S. high school and colleges, students change classes, and the teachers stay in the rooms. New Hispanic immigrants are often late because they have not been conditioned to move between classes in a short time. In addition, they are used to spending more time on social interaction and less time on getting from one place to another (de Hainier & Lake, 1978).

Cooperation and acceptance are also highly valued in Hispanic culture. In the educational setting, Hispanic students avoid individual achievement and competitiveness because these qualities place them in conflict with friends and with the teacher (Cortes, 1978; Vasquez, 1988). "Showing off" knowledge undermines loyalty and respect, which must be accorded to others. On the other hand, Hispanics appreciate oral praise when it is given for shared accomplishments (de Hainier & Lake, 1978).

Finally, as one would anticipate from this discussion, the learning style of Hispanic students is often field sensitive rather than field independent (Cortes, 1978; Ramirez, 1973). They prefer working with others rather than working alone to achieve educational goals; they enjoy more personal, interactive, and verbal activities in their learning; and they are more comfortable working on global aspects of the curriculum rather than isolated details or parts. They also succeed more quickly when concepts from math and science are presented in an experimental context or even in story form as, for example, in the film *Stand and Deliver*, which dramatizes how a dedicated math teacher successfully uses a field-sensitive learning style with a group of Hispanic students from a Los Angeles barrio.

Cultural variations and exceptions among Hispanic groups center on the reasons for entering the United States or on demographic patterns. Mexican immigrants enter the United States for mainly economic reasons such as poverty or lack of steady employment. Central Americans immigrate more often for political reasons. Some have been forced to join the Contras in El Salvador whereas others may be targets of death squads in Guatemala. Many Central American refugees have a strong work ethic and want to provide better educational opportunities for their children. These individuals persevere in their schooling because of responsibilities to family they have left back home or because of the many sacrifices their parents make for them (Suarez-Orozco, 1987). Cultural variations can also be traced to other demographic factors both within and between Hispanic groups. These factors include such categories as length of residence, socioeconomic status (SES), reasons for entering the United States, languages spoken at home, the educational level of their parents, and degree of identification with a particular country or national group (de Hainier & Lake, 1978).

ISSUES, CONSIDERATIONS, AND STRATEGIES FOR TEACHING READING AND WRITING

Working with ESL students in the reading and writing classroom requires both a knowledge of key issues and the application of effective teaching strategies that improve these students' chances for success in higher education. The following is a brief discussion of some of these issues and strategies:

Cultural Understanding

Hwang (1978) asserted that in a true multicultural democracy "the way a person communicates, relates to others, seeks support and recognition from his environment and thinks and learns is a product of the value system of his home and community" (p. 96). Although this statement was made in the late 1970s, it remains relevant today. Consequently, understanding the cultural backgrounds of second-language students is one of the key considerations that must be addressed in the college reading or writing classroom.

Teachers and learning center personnel should develop sensitivity to the varied cultural backgrounds of second-language learners. In other words, we should do our cultural homework when working with these students (Knott, 1991). For example, students used to excelling in a culture that values rote memorization may find our reading–writing-based college culture challenging. Males and females taught separately in other cultures may feel discomfort in mixed gender classrooms in the United States.

Avenues to cultural awareness consist of print resources, Internet Web sites, or simply asking your students. Teachers and tutors working with these students can also participate in on-campus staff development workshops using the expertise of international faculty and students, ESL faculty, faculty from the Departments of Foreign Language, Anthropology, and Geography, and members of cultural and community organizations. Shiels-Djouadi (1978) provided a useful questionnaire for second-language students that covers such areas as educational background, social attitudes, and language characteristics. The *New Faces of Liberty Guide* (1988) is also helpful.

Acculturation

As international and immigrant students begin their college courses, they often experience culture shock. They are adjusting to the values and practices that are common to the culture of the United States, thus engaging in a process called "culture learning" (Damen, 1987). Whether they are in a honeymoon stage in their new country, hostile toward our consumer-oriented society, or homesick for their favorite food, adjusting to a new society can cause anxiety and takes time. Consequently, learning new belief systems both inside and outside the classroom can evoke various responses from second-language students ranging from humor to shock.

What strategies are useful for helping ESL students acculturate to the college classroom and to the larger community in which they live? Some suggestions follow:

Provide an Orientation to the Culture of the United States. This orientation can be a workshop before the semester starts, a small group session with international advisers or teachers, or periodic chat sessions with native speakers or more seasoned international students. Topics covered could include food, clothing, customs, attitudes about time, space, and authority; family relationships; gender relationships; expectations and practices in the college classroom; relationships with teachers; gestures; and taboos (Damen, 1987; McClendon & Keller, 1995).

Assign the ESL Student a Partner in the Reading or Writing Classroom. This partner should be of the same gender and preferably from a different cultural background. A native speaker interested in other cultures could also be a possible choice. This partner can help to bridge understanding of course content and assignments. In addition, a second-language student may be more likely to express concerns or ask questions about course work or personal issues with a peer than with a professor. Ultimately, college orientation courses are valuable experiences for native English speakers as well as second-language students.

Encourage Second-Language Students to Enroll in Freshman Year Experience Courses or College Orientation Seminars.   College orientation courses can assist second-language learners in addressing their personal, social, and academic issues and concerns. These courses can provide a smoother transition into the culture and language of the college campus. In fact, special sections of freshman seminars devoted to the needs and issues of second-language students may be helpful. Topics frequently covered in such seminars include the value of a college education, time management, money management, study and reading strategies, notetaking, test taking, research skills, health, relationships, campus activities and organizations, and career planning.

Testing and Assessment

According to Law and Eckes (1995), testing both frees teachers and hogties them at the same time. Tests simply and conveniently summarize how much a student has learned. We can easily record scores and percentages in our grade books. At the same time, standardized reading and writing tests often fragment knowledge because they tend to measure specific skills in isolation such as vocabulary and grammatical structures. Cutoff scores are often arbitrary, and we do not know for sure whether the student guessed or really knew the answer. We do not even know the thought process a student used in choosing the answer. Most importantly, standardized tests do not clearly tell us whether a second-language student can succeed in a world history or college composition course (Baker, 1992; Law & Eckes, 1995).

Nonetheless, because of national and international concerns about higher education's accountability coupled with the need for standard measures of academic proficiency for second-language students, normed tests are often used as admission criteria in colleges and universities as well as for determining the academic competence of second-language learners. In addition, these tests are also used to identify students who need courses in developmental reading and writing. Among these tests are the Test of English as a Foreign Language (TOEFL), the Michigan Test of English Language Proficiency (MTELP), and the Comprehensive English Language Test (CELT). All three tests measure English language proficiency in such areas as listening, vocabulary, grammar, reading comprehension, and writing using a multiple-choice format (Alderson, Krahnke, & Stansfield, 1987). State- or university-developed tests are also used to place students in developmental reading and writing classes or in an ESL program.

If they have access to the scores on these standardized placement tests, teachers in college developmental or learning support programs can analyze these scores to determine a second-language student's beginning proficiency level in reading or writing. The scores can then become the basis for curriculum and activities that the teacher can develop for second-language learners.

Although standardized proficiency and placement tests are helpful for preliminary identification of language difficulties in reading and writing, assessment is a broader and more comprehensive strategy because the instructor can observe the second-language student's progress over time in multiple contexts (Brindley, 1995; Law & Eckes, 1995; Vacca & Vacca, 1996). Another benefit of assessment is an opportunity to instill basic standards for reading and writing by reviewing various samples of a student's work. An excellent guide for helping students prepare for college-level standards in reading and writing is the ESL standards and vignettes for Grades 9 to 12 in *ESL Standards for Pre-K–12 Students* (1997). A final benefit of assessment is the continual interaction of teacher and student as they learn together in the holistic and authentic setting of the classroom.

The instructor can utilize a variety of methods of assessment for identifying and meeting the linguistic needs of limited English speakers. Formal methods of assessment could include alternate forms of placement tests, criterion-referenced tests and quizzes typically used in the college classroom (multiple-choice, true–false, matching, etc.), and reports and presentations that would be required periodically during the semester. Informal methods of assessment could consist of several or all of the following:

Home Language Survey. The purpose of a home language survey is to determine the language proficiency of your second-language students. It can be administered either orally or in written form and can be given in English or in the student's first language. Key questions to ask would be: What is the student's first language? What language is most frequently used by the student at home? At work? Can the student read or write in English? To what extent? How many years of schooling did the student have in the home country? How long has the student lived in the United States? Did the student have any schooling in the United States? To what extent? Does the student understand what you say? What other languages does the student speak? (This question is helpful if you cannot find a translator for the student's first language; *Georgia ESOL Resource Guide*, 1996; Law & Eckes, 1995.)

Reading–Writing Inventories, Interviews, and Checklists. Both commercial and teacher-made versions of these informal assessments can be used. They consist of preselected questions about reading and study tasks, writing competencies, or attitudes about reading and writing (Lavadenz, 1996; Vacca & Vacca, 1996). The instructor can use the results of these inventories in planning curriculum and teaching approaches. They can be administered orally or in written versions, and the open-ended format of the questions encourages the second-language student to share genuine views about reading and writing. Students respond on a variety of topics such as reading likes and dislikes, favorite books, author's message, knowledge of words, and study habits. Examples of inventories and checklists useful for limited English proficient students are readily accessible (Brindley, 1995; Day, 1993; Law & Eckes, 1995; Vacca & Vacca, 1996).

Observations and Anecdotes. *Observations* and *anecdotes* are written commentaries by the teacher about the second-language student's responses and reactions in the learning environment. These field notes provide valuable information about each student's self-image, learning progress, capabilities, social interactions, and work habits (Lavadenz, 1996; Vacca & Vacca, 1996). These observations and anecdotes also help the instructor in evaluating the effectiveness of classroom activities.

Cloze Procedure. The *cloze procedure* is another way to assess a student's ability to read written material. Every fifth word is removed from the text, and the students are required to supply the words that were deleted. A cloze test offers the instructor a way of evaluating a student's knowledge of vocabulary, grammar, and reading comprehension, but it should be administered several times during the semester so students have ample time to practice and become familiar with the format (Day, 1993; Lavadenz, 1996; Vacca & Vacca, 1996).

Portfolio.   A *portfolio* is an organized collection of a student's work in a given area over time. The student and the teacher are involved in choosing the content of the portfolio and in deciding on the criteria for selecting and judging the work samples. In addition, there must be evidence of student reflections about the contents (Law & Eckes, 1995; Lavadenz, 1996; Pintozzi & Valeri-Gold, in press; Vacca & Vacca, 1996). Portfolios can contain any or all of the following examples: reading–writing inventories, daily work samples, vocabulary or comprehension tests and quizzes, writing samples, journal entries, holistic writing scores, group reports, computer-generated assignments, self- evaluations, or peer evaluations (Pintozzi & Valeri-Gold, in press; Vacca & Vacca, 1996).

According to Vacca and Vacca (1996) and Valencia (1990), the advantages of portfolio assessment over conventional testing are numerous. Among these advantages are an emphasis on learning as a process as well as a product of instruction, learning as a collaborative effort among teacher, student, and peers; and the incorporation of the cognitive, affective, and social dimensions of the learner into the daily activities of classroom instruction. Thus, assessment becomes a more authentic way of interpreting and evaluating the achievement of second language students.

Instruction.   Most college learning support specialists agree that instruction is the central issue that must be addressed in working with second-language learners in the reading or writing classroom. In fact, second-language research suggests that in the teaching situation it is the methods used, more than any other factor, that determine the results achieved (p. 17). Experienced reading and writing teachers adapt their most effective methods to the needs of the second-language learners in their class. If instructors need further professional development working with second-language students, they seek the support and assistance of ESL teachers, participate in staff development workshops and conferences, or consult the many books and periodicals that address instructional strategies for second-language learners. Because of the myriad number of reading and writing strategies cited in the research, this chapter limits the discussion to the strategies that are personally effective in the reading or writing classroom. The innumerable other methods and strategies can be accessed through the references at the end of this chapter, through the ERIC Clearinghouse, or through the many print and computerized resources in college libraries and bookstores.

Build Positive Relationships With Second-Language Students.   R e a d - ing and writing teachers should be sensitive to the cultural and linguistic differences of all students and be willing to understand and appreciate those differences. The presence of limited English speakers enriches the classroom experiences of the instructor and the other students. For example, assignments could center on similarities and differences between the United States and other countries in such areas as family life, clothing, food, and gender relationships. Most of all, reading and writing instructors should create an atmosphere of caring and affirmation toward second language learners. In this way, the students are willing to participate and communicate freely in the classroom. Remember that language differences should not be equated with language deficits (Vacca & Vacca, 1996).

Use Cooperative Learning.

Cooperative learning is an effective learning strategy that can help second-language students extend and deepen their understanding of reading and writing. Second-language students and native speakers work together in small, heterogeneous groups to complete learning tasks. The advantages of cooperative learning for second-language students are greater use of English, especially speaking and listening, increased participation and interaction between students and between the students and the teacher, greater self-confidence and respect for other students' points of view, the generation of more ideas, and greater academic achievement (Johnson, Johnson, & Holubec, 1990; Pintozzi & Valeri- Gold, in press; Vacca & Vacca, 1996).

Various forms of cooperative learning can be useful such as *jigsaw groups* (Aronson, 1978), in which students learn and teach each other a topic in a small group and then share this topic with other groups, *learning circles* (Johnson et al., 1990), which involve reading and writing activities in both large groups and small group formats, and *dyads* (Larson & Dansereau, 1986) in which pairs of students work together to read and study texts or to write collaboratively.

Cooperative learning can be very effective with field-dependent Hispanic students who value group interaction. Cooperative learning coupled with the language experience approach also works well with many second-language students because their reading and writing activities are based on familiar experiences, their writing does not have to be perfect to be acceptable, and they feel the support of their peers and the teacher (Thomas, 1993). Reading or writing about personal experiences in a new country or about ways the world is changing promote positive attitudes about the language, which in turn generate greater fluency through discussion and writing.

Apply Communicative Principles.

Provide ESL learners with a variety of opportunities to engage in assignments, projects, and activities that integrate reading, writing, speaking, and listening as interrelated disciplines. Instructors can build on the students' prior knowledge of experiences to help them monitor and evaluate their own comprehension. For example, an instructor might choose a thematic reader that encourages second-language learners to read, write, reflect, and talk about what they have read based on their own background knowledge and experiences. These selected readings should contain works written by authors representing various cultures. Instructors can also promote an appreciation of diversity by incorporating into the classroom a plethora of literary genre that represents a multitude of cultures, traditions, and customs. By reading, discussing, and writing about poetry, vignettes, short stories, novels, autobiographies, and nonfiction, students can develop better comprehension and higher level thinking and communication skills.

An interesting example of a novel that promotes reading, thinking, and writing about the culture of the United States is *To Do Justice* (Thornton, 1998). This novel revolves around a community college ESL teacher who becomes an assistant to the college president and finds herself confronting unethical behaviors, criminal activities, and political scandals in the state capital. When she is discovered with a playboy senator, her marriage collapses and a court battle for the custody of her children begins. Thornton, who is a reading and writing teacher herself, stated that *To Do Justice* introduces ESL students to bits of Americana which can lead to lively discussions in the classroom" (p. iii). In addition, a teacher's guide with sample tests, discussion questions, and writing topics accompanies the novel.

Use Holistic Approaches for Teaching Reading and Writing.   Instructors should demonstrate to second language learners that reading and writing are both holistic acts that are part of an ongoing process of constructing meaning (Tierney & Pearson, 1983). A reader tries to make sense out of a text, and a writer tries to compose ideas into text. Vacca and Vacca (1996) indicated that reading and writing "involve purpose, commitment, schema activation, planning, working with ideas, revision and rethinking, and monitoring" (p. 285). Writing, then, becomes a process with a continuum of strategies starting with brainstorming, clustering, and freewriting; continuing into thesis formation, introduction, and rough draft; and ending with peer feedback, revising, editing, and final copy (Celce-Murcia, 1991; Gee, 1996). Likewise, reading becomes an interactive process between reader and text. Prior knowledge, prereading, comprehension monitoring, and postreading strategies become the framework for learning the text (Celce-Mucia, 1991; Vacca & Vacca, 1996).

Second-language students can use two interactive study–reading systems to improve reading comprehension. OASE stands for organizing, analyzing, synthesizing, and extending your reading (Pintozzi & Valeri-Gold, in press). *Organizing* involves predicting and previewing strategies such as anticipation guides, think ahead and write (TAW), and several brainstorming strategies. *Analyzing* consists of comprehension monitoring strategies such as think alouds, annotating, and underlining. *Synthesizing* is a postreading strategy in which students learn to use semantic maps, advance organizers, concept cards, and split-half sheets to recall and retain the key ideas in the text. *Extending* includes the use of such strategies as journaling, collaboration, computers, and library research to deepen and broaden understanding of the text. In addition, students build vocabulary within the framework of the text they are reading using such strategies as context clues, semantic word maps, and graphic organizers. SQ3R stands for survey, question, read, recite, and review (Robinson, 1961). *Survey* involves a skimming of the text to gain an overview of the material. In the question step, the student forms questions that can be answered by *reading* the material, which is the next step. *Recite* consists of answering the questions from the second step. The reader should then *review* the text and the questions and answers.

Know How to Communicate in English With Second-Language Students.   Speak at a normal speed and volume. Do not raise your voice when the student does not understand, but do speak in distinct syllables. Repeat instructions and phrases, and ask your students to repeat or rephrase instructions as well. Pause between sentences periodically so students can process what you are saying. Avoid complex sentences, slang, or idioms unless you can explain them clearly. Use body language, gestures, props, and pictures to explain words and concepts. Student reluctance to respond may be based on culture and not ignorance.

Initially ask yes–no and five W (who, what, when, where, why) questions until students show more confidence with English. This encourages students to paraphrase and summarize what they are learning.

Allow students extra time to respond to questions. Silence is acceptable. Write or print instructions, words, and assignments on the board and reinforce them orally.

Summarize what was taught at the end of class and teach ESL students how to take good notes by reviewing yours or those of your students. Make sure your instruction is direct, explicit, and structured step by step. Have students write a response journal periodically on their problems and progress.

Provide second-language students with additional time to complete tests. Allow second-language learners to retake a test if the results seem inconsistent with general performance. Use authentic assessment whenever possible. Finally, affirm the progress and contributions of second language students frequently and avoid being overly critical (Knox, 1996; McClendon & Keller, 1995; Wang, 1998).

IMPLICATIONS FOR TEACHING READING AND WRITING TO ESL STUDENTS

Knowledge about cultural and linguistic issues as well as the most effective reading and writing strategies to use with second-language learners are essential for higher educators as more of these students enter our colleges and universities. Fortunately, there are a number of professional resources that provide information and networking services. Among these are TESOL, which also has chapters in each state and ESL interest groups in National Association for Developmental Education (NADE), International Reading Association (IRA), National Council of Teachers of English (NCTE), and College Reading and Learning Association (CRLA). All of these organizations offer conferences and workshops on second-language issues and teaching strategies. In addition, clearinghouses for second-language issues and instructional strategies on the national level include the Center for Applied Linguistics, the Center for Bilingual Education, and ERIC Clearinghouse. Many colleges and universities offer courses and programs in second-language teaching featured in the directory of the Institute of International Education (DeAngelis & Battle, 1994).

Numerous publishers provide teaching resources and materials for second-language students such as Addison-Wesley Longman, Alta Publications, Heinle and Heinle, McGraw-Hill, Oxford University Press, Prentice-Hall, Steck-Vaughn, St. Martin's Press, and TESOL Publications. Several periodicals contain articles, tips, and book reviews on teaching reading and writing to limited English proficient students. Among these journals are *American Language Review, Applied Linguistics, ELT (English Language Teaching) Journal, English Today, Journal of Reading, Language Arts Journal, RELC (Regional Language Centre)* in Singapore, *TESOL Journal,* and *TESOL Quarterly.* Professional resources on the Internet are expanding as well. Several of the previously mentioned journals are now online, and their Web addresses are cited in the hard copy versions. In addition, *The Prentice Hall Directory of Online Education Resources* contains lists and descriptions of Web sites devoted to language, reading, and ESL. Dave's ESL Cafe and its many links to other Web sites is one of the best online resources for second-language teachers and students.

IMPLICATIONS FOR FUTURE RESEARCH

The number of ESL students continues to increase in the 21st century. As a result, more and more college reading and writing instructors need to identify issues and implement effective teaching strategies in an increasingly diverse classroom environment. Consequently, questions for future research with this population include:

1. Do teacher training and preparation have an effect on the instruction of second-language learners? To what extent?
2. Are integrated or literature-based approaches to teaching second-language students more effective than traditional approaches? Why or why not?
3. Do culture or language background play a more significant role in learning reading and writing?
4. To what extent does the learning style of limited English-speaking students affect the successful completion of reading and writing tasks?
5. To what extent does collaboration increase language proficiency? Are there any disadvantages to collaboration?
6. What other formal and informal means of assessment should be developed to identify areas of language deficiency?
7. Should college reading and writing be taught to second-language students in one integrated course or as two separate courses? Why or why not?
8. Do the study and learning strategies of limited English speakers differ from those of native-born speakers of English? Will the teaching of these strategies help limited English speakers be more successful students?

These questions provide a basis for future research about the teaching and learning of second-language students in college reading and writing classes. As research provides more insights into these questions, the benefits to second-language students and their instructors are invaluable.

SUMMARY

National demographics indicate increasing cultural and linguistic diversity in our classrooms and learning centers as we begin the 21st century. Second-language students constitute a major portion of this diversity. Providing effective learning experiences for these students requires an understanding of their culture and its implications for learning. In addition, college reading and writing teachers must build an awareness of the issues, considerations, and strategies that affect the delivery of instruction to these students. Therefore, continuing professional development and research are needed in this important area of education so that our knowledge increases and second-language students are better served.

REFERENCES AND SUGGESTED READINGS

Adamson, H. D. (1990). ESL students' use of academic skills in content courses. *English for Specific Purposes*, 9, 67–87.

*Alderson, J. C., Krahnke, K. J., & Stansfield, C. W. (Eds.). (1987). *Reviews of English language proficiency tests*. Washington, DC: TESOL Publications.

Altwerger, B., & Ivener, B. L. (1994). Self-esteem: Access to literacy in multicultural and multilingual classrooms. In K. Spangenberg-Urbschat & R. Pritchard (Eds.), *Kids come in all languages: Reading instruction for ESL students* (pp. 65–81). Newark, DE: International Reading Association.

Arani, M. T. (1993, April). *Inconsistencies in error production by non-native English speakers and in error gravity judgment by native speakers*. Paper presented at the annual meeting of the Teachers of English to Speakers of Other Languages, Atlanta.

*Aronson, E. (1978). *The jigsaw classroom*. Beverly Hills, CA: Sage.

Asher, J. J. (1977). *Learning another language through action: The complete teacher's guide*. Los Gatos, CA: Sky Oaks Productions.

Baca, L. M., & Almanza, E. (1991). *Language minority students with disabilities*. Reston, VA: Council for Exceptional Children.

Baker, Eva L. (1992). *Proceedings of the second national research symposium on limited English proficient student issues: focus on evaluation and measurement* (Vol. 2). Washington, DC: United States Department of Education, Office of Bilingual Education and Minority Languages Affairs.

Bardovi-Harlig, K. (1994). Reverse-order reports and the acquisition of tense: Beyond the principle of chronological order. *Language Learning, 44*(2), 243–282.

Barringer, P. (1993). Immigration in 80's made English a foreign language for millions. *The New York Times*, Vols. Al, A10.

Bell, J. S. (1995). The relationship between L1 and L2 literacy: Some complicating factors. *TESOL Quarterly, 29*(4), 687–704.

Benware, M. A. (1989). *Bridging the gap: A transitional program from ESL to ABE. Research and curriculum*. Harrisburg, PA: Pennsylvania State Department of Education (ERIC Document Reproduction Service No. ED 377 741)

Bertrand, J. E., & Stice, C. F. (Eds.). (1995). *Empowering children at risk at school failure: A better way*. Norwood, MA: Christopher-Gordon.

Best, L. (1987, March). *Sociolinguistic theories as means to understand and meet the needs of ESL college writers*. Paper presented at the annual meeting of the Conference on College Composition and Communication, Atlanta.

*Bird, L. B. (1989). The art of teaching: Evaluation and revision. In K. S. Goodman, Y. M. Goodman, & W. J. Hood (Eds.), *The whole language evaluation book* (pp. 15–24). Portsmouth, NH: Heinemann.

Blanton, L. L. (1992). A holistic approach to college ESL: Integrating language and content. *ELT Journal, 46*(3), 285–293.

Bonilla, C., & Goss, J. (Eds.). (1997). *Students at risk: The teachers call to action!* Stockton, CA: ICA.

Braine, G. (1994, March). *A comparison of the performance of ESL students in ESL and mainstream classes of freshman English*. Paper presented at the annual meeting of the Teachers of English to Speakers of Other Languages, Baltimore.

Brenner, C. A. (1989). *Teaching the research paper to ESL students in American college and universities*. Unpublished masters thesis, School for International Training, Bratelboro, VT.

Brice, C. (1995, March). *ESL writers' reactions to teacher commentary: A case study*. Paper presented at the annual meeting of the Teachers of English to Speakers of Other Languages, Long Beach, CA.

*Brindley, G. (Ed) (1995) *Language assessment in action*. Sydney, Australia: National Centre for English Language Research, Macquarie University.

Brinton, D. M., Snow, M. A., & Wesche, M. B. (1989). *Content-based second language instruction*. New York: Newbury House.

Brock, M. (1990). The case for localized literature in the ESL classroom. *English Teaching Forum, 28*(3), 22–25.

Brooks, E. (1985). *Case studies of unskilled ESL college writers: An hypothesis about stages of development*. Unpublished doctoral dissertation, New York University, New York

Calderon, M. (1989). Cooperative learning for LEP students. International Development Research Association Newsletter, *16*(9), 1–7.

*Carroll, P. S., Blake, F., Camalo, R. A., & Messer, S. (1996). When acceptance isn't enough: Helping ESL students become successful writers. *English Journal, 88*(8), 25–33.

Carson, J. G. (1993). Reading for writing: Cognitive perspectives. In J. G. Carson & I. Leki (Eds.), *Reading in the composition classroom* (pp. 85–104). Boston: Heinle & Heinle.

*Celce-Murcia, M. (Ed.). (1991). *Teaching English as a second or foreign language*. Boston: Heinle & Heinle.

Chamot, A. U., & O'Malley, J. M. (1994). Instructional approaches and teaching procedures. In K. Spangenberg-Urbschat & R. Pritchard (Eds.), *Kids come in all languages: Reading instruction for ESL students* (pp. 82–107). Newark, DE: International Reading Association.

Chamot, A. U., & Steiner-Manzanares, G. (1985). *ESL instructional approaches and underlying language theories*. Washington, DC: National Clearinghouse for Bilingual Education.

Charry, M. B. (1988, April). *Teaching English as a second language students to paraphrase what they read*. Paper presented at the annual meeting of the New York College Learning Skills Association, New York.

Chaudron, C. (1983, March). *Evaluating writing: Effects of feedback on revision*. Paper presented at the annual Teaching English to Students of Other Languages Convention, Ontario, Canada.

*Clarke, M. A. (1994). Mainstreaming ESL students: Disturbing changes. *College ESL 4*(1), 1–19.

Claxton, C. S. (1990). Learning styles, minority students, and effective education. *Journal of Developmental Education, 14*(1), 6–8, 35.

Commission on Minority Participation in Education and American Life. (1988). *One-third of a nation*. Washington, DC: American Council on Education.

Cortes, C. (1978). Chicano culture, experience, and learning. In L. Morris (Ed.), *Extracting learning styles from sociocultural diversity*. Washington, DC: Southwest Teacher Corp. Network.

Crandall, J. A.(Ed) (1987) *ESL through content-area instruction: Mathematics, science, social studies*. Englewood Cliffs, NJ: Prentice Hall.

Cummins, J. (1980) The cross-lingual dimensions of language proficiency: Implications for bilingual education and the optimal age issue. *TESOL Quarterly, 14*(2), 175–187.

*Damen, L. (1987). *Culture learning*. Reading, MA: Addison-Wesley.

Dave's esl café. http://www.eslcafe.com

*Day, R. R.(Ed.). (1993). *New ways in teaching reading*. Alexandria, VA: TESOL Publications.

*DeAngelis, C., & Battle, E. (Eds.). (1994). *English language and orientation programs in the United States*. New York: Institute of International Education.

de Hainier, E., & Lake, E. (1978). Hispanic learners and Anglo teachers: Insights for cross-cultural understanding. Arlington, VA: Arlington Public Schools Project.

ESL standards for pre–k–12 students. (1997) Alexandria, VA: TESOL Publication

*Gee, R. W. (1996). Reading/writing workshops for the ESL classroom. *TESOL Journal*, Spring, 4–9.

*Díaz, D. M. (1988). ESL college writers: Process and community. *Journal of Developmental Education, 12*(2), 6–8.

*Díaz, D. M. (1991). Writing, collaborative learning, and community. *College ESL, 1*(1), 19–29.

Dolson, D. (1985). Bilingualism and scholastic performance: The literature revisited. *NABE Journal, 10*(1), 1–35.

*Dubin, F. (1983). *How to succeed in college courses: A guide for the ESL student*. New York: Association of American Publishers.

*Dupuy, B. (1996). Bringing books into the classroom: First steps in turning college ESL students into readers. *TESOL Journal, 5*(4), 10–15.

Early, M. (1990). Enabling first and second language learners in the classroom. *Language Arts, 67*, 567–575.

Edelsky, C., Altwerger, B., & Flores, B. (1991). *Whole language: What's the difference?* Portsmouth, NH: Heinemann.

El Banna, A. (1989). *Language anxiety and language proficiency among EFL/ESL learners at university level: An exploratory investigation*. Egypt: Tanta University. (ERIC Document Reproduction Service No. ED 308 698)

*Elliott, R. (1990). Encouraging reader-response to literature in ESL situations. *ELT Journal, 44*(3), 191–203.

Ferris, D., & Tagg, T. (1996). Academic oral communication needs for EAP learners: What subject-matter instructors actually require. *TESOL Quarterly, 30*(1), 31–55.

Flores, N. L. (1991, November). *Meeting the challenge of improving the oral communication of at-risk Latino students*. Paper presented at the annual meeting of the Speech Communication Association, Atlanta.

*Gaies, S. J. (1991). ESL students in academic courses: Forging a link. *College ESL, 1*(1), 30–36.

Gajdusek, L., & vanDommelen, D. (1993). Literature and critical thinking in the composition classroom. In J. G. Carson & I. Leki (Eds.), *Reading in the composition classroom* (pp. 197–215). Boston: Heinle & Heinle.

Gantzer, J. (1996). Do reading tests match reading theory? *College ESL*, 6(1), 29–48.

García, G. E. (1988). *Factors influencing the English reading test performance of Spanish-speaking Hispanic students.* Unpublished doctoral dissertation, University of Illinois, Urbana.

*García, G. E. (1991). Factors influencing the English reading test performance of Spanish-speaking Hispanic students. *Reading Research Quarterly, 26,* 371–392.

García, G. E. (1994). Assessing the literacy development of second-language students: A focus on authentic assessment. In K. Spangenberg-Urbschat & R. Pritchard (Eds.), *Kids come in all languages: Reading instruction for ESL students* (pp. 180–205). Newark, DE: International Reading Association.

García, G. E., & Pearson, P. D. (1991). The role of assessment in a diverse society. In E. Hiebert (Ed.), *Literacy for a diverse society: Perspectives, practices, and policies* (pp. 253–278). New York: Teachers College Press.

Garibaldi, A. V. (1994). Selecting materials for the reading instruction of ESL children. In K. Spangenberg-Urbschat & R. Prichard, (Eds.), *Kids come in all languages: Reading instruction for ESL students* (pp. 108–134). Newark, DE: International Reading Association.

Gayle, S. (1992, June). *Windows to the world.* Paper presented at the annual National Educational Computing Conference, Dallas.

Georgia ESOL resource guide. (1995) Atlanta: Georgia Department of Education.

Gillespie, M. K. (1994). *Native language literacy instruction for adults: Patterns, issues, and promises.* Washington, DC: Office of Educational Research and Improvement. (ERIC Document Reproduction Service No ED 379 969)

Goldman, S. R., & Murray, J. D. (1992). Knowledge of connectors as cohesion devices in text: A comparative study of native-English and English as a second language speakers. *Journal of Educational Psychology, 84*(4), 504–519.

Gray, M. J., Vernez, G., & Rolph, E. (1996). Student access and the new immigrants. *Change.* September/October, 41–47.

Guadalupe, D. R. (1993). *Integrated methods for pupils to reinforce occupational and verbal effectiveness (Project IMPROVE).* Washington, DC: Department of Education. (ERIC Document Reproduction Service No. 370 374)

Halford, J. M. (1996). *Bilingual education: Focusing policy on student achievement.* Alexandria, VA: Association for Supervision and Curriculum Development.

*Harmer, J. (1991). *The practice of English language teaching.* London: Longman.

Hamp-Lyons, L. (Ed.). (1991). *Assessing second language writing in academic contexts.* Norwood, NJ: Ablex.

*Hamp-Lyons, L. (1994). Interweaving assessment and instruction in college ESL writing. *College ESL, 4*(1), 43–55.

Harp, B. (Ed.). (1993). *Assessment and evaluation in whole language programs.* Norwood, MA: Christopher-Gordon.

*Heald, T. G. (1986). *Whole language strategies for ESL students: Language and literacy series.* Toronto, Canada: Ontario Institute for Studies in Education. (ERIC Document Reproduction Service No. ED 280 287)

*Hedge, T. (1988) *Writing.* Oxford: Oxford University Press.

Hernandez-Chavez, E. (1984). The inadequacy of English immersion education as an educational approach for language minority students in the United States. In *Studies on immersion.* Sacramento: California Department of Education.

Hiebert, E. (1991). Literary contexts and literary processes. *Language Arts, 68,* 134–139.

Hodgkinson, H. (1985). *All one system: Demographics of education, kindergarten through graduate school.* Washington, DC: Institute of Educational Leadership.

*Hwang, B. (1978). Exemplars of institutional units for cultural diversity. In L. Morris (Ed), *Extracting learning styles from sociocultural diversity.* Washington, DC: Southwest Teacher Corp Network.

Hyland, K. (1992). Genre analysis: Just another fad? *English Teaching Forum, 30*(2), 14–17, 27.

Irizarry, J. (1994). Issues in ESL: The question of content. *College ESL, 4*(1), 28–34.

Iwamura, S. G. (1981, March). *A multi-skill approach to ESL in bilingual education.* Paper presented at the Teachers of English to Students of Other Languages Conference, Detroit.

Jackson, R., & Berkshire, M. (1996, November). *Speaking and listening across the curriculum: Teaching teachers. K–12 teachers short course.* Paper presented at the annual meeting of the Speech Communication Association, San Diego, CA.

Johnson, D. (1991). Some observations on progress in research in second language learning and teaching. In M. McGroaty & C. Faltis (Eds.), *Language in school and society: Politics and pedagogy* (pp. 38–46). Berlin: de Gruyter.

*Johnson, D., & Steele, V. (1996). So many words, so little time: Helping college ESL learners acquire vocabulary-building strategies. *Journal of Adolescent & Adult Literacy, 39*(5), 347–348.

*Johnson, D. W., Johnson, R. T., & Holubec, E. J. (1990). *Circles of learning: Cooperation in the classroom* (3rd ed). Edina, MN: Interaction Book Company.

*Kasper, L. F. (1994). Improved reading performance for ESL students through academic course pairing. *Journal of Reading, 37*(5), 376–384.

*Kasper, L. F. (1996). Using discipline-based texts to boost college ESL reading instruction. *Journal of Adolescent & Adult Literacy, 39*(4), 298–306.

Kayfetz, J. (1998). *Improving ESL instruction for college-bound students.* Fountain Valley, CA: California Community College Fund for Instructional Improvement. (ERIC Document Reproduction Service No. ED 307 946)

Kim, B. W. (1988, October). *Why students fail in ESL and what should be done.* Paper presented at the annual meeting of the Japan Association of Language Teachers International Conference on Language Teaching/Learning, Port Island, Kobe, Japan.

*Knott, E. (1991). Working with culturally diverse learners. *Journal of Developmental Education, 15*(2), 14–18.

Knox, L. (1996, April 4). *Communicating in English with non-native speakers.* Presentation at Kennesaw State University, Kennesaw, GA.

Krapels, A. R. (1990). An overview of second language writing process research. In B. Kroll (Ed.), *Second language writing* (pp. 37–56). New York: Cambridge University Press.

Krashen, S. D. (1985a). *Input in second language acquisition.* Oxford, UK: Pergamon.

Krashen, S. D. (1985b). *Inquiries and insights.* Hayward, CA: Alemany Press.

Krashen, S. D. (1989). We acquire vocabulary and spelling by reading: Additional evidence for the input hypothesis. *The Modern Language Journal, 73,* 440–464.

*Larson, C. O., & Dansereau, D. (1986). Cooperative learning in dyads. *Journal of Reading, 30,* 516–520.

Lavadenz, M. (1996) Authentic assessment: Toward equitable assessment of language minority students. *New Schools, New Communities. 12*(2), 31–35.

Law, B., & Eckes, M. (1990). *More than just surviving ESL for every classroom teacher.* Winnipeg, Manitoba: Peguis.

*Law, B., & Eckes, M. (1995). *Assessment and ESL.* Winnipeg, Manitoba: Peguis.

*Lay, N. S. (1995). Enhancing vocabulary: Using eyes and minds as a microscope. *College ESL, 5*(1), 36–46.

Lee, J. F. (1986). On the use of the recall task to measure L2 reading comprehension. *Studies in Second Language Acquisition, 8,* 201–211.

Leki, I. (1993). Reciprocal themes in ESL reading and writing. In J. G. Carson & I. Leki (Eds.), *Reading in the composition classroom* (pp. 9–32). Boston: Heinle & Heinle.

*Leki, I. (1995). Coping strategies of ESL students in writing tasks across the curriculum. *TESOL Quarterly, 29*(2), 235–260.

*Lightbown, P. M., & Spada, N. (1993). *How languages are learned.* Oxford, England: Oxford University Press.

*MacGowan-Gilhooly, A. (1991). Fluency before correctness: A whole language experiment in college ESL. *College ESL, 1*(1), 37–47.

Madden, H. S., & Murray, N. (1984, March). *Retrospective evaluation of testing in ESL content and skills courses.* Paper presented at the annual meeting of the Teachers of English to Speakers of Other Languages, Houston.

*Mandel M., Glazer, S., & Smullen Brown, C. (1993). *Portfolios and beyond: Collaborative assessment in reading and writing.* Norwood, MA: Christopher-Gordon.

Manzo, A. V., & Manzo, U. C. (1990). A comprehension and participation training strategy. *Journal of Reading, 33,* 608–611.

Marshall, H. W. (1981, October). *A useful concept for eliminating fragments and run-ons.* Paper presented at the annual conference of the New York State English to Speakers of Other Languages and Bilingual Educators Association, Rochester, NY.

*McClendon, L., & Keller, R. (1995). *Teacher handbook: ESOL students in the classroom.* Atlanta: Fulton County Board of Education.

Mohan, B. A. (1986). *Language and content.* Reading, MA: Addison Wesley.

Murphy, J. M. (1985, April). *An investigation into the listening strategies of ESL college students.* Paper presented at the annual meeting of the Teachers of English to Speakers of Other Languages, New York.

Nation, I. S. P. (1990). *Teaching and learning vocabulary.* New York: Newbury House.

New faces of liberty. (1988). Berkeley, CA: New Faces of Liberty Project.

Norris, S. (1995, March). *Responding to the adult ESL writer: A teacher-as-researcher case study.* Paper presented at the annual meeting of the Sunshine State Teachers of English to Speakers of Other Languages, Jacksonville, FL.

O'Brien, T. (1989). Language comprehension strategies through a Canadian cultural context. TESL Talk, *19*(1), 86–109.

Ogbu, J. (1987). Variability in minority school performance. *Anthropology & Education Quarterly, 18*(4), 312–334.

*O'Hearn, C. C. (1998). *Half and half: Writers on growing up biracial and bicultural.* New York: Pantheon.

*Ovando, C., & Collier, V. (1985). *Bilingual and ESL classrooms.* New York: McGraw-Hill.

Oxford, R., & Crookall, D. (1989). Research on language learning strategies. *The Modern Language Journal, 73,* 404–419.

Parish, C., & Perkins, K. (1984, March). *Using tests of anaphoric reference in ESL reading.* Paper presented at the annual meeting of the Teachers of English to Speakers of Other Languages, Houston.

Pedersen, E. M. (1993, April). *Folklore in ESL/EFL curriculum materials.* Paper presented at the annual meeting of the Teachers of English to Speakers of Other Languages, Atlanta.

*Peregoy, S., & Boyle, O. (1993). *Reading, writing, and learning in ESL: A resource book for teachers.* White Plains, NY: Longman.

Peyton, J., & Crandall, J. (1995). *Philosophies and approaches in adult ESL literacy instruction.* Washington, DC: Office of Educational Research and Improvement. (ERIC Document Reproduction Service No. 386 960)

Pintozzi, F. J. (1995). Culture and its implications for learning among second language students. *Journal of College Reading and Learning, 26*(2), 45–53.

*Pintozzi, F. J., & Valeri-Gold, Maria. (in press). *Taking charge of your reading.* White Plains, New York: Longman.

*Polio, C., & Glew, M. (1996). ESL writing assessment prompts: How students choose. *Journal of Second Language Writing, 5*(1), 35–49.

Prentice-Hall directory of online education resources. (1998). Paramus, NJ: Prentice-Hall.

Raimes, A. (1987). Language proficiency, writing ability, and composing strategies: A study of ESL college student writers. *Language Learning, 37*(3), 439–468.

Ramirez, M. (1973). Cognitive styles and cultural democracy in education. *Social Science Quarterly, 53*(4), 895–904.

Raphan, D., & Moser, J. (1994). Linking language and content: ESL and art history. *TESOL Journal, 3*(2), 17–21.

*Reid, J. (1993). Historical perspectives on writing and reading in the ESL classroom. In J. G. Carson & I. Leki (Eds.), *Reading in the composition classroom* (pp. 33–60). Boston: Heinle & Heinle.

Rhodes, N. (Ed.). (1993). *Project-assessing academic language of language minority students.* Washington, DC: Center for Applied Linguistics.

Robinson, F. (1961) *Effective study.* New York: Harper and Row.

*Rodriguez, R. (1982). *Hunger of memory: The education of Richard Rodriguez.* New York: Bantam Books.

Rubin, A. M. (1997). Intensive English programs are lucrative for universities. *Chronicle of Higher Education, 44,* 16, A48.

Russell, D. R. (1990). Writing across the curriculum in historical perspective: Toward a social interpretation. *College English, 52,* 262–276.

Ryan, C. (1995, March). *Debate is perfect for integrated skills.* Paper presented at the annual meeting of the Teachers of English to Speakers of Other Languages, Long Beach, CA.

Schifini, A. (1994). Language, literacy, and content instruction: Startegies for teachers. In K. Spangenberg-Urbschat & R. Pritchard (Eds.), *Kids come in all languages: Reading instruction for ESL students*. Newark, DE: International Reading Association.

Schilling, J. (1992). *Cultural behavior*. Norcross, GA: International Newcomer Center.

Schnackenberg, H. L. (1997, February). *Learning English electronically: Formative evaluation in ESL software*. Paper presented at the annual meeting of the Association for Educational Communication and Technology, Albuquerque, NM.

Schwartz, J., & Exter, T. (1989). All our children. *American Demographics, 12*(1), 34–37.

Sheorey, R. (1986). Error perceptions of native-speaking and non-native speaking teachers of ESL. *ELT Journal, 40*(4), 306–312.

Shiels-Djouadi, M. (1978). *Easing the transition: a guide for learning more about foreign-born students*. Arlington, VA: Arlington Public Schools Project.

Smith, F. (1983). Reading like a writer. *Language Arts, 60*, 558–567.

Snow, M. A., & Brinton, D. M. (1988). Content-based language instruction: Investigating the effectiveness of the adjunct model. *TESOL Quarterly, 22*, 553–574.

*Snow, M. E., Met, M., & Genesee, F. (1989). A conceptual framework for the integration of language and content in second/foreign language instruction. *TESOL Quarterly, 23*, 553–574.

Stefanakis, E. H. (1998). *Whose judgment counts?: Assessing bilingual children, K–3*. Portsmouth, NH: Heinemann.

*Stroller, F., & Grabe, W. W. (1993). Implications for L2 vocabulary acquisition and instruction from L1 vocabulary research. In T. Huckin, M. Haynes, & J. Coady (Eds.), *Second language reading and vocabulary learning* (pp. 24–45). Norwood, NJ: Ablex.

Suarez-Orozco, M. (1987). Becoming somebody: Central American immigrants in U.S. inner-city schools. *Anthropology & Educational Quarterly, 18*(4), 287–299.

*Tannacito, D. J. (1995). *A guide to writing in English as a second or foreign language: An annotated bibliography of research and pedagogy*. Alexandria, VA: Teachers of English to Speakers of Other Languages (TESOL).

Tegey, M. (1985). A structured approach to teaching composition. *WATESOL Working Papers, 2*, 1–12.

Templin, S. A. (1995, March). *Reliable and valid testing of productive vocabulary: Speaking vocabulary test*. Paper presented at the annual meeting of Teachers of English to Speakers of Other Languages, Long Beach, CA.

Terdy, D. (1984, April). *So what do you do in there anyway?* Paper presented at the annual state convention of the Illinois Teachers of English to Speakers of Other Languages/Bilingual Education, Chicago.

*Thomas, J. (1993). Countering the "I can't write English" syndrome. *TESOL Journal, 2*(3), 12–15.

Thonis, E. W. (1994). The ESL student: Reflections on the present, concerns for the future. In K. Spangenberg-Urbschat & R. Pritchard (Eds.), *Kids come in all languages: Reading instruction for ESL students* (pp. 207–218). Newark, DE: International Reading Association.

*Thornton, E. (1998). *To do justice*. New York: McGraw-Hill.

Tierney, R. J., & Pearson, P. D. (1983). Toward a composing model for reading. *Language Arts, 60*(5), 568–580.

*Tierney, R., Carter, M., & Desai, L. (1991). *Portfolio assessment in the reading–writing classroom.* Norwood, NJ: Christopher-Gordon.

Tong, B. (1978). Warriors and victims: Chinese American sensibility and learning styles. In L. Morris (Ed), *Extracting learning styles from sociocultural diversity* (pp. 17–24). Washington, DC: Southwest Teacher Corp Network.

*Vacca, R. T., & Vacca, J. L. (1996). *Content area reading* (5th ed.) New York: HarperCollins.

*Valencia, S. (1991). A portfolio approach to classroom reading assessment: The whys, whats, and hows. *The Reading Teacher, 43,* 338–340.

*Valencia, S. W., Hiebert, E. H., & Afflerbach, P. P. (Eds.). (1994). *Authentic reading assessment: Practices and possibilities.* Newark, DE: International Reading Association.

*Vandrick, S. W. (1996). Using multicultural literature in college ESL writing classes. *Journal of Second Language Writing, 6*(3), 253–269.

*Vasquez, J. (1988). Teaching to the distinctive traits of minority students. *Clearing House, 63,* 299–304.

Vriend, D. L. (1988, April). *Chinese speakers and English prepositions: Problems and solutions.* Paper presented at the annual meeting of the California Teachers of English to Speakers of Other Languages, San Francisco.

*Wang, Y. (1998). *A user friendly ESL guide for the mainstream teacher.* Portsmouth School District: Portsmouth, NH.

*White, R. V. (1995). *New ways in teaching writing. New ways in TESOL series: Innovative classroom techniques.* Alexandria, VA: Teaching English to Speakers of Other Languages.

Witkin, H. A. (1967). A cognitive-style approach to cross-cultural research. *International Journal of Psychology, 6,* 4–87.

Wong, S. C. (1983). Handles for teaching grammar. *CATESOL Occasional Papers, 9,* 86–97.

Woodruff, B. B. (Ed.). (1988). Inside English. *Journal of the English Council of California Two Year Colleges, 15,* (1–4), 1–55.

Yang, N. D. (1995, March). *Effective awareness-raising in language learning strategy training.* Paper presented at the annual meeting of the Teachers of English to Speakers of Other Languages, Long Beach, CA.

*Zhang, Z. (1994, March). *The development and use of a reading strategy inventory for ESL college students.* Paper presented at the annual meeting of the Mid-South Educational Research Association, Nashville.

*Zimmerman, C. B. (1997). Do reading and interactive vocabulary instruction make a difference? An empirical study. *TESOL Quarterly, 31*(1), 121–139.

11

Technology
and College Reading

❧§§❧

David C. Caverly
Cynthia L. Peterson
Southwest Texas State University

Readers have always used technology to improve their learning, whether it be clay tablets 5,000 years ago, books 500 years ago, or computers beginning 50 years ago. Today, computer technology is integrated into almost every aspect of learning in higher education: textbooks arrive with CD-ROMs; homework is delivered and graded on the World Wide Web (WWW); and assignments are designed to be completed collaboratively through electronic mail (e-mail). Facility with computer technology is essential for college (Lemke, 1993) as well as career success (Groff, 1996; Oblinger & Rush, 1997).

Developmental educators have also looked to computer technology to provide an instructional boost for underprepared students who have difficulty understanding text. Yet, research on the effect of technology on reading achievement shows mixed results (Caverly, 1995; Jamison, Suppes, & Wells, 1974; Kulik & Kulik, 1985; Kulik, Kulik, & Cohen, 1980). These results come from a period of technology research that focused on the machine as the agent of instructional change. Clark (1983) noted that technology is merely a delivery vehicle which does not influence student achievement "any more than the truck that delivers our groceries causes changes in our nutrition" (p. 445).

How, then, to best review the research on the effectiveness of computer technology in developmental reading? The effectiveness of any technology depends on a number of factors. From the literature in technology and reading, we have identified three. For a typical college developmental reader, "Jenny Exe," these factors are: (a) her role as a learner in using the computer, (b) the instructional approach of the software or the developmental reading instructor, and (c) the cognitive complexity of her learning task.

We propose that these factors interact to form a technology support model for developmental reading (see Fig. 11.1) that aids our understanding of the effectiveness of technology for developmental readers.

We begin the chapter with the theoretical rationale for the technology support model. The model guides our review of research on the effectiveness of computer technology in developmental reading. One dimension of the model, the reader's educational use of the computer, serves as an organizing framework from which we consider the research in terms of the other two dimensions. When possible, we address the relationship between technology and attitude. Next, we explore the impact of technology delivered, distance education. We conclude with a summary and a discussion of the implications of the review for practice and future research in developmental reading instruction.

TECHNOLOGY SUPPORT MODEL FOR DEVELOPMENTAL READING

A utilitarian model for considering technology in developmental reading is presented in Fig. 11.1.

The breadth dimension of this model is a categorization of the educational role of the computer as a *tutor, tool,* or *tutee.* (Ayersman, 1996, Broderick & Caverly, 1988, 1992a, 1992b; Caverly & Broderick, 1988, 1989, 1993; Taylor, 1980). The depth dimension depicts how the uses of technology vary by instructional perspectives, ranging from *behaviorist* (related to the terms objectivist, mastery learning, and skills) to *social constructivist* (related to the terms subjectivist, whole language, and holistic) perspectives that represent different degrees of learner control of the learning environment. The height dimension of this model represents the cognitive task demands of the college reader (cf. Spiro, Coulson, Feltovich, & Anderson, 1994). *Simple* and well-structured

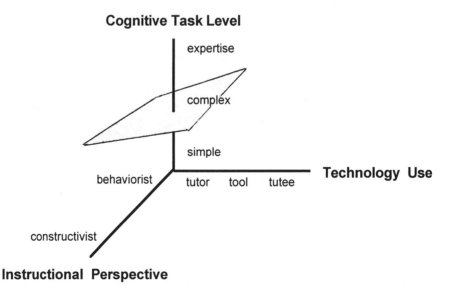

FIG. 11.1. A technology support model for developmental reading.

reading demands support the introductory level of knowledge required in lower division courses, but this knowledge must be transferred to the more *complex* task demands of upper division coursework. In some areas, students need or choose to attain *expertise*.

The Breadth Dimension: Uses of Technology

The uses of computer technology in education often have been described as tutor, tool, and tutee (Ayersman, 1996, Broderick & Caverly, 1988, 1992a, 1992b; Caverly & Broderick, 1988, 1989, 1993; Taylor, 1980). Here, we define the computer as tutor as the computer teaching students; the computer as tool as students teaching themselves through the computer; and the computer as tutee as students teaching themselves by using the computer to teach others.

Computer As Tutor. As a tutor, the computer delivers a software program written by instructional designers to improve specific reading skills or strategies. This function has been labeled computer-assisted instruction (CAI), computer-managed instruction (CMI), or computer-based instruction (CBI). Examples of the computer as tutor are tutorials, drill and practice, and simulations. Tutorials present a skill or strategy, followed by practice, and are used to supplement other instruction, or, when used in place of developmental educators, to supplant instruction. Drill and practice programs reinforce a skill or strategy previously introduced, often monitoring student progress and regulating exercises based on student answers. Practice exercises, programmed instruction, and games for comprehension and vocabulary are the most common of these for developmental reading. Simulation programs present a scenario, through text and more recently through multimedia, to which the reader responds and receives feedback.

More recently, software programs have been packaged into an integrated learning system (ILS). Here, a technology firm collects a group of computer tutorials into one system for delivery over a *local area network* (i.e., a group of computers networked together with the software accessed from a server) with the computer managing the instruction (i.e., a diagnostic-prescriptive system for identifying the developmental student's deficiencies, computer-directed remediation, monitoring, reteaching if necessary, and report generation of student performance and attendance). Some specific ILSs include CCC (1998), INVEST Learning (1998), Learning Plus (1998), and Plato (1997).

Sophisticated tutorials have begun to incorporate *multimedia* (linear programs presenting instruction via audio, video, graphics, and text controlled by the producer), *hypermedia* (offline, nonlinear programs with multimedia, but controlled by the user), and the WWW (online hypermedia programs). These applications can represent domains of knowledge as "ill-structured" (Spiro et al., 1994); that is, in authentic, nonprototypical form. Here, instructional designers create tutorial programs that scaffold readers in constructing meaning from difficult text by assessing their level of prior knowledge, by providing links to concept definitions or text structure, and by embedding questions to monitor comprehension (for a review of this research, see Ayersman, 1996). In a word, the "computer as tutor" is the computer teaching the developmental student.

Computer As Tool. A second function of computer technology is its most common use, that of a tool, for gathering, arranging, and presenting through word processors, databases, spreadsheets, outliners, graphic designers, desktop publishing, e-mail, and WWW search engines. Technology as a tool has been defined as a knowl-edge-based, systematic method of achieving a practical purpose (Puk, 1992). Just as a hammer is a means for building a bookcase, the computer is a means for reading, writing, and computing. By handling mundane and routine tasks, the computer tool frees the reader to engage in higher level thinking.

Developmental readers use the computer as a tool for manipulating words, num-bers, and images as they read and write in the context of instruction. More sophisticated computer tool applications require the reader to determine a purpose, set preferences within the program, and possibly to integrate information across linear and multilinear applications. Web browsers and video telecommunications programs make it possible for developmental students to interact with live tutors across distances.

The computer as tool can support readers in transforming information into knowl-edge as they gather, arrange, and present: a process Caverly (1996) called GAP. Students learn to *gather* information from lectures, texts, and the WWW, using search engines for finding information and databases for storing it. They learn to *arrange* the material to-ward understanding by using computer tools, such as outlining or mapping programs, and then to *present* that material to peers through multimedia and hypermedia, reflecting on the feedback they receive. What students learn as they move through this process are thinking strategies needed to move from simple to complex knowledge of the reading process. In a word, developmental readers use the computer as a tool to teach them-selves.

Computer As Tutee.   A third function of the computer is that of a tutee. The computer as tutee has been defined as students teaching the computer to do their bidding through programming languages such as BASIC and LOGO (Caverly & Broderick, 1989, 1993; Luehrmann, 1980; Papert, 1993; Taylor, 1980). Although LOGO might be an effective tool for developing problem-solving abilities in young chil-dren (Roblyer, Edwards, & Havriluk, 1997), new technology has limited the utility of learning a programming language.

Here, we have redefined the computer as tutee as the devlopmental reader using the computer to aid in the tutoring of others. Learning through tutoring is well docu-mented in the literature (cf. Cohen, Kulik, & Kulik, 1982; Goodland & Hirst, 1989; Hedin, 1987; Juel, 1996), typically with comparable achievement gains found for tutor and tutee, but often greater attitude gains by the tutor. Building on the positive effects of tutoring, developmental readers can construct multimedia and hypermedia tutorials, slide shows, and Web pages to be read and viewed by other developmental readers (Ayersman, 1996; Caverly & Broderick, 1989, 1990, 1991, 1993; Marchionini, 1988; Tierney et al., 1992). In doing so, students are led to articulate their understanding of the skills and strategies they are teaching others. In a word, the computer as tutee is the de-velopmental reader using the computer as a tool for the purpose of teaching others and improving his or her own reading in the process.

The Depth Dimension: Instructional Approach

Instructional uses of technology in developmental education fall along a second contin-uum as well; that of views as to how one learns (Caverly & Peterson, 1996). From a *be-haviorist* view (Skinner, 1968), the computer provides an instructional stimulus and then reinforces the learner's response. Computer technology has made it possible to fully implement and to evaluate behaviorist models such as mastery learning (Bloom, 1976). The elements of individualized diagnosis, sequenced instruction, controlled pacing, extensive drill and practice, and immediate feedback can be delivered easily via computer technology. A posttest measure can be closely aligned with clearly identified learning objectives and the content of the instruction. Although modest learning gains are consistently reported, these gains have not been demonstrated on standardized tests (Joyce & Weil, 1996), suggesting a limited positive effect on reading ability.

More recent information processing theories of learning (Ausubel, 1968; Gagne, 1985) led to instructional technology that considered how the material is best structured and sequenced for learning to occur. Both behaviorist and information processing perspectives result in a high degree of direction and control by the instructional program, rather than control by the learner.

Opposite to behaviorism on the continuum of instructional perspectives is *social constructivism*. Along this view, learners actively "construct" their own understanding (cf. Brooks, 1990; Duffy & Bednar, 1991; Duffy & Jonassen, 1992) rather than passively respond to a predetermined protocol or receive a "pre-packaged schema" (Spiro et al., 1994, p. 605). Reading strategies learned from either instructional perspective might differ in sequence or in how performance is measured. Social constructivism holds that higher mental functioning originates in social activity—that for complex knowledge to be internalized, the learner must reconstruct (as "inner speech") an external (social) exchange. That is, social interaction awakens internal thinking processes (Vygotsky, 1962). Algorithms and heuristics about the reading process can be constructed by the reader after multiple and varied experiences with text and after extensive discussion with peers (including other developmental readers) and experts (including developmental educators). For example, students might access digitized video clips to watch expert readers modeling how to determine organizational structure in text. After discussing the expert modeling in cooperative e-mail groups, students could submit to their instructor a group consensus statement about the strategy. The social learning becomes internalized as they independently apply and adapt the strategy to multiple sources in other classes, and then report back to their instructor and to their group on its effectiveness (Caverly, Sundin, Nicholson, & Oelke, 1990). Specific constructivist instructional approaches that have been successful in promoting learning through technology include cognitive apprenticeship and situated cognition (Collins, Brown, & Newman, 1989), cooperative learning (Johnson & Johnson, 1990), and inquiry learning (cf. Dodge, 1998; Laffey, Tupper, Musser, & Wedman, 1998). These approaches require a high degree of direction and control by the learner, rather than control by the program.

The Height Dimension: Cognitive Task Demands of the College Reader

The instructional uses of technology interact with the reading comprehension task demands of the college reader. Cognitive flexibility theory (CFT; Spiro et al., 1994) is a major theory of comprehension often invoked to explain the acquisition of the advanced or complex knowledge and expertise required of students in and beyond college in an information age (Greening, 1998). Here we apply CFT to the use of technology to support developmental reading instruction.

Simple Knowledge.   Acquisition of declarative and procedural knowledge, according to CFT, begins with a general category orientation, and grows to a simple or introductory level. Developmental reading instruction can leave students with a simple understanding of expert reading strategies for word recognition, vocabulary development, comprehending, metacomprehending, and rate if taught only in well-structured, prototypical text. Yet, college success requires academic literacy (Pugh, Pawan, & Antommarchi, chap. 2, this volume). It is only by reasoning with simple knowledge and applying it flexibly in diverse contexts that advanced or complex knowledge of reading can be acquired.

Complex or Advanced Knowledge.   Complex knowledge acquisition requires seeing knowledge domains as "ill-structured"; that is, understanding how patterns of concepts, heuristics, and rules (i.e., strategies) may be inconsistent across different task demands and then learning how to adapt them appropriately (Spiro et al., 1994). Reading, like writing, arithmetic, and probably technology, is a tool domain, characterized by some domain-specific concepts, tactics, and strategies. As such, it is ill-structured, as are the content domains (such as biology or history) to which reading is applied. In reading to learn, college readers must orchestrate strategic approaches (Caverly, Mandeville, & Nicholson, 1995), exercising cognitive flexibility.

Expertise.   According to CFT, expertise is characterized by flexible thinking, acquired through extensive experience, and practiced in diverse situations. Expertise in reading results from extensive experience in adapting reading strategies to varied and difficult text. Although technology can support readers, it has also created new text formats that require the adaptive thinking of reading expertise.

As students move into upper division courses, cognitive demands become more complex, requiring knowledge of the procedural strategies of reading and experience with varied and difficult text (Caverly & Orlando, 1991; Orlando, Caverly, Swetman, & Flippo, 1989). At this point, many developmental readers are at risk of failing. For example, a phenomenon known as "transfer shock" for 2-year college students who begin junior level work has been well documented (Cejda, 1997). The research reviewed in the following sections demonstrates that although simple to complex knowledge of reading can be mastered from a technology supported, behaviorist instructional approach, developmental readers may overgeneralize that knowledge when faced with more challenging, "ill-structured" text and more rigorous task demands. The research also demonstrates the potential of constructivist instructional approaches with a technology scaffold to move developmental readers to independent reading expertise.

RESEARCH ON THE COMPUTER AS TUTOR

Minimal Achievement Gains

Prior to the advent of microcomputers in the early 1980s, meta-analyses of research on computer tutorials generated average effect sizes of +.31 for reading achievement (cf.

Kulik et al., 1980). This effect size represents a gain of about 10 percentile points on a standardized test: positive and encouraging, but minimal. A closer look at the posttest scores of those studies reviewed reveals that where improvement was found, the posttest scores still averaged only at the 60th percentile for computer tutorials, inadequate for even the simplest level of task demands required by higher education.

The shift to microcomputer use brought renewed hope for significant gains from the computer as tutor. Yet meta-analyses completed since the mid-1980s (Kulik, 1993; Kulik & Kulik, 1985, 1987, 1991) found similar, minimal effect size gains.

Individual studies have explored this limited gain. Schnitz (1983), used the Individualized Reading and Instruction System (IRIS), an ILS, and found immediate posttest gain, but after 2 years there was no effect. Balajthy, Bacon, and Hasby (1985) and Balajthy (1988) attempted to improve developmental readers' vocabulary through drill and practice computer tutorials, but found little gain. Wepner and Feeley (1987) found no differences in speed reading learned from a computer tutorial or from traditional textbooks. Taylor and Rosecrans (1986) found no difference between traditional instruction and a computer tutorial when teaching word recognition skills. In a controlled evaluation study of the CCC-based ILS, Underwood, Cavendish, Dowling, Fogelman, and Lawson reported significant learning gains on standardized tests of math achievement, but none for reading. Peterson, Burke, and Segura (1999) as well as McCreary and Maginnis (1989) compared lab and text-based instruction to computer-presented instruction and found no advantage in student achievement for the computer delivery. Read (1992) used an ILS with low-level English as a second language (ESL) students. Compared to a control group, no significant gains were found on posttest scores or on the percentage passing the course based on attaining a specific grade level on a standardized reading test.

Other studies (MacGregor, 1988; Reinking, 1988; Reinking & Schreiner, 1985) found that lack of computer expertise negatively affected academic performance on computer tutorials. Adequate instruction in computer use might improve student success with the computer as tutor.

Significant Achievement Gains for Computer As Tutor

Some of the weak effects of computer as tutor on reading achievement can be explained by a failure to consider the importance of the instructional perspective of the computer tutorials. If the computer *supplants* traditional instruction, as is often the case when used from a behaviorist instructional perspective, only simple levels of knowledge seem to be attained.

Many studies have found significant gains from the use of an ILS (Havlicek & Coulter, 1982; Lang, 1992; Moore, 1993; Peterson & Williams, 1990; Reinking & Bridwell-Bowles, 1992; Seaman & McCallister, 1988; Walker, 1992). The less skilled (i.e., lower level readers) typically improved more than the higher skilled readers, an important benefit. Project LEAP, a recent evaluation study of the INVEST Learning ILS (Johnson & Perez, 1997) in nine community colleges, concluded that the ILS positively affected student persistence at the learning task and was successful in meeting the objectives of the developmental reading program. However, there was no control group, so results are questionable.

In these studies, gains were found on ILS posttests and on developmental course grades, but no transfer to improved performance on standardized reading tests or to future reading task demands was reported. Only Dixon (1993), using a behaviorist instructional approach with computer tutorials in developmental reading classes, found improved transfer as defined by performance on a standardized test and enrollment retention. Attributing those gains directly to computer tutorials is confounded by attendance in a developmental reading course, which alone improves retention (Hennessey, 1990; Tedrow & Rust, 1994; Weissman et al., 1994).

Computer ILS have often been used inappropriately. For low-achieving students the ILS experience was found to be haphazard and not integrated into instruction (Becker, 1992b), resulting in limited gains (Becker, 1992a). Ginsburg and McCormick (1998) found high SES students spent more time on computers, completing more sophisticated activities, while their low SES peers were relegated to unsophisticated drill and practice programs or games. Waxman (1992) described this use of computer tutorials as promoting a "Matthew Effect" (Stanovich, 1986), meaning the academically rich get richer and the academically poor get poorer.

On the other hand, significant gains in reading achievement have been found when computer tutorials are used to *supplement* regular classroom instruction, particularly when used from a constructivist instructional perspective. Mikulecky and Adams (1988) developed two computer tutorial programs to teach students how to recognize main ideas through mapping within biology and psychology textbooks. This program was provided by the learning center using a supplemental instruction (SI) intervention model (Martin & Arendale, 1992). Improved student performance was attributed to the combined effect of SI, the computer tutorials, and the support by instructors to help developmental students make immediate transfer to course task demands. Others have found similar gains when computer tutorials were used to supplement other content courses (Brothern, 1992; Price, 1992; Reed-Sanders, & Liebowitz, 1991). Wepner (1990), supplemented a computer tutorial program with college developmental readers and found significant speed-reading performance gains when students applied speed-reading strategies to recreational reading.

Computer As Tutor and Instructional Time

When instructional time is the dependent variable, rather than achievement, meta-analyses on computer tutorials have found significant reductions in the time necessary to learn the same skills or strategies compared to instruction without computers. Kulik and Kulik (1987), for example, found that instructional time was reduced by 32%. In a study of undergraduate psychology students, Taraban and Rynearson (1998) concluded that self-paced computer tutorials were as effective as traditional lecture on student achievement, but more efficient in terms of student time. When the instructional perspective is the same, we might expect the computer to be more engaging. Attention has long been recognized as a necessary prerequisite to reading (cf. LaBerge & Samuels, 1974). Whether the computer is effective in focusing reader attention to text is addressed in part by studies of the effect of computer technology on attitude and motivation. Although greater frequency of use is associated with more positive attitudes toward technology (Yaghi, 1997), these positive effects decline with the perception of its novelty (Goodwin,

Goodwin, Nansel, & Helm, 1986; Lee & Boling, 1996; McCall, 1984; Saracho, 1982). Moreover, computer use has not been shown to affect attitudes toward the content being studied. These diminishing returns require either a new technological innovation, or a more inherently engaging instructional model.

Social constructivist instructional models may be more inherently engaging; they also have been successful in maximizing student use of technology-supported instructional time. Cavalier and Klein (1998) found that a cooperative learning approach was more efficient for readers than either traditional instruction or computer tutorials. Students working independently were more easily distracted and exhibited more off-task behavior. Although students working on computer tutorials with drill and practice spent significantly more time on the task than students working in cooperative pairs, there was no difference in their performance. Other studies have demonstrated higher levels of individual achievement when students worked on computer tutorials within cooperative learning groups (Brush, 1997; Dalton, Hannafin, & Hooper, 1989; Mevarech, Silber, & Fine, 1991).

The literature reviewed here suggests that achievement gains through the use of computer tutorials to improve reading achievement can be explained by the technology support model presented in Fig.11.1. Where computer tutorials followed a behaviorist instructional perspective, gains were found, albeit minimal, on end-of-course grade, reduced dropout rates, and performance on a posttest. Gains were not necessarily found on transfer-dependent variables such as improved performance on standardized tests or future course performance. Computer tutorials from a behaviorist instructional perspective seem to lead students only to simple levels of knowledge about reading. Although this is necessary, it is not sufficient for the advanced literacy requirements of higher education. The computer as tutor from social constructivist instructional perspectives shows solid achievement gains and the potential for students to attain more complex levels of knowledge acquisition.

Hypermedia

More sophisticated computer tutorials have emerged in the last 20 years in the form of hypermedia. Hypermedia tutorial software provides either the same instruction in the same sequence to all learners (i.e., program control) or allows the learner to make choices as to the amount or type of instruction to receive (i.e., learner control). Williams (1993) noted that instructional design research comparing the benefits of program versus learner control has been equivocal, due to the many other factors intervening with achievement (e.g., metacognitive skills, motivation, task persistence, self-efficacy, and attributional style). Little research has been done to relate these factors to technology supported reading.

In a meta-analysis, Liao (1988) found a moderate effect size (+.48, representing an achievement gain of about 18 percentile points) for the use hypermedia computer tutorials over traditional lecture and demonstration instruction. Notably, the effect size was +.26 higher when hypermedia was used to supplement rather than supplant teacher-led instruction.

There are two lines of research on instructional hypermedia: how to support readers through the strategic use of hypermedia, and how it can represent real-world complexity for complex knowledge acquisition. The first line of research addresses the design and effectiveness of organizational aids to help the naïve reader recognize text structure and thus help them comprehend. In a review of empirical studies of learning with hypertext, Rouet and Levonen (1996) concluded that providing structural cues in the form of interactive organizers, hierarchical maps, and structure overviews is important to reader success. Dee-Lucas and Larkin (1995), for example, demonstrated that users of hypermedia tutorials exposed to interactive overviews outperformed learners who studied the same materials using traditional text when tested for breadth of recall and memory of text topics.

Level of metacognitive strategy knowledge and background knowledge about the hypermedia tutorial affects learners' success in programs written for learner control. Shin, Shallert, and Savenye (1994) found that readers learned more and liked it better when advice and structure was suggested to aid in key decisions about (a) when they were successful, (b) when more study was necessary, and (c) when to access program assistance—in other words, when metacognitive decisions were facilitated. Undergraduate archaeology students who did have knowledge of learning strategies were able to adapt them to a hypermedia tutorial, in a study by Relan and Smith (1996), but they expressed a desire for more contact with a human instructor. Schroeder 1994) found that background knowledge (but not verbal ability) affected a readers' use of a structural map to a hypermedia document. Those with high prior knowledge were better able to access the maps and also gained the most in a measure of the structural knowledge.

The importance of structural cues seems also to be affected by the nature of the reading task. Rouet and Levonen (1996) cited a number of studies to support this relationship, including one by Dee-Lucas and Larkin (1995) who found that the more focused the reading task demand (e.g., to write a summary), the less important the presentation format. Their conclusions argue for readers of hypertext to read with task awareness. Metacognitive learning strategies, and, likely, knowledge of and practice in the new text structures of hypermedia, seem to be necessary for developmental readers to make appropriate decisions in hypermedia tutorials that require learner control.

A second line of research is the potential of hypermedia environments to present complex material in multiple contexts, in ways that highlight the interconnections of abstract and case-specific information for complex knowledge acquisition. Spiro et al. (1994) proposed that hypermedia based on cognitive flexibility theory might capture real-world complexities on which abstract and expert conceptual knowledge could be developed. In a study by Jacobson and Spiro (1995), a control group that accessed traditional text performed better on factual knowledge measures, whereas a group accessing hypermedia performed better on knowledge transfer measures, suggesting they acquired more advanced knowledge. For additional examples of instructional uses of hypermedia, see the review by Ayersman (1996).

RESEARCH ON THE COMPUTER AS TOOL

Increasingly, developmental educators are exploring the use of the computer as a tool, although more recommendations than research have been reported. As a tool, the computer can be a cognition enhancer (Dede, 1987) particularly when linked to instruction. The use of word processing, for example, does not necessarily improve student writing (Daiute, 1985). Student writing does improve when word processing supports instruction in effective writing strategies (Reynolds & Hart, 1990). Computer tools may support a be-haviorist instructional program, but the learner-controlled uses of computer tools for scaffolding reading most likely represent a constructivist instructional perspective.

Comprehension of linear text has been shown to be no different when reading from a computer screen than when reading from the printed page, although quality of screen resolution has been found to be important for reader success (Chen et al., 1996; Gould et al., 1987). Hypermedia (including text and multimedia) presents a nonlinear text structure, prompting research into the cognitive skills needed for the reader to be successful (cf., Rouet & Levonen, 1996). The next section applies the technology support model to the use of computer tools for scaffolding the reader in the processes of gathering and arranging information and then presenting one's understanding, or GAP (Caverly, 1996).

Computer As a Tool for Gathering Information

The computer can be used as a comprehending tool as the reader gathers information from a single source (typical of simple or introductory knowledge tasks) or multiple sources (often necessary for complex knowledge acquisition). It can provide models, support tools, and guides to aid the reader in accessing and identifying information.

First, a computer tool can provide a clear model to introduce a reading strategy, which may be particularly useful for at-risk readers. For example, after computer training with speech feedback, dyslexic students gained more in reading comprehension and spelling performance than did a control group of students in a conventional special education setting (Lundberg, 1995). Knox-Quinn and Horney (1998) found that learning disabled students took better lecture notes when they could read the model notes of an expert tutor on the split screen of their networked laptops.

Support tools, in the form of online definitions, outlines, and background information, have advantages for reading comprehension (Reinking, 1988). The least structured of these support tools are hypermedia links to vocabulary definitions, databases of information, audio narration, graphics, sound and video, and critical analyses that are not connected to the text structure. Geske (1991) found that although these links help compensate for a reader's low prior knowledge, some readers believe that they interrupt the process of comprehension. This perceived interruption relates to findings that readers spend more time working with computer-mediated text that provides support options for readers to access (Reinking, 1989). Shin et al. (1994) documented how readers with low background knowledge for the content of hypermedia text became disoriented when allowed free access to links and made poor strategic decisions about what to do next. Moreover, the use of links not connected to the text structure resulted in lower achievement in a study by Schroeder (1994). As with hypermedia tutorials, developmental students need the metacognitive strategies to know when and where to access these computer support tools.

Interactive guides are a more structured computer support tool that can aid the reader in developing metacognition and comprehension strategies. Salomon, Globerson, and Guterman (1989) studied secondary students' use of a computer "Reading Partner" tool that allowed them to access explicit metacognitive guidance during reading. These students performed significantly higher on a standardized reading measure, a measure of metacognitive transfer, and a self-report measure of mental effort expended than did students who received computer-presented postreading questions or students who received no support. Readers engaged in online communities(called MOOs and MUDs) where participants take on roles) may interact with a "Client-Bot," a program that responds to questions, guides the user, and offers advice (Foner, 1998). The computer as tool is potentially an effective "guide on the side" (Brooks & Brooks, 1993) from a constructivist instructional perspective, providing for the reader "a more capable peer" in a zone of proximal development for reading (Salomon et al., 1989). Developmental educators who use computer tool scaffolds need also to promote reader independence by considering when to remove them.

Computer As a Tool for Gathering Information From Multiple Sources

Although hypermedia is the most recent "power tool," the idea is not new. As far back as 1945, Bush proposed a "memex" (Bush, 1945) of all books, records, and communications stored in an electronically searchable format. Bush envisioned that as the reader proceeded through the memex, accessing pages from one text or another, an electronic trail could be blazed. Bush's "electronic trail" recognized a potential research tool for obtaining direct evidence of readers' cognitive strategies (Britt, Rouet, & Perfetti, 1996).

Gathering information from multiple sources is a college task demand that takes heightened importance with the availability of the WWW (Dodge, 1998; McKenzie, 1998). The WWW offers interesting, authentic text, but also challenges the reader with the opportunity to pursue multiple pathways (Caverly & Broderick, 1995). Readers are aided in gathering information by computer tools such as search engines and databases, but they must be taught critical reading skills for constructing and executing a search (Peterson & St. Clair, 1997). The reader's ability to gather information is extended by a computer tool such as a remembrance agent (RA), which augments human memory by displaying a list of documents that might be relevant to the user's current context (Rhodes, 1996). Unlike most information retrieval systems, an RA runs continuously in the background without user intervention. Its unobtrusive interface (a message running across the bottom of the screen) allows the reader to pursue or ignore the RAs suggestions. These "intelligent agents" can search the WWW based on the reader's previous searches bringing up links of interest (Foner, 1998; Negroponte, 1995), or augmenting current work. Although agents allow the reader to make sense of the morass of information from the WWW, they are only as good as the user queries. Thus, the WWW can be a tool for complex knowledge acquisition if developmental readers are taught questioning strategies for accessing multiple sources.

Computer As a Tool for Arranging Information Into Knowledge

Reading comprehension has long been argued to be a reasoning ability (Thorndike, 1917; Todd, 1854). Formulating a conceptual model, breaking down a problem into a series of steps, and testing ideas with simulations are mental processes that successful students engage in while reading. Some researchers (Papert, 1980; Taylor, 1980) have argued that programming the computer can generate this type of thinking. The value of students programming the computer (originally Taylor's notion of tutee) has received mixed reviews (Lepper, 1985), and it raises the question of whether those reasoning skills transfer to other contexts (Perkins & Salomon, 1989). At the time of Taylor's research, students were taught programming languages. Now, computer tools such as authoring languages exist to support students in those problem-solving tasks (Broderick & Caverly, 1990, 1994). Using an authoring language within a hypermedia application may not be strong enough to affect general problem-solving ability (Reed & Liu, 1994). Yet if StarLogo, a parallel programming environment, can expand our ability to use mathematical thinking to understand the world (as suggested by Resnick, 1995), there is the potential for programming tools to expand our ability to comprehend.

The computer can be an effective tool for readers to reason with text as they make decisions about how to organize information, make inferences, and draw conclusions. Britt et al. (1996) argued that the ability to access, organize, manipulate, and comprehend information may be the most important function of hypermedia tools. After reading each unit of hypermedia information, the reader must select and click on a node in order to progress. Most hypermedia research has focused on documenting and explicating those decisions; Rouet and Levonen (1996) noted it has been from the perspective of design elements, rather than on the cognitive processes involved in reading hypermedia. With few controlled evaluations of the impact of hypermedia on learning, little is known about its effectiveness as a learning tool.

Still, we know that hypermedia imposes a higher cognitive load on the reader who must keep track in this new and different text structure. In order to comprehend, the reader must develop strategies for building coherence out of loosely structured materials. Foltz (1996) and Rouet and Levonen (1996) explored novice and expert strategies in building coherence from multiple historical documents related through hypertext. Novice history students with lower background knowledge read documents in the order presented on an overview screen, whereas the expert history graduate students approached the task more strategically, by selecting the document that seemed most important before branching through the links. These studies suggest that hypermedia tools require developmental readers to have strategies for comprehension monitoring and for strategically selecting text.

Another way in which computer tools can aid the reader in reasoning with text is through outlining and concept mapping for determining the ordination and relationships among ideas. Computer-mapping tools have been used successfully to support reading comprehension (Anderson-Inman & Zeitz, 1993; Caverly et al., 1990) and for brainstorming and then synthesizing different sources during prewriting (Anderson-Inman, Horney, Knox-Quinn, Corrigan, & Ditson, 1996). Using the computer as a tool with low-ability students to teach problem solving may be particularly effective when students work collaboratively in small groups (Derry, Tookey, & Roth, 1993).

Other specific advantages for developmental readers using the computer as tool have been reported. Mehan, Moll, and Riel (1985) gave at-risk students complex problems to solve in a group via computer tools. Through the rich language environment encouraged by group problem solving, the students were successful at solving the problems and improving their language skills. Brothern (1992, 1994, 1996) found that developmental students could become more self-regulated learners by accessing a computerized gradebook and a practice final exam. VanOostendorp (1996) found improved comprehension for electronic notetaking while reading electronic texts. Betza's (1997) description of how students become active learners by adding to and deleting from a word processor spelling checker demonstrates how arranging information into knowledge is fostered by computer tools. Successful uses of word processing, outlining, concept mapping, summarizing text, developing cohesion in writing, and self-testing are also reported by Anderson-Inman and Zeitz (1993) and Bernhardt (1994). Despite this limited research on the computer as a tool for arranging information into knowledge, the reports from practice are encouraging.

Computer As a Tool for Presenting Knowledge

As a tool for presenting new knowledge, the computer can develop literacy skills. One documented example is e-mail. Sinagra, Battle, and Nicholson (1998) looked at developmental reading students' use of e-mail to respond to literature. Students from each university were paired as "booktalk" partners for 8 weeks. Qualitative data analysis provided a detailed view of the nature of students' engagement and showed that using quality literature, e-mail, and authentic audiences engaged many of these developmental students in academic discourse. Other successful reports of improving developmental ESL students use of writing skills via e-mail journaling come from Meyer (1995) and Wang (1996). Real-time electronic chat was also found to be successful in engaging students with booktalking (Jody & Saccardi, 1996). Russell (1995), working with adults learning e-mail communication, reported that providing them with realistic expectations of the time required to become proficient users resulted in their more positive technology attitudes towards technology.

Summary of the Computer As Tool

Although the effective use of computer tools is arguably a new basic skill, developmental students need to learn how to apply these tools to their college classes. The research suggests that when developmental readers use the computer as a tool from a more constructivist instructional perspective they can attain more advanced levels of reading knowledge. Moreover, this use can result in an increased sense of control over and intrinsic motivation for learning (Becker & Dwyer, 1994).

RESEARCH ON THE COMPUTER AS TUTEE

As noted earlier in this chapter, we redefined Taylor's conception of tutee to accommodate new possibilities in technology and instruction. From a social constructivist perspective, computer tools enable interaction around a shared learning task between a more knowledgeable tutor and a tutee who has particular learning needs. Tutors benefit from teaching others, a well-documented conclusion in the literature on tutoring (Cohen et al., 1982). The meta-analysis effect size on achievement (+.33) for tutors was similar for tutees (+.40), but tutors had significantly greater benefits in attitude toward the subject matter (effect size of +.42 for tutors vs. +.20 for tutees). Juel (1996) reported that at-risk college student athletes who tutored elementary students in reading scored significantly higher on a reading posttest than those who did not tutor.

Several studies have explored why tutoring is so effective. Annis (1983), McKellar (1984), as well as Gartner and Riessman (1993) concluded that the primary factor accounting for these gains is the process of organizing and reworking concepts in order to teach or tutor. In reviewing the research on the computer as a tutee, we look at how students produce multimedia or hypermedia as they teach their peers concepts about reading and study strategies they are learning (Ayersman, 1996; Caverly & Broderick, 1989, 1993; Tierney & Pearson, 1994).

Achievement

Some studies have documented the cognitive benefits of students producing interactive multimedia for others. When Riskin (1990) had undergraduate sociology students produce interactive multimedia for other sociology students, the student producers gained in nonlinear, creative thinking about the interdisciplinary nature of sociology. Sayers (1989) engaged ESL students in soliciting themed articles from other at-risk students around the world to create, edit, and produce an online newspaper. From this complex, social constructivist computer task, the students improved skills in both native and English languages. Diaz (1984) found similar gains among at-risk ESL high school students who tutored Anglos in complex computer skills. Other studies (Griffin, 1994; Hay, Guzdial, Jackson, Boyle, & Soloway, 1994; Reinking & Watkins, 1996; Rodrigues, 1997) demonstrated content knowledge gains in elementary- and secondary-level students. These results suggest that when students produce multimedia or hypermedia for other students, they can improve their own understanding of the material and their confidence as learners.

There is solid support for investigating the effects of developmental readers producing multimedia or hypermedia for others toward improving their own procedural knowledge of reading. Some studies (Tierney et al., 1992; Turner & Dipinto, 1992) are beginning to verify that students who engage in hypermedia authoring *specifically for an audience* shift in how they represent and integrate new ideas. They also communicate more effectively, improve their content knowledge, and accomplish tasks they could not have done without the technology. Specifically with developmental readers, Caverly, Nicholson, Peterson, and Wright (1997) found that students' procedural knowledge of reading improved after they produced hypermedia to teach reading strategies to other developmental students. Peterson, Nicholson, Murray, and Caverly (1995) found that at-risk student athletes were able to articulate internalized study strategies by constructing a hypermedia slide show for future first-year students.

DISTANCE READING EDUCATION

Many postsecondary institutions have expanded the delivery of courses through distance education in general and distance reading education in particular (Caverly & McDonald, 1998; McDonald & Caverly, 1997). Romiszowski (1993) characterized the variety of delivery systems as generational as higher education institutions evolve in their use of distance education. A first-generational delivery system for distance education is correspondence courses, delivered from a behaviorist instructional perspective, as students work independently to complete a sequence of lessons, and submit assignments and exams by mail. A second evolution of distance education delivery occurred with video- or audiotaped lecture supplements to the print material, also sent through the mail, and also real-time broadcasts, when students can call in with questions. Internet access has substantively changed distance education, causing a third generation characterized by more student interactivity. Instructors teleconference through one-way or two-way audio or video transmission and students interact with them and with other students over e-mail bulletin boards or listserves for asynchronous communication, or chat rooms, MOOs, and MUDs for synchronous communication. Many institutions have moved into a fourth generation of distance education delivery, making possible a social constructivist instructional approach (Thorpe, 1995). Here students participate in multimedia and hypermedia teleconferencing, usually over the WWW, access interactive tutorials, download course materials, search online databases, and collaborate over e-mail and within chat rooms. This paradigm shift can lead to more complex knowledge construction through distance education (Jonassen, 1995).

The new electronic delivery systems have spawned a myriad of course offerings. A survey of 153 institutions found that science and engineering, economics and business, and education courses were the largest contributors to distance education with computer science and health science/medicine not far behind (Golladay, Copeland, & Wu, 1998). Video conferencing was the most typical delivery mechanism, followed by video tapes and information posted on the Internet. Most of these programs (94%) offered instructor assistance outside of class time with a majority (54%) providing additional learning assistance ranging from help desks, labs, and peer assistance for technical problems, to academic, library, and career support.

Although distance education presents challenges and advantages for all students, some are particularly acute for the developmental reader. Benefits of distance education include flexibility of scheduling, time and location; compatibility of computer platforms; and reduced gender, ethnicity, or disability bias (Andrews & Hall, 1991; Kerka, 1996; Thompson, 1996). Learning effectiveness can be impeded by the social isolation of students, information overload, lack of nonverbal cues in communication, opportunity for student passivity, limited bandwidth (i.e., the capacity of the communication connection), inaccessibility in some rural areas, and lack of technical coping skills (Filipczak, 1995; Wiesenberg & Hutton, 1996). Although some of these barriers to learning effectiveness can be overcome by more constructivist approaches, developmental readers in particular need adequate support for learning in a distance education environment (Caverly & McDonald. 1998).

Distance Developmental Reading Education

Early on, colleges offered distance developmental reading education courses (Engler, 1978; Morris, 1992), and as the technology evolved, added study strategy courses and tutoring using fourth-generation distance education delivery systems. Groomes (1994), for example, describes interactive tutorials, test banks for practice questions, online databases, and online developmental reading, writing, and study strategy support in a technical college. The most comprehensive distance developmental reading programs are borne out of necessity in rural environments, such as the one delivered by the University of Alaska, Fairbanks (Illingworth & Illingworth, 1998). Many learning centers provide distance education through e-mail or WWW pages with links to reading tutorials or study strategy tutorial handouts in-house and at other institutions. For a descriptive list of those centers, see Caverly (1998). Most of these applications have yet to be evaluated to determine the effect on developmental readers.

Research on Distance Education

Students using computers as a tutor or tool in distance education courses perform at the same rates as in comparable on-campus courses, with no significant differences on achievement as measured by grade point average (GPA) or course completion rates (Blanchard, 1989; Moore, Thompson, Quigley, Clark, & Goff, 1990; Nixon, 1992; Searcy, Howton, & Yarbrough, 1993). This finding is consistent with Clark's (1983, 1994) point that technology as a delivery vehicle does not improve achievement.

Several factors are reported to be particularly important for success in a distance learning environment: metacognitive strategy knowledge, effective learning strategies, and social interaction, factors that are developed to a more complex level from a social constructivist instructional perspective. Bernt and Bugbee (1990), in a discriminate analysis of high and low passers compared to those who failed a distance education course, found that the best predictors of student success were metacognitive monitoring and strategic test-taking skills. Ekins (1992a, 1992b) survey of Chinese students learning English found that success depended on complex levels of study strategy knowledge. Naidu and Bernard (1992) reported that distance education nursing students who created concept maps outperformed those who responded to inserted questions. Zirkin and Sumler (1995) identified interaction among students as well as between teachers and students as important to learner success.

The research on distance education with developmental readers is sparse. The technology support model predicts that constructivist instructional perspectives are more likely to result in complex levels of reading and study strategy knowledge. New technology enables more constructivist approaches to distance education and promises that the student passivity inherent in earlier behaviorist approaches can be overcome. Just as in nondistance education environments, developmental readers must have additional scaffolds, such as support tools, models, and guides, if they are to become active, strategic readers.

RECOMMENDATIONS FOR INSTRUCTION AND RESEARCH

Conclusions

Technology effectiveness in developmental reading instruction depends on its context and how it is used. We have looked at the context of technology in developmental reading in terms of the instructional approach, on a continuum of behaviorism to social constructivism, and on a continuum of the cognitive task demands of the college reader, from simple to complex to expert knowledge. In looking at how the technology is used, we modified Taylor's (1980) categorization of tutor, tool, or tutee to account for the other two dimensions and for new technology applications. Teaching the computer to do one's bidding (Taylor's notion of the computer as tutee) is more accurately a tool. The computer as tool is used in the process of transforming information into knowledge, through gathering, arranging, and presenting (GAP). The computer as tutee is a powerful way for the developmental reader to learn by using the computer to teach others. The interaction of the three dimensions presented here forms the technology support model for developmental reading.

Computer technology has been reasonably effective when used for reading instruction from behaviorist instructional perspectives, when student improvement is measured by a test aligned with program goals (i.e., in simple knowledge domains). But, those goals are often too limited for the task demands of the college reader who must perform further along the continuum of comprehension toward more complex knowledge acquisition. The college developmental student must have expertise as a reader in order to use reading to learn in other ill-structured knowledge domains.

There is a limited utility to the behaviorist instructional model on which most technology use as tutor and tool has been based. When computer as tutor and tool supplant instruction, we see acquisition of simple levels of knowledge of reading, as evidenced by gains on ILS posttests, but little evidence of gains in complex knowledge. Still, social constructivist instructional approaches have yet to be fully evaluated, particularly in developmental education.

This review also suggests that Clark's (1983, 1994) argument that media is merely the delivery vehicle is not completely accurate. Hypermedia and WWW access have expanded the power of computer tutorials and tools, elevated the task demands of college students, and allowed for more constructivist instructional models to be implemented.

Implications for Instruction

Computer tutorials have been effective in supporting the work of the developmental educator, but they have not been effective as stand-alone interventions. By supporting students in the use of computer tools, developmental reading instruction can lead students to be successful in complex reading tasks that are beyond the simple level of the tutorial. Through GAP, we explained how computer tools can support complex learning task demands. The addition of computer tools to developmental reading instruction suggests shifts in instructional emphasis. Metacognitive strategy instruction, for example, seems to be essential for students to work in hypermedia tool environments. Use of the computer as a tutee for developmental reading seems fruitful, although is still unevaluated. Each of the three instructional uses of the computer, tutor, tool, and tutee, has a place in the college developmental reading program.

What does the future hold? New computing paradigms like object-oriented programming, constraints, logic, and parallelism, have expanded the possibilities of the computer as tool. *Digital manipulatives* (Resnick et al., 1998), computationally enhanced versions of traditional children's toys that have been used to introduce all levels of students to abstract math concepts, might be applied to support the development of reading expertise. Remembrance agents (Rhodes, 1996) might serve to meet a student's particular needs by providing course and assignment schedules, status reports, digests of background knowledge, and selected sources of information. With expanded computer tools, the possibilities for the computer as tutor and as tutee will grow.

What does the future hold for the developmental student we introduced at the beginning? Jenny Exe might begin a developmental reading program (either on campus or through distance education) led by a developmental educator who supplements instruction with a hypermedia tutorial that is a work in progress, as several of the paths have been constructed by previous students in the class. She will collaborate with classmates to determine the best structure for a piece of hypermedia in order to create online metacognitive advice and support guides for the next group of developmental reading students. At the learning center, she becomes proficient in use of computer tools to aid her in gathering, arranging, and presenting knowledge of the content of a difficult course. Every semester, Jenny receives support through the learning center, which provides hypermedia tutorials for particular topics and skills that include contributions from previous students who have taken the course. There, she joins online academic support groups for some of her classes. Her college requires a service component for all students. Because she has completed the developmental reading course, she is given service options related to tutoring younger at-risk students in reading strategies, who look to her as the expert.

Implications for Future Research

The research reviewed here leaves many questions unanswered. From the instructional dimension, the technology support model calls for research into social constructivist perspectives; in particular, the effectiveness of developmental readers using the computer as a tool in tutoring others. From the dimension of cognitive task demands, the model calls for research into the cognitive strategies necessary for developmental readers to interact in hypermedia. How can these strategies be developed? In particular, how can developmental readers acquire the metacognitive strategy awareness to become expert readers of multiple texts? From the dimension of educational uses of the computer, the model calls for assessing how hypermedia, and technology as yet unknown, will change our definitions of computer as tutor, tool, and tutee. Finally, levels of engagement emerged as an important factor that may belong as a fourth dimension in the model. What is the level of engagement developmental readers must attain to be successful using the computer as tool, tutor, or tutee?

In writing this chapter, we often had to rely on research from elementary and secondary populations because of the scarcity of published sources on the uses of technology with college developmental readers. We need to learn more about how technology supports the acquisition of reading expertise and how developmental readers can use that expertise for complex knowledge acquisition. The technology support model can guide future studies and reports.

REFERENCES AND SUGGESTED READINGS

Anderson-Inman, L., Horney, M. A. Knox-Quinn, C., Corrigan, B., & Ditson, L. (1996). Computer-based study strategies for students with learning disabilities: Individual differences associated with adoption level. *Journal of Learning Disabilities, 29*(5), 461–484.

*Anderson-Inman, L., & Zeitz, L. (1993). Computer-based concept mapping: Active studying for active learners. *Computing Teacher, 21*(1), 6–8.

Andrews, M. B., & Hall, D. E. (1991). *Arctic College/Athabasca University transfer program: A review. A study conducted on behalf of Arctic College.* (ERIC Document Reproduction No. ED 348 080)

Annis, L. F. (1983). *The processes and effects of peer tutoring.* (ERIC Document Reproduction No. ED 228 964)

Ausubel, D. P. (1968). *Educational psychology: A cognitive view.* New York: Holt Rinehart and Winston.

*Ayersman, D. J. (1996). Reviewing the research on hypermedia-based learning. *Journal of Research on Computing in Education, 28*(4), 500–525.

Balajthy, E. (1988). An investigation of learner-controlled variables in vocabulary learning using traditional instruction and two forms of computer-based instruction. *Reading Research and Instruction, 27*(4), 15–24.

Balajthy, E., Bacon, L., & Hasby, P. (1985). *Introduction to computers and introduction to word processing: Integrating content area coursework into college reading/study skills curricula using microcomputers.* (ERIC Document Reproduction No. ED 273 941)

Becker, D. A., & Dwyer, M. M. (1994). Using hypermedia to provide learner control. *Journal of Educational Media and Hypermedia, 3*(2), 155–172.

Becker, H. J. (1992a). Computer-based integrated learning systems in the elementary and middle grades: A critical review and synthesis of evaluation reports. *Journal of Educational Computing Research, 8*(1), 1–41.

Becker, H. J. (1992b). A model for improving the performance of integrated learning systems: Mixed individualized/group/whole class lessons, cooperative learning, and organizing time for teacher-led remediation of small groups. *Educational Technology, 32*(9), 6–15.

Bernhardt, B. (1994). Reading and writing between the lines: An interactive approach using computers. *Journal of Reading, 37*(6), 458–463.

Bernt, F. M., & Bugbee, A. C., Jr. (1990). *Study practices of adult learners in distance education: Frequency of use and effectiveness.* (ERIC Document Reproduction No. ED 323 385)

Betza, R. E. (1987). Online: Computerized spelling checkers: Friends or foes? *Language Arts, 64*(4), 438–443.

Blanchard, W. (1989). *Telecourse effectiveness: A research-review update.* (ERIC Document Reproduction No. ED 320 554)

Bloom, B. S. (1976). *Human characteristics and school learning.* New York: McGraw-Hill.

Britt, M., Rouet, J. F., & Perfetti, C. (1996). Using hypertext to study and reason about historical evidence. In J. F. Rouet, J. Levonen, A. Dillon, & R. Spiro (Eds.), *Hypertext and cognition* (pp. 43–72). Mahwah, NJ: Lawrence Erlbaum Associates.

*Broderick, B., & Caverly, D. C. (1988). The computer as tool. *Journal of Developmental Education, 12*(1), 30–31.

Broderick, B., & Caverly, D. C. (1990). Creating your own courseware with software authoring programs. *Journal of Developmental Education, 14*(1), 32–33.

Broderick, B., & Caverly, D. C. (1992a). Another look at the computer as tool. *Journal of Developmental Education, 16*(1), 36–37.

*Broderick, B., & Caverly, D. C. (1992b). Another look at the computer as tutor. *Journal of Developmental Education, 16*(2), 34–35.

Broderick, B., & Caverly, D. C. (1994). Creating your own courseware. *Journal of Developmental Education, 18*(1), 36–37.

Brooks, J. G. (1990). Teachers and students: Constructivists forging new connections. *Educational Leadership, 48*(6), 68–71.

*Brooks, J. G., & Brooks, M. G. (1993). *The case for constructivist classrooms.* Alexandria, VA: Association for Supervision and Curriculum Development.

Brothern, T. (1992). Ideas in practice: A developmental education approach to computer-assisted content instruction. *Journal of Developmental Education, 15*(3), 32–35.

Brothern, T. (1994). A computer-assisted exercise that increases self-regulated learning. *Journal of Developmental Education, 18*(2), 18–21.

Brothern, T. (1996). A student-accessible computerized gradebook that facilitates self-regulated studying behavior. *Teaching of Psychology, 23*, 127–130.

Brush, T. A. (1997). The effects of group composition on achievement and time on task for students completing ILS activities in cooperative pairs. *Journal of Research on Computing in Education, 30*(1), 2–17.

Burke, M., Peterson, C., Segura, D., & Johnson, L. (1992). *Computer-assisted vs. text-based practice: Which method is more effective?* (ERIC Document Reproduction No. ED 350 046)

*Bush, V. (1945, July). *As we may think* [Online]. Available: http://www.ps.uni-sb.de/~duchier/pub/vbush/

Cavalier, J. C., & Klein, J. D. (1998). Effects of cooperative versus individual learning and orienting activities during computer-base instruction. *Educational Technology Research and Development, 46*(1), 5–17.

Caverly, D. C. (1995). *Technology and the learning assistance center: Past, present, and future* [Online]. Available: http://www.ci.swt.edu/Dev.ed/Technology/PastPresFuture.html

Caverly, D. C. (1996, March). *Technology in developmental education: Past, present, and future.* Paper presented at the annual meeting of the Pennsylvania State University Academic Assistance Program Spring Conference, University Park, PA.

Caverly, D. C. (1998). *Whole language college reading.* [Online]. Available: http//www.ci.swt.edu/Whole_Language.html

*Caverly, D. C., & Broderick, B. (1988). The computer as tutor. *Journal of Developmental Education, 12*(2), 32–33.

*Caverly, D. C., & Broderick, B. (1989). *The computer as tutee. Journal of Developmental Education, 12*(3), 30–31.

*Caverly, D. C., & Broderick, B. (1990). Hypermedia in developmental education. *Journal of Developmental Education, 14*(2), 32–33.

*Caverly, D. C., & Broderick, B. (1991). Learning through hypermedia. *Journal of Developmental Education, 14*(3), 32–33.

*Caverly, D. C., & Broderick, B. (1993). Another look at the computer as tutee. *Journal of Developmental Education, 16*(3), 38–39.

Caverly, D. C., & Broderick, B. (1995). World Wide Web and developmental education. *Journal of Developmental Education, 19*(2), 36–37.

*Caverly, D. C., Mandeville, T. P., & Nicholson, S. A. (1995). PLAN: A study-reading strategy for informational text. *Journal of Adolescent & Adult Literacy, 39*(3), 190–99.

*Caverly, D. C., & McDonald, L. (1998). Distance developmental education. *Journal of Developmental Education, 21*(3), 37–38.

Caverly, D. C., Nicholson, S. A., Peterson, C. L., & Wright, N. (1997, October). *Developmental students creating WWW pages.* Paper presented at the annual conference of the College Reading and Learning Association, Sacramento, CA.

Caverly, D. C., & Orlando V. P. (1991). *Text demands of upper division classes* : Unpublished manuscript, Metropolitan State College, Denver, CO.

Caverly, D. C., & Peterson, C. L. (1996). *Foundations for a constructivist, whole language approach to developmental college reading* [Online]. Available: http://www.umkc.edu/cad/nade/nadedocs/96monpap/cpmpap96.htm

Caverly, D. C., Sundin, S., Nicholson, S., & Oelke, E. (1990, October). *Empowering T.A.S.P. developmental readers through computers.* Paper presented at the annual conference of the Conference on Academic Support Programs, San Antonio, TX.

CCC *SuccessMaker.* (1998). [Computer software]. Sunnyvale, CA: Computer Curriculum Corporation.

Cejda, B. D. (1997). An examination of transfer shock in academic disciplines. *Community College Journal of Research and Practice, 21,* 279–288.

Chen, M. P., Jackson, W. A., Parsons, C., Sindt, K. M., Summerville, J. B., Tharp, D. D., Ulrich, R. R., & Laflarella, E. P. (1996). *The effects of font size in a hypertext computer-based instruction environment.* (ERIC Document Reproduction No. ED 397 784)

Clark, R. E. (1983). Reconsidering research on learning from media. *Review of Educational Research, 53*(4), 445–459.

Clark, R. E. (1994). Media will never influence learning. *Educational Technology Research and Development, 42*(2), 21–29.

*Cohen, P. A., Kulik, J. A., & Kulik, C. C. (1982). Educational outcomes of tutoring: A meta-analysis of findings. *American Educational Research Journal, 19*(2), 237–248.

*Collins, A., Brown, J. S., & Newman, S. E. (1989). Cognitive apprenticeship: Teaching the crafts of reading, writing, and mathematics. In L. B. Resnick (Ed.), *Knowing, learning, and instruction: Essays in honor of Robert Glaser* (pp. 453–494). Hillsdale, NJ: Lawrence Erlbaum Associates.

Daiute, C. (1985). *Writing and computers.* Reading, MA: Addison-Wesley.

Dalton, D. W., Hannafin, M. J., & Hooper, S. (1989). Effects of individual and cooperative computer-assisted instruction on student performance and attitude. *Educational Technology Research and Development, 37*(2), 15–24.

*Dede, C. (1987). Empowering environments, hypermedia and microworlds. *The Computing Teacher, 15*(3), 20–24.

Dee-Lucas, D., & Larkin, J. H. (1995). Learning from electronic texts: Effects of interactive overviews for information access. *Cognition and Instruction, 13*(3), 431–468.

Derry, S., Tookey, K., & Roth, B. (1993). *The effects of collaborative interaction and computer tool use on the problem-solving processes of lower-ability students.* (ERIC Document Reproduction No. ED 374 776)

Deutsch, L. (1988). *Word processing: A motivational force in developmental English. A comparison of two developmental English classes.* (ERIC Document Reproduction No. ED 295 702)

Diaz, S. (1984, November). *Bilingual-bicultural computer experts: Traditional literacy through computer literacy.* Paper presented at the annual conference of the American Anthropological Association, Denver, CO.

Dixon, R. A. (1993). *Improved reading comprehension: A key to university retention?* (ERIC Document Reproduction No. ED 359 498)

*Dodge, B. (1998). *The WebQuest page* [Online]. Available: http://edweb.sdsu.edu/webquest/webquest.html

Duffy, T. M., & Bednar, A. K. (1991). Attempting to come to grips with alternative perspectives. *Educational Technology, 31*(9), 12–15.

*Duffy, T. M., & Jonassen, D. H. (1992). *Constructivism and the technology of instruction: A conversation.* (ERIC Document Reproduction No. ED 364 198)

Ekins, J. M. (1992a). *The development of study processes in distance learning students.* (ERIC Document Reproduction No. ED 355 402)

Ekins, J. M. (1992b). *Study approaches of distance learning students, studying in a second language.* (ERIC Document Reproduction No. ED 355 810)

Engler, N. (1978). An A for ASEP. *Appalachia, 11*(5), 26–32.

Filipczak, B. (1995). Putting the learning into distance learning. *Training, 32*(10), 111–118.

Foltz, P. W. (1996). Comprehension, coherence, and strategies in hypertext and linear text. In J-F. Rouet, J. J. Levonen, A. Dillon, & R. J. Spiro (Eds.), *Hypertext and cognition* (pp. 109–136). Mahwah, NJ: Lawrence Erlbaum Associates.

*Foner, L. (1998). *What is an agent, anyway?* [Online]. Available: http://foner.www.media.mit.edu/people/foner/Julia/Julia.html

Gagne, R. M. (1985). *The conditions of learning and theory of instruction.* New York: Holt, Rinehart & Winston.

Gartner, A., & Riessman, F. (1993). *Peer-tutoring: Toward a new model.* (ERIC Document Reproduction No. ED 362 506)

Geske, J. (1991). Hypercard: Another computer tool. *Communication: Journalism Education Today, 24*(4), 14–17.

Ginsburg, R., & McCormick, V. (1998). Computer use in effective schools. *Journal of Staff Development, 19*(1), 22–25.

Golladay, R. M., Copeland, B. R., & Wu, F. H. (1998, Spring). Current state of distance education. *Journal of Computer Information Systems,* 11–14.

Goodlad, S., & Hirst, B. (1989). *Peer tutoring. A guide to learning by teaching.* (ERIC Document Reproduction No. ED 311 006)

Goodwin, L. D., Goodwin, W. L., Nansel, A., & Helm, C. P. (1986). Cognitive and affective effects of various types of microcomputer use by preschoolers. *American Journal of Educational Research, 23,* 348–356.

Gould, J. D., Alfaro, L., Barnes, V., Finn, R., Grischkowsky, N., & Minuto, A. (1987). Reading is slower from CRT displays than from paper: Attempts to isolate a single variable explanation. *Human Factors, 29*(3), 269–299.

*Greening, T. (1998). Building the constructivist toolbox: An exploration of cognitive technologies. *Educational Technology, 38*(2), 23–35.

Griffin, I. A. (1994). *Utilizing computer and multimedia technology in generating choreography for the advanced dance student at the high school level.* (ERIC Document Reproduction No. ED 385 247)

Groff, W. H. (1996). *Creating and sustaining learning communities in the digital era.* (ERIC Document Reproduction No. ED 396 188)

Groomes, M. R. (1994). *Comprehensive learning centers: Using technology to supplement the classroom.* (ERIC Document Reproduction No. ED 371 795)

Havlicek, L. L., & Coulter, T. (1982). *Development of a junior college CMI-computer-managed instruction reading instruction program.* (ERIC Document Reproduction No. ED 214 613)

Hay, K., Guzdial, M., Jackson, S. Boyle, R. A., & Soloway, A. (1994). Students as multimedia composers. *Computers & Education, 23*(4), 301–17.

Hedin, D. (1987). Students as teachers: A tool for improving school climate and productivity. *Social Policy, 17*(3), 42–47.

Hennessey, J. H. (1990). At-risk community college students and a reading improvement course. *Journal of Reading, 34,* 114–120.

Illingworth, R. D., & Illingworth, M. L. (1998, March 6). *Developmental education: WWW student support.* Paper presented at the annual conference of the National Association of Developmental Education, Atlanta.

INVEST Learning. (1998). [Computer software]. San Diego, CA: Invest Learning.

Jacobson, M. J., & Spiro, R. J. (1995). Hypertext learning environments, cognitive flexibility theory, and the transfer of complex knowledge: An empirical investigation. *Journal of Educational Computing Research, 12*(4), 301–333.

Jamison, D., Suppes, P., & Wells, S. (1974). Effectiveness of alternative instructional media. *Review of Educational Research, 44,* 1–67.

Jody, M., & Saccardi, M. (1996). *Computer conversations: Readers and books online.* (ERIC Document Reproduction No. ED 392 069)

Johnson, D. W., & Johnson, R. T. (1990). *Cooperation and competition: Theory and research.* Edina, MN: Interaction Book Company.

Johnson, L., & Perez, S. (1997). *Final report of the computer-based developmental education project measured* [Online]. Available: http://www.investlearning.com/Stories/league.htm

Jonassen, D. H. (1995). Supporting communities of learners with technology: A vision for integrating technology with learning in schools. *Educational Technology, 35*(4), 60–63.

Joyce, B., & Weil, M. (1996). *Models of teaching.* Boston: Allyn & Bacon.

*Juel, C. (1996). What makes literacy tutoring effective? *Reading Research Quarterly, 31*(3), 268–289.

*Kerka, S. (1996). *Distance learning, the Internet, and the World Wide Web. ERIC digest.* (ERIC Document Reproduction No. ED 395 214)

*Kleifgen, J. A. (1989). *Computers and opportunities for literacy development.* (ERIC Document Reproduction No. ED 311 120)

*Knox-Quinn, C., & Horney, M. A. (1998). *Project ASSIST: Academic Study Strategies using Interactive Support Technology* [Online]. Available: http://www.ces.uoregon.edu/assist/

*Kulik, C. L., & Kulik, J. A. (1985). *Effectiveness of computer-based education in colleges.* (ERIC Document Reproduction No. ED 263 890)

*Kulik, C. L., & Kulik, J. A. (1991). Effectiveness of computer-based instruction: An updated analysis. *Computers in Human Behavior, 7*(1), 75–94.

*Kulik, J. A. (1983). *Effects of computer-based reading on learners.* (ERIC Document Reproduction No. ED 246 877)

*Kulik, J. A., & Kulik, C. L. (1987). Review of recent research literature on computer-based instruction. *Contemporary Educational Psychology, 12*(3), 222–230.

Kulik, C. L., & Kulik, J. A. (1991). Effectiveness of computer-based instruction: An updated analysis. *Computers in Human Behavior, 7*(1), 75–94.

*Kulik, J. A., Kulik, C. L., & Cohen, P. (1980). Effectiveness of computer-based college teaching: A meta-analysis of findings. *Review of Educational Research, 50*(4), 525–544.

LaBerge, D., & Samuels, S. J. (1974). Toward a theory of automatic information processing in reading. *Cognitive Psychology, 6*(4), 293–323.

Laffey, J., Tupper, T., Musser, D., & Wedman, J. (1998). A computer-mediated support system for project-based learning. *Educational Technology Research and Development, 46*(1), 73–86.

Lang, S. (1992). *Creating a community of learners using hypertext.* (ERIC Document Reproduction No. ED 350 600)

LEARNING PLUS (1998). [Online]. Available: http://etsis1.ets.org/learnplus/

Lee, S. H., & Boling, E. (1996). *Motivational screen design guidelines for effective computer-mediated instruction.* (ERIC Document Reproduction No. ED 397 811)

Lemke, J. L. (1993). Hypermedia and higher education. [Online]. Available: http://infosoc.uni-koeln.de/etext/text/lemke.93b.txt

Lepper, M. R. (1985). Microcomputers in education: Motivational and social issues. *American Psychologist, 40*, 1–18.

*Liao, Y. C. (1998). Effects of hypermedia versus traditional instruction on students' achievement: A meta-analysis. *Journal of Research on Computing in Education, 30*(4), 341–359.

Luehrmann, A. (1980). Should the computer teach the student, or vice-versa? In R. Taylor (Ed.), *The computer in the school: Tutor, tool, tutee* (pp. 129–135). New York: Teachers College Press.

Lundberg, I. (1995). The computer as a tool of remediation in the education of students with reading disabilities: A theory-based approach. *Learning Disability Quarterly, 18*(2), 89–99.

MacGregor, S. K. (1988). Use of self-questioning with a computer-mediated text system and measures of reading performance. *Journal of Reading Behavior, 20*, 131–148.

*Marchionini, G. (1988). Hypermedia and learning: Freedom and chaos. *Educational Technology, 28*(11), 8–12.

Martin, D. C., & Arendale, D. R. (1992). *Supplemental instruction: Improving first-year student success in high-risk courses.* (ERIC Document Reproduction No. ED 354 839)

*McCall, C. (1984). *Not since Gutenberg: Microcomputers and reading.* (ERIC Document Reproduction No. ED 262 771)

McCreary, R., & Maginnis, G. (1989). *The effects of computer-assisted instruction on reading achievement for college freshman.* (ERIC Document Reproduction No. ED 311 402)

*McDonald, L., & Caverly, D. C. (1997). *Distance education and the developmental educator. Journal of Developmental Education, 21*(2), 37–38.

McKellar, N. A. (1984). *Locus of cognitive gains from tutoring.* (ERIC Document Reproduction No. ED 249 189)

*McKenzie, J. (1998). *From now on: The educational technology journal* [Online]. Available: http://www.fromnowon.org/www.html

Mehan, J., Moll, L. C., & Riel, M. (1985). *Computer in the classrooms: A quasi-experiment in guided change.* National Institute of Education, Washington, DC.

*Mevarech, Z., Silber, O., & Fine, D. (1991). Learning with computers in small groups: Cognitive and affective outcomes. *Journal of Educational Computing Research, 7*(2), 233–234.

Meyer, M. D. (1995). Classroom research: A new frontier Part II. *Research and Teaching in Developmental Education, 12*(1), 61-70.

*Mikulecky, L., & Adams, S. M. (1988). *The effectiveness of using interactive computer programs to model textbook reading strategies for university and community college psychology and biology students.* (ERIC Document Reproduction No. ED 302 810)

Moore, A. (1993). *Computer assisted instruction (ILS) for adults.* (ERIC Document Reproduction No. ED 377 897)

Moore, M. G., Thompson, M. M., Quigley, A. B., Clark, G. C., & Goff, G. G. (1990). *The effects of distance learning: A summary of the literature. Research Monograph No. 2.* (ERIC Document Reproduction No. ED 330 321)

Morris, W. (1992). *Cooperative learning in a developmental reading course.* (ERIC Document Reproduction No. ED 348 118)

Naidu, S., & Bernard, R. M. (1992). Enhancing academic performance in distance education with concept mapping and inserted questions. *Distance Education, 13*(2), 218–233.

*Negroponte, N. (1995). *Being digital.* New York: Vintage Books.

Nixon, D. E. (1992). Simulteaching: Access to learning by means of interactive television. *Community Junior College Quarterly of Research and Practice, 16*(2), 167–175.

Oblinger, D. G., & Rush, S. C. (1997). *Challenges of the learning revolution.* (ERIC Document Reproduction No. ED 404 957)

*Orlando, V. P., Caverly, D. C., Swetman, L. A., & Flippo, R. F. (1989). *Text demands in college classes. Forum for Reading, 21*(1), 43–48.

*Papert, S. (1993). *The children's machine: Rethinking school in the age of the computer.* New York: HarperCollins.

*Papert, S. A. (1980). *Mindstorms: Computers, children, and powerful ideas.* New York: Basic Books.

Perkins, D. N., & Salomon, G. (1989). Are cognitive skills context-bound? *Educational Researcher, 18*(1), 16–25.

Peterson, C., Nicholson, S. A., Murray, M., & Caverly, D. C. (1995, April). *Helping at-risk college readers through a holistic use of technology*. Paper presented at the annual meeting of the College Reading and Learning Association, Tempe, AZ.

Peterson, C. L., & St. Clair, L. (1997, October 22). *Pearls of wisdom: Hunting & gathering on the WWW.* Paper presented at the annual meeting of the College Reading and Learning Association, Sacramento, CA.

Peterson, C. L., Burke, M. K., & Segura, D. (1999). Computer-based practice for developmental reading: Medium and message. *Journal of Developmental Education, 22*(3), 12–14.

Peterson, D. L., & Williams, D. A. (1990). *PALS: An advanced technology literacy experiment with delinquent youth.* (ERIC Document Reproduction No. ED 337 319)

PLATO Learning System. (1997). [Computer software]. Edina, MN: TRO Learning, Inc.

Price, R. L. (1992). Computers can help student retention in introductory college accounting. *Business Education Forum, 47*(1), 25–27.

*Puk, T. (1992). Technology, technology education, and teacher education: A rose by any other name? In D. Carey, R. Carey, D. A. Willis, & J. Willis (Eds.), *Technology and teacher education annual* (pp. 115–118). Charlottesville, VA: Association for the Advancement of Computing in Education.

Read, G. (1992). *Use of CSR for reading.* (ERIC Document Reproduction No. ED 345 804)

Reed, W. M., & Liu, M. (1994). The comparative effects of BASIC programming versus HyperCard programming on problem solving, computer anxiety, and performance. *Computers in the Schools, 10*(1–2), 27–46.

Reed-Sanders, D., & Liebowitz, S. (1991). An empirical test of integration of computers in introductory sociology. *Teaching Sociology, 19*(2), 223–230.

*Reinking, D. (1988). Computer-mediated text and comprehension differences: The role of reading time, reader preference, and estimation of learning. *Reading Research Quarterly, 23*(4), 484–498.

Reinking, D. (1989). Misconceptions about reading that affect software development. *Computing Teacher, 16*(4), 27–29.

*Reinking, D., & Bridwell-Bowles, L. (1992). Computers in reading and writing. In P. D. Pearson (Ed.), *Handbook of reading research* (pp. 310–340). White Plains, NY: Longman.

*Reinking, D., & Schreiner, R. (1985). The effects of computer-mediated text on measures of reading comprehension and reading behavior. *Reading Research Quarterly, 20*, 536–552.

*Reinking, D., & Watkins, J. (1996). *A formative experiment investigating the use of multimedia book reviews to increase elementary students' independent reading. Reading Research Report No. 55.* (ERIC Document Reproduction No. ED 398 570)

*Relan, A., & Smith, W. C. (1996). Learning from hypermedia: A study of situated versus endemic learning strategies. *Journal of Educational Multimedia and Hypermedia, 5*(1), 3–21.

Resnick, M. (1995). New paradigms for computing, new paradigms for thinking. In A. diSessa, C. Hoyles, & R. Noss (Eds.), *Computers and exploratory learning.* (pp. 31–43). Berlin: Springer-Verlag.

*Resnick, M., Martin, F., Berg, R., Borovoy, R., Colella, V., Kramer, K., & Silverman, B. (1998). *Digital manipulatives: New toys to think with* [Online]. Available: http://el.www.media.mit.edu/groups/el/

Reynolds, S. B., & Hart, J. (1990). Cognitive mapping and word processing: Aids to story revision. *Journal of Experiential Education, 58*(4), 273–279.

*Rhodes, B. J. (1996). *Remembrance agent* [Online]. Available: http://hodes.www.media.mit.edu/people/rhodes/research/Papers/remembrance.html

*Riskin, S. R. (1990). *Teaching through interactive multi-media programming. A new philosophy of the social sciences and a new epistemology of creativity.* (ERIC Document Reproduction No. ED 327 133)

*Roblyer, M. D., Edwards, J., & Havriluk, M. (1997). *Integrating educational technology into teaching.* Upper Saddle River, NJ: Merrill.

Rodrigues, S. (1997). Using multimedia authoring tools in primary science. *Primary Science Review, 48,* 21–24.

*Romiszowski, A. (1993). *Telecommunications and distance education.* (ERIC Document Reproduction No. ED 358 841)

*Rouet, J. F., & Levonen, J. (1996). Studying and learning with hypertext: Empirical studies and their implications. In J. F. Rouet, J. J. Levonen, A. Dillon, & R. J. Spiro (Eds.), *Hypertext and cognition* (pp. 9–23). Mahwah, NJ: Lawrence Erlbaum Associates.

Russell, A. (1995). Stages in learning new technology: Naive adult email users. *Computers and Education, 25*(4), 173–178.

*Salomon, G., Globerson, T., & Guterman, E. (1989). The computer as a zone of proximal development: Internalizing reading-related metacognitions from a reading partner. *Journal of Educational Psychology, 89*(81), 620–627.

Saracho, O. N. (1982). The effects of a computer-assisted instruction program on basic skills achievement and attitudes toward reading instruction of Spanish-speaking migrant children. *American Educational Research Journal, 19,* 201–219.

Sayers, D. (1989). Bilingual sister classes in computer writing networks. In D. M. Johnson & D. H. Roen (Eds.), *Richness in writing* (pp. 120–133). New York: Longman.

Schnitz, J. E., Maynes, D., & Revel, L. (1983). *High technology and basic skills in reading.* (Contract No. 300-80-0844). Washington, DC: U.S. Department of Education.

Schroeder, E. E. (1994). *Navigating through hypertext: Navigational technique, individual differences, and learning.* (ERIC Document Reproduction No. ED 373 760)

Seaman, D. F., & McCallister, J. M. (1988). *An evaluation of computer-assisted instructional systems used to deliver literacy services for J.T.P.A. participants at Houston community college.* (ERIC Document Reproduction No. ED 311 226)

Searcy, R. D., Howton, C., & Yarbrough, M. (1993). *Grade distribution study: Telecourses vs. traditional courses.* (ERIC Document Reproduction No. ED 362 251)

Shin, C. E., Schallert, D. L., & Savenye, W. C. (1994). Effects of learner control, advisement, and prior knowledge on young student's learning in a hypertext environment. *Educational Technology Review and Development, 42*(1), 33–46.

Sinagra, M., Battle, J., & Nicholson, S. (1998). E-mail "booktalking": Engaging developmental readers with authors and others in the academic community. *Journal of College Reading and Learning, 29*(1), 30–40.

Skinner, B. F. (1968). *The technology of teaching.* New York: Appleton.

*Spiro, R. J., Coulson, R. L., Feltovich, P. J., & Anderson, D. K. (1994). Cognitive flexibility theory: Complex knowledge acquisition in ill-structured domains. In R. B. Ruddell, M. R. Ruddell, & H. Singer (Eds.), *Theoretical models and processes of reading* (4th ed., pp. 602–615). Newark, DE: International Reading Association.

*Stanovich, K. E. (1986). Matthew effect: Some consequences of individual differences in the acquisition of literacy. *Reading Research Quarterly, 21*(4), 360–407.

Taraban, R., & Rynearson, K. (1998). Computer-based comprehension research in a content area. *Journal of Developmental Education, 21*(3), 10–18.

*Taylor, R. (1980). *The computer in the school: Tutor, tool, tutee.* (ERIC Document Reproduction No. ED 207 670)

Taylor, V. B., & Rosecrans, D. (1986). *An investigation of vocabulary development via computer-assisted instruction (CAI).* (ERIC Document Reproduction No. ED 281 168)

Tedrow, J. W., & Rust, J. O. (1994). Retention and graduation rate of student from a college developmental reading program. *Reading Improvement, 31*(4), 205–10.

Thompson, M. M. (1996). Distance delivery of graduate-level teacher education: Beyond parity claims. *Journal of Continuing Higher Education, 44*(3), 29–34.

*Thorndike, E. L. (1917). Reading as reasoning: A study of mistakes in paragraph reading. *Journal of Educational Psychology, 8,* 323–332.

Thorpe, M. (1995). Reflective learning in distance education. *European Journal of Psychology of Education, 10*(2), 153–167.

*Tierney, R. J., Kieffer, R., Stowell, L., Desai, L. E., Whalin, K., & Moss, A. G. (1992). *Computer acquisition: A longitudinal study of the influence of high computer access on students' thinking, learning, and interactions.* (ERIC Document Reproduction No. ED 354 856)

Tierney, R. J., & Pearson, P. D. (1994). A revisionist perspective on learning to learn from text: A framework for improving classroom practice. In R. B. Ruddell, M. R. Ruddell, & H. Singer (Eds.), *Theoretical models and processes of reading* (pp. 514–519). Newark, DE: International Reading Association.

*Todd, J. (1854). *The student's manual.* New York: Baker and Taylor.

*Turner, S. V., & Dipinto, V. M. (1992). Students as hypermedia authors: Themes emerging from a qualitative study. *Journal of Research on Computing in Education, 25*(2), 187–199.

*Underwood, J., Cavendish, S., Dowling, S., Fogelman, K., & Lawson, T. (1996). Are integrated learning systems effective learning support tools? *Computers in Education, 26*(1), 33–40.

vanOostendorp, H. (1996). Studying and annotating electronic text. In J. Rouet, J. J. Levonen, A. Dillon, & R. Spiro (Eds.) *Hypertext and cognition* (pp. 137–147). Mahwah, NJ: Lawrence Erlbaum Associates.

*Vygotsky, L. S. (1962). *Thought and language.* Cambridge, MA: MIT Press.

Walker, D. (1992). *Use of PLATO for reading.* (ERIC Document Reproduction No. Ed 345 804)

Wang, Y. (1996). *E-mail dialogue journaling in an ESL reading and writing classroom.* (ERIC Document Reproduction No. ED 397 845)

Waxman, H. C. (1992). Restructuring urban schools with technology: Implications for students at risk of failure. In D. Carey, R. Carey, D. A. Willis, & J. Willis (Eds.),

Technology and teacher education annual (pp. 132–136). Charlottesville, VA: Association for the Advancement of Computing in Education.

Weissman, J., Silk, E., & Bulokkowski, C. (1994). *Assessing developmental education through student tracking.* (ERIC Document Reproduction No. ED 386 983)

*Wepner, S. B. (1990). Do computers have a place in college reading courses? *Journal of Reading, 33*(5), 348–354.

Wepner, S. B., & Feeley, J. T. (1987). *College students' reading efficiency with computer-presented text.* (ERIC Document Reproduction No. ED 281 190)

Wiesenberg, F., & Hutton, S. (1996). Teaching a graduate program using computer-mediated software. *Journal of Distance Education, 11*(1), 83–100.

Williams, M. (1993). *A comprehensive review of learner-control: The role of learner characteristics.* (ERIC Document Reproduction No. ED 362211)

Williamson, B. L. (1993). *Writing with a byte. Computers: An effective teaching methodology to improve freshman writing skills.* (ERIC Document Reproduction No. ED 362 245)

Yaghi, H. M. (1997). Pre-university students' attitudes towards computers: An international perspective. *Journal of Educational Computing Research, 16*(3), 237–249.

Zirkin, B. G., & Sumler, D. E. (1995). Interactive or non-interactive? That is the question: An annotated bibliography. *Journal of Distance Education, 10*(1), 95–112.

12

College Reading Programs

࿊ఏఏ࿊

Linda L. Johnson
Kirkwood Community College

Kathy Carpenter
Kearney State College

Almost since their beginnings, colleges and universities in the United States have provided reading and study skills programs for their students. Today, reading and study skills are taught on most college campuses, either as individual courses or as part of large learning assistance programs. Colleges provide these services for students who request assistance and for students who are likely to have difficulty with college studies as identified by admissions officers.

The variety of programs on college campuses today speaks to the innovative spirit of college reading and learning professionals as well as to the exponential increase in technology now widely available. This chapter describes current programs and addresses organizational and programmatic factors related to their success.

It is impossible to discuss reading and study skills in postsecondary institutions without connecting them to the broader range of *learning assistance programs*. Learning assistance programs include any remedial or developmental program intended to help students succeed academically in college. They range from a single course in reading offered by the English department to comprehensive programs, including basic skills and counseling, housed in a developmental reading studies department.

Institutions refer to learning assistance programs under a variety of names (e.g., learning center, reading lab, learning assistance center, academic skills center, learning skills center). We use the terms *learning center* or *learning assistance program* to refer to all of these programs. The term *developmental education*, although appropriate for nonremedial courses, has yet to catch on outside the field. Furthermore it is now considered by many people as interchangeable with *remedial*, a word suggesting a limited focus or considered embarrassing or humiliating to some students. Learning assistance seems to be the most neutral or euphemistic term to refer to programs that address the learning needs of all students, not just those with special needs (Maxwell, 1994).

Learning assistance programs can be successful in increasing students' grades and improving student retention. Their success, however, depends on the variety of services colleges provide, the degree to which programs address the actual causes of students' difficulties, and the extent to which programs reach students who need them. Many programmatic and organizational factors are involved in assuring that learning assistance programs succeed.

This chapter first reviews the need for learning assistance programs by examining historical trends in their development and the distribution of programs in colleges and universities across the country. Then it examines the organizational features of current programs and the factors that influence them. Next, it describes types of programs now in existence with reference to research findings. Finally, it draws conclusions based on analysis and research.

THE RATIONALE FOR LEARNING ASSISTANCE PROGRAMS

The existence of college learning assistance programs indicates that high schools are not in a position to prepare all their graduates for the intense independent learning required in college. The need for learning assistance is not a by-product of open admissions, not a need exclusive to underprepared students, and it is not a recent arrival to U.S. shores. From the earliest colleges in the United States to the newest, from open admission 2-year colleges to highly selective universities, and from high-risk students to straight-A students, all have some need for programs in learning assistance.

Historical Background

College learning assistance has a long history in this country, dating back to our earliest postsecondary institutions. Since colonial America, colleges and universities have acknowledged, however reluctantly, the need for some form of assistance to underprepared students. For Harvard, the oldest college in America, an underprepared student meant a student who did not know Latin, the language of instruction. In the 17th century, Harvard instituted a remedial program in that language (Boylan & White, 1987). Colleges were seen then as training ground for clergy and the elite, instituted primarily to carry on the traditions and culture of Europe. Little interest was shown in educating Native Americans or working class European Americans. Because colleges were unwilling to admit nontraditional students, enrollment was small. In 1710, Harvard had 123 students and Yale had 36 (Brier, 1984).

In the 18th century, colleges remained reluctant to broaden their enrollment beyond the elite and their curriculum beyond European languages and culture. But when colleges increased in number, more students were needed and colleges found themselves admitting less-prepared students. Some colleges offered alternative degrees, such as the bachelor of philosophy and the bachelor of science, but this was considered to be a lowering of standards. Another way to deal with underprepared students was to offer courses in the professions and government leadership. These were proposed and at least considered, although they, too, were seen as a lowering of standards.

Remedial programs did not appear on college campuses until the middle of the 19th century with the establishment of *land grant colleges* (Boylan & White, 1987). These new colleges taught agriculture and mechanics rather than classics in Latin and Greek. Because there were insufficient numbers of qualified students even for these nonclassical courses, colleges opened their doors to underprepared students. To help such students, colleges frequently instituted preparatory departments. Resembling secondary schools, these departments offered courses in mathematics, reading, and writing to students who might take 6 years to complete a 4-year college program. Secondary schools at that time were weak, probably because state funding went primarily to elementary schools.

By 1915, about 350 colleges had established preparatory departments. After that peak, the number of colleges with such programs began to decline. Some colleges simply renumbered their courses and preparatory courses became college-level courses. Other reasons for the decline were better admissions procedures and secondary schools and colleges increased their cooperation. Furthermore, the College Entrance Examination Board, founded in 1890, enabled colleges to set cutoff points for admissions. Students began arriving who were better prepared. However, these new and changing standards made it difficult for some students to achieve them. In 1907, for instance, more than half the students attending Harvard, Princeton, and Yale had failed to meet entrance requirements (Maxwell, 1997). Lower scoring students were admitted anyway because colleges competed for the still small supply of well qualified students.

Programs specifically for reading and study skills began appearing in the early 20th century when remedial reading courses became prevalent in the pubic schools. Kingston (1990) surveyed the literature and found that experimental college remedial reading programs could be identified as early as the 1920s. He found descriptions of short reading courses in several studies published in the 1930s. By then, the courses included instruction in study skills as well as in basic skills such as reading. Students studied the same topics that students study today—time management, concentration, notetaking, and test taking (Enright & Kerstiens, 1980).

In the 1930s, colleges and universities established remedial reading clinics to help students cope with the lengthy reading assignments required in their general survey courses. According to Maxwell (1997), reading laboratories owe their existence to Stella Center who in 1936 established the Reading Laboratory in the extension department of New York University. Pioneer reading programs at Minnesota and Harvard started 2 years later. After 1941, when Robert Bear of Dartmouth published a pamphlet called *How to Read Rapidly and Well*, many developmental reading programs began to appear. Maxwell (1997) additionally attributed the growth in reading services to the development of undergraduate survey courses in 1929. Courses such as Introduction to Contemporary Civilization demanded extensive reading.

The focus of reading instruction in the 1940s was a diagnostic-prescriptive approach with individualized practice. Triggs (1942) noted a lack of commercial materials, diagnostic tools, and trained instructors for his reading clinic at the University of Minnesota. Although his ideal was to work with individual cases, his compromise solution was small groups in combination with clinical work.

The machines that gave the name "laboratory" to the new centralized reading programs were brought over from psychology laboratories where researchers were experimenting with eye movements. By 1946, such machines as tachistoscopes, the Keystone Ophthalmic Telebinocular, Ophthalm-O-Graph, and the Metronoscope were in fairly common use (Enright & Kerstiens, 1980). Today, we find the descendents of these machines in speed-reading courseware intended for computer laboratories in learning centers.

After World War II, government funding enabled colleges to establish programs to assist veterans, many of whom had little high school preparation for college work or who had been out of high school for many years. These centers offered reading, writing, and study skills programs, as well as tutoring services. As they are today, programs were highly varied, with some requiring enrollment based on placement tests, whereas others were voluntary. Some were housed in the education department whereas others were housed in the mathematics, psychology or English departments. Some consisted of courses whereas some were tutoring or counseling programs. The latter types of programs expanded with the growth of divisions of student personnel services during the 1950s and into the 1960s (Kingston, 1990). At the same time, learning assistance programs became institutionalized and expanded their services (Maxwell, 1979).

The greatest growth in learning assistance occurred during the 1960s and 1970s when many 2-year colleges and some universities implemented open admissions policies. A surge of open admissions policy changes occurred after passage in 1973 of Section 504 of Public Law 93–112 (Rehabilitation Act). The section prohibited discrimination against individuals as to gender, race, or handicap. The 1970s became the era of the adult learner. Large numbers of older students, particularly women, enrolled as undergraduate students. Many students were unprepared for academic studying, and soon the open doors became revolving doors.

In response, institutions established remedial programs that offered innovative services such as academic counseling, individualized programs, and self-paced courses. Many institutions established these programs primarily to assist the nontraditional student population. Concurrently, federal funding became available to promote educational opportunity for disadvantaged students. This federal commitment to Affirmative Action (AA) and equal educational opportunity stimulated rapid expansion of programs to help students succeed. As a result, the number of learning assistance centers doubled between 1974 and 1979 (Sullivan, 1980).

Unfortunately, many of these programs failed to improve the retention rate of high-risk students (Roueche & Snow, 1977). Gradually programs began to come under closer evaluation, and some improvements were made (Smith & Smith, 1988). By the mid-1990s, Maxwell (1997) was able to cite a number of studies demonstrating that learning assistance programs "can be effective in increasing student retention and graduation rates" (p. 19). (For a further review of the history of college reading, see Stahl & King, chap. 1, this volume.)

Students' Need for Learning Assistance

Students' need for learning assistance is apparent from both questionnaire data and from anecdotal evidence. Today, learning assistance programs are frequently geared to all students, not just the underprepared—and with good reason.

Students today may be "misprepared," earning high grades in high school from courses that do not prepare them for college. Even if students take college preparatory courses, grade inflation and lack of rigor may lead them to think they are prepared when they are not. Other students who may require learning assistance include nonnative speakers of English, who often need extra help in dealing with cultural differences and language comprehension. Many students need learning assistance not to improve their reading and study skills but because they are burdened by noncollege concerns. Some are working 30 hours a week or more and still trying to take a full load of courses. Some students are single mothers or fathers, and they may have a family to support. Students may have learning disabilities (LD) or attention deficit disorder (ADD), which make it hard for them to study. Physical disabilities such as hearing, speech, and vision impairments do not keep students from attending college. Students with alcohol and drug problems try to attend college. The full range of problems and challenges in the larger society exists on college campuses more than ever before. Rather than underprepared, many students are now called *at risk,* a broader, more descriptive term (Maxwell, 1997).

The study skills and strategies students devise for themselves or learn from each other may work for students who are not at risk. But when students face one or more of these other problems, the typical learning strategies students use may not be adequate. Reading and study skills instructors need to address serious problems in time-management and such problems as motivation, self-esteem, and self-confidence. Instructors must somehow help students deal with studying amidst estranging environments. Moreover, college is not getting any easier. Even students who are not at risk may lack reading and study skills necessary for success in highly demanding courses. Evidence of the need for learning assistance is easy to find even in highly selective colleges and universities.

Perry (1959) described the need for reading improvement at Harvard University in the 1940s. In 1946 all entering freshmen took a reading test, and the bottom scorers were assigned remedial reading—although the lowest scoring student still scored above the 85th percentile according to national norms. When these results were revealed, the course was made more difficult, and 800 students enrolled. Perry discovered that these students did not lack the mechanics of reading, but they needed to improve their ability to set purposes for reading as well as improve their flexibility in achieving their purposes.

In a study of 1,029 Western Michigan University freshmen (Carter, 1959), 66% reported that they had not been taught to read a textbook chapter in high school, and 62% said they had received no reading instruction from their high school teachers at all. Most said they would have benefited from a high school developmental reading course. Shaw (1961) estimated that 95% of entering students lacked study skills.

The situation has not changed. Simpson (1983) surveyed 395 freshmen at a midwestern university and found that they could report using few study strategies. Students frequently could not explain why a strategy might be effective, often used the same study strategy regardless of the subject, and were unable to explain how they knew whether they were prepared for an upcoming test. She concluded that the general college student population would benefit from study skills instruction.

Clearly, many average and even high-achieving students need reading and study skills instruction. Although many students figure out for themselves how to study, some otherwise well-prepared students may find themselves on academic probation because of inadequate study skills. Most learning assistance programs were established to increase the retention rate of underprepared students. Despite this stated goal, however, many colleges and universities have been able to serve both populations with independent or coordinated programs. Stanford University's learning assistance center is a good example. At one point at least, the center served more than 50% the freshmen each year (Roueche & Snow, 1977). Even straight-A students, many of whom were found to have inefficient study methods, benefited from the program.

Prevalence of Learning Assistance Programs

According to several nationwide surveys, most degree-granting institutions now offer some kind of program that provides learning assistance. In 1974, Smith, Enright, and Devirian (1975) mailed surveys to 3,389 U.S. colleges and universities, and 1,258 of them (38%) returned a completed form. Of these, 759 (60%) reported that they operated a learning assistance center, and an additional 115 planned to establish one within the next 2 years. Only 10% of these learning centers existed before 1960. Although the authors did not report how often the learning centers offered reading instruction, they did report that 79% offered study skills courses. The number of college learning assistance programs grew steadily since the time of that report until a peak was reached in the mid-1980s (Cranney, 1987).

Sullivan (1980) surveyed 2,872 U.S. and Canadian postsecondary institutions that offered at least an associate's degree. Of 2,713 U.S. institutions, 50.6% operated at least one learning assistance program. More than 75% of the surveyed 4-year public institutions in the United States operated learning centers. Roueche (1983) surveyed 2,508 U.S. colleges and universities. Of the 58% responding, only 160 (11%) lacked programs, courses or other alternatives for responding to the needs of low-achieving students.

The National Center for Education Statistics (NCES) conducted three statistical studies of remedial education at postsecondary institutions since the early 1980s, focusing on reading, English, and mathematics. Compared to the other basic skills, the percentage of institutions offering reading instruction was fairly low. In the 1983–1984 academic year, NCES reported that 66% of all colleges and universities offered remedial reading courses (Wright, 1985). By 1995, the number had dropped to 57% (NCES, 1996).

When English and mathematics were factored in, there were increases in the number of institutions providing remedial programs. In 1991, 74% of colleges and universities offered at least one of the three remedial courses (Boylan, 1995), and by fall of 1995, 78% offered at least one of the courses. Furthermore, 99% of 2-year institutions offered remedial courses (NCES, 1996).

With all these courses in place, a relatively large number of students were enrolled in them. In 1989, NCES reported that 30% of all entering freshmen took at least one remedial course in English, reading, or mathematics (Boylan, 1995). In 1995, this percentage remained virtually the same (NCES, 1996). Boylan estimated that more than 2 million students participate in learning assistance programs or developmental courses each year.

Cranney (1987) postulated that peak enrollment in learning assistance programs had been reached, and that budget cutbacks would force learning assistance professionals to struggle to maintain the gains they had made. He noted that although community colleges might be able to hold their own, university programs would be more subject to cuts. The reduction in remedial reading courses from 66% in 1983 (Wright, 1985) to 57% in 1995 (NCES, 1996) may suggest the start of that trend. However, although reading courses were decreasing, colleges increased minimally their offerings of remedial mathematics. Otherwise, offerings and enrollments in remedial instruction appear to be fairly constant since the early 1980s. When many qualified students are enrolling in postsecondary institutions, institutions may not work to attract underprepared and at-risk students. As a result, funding for learning assistance programs aimed at these students may be cut back.

Most researchers conclude that the need for reading and learning assistance on college campuses will continue indefinitely, whether or not programs for students are fully funded. Williams (1989), for example, predicted that increased numbers of nontraditional students in the 21st century will necessitate the continuing critical role of learning assistance programs in postsecondary institutions.

Inevitably, some students lack effective study procedures or adequate background in a subject, no matter how outstanding their schooling has been. Other students simply wish to improve their already adequate study skills.

ORGANIZATIONAL INFLUENCES AND FEATURES

The nature of a learning assistance program is dependent on a number of philosophical and practical influences. These influences determine both the diversity of programs and the direction they take.

Influences on Program Configuration

The way learning assistance programs are created, revised, and expanded are subject to a number of influences. The most telling of these are school philosophy, the academic background of the program's staff, funding issues, government policies, and the type of institution involved.

School Philosophy. Both the services a learning assistance program provides and the activities it sponsors are influenced by the philosophical orientation of the postsecondary institution. If the institution has a liberal, humanistic orientation, it seeks to offer a variety of services to help all students reach their academic goals. If the orientation is academically conservative, departmental faculty and administrators may believe that students should rely on their own resources. Under these conditions, learning assistance programs may be limited or less effective than those with strong support.

Academic Background.   The training, experience, and educational beliefs of learning assistance personnel determine in part how resources are allocated. The theoretical perspective of those responsible for the program may determine the nature and range of activities they undertake. For example, if instructors are trained through a guidance and counseling department, they are likely to include individual and small group academic counseling in the program. If they studied reading from a professor espousing whole-language theories, they likely encourage students to read full-length books and articles rather than excerpts from longer works, and they are less likely to use machines in their learning center to teach learning strategies.

Funding.   Funding for a learning assistance program may be linked to the emphasis placed on certain programs or activities. Funding agency stipulations may determine the scope and direction of the program. If funding is available from only one source, the program's goals may reflect the requirements of the funding agency; other concerns may be neglected until additional funds are found.

Policies and Statutes.   Governmental or administrative policies may place restrictions on a learning assistance program. Conversely, an agency may mandate testing and the establishment of programs to help students who fail the test. The NCES (1996) reported from its survey that one third of the institutions that offer remedial courses were affected by state law or state policies. These mandates dictated some of their offerings, most often requiring that such courses be offered. In Texas, for example, college students must pass the Texas Academic Skills Program (TASP) test in order to take upper division college classes or to graduate from a degree program. Texas colleges must provide courses or other learning assistance to help students learn basic skills in reading, writing, and mathematics (Boylan, 1996).

Type of Institution.   Tax-supported institutions may require a different orientation than private colleges, and universities may desire a completely different format from what a community college would prefer.

In order to meet the varying needs and expectations of students, faculty, and administrators on their individual campuses, learning assistance educators build customized programs and centers. Program administrators must address a variety of issues, including how students are directed toward services, courses, and activities. Then, they must address whether students receive individualized or group instruction, where and when they receive tutoring, whether they are enrolled in regular classes, how extensive the drop-in and outreach services are, and how services are evaluated. The goal is to try to provide students with the best possible learning assistance based on the available resources and professional expertise.

Philosophical Perspectives

Those working in learning assistance settings have evolved various philosophical perspectives that heavily influence the structure of their programs. Practitioners identified with specific perspectives in the following pages may argue that they are not limited to one perspective, and certainly most learning assistance educators create a blend of activities from many perspectives. However, the writings of these practitioners often suggest a particular orientation or preference. We intend the following discussion only to identify and clarify trends in theoretical orientations, not to classify rigidly the beliefs of any individuals.

Counseling Perspective.   Many learning assistance programs, particularly those associated with student services, operate under the belief that learning emerges through a heavy emphasis on personal counseling. Counseling proponents regard individual counseling and regular conferences with professional staff members as a way to help students break emotional barriers and negative attitudes toward learning, which traditional classroom and familiar lecture, practice, and homework programs may fail to address. Students may approach learning with a background of negative experiences, fear of failure, and self-dissatisfaction. Even if students' attitudes toward learning are positive, students may still find that personal difficulties interfere with learning and even with staying in school. A counseling approach combines work on improving learning attitudes, self-image, and other emotional stresses with instruction in reading and study skills.

Raygor (1977) identified emotional problems that manifest themselves in reading and study behaviors and listed 10 characteristics that an ideal learning center should include to address those problems. The emotional problems he noted were distortion of reality, unwillingness to take risks, compulsive reading, nervousness and tenseness during instruction, refusal to read, lack of concentration, fear of discovery, transference symptoms, giving up, escapism, blame-placing, and examination panic. He concluded that the ideal learning center program should include individualized instruction, diagnosis and treatment models, counseling, flexible schedules, self-paced instruction, flexible grades and credits, competency-based objectives, appropriate program evaluation, services that reflect the academic goals of the institution, and a trained staff.

Robyak and Patton (1977) cited research suggesting poor academic performance results from emotional factors as well as from skill deficits. They argue that students should receive academic advice and counseling—preferably on a one-to-one basis—as well as assistance in developing reading, writing, and study skills. Forums and workshops should be offered on specific topics throughout each semester, and students should be encouraged to participate. For instance, small groups might focus on stress, test taking, test anxiety, time management, or effective listening.

Counseling is still considered an important component in programs today. For example, Hancock and Gier (1991) presented a rationale for training tutors in basic counseling skills and techniques. They note that many tutoring programs expect tutors to display sensitivity to others and help them to build self-esteem. Tutors and counselors have much in common. Both help their clients learn to deal effectively with outside conflicts and problems that they confront.

In the published literature, we found several articles describing learning assistance programs that either had counseling components or were administered by counselors. One program with a counseling orientation emphasized academic enrichment for entering high-risk students. Academic counselors with master's degrees in educational psychology taught a course involving both group discussions and individual counseling (Landward &

Hepworth, 1984). Pollock and Wilkinson (1988) described a program at Brock University in which, when necessary, study skills were taught through individual counseling.

More recently, peer-mentoring programs have been established in learning centers as a way to improve student retention. Trained peer mentors are usually upper division students recommended by their instructors. Their function is to help students adjust to the campus, answer questions, direct students to appropriate resources, and sometimes do direct tutoring. At the University of North Carolina–Charlotte, the William States Lee College of Engineering has established a mentoring program (William States Lee, 1999). Peer mentors are upper division engineering students who help work individually with new students to identify goals, teach specific academic strategies, and introduce students to campus organizations and resources. Students also can enroll in small group mentoring sessions for peer mentoring and for networking with other students enrolled in similar classes.

A mentoring program at Rowan College in New Jersey (formerly known as Glassboro State College) is one of a large number of services at the Academic Advancement Center intended to help students make it to graduation. After taking a freshman seminar course, students receive follow-up mentoring. Peer mentoring is available among the many other services. The entire program has been found to improve retention rates (Harris, 1990).

Administrative Perspective. Learning center directors often take an administrative perspective that they have adapted from theories for business management. Because management theories change over the years, we can see changes in the administrative style of learning centers as well. During the 1970s, many administrators of learning centers adopted management by objectives (MBO). Directors with this perspective tested students and used the results to develop an individualized plan with specific learning objectives. A learning contract established what the educator expected and elicited a commitment from the student. Materials and center facilities were usually provided to assist in the completion of each learning objective, and student progress was monitored periodically. Educators who argued that effective learning came from an MBO approach include Roueche and Snow (1977) and Boylan (1982).

More recently, many administrators take a total quality management (TQM) approach, based on the work of W. Edwards Deming, an automobile manufacturing manager whose theories were first successfully applied in Japan after World War II. To apply TQM, administrators must first acquire thorough knowledge of "systems, statistics, psychology and the nature of knowledge itself" (Porter, 1993, p. 17). Applied to education, program administrators must thoroughly understand student learning. Furthermore, they must understand their customers, who are students, the future employers of their students, and even the state legislature. Administrators also must have trust and understanding of their workers. Learning center administrators, then, must focus on finding out exactly what students need in order to be successful, train their staff, and find ways to encourage the staff to take pride in what they do. The key word is teamwork. People who work in the learning center must trust each other and work together to help students achieve. An example of one TQM learning assistance program is the Air Force Academy program that Porter directs.

Maxwell (1997) identified other management approaches for learning centers. One is called *benchmarking*, having program personnel observe learning centers at other institutions and identify their secrets of success. Another is the quality assurance model (QAM), which focuses on finding, recognizing and rewarding good staff members.

Within the management perspective, different programs take different approaches. Castelli and Johnson (1983), working at two different kinds of universities, took an administrative perspective when they proposed that the learning center should take a leadership role in predicting and responding to change. They recommended that learning center directors "cultivate and use the channels of power" (p. 31) and develop an understanding of how universities work in order to avoid being subject to the whims and trends of college decision making.

Earlier programs with administrative perspectives took diagnostic-prescriptive or contractual approaches, among others, which are briefly described in Carpenter and Johnson (1991). According to proponents, an administrative perspective not only enhances learning but also facilitates the administration of the program as a whole, particularly the data collection and program evaluation aspects. Program administrators write objectives and goals for the program and gather data. Through periodic evaluations, they decide which objectives are being met as well as which ones need further effort.

Mechanistic Perspective.

Content tutoring and appropriate materials selection to ameliorate specific skill deficiencies are the major components of the mechanistic perspective. Christ (1971) stressed that the materials do the actual teaching. Instructors are "learning facilitators" who identify weaknesses and assign students to materials. Students also might be assigned to specific learning center classes and subject-specific tutoring groups, or assistance might be provided on an individual basis through self-instructional packets.

Proponents of the mechanistic perspective maintain that the use of technology can improve the work of learning facilitators through the systematic identification, development, organization and utilization of a full range of learning resources. Using the learning options made available through technology, students can learn more in less time.

Mechanistic programs using self-instruction with programmed materials were abundant in the early 1970s (Reedy, 1973). In the 1980s, programs that combined a mechanistic approach with tutoring or direct instruction were more common (e.g., McMurtrie, 1982). Townsend (1983) described a self-instructional program for underprepared Pennsylvania college students in which students were given competency-based pre- and posttests in 11 skill areas. Students studied from individualized reading programs determined by test results. Because students had problems setting personal as well as academic goals, Townsend planned to include counseling techniques in the future.

A mechanistic diagnostic-prescriptive approach is still used today in some colleges. Often it is used in conjunction with computer-assisted instruction (CAI). At Jefferson State Community College in Birmingham, Alabama, students take a regular course in study skills or a computer-assisted module. In either module, students take the Learning and Study Strategies Inventory (LASSI; Weinstein, Schulte, & Palmer, 1987) as a pretest and a posttest. In the computer course, analysis of the LASSI subscores is used to prescribe lessons in the computer program. The computer does the teaching. Topics covered include managing time, improving memory, taking lecture notes, reading textbooks, taking examinations, writing themes and reports, making oral reports, improving scholastic motivation, improving interpersonal relations, and improving concentration (R. Sartori, lrnasst, August 22, 1995).[1]

Basic Skills Perspective.   The basic skills perspective presupposes that deficiencies in the basic skills of reading, writing, and mathematics are the major contributors to academic difficulties. Proponents believe that if students improve their basic skills, they are more likely to succeed in college. Materials and instruction in programs with this focus may or may not be closely related to the reading and writing required in the college curriculum.

Maxwell (1997) suggested that underprepared college students can upgrade their skills and attain their educational goals by taking basic skills courses in writing and mathematics, although she is less enthusiastic about the success of current reading courses. To be effective, she said, reading courses need to be part of the regular curriculum and teach skills relevant to success in content courses.

A voluntary program for high-risk students at the City University of New York (CUNY) typifies basic skills programs in the 1980s (Bengis, 1986). In this program, students with low scores on skills assessments of reading, writing, and mathematics enrolled in a 6-week summer session. They received basic skills instruction as well as tutoring and counseling. Instructors worked together to plan instruction and share effective teaching methods.

Students who enroll in a basic skills reading course at a New York state community college had previously taken the Computerized Placement Tests (CPT, published by the College Entrance Examination Board and the Educational Testing Service) and scored well below college level, requiring them to take the course. Students learn to identify main ideas, make inferences, recognize paragraph structures, draw conclusions, and develop other study-reading skills. Besides classwork, students spend 1 hour per week in the academic skills center where they work on self-paced materials and receive one-on-one instruction. Students taking the course achieved significantly higher grade point averages (GPAs) than students who did not take the course. CPT posttest scores were significantly higher than pretest scores of the same students (Napoli & Hiltner III, 1993).

As the programs illustrate, most learning assistance programs that stress one theoretical perspective recognize the need for additional services that may be more congruent with a different perspective.

ORGANIZATIONAL TRENDS

Because of the numerous influences on learning assistance programs, it is unlikely that any two programs are identical. Goals, structure, and activities are institution-specific,

---

[1]To subscribe to lrnasst listserv, send an e-mail message to the following address: LISTSERV@LISTSERV.ARIZONA.EDU Leave the subject header blank. In the body message, type the following, substituting your first and last name for the lower case words: SUBSCRIBE LRNASST Firstname Lastname Make sure nothing else appears in your message and nothing appears next to the subject header. Soon you will receive a welcome message from the person in charge of the listserv.

and each program exploits whatever resources and expertise are available to provide needed services. However, we can classify programs in general according to their location in the college hierarchy, whether they are dispersed throughout the institution or are located in one central facility. We can classify programs as to whether they require at least some students to enroll in at least some of their programs. Finally we can classify programs as to whether they are aimed at all students or only to high-risk, minority, or first-year students.

Location of Programs in the College Organizational Structure

Often the responsibility for providing learning assistance is divided among several schools or departments within a university. The school of education may provide study skills training, peer counseling, remedial reading instruction, and tutoring. The English department may teach developmental reading and writing. The linguistics department may teach writing courses for international students. The law school may sponsor reading and writing courses for law students. Administrative personnel may offer writing and time management courses for faculty and staff. The dean of graduate studies may provide tutoring for graduate students. The office of student affairs may offer counseling and tutoring.

According to a survey by Smith et al. (1975), learning centers in the early 1970s tended to be administered by English departments in 2-year colleges and by counseling or education departments in universities. By the early 1980s, nearly 50% of the respondents to a Gordon and Flippo (1983) survey were located in their own department, whereas another 33% were in English departments and 22% were in the college of education. In the 1980s, the national trend was to form a central service unit for the entire institution (Walker, 1980; Wright, 1985).

In the 1990s, remedial courses continue to be offered in academic departments, most often in the English and mathematics departments. Only about 20% of institutions offer courses in a separate division, and learning centers seldom provide courses, whether credit or noncredit (NCES, 1996). These same institutions might contain all other learning assistance services in a single unit, but courses were administered by the individual departments.

If learning assistance programs are to meet the demands of today's postsecondary students, there are many reasons why they should be placed in one central facility. A single center provides credibility and continuity for programs and promotes cooperation among staff members. There are additional reasons why a college or university is best served by a central unit.

1. Developmental activities are closely related, and each service—reading, writing, study skills, tutoring—is strengthened by proximity to others. Course content sometimes overlaps, and consultation between instructors improves the quality of all courses. In addition, a central unit allows the staff to help train new staff members.

2. Many learning centers have large drop-in populations. Students seldom know where to go for needed assistance if no designated center exists. Those who are

not enrolled in developmental classes are more likely to visit if the learning center is visible and identified.

3. A central unit lends name and place recognition to a program. The more students know about the center, the more able the center is to reach students in need.

4. Identification of the center as a cohesive entity with a special focus gives the staff a sense of direction. As a unit, the center can give its teaching staff the kind of support that a lone person teaching study skills in a school of education might not have.

5. The existence of a designated center emphasizes the institution's commitment to reading, study skills, writing, and tutoring. Delegating these services to the school of education or to a freshman English class may make these activities seem less important.

6. Administrative time is better employed if three or four subunits are grouped together than if each is functioning separately in diverse locations. This structure makes central accountability and standardized evaluation much more feasible.

Another important factor in determining the best location for a learning center within the institution's organization is whether the center offers courses for credit. Roueche and Snow (1977) and Sullivan (1980) found that an increasing number of colleges were offering credit for learning center classes. Roueche (1983) noted that successful programs offered courses for credit and made sure that they appeared as such on the students' transcripts.

If the center does not offer classes for credit, it may be viewed as having a student service function rather than an academic function. In this case, the learning center program is administered through a student service office, such as the counseling unit, which acts on the belief that students' academic problems are seldom purely academic. If the center is associated with the counseling unit, referrals between program services are easier, and the student service orientation of the center is maintained.

Usually, if developmental classes are offered for credit, the learning center is under the supervision of an administrator in academic affairs because some postsecondary administrative units (such as student affairs or student services) do not grant credit for developmental activities (Walker, 1980).

If a program offers credit, then reporting to an academic department, divisional chair, dean of undergraduate studies, vicepresident for academic affairs, or some other academic administrator may enhance the learning center's credibility to the faculty. A center might be a part of the school of education and report directly to its dean. This would give it the power and strength of being part of the school. Teaching staff would be education faculty, and courses would be listed under education. However, the question arises as to whether the student service orientation of the center might be lost in a school or department whose primary interests are research and teacher training. Certainly, the center would lose some of its separate identity and assume the flavor and reputation of its administrative home. A similar discussion of advantages and disadvantages would occur if the center became part of the English department.

If the center serves the entire academic community, it is beneficial if it is not tied to any one department or school. If the center is independent, students in all major areas would realize that the center is there to serve their needs, as would faculty and administrators. Tutoring in various areas and working relationships with faculty members in diverse departments would be enhanced. Financially, no one department or school would be required to shoulder the monetary burden of a center designed to serve the entire institution. A direct administrative relationship to the vice-president for academic affairs or the dean of undergraduate studies would eliminate many of the undesirable outcomes associated with a departmental or school association. If the center offers services for graduate students, a separate reporting relationship for those activities could be established with the dean of graduate studies.

Successful programs have been found to be organized as a single unit on a campus, whether a department or division of developmental studies (Roueche & Kirk, 1973). According to Boylan et al. (1994), the preponderance of research suggests that programs located under one roof work better than ones scattered all over the campus. Programs, courses, and other activities in close proximity are easier to coordinate. Such coordination allows professionals to work together on common themes, goals and objectives.

Placing the center for learning assistance programs directly under the chief academic officer in the administrative structure also allows the center to develop programs with an institution-wide appeal, rather than catering to the interests of one academic view or a student services orientation. Ideally, the center should be administratively responsible to the highest ranking academic officer to ensure autonomous and diversified assistance for all registered students.

Remedial Programs and Developmental Programs

Cross (1976) divided learning assistance programs into two types: *remedial* and *developmental*. She defined remedial programs as those whose purpose is to overcome students' academic deficiencies. Many institutions still view the mission of their learning centers in this light. Open admission policies and federal funding that enables a wide diversity of students to participate in higher education have led many institutions to offer remedial services for their high-risk students. In some cases, the remedial courses are mandatory and must be successfully completed in order to continue enrolling at the institution (Cashen, 1983). In other cases, students attend regular college classes in addition to their remedial activities (Roueche & Snow, 1977). Often remedial courses do not carry academic credit; if credit is available, it is sometimes institutional or internal credit, in which case it counts toward the students' load and GPA but not toward graduation requirements (Helm & Chand, 1983).

Cross (1976) defined developmental programs as those whose activities are designed to develop students' diverse academic talents. Boylan (1983) agreed and further defined developmental education as a professional specialty concerned with promoting educational opportunity, academic skills development, and educational efficiency at the postsecondary level. Maxwell's (1997) definition is similar to Boylan's. She also observed that developmental education rose from the attempts by student services offices to unite academic and student affairs personnel with the goal of supporting student learning. Some learning centers offer both remedial and developmental services, clearly delineating the difference by offering credit for the developmental classes but not for the remedial activities (Rosen, 1980). Often, high-risk students must successfully complete their remedial programs before they are allowed to participate in developmental activities.

A large number of learning centers label their programs developmental to avoid placing the stigma of remedial on their students. Financial considerations often dictate use of the term developmental because state legislatures may discourage or even prohibit institutions from offering remedial courses at the postsecondary level. (Ironically, these same legislatures expect their institutions of higher learning to successfully educate all who enroll.)

Increases and declines in postsecondary enrollment over the years stimulate swings in interest in student retention by the larger institution. When enrollments decline because of fewer high school graduates, institutions do all they can to retain the students who do enroll on their campuses. Learning assistance programs have been the mainstay of higher education's retention efforts. When large numbers of qualified students apply, support for learning assistance tends to decrease.

All kinds of students, even high achieving ones, have problems adjusting to the academic demands of college (Walker, 1980). Therefore, whenever possible, learning centers offer a variety of services: remedial support, developmental education, and enrichment opportunities. By offering learning opportunities at all levels, learning assistance educators provide intervention and support for all students in developing their learning strategies and abilities to the fullest.

Student Placement and Enrollment

Colleges and universities use a variety of methods to determine whether students should enroll in basic skills classes or learning assistance programs. Some schools make enrollment mandatory for certain students; others recommend but do not require that students enroll.

Placement by Testing.　　　About 60% of postsecondary institutions test all entering freshmen in reading, writing, and mathematics (Roueche, Baker, & Roueche, 1984). That same figure held in 1995 (NCES, 1996). About 75% of institutions administering placement tests went on to require students needing remediation to enroll in remedial courses. Two-year colleges tended to recommend rather than require more often than did 4-year colleges. Many community college students are enrolled part time and are not pursuing a degree, which may explain why the colleges do not always require enrollment in basic skills courses.

In four regional and national studies analyzed by Gabriel (1989), the Nelson–Denny Reading Test was the most commonly administered test for reading, while essays or locally developed tests were more common for writing and mathematics. Learning center personnel also may administer pretests, but generally they are more interested in using tests as diagnostic instruments to direct students to the most appropriate services.

Gabriel's findings still hold true today, although there is a broader variety of tests used for placement. At a Philadelphia technical college (F. Ross, lrnasst, August 5, 1997), learning center personnel conduct placement testing for all degree-seeking day students, whether full or part time, in mathematics, writing, and reading. For reading, students take Form E of the Nelson–Denny. If on one of more of the placement tests, students score below the cutoff score, they are placed in the relevant developmental courses. On the first day of class, students take a campus-developed placement test, and a student can "test out" based on that test. This reading test is quite different from the Nelson–Denny. Students write a summary of a short passage, then write the topic and main idea for five paragraphs.

A Florida community college administers the state-mandated College Placement Test to all students aiming for an associates degree and to all entering freshmen. If students' relevant scores are not high enough, they are required to take one of the semester-long courses in reading, mathematics, or writing (D. Warford-Alley, lrnasst, August 5, 1997). In order to enroll in one Missouri community college, students must take the ACT or ASSET tests (both published by ACT, Inc.). Advisors recommend but do not require that students take developmental courses in reading and study skills based on a cutoff score. Once enrolled in the course, students take the Nelson–Denny Reading Test as a pre- and posttest (E. G. Clark, lrnasst, February 6, 1996).

Some institutions now use the computer for placement. At a Wyoming college, COMPASS (ACT, Inc., Computer-Adaptive Placement Assessment and Support System) is used for placement into developmental or honors sections of English, mathematics, and reading (P. Killebrew, lrnasst, September 5, 1997). The computer test does not require time limits, and students can work on it for a while and then come back to it later if need be. Students in the developmental classes may retake the COMPASS test at the end of the semester in order to raise their scores, because many regular courses have a prerequisite of a certain reading or composition level on this test. Accuplacer (published by the College Board) tests students in reading comprehension, sentence skills, and three levels of mathematics. A North Carolina community college chose the Accuplacer program for its convenience in administration and grading by the computer. Students average 20 minutes in taking the test, which is untimed (S. Paterson, lrnasst, September 15, 1997).

Often, a combination of information is used to place entering freshmen in classes where they can function academically. In the absence of a locally administered testing program, institutions often rely on the ACT or the Scholastic Aptitude Test (SAT) scores along with high school records in making class assignments. Academic advisors may ask students for a self-assessment and use this information as an aid in making class selection decisions.

Maxey and Sawyer's (1981) study indicated that ACT test scores and high school grades are useful predictors of freshman GPA in college, although they are very slightly less accurate for minorities. The authors also determined that the combination of test scores and self-reported high school grades predict college freshman GPA with greater accuracy than does either measure alone.

Research by McDonald and Gawkoski (1979) supported the use of SAT tests for predicting the performance of incoming freshmen. Chissom and Lanier (1975) produced similar results earlier. In a more recent study, however, King, Rasool, and Judge (1994) found that verbal SAT scores did not predict GPA for reading-intensive courses taken by freshmen at a Massachusetts state college. In fact, neither did the Nelson–Denny Reading Test nor did the Degrees of Reading Power. The mathematics portion of SAT did prove to be statistically related to mathematics course grades. Because such a weak relationship existed, however, the authors did not recommend placing students in mathematics courses based on the SAT.

Many institutions have guidelines for mandated placement in remedial classes or learning center programs. A student who scores below a certain level on the ACT or SAT, has a high school GPA below a specified minimum, or scores below a designated score on a preenrollment placement test may be required to participate in specific courses or learning center activities before the student is permitted to enroll in regular courses. At some institutions, the student may be allowed to enroll in regular classes while still being required to take specific remedial classes (Committee on Learning Skills Centers, 1976; Maxwell, 1979). Roueche (1983) reported that mandatory completion of specific developmental courses assigned on the basis of basic skills achievement levels is one of the earmarks of a successful learning center.

The procedure at a 4-year liberal arts school in upstate New York is a recent example (N. M. Bailey, lrnasst, September 11, 1997). First year students who score below nineth-grade level on both the vocabulary and comprehension sections of the Nelson-Denny are required to take the college reading and study skills class. Students are permitted to refuse to take this developmental course, but this happens rarely. (For a full review and for further discussion of reading tests, see Flippo & Schumm, chap. 14, this volume.)

Voluntary Placement.   At some institutions, entering students are not required to participate in learning center programs, no matter how low their test results or previous grades are. Students are advised of the available opportunities, but use of the learning center is voluntary. Jones (1959) proposed that involvement in developmental activities be completely voluntary, maintaining that students are successful only if they want to be and not because they are forced. But when skills assistance is offered solely on an elective basis, programs may not reach all student who need them. In a study conducted at an open-admissions junior college, Reed (1989) found that 62% of students scoring below the ninth-grade level on the Nelson-Denny Reading Test said that they did not need help with their reading. Students' inaccuracy in assessing their need for help was made evident at the end of the year. Of the students reading below the ninth-grade level, those who had said they needed help with their reading achieved higher GPAs than students who had said they might need help, who in turn achieved higher GPAs than students who had said they did not need help.

After experience with both required and voluntary programs, Shaw (1961) concluded that freshmen generally were incapable of determining if they should enroll in a skills course. He further noted that, once enrolled, students were unable to determine whether they needed to continue. On the other hand, he said, if students resist taking the course, they should be allowed to drop it as they would any other course.

Whenever possible, learning centers offer credit for regularly scheduled classes. Those who support required programs generally recommend that credit be granted for developmental classes (Roueche & Snow, 1977). Faculty and administrative politics sometimes make granting credit for a course difficult; however, research indicates that awarding credit for developmental classes increases the overall effectiveness of the program. Boylan (1983), reviewed the effectiveness of programs through an analysis of program reports, research, and literature. He found that the programs reporting the greatest gains all offered credit for developmental courses.

In a national study, Roueche (1983) used survey questions to identify program and course elements common to institutions that reported the most positive outcomes. He found that among the skills development programs reporting the most complete and encouraging retention data, all awarded credit for developmental courses and all counted the credit as degree credit (counting toward graduation requirements).

Despite results like these, many postsecondary institutions are still reluctant to offer degree credit for developmental courses. About 70% of institutions now offer some type of credit for developmental courses (NCES, 1996). Of these, institutional credit (credit that counts toward financial aid, ability to live on campus, or that counts toward full-time status) is the most frequently given type. Institutions offering institutional credit are increasing over the years, whereas the percentage of colleges offering elective degree credit for developmental courses is decreasing. Elective degree credit for remedial mathematics, for example, is awarded by 11% of colleges and universities; 71% award institutional credit, and 13% give no credit. This pattern was similar for English and reading courses. Of postsecondary institutions, community colleges are most likely to provide institutional credit, 80%. Only about 50% of private 4-year colleges offer any credit.

The advantage of offering degree credit for developmental courses is considerable. If students are required to take developmental or skills courses before they enroll in regular courses, they may give up and drop out of college. If they cannot earn credit until they have taken courses for a year or longer, they must certainly become discouraged. Degree credit is an inducement to remain in college longer. Even institutional credit makes it possible for some students to attend. If colleges are truly interested in helping at-risk students make their way through the tangle of difficulties they face in attending college, they should offer credit for their developmental courses.

TYPES OF PROGRAMS

Colleges have many options in organizing learning assistance programs. An institution might create a large-scale program directed specifically at improving the retention of high-risk students. It might offer programs for students on academic probation. It might provide a learning center or course work for students who want to improve their already adequate reading and study skills. These programs may be housed in several different departments or in one department under a single administrator. They may be controlled by one or more departments, an office of academic affairs, or by the student affairs office. The internal structure may consist of any or all of a number of elements, including a lab, a series of courses, peer tutoring, drop-in services, small group instruction, individualized self-instruction, or counseling services.

Students Served

Learning assistance programs may be categorized according to the kinds of students they are intended to help—whether at-risk students, minority or nontraditional students, first-year students, or any students. Some programs that are aimed at particular groups of students may overlap. If a student is both a freshman and an at-risk student, for example, he or she may be eligible for programs aimed at either or both.

Programs for First-Year Students.

New or freshman students are the main focus of most postsecondary institutions in their desire to retain students and see them on their way to graduation. These first-year students are the ones at highest risk for failure or for dropping out. They are the ones that most need acculturation to services, academic life, and to the new demands on their time and self-discipline.

A widespread program for first year students is the Freshman Seminar. According to Sims' (1977) data, about 70% of U.S. colleges and universities offer a seminar or course for entering students. Seminars vary in content and goals but most are intended to increase retention and promote academic and social adjustment. At the University of South Carolina, the home of the National Resource Center for the Freshman Year Experience, about 70% of the freshman class voluntarily enroll for the three-credit course. Students who participate are disproportionately females, athletes, high-risk students, minorities, provisionally admitted students, students with disabilites, on-campus residents, and out-of-state students. Those voluntarily taking the courses are more likely to seek out other campus services, earn higher grades, and graduate than those who do not take the course.

Programs for Minority and High-Risk Students.

Roueche et al. (1984) found that more than 50% of the postsecondary institutions provided orientation programs specifically for high-risk students. Most institutions preferred structured courses for these students, although drop-in facilities were frequently available.

At the University of California–Berkeley, eight different academic support programs target minority retention as their goal (Robert & Thomson, 1994). Several programs are intended for specific majors; for example, Professional Development works with 600 minority student in mathematics. The Academic Achievement Division supports academic assistance for low-income, first-generation college students. The Athletic Study Center provides academic support for athletes, many of whom are minorities. Summer Bridge is offered to some specially admitted students. Retention rates for Summer Bridge students are 12% higher than for eligible students who did not enroll in the program. The largest program is the Student Learning Center, available to all lower division students. The Student Learning Center offers adjunct classes, writing workshops, study groups, and tutoring. Priority in getting service is given to at-risk students. The authors attribute the success of the programs to making them attractive rather than stigmatizing, to creating a strong supportive community, and to encouraging collaborative learning.

As with the Berkeley program, programs for high-risk students often begin the summer between high school graduation and enrollment at the postsecondary institution. Called *summer bridge programs*, these usually include intensive courses in basic skills, orientation seminars, career counseling, and academic advising, among other components. A 6-week program at a New York City community college is typical. Aimed at minorities and low-income students, it was evaluated with questionnaire, retention, and GPA data (Santa Rita & Bacote, 1997). The authors concluded that participation in the program helped facilitate students' adjustment to campus life and improved their persistence, which was a higher percentage than obtained by students entering the same semester but not participating in the summer program.

A similar bridge program at the University of Virginia is aimed primarily at minority students. Called the Summer Transition Program, students are invited to participate based on admission test scores. They must complete the 6-week program in order to be admitted to the university in the fall. On the basis of placement tests, students enroll in special writing, mathematics, and reasoning courses. The reasoning courses emphasize reading comprehension and are coordinated with the writing courses. In addition to the courses, daily tutorials and study groups are available to students. In the evening, students may seek help from tutors, faculty advisors, graduate students, and administrators, all of whom live in the residence halls. Adult mentoring and group projects play an important role in the experience. Taken together with two other precollege programs in which the students participated, retention rates were at the 76% level compared to 55% retention for at-risk nonparticipants in the three programs (Simmons, 1994).

High-risk African American students attended freshman seminar courses at the University of South Carolina. In 9 of the 13 years of the program, these students attained a higher retention rate than African American students who did not enroll in the courses (Fidler & Godwin, 1994). The authors attributed the success to various components of the seminar, especially introduction to campus facilities and the support students receive from the faculty member heading the group.

Programs for Those on Academic Probation.

Needs of students on academic probation confront academic advisors, who suggest these students seek help at learning centers or other services on campus. Occasionally, programs addressed particularly to probationary students are established.

Students on academic probation cite a variety of causes for their poor performance in college classes. A new academic probation success-oriented program required of all 278 students then on probation at a community college in a Chicago suburb, was evaluated by Lucas (1991). About 73% of participants returned the following semester. Besides analyzing students' academic records, Lucas performed a follow-up telephone survey. Students attributed their poor grades to poor study habits and working too many hours (35%). Students who had decided not to return after the intervention program blamed job responsibilities (35%), personal and family responsibilities (25%), and a need for time away to rethink their goals (21%). Lucas concluded that the intervention program influenced students' work habits more than their goals.

At a Los Angeles community college, a drop-out prevention program was initially targeted at students on academic probation. The Magic of the Mind (MOM) program was aimed at improving students' learning skills, self-efficacy, and stress management. The predominantly Mexican American students in the study experienced a dropout rate of 16%. The control group's dropout rate was 56%. The researchers attributed the success of the program to its ability, through immediate feedback, to develop a strong belief in both students and instructors that they could succeed (Barrios, 1997).

Programs for Athletes.

Study tables have long been a feature of academic support programs for college athletes. With physical training and practice as well as time away from the campus for games, student athletes need extra assistance. Furthermore, some athletes are admitted although they do not meet other admissions criteria. The Student-Athlete Academic Support Program (SAASP) at one college is intended to improve academic performance, retention, and graduation rate of all student athletes (Smith & Herman, 1996). Career exploration is an important part of the program. Attaining study skills competence and forming a self-image as an athlete–scholar are among other goals. Required study time, study skills workshops, and tutoring services are components of the program.

Services Provided

Programs can be categorized as to the services and instruction they provide—tutoring, mentoring, skills classes, adjunct or paired classes, linked classes, learning communities, counseling, workshops, outreach programs, and computer-based programs. Learning assistance programs may consist of classes that are similar to other college classes in appearance and that meet in regular classrooms. Alternately, programs may be located in a learning center that students visit individually or in small groups. As a third option, facilities may consist of several rooms housing a variety of learning assistance programs. At some universities, all of these types of programs may operate simultaneously in different parts of the campus. The structure of the program often dictates the services offered.

Tutoring.   Tutoring is one of the most widespread learning assistance programs across the nation (Rouche & Snow, 1977). About 70% of 2-year institutions and 77% of 4-year institutions offer tutoring; the latter institutions were much more likely to train the tutors (Boylan et al., 1994).

The exact nature of a tutoring program affects its success. As Boylan et al. (1995) found, tutor training is associated with the success of tutoring programs. These researchers found that most institutions, about 90%, trained their tutors. Less than 50%, however, trained tutors in skills specifically needed by at-risk students. Even fewer offered training about the nature and needs of these students. Maxwell (1990) did not find consistent evidence that at-risk students who receive tutoring improve their grades. In a review of the literature, Maxwell found that tutoring helped those who were better prepared for college. There was evidence that at-risk students like peer tutoring and feel that it helps their grades. Furthermore, they tend to remain in college longer than students who are not tutored.

Learning centers often provide content-area tutoring to assist students with specific academic classes (Beal, 1980; Clymer, 1978). Often the institution pays the tutors, and the learning center is responsible for selecting, training, and monitoring them. At some colleges, students must pay for tutor assistance, and learning center personnel act as program administrators and brokers, bringing the student together with a tutor who is proficient in the required subject area. Tutors also may be available to help students engage in the center's activities, such as using workbooks, videos, and computers.

Researchers at Los Angeles City College found that students who worked with tutors showed a higher rate of achievement than students who did not (Gold, 1980). The same study reported strong support from faculty for the tutoring program. Similar results were reported at Los Angeles Pierce College (Schulman, 1981), where 50% of the students indicated that they would have failed or dropped courses without tutoring help.

Tutoring is a familiar component of large comprehensive programs for high-risk students. McHugh et al. (1986) employed tutoring in a multifaceted program that included study skills and writing courses along with regular freshman courses. Anderson and Smith (1987) used peer tutors in a developmental college reading laboratory.

Tutoring for a particular course most often is done on an individual basis. Many students need to contact a tutor only once for help with a specific problem. However, students often return to a tutor weekly for continuing assistance with a difficult subject. In these circumstances, a learning center staff member or the tutor may form tutoring groups, encouraging all individuals who need help with a specific class to meet weekly at a regular time and place.

Tutors may be graduate students or upper division students with expertise in a specific subject, full- or part-time teachers, members of the community, or retired faculty members. Continuous training in the skills areas, empathy, assertiveness, and record-keeping ability enable tutors to be of maximum assistance (Carpenter, 1984).

Although adult tutors have many advantages, peer tutors can be effective. Peer tutors in the Anderson and Smith (1987) study helped students achieve higher grades, increase attendance in the reading laboratory, and improve reading posttest scores. Maxwell (1991) concluded that students earned higher grades when they worked with peer tutors of the same gender. They also earned higher grades when their peer tutor was from a different ethnic background.

Tutoring has positive benefits for tutors as well as the tutees. Tutoring is a type of overlearning in that teaching someone else about a subject forces the tutor to learn the material well, and this leads to long-term retention of the knowledge (Semb, 1993).

Sometimes peer tutoring is offered in association with a particular skills course. In a study skills course at Northern Michigan University, a peer tutor meets weekly for 30 minutes with each student to help students immediately apply the strategies they are learning (Soldner, 1992). Tutors work with no more than 10 students and help each student set goals. Because tutors are taking courses and applying the strategies themselves, they are credible to the students they are tutoring.

Presently, online tutoring usually involves answering students' questions over e-mail, usually within a 24-hour turnaround time. The learning center at Chemeketa Community College in Salem, Oregon is an example (L. MacDonald, lrnasst, December 3, 1995). MacDonald reports that the evening tutoring sessions are often slow, a good time for tutors to respond to e-mail requests. These requests usually come from one of the five satellite campuses or from students' homes.

Online, real-time tutoring is becoming available at a few college learning centers. Using videoconferencing software, video cameras, a network server, among other computer equipment, participants can see and hear one another over the Internet. The equipment and software is expensive, though. At one California State University campus, the learning center applied for a grant to fund the equipment to contact satellite campuses and secondary schools for tutoring students at those locations (S. T. Wentworth, lrnasst, February 9, 1998). Online tutoring may help distance learners with other online courses and with correspondence courses.

Laboratory Instruction.   Laboratory instruction may be offered to the entire college community or only to those in special programs for at-risk students. It may be required of students taking regularly scheduled learning assistance classes or be offered on a drop-in basis. Finally, it may be the only learning assistance provided on a campus.

Many learning centers are housed in a centralized, well-advertised laboratory setting where students are encouraged to drop in for assistance at any time during the semester. Students enter the center, sign in, and are interviewed for their needs. Some diagnostic testing may take place. Students may take part in the tutoring program, enroll in short noncredit courses or workshops, get directed to counseling or career guidance across campus, or work with a tutor in the lab. In the same cluster of rooms, there may be labs for reading and study skills, for writing, and for mathematics (Beal, 1980). More recently, there is often a computer lab where students may find help with any of the basic skills. In the lab, a tutor might help students get started on a computer, identify some appropriate workbook material, or work individually with the student on immediate needs.

At Monroe Community College in southeastern Michigan (Holladay & Zwayer, 1992), students troubled with writing in certain courses get help at the learning assistance center. As part of a writing across the curriculum project (WAC), specially trained peer writing fellows work with students enrolled in WAC courses. Fellows, students, WAC instructors, and learning assistance personnel found the program beneficial. Frequency use data for the learning center improved.

Louisiana State University at Alexandria is a 2-year commuter campus with a comprehensive learning center (LSUA, 1998). It provides free peer tutoring, a collection of audio- and videotapes, and CAI. The center offers learning skills classes, workshops, and seminars on such topics as taking notes, managing time, test taking, and managing stress.

Regularly Scheduled Classes.   Learning assistance programs often consist of regularly scheduled classes because many underprepared students require more structure than that provided in drop-in programs (Roueche et al., 1984). In addition, these courses are, in the short run, less costly for the college to provide. Classes may be structured similarly to regular courses, running for a full quarter or semester, counting for 2 or 3 credit hours, and involving comprehensive development of reading and study skills. Conversely, they may be a series of short, 1-hour credit classes that emphasize specific skills such as listening and notetaking, test taking, or spelling improvement. The classes often have a laboratory component associated with them, and additional assistance from tutors or faculty may be readily available.

A program in New Mexico exemplifies a novel approach in which local public school reading specialists taught at the university without outside laboratories or tutoring (Hamberg & Rubin, 1986). Using the Nelson-Denny Reading Test for placement, the public school teachers employed commercial materials, magazine articles, the students' regular course materials, and sustained silent reading (SSR) in their instruction. The teachers applied direct teaching of reading and study skills instead of individualized work packets.

At a Louisiana university, students received 5 hours credit for recitation and lecture sections of either a lower or upper level course in developmental reading (Dillard, 1989). In the lower level courses, students read and reported on material on their major and on fiction. They also learned test-taking skills, developed vocabulary and reading rate, and received lessons from the instructor. When students reached the upper level course, they learned to use a study plan, text structures, and writing patterns. The instructors provided individual guidance and small group work in the classroom and in the library. Students used both regular state-adopted textbooks and texts designed for reading classes.

With the increase in computer technology, instructors are exploring ways to implement it in their classrooms. Classes, especially in writing, but also in other subjects, sometimes link through e-mail with other classes around the country. Lrnasst, the listserv for learning assistance professionals, occasionally contains messages from one instructor seeking to link classes of similar interests. For example, an instructor of a college success seminar at a New York community college sought students in a similar course for participation in a discussion group over e-mail (K. Wunderlich, lrnasst, January 16, 1998).

As to whether individual courses improve GPAs or retention rates is open to question. Research by Beal (1980) revealed that students who participate in regularly scheduled classes show improved study habits and attitudes. Students also improved their GPAs and expressed positive feelings toward the institution and education.

At an Iowa community college (Pierson & Huba, 1997), GPAs were compared between students who completed all recommended developmental courses, those who did not enroll in or did not complete one or more of the recommended courses, and those who were exempt (no developmental courses were recommended to them). Of the 314 students in the analysis, only 17 completed the recommended courses. The other 252 did not complete the courses and 45 were exempt from them. As might be expected, those who were exempt earned higher GPAs than those who did not complete the recommended courses. That was the only significant difference among the three groups in GPA. Those who completed the courses did not earn significantly higher grades than those who did not complete the recommended courses. The authors hypothesized that other services on campus—including a learning center, tutoring, mentoring by faculty and staff, and a counseling center—may have offset lack of completion of the developmental courses. There were no differences among the groups on retention or credits earned.

In a large-scale study of the effects of courses in reading, writing, and mathematics, Boylan and Bonham (1992) examined transcripts of 5,166 students enrolled in 150 institutions around the United States. For developmental mathematics, 77.2% of the students passed with a C or better the college mathematics course that followed. For developmental English, 91.1% attained a C or better in the following college English course. For developmental reading, 83% attained at least a C in a college-level social science course that followed. The researchers concluded that because the goal of developmental courses is to prepare students to pass later college courses, these results suggest they do their job very well, indeed.

Paired or Adjunct Classes. Special classes are sometimes initiated in conjunction with a specific academic department (Dempsey & Tomlinson, 1980; Elliott & Fairbanks, 1986). Called *paired or adjunct classes*, they help student pass a particular content course. For instance, an adjunct course designed to aid students in a nursing course would be specifically aimed at teaching the learning strategies required for that course. Students register for both classes and take quizzes and exams in both classes. The aim is to teach learning strategies and study skills in an environment where they can be immediately applied. Presumably, the students are able to adapt what they learn in the adjunct class to other classes they take as well.

At the University of Cincinnati, a psychology professor and two faculty members from the reading and study skills program collaborated on delivering two courses, one in psychology and one in reading and study skills. The two classes offered five credits and were given a single course number to facilitate scheduling (Bullock, Madden, & Harter, 1987). Students taking the adjunct course had a better perception of their reading and study abilities and a higher standardized reading test score than their counterparts who took psychology without the adjunct course.

At St. Cloud State University in Minnesota, students whose high school grades are below the 50th percentile in their class must take a paired class for two quarters of their freshman year (Rauch, 1989). In conjunction with Modern Technology and Civilization, for example, they take a reading and study skills course. The program also includes a voluntary tutorial service.

Tomlinson and Green (1976) reported the beneficial outcomes of integrating reading and study skills adjunct classes with the content areas. Dempsey and Tomlinson (1980) described different formats used to teach adjunct classes and maintained that the concurrent development of process skills and content understanding achieved by adjunct programming is a powerful tool for the improvement of instruction and student academic performance.

An adjunct course at Georgia State University was taught with a difficult course in introductory U.S. history. Statistically, the developmental students taking the adjunct course attained grades that did not differ significantly from the grades of the regular students (Commander, Stratton, Callahan, & Smith, 1996). Students in the two courses earned equal credit hours, although the adjunct credits did not count toward graduation. Ordinarily, the developmental students would not have been permitted to enroll in the history course until after they had passed two reading courses.

Adjunct courses work to the extent that the courses they are paired with are difficult courses. If a course is already well taught by faculty interested in the success of underprepared students and the course is supported by other learning assistance facilities, pairing an adjunct course with it is not likely to make much difference.

Supplemental Instruction.   The widely implemented supplemental instruction (SI) program has some similarities to adjunct courses. The focus is on strategies to help students do well in a particular course. No credit is given and attendance is not required, however. A trained student leader rather than an instructor usually facilitates rather than teaches. The student leader acts as a model student, attending all classes and taking notes. Three or four SI sessions per week usually are scheduled to volunteer students. Students in need of further assistance are given tutoring.

Originating at the University of Missouri–Kansas City, SI has been adopted in 34 states (Blanc, DeBuhr, & Martin, 1983; Wolfe, 1987). Compared to the performance of students who wished to take the SI sessions but could not because of schedule conflicts, students who attended one or more times achieved significantly higher course test grades, course final grades, and overall GPA for the semester (Blanc, DeBuhr, & Martin, 1983).

Unlike adjunct courses where students must attend, SI sessions depend on the motivation of the students and whatever attractions the individual student SI leader can bring to the sessions to achieve regular attendance. In a study conducted at Georgia State University, for example, three or more SI sessions were attended by 52 students, 40 students attended one or two sessions, and 169 students did not attend any sessions (Commander et al., 1996). SI students attained significantly higher mean grades than students who did not participate in SI. The grades were one whole grade higher. Wolfe (1987) conducted a pilot study in a history class at Arundel Community College in Arnold, Maryland. She found that participants in the SI program had lower SAT scores than nonparticipants, yet they achieved significantly higher GPAs and final course grades in history than nonparticipants. The administrators of both of the just-mentioned programs received training from the University of Missouri program staff.

Many other studies have produced similar results. Perhaps because the program has been so widely implemented, it has been subject to some criticism. Like all voluntary programs, criticism centers on uncontrolled differences in motivation between those who attend these voluntary sessions versus those who do not. The significantly higher course grades could be due to the higher motivation of the students attending. In reply, researchers have conducted studies in which they have attempted to control for motivation.

In one such study at California State University–Long Beach, Ramirez (1997) grouped students by high and low SAT scores and, to control for motivation, high and low prior GPAs, but the SI program was changed significantly from the recommended format. Whereas students voluntarily enrolled in the class as it is customary, the course itself earned them one hour of institutional credit. Furthermore, the class met three times a week immediately following the course with which it was associated. In other words, at this college, SI sessions began more closely to resemble adjunct courses.

Outreach Programs. A large learning assistance center may offer a variety of outreach programs. Instructors may offer workshops to various groups on campus such as classes, fraternities and sororities, and residence hall gatherings. They may work with faculty members on dealing with reading and learning in their classes. For example, McKinley (1990) obtained released time from teaching to meet individually with the 65 full-time faculty members of Laramie County Community College in Cheyenne, Wyoming. She provided readability information about the textbooks they were using and informed them about the reading classes students could take. In some cases she shared some techniques they could use to help students comprehend their textbooks.

Distance Learning. Electronic technology has vastly increased the variety of instructional delivery systems. Distance learning used to refer to correspondence courses, but now it can refer to audio and television networks, interactive television, and online tutoring and instruction. The advantage of distance learning is that students who live far from the nearest college campus can still complete all or part of their education without having to drive long distances or move away from home. Learning assistance centers offer many of these services.

Broderick and Caverly (1996) described several computer-based courses that are taught online. Students use the computer and a modem to access the instructor's syllabus, lessons, and tests as appropriate throughout the semester. Instructor and student may never meet. To take such courses, students should already be versed in computers, modems, and the Internet. Alternately, instructors may design courses in which only part of instruction is online. They may spend a class period explaining how to use the technology. Except for tests, the rest of the class may be conducted online. Some of the instruction may consist of commercial computer courseware, or it could simply be lectures and assignments. Students submit completed written assignments via e-mail. Broderick and Caverly predict that online courses will increase in the years ahead because of cost effectiveness and the quality of instruction.

Delivery of Instruction

Learning assistance programs can be classified on the delivery of instruction within a classroom or lab (e.g., small group or individualized instruction). According to Roueche et al. (1984), 60% of respondents to their survey employed some form of individualization in learning assistance instruction. Forty percent employed whole-class activities such as lectures, class discussion, and small group activities. Whether instructors work within a classroom or learning center lab, however, they may employ one or more variations of these instructional delivery systems.

Small Group. At times a number of students need to gain expertise in the same skills (Spaulding, 1975). Small groups may be used to teach time management, effective listening skills, efficient notetaking, or a variety of other developmentally oriented skills. Students receive feedback not only from the teacher but from other group members. These groups may be advertised campuswide or formulated specifically for students already enrolled in learning center activities. Such small groups or workshops are usually short-term associations, but students often participate in more than one workshop group in order to strengthen academic abilities. Heerman (1984), for example, employed small groups in an individualized lab setting.

Dempsey and Tomlinson (1980) suggest that small groups can provide a place for experimentation, creativity, and innovation. Small groups also enable the learning center staff to provide some very specific help to a wide variety of students without the expenditure of time required for an ongoing class or for individual counseling.

Small groups are often effective for the delivery of instruction as opposed to the lecture method. After instruction via small groups, McMillon (1994) found that her African American students' tests scores and attitudes were higher than achieved by students receiving lectures. Students in the small groups worked together on process-oriented activities.

Individualized Instruction. Based on a pretest, diagnostic test, or professional evaluation, students may be given an individualized program designed to correct specific skill deficiencies or develop educational efficiency. The program may include readings, workbook pages, lab assignments, CAI or a combination of these activities in conjunction with other instructional materials. These types of programs date back to as early as the 1940s (Triggs, 1942). This type of program is much less used today, if judged by the number of descriptions in the learning assistance literature.

In a traditional individualized course with a strong CAI component, students participated in planning individualized programs of study with their instructors (Kincade, Kleine, Johnson, & Jacob, 1989). A total of 423 students enrolled in 24 sections of a one-semester college reading improvement course that was evaluated over a six-semester period. In addition to using computer programs that provided vocabulary practice and diagnostic information on 25 comprehension skills, students worked with comprehension kits, workbooks, and audiotapes. Researchers found significant gains in reading ability according to the Nelson–Denny Reading Test.

One of the problems of CAI in the college reading and learning center is the dearth of materials. The expense in time and money can be prohibitive. Computer courseware on using college biology and psychology textbooks, however, was developed and evaluated at Indiana University (Adams & Mikulecky, 1989). Students at a community college and a 4-year college completed three lessons over a 3-week period. They learned to determine key concepts, compare–contrast these concepts, and represent graphically the relationships among them. Treatment groups significantly outperformed control subjects on chapter tests. The authors concluded that certain reading and learning strategies could be taught effectively with CAI.

In the 1990s, many learning centers have computers, some of which are used for individualized instruction. Learning Plus (Educational Testing Service, 1993) is a well-known computer program. Its individualized instructional programs in reading, writing, and mathematics include diagnostic tests and ongoing assessments. Its courseware applies cognitive apprenticeship—incorporating modeling, scaffolding, fading and coaching. At the University of Texas–El Paso, students use Learning Plus in the CAI lab to prepare for the state-mandated skills test all students must take (T. D. Hibbert, lrnasst, July 3, 1997). In a large learning center at the Community College of Denver, instructors use Learning Plus to support instruction. The instructor introduces the subject and the students use the program for review and practice (S. Mahan, lrnasst, July 3, 1997). Skills Bank 4 (McDaniels et al., 1997) is another well-known program for individualizing instruction. It is aimed at slightly lower reading levels.

With sequenced individualized assistance, students complete designated sequences of a program before they are assessed to determine whether they should continue in the same sequence. They are given instructional supervision, tutorial help, or aid from lab assistants. Often they are expected to complete the assignments with little supervision and to meet with faculty only for evaluation purposes. Rupley, Clark, and Blair (1979) provided an example of an individualized program that differentiated and coordinated personnel, time, and available resources to maximize the reading development of all learners.

INGREDIENTS OF SUCCESSFUL PROGRAMS

Investigating Successful Programs

Many published program descriptions now report some form of evaluation, and the sophistication of program evaluation appears to be improving. Components of successful learning assistance programs as determined by several research reviews are listed in Table 12.1.

TABLE 12.1
Components of Successful Learning Assistance Programs

Qualities	Donovan (1975)	Roueche & Snow (1977)	Grant & Hoeber (1978)	Maxwell (1979)	Boylan (1983)	Roueche (1983)	Van (1992)	Boylan et al. (1994)	Garza (1996)
Strong administrative support	X					X	X		X
Single administrative unit								X	
Assessment, diagnosis, placement		X	X	X	X	X	X	X	X
Orientation program									X
Structured courses						X		X	X
Academic skills development	X	X		X	X				X
Whole-language approach		X							X
Attention to how students transfer knowledge									
Program required of those who need it						X	X		
Award of credit					X	X			
Flexible course completion policies, individualization						X	X		
Multiple learning systems			X			X			
Written disseminated objectives			X				X		X

Programs

Qualities	Donovan (1975)	Roueche & Snow (1977)	Grant & Hoeber (1978)	Maxwell (1979)	Boylan (1983)	Roueche (1983)	Van (1992)	Boylan et al. (1994)	Garza (1996)
Continuous faculty trainng		X	X			X			
Well-trained and committed faculty						X	X		X
Use of peer tutors			X	X		X		X	
Student contact, monitoring	X	X	X	X	X	X			X
Strict attendance policy						X			X
Program evaluation, research, revision		X	X	X		X	X	X	X
Variety of services	X	X	X	X	X	X	X		X
Personal counseling	X	X	X	X		X	X	X	X

One of the first major efforts to investigate the components of successful developmental programs resulted from the federally funded National Project II: Alternatives to the Revolving Door, which involved a consortium of institutions with successful developmental programs. In his report of project activities, Donovan (1975) found that the more successful programs included (a) a wide variety of personal and academic developmental services, (b) a dual emphasis on personal counseling and academic skills development, and (c) frequent staff contact with students.

Roueche and Snow (1977) attempted to identify model developmental programs using the survey technique. In programs identified as being particularly effective, they found the following components: (a) diagnostic services, (b) an emphasis on learning skills development, (c) personal counseling to support learning skills development, and (d) individualized learning opportunities provided through small classes or laboratories.

Grant and Hoeber (1978) investigated the effectiveness of developmental programs through an extensive review of the literature and research. Their findings were reported in two categories: instructional and programmatic. Under instructional components, the authors listed five important features: (a) clearly written, well-articulated objectives made available to the students; (b) continuous and systematic planning based on feedback and program monitoring; (c) attention to individual needs, personal styles of learning, and rates of growth; (d) close attention to appropriate matches of learners, teachers, methods, and materials; and (e) intensive efforts to identify how and under what learning conditions students transfer knowledge.

Under the heading of programmatic considerations, the authors found the following to be important: (a) faculty development in specific awareness skills and teaching-learning strategies, (b) development and refinement of diagnostic instruments, (c) sophisticated and sensitive research designs, and (d) comprehensive curricular revision.

Based on her own experience in working with developmental students as well as a review of the literature, Maxwell (1979) recommended that effective learning assistance programs include (a) diagnosis of students' strengths and weaknesses as learners, (b) tutorial services, (c) personal counseling, (d) basic reading and study skills instruction, and (e) built-in evaluation activities. Maxwell concluded that the increasing amount of research in learning assistance programs indicated that improving student learning skills was a unified process rather than a set of individual activities. Those programs that included isolated and unrelated services were far less likely to be successful than those that were comprehensive and systematic. Furthermore, those programs that emphasized personalization of the learning process and attended to affective as well as cognitive dimensions of learning were also more likely to be successful.

Boylan (1983) based his review of the effectiveness of developmental programs on an analysis of program reports, research, and literature. He found that programs reporting the greatest student gains (a) provided a comprehensive array of services, (b) had a high degree of student participation, (c) made participation mandatory at the outset of the college careers of high-risk students, (d) offered credit for developmental courses, and (e) emphasized the development of students' reasoning skills in addition to basic content skills.

Roueche (1983) conducted a national study to determine how colleges and universities responded to underprepared students. Among other objectives, Roueche sought to identify which program and course characteristics were shared by the institutions that reported the most positive outcomes. Roueche identified 11 common elements: (a) strong administrative support; (b) mandatory assessment and placement; (c) structured courses having scheduled days and times with attendance requirements; (d) award of credit without exception; (e) flexible completion strategies, including the use of incompletes; (f) multiple learning systems; (g) volunteer instructors who receive special training in developmental studies and consider counseling an integral part of the instructional effort; (h) use of peer tutors; (i) monitoring of student behaviors; (j) preparation for subsequent courses, including awareness of their demands; and (k) program evaluation.

Van (1992) conducted a review of the literature on developmental education, student development, and college retention. She identified nine variables associated with effective practices in learning assistance: (a) program planning was based on students' needs; (b) written policies and goals demonstrated commitment by the university to educating underprepared students; (c) programs were adequately staffed and funded by the larger institution, again demonstrating commitment to the students; (d) the program was staffed by well-qualified and committed educators; (e) the program included individualized instruction, paired learning, and flexible programs which enabled students to progress at their own pace; (f) supportive services that developed students' self-concept and internal locus of control; (g) assessment that placed students in appropriate courses; and (h) program evaluation that included formative and summative data.

Boylan et al. (1994) identified six variables that earlier researchers considered essential for a successful developmental program. Successful programs (a) provided developmental courses, (b) were organized under a single administrative unit, (c) required mandatory assessment of entering students, (d) offered a tutoring program, (e) included counseling and advising as part of the learning assistance program, and (f) conducted program evaluation.

Garza (1994) identified eight successful developmental reading programs in Texas community colleges. She chose programs having at least 20% Hispanic or African American students enrolled. The community colleges with highest aggregate scores on the TASP Reading Test for students in these two categories were selected. Following interviews with developmental studies administrators, she identified important similarities among the programs. Organizationally, 60% of the programs received administrative support, provided a written mission statement or philosophy, were housed in academic departments, and included evaluation apparatus. At least 60% of the programs included some form of student assessment followed by academic counseling and placement in appropriate classes. Follow-up assessment was conducted once students were placed in classes. Courses were restricted by reading level. All programs adhered to a strict attendance policy. Additionally, all provided an orientation for their students. Administrators described their reading faculty as highly motivated and actively collaborative. In fact, they said that collaboration was evident across the entire college. In addition to reading, programs included study skills and tutoring. Within reading classes, instructors used a whole-language approach. Again, comprehensive programs were the rule. Garza found that the programs included learning centers, support services for minorities, and child care. Finally, each college monitored student progress with evaluations at the student, faculty, and program level.

Investigating the Investigations

Inspection of Table 12.1 and the literature reviews brings to mind several observations. First, without some objective means of identifying which reports of program evaluations to include, the analyses might be subject to bias, either intentional or inadvertent. Second, some important factors may have failed to make the list or were identified in only one or two analyses. Third, the content of instruction often seems to be irrelevant to the success of a program, although this appearance may be due simply to difficulty in defining reliably what the content was. Fourth, some components of successful programs may be components of nearly all programs, successful or unsuccessful. Even components that are associated only with success may not be the reason for the success. For instance, whole-language instruction is notoriously hard to define. Those who say they employ whole language may only be indicating that they are informed of the recent reading literature. Other knowledge acquired in the literature or simply the interest in acquiring it may be what is truly a factor in the success of the program.

A meta-analysis of studies selected according to strict criteria is the logical alternative to informal procedures. In their meta-analysis, Kulik, Kulik, and Shwalb (1983) found only 60 studies that met their criteria out of more than 500 available in the research literature. They found that college programs for high-risk and disadvantaged students produced a small but positive effect on GPA and retention rates. Effects were stronger for new programs than for older ones, which led them to postulate that much of the effect was due to the novelty of the program rather than its instructional effectiveness. In community colleges, learning assistance programs were relatively ineffective. Because the effects reported in published journal articles were larger than those reported in ERIC documents, the researchers concluded that even the small overall improvement found in GPA and retention rates might have been overly optimistic, noting that many studies without significant effects might not have been published at all.

These review studies suggest that for learning assistance programs to be effective, much care must be taken in their design, implementation, and evaluation. Apparently, it is all too easy for programs to have little lasting effects on the students they serve.

Assessing Program Effectiveness

The consensus in the increasing body of research in developmental education, flawed as it may be, is that improving student survival in college is a unified process rather than a set of individual activities spread out over a campus. Programs with isolated and unrelated services are far less likely to be successful than those with a comprehensive and systematic approach. Furthermore, programs that emphasize personalization of the learning process and attend to the affective as well as the cognitive dimensions of learning are more likely to succeed (Maxwell, 1979).

Research reports also suggest that the greater the variety of services provided, the more likely students are to show gains in test scores, GPAs, and retention. Skill development groups or classes are effective if they are coupled with counseling or tutoring (Appel, 1977; Martin & Blanc, 1981; Randlett, 1983; Starks, 1982).

Learning centers in higher education need to assess the value of their programs and services. Formative and summative evaluations of each aspect of existing programs should lead to valuable information for growth and change (see Boylan, Bonham, White, & George, chap. 13, this volume). Longitudinal research that tracks student GPA, perseverance, and graduation might indicate which types of programs are the most successful, which approaches yield the best results, and which instructional practices produce the most efficient learners (Morante, 1986). These studies are beginning to appear in the literature.

Although aiding students in becoming efficient learners is the main objective of developmental educators, school administrators might be more impressed if researchers followed Tucker's (1982) lead and initiated projects that would justify the cost of developmental programs. For instance, studies comparing matched groups of students suggest that the attrition rate is lower among students who participate in developmental programs than among those who do not (Kulik et al., 1983; Obler, 1980; Starks, 1982).

Programs that cater specifically to high-risk students particularly need to conduct careful research projects to determine the effectiveness of the services provided. Because some educators believe that money would be better spent in other endeavors that show visible benefits, those involved in high-risk student retention must carefully justify the worth of their programs.

CONCLUSIONS AND IMPLICATIONS

Learning assistance has been a part of U.S. higher education since at least the 19th century. Then, as now, institutions provided specific educational programs to assist their academically underprepared students. Learning assistance programs were not spawned because of open admission policies; bridging the academic preparation gap has long been part of the traditional, if not the formal, mission of higher education.

Differences in philosophical perspective, program organization, and external and internal structure are as numerous as learning centers themselves. No two programs are identical because each is tailored to fit the requirements of the institution, the needs of the students, and the expertise of the professional staff. Educators in learning assistance programs continue to search for more efficient teaching strategies, a more effective structuring model, and an ideal pattern of program organization that fits their unique circumstances.

Because research has not yet indicated the desirability of one theoretical model over all others or even the best combination of several models, individuals who are just beginning to work in learning assistance or who wish to expand their services in a learning center must make the best of what research and information is available. Adopting successful activities into new or expanding centers could strengthen programs while eliminating the trial-and-error approach necessarily employed by professionals who began their learning centers in earlier years.

When initiating or expanding a learning center, administrators need to assess the needs of their students, their faculty, and their institution (Castelli & Johnson, 1983). One of the theoretical models previously discussed might serve as a guide for development; on the other hand, a combination of models might more nearly address the needs of these groups. Only those actively involved in the project can adequately determine what the most pressing needs are and initiate activities to meet them. Attempting to duplicate the programs of another learning center may not be the most effective approach.

Whatever approach administrators use, they should take care not to promise more than their program can deliver. They should initiate activities based on the resources available, adding additional services as they become feasible. It is important to perform advertised activities well in order to build confidence in the center's ability to increase student learning and achievement. If a program offers too many services in relation to the resources available, the center's staff may not be able to perform any of the promised activities adequately. Students, as well as the reputation of the center, will suffer.

Whenever possible, input from students, faculty, and mid-level administrators should be encouraged. Regular meetings of an advisory board comprising several students, faculty from each area of the institution, and interested administrators strengthen the center, generate new ideas, and make programs more visible. In addition, keeping supervisory administrators informed and involved should increase their commitment and support to the center and its activities.

Formative and summative evaluations (Peterson, 1983) can further increase support from the administrative and academic communities. These evaluations should be conducted on a regular basis, involve all aspects of the center's activities, and be made available to the public. Evaluations are a valuable tool in assessing the quality of the services being offered as well as indicating areas of concern. The type of evaluation tools should be varied, as should the evaluators, in order to acquire reliable, new, and useful information (Clowes, 1984; Somers, 1987).

In addition to conducting regular and periodic evaluations, we encourage professionals to become involved in research activities. Research in the field of postsecondary learning assistance is relatively new, and little information was published prior to 1960. Since that time, much of what has been written has been descriptive. Some excellent survey research has described what is being done in learning centers; however, more empirical research is needed.

Empirical research examining the different types of programs would aid professionals in determining the most effective delivery systems and instructional methods. Both qualitative and quantitative research that could be replicated would provide useful information to educators in learning assistance. Past research has provided some basic information, but it is now time to test hypotheses about models of organization and methods of instruction. What is determined through research could assist educators in all academic areas in providing quality educational opportunities to all students.

Professionals in learning centers have a responsibility to assist students in achieving their academic goals. They also can become campus leaders in initiating new learning experiences, sharing teaching techniques, and providing developmental activities for teachers as well as students. By offering insights and expertise to other faculty members in a nonthreatening atmosphere, they can make a narrowly focused learning assistance program a true learning center where learning is enhanced for everyone.

REFERENCES AND SUGGESTED READINGS

Adams, S. M., & Mikulecky, L. (1989). Teaching effective college reading and learning strategies using computer assisted instruction. *Journal of College Reading and Learning, 22*, 64–70.

Anderson, O. S., & Smith, L. J. (1987). Peer tutors in a college reading laboratory: A model that works. *Reading Improvement, 24,* 238–247.

Appel, A. W. (1977). Academic achievement of a voluntary reading program. *Journal of Reading, 19,* 644–646.

Barrios, A. A. (1997). *The magic of the mind (MOM) program for decreasing school drop-outs.* (ERIC Document Reproduction Service No. ED 405 436)

Bengis, L. (1986, April). *College discovery prefreshman summer program, 1985: An evaluation.* New York: City University of New York, Office of Student Affairs and Special Programs. (ERIC Document Reproduction Service No. ED 278 287)

*Beal, P. E. (1980). Learning centers and retention. In O. T. Lenning & R. L. Hayman (Eds.), *New roles for learning assistance* (pp. 59–73). San Francisco, CA: Jossey-Bass.

Blanc, R. A., DeBuhr, L. E., & Martin, D. C. (1983). Breaking the attrition cycle: The effects of supplemental instruction on undergraduate performance and attrition. *Journal of Higher Education, 54,* 80–90.

Boylan, H. R. (1982). The growth of the learning assistance movement. In H. R. Boylan (Ed.). *Forging new partnerships in learning assistance* (pp. 5–16). San Francisco, CA: Jossey-Bass.

Boylan, H. R. (1983). *Is developmental education working? An analysis of research.* A research report prepared for the National Association for Remedial and Developmental Studies in Postsecondary Education, Appalachian State University, Boone, NC.

Boylan, H. R. (1995). The scope of developmental education: Some basic information on the field. *Research in Developmental Education, 12*(4), 1–6.

Boylan, H. R. (1996, September). *An evaluation of the Texas academic skills program (TASP).* A report prepared by The National Center for Developmental Education Appalachian State University, Boone, North Carolina Under Contract to The Texas Higher Education Coordinating Board [Online]. Available: http://www.thecb.state.tx.us/divisions/univ/tasp/boylans/boynof.htm#findings

*Boylan, H. R., & Bonham, B. S. (1992). The impact of developmental education programs. *Review of Research in Developmental Education, 9*(5), 1–6.

Boylan, H. R., Bonham, B. S., & Bliss, L. B. (1994). Characteristic components of developmental programs. *Research in Developmental Education, 11*(1), 1–6.

Boylan, H. R., Bonham, B. S., Bliss, L. B., & Saxon, D. P. (1995). What we know about tutoring: Findings from the national study of developmental education. *Research in Developmental Education. 12*(3), 1–4.

Boylan, H. R., & White, W. G. (1987). Educating all the nation's people: The historical roots of developmental education (Part 1). *Research in Developmental Education, 4*(4), 1–4.

Brier, E. (1984). Bridging the academic preparation gap: An historical view. *Journal of Developmental Education, 8,* 2–5.

Broderick, B., & Caverly, D. C. (1996). Techtalk: On-line developmental education. *Journal of Developmental Education, 19*(3), 34–35.

Bullock, T., Madden, D., & Harter, J. (1987). Paired developmental reading and psychology courses. *Research and Teaching in Developmental Education, 3,* 22–31.

Carpenter, K. (1984). *Tutor selection, training and supervision.* Unpublished manuscript, Kearney State College, Kearney, NE.

Carpenter, K., & Johnson, L. L. (1991). Program organization. In R. F. Flippo & D. Caverly (Eds.), *College reading & study strategy programs* (pp. 28–69). Newark, DE: International Reading Association.

Carter, H. L. J. (1959). Effective use of textbooks in the reading program. In O. S. Causey & W. Eller (Eds.), *Starting and improving college reading programs* (pp. 155–163). Fort Worth, TX: Texas Christian University Press.

Cashen, C. J. (1983). The University of Wisconsin-Parkside college skills program. In J. E. Roueche (Ed.), *A new look at successful programs* (pp. 49–58). San Francisco, CA: Jossey-Bass.

Castelli, C., & Johnson, D. (1983). Learning center assessment: Managing for change in the 80's. *Journal of College Reading and Learning, 17,* 30–42.

Chissom, B. S., & Lanier, D. (1975). Prediction of first quarter freshman GPA using SAT scores and high school grades. *Educational and Psychological Measurement, 35,* 461–463.

Christ, F. L. (1971). Systems for learning assistance: Learners, learning facilitators, and learning centers. In F. L. Christ (Ed.), *Proceedings of the fourth annual conference of the Western College Reading Association* (pp. 32–41). Whittier, CA: College Reading and Learning Association.

Clowes, D. A. (1984). The evaluation of remedial/developmental programs: A stage model of program evaluation. *Journal of Developmental Education, 8,* 14–15, 27–30.

Clymer, C. (1978). A national survey of learning assistance evaluation: Rationale, techniques, problems. In G. Enright (Ed.), *Proceedings of the Eleventh Annual Conference of the Western College Reading Association* (pp. 21–30). Whittier, CA: College Reading and Learning Association.

Commander, N. E., Stratton, C. B., Callahan, C. A., & Smith, B. D. (1996). A learning assistance model for expanding academic support. *Journal of Developmental Education, 20*(2), 8–10, 12, 14, 16.

Committee on Learning Skills Centers. (1976). *Learning skills centers: A CCCC report.* Urbana, IL: National Council of Teachers of English.

Cranney, A. G. (1987). The improving professionalization of postsecondary developmental reading. *Journal of Reading, 30,* 690–700.

*Cross, K. P. (1976). *Accent on learning.* San Francisco, CA: Jossey-Bass.

Dempsey, J., & Tomlinson, B. (1980). Learning centers and instructional/curricular reform. In O. T. Lenning & R. L. Nayman (Eds.), *New roles for learning assistance* (pp. 41–58). San Francisco, CA: Jossey-Bass.

Dillard, M. L. (1989). Changing a college developmental reading program from three to five semester hours credit: What's involved? *Forum for Reading, 20,* 26–31.

Donovan, R. A. (1975). *National Project II: Alternatives to the revolving door.* Unpublished manuscript, Bronx Community College, New York.

Educational Testing Service. (1993). *Learning Plus: Computer based learning of skills and strategies* (Version 1.1). [Computer software]. Princeton, NJ: Educational Testing Service.

Elliott, M. K., & Fairbanks, M. (1986). General vs. adjunct reading/study skills instruction for a college history course. *Journal of College Reading and Learning, 19,* 22–29.

Enright, G., & Kerstiens, G. (1980). The learning center: Toward an expanded role. In O. T. Lenning & R. L. Nayman (Eds.), *New roles for learning assistance* (pp. 1–24). San Francisco, CA: Jossey-Bass.

Fidler, P. P., & Godwin, M. A. (1994). Retaining African-American students through the freshman seminar. *Journal of Developmental Education, 17*(3), 34–36, 38, 40.

Gabriel, D. (1989). Assessing assessment. *Review of Research in Developmental Education, 6*(5), 1–5.

Garza, N. R. (1994). A description and analysis of selected successful developmental reading programs in Texas community colleges. Doctoral dissertation, University of Texas, Austin. *Dissertation Abstracts International, 55*(06), 1433.

Gold, B. K. (1980). *The LACC tutoring program: An evaluation.* (Research Study No. 80-4). Los Angeles, CA: Los Angeles City College. (ERIC Document Reproduction Service No. ED 182 465)

Gordon, B., & Flippo, R. F. (1983). An update on college reading improvement programs in the southeastern United States. *Journal of Reading, 27*, 155–163.

Grant, M. K., & Hoeber, D. R. (1978). *Basic skills programs: Are they working?* Washington, DC: American Association for Higher Education.

Hamberg, S., & Rubin, R. (1986). Profiles of a successful college reading program. *New Mexico Journal of Reading, 7*, 25–27.

Hancock, K., & Gier, T. (1991). Counseling skills: An important part of tutor training. *Journal of College Reading and Learning, 23*, 55–59.

Harris, D. M. (1990). *The Glassboro State College retention program.* (ERIC Document Reproduction Service No. ED 321 640).

Heerman, C. E. (1984). Reading gains of students in a college reading laboratory. *Reading Horizons, 24*, 186–192.

Helm, P. K., & Chand, S. (1983). Student success at Triton College. In J. E. Roueche (Ed.), *A new look at successful programs* (pp. 43–48). San Francisco, CA: Jossey-Bass.

Holladay, J. M., & Zwayer, S. (1992). *Monroe County Community College [Michigan] writing across the curriculum, annual reports 1990–1991 and 1991–1992.* (ERIC Document Reproduction Service No. ED 353 014)

Jones, E. (1959). Selection and motivation of students. In O. S. Causey & W. Eller (Eds.), *Starting and improving college reading programs* (pp. 25–34). Fort Worth, TX: Texas Christian University Press.

Kincade, K. M., Kleine, P. F., Johnson, I. T., & Jacob, C. T., Jr. (1989). Individualizing a college reading course with the aid of computers. *Journal of College Reading and Learning, 23*, 71–80.

King, B. W., Rasool, J. A., & Judge, J. J. (1994). The relationship between college performance and basic skills assessment using SAT scores, the Nelson Denny Reading Test and Degrees of Reading Power. *Research on the Teaching of Developmental Education, 11*, 5–13.

*Kingston, A. J. (1990). A brief history of college reading. *Forum for Reading, 21*(2), 11–15.

*Kulik, C. C., Kulik, J. A., & Shwalb, B. J. (1983). College programs for high-risk and disadvantaged students: A metaanalysis of findings. *Review of Educational Research, 53*, 397–414.

Landward, S., & Hepworth, D. (1984). Support systems for high risk college students: Findings and issues. *College and University, 59*, 119–128.

LSUA general information. (1988, January). [Online]. Available: http://pc01.lsua.edu/genlinfo.htm#lrn_cntr

Lucas, J. A. (1991). *Evaluation of new probation intervention program at Harper College—1990.* Volume XX, No. 4. (ERIC Document Reproduction Service No. ED 348 122)

Martin, D. C., & Blanc, R. (1981). The learning center's role in retention: Integrating student support services with departmental instruction. *Journal of Developmental & Remedial Education, 4*, 2–4.

Maxey, J., & Sawyer, R. (1981). *Predictive validity of the ACT assessment for Afro-American/black, Mexican-American/Chicano, and Caucasian-American/white students.* (Research Bulletin No. 81-1). Iowa City, IA: American College Testing Program.

Maxwell, M. (1979). *Improving student learning skills.* San Francisco, CA: Jossey-Bass.

Maxwell, M. (1990). Does tutoring help? A look at the literature. *Review of Research in Developmental Education, 7*(4), 1–5.

Maxwell, M. (1991). The effects of expectations, sex, and ethnicity on peer tutoring. *Journal of Developmental Education, 15*(1), 14–16, 18.

Maxwell, M. (Ed). (1994). *From access to success: A book of readings on college developmental education and learning assistance programs.* Clearwater, FL: H&H Publishing Company.

*Maxwell, M. (1997). *Improving student learning skills: A new edition.* Clearwater, FL: H&H Publishing Company.

McDaniels, G., Gombeert, J., & Hall, L. (1997). *Skills Bank 4.* [Computer software]. Baltimore, MD: SkillsBank Corporation.

McDonald, R. T., & Gawkoski, R. S. (1979). Predictive value of SAT scores and high school achievement for success in a college honors program. *Educational and Psychological Measurement, 39*, 411–414.

McHugh, F., Jernigan, L., & Moses, K. (1986). Literacy first: A successful opportunity program. *College Teaching, 34*, 83–87.

McKinley, N. (1990). Reach out to community college faculty. *Journal of Reading, 33*, 304-305.

McMillon, H. G. (1994). Small groups: An instructional approach to learning. *Research and Teaching in Developmental Education, 20*, 71–80.

McMurtrie, R. S. (1982). Effects of training in study skills for specific content courses as reflected in actual course enrollment, grades and withdrawals of high-risk college freshmen. *Yearbook of the American Reading Forum, 2*, 64–65.

Morante, E. A. (1986). The effectiveness of developmental programs: A two-year follow-up study. *Journal of Developmental Education, 9*, 14–15.

Napoli, A. R., & Hiltner, G. J., III. (1993). An evaluation of developmental reading instruction. *Journal of Developmental Education, 17*(1), 14–16, 18, 20.

National Center for Education Statistics. (1996). *Remedial Education at Higher Education Institutions in Fall 1995.* Washington, DC: U.S. Department of Education, Office of Educational Research and Improvement [Online]. Available: http://nces.ed.gov/pubs/97584.html

Obler, S. S. (1980). Programs for the underprepared student. In J. E. Roueche (Ed.), *A new look at successful programs* (pp. 21–30). San Francisco, CA: Jossey-Bass.

*Perry, W. G. (1959). Students' use and misuse of reading skills: A report to the faculty. *Harvard Educational Review, 29*, 193–200.

Peterson, P. (1983). Success: A model for the planning and evaluation of college learning. *Journal of College Reading and Learning, 16*, 39–54.

Pierson, K. P., & Huba, M. E. (1997). Assessment of developmental course outcomes at a community college. *Community College Journal of Research and Practice, 21*, 661–673.

Pollock, J. E., & Wilkinson, B. L. (1988). Enrollment differences in academic achievement for university study skills students. *College Student Journal, 22*, 76–82.

Porter, D. (1993). Total quality education: Implications and opportunities. *Journal of College Reading and Learning, 26*(1), 16–27.

Ramirez, G. M. (1997). Supplemental instruction: The long-term impact. *Journal of Developmental Education, 21*, 2–4, 6, 8, 10, 28.

Randlett, A. L. (1983). Peer tutor training in reading and study skills: A research review. *Yearbook of the American Reading Forum, 3*, 53–57.

Rauch, M. (1989). Encouraging students to use tutorial services. *Journal of Reading, 32*, 55.

Raygor, A. L. (1977). Keynote address: Meeting the individual needs of students. In G. Enright (Ed.), *Proceedings of the 10th annual conference of the Western College Reading Association* (pp. 6–10). Whittier, CA: College Reading and Learning Association.

Reed, K. X. (1989). Expectation vs. ability: Junior college reading skills. *Journal of Reading, 32*, 537–541.

Reedy, V. (1973). Maximized individualized learning laboratory. *Community and Junior College Journal, 43*, 34.

Robert, E. R., & Thomson, G. (1994). Learning assistance and the success of underrepresented students at Berkeley. *Journal of Developmental Education, 17*(3), 4–6, 8, 10, 12, 14.

Robyak, J. E., & Patton, M. J. (1977). The effectiveness of a study skills course for students of different personality types. *Journal of Counseling Psychology, 24*, 200–207.

Rosen, S. S. (1980). College level developmental reading and study skills programs: Survey report and overview. *Forum for Reading, 12*, 3–12.

Roueche, J. E., Baker, G. A., III, & Roueche, S. D. (1984). College responses to low-achieving students: A national study. *American Education, 20*, 31–34.

Roueche, J. E., & Kirk, W. (1973). *Catching up: Remedial education.* San Francisco, CA: Jossey-Bass.

Roueche, J. E., & Snow, J. J. (1977). *Overcoming learning problems.* San Francisco, CA: Jossey-Bass.

Roueche, S. D. (1983). Elements of program success: Report of a national study. In J. E. Roueche (Ed.) *A new look at successful programs* (pp. 3–10). San Francisco, CA: Jossey-Bass.

Rupley, W. H., Clark, F. E., & Blair, T. R. (1979). A model for individualizing instruction. In G. Enright (Ed.), *Proceedings of the 12th annual conference of the Western College*

Reading Association (pp. 117–121). Whittier, CA: College Reading and Learning Association.

Santa Rita, E. D., & Bacote, J. B. (1997). The benefits of college discovery prefreshman summer program for minority and low-income students. *College Student Journal, 31,* 160–167.

Schulman, S. (1981). *A description of a developmental program for high risk students in a community college.* Los Angeles Pierce College, Woodland Hills, CA. (ERIC Document Reproduction Service No. ED 208 928)

Semb, G. B. (1993). Long-term memory for knowledge learned in school. *Journal of Educational Psychology, 85,* 305–316.

Shaw, P. (1961). Reading in college. In N. B. Henry (Ed.), *Development in and through reading* (pp. 336–337). Chicago, IL: University of Chicago Press.

Simmons, R. (1994). Precollege programs: A contributing factor to university student retention. *Journal of Developmental Education, 17*(3), 42–45.

Simpson, M. L. (1983). Recent research on independent learning strategies: Implications for developmental education. *Forum for Reading, 15,* 22–29.

Smith, D. A., & Herman, W. E. (1996, August). *A Division III student-athlete academic support program model.* Paper presented at the meeting of the American Psychological Association, Toronto, Canada. (ERIC Document Reproduction Service No. ED 401 256)

Smith, G. D., Enright, G. D., & Devirian, M. (1975). A national survey of learning and study skills programs. In G. H. McNinch & W. D. Miller (Eds.), *Reading: Convention and inquiry* (pp. 67–73). Clemson, SC: National Reading Conference.

Smith, L., & Smith, G. (1988). A multivariate analysis of remediation efforts with developmental students. *Teaching English in the Two-Year College, 15,* 45–52.

Soldner, L. B. (1992). Managing peer tutors with letters and anecdotal records. *Journal of Reading, 36,* 135.

Somers, R. L. (1987). Evaluation of developmental education programs: Issues, problems, and techniques. *Research in Developmental Education, 4,* 1–4.

Spaulding, N. V. (1975). Five minicourses in study skills. In R. Sugimoto (Ed.), *Proceedings of the 8th annual conference of the Western College Reading Association* (pp. 179–181). Whittier, CA: College Reading and Learning Association.

Starks, G. (1982). *Community college retention in the 70's and 80's: Reasons for the withdrawal and effects of remedial and developmental programs.* Unpublished manuscript, University of Minnesota, Crookston.

Sullivan, L. L. (1980). Growth and influence of the learning center movement. In K. V. Lauridsen (Ed.), *New directions for college learning assistance: Examining the scope of learning centers* (pp. 1–8). San Francisco, CA: Jossey-Bass.

Tomlinson, B. M., & Green, T. (1976). Integrating adjunct reading and study classes with the content areas. In R. Sugimoto (Ed.), *Proceedings of the 9th annual conference of the Western College Reading Association* (pp. 199–203). Whittier, CA: College Reading and Learning Association.

Townsend, B. S. (1983). Assessment of a college reading course for academically deficient students. *Yearbook of the American Reading Forum, 3,* 41–42.

Triggs, F. O. (1942). Remedial reading programs: Evidence of their development. *Journal of Educational Psychology, 33,* 678–685.

Tucker, J. (1982). The cost-effectiveness of programs that teach people how to learn: An economic perspective. *Journal of Learning Skills, 4,* 28–34.

Van, B. (1992). College learning assistance programs: Ingredients for success. *Journal of College Reading and Learning, 24*(2), 27–39.

Walker, C. (1980). The learning assistance center in a selective institution. In K. V. Lauridsen (Ed.), *Examining the scope of learning centers* (pp. 57–68). San Francisco, CA: Jossey-Bass.

Weinstein, C. E., Schulte, A. C., & Palmer, D. R. (1987). *Learning and study strategies inventory (LASSI).* Clearwater, Fl: H&H Publishing.

William States Lee College of Engineering MAPS Program. (1999, February). [Online]. Available: http://www.coe.uncc.edu/~mentor/

Williams, A. (1989). Mission possible: Recent developments in college learning assistance programs. In A. M. Frager (Ed.), *College reading and the new majority: Improving instruction in multicultural classrooms* (pp. 22–31). Easton, PA: College Reading Association.

Wolfe, R. F. (1987). The supplemental instruction program: Developing learning and thinking skills. *Journal of Reading, 31,* 228–233.

Wright, D. A. (1985). *Many college freshmen take remedial courses.* (Report No. NCES-85-211b). Washington, DC: National Center for Educational Statistics. (ERIC Document Reproduction Service No. ED 262 742)

13

Evaluation of College Reading and Study Strategy Programs

ᭁᣔᣔᭀ

Hunter R. Boylan
Barbara S. Bonham
James R. White
Appalachian State University

Anita P. George
Mississippi State University

In its most basic sense, *evaluation* means to establish the value of something. In the sense of *educational evaluation*, the term generally refers to establishing the value of a particular program, technique, or set of materials on the basis of some known criteria.

In recent years the term *outcomes assessment* has become popular and used by many as a synonym for evaluation. Initially, outcomes assessment was part of the movement among legislators and other policymakers to promote greater accountability in education. Its focus was on measuring the results of educational practice, frequently in terms of the funds allocated to support practice. It emphasized outputs, at the expense of inputs and processes. As the limitations of this became apparent, many authors attempted to redefine outcomes assessment. Astin (1991), for instance, distinguished between *measurement*, the gathering of information, and *assessment*, the use of this information to improve programs. He defines assessment as an activity that combines the processes of both measurement and evaluation and requiring attention to inputs, environments, and outcomes.

Shadish, Cook, and Leviton (1991) defined evaluation as a process involving: (a) identifying a problem, (b) generating alternative solutions to the problem, (c) analyzing these alternatives, and (d) adopting the most satisfactory alternatives. Upcraft and Schuh (1996) used the term *assessment* to describe all of the components in this process.

Other authors define evaluation and assessment in terms of their purposes. Rossi and Freeman (1985) considered the major purpose of *evaluation* to be "to judge and to improve the planning, monitoring, and efficiency of educational services" (p. 19). Astin (1991) stated that the purpose of *assessment* activities are "to improve the functioning of the institution and its people" (p. 2). Cronbach (1983) suggested that the intent of *evaluation* is to influence thought or action in both the short and the long term. Banta, Lund, Black, and Oblander (1996) identified the purpose of *assessment* as enhancing our understanding of how programs work in an effort to improve them. Anderson and Ball (1978) listed six purposes of educational program evaluations: (a) to make decisions about program installation, (b) to make decisions about program continuation, (c) to rally support for a program, (d) to rally opposition to a program, (e) to revise or refine a program, or (f) to understand basic processes. They further suggested that evaluation activities may be directed to several of these purposes at the same time.

The distinctions between *evaluation* and *assessment* are not always clear. Evaluation tends to be used more often by social scientists and assessments is used more often by educators, with both groups frequently using the term to describe many of the same purposes and processes. Assessment is used more often by modern educational writers and evaluation is used more often by those who wrote prior to the 1990s. It may be that the past misuses of evaluation (Vroom, Colombo, & Nahan, 1994) have caused authors to use assessment instead in an effort to avoid its potential negative connotations.

Casazza and Silverman (1996) distinguished between assessment and evaluation by saying that "assessment is used to refer to the appraisal of individuals and evaluation to the appraisal of groups or programs" (p. 93). For the purposes of this chapter, the just-mentioned definition is used for the word evaluation. To extend that definition further, although all of the definitions offered for assessment and evaluation differ somewhat, several elements are common to each. First, evaluation describes *what* is being done. Second, it describes *how* it is being done. Third, it describes *how well* it is being done as measured against some relevant criteria. Finally, it provides information that may be used in *decision making*. When all these elements are present for the purpose of establishing the value of an activity or a program, it represents evaluation.

This chapter provides information on methods representing evaluation as just defined. The information provided is designed to assist practitioners who are considering the implementation of evaluation activities as well as those who are actively engaged in such activities. (Readers also interested in selecting appropriate reading tests, and reviews of current reading texts, may refer to Flippo & Schum, chap. 14, this volume.)

The first section of the chapter provides an overview of the changing role of educational evaluation during the past 50 years. It explains some of the reasons why evaluation has become such an important issue for college reading programs. Next, the chapter discusses different types of evaluation and when they should be used. This discussion is followed by a review of several theoretical models of evaluation. The third section is designed to explore the strengths and weaknesses of various models commonly applied to the evaluation of postsecondary education programs. The fourth section discusses attempts by reading- and study-skills professionals to apply some of these models to the evaluation of their activities. Examples of the research and literature in the field are described and critiqued. In the fifth section, implications for practitioners of both the theoretical and the praxeological literature are discussed. Based on this review, recommendations are offered for those who are engaged in program evaluation activities. The concluding section explores future trends in the evaluation of postsecondary reading and study skills. We expect these trends to affect the ways in which evaluation is carried out in college reading and study strategies programs and the issues that such evaluation will explore in the future.

FACTORS CONTRIBUTING TO THE CHANGING ROLE OF EVALUATION

Efforts to evaluate college reading programs are a relatively recent phenomenon. In fact the emergence of the field of educational evaluation can be traced to the 1960s (Anderson & Ball, 1978). Prior to the 1960s, few people in education bothered to evaluate what they were doing in any formal or systematic way. It was taken for granted that those teaching or managing educational programs were able to determine how well things were working based on observation and experience. This was made possible by the fact that institutions and individuals in postsecondary education were much more autonomous then than they are now. Not only were there few external forces advocating evaluation, few were holding institutions and their faculties accountable for their actions.

Even when some form of evaluation was deemed desirable, few commonly accepted tools and models were available. Those that were available were borrowed from the biological sciences and were heavily oriented toward testing and statistics (Clowes, 1981; Shadish et al., 1991). Such models often required data that were difficult to obtain and calculations that were difficult to perform. Obviously, times have changed. Evaluation has become almost a cottage industry in most postsecondary institutions. The evaluation of reading and study skills programs is only one component of a vast array of evaluation activities taking place on college and university campuses.

At least four forces have had a major impact on the increasing volume and sophistication of evaluation activity. The first is the rise of state higher education systems and the federal government's increasing investment in the funding of postsecondary education. Both of these have expanded the oversight of higher education. The second is the increased demand by legislative and government agencies for accountability in all segments of education (Astin, 1991; Upcraft & Schuh, 1996). The third is the recognition by faculty, staff, and administrators that evaluation can be a primary tool for program improvement (Banta et al., 1996). The fourth is the availability of computer technology to simplify the process of collecting, storing, retrieving, and analyzing data. Each of these factors has contributed to the importance of describing what we do, measuring its impact, and using evaluation data in the process of program development, improvement, and refinement.

The Rise of State Postsecondary Education Systems

As the number of colleges and universities grew in the 1950s and 1960s, most state legislatures established coordinating agencies for postsecondary education. Although the roles of these agencies varied widely from state to state, all of them exercised some responsibility for assessment of educational activities. As these agencies grew, so did their desire for data and evaluative assessment. The information these agencies required included such descriptive information as the number of minority students enrolled, the types of courses and services offered, and the number of faculty with terminal degrees. The purpose of collecting this information was consistent with Anderson and Ball's (1978) notion of gathering data to understand basic processes. Without this information on what was being accomplished with state tax revenues, it was practically impossible for coordinating agencies to discharge their legislatively mandated responsibility for oversight of postsecondary education activities.

Because these agencies did not have the staff to collect their own data, they relegated this responsibility to the institutions under their control. Pressure for evaluation at the state level was, therefore top–down. Initially, coordinating agencies only wanted data that described what was taking place at the institutional level so they could understand basic processes and develop a statewide picture of postsecondary education activity. Later, this information was used in a more sophisticated fashion consistent with Rossi and Freeman's (1985) notion of incorporating evaluation data into program planning and development. The information was also used to make decisions about program expansion, continuation, or elimination. Individual institutions, therefore, had to provide information in order to ensure that their needs were considered in statewide planning efforts.

The establishment of state coordination agencies had two effects on evaluation. First, it made individual institutions accountable for providing information to a higher authority. Within the institution, central administrators held department chairs and program directors accountable for providing this information. Thus, gathering data for evaluation purposes was added to the job description of middle managers throughout postsecondary education.

A second effect was that college administrators began to use evaluation for more than just descriptive purposes. They, too, began to gather information for decision making. They also began to see evaluation as being linked to decisions made by state coordinating agencies about the funding of their particular institution.

The Growing Role of the Federal Government in Postsecondary Education

A second force in the expansion of evaluation activities was the growth of the federal role in funding postsecondary education during the latter half of the 20th century. Although the federal government has a long history of funding postsecondary education (e.g., the Morrill Acts of 1862 and 1890, the National Defense Education Act of 1958) the Higher Education Act of 1965 was the most comprehensive piece of modern legislation involving federal funding for colleges and universities. The act's various titles authorized hundreds of millions of federal dollars for financial aid and the support of educational opportunity, campus building programs, library improvement, and special programs for women, minorities, and adults. After 1965, the federal education bureaucracy expanded dramatically to monitor and manage these programs. With this expansion came an increased need for information to help in coordinating, refining, and improving this vast array of postsecondary education endeavors. Again, initial evaluation activity was undertaken to describe what existed or to understand basic processes—in this case, to quantify what the public was receiving for its tax dollars. Federal programs were expected to provide data on the numbers of students served, the types of services provided by these programs, and the gains made by students as a result of their participation in various programs. Like state coordinating agencies, federal agencies needed data to demonstrate the returns for monies spent.

Later, as new programs were proposed under the Higher Education Act and new budget authorizations debated, evaluative data was needed for political and decision-making purposes. Officials who supported the expansion of federal postsecondary programs wanted evaluation data to rally support for their position. Those who opposed these programs looked for evaluation data as a means of establishing that such programs were ineffective and should not be supported.

At the same time, legislative mandates for improved planning and management of federal education programs caused those responsible for monitoring them to seek even more evaluation data. Their needs were to determine exactly what was being provided in various federal programs so that efforts could be coordinated and refinements planned

In both cases, the burden of providing data was placed on the institutions receiving federal funding. Again, the pressure for evaluation came from the top (the federal bureaucracy) down (to the individual institutions). By the end of the 1970s, most public colleges and universities were providing data for two levels of bureaucracy—state and federal. Both reinforced the notion that evaluation activity was important. Now, however, the importance of evaluation was not only to describe and understand basic processes but also to justify continued federal and state funding of postsecondary education programs.

The Recognition That Evaluation Is Linked to Improvement

Since the 1970s, researchers have understood that program evaluation is linked to program effectiveness (Astin, 1991; Boylan, Bliss, & Bonham, 1997; Casazza & Silverman, 1996; Roueche & Snow, 1977). Any organized academic activity, be it a course, a program, or a curriculum, requires evaluation in order to improve. Unless instructors or administrators know how well an academic activity is being done and what its outcomes are, it is impossible to know how to improve it.

Although the link between evaluation and program effectiveness was suspected in the 1970s, there was little momentum for systematic program evaluation until the 1980s. Most of this momentum came, initially, from state and federal bureaucracies' need for information. Eventually, however, the academic community realized that much of the information required for top–down reporting could also be modified and used for bottom–up program improvement.

At the same time, many academics began to challenge the traditional view of institutional excellence as a combination of resources and reputation. Instead, they argued, institutional excellence was a function of how well it developed the talents of the students it admitted (Astin, 1993; Pascuarella & Terenzini, 1992). If, in fact, the quality of a college or university was based on how much its students developed in the cognitive and affective domains, then it was essential for an institution valuing quality to measure these gains.

This gave rise to the outcomes assessment movement of the late 1980s and early 1990s (Astin, 1991; Banta et al., 1996), based on the recognition that evaluation was linked to effectiveness and effectiveness in promoting student development was a measure of institutional quality. The resulting movement coupled with increasing state and federal demands for accountability brought the concept of evaluation to the forefront of U.S. postsecondary education.

The Availability of Computer Technology

Among the many factors contributing to an increase in evaluation activity in U.S. postsecondary education is the availability of computer technology as an aid in collecting, storing, managing, and retrieving data. As recently as the early 1980s, few reading and study skills instructors or programs had access to desktop computers. Even for those who did, the design of databases, the entry of information into these databases, and the retrieval and analysis of information was a cumbersome process.

By the early 1990s, however, two trends contributed to greatly simplifying the processes of data collection and analysis. One was the wide dissemination of computer technology throughout U.S. college and university campuses. By the beginning of the 1990s, practically every full-time reading and study skills faculty member had access either to a nearby computer laboratory or to their own personal computer.

In addition, computer software had become more user friendly by the 1990s, particularly with the development of Windows™-based software programs. Even those who considered themselves technophobic were able to use computer tools such as word processing, spreadsheets, and e-mail. For those who used computer-managed instruction (CMI), most of the data needed for course and program evaluation was built right into the management software.

These two trends combined to simplify the process of collecting and storing data well as the process of data retrieval and analysis. Evaluation activities that would have been next to impossible in the 1970s without the assistance of a mainframe and a computer programmer were, by the 1990s, able to be accomplished with comparative ease on a personal computer (PC).

As a result of the confluence of these four forces, evaluation that was once a top–down and episodic activity had changed dramatically. Evaluation is now seen as an activity that can help individual reading instructors and program administrators measure the impact of their work, explore the effectiveness of their interventions, and monitor and revise their activities while planning for future changes.

Fortunately, as the amount of evaluation undertaken in U.S. postsecondary education has increased, the amount of theory, research, and literature on the topic has also expanded. The next section reviews the more salient aspects of this body of knowledge as a guide to those who are contemplating either initiation or revision of evaluation activities.

TYPES OF EVALUATION

On the topic of evaluation types, two areas bearing review are formative and summative and quantitative and qualitative evaluation activities. Although formative and summative evaluation are often thought to be at opposite ends of a continuum, the line between them is frequently difficult to draw. Similarly, in current practice, quantitative and qualitative evaluation methods are no longer regarded as polar opposites but as complementary activities.

Formative and Summative Evaluation

The notions of *formative* and *summative* evaluation are useful in deciding which evaluation activities are appropriate at any given time in a program's development. According to Stake (1967), one of the originators of the concept, summative evaluation is "aimed at giving answers about the merits and shortcomings of a particular curriculum or a specific set of instructional materials" (p. 24). Such an evaluation provides a summary of the program's real, rather than potential accomplishments and benefits. Summative evaluation, therefore, is most appropriate when a technique or program has been fully implemented. The strengths and weaknesses of a particular program or method can be accurately determined only after it has been in place long enough for it to be revised, refined, and adjusted to meet local needs and realities. In other words, summative evaluation of a program or approach should be undertaken only after the "bugs" have been worked out (Vroom et al., 1994).

Frequently, a novel approach to instructional delivery or a new set of instructional materials are either unsuccessful or unable to attain the desired outcomes at first. Methods or materials borrowed from other programs often need major adjustment and fine-tuning to work in a new setting. Similarly, methods and materials that should work in theory often need considerable revision before they work in practice.

Too often, new programs are subjected to summative evaluation before these adjustments have been made. As a general rule, new programs, methods, or materials should not be the subject of summative evaluation until they have been fully implemented. Full implementation does not occur until enough time has passed for the innovation to be reviewed, refined, and adjusted. Until then, innovative programs, methods, or materials are most appropriately evaluated for formative purposes. In fact, the formative evaluation is a key component of the review, refinement, and adjustment process.

Stake (1967) referred to formative evaluation as that which "seeks information for the development of a curriculum or instructional device," further noting that "the developer wants to find out what arrangements to make or what amounts of something to use" (p. 25). Formative evaluation should be undertaken to understand how new programs, techniques, or materials are working and use this understanding to modify and improve them. Formative evaluation, therefore, generally should precede summative evaluation. In fact, results from formative evaluation activities tell program directors, faculty, and staff when it is appropriate to conduct summative evaluation. This does not mean that formative evaluation should cease once an innovation has been fully implemented. In fact, a major purpose of formative evaluation is to encourage the constant scrutiny of an activity. It should encourage faculty, staff, and administrators to regularly rethink their objectives and the methods they employ to attain these objectives.

Formative evaluation addresses one of the major purposes for evaluating college reading programs: It provides information to be used in modifying and improving the program. It can also provide information about exactly what the program is doing. Although formative evaluation provides information about how well a program is doing, it provides this information only for a given point in time. It does not provide information about the program's full potential.

Summative evaluation addresses another major purpose for evaluating college reading programs: It determines how well the program, its techniques, and its materials are working once they have been implemented. Summative evaluation is, therefore, more generalizable than formative evaluation. It provides publishable information that can be used to make institutionwide or systemwide decisions about the efficacy of various approaches. Summative evaluation reports should include the best and most credible evaluation information available to enable decision makers to accurately assess the value of a particular approach or set of approaches.

Qualitative and Quantitative Evaluation

In recent years, much debate has occurred in the evaluation community over the *qualitative* and *quantitative* traditions of evaluation. Until the 1980s, the dominant approach to evaluation was quantitative (Crowl, 1996). Prior to that time, many researchers and evaluators believed that scientific, experimental, and statistical approaches represented the only valid way to collect, analyze, and interpret phenomenon. This belief governed the conduct of most of the educational research and evaluation that took place prior to the 1980s and, to a great extent, much of what takes place today.

The quantitative approach emphasizes numerical expression based on numbers, measurement, relationships, and experiments (MacMillan, 1996). Qualitative methods, on the other hand, emphasize the perceptions, feelings, and reactions of individuals involved in the experience being evaluated (Ely, Anzul, Friedman, Garner, & Steinmetz, 1991).

Quantitative evaluation methods are used primarily to examine questions that can best be answered by collecting and statistically analyzing data in numerical form. Descriptive and inferential statistics are a common tool of quantitative methodology.

Qualitative evaluation methods are used to examine questions that can best be answered by verbally describing how participants in an evaluation perceive and interpret various aspects of their environment. It can refer not only to research about persons' lives, stories, and behavior, but also about organizational functioning, social movements, or interactional relationships. Observations, interviews, and case studies are common tools of qualitative methodology. It should also be noted that the terms *qualitative, naturalistic,* and *ethnographic* are used more or less synonymously by many researchers and evaluators (Crowl, 1996; Tesch, 1990). It should also be noted that there exists considerable diversity in the models, techniques, and approaches to qualitative evaluation (Pitman & Maxwell, 1992).

Most evaluation projects place their emphasis on either qualitative or quantitative methods. However, the two can be combined. One might use qualitative data to illustrate or clarify quantitatively derived findings; or one could quantify demographic findings. Or, some other form of quantitative data could be used to partially validate one's qualitative analysis.

In essence, quantitative methodology is an excellent way to determine what is taking place in a course or program and accurately assess outcomes. Qualitative methodology is an excellent way to determine the meaning of what is taking place and how it is perceived by the participants in a course or program. Consequently, modern program evaluation methods should usually involve a combination of quantitative and qualitative analysis (Straus & Corbin, 1990).

EVALUATION TYPOLOGIES

Several authors have attempted to describe typologies of evaluation theories or models. Stufflebeam et al. (1971) identified four types of evaluation based on the purpose each was designed to serve: context, input, process, and product. *Context evaluation* determines objectives for planning, *input evaluation* helps to determine project designs, *process evaluation* helps to determine project operations and policies, and *product evaluation* helps to refine and improve project operations. These categories do not represent evaluation models so much as purposes for evaluation. In many respects, they can be likened to Anderson and Ball's (1978) purposes cited earlier.

Cronbach (1983) suggested that two types of evaluation methodologies exist, one supporting the *scientific* ideal and the other supporting the *humanistic* ideal. The former uses the scientific method and is concerned with objectivity, whereas the latter uses qualitative methods and allows for subjective impressions. Cronbach further suggests that most evaluation designs can be plotted on a continuum between these two connecting schools of thought.

Campbell and Stanley (1966) are the most frequently cited proponents of the scientific school of evaluation based on the research model. They argue that "true" scientific designs fall into one of two categories, *experimental* or *quasi-experimental*. Experimental designs provide for full control of the factors that affect results, such as internal and external validity and reliability. Quasi-experimental designs are used in situations in which full control is not possible. It must be noted that Campbell and Stanley's models were designed to govern research activities, not evaluation activities. Although much of what they say is relevant to evaluation, particularly evaluation designed to understand basic processes, their work was never intended as a guideline for program evaluation.

Popham (1988) developed five classes of educational evaluation models. The five classes include the following:

1. goal attainment models,
2. judgmental models emphasizing inputs,
3. judgmental models emphasizing outputs,
4. decision-facilitating models, and
5. naturalistic models.

Although these categories are neither exhaustive nor mutually distinctive, this classification scheme presents a sampling of some of the currently available evaluation models without overwhelming the reading with an endless set of categories and models. The implications based on these models are geared generally to educational evaluation and measurement with some applicability and use in program evaluation.

Moore (1981) developed a typology of 10 evaluation frameworks based on the ways evaluators assess programs. His typology, which combines several of the models presented by other authors, includes the following categories: experimental research design, quasi-experimental research design, professional judgment, measurement methods, congruency comparison, cost-effectiveness approaches, behavioral taxonomies, systems analysis, informal evaluation, and goal-free or responsive evaluation.

Moore's typology appears to be one of the more comprehensive in the literature; it includes the works of most major authors in the field of evaluation. Although all these models have been applied to some degree in the college reading and study strategies programs, six of them are particularly applicable for the purposes of this chapter. Table 13.1 summarizes the advantages, disadvantages, and uses of each of these six models.

TABLE 13.1

Comparison of Evaluation Models

Model	Advantages	Disadvantages	Purposes/Uses
Professional Judgment Subjective ratings by peers, panels, or individual experts	Direct and easy; usually results in clear recommendations for action	Lacks reliability and generalizability; is not an objective model	Answers specific questions when other models are inappropriate and provides good formative information
Experimental Scientific approach providing control of specific factors that may affect results	Controls for internal and external validity	Requires quantifiable and measurable data, specific sample size, selection procedures; focuses only on reliable, objective data	Is appropriate for answering specific questions regarding and individual program components; is most appropriate when program is in a mature state of development
Quasi-Experimental Similar to experimental model but lacks full experimental control	Controls some factors affecting validity; uses similar to those used in experimental designs	Includes potential sources of internal and external invalidity	Useful in determining causal relationships in situations requiring more formal research in natural social settings
Congruency Comparison Based on comparison of program objectives with observed outcomes	Is easy and direct as well as reliable and generaliz able; can be integrated with instructional processes	Has a rather narrow focus that may overlook certain desirable effects	Useful in refining programs and determining program effectiveness; is particularly appropriate for competency-based programs
Cost-Effectiveness Used to determine the financial benefits of a total program and/or its components	Provides cost factors for program components and the total proram; provides useful data for program budgeting and accountability	Excludes program activities that are not observable and measurable in terms of cost; requires some specific training in cost accounting procedures	Useful in assessing program benefits versus costs
Goal-Free and Responsive Reviews program from a broad perspective including all areas and activites; emphasizes actual outcomes independent of program goals or objectives	Useful for programs with varied purposes and activities; is flexible and adaptable to unstructured situations	Does not provide information that may be required for reporting purposes, such as program intent, goals, or objectives	Useful for investigating strategies that work best for particular individuals or groups of students

Professional Judgment Designs

Professional judgment designs rely on the subjective ratings of individuals or panels of experts and peers. Before the advent of more scientific evaluation designs in the 1960s, professional judgment was the primary method of evaluation in postsecondary education (Walvekar, 1981). Today, it is widely used, particularly among federally funded programs.

Individual program reviewers, grant proposal reviewers, or professional journal referees all represent examples of the professional judgment design. One of the most common examples of professional judgment design is the use of an expert external consultant to review a particular course, program, or program element. This is generally done when decision makers believe that a course or program is not delivering all the outcomes desired or delivering them as well as desired. The intention of such evaluation, then, is to use the professional expertise of an external evaluator to identify problems and suggest solutions.

The expert judgment design may also be applied by local reviewers or program staff through the use of the literature and research in the field. In this case, a body of research and literature is used to identify (a) the typical or baseline outcome for a given activity and (b) the best practices available to conduct that activity. Given this information, local evaluators compare course or program outcomes and activities to typical outcomes and recommended the best practices. In this case, the expert being consulted is not an external reviewer but the opinions and research of experts available through the literature in the field. This model might also fit under the category of congruency comparison designs.

Another example is the panel method, described by Campbell and Stanley (1966) as "observations made at a single point in time" and strengthened by "waves of interviews," thus providing individual observations over a span of time (pp. 66–67). Accreditation teams or program review teams represent examples of this method of applying expert judgment.

The latter represents a complete model of evaluation because teams of experts can reconcile their differences in judgment, producing an expert consensus. This, in theory, brings about a more scientific application of professional judgment. However, as Provus (1971) pointed out, even this sort of evaluation is subject to questions about the standards used for such judgment—those of the judges and those of the programs being evaluated.

Two other forms of evaluation that fall within the category of professional judgment are the opinions of program staff and the opinions of those affected by a program. Maxwell (1997) suggested that evaluations based on the opinions of a program's participants put those persons in the role of participant–observer. She describes the evaluation process as follows: each participant systematically records his or her reactions to a program, after which all the reactions are combined and used to assess the program's strengths and weaknesses.

Used alone, this design would not meet the total evaluation needs of a college reading and study strategies program, particularly one subject to the scrutiny of colleagues oriented toward scientific evaluation. Its lack of sophistication, reliability, objectivity, and generalizability are obvious disadvantages (Maxwell, 1997). Nevertheless, there appears to be some merit to the inclusion of expert, subjective judgments in program evaluation, particularly when some of the questions asked are unanswerable by other methods. In this context, professional judgment is, perhaps, better included as one component of a systematic evaluation design than a design in itself.

Experimental Research Designs

Program evaluation designs that employ the research model derive from experimental or scientific research designs. Campbell and Stanley's (1966) classic work on this topic maintains that only three true experimental research designs exist: the pretest–posttest control group design, the Solomon four-group design, and the posttest-only group design. These designs are supposedly true because they provide controls for internal and external validity and random assignment of subjects to groups.

Campbell and Stanley's (1966) work also explored pre-experimental designs. Such designs lack some of the major controls necessary for statistical validity. Although these designs are used frequently, Campbell and Stanley consider them to be of little scientific value. This, however, may reflect the quantitative bias that pervaded the research and evaluation literature of the time (Patton, 1990).

The issue of experimental designs versus qualitative designs, or hard versus soft evaluation data, has been a source of considerable debate among evaluation experts over the years. Current opinion, however, suggests that all these forms of design have a place in comprehensive evaluation (Upcraft & Schuh, 1996). Maxwell (1997), for instance, asserted that experimental research designs are generally used for determining causal relationships; for collecting objective, reliable, and valid data; and for analyzing data suitable to statistical treatment. She cautions against the inclination of some to stereotype hard and soft evaluation and suggests that evaluation techniques be chosen according to their appropriateness for specific evaluation questions. For example, qualitative or soft information such as student evaluations of instruction or colleagues' impressions may be entirely appropriate for assessing students' perceived quality of experience during their participation in a program. Quantitative or hard data, such as analysis of score points on standardized instruments may be more appropriate for assessing program impact on student performance.

There are several arguments that may be used against complete reliance on experimental research designs. As Patton (1990) pointed out, experimental design methodology is borrowed from the biological sciences where approximations of the truth may be obtained by carefully manipulated and controlled experiments. Such careful manipulation and control is rarely possible when the subjects are groups of students who spend little time in classrooms and the majority of their time being influenced by extracurricular factors. In other words, classic experimental design is devoid of context. Instead, most variables are controlled by the experimenter. In real-life situations, human beings are influenced by a variety of context variables that cannot be controlled by the experimenter.

Rossi and Freeman (1985) also pointed out that important information about a program during its formative stages is missed if an evaluation employs and experimental design. Experimental designs are much more appropriate to summative evaluation. In effect, many good programs are found to have no significant effects because they were evaluated before they were fully implemented.

Sample size and selection in college reading and study strategies programs also contribute to problems with experimental research designs. Frequently, the numbers of students involved in a course or a program are insufficient to provide an appropriate sample. Small sample size has consistently contributed to findings of "no significant difference" in comparative studies even in cases where the experimental treatment actually works (Scriven, 1993). As Stufflebeam et al. (1971) wisely noted, "When a technique continually produces findings that are at variance with experience and common observation, it is time to call that technique into questions" (p. 8). This appears to be the case in many instances in which evaluators have relied on the experimental model to assess college reading and study strategy programs.

These designs are not always appropriate for evaluating such programs. When conditions exist allowing the use of experimental models, when sample size is sufficient, and when a program is in a mature state of development, experimental models may be appropriate. Otherwise, they are unlikely to produce either significant findings or useful information.

Quasi-Experimental Research Designs

The application of quasi-experimental research techniques to answer specific questions or to evaluate specific components of a program has been proposed by several authors. Campbell and Stanley (1966) recommend quasi-experimental designs for use in natural social settings where full experimental control is impossible. They propose 10 such models, emphasizing the importance of understanding the variables for which these models fail to control.

Myers and Majer (1981) provided a rationale for the use of a quasi-experimental research methodology to answer practical questions in evaluating learning assistance centers. They propose that the overall purpose of evaluation is to answer important questions concerning program improvement, accountability, funding, and knowledge. They also provide several examples of such questions and suggest experimental and quasi-experimental techniques as ways to answer these questions.

Akst and Hecht (1980) stressed that preprogram and postprogram measures must be a part of an objective evaluation of college remedial programs. In their opinion, the measurement and evaluation of learning are critical to program evaluation. Measurement of learning involves determining how well the content has been mastered, whereas the evaluation of learning entails judging the quality of learning against some standard.

Akst and Hecht recommend four comparative evaluation designs for measuring learning in which groups are compared to those qualifying for but not participating in programs. These are: single-group pretest–posttest, remediated–unremediated, marginally remedial, and marginally exempted designs. For evaluation learning, the authors suggest remediated–exempted, cross-program, historical, norm-group, and regression–discontinuity comparison. Akst and Hecht also provide a summary table with ratings of each design, appropriate preprogram and postprogram measures, feasibility problems, possible biases, and a judgment of design suitability.

Quasi-experimental designs may be appropriate for the assessment of selected components of a particular program. Maxwell (1997) suggested that the various purposes of program evaluations may determine the areas where quasi-experimental designs are appropriate. She provides a chart outlining which research designs may yield the best results with certain applications. She recommends the use of quasi-experimental designs for the following activities:

- making decisions about program continuation, expansion, or accreditation,
- determining the effectiveness or sequencing of curriculum components,
- determining the effectiveness of presentation methods, pacing, and length,
- selecting and placing students,
- training and evaluating instructors and administrators,
- obtaining evidence to rally support for or opposition to a program, and
- contributing to the understanding of basic processes in educational, social, psychological, or economic areas.

It is important to note that many of the objectives of college reading and study strategy programs relate to affective and personal growth factors, many of which are not typically assessed through quasi-experimental approaches. Caution must be exercised to ensure that these factors are not overlooked in the evaluation process. A research-based judgment, although preferred by many, may be inappropriate for assessing many worthwhile program components (Dressel, 1976). Other designs, such as congruency comparison, cost-effectiveness models, or goal-free responsive designs may be more effective in such cases.

Congruency Comparison Designs

Congruency comparison designs are included in the large class of general evaluation models that are applicable to many contexts and users (Borich, 1974). They involve comparing a program's objectives or standards with data derived from observation of the program to determine congruence or lack of congruence. A measure of congruence reveals whether intended transactions or outcomes did occur (Stake, 1967).

The discrepancy evaluation model (Provus, 1971) is one of the best-known examples of a congruency comparison design. Since its original development, it has been revised substantially to accommodate explorations and critiques from several sources. The revised model is described in terms of five stages, design, installation, process, product, and program comparison.

Stages 1 through 4 are used to evaluate programs that are already under way. Stage 5 is an optional step that allows for comparisons of two or more programs. The process of this design involves working through the stages while simultaneously examining the program's input, process, and output. In other words, program design and installation are assessed to determine who is entering the program, what is happening in the program, and what outcomes the program produces.

This model is quite similar to Astin's (1991) model of input–environment–output or IEO assessment. This more recent model was developed specifically for use in college and university settings as part of the outcomes assessment movement.

Boylan (1997a) suggested that the comparison of current program practices with identifiable best practices represents another, albeit less sophisticated, form of congruency–comparison design. In this method, the literature and research is used to establish a theoretical model of best possible practices. Program activities are then compared to this theoretical model to identify congruities and incongruities. Given local circumstances, constraints, and resources, the program is then modified to reflect appropriate best practices.

A significant feature of congruency observations, comparison, and judgments is that they are replicable, generalizable, and appropriate for competency-based programs (Moore, 1981). Moore provides the example of comparing student outcomes against stated behavioral objectives as a straightforward application of the congruency approach.

Stufflebeam et al. (1971) considered this model to have advantages and disadvantages. The disadvantages include placement of the evaluator in a technical role, the focus on evaluation as a terminal process, and a narrow focus on objectives, as well as the elevation of "behavior as the ultimate criterion of every instructional action." The model's advantages include a "high degree of integration with the instructional process, data available on both student and curriculum, possibility of feedback, objective referent and built-in criteria, and the possibility of process as well as product data" (Stufflebeam, 1971, p. 15).

This type of evaluation appears to be relatively easy and direct, which are distinct advantages, although this directness means that such evaluation may not address incidental but desirable effects not specified in a program's objectives. This technique may be appropriate for evaluations designed to refine programs as well as those designed to determine program effectiveness. In addition, the opportunity for feedback makes this model appropriate for administrators of college reading and study skills programs who want to revise program content and processes. Those who want to determine the financial benefits of their activities, on the other hand, may be better served by cost-effectiveness design.

Cost-Effectiveness and Cost-Benefit Designs

Cost-effectiveness designs are considered by some to be among the most effective approaches to program evaluation. The notion of evaluating program effectiveness in terms of costs has its origins in business and industrial evaluation, where costs and products are easier to measure. Nevertheless, when used properly, this model can be applied to teaching, learning, and human behavior.

Land (1976) delineated a problem classification schema in applying the cost-effectiveness approach to the evaluation of education programs. His classification includes discussions relating to the problems of estimation, investment decisions, measurement of achievement, cost allocation, and program control. These are all essential issues in the literature of cost-benefit analysis as a program evaluation tool.

The most often cited research on cost-effectiveness is that of Levin (1991). He traces the origins and history of cost-effectiveness studies, explains the methodology, describes its application to policy analysis, and how it may be integrated into educational evaluation. Levin points out that cost-effectiveness studies are usually a secondary analysis included as part of a larger evaluation study. This is because cost-effectiveness is difficult to carry out without access to the data collected and evaluated through a primary analysis. Levin (1991) also introduced the notion of cost-benefit analysis as a component of cost-effectiveness studies.

Haller (1974) described cost-benefit analysis as an expanded notion of program costs that goes beyond the usual definition of dollars and cents. In this model, costs are considered to be "benefits lost" (p. 408). In other words, what might have happened had a particular program or intervention not been in existence? Three implications arise from this point of view. First, the costs of a given action or inaction are directly related to the decision about whether to take that action. Second, the consequences of doing or not doing something must be adequately defined in order for cost-effectiveness to be measured. Third, because absolute accuracy in measuring costs is impossible, approximate measures must be accepted in determining cost-effectiveness.

This design would certainly be attractive to college administrators who are responsible for fiscal accountability and planning because it provides cost factors for discrete program components as well as for the total program. Cost effectiveness evaluations do present certain problems, however.

The disadvantages of this approach, noted by Moore (1981) and Land (1976), relate to the fact that it is frequently used ineffectively. Ineffectiveness results from time constraints and the exclusion of program components from the evaluation process because they may not be directly observable.

We do not recommend this design for college reading and study skills programs because many worthwhile components are not observable or measurable. In addition, few program directors have the expertise or fiscal training to apply this type of design successfully to an overall program evaluation.

The cost-effectiveness design is discussed here because administrators and legislators often pressure reading and study strategy programs to apply this design. Although this model may satisfy the needs of administrators to document what is gained from dollars spent, it does not satisfy the needs of program personnel to determine the impact of program activities and ways in which this impact may be enhanced. A more effective method to accommodate this need might be to apply goal-free or responsive evaluation designs.

Goal-Free and Responsive Designs

A sixth evaluation design model represents a "laissez-faire perspective" of evaluation unencumbered by the language of intent, goals, and objective (Borich, 1974). Moore (1981) combined goal-free and responsive designs because of the similarity of these two models. They are combined in this review for the same reason.

Goal-free and responsive designs are distinguished by their emphasis on the importance of an external, objective evaluator. This evaluator looks for the actual results or outcomes of a program, not its intent. Borich (1974) described the goal-free evaluator as viewing program development and evaluation from a broad, general perspective that includes all of a program's areas and activities. This view differs only slightly from the professional judgment model of evaluation discussed earlier. The major difference is that with a goal-free approach, evaluators base their judgments not on their own expertise but on the extent to which all program activities are integrated into some meaningful whole.

Scriven (1993)—a proponent of goal-free evaluation—distinguished between evaluation that incorporates values into a model, thus giving weight to both description and judgment, and the casting of the evaluator in a decision-making role. Stake (1967), on the other hand, believed that the evaluator should not be a part of the decision-making team. Although this may be true in theory, the fact is that the evaluator is often called on to make decisions. It seems more sensible to acknowledge this role by formally including the evaluator in the decision-making process than to pretend that such a role does not exist.

A possible problem encountered by administrators who receive goal-free reports is that such reports may be difficult to relate to their goals for a program. In spite of this difficulty, the varied purposes and intents of college reading and study strategy programs make goal-free and responsive evaluation more suitable than other evaluation approaches. These designs are flexible and adaptable to relatively unstructured situations. Moore (1981) commented that all "processes, outcomes, resources, and objectives are potentially relevant" in goal-free and responsive evaluation, and that these models are people-centered rather than system-centered (p. 41).

Ethnographic approaches that evaluate program effectiveness for individuals and groups also should be included in this category. Guthrie (1984) explained ethnographic methods in terms of participant observation, interviews, quantification schemes, diary studies, case studies, and the use of technology. He particularly recommends ethnographic designs for the evaluation of reading programs when the objective is to determine what is really happening between the teacher and individual students or a particular group of students. These methods, of course, are representative of the qualitative approach to evaluation (Shadish et al., 1991).

Essentially, goal-free and responsive designs enable evaluators to review programs from a broad perspective including all areas and activities and emphasize actual outcomes independent of program goals and objectives. This encourages attention to a wider range of program outcomes. It is useful for investigating strategies that work best for particular individuals or groups of students. It focuses on intended as well as unanticipated outcomes and is recommended as a supplement to more goal oriented frameworks.

It is certainly important for the staffs of college reading and study strategy programs to understand what works best for each group of students enrolled in their programs. Ethnographic and other goal-free and responsive evaluation research may be a valuable tool for investigating such programs. Unfortunately, the literature does not, at present, provide any examples of its use in college reading programs.

TYPICAL EVALUATION STUDIES OF COLLEGE-LEVEL PROGRAMS

The literature reflects relatively few examples of the various evaluation methodologies that can be applied to college reading and study skills programs. A review of the last five volumes of the four major reading journals and three developmental education journals, as well as a detailed Educational Resources Information Center (ERIC) search, yielded a substantial number of articles on the evaluation of college reading and study strategy programs.

However, this literature reflects a fairly narrow range of evaluation strategies applied to college reading and study strategies programs. Of those reported in the literature, the vast majority are either experimental or quasi-experimental in design. This preponderance is probably the result of two factors. First, many journals show a preference for research articles using experimental or quasi-experimental methods. Second, many articles discussing program evaluation activities using alternative methodologies do not yield statistically quantifiable results. In spite of the increased use of qualitative methodology in program evaluation, many professional journals still favor quantitative studies. These factors militate against the publication of articles dealing with alternative evaluation models.

We did not find any studies that compared the effectiveness of various evaluation designs for college reading and study skills programs. The studies that follow represent a sampling of the published accounts of systematic efforts to apply either experimental or quasi-experimental designs to the evaluation of these programs.

Experimental Research Studies

One of the earliest articles featuring the experimental approach is provided by Behrens (1935). He investigated the effects of a course on how to study, comparing students who had taken the course with those who had not. He found that students in the experimental group that took the course obtained better grades than students in the control group.

In a later and more extensive study, Mouly (1952) attempted to assess the effects of a university remedial reading program on student grades. The experimental group consisted of 155 students who took remedial reading for one semester. This group was further divided into two subgroups: students who successfully completed the course and student who either failed or did not complete the course. The control group was made up of students who did not take the remedial course. This group was subdivided into those who were advised to take the course and decided not to and those who were randomly selected to be excused from the course.

Only slight differences were reported in the combined grade point averages (GPAs) of the total experimental and the total control group; in addition, these groups' dropout rates and average number of credits accumulated during the period under study were almost identical. When the results were broken down by subgroup, however, a different picture emerged. The experimental subgroup that successfully completed the remedial course earned a significantly higher combined GPA than the total control group. Mouly (1952) concluded that "a remedial reading program can result in improvement in academic grades for those persons who take the course seriously" (p. 466). Mouly noted further that in institutions where enrollment in remedial courses is voluntary, the benefits of such courses are lost to many students. In considering the results of this study, however, it should be noted that it did not control for possible pretreatment differences between experimental and control groups.

Simpson and Nist (1990) provided another example of a common experimental design in reading research. This design involves providing one treatment to the experimental group and another treatment to the control group. The authors provided training in previewing and question formulation to one group of students and training in text annotation to another. Using two different outcome measures, raw scores on tests and study times, they found that the annotation group performed better on tests and was more efficient in learning. The authors concluded that training students to annotate their texts enabled them to perform more effectively in the long run.

Baker and Mulcahy-Ernt (1993) compared the performance of students randomly assigned to either an experimental or a control group in an attempt to identify the impact of weekly learning logs. Control group students were assigned to a traditional basic skills course and the experimental group students were taught to develop learning logs in response to their assigned readings. Both groups were tested at the end of the term with the *Reading Assessment Test* as well as a required course exit test. The students who were taught the learning log process showed significant gains in comprehension.

Maring, Shea, and Warner (1987) compared three experimental groups taking reading and study strategy courses with two control groups not taking these courses. Their purpose was to assess the impact of the courses on such factors as student GPA, retention, and satisfaction. Although a major part of the study used an experimental design featuring objective statistical data, the authors also collected subjective data from students. They found no significant difference between the GPAs of the experimental and the control groups. However, students in the experimental groups had higher retention rates and expressed greater satisfaction with their college experience than did students in the control groups.

The Maring, Shea, and Warner (1987) study provided an excellent example of an experimental design using it in conjunction with subjective data and qualitative analysis. The authors offer a number of recommendations for those who wish to implement this design in evaluating reading, study strategy, and learning assistance programs. This design appears to be one of the most powerful evaluation models reported in the recent reading literature.

Quasi-Experimental Design Studies

Several reading and study skills programs at the college level have been evaluated using quasi-experimental designs. Studies are classified as quasi-experimental when the subject are not randomly assigned to groups or when full control of variable is not possible (Cook & Campbell, 1979).

In one quasi-experimental study, Borich (1974) analyzed the relationships of selected intellective and nonintellective variables to the academic success of educationally and economically disadvantaged freshmen. The subjects participated in a special summer transitional program before enrolling as freshmen the following fall semester. The special program involved instruction in regular freshman English and history courses, remedial courses in mathematics and reading and study skills, peer counseling, and professional counseling. Academic achievement was measured by changes in pretest and posttest scores during the special summer program. Measures of achievement, study habits and attitudes, self-concept, and intelligence were administered. Other variables studied were IQ, high school GPA, gender, preliminary American College Testing (ACT) score, and selected demographic variables.

Significant predictors of post-program achievement were reported to be pretest scores and IQ. The best predictors of fall GPA were found to be high school GPA, gender, IQ, and self-concept. The study also concluded that successful and unsuccessful students showed significant differences on cognitive variables but not on self-concept or demographic variables.

Freeley, Wepner, and Wehrle (1987) conducted a quasi-experimental study designed to test the impact of direct exposure to test items on the performance of students taking the reading section of the New Jersey College Basic Skills Placement Test. The experimental group took a reading course that used direct quotations from the test as reading passages. The control group was given reading passages that covered topics similar to those on the test but that were not direct quotes. The authors found that although the scores of both groups on the New Jersey College Basic Skills Placement Test improved significantly over pretest scores, there was no significant difference between the two groups' posttest scores. These results suggest that a reading and study strategy program focusing on preparing students for standardized tests need not involve direct "teaching to the test" to be successful.

A recent study by Taraban (1997) used database analysis to monitor students who had failed a statewide test of basic readings skills. These students were then divided into two groups: an experimental group that took a noncredit developmental reading course and a control group that did not take developmental courses. No significant differences were found between the two groups in terms of their later pass rates on the statewide test. In essence, those who simply took regular college courses did as well on retaking the reading test as those who took a developmental reading course. The author concluded that participation in regular college courses can often build reading skills as well as taking a developmental reading course.

Although the studies cited here provide data that can be used for program evaluation purposes, they also represent examples of research designed to understand basic processes. The Borich (1974) study, for instance, was clearly designed to explore the effect of intellective and nonintellective variables on student performance—not necessarily to assess the quality of the program in which the students were enrolled. Similarly, the Taraban (1997) and Freeley et al., (1987) studies were designed to assess a particular strategy for improving student performance. Nevertheless, each study provides a good example of how quasi-experimental design can be used to assess the impact of program components.

Other Evaluation Studies and Models

Although the literature clearly favors studies that take an experimental or quasi-experimental approach to program evaluation, we did find several examples of other approaches. Spivey (1981) provided an example of a congruency comparison model for program evaluation. Using a system known as *goal attainment scaling*, students in a learning center were asked to establish goals for their participation in the center. The goals were discussed with a counselor, quantified in terms of measurable outcomes, and then reviewed at the end of each semester. Students and counselors then jointly agreed on the extent to which these goals had been accomplished or the degree to which student performance matched expectations. In addition to serving as a program evaluation tool, this system had a positive impact on student performance.

Smith and Brown (1981) used a version of congruency comparison to evaluate staff performance in a reading and study strategies program. Using a modified version of management by objectives (MBO; McConkey, 1975), staff members negotiated their performance objectives with supervisors. These objectives were then quantified and weighed. At the end of each year, staff members met individually with supervisors to determine the extent to which these objectives had been accomplished. The authors concluded that this system not only improved the quality of program management but also boosted staff motivation.

An evaluation using goal-free methodology was carried out by Ley, Hodges, and Young (1995). The authors sought to obtain information on the advantages and disadvantages of a particular cooperative learning strategy. Data was obtained through a combination of the observations of instructors and feedback from students. Following analysis of this information, the authors concluded that the strategy under consideration offered the advantages of providing opportunities for students to learn collegiality and the value of working in a group. Among the strategy's disadvantages were that it required more test-taking time.

Silverman (1983) used a goal-free and responsive evaluation approach in attempting to determine which variables affected students' self-esteem and academic performance. Using student interviews combined with performance data, she determined that positive academic self-concepts were directly related to academic performance. Additional factors such as motivation, peer influence, and faculty influence also affect self-concept. The information collected with this evaluation approach has useful implications for the design and refinement of basic skills programs as well as for counseling interventions designed to support them.

The work of Boylan et al. (1996) provided an example of a congruency–comparison design to a statewide testing and instruction program. In this study the Texas Academic Skills Program (TASP), a statewide assessment test followed by mandatory remediation of basic skills in reading, English, and mathematics, was evaluated to determine its effectiveness and to make recommendations for improvement. As a part of this study, a theoretical model of an ideal developmental education program representing best practices was identified through the research and literature. A combination of surveys and observations conducted during site visits was used to match what was done at local institutions with the theoretical model of best practices. The study found that Texas developmental programs reflected a wide range of practice, some of it inconsistent with the available research and literature. This was particularly true in the areas of faculty and staff training, program coordination, and program evaluation.

An example of cost-effectiveness evaluation is found in the work of Levin, Glass, and Meister (1987). These authors attempted to determine the cost-effectiveness of computer-assisted reading instruction—as measured against peer tutoring, increased instructional time, and reduced class size—as a means of improving scores on reading tests. Results were reported as the score gains achieved for each $100 spent per student. Peer tutoring was found to be the most cost-effective approach, with computer-assisted instruction (CAI) just slightly behind. Increasing instructional time and reducing class sizes were found to be the least cost-effective methods.

Boylan (1997a) suggested a cost effectiveness evaluation model that takes into consideration the benefits lost through student attrition. This model advocates the assignment of a monetary value to the loss of a single student and the compilation of monetary benefits gained through the retention of a single student. If participation in any reading or study strategies activity can be shown to result in a percentage increase in retention for one or more terms, this percentage increase can be translated into dollar amounts. These dollar amounts represent cost benefits accrued to the institution.

Another form of cost-analysis is provided by Breneman (1998). At the request of the Brookings Institute, he attempted a cost analysis of developmental education, including reading and study strategies courses, across the United States. Using data from two representative states, Maryland and Texas, the author extrapolated from their expenses on developmental education to the other 48 states in the Union. He found that only about 1% of the total of state higher education budgets, or just over $1 billion, was expended on developmental education. He concluded that "the cost of remediation is probably less than the cost of an average year of American secondary school" (p. 379) and that prohibiting colleges from offering remediation was "not the right policy" (p. 381). Although this was a national study of the costs of developmental education, it provides the sort of baseline cost data that allows college reading and study strategies programs to justify the cost-effectiveness of their offerings.

One example of qualitative evaluation is provided by Payne (1995), who explored high-risk students' perceptions of study demands. Using a combination of interview and survey questionnaires, the author examined student perceptions of their own strengths and weaknesses and their plans for study activities. The author found that students perceived their strongest skills to be in English and their weakest to be in mathematics. The study also found that high-risk students tend to have unrealistic perceptions of the amount of work required for success in college. Although this was, in essence, a research study, it provides justification for a greater emphasis on study strategies for high-risk students. This is the sort of qualitative data that can help to establish the need for reading and study strategies courses or programs.

Another examination of qualitative evaluation is provided by Chase, Gibson, and Carson (1994). Using survey and interview techniques, this study attempted to determine the level and extent of reading requirements across the curriculum in history, political science, biology, and English. The authors concluded that college-level reading requires a much greater degree of synthesis and retrieval than is typical of high school requirements. This provides an example of formative evaluation activity that might assist college reading and study strategies programs in determining the content of their curriculum.

IMPLICATIONS FOR PRACTICE

General Guidelines for Evaluation

The studies reviewed in this chapter include evaluations of a variety of program components, reading courses, techniques, and approaches. Few of these studies are comprehensive because they focus on one of more aspects of a given course or program. Most of these studies used either quantitative or qualitative data. We believe that comprehensive program evaluation should include both quantitative and qualitative data.

This notion is consistent with the views of Cronbach (1983), who suggested that evaluators need not choose between humanistic and scientific schools of thought. Certain settings require objective, reproducible, concentrated evaluation, whereas others demand broad, phenomenological, flexible evaluation. The choice of approach should reflect the purpose of the evaluation. There appears to be no agreement among experts in the field as to the best design for evaluation. This lack of consensus is particularly true for college reading and study strategy programs, whose goals, objectives, and methods are so diverse.

Although it is impossible to recommend a single evaluation model for college reading and study skills programs, those who must select and implement evaluation activities for their programs may find the following general guidelines useful.

1. A clear statement of realistic, attainable objectives is essential to program development and, consequently, to program evaluation.
2. Both formative and summative evaluations are necessary for successful overall program evaluations.
3. Evaluations conducted by external experts who know and understand various reading and study strategies and their functions should be a substantial part of formative evaluations.
4. A summative evaluation at the end a program is probably the best place for objective, quantitative, data-based information regarding program effectiveness.
5. Traditional experimental designs are less appropriate than other designs for evaluation reading programs because these programs are typically unable to assign students randomly.
6. Evaluations should consist of multiple criteria; evidence of success should be sought on several dimensions.
7. Because of the range of readers who review evaluation reports of reading and study strategies programs, simple statistics and graphics such as frequencies and percentages, bar graphs and pie charts are the most effective ways of describing evaluation results.

An essential set of guidelines designing evaluation is also provided by the American Association for Higher Education's (AAHE) document entitled *Principles of good practice for assessing student learning* (AAHE, 1992). No current discussion of outcomes assessment would be complete without listing the following principles (AAHE, 1992, pp. 2–3):

1. The assessment of student learning begins with educational values.
2. Assessment is most effective when it reflects an understanding of student learning as multidimensional, integrated, and revealed in performance over time.
3. Assessment works best when the programs it seeks to improve have clear, explicitly stated purposes.
4. Assessment requires not only attention to outcomes but also and equally to the experiences that lead to these outcomes.
5. Assessment works best when it is ongoing, not episodic.
6. Assessment fosters wider improvement when representatives from across the educational community are involved.
7. Assessment makes a difference when it begins with issues of use and illuminates questions that people really care about.
8. Assessment is most likely to lead to improvement when it is part of a larger set of conditions that promote change.
9. Through assessment, educators meet responsibilities to students and to the public.

Aside from choosing an evaluation model and attending to good principles of assessment, those involved in reading and study strategy programs must consider several other issues before beginning an evaluation. Important considerations include choosing an evaluation strategy that encourages use by decision makers, deciding how much information to include, and determining the evaluation criteria.

Vroom et al. (1994) provided a number of guidelines for avoiding the possibility of misuse of evaluation. They suggest that any evaluation activity should involve (a) an exploration of the basic assumptions behind program activities, (b) periodic meetings with program staff and managers to provide ongoing feedback to evaluators, (c) clear determination of the decision-making structure that makes use of evaluation data, (d) explicit determination of desired program changes to result from evaluation, and (e) consistent confrontation of attempts to evade issues or problems critical to the evaluation.

Encouraging Utilization of Evaluation Reports

If the personnel of a reading and study strategy program have gone to the trouble of completing an evaluation and reporting their findings, they naturally want administrators to use those findings in making decisions that affect the program. In an extensive study on the use of evaluation reports, Cousins and Leithwood (1986) found that decision makers are more apt to utilize evaluation information under the following circumstances: (a) evaluation activities are considered appropriate in approach and methodology to the issues being investigated, (b) the decisions to be made directly affect the users of evaluation information and are of the sort normally made on the basis of evaluation data, (c) evaluation findings are consistent with the beliefs and expectations of the decision makers, (d) decision makers have been involved in the evaluation process and have shown commitment to the benefits of evaluation, (e) decision makers consider data reported in the evaluation to be relevant to the problem being explored, and (f) information from other sources conflicts minimally with the results of evaluation.

These findings are consistent with those of several other authors (Casazza & Silverman, 1996; Clowes, 1983; Keimig, 1984) regarding the importance of administrator involvement in the planning of program evaluation. These authors note that it is essential for institutional decision makers to be involved in the evaluation. The principles noted are also consistent with the AAHE's (1992) *Principles of good practice for assessment of student learning*. The evaluation literature makes it clear that it is essential for institutional decision makers to be involved in the evaluation process from the outset. Such decision makers should be thoroughly familiar with the purposes of evaluation, the issues to be evaluated, the methodologies to be used, and the objectives to be accomplished through evaluation. They should be consulted at each step in the evaluation process, and the results of the evaluation should be presented in a manner consistent with the need for information.

Keeping It Simple

In determining how much information to present in an evaluation report and how this information should be presented, there is a fine line between too little and too much. The information should be sufficient to provide administrators with appropriate data to make decisions or to understand the program being evaluated. It should not, however, be so extensive that it becomes difficult to extract necessary information.

A 100-page report filled with graphs, charts, and statistical analysis may be appropriate if administrators want to know the exact status of every program activity. On the other hand, if the only decision to be made on the basis of the report is whether to change diagnostic instruments, such a thorough view is too cumbersome to be useful. In essence, the amount and sophistication of evaluation information presented should be directly related to the extent and complexity of the decisions to be made as a result of this information.

Care should be taken to ensure that those reading the evaluation reports are able to understand them. Not all administrators are statisticians. It may take a fairly sophisticated statistical analysis to determine which of two techniques is more effective in raising student scores on a standardized instrument, but the key part of this information is simply that different groups of students scored differently. Although a t test or an ANOVA procedure might be conducted to determine statistical significance, decision makers do not normally need to read the calculations or see the charts and tables used to arrive at the final figures. They really only need to know that one technique worked better than another and that a valid technique was used to determine these results.

The point here is that it is possible to obscure important findings by spending too much time presenting statistical analysis and not enough time dealing with the implications of the analysis. As a general rule, raw data should be explained in the simplest terms possible, regardless of how sophisticated the methods of analyzing them were. The purpose of evaluation is, after all, to generate useful information—not to impress superiors with one's ability to perform statistical calculations.

Evaluation Criteria

One of the major tasks in designing a program evaluation is the selection of evaluation criteria. Maxwell (1997) listed eight common criteria for evaluating college reading and study strategies:

1. extent to which students use the program,
2. extent to which users are satisfied with the program,
3. grades and grade point averages of those who use the program,
4. year-to-year retention rates of students in the program,
5. test scores and gain scores of those who use the program,
6. faculty attitudes toward the program,
7. staff attitudes toward the program, and
8. impact of the program on the campus as a whole.

In addition to these criteria Boylan (1997b) recommended the use of student course completion rates, grades in follow-up courses, and number of attempts required for students to pass courses. He also recommends the collection of student demographic information as an aid to program evaluation. His list of demographic factors include: (a) age, (b) socioeconomic status (SES), (c) degree–nondegree status, (d) race, (e) gender, and (f) enrollment status (full time vs. part time).

The authors recommend that particular attention be paid to the criteria of grades in follow-up courses, course completion rates, and other benefits. If a reading and study strategy program is designed to improve student performance, its effectiveness can best be measured by assessing the grades students receive in subsequent reading-oriented courses. If students who complete the program do well in later courses requiring advanced reading skills, the program has accomplished its objective.

The extent to which students who enter reading and study strategy courses complete these courses is another valid indicator of program success. Low course completion rates often indicate that something is wrong with the delivery of the course. High completion rates usually indicate that students see the course as valuable and perceive that they are obtaining benefits as a result of their participation. It also should be noted that those who participate in a reading and study strategy program but do not complete it should not be counted in measuring the program's subsequent impact. The impact of a given treatment can be measured accurately only for those students who experienced the full treatment.

It is also important for program evaluation activities to take the possibility of "serendipitous benefits" (Boylan, 1997a) into consideration. Serendipitous benefits are unanticipated positive results from a program. By their very nature, evaluation of these benefits cannot be planned. A good evaluator should be constantly aware of potential benefits that may not be part of an evaluation plan. An unanticipated benefit of a college reading and study strategy program, for instance, might be increased faculty awareness of the reading levels of texts used in their courses. Instructors in community college General Equivalency Diploma (GED) programs have found that participants often use their newly acquired reading skills to teach other family members how to read. Benefits of this type are unlikely to be listed as program evaluation objectives. Nevertheless, they are valid measures of program impact.

The State of the Art in Program Evaluation

For a variety of reasons, reading and study strategies programs are more frequently called on to evaluate their efforts than are most other academic units on a college or university campus. In spite of the current emphasis on accountability, the sociology department is seldom asked to prove that students know more about sociology after completing introductory courses than they did beforehand. On the other hand, this type of request accompanies practically all efforts to improve the basic skills of underprepared college students. In terms of quantity of evaluation, college reading and study strategy programs probably rank near the top among postsecondary programs.

Nevertheless, this quantity is still not particularly high. In their national study of developmental education programs, Boylan et al. (1997) found that only 14% of 2-year programs and 25% of 4-year programs engaged in ongoing, systematic evaluation activity. It should be noted that ongoing and systematic evaluation as defined in this study included only those evaluation activities that took place on an annual basis and that were used for the purposes of program improvement as well as program accountability. It is reasonable to assume that college reading and study strategies programs are not superior to developmental programs generally in this regard. They are evaluated more frequently than other types of programs but the frequency of this evaluation activity is still not impressive.

It should also be noted that the quality of these evaluation efforts often leaves much to be desired. Control groups are seldom used in assessing the relative merits of program activities. Too much emphasis is placed on either quantitative data or qualitative data without an appropriate mix of each. Programs either report gain scores and retention rates without asking students their opinion of the program or they rely on student testimonials without reporting sufficient data on student performance. Where statistical treatment of data takes place, it is often inappropriate—either too sophisticated for the issues being considered or not sophisticated enough to generate valid conclusions. Frequently, evaluation reports are prepared without the benefit of adequate data collection systems. Consequently, the results are either fragmentary of meaningless. In their meta analysis of remedial programs for high-risk college students, Kulik, Kulik, and Shwalb (1983) had to discard the results of 444 out of 504 program evaluation reports because they suffered from "serious methodological flaws."

O'Hear and MacDonald (1995) reviewed the quality of evaluation in developmental education, including reading and study strategies programs. Based on a review of professional journals, ERIC, and conference presentations, they concluded that most of the research and evaluation activity that appeared either in print or in conference presentations was "quantitative and most of those quantitative studies are seriously flawed" (p. 2). This emphasis on quantitative evaluation is consistent with the authors' own experience in reviewing the evaluation literature in college reading and study strategies programs.

In addition, many college reading programs attempt summative evaluation at inappropriate points without enough formative data to inform the evaluation. Often these programs are called on to provide annual reports for institutional, state, or federal administrators. Their reports summarize what the program is doing and assess the program's activities as if all of them were fully developed. Program staff and institutional administrators alike treat these reports as summative evaluations.

This misguided approach can produce seriously flawed results. A newly acquired computer-assisted reading package is evaluated in the same way and against the same criteria as a set of reading textbooks that have been used successfully for 10 years. A newly implemented learning laboratory is assessed in the same manner and using the same standards as reading classes that have been in operation for 20 years. As a results, many promising innovations are judged as failures because they have been subjected to summative evaluation standards before they have been fully implemented. A word of caution is in order. As a general rule, one should never conduct a summative evaluation until a program has been properly implemented.

In essence, then, the state of the art in college reading and study strategy program evaluation is generally poor. Although a great deal of evaluation activity takes place in these programs, much of it is done poorly, much of it is unsystematic, and much of it yields inaccurate or misleading results. Furthermore, evaluations often take place at the wrong time for the wrong reasons and ask the wrong questions. As a result, judgments regarding the effectiveness of college reading and study strategy programs are often inaccurate.

There is much room for improvement in the quality of evaluation in these programs. Nevertheless, the personnel involved in college reading and study skills programs are to be commended for being among the first in academia to take evaluation seriously.

They are also to be commended for having increased the amount of their evaluation activity in recent years. In conducting the literature review for this chapter, it was apparent that the number of published evaluation reports describing college reading and study strategies programs had increased substantially since the original version of this chapter was published in 1991 (Boylan, George, & Bonham, 1991). The early experiences and pioneering efforts of college reading programs in this area will serve them well in the future as evaluation becomes an increasingly critical component of all postsecondary evaluation ventures.

FUTURE ISSUES IN THE EVALUATION OF COLLEGE READING PROGRAMS

During the remainder of this century, college reading and study strategy programs must come to grips with a number of issues relating to program evaluation. Some of the more important of these issues are discussed here.

Focus on Purpose

College reading and study strategies programs have a variety of origins. Some stemmed from attempts by counseling centers to help students who were doing poorly in school. Some grew out of efforts to facilitate the adjustment of military veterans returning to campus. Some began as a component of college learning assistance centers. Some originated as content area courses—either independent courses or segments of basic skills or remedial and developmental courses. Regardless of their origins, however, many of these programs stated their goals in "broad and rather vague terms" making it unlikely that an evaluation plan [could] be implemented consistent with these goals" (Rossi & Freeman, 1985, p. 65).

In many cases, programs were established in response to some local condition such as an increase of nontraditional students in the campus population or a shortfall in enrollment leading to a desire for greater student retention. Frequently, these local conditions have changed but the content and processes of the reading and study strategy program have remained the same. In many cases, little thought has been given to program purpose since the program was originally established.

As higher education changes, it is reasonable to expect that college reading and study strategy programs also will change. In the coming years, it will become increasingly important for these programs to focus on their purposes. Program coordinators and staff need to rethink what their programs are supposed to accomplish, how they plan to do it, and how they assess whether they are successful.

This rethinking undoubtedly will result in new roles, new goals, and new objectives for these programs. Evaluation designs must reflect these changes. An evaluation designed to assess gain scores from pretest to posttest, for instance, is perfectly appropriate if the goal of the program is to improve students' reading rates. If the goal of the program changes to enhancing retention, however, such a design is no longer appropriate. A major issue for personnel in college reading and study strategy programs will be to reconsider their focus and perhaps to redesign their activities. A refocus and redesign will have a substantial impact on the nature of evaluation activities, the type of data collected, and the analysis techniques used in these programs.

Focus on Integration

College reading and study strategy programs often function independently rather than as part of a larger effort to assist underprepared students. For instance, a great many college reading and study strategy programs were designed exclusively to teach reading skills independently of other activities and courses. As Thomas and Moorman (1983) noted, "The most striking characteristic of most programs is the isolation of reading from the rest of the curriculum" (p. 15). More than 10 years later, Boylan et al. (1996) found that reading and study strategies programs in Texas were still isolated from the academic mainstream at most institutions. As a result, the activities of these programs often were not well integrated into the total structure of campus academic support activities.

As pressures for college and university accountability mount, college reading and study strategy programs will be asked to document not only what they do but also how their activities contribute to overall campus efforts to assist students. If the efforts of these programs take place in a vacuum, their contributions will be extremely hard to document. It will become increasingly important, therefore, for such programs to be integrated with other campus activities designed to assist underprepared students. These programs must be conceived of and operated as one component of a larger effort rather than as independent units.

The personnel of reading and study strategy programs must interact with their colleagues more often, participate in joint planning efforts on a more regular basis, and conceive of their efforts from a more global perspective. When this is done, the nature of evaluation activity may change. The direction of this change—from assessment of a single activity to assessment of the activity as part of a series—will have a significant impact on evaluation designs. Such designs will, of necessity, explore more variables, investigate more interactions, and pool larger amounts of data to determine a total picture of the forces that affect student performance (see Johnson & Carpenter, chap. 12, this volume, for more information concerning college reading program organization).

Focus on Long-Term Outcomes

As Robinson (1950) pointed out more than 40 years ago, "Academic performance is clearly the sine qua non for the validation of remedial courses. In the final analysis remedial instruction must necessarily stand or fall on the basis of this single criterion" (p. 83). In recent years, the definition of student performance has expanded from performance measured at a given time to performance measured over a period of time (Levitz, 1986).

In spite of this change, most college reading and study strategy programs are evaluated according to short-term performance criteria such as gain scores or GPAs for a given semester. If student performance is the major evaluation criterion for these programs, performance must be measured over time rather than at a single point in time. Thus, long-term and longitudinal evaluation must be undertaken to assess the impact of programs.

Such longitudinal evaluation should involve tracing student performance over several semesters—preferably through graduation. Particular attention should be paid to student performance in the semester immediately following participation in a reading and study strategy program. Attempts should be made to determine not only whether participation in such programs has some immediate impact but also whether the skills learned in these programs are transferred to other courses.

Focus on the Affective Dimension

Previous researches (Bliss & Mueller, 1987; Haburton, 1977; Mouly, 1952) noted the lack of correlation between what students know about study skills and how they actually study. As Maxwell (1997) noted if students are instructed to respond to study skills inventories as if they were excellent students, their responses will indicate a fairly sophisticated knowledge of good study habits. This suggests that the affective dimension of reading and study habits is at least as important as the cognitive dimension. The key is not only to teach students how to study but also to get them to put to use what they learn.

An effective program, therefore, must be concerned not only with teaching reading and study strategies but also with developing the attitudes, beliefs, and values that shape how students use those skills. Although some efforts to accomplish this goal already have been made (Brozo & Curtis, 1987; Butkowski & Willow, 1980), more research in this area is needed. As the results of this research become available, the current focus on measuring and evaluating cognitive skills may be replaced by a focus on measuring a combination of cognitive skills and affective development.

Focus on Component Analysis and Ethnographic Evaluation

For much of the past 30 years, evaluation reports have dealt with the issues of whether a program works to improve reading or study skills, to what degree it works, and the extent to which its outcomes benefit students. In the next several years, attention will be given to the question, "what works for whom?" As Cross (1976) pointed out, we move from a concept of education for all to one of "education for each" (p. 129).

In order to discover what works for whom, we will have to explore a number of issues more fully and use our existing knowledge more effectively. Areas that need this type of work include the specific characteristics of students and the extent to which these characteristics influence learning, the degree to which demographic factors may influence the effectiveness of certain kinds of instructional programs, and the components of such factors as motivation and aptitude.

The acquisition and use of this information requires the analysis of individual program components and treatments as well as expanded use of ethnographic evaluation techniques. Also, more advanced statistical treatments such as factor and regression analysis are required in program evaluation. This change may result in a shift of program works to improving our understanding of the basic processes that make it work. We know that reading and study skills programs tend to work. In the future, we may place more emphasis on discovering why they work, and who they work for, as part of the overall evaluation process.

Focus on Eclectic Evaluation Methodologies

As this analysis makes clear, there is no best method of evaluating college reading and study strategy programs. Evaluators employ a wide range of methods in assessing such programs, and there is little agreement among experts as to which designs have the most promise. Furthermore, college reading and study strategy programs (like all programs concerned with human learning) involve extremely complex sets of personal, contextual, content, and process variables. No single evaluation design can explore all these variables and find definitive answers.

It appears that the most promising designs incorporate a combination of several research methods. At present, selection of evaluation methods for reading and study strategy programs is generally random. Often the choice is based on which method a particular program administrator happens to know about or which one a particular consultant recommends. Evaluation activities of the future will likely be far more systematic as well as far more eclectic than those in use today.

As our understanding of evaluation grows, designs will become tools of the evaluation process as opposed to structures for that process. No standard design will exist for the evaluation of college reading and study strategy programs of the future. Instead, there will be a series of choices to be made about the purposes, intent, goals, and objectives of a program or course in the planning of evaluation activities.

Evaluation practitioners have to become more familiar with the many design tools available to them or be able to select the most appropriate ones for their purposes. This eclectic approach to evaluation enables individual programs to explore issues specific to their particular needs, contexts, and circumstances.

Focus on Diversity

It is only necessary to read the popular press or glance through the pages of the *Chronicle of Higher Education* or *Education Weekly* to recognize that the population of the United States has become increasingly diverse. The students served through college reading and study strategies programs reflect this diversity.

Those involved with college reading and study strategies programs are not only serving students of increasingly diverse ethnicity, they are also serving students from increasingly diverse socioeconomic and cultural backgrounds. There are not only more African American, Latino, Native-American, and Asian students attending college, there are also more European immigrants, more students with physical or psychological impairments, and more students from disadvantaged social and economic backgrounds (Richardson & Skinner, 1991).

The presence of these students on our campuses requires that we rethink the models, methods, and techniques traditionally used to teach college reading and study strategies. Anderson (1996) for instance, suggested that traditional teaching techniques may be more or less appropriate for different groups of nontraditional students. Nora and Cabrera (1996) suggested that minority students' perceptions of the classroom environment may have a positive or negative impact on their academic performance. Richardson and Skinner (1991) pointed out that efforts to improve instructional environments for diverse students require a comprehensive and systematic rethinking of instructional goals, processes, and techniques. Random or episodic interventions are rarely sufficient to achieve quality while retaining diversity.

Faculty and staff of college reading and study strategies programs cannot, by themselves, improve the retention of diverse students. They can only improve the instructional environments over which they have direct control. In the future, however, they will be called on more frequently to demonstrate that they have done this. They will also be called on to participate in campuswide efforts to create environments conducive to the success of increasingly diverse student populations.

Based on findings from the National Study of Developmental Education (Boylan, Saxon, White, & Erwin, 1994) and the dissertation research of White (1997), the National Center for Developmental Education generated an overview of 12 recommendations for improving the performance of minorities (specifically African Americans and Latinos) in developmental education. This study was funded by the Alfred P. Sloan Foundation and based on findings from the review of the literature suggested ways in which developmental educators can contribute to the retention of minorities. Areas pertinent to college reading and study strategies programs are (a) commitment from administration, (b) resource allocation, (c) institutional climate (e.g., positive environment), (d) student support services (e.g., special programs, personal support and other services), (e) financial assistance and management, (f) faculty involvement, (g) diversity in staffing, and (h) diversity in programming. (Also see Pintozzi and Valeri-Gold, chap. 10, this volume, for a discussion regarding teaching language and diverse students.)

Focus on Accountability

As Astin (1991) pointed out, accountability has become a key word for the 1990s. State legislators are demanding that college programs show results for the resources assigned to them. College administrators are demanding that programs show results in order to lay claim to scarce institutional resources. Students are becoming consumer-oriented in their education and want to know what benefits they will attain through participation in a particular course or program. As Upcraft and Shuh (1996) pointed out, "the public is gaining the impression that higher education is not producing what it promises: educated persons prepared for the world of work. Thus, accountability becomes an issue" (p. 6). At the same time, according to Upcraft and Schuh (1996), the public is expressing increased dissatisfaction with the rising costs of higher education. Consequently, the public impression exists that attending a college or university has gotten more expensive while its benefits have declined.

All of these factors contribute to an increased emphasis on accountability for results accrued as a result of dollars invested. In this environment, those involved in college reading and study strategies programs must realize that their programs will be judged not only in terms of how well their services are delivered but also on the outcomes of these services. If they cannot measure the outcomes in ways that are clearly understood by legislators, parents, administrators, and students, they will not fare well in competition for scarce resources. Neither will they instill confidence in the students who participate in these programs or the administrators who oversee them.

Furthermore, the demonstration of accountability should not be perceived as an additional burden that has been inflicted on college reading and study strategies professionals by external political forces. Although pressures for accountability may, indeed, have originated from political considerations, holding oneself and others accountable for quality professional practice has traditionally been one of the obligations and hallmarks of a professional. If the faculty and staff of college reading and study strategies programs wish to be seen as professionals, they must exercise their professional responsibility for demonstrating accountability.

Conclusion

It is apparent that the evaluation of college reading and study strategy programs is an extremely complex enterprise. It is a field with few standard models and little agreement on what variables, techniques, or questions should take precedence. In addition, evaluation is not an area in which many reading specialists are well trained. Program evaluation is becoming a profession in and of itself. It is no longer a task that anyone with graduate training can do. The available evaluation methods have become too diverse, the application of these methods too specific, the statistical methods for analyzing data too complicated, and the planning and implementation decisions involved too numerous.

As pressure for program evaluation continues to expand, as the need for understanding basic processes becomes more apparent, and as the population of U.S. colleges and universities becomes more diverse, reading professionals face several new challenges. They need to improve their own knowledge of the research and evaluation literature. They need to place more emphasis on investigating what they do, analyzing and reporting what they find, and sharing their results with others. They need to establish links with colleagues in other related areas—particularly those in graduate schools of education and university research centers—to ensure that basic research on the evaluation of college reading programs continues and the results are disseminated.

As Christ (1985) pointed out, "any activity worth doing should be evaluated" (p. 3). If we truly value what we do, we should want to know how well we do it. We should take an interest in the impact of what we do. We should be able to describe and measure what we do. We should be able to explore what works and why. In essence, we should exercise the responsibilities of professionals to enhance our professional body of knowledge through evaluation.

These are the challenges presented by program evaluation. They are challenges that can only enhance the professionalization of those who work in college reading and study strategy programs.

REFERENCES AND SUGGESTED READINGS

Akst, J., & Hecht, M. (1980). Program evaluation. In A. S. Trillin & Association, *Teaching basic skills in college* (pp. 261–296). San Francisco, CA: Jossey-Bass.

*American Association for Education. (1992). *Principles of good practice for assessing student learning.* Washington, DC: AAHE.

Anderson, J. (1996, October). *Retention strategies for diverse populations.* Address at the second National Conference on Research in Developmental Education, Charlotte, NC.

Anderson, S., & Ball, D. (1978). *The profession and practice of program evaluation*. San Francisco, CA: Jossey-Bass.

*Astin, A. W. (1991). *Assessment for excellence*. New York: American Council on Education/ Macmillan.

Astin, A. W. (1993). *What matters in college: Four critical years revisited*. San Francisco, CA: Jossey-Bass.

*Banta, T. W., Lund, J., Black, K. E., & Oblander, F. W. (1996). *Assessment in practice: Putting principles to work on college campuses*. San Francisco, CA: Jossey-Bass.

Baker, I., & Mulcahy-Ernt, P. (1993). The case for expressive writing for developmental college readers. In D. Leu & C. Kinzer (Eds.), *Examining central issues in literacy research, theory, and practice* (pp. 55–65). Chicago, IL: National Reading Conference.

Behrens, H. (1935). Effects of a "how to study" course. *Journal of Higher Education, 6*, 195–202.

Bliss, L., & Mueller, R. (1987). Assessing study behaviors of college students: Findings from a new instrument. *Journal of Developmental Education, 11*(2), 14–19.

Borich, G. (Ed.). (1974). *An investigation of selected intellective and nonintellective factors as predictors of academic success for educationally-economically disadvantaged college freshmen*. Unpublished manuscript, Mississippi State University, Starkville.

Boylan, H. (1997a). *Cost effectiveness/cost benefit analysis in developmental education*. Presented at the 1997 Kellogg Institute for the Training and Certification of Developmental Educators, July 22, Boone, NC.

Boylan, H. (1997b). Criteria for program evaluation. *Research in Developmental Education, 14*(1), 1–4.

Boylan, H. R., Bliss, L., & Bonham, B. S. (1997). The relationship between program components and student success. *Journal of Developmental Education, 20*(2), 2–9.

Boylan, H., Bonham, B., Abraham, A., Allen, R., Anderson, J., Morante, E., Ramirez, G., Vadillo, M., & Bliss, L. (1996). *An evaluation of the Texas Academic Skills Program*. Austin: Texas Higher Education Coordinating Board.

Boylan, H. R., George, A. P., & Bonham, B. S. (1991). Program evaluation. In R. F. Flippo & D. C. Caverly (Eds.), *College reading & study strategy programs* (pp. 70–117). Newark, DE: International Reading Association.

Boylan, H. R., Saxon, D. P., White, J. R., & Erwin, A. (1994). Retaining minority students through developmental education. *Research in Developmental Education, 11*(3), 1–4.

Breneman, D. (1998). Remediation in higher education: Its extent and costs. D. Ravitch (Ed.), *Brookings papers on educational policy* (pp. 359–383). Washington, DC: Brookings Institute.

Brozo, W., & Curtis, C. (1987). Coping strategies of four successful learning disabled college students: A case study approach. In J. Readance & R. Baldwin (Eds.), *Thirty-Sixth Yearbook of the National Reading Conference* (pp. 237–246). Rochester, NY: National Reading Conference.

Butkowski, I., & Willow, D. (1980). Cognitive-motivational characteristics of children varying in reading ability: Evidence of learned helplessness in poor readers. *Journal of Educational Psychology, 72*, 408–422.

Campbell, D., & Stanley, J. (1966). *Experimental and quasiexperimental designs for research*. Chicago, IL: Rand McNally.

*Casazza, M., & Silverman, S. (1996). *Learning assistance and developmental education.* San Francisco, CA: Jossey-Bass.

Chase, N., Gibson, S., & Carson, J. (1994). An examination of reading demands across four college courses. *Journal of Developmental Education, 18*(1), 10–16.

Christ, F. (1985, August). *Managing learning assistance programs.* Symposium conducted at the Kellogg Institute for the Training and Certification of Developmental Educators, Boone, NC.

Clowes, D. (1981). Evaluation methodologies for learning assistance programs. In C. Walvekar (Ed.), *New directions for college learning assistance, Vol. 5, Assessment of learning assistance services* (pp. 17–32). San Francisco, CA: Jossey-Bass.

Clowes, D. (1983). The evaluation of remedial/developmental programs: A stage model for evaluation. *Journal of Developmental Education, 8*(1), 14–30.

Cook, T., & Campbell, D. (1979). *Quasiexperimentation: Design analysis for field settings.* Chicago, IL: Rand McNally.

Cousins, B., & Leithwood, K. (1986). Current empirical research on evaluation utilization. *Review of Educational Research, 56,* 331–364.

Cronbach, J. (1983). *Designing evaluations of educational and social programs.* San Francisco, CA: Jossey-Bass.

Cross, K. P. (1976). *Accent on learning.* San Francisco, CA: Jossey-Bass.

Crowl, T. (1996). *Fundamentals of educational research.* Dubuque, IA: Brown & Benchmark.

Dressel, P. (1976). *Handbook of academic evaluation.* San Francisco, CA: Jossey-Bass.

Ely, M., Anzul, M., Friedman, T., Garner, D., & Steinmetz, A. (1991). *Doing qualitative research: Circles within circles.* London: The Falmer Press.

Freeley, J., Wepner, S., & Wehrle, P. (1987). The effects of background information on college students' performance on a state developed reading competency test. *Journal of Developmental Education, 11*(2), 2–5.

Guthrie, J. (1984). A program evaluation typology. *The Reading Teacher, 37*(8), 790–792.

Haburton, E. (1977). Impact of an experimental reading-study skills course on high risk student success in a community college. In P. D. Pearson (Ed.), *Twenty-sixth yearbook of the National reading conference* (pp. 110–117). Clemson, SC: National Reading Conference.

Haller, E. (1974). Cost analysis for program evaluation. In W. J. Popham (Ed.), *Evaluation in education* (pp. 3–19). Berkeley, CA: McCutchan.

Keimig, R. (1984). *Raising academic standards: A guide to learning improvement* (Report No. 3). Washington, DC: American Association for Higher Education.

Kulik, J., Kulik, C., & Schwalb, B. (1983). College programs for high-risk and disadvantaged students: A meta-analysis of findings. *Review of Educational Research, 53,* 397–414.

Land, F. (1976). Economic analysis of information systems. In F. Land (Ed.), *We can implement cost-effective systems now* (pp. 2–17). Princeton, NJ: Education Communications.

Ley, K., Hodges, R., & Young, D. (1995). Partner testing. *Research & Teaching in Developmental Education, 12*(1), 23–30.

*Levin, H. (1991). Cost-effectiveness at quarter century. In D. Milbrey & D. Phillips (Eds.), *Evaluation and education at quarter century* (pp. 190–209). Chicago: University of Chicago Press.

Levin, M., Glass, G., & Meister, G. (1987). Cost-effectiveness of computer-assisted instruction. *Evaluation Review, 2,* 50–72.

Levitz, R. (1986, March). *What works in student retention.* Keynote address presented at the annual conference of the National Association for Developmental Education, New Orleans.

MacMillan, J. (1996). *Educational research: Fundamentals for the consumer.* New York: HarperCollins.

Maring, G. H., Shea, M. A., & Warner, D. A. (1987). Assessing the effects of college reading and study skills programs: A basic evaluation model. *Journal of Reading, 30,* 402–408.

*Maxwell, M. (1997). *Improving student learning skills.* Clearwater, FL: H & H. Publishing Company.

McConkey, D. (1975). *MBO for nonprofit organizations.* New York: American Management Associates.

Moore, R. (1981). The role and scope of evaluation. In C. Walvekar (Ed.), *New directions for college learning assistance, Vol. 5: Assessment of learning assistance services* (pp. 33–50). San Francisco, CA: Jossey-Bass.

Mouly, C. (1952). A study of the effects of remedial reading on academic grades at the college level. *Journal of Educational Psychology, 43,* 459–466.

Myers, C., & Majer, K. (1981). Using research designs to evaluate learning assistance programs. In C. Walvekar (Ed.), *New directions for college learning assistance, Vol. 5: Assessment of learning assistance services* (pp. 65–74). San Francisco, CA: Jossey-Bass.

Nora, A., & Cabrera, A. (1996). The role of perceptions of prejudice and discrimination and the adjustment of minority students to college. *Journal of Higher Education, 67*(2), 119–148.

O'Hear, M., & MacDonald, R. (1995). A critical review of research in developmental education: Part 1. *Journal of Developmental Education, 19*(2), 2–6.

*Patton, M. (1990). *Qualitative evaluation and research methods.* Newbury Park, CA: Sage.

*Pasquarella, E., & Terenzini, P. (1992). *How college affects students: Findings and insights from 20 years of research.* San Francisco, CA: Jossey-Bass.

Payne, E. (1995). High risk students' study plans. *Research and Teaching in Developmental Education, 11*(2), 5–12.

Pitman, M., & Maxwell, J. (1992). Qualitative approaches to evaluation: Models and methods. In M. Lecompte, W. Millroy, & J. Preisle (Eds.), *The handbook of qualitative research in education* (pp. 729–770). San Diego, CA: Academic Press.

Popham, W. J. (1988). *Educational evaluation.* Englewood Cliffs, NJ: Prentice-Hall.

Provus, M. (1971). *Discrepancy evaluation for educational program improvement and assessment.* Berkeley, CA: McCutchan.

Richardson, R., & Skinner, E. (1991). *Achieving quality and diversity: Universities in a multicultural society.* New York: MacMillan.

Robinson, F. (1950). A note on the evaluation of college remedial reading courses. *Journal of Educational Psychology, 41*, 83–96.

Rossi, P., & Freeman, H. (1985). *Evaluation: A systematic approach.* Beverly Hills, CA: Sage.

Roueche, J., & Snow, J. (1977). *Overcoming learning problems.* San Francisco, CA: Jossey-Bass.

Scriven, M. (1993). *Hard-won lessons in program evaluation.* San Francisco, CA: Jossey-Bass.

Shadish, W., Cook, T., & Leviton, L. (1991). *Foundations of program evaluation.* Newbury Park, CA: Sage.

Silverman, S. (1983). Qualitative research in the evaluation of developmental education. *Journal of Developmental and Remedial Education, 6*(3), 16–19.

Simpson, M., & Nist, S. (1990). Textbook annotation: An effective and efficient study strategy for college students. *Journal of Reading, 34*(2), 122–129.

Smith, K., & Brown, S. (1981). Staff performance evaluation in learning assistance centers. In C. Walvekar (Ed.), *New directions in college learning assistance, Vol. 5: Assessment of learning assistance services* (pp. 95–110). San Francisco, CA: Jossey-Bass.

Spivey, N. (1981). Goal attainment scaling in the college learning center. *Journal of Developmental and Remedial Education, 4*(2), 11–13.

Stake, R. (1967). The countenance of educational evaluation. *Teachers College Record, 68*, 523–540.

Straus, A., & Corbin, J. (1980). *Basics of qualitative research.* Newbury Park, CA: Sage.

Stufflebeam, D., Foley, W., Gephard, W., Guba, E., Hammond, R., Merriam, H., & Provus, M. (1971). *Education evaluation and decision making.* Itasca, IL: F.E. Peacock.

Taraban, R. (1997). Using statewide data to assess the effectiveness of developmental reading programs. *Journal of College Reading and Learning, 27*(3), 119–128.

Tesch, R. (1990). *Qualitative research: Analysis type and software tools.* London: Falmer Press.

Thomas, K., & Moorman, G. (1983). *Designing reading programs.* Dubuque, IA: Kendall/Hunt.

Upcraft, M., & Schuh, J. (1996). *Assessment in student affairs.* San Francisco, CA: Jossey-Bass.

Vroom, P., Colombo, M., & Nahan, N. (1994). Confronting ideology and self-interest: Avoiding misuse of evaluation. In C. Stevens & M. Dial (Eds.), *Preventing the misuse of evaluation,* (pp. 23–31). San Francisco, CA: Jossey-Bass.

Walvekar, C. (1981). Educating learning: The buck stops here. In C. Walvekar (Ed.), *New directions in college learning assistance, Vol. 5: Assessment of learning assistance services* (pp. 75–94). San Francisco, CA: Jossey-Bass.

White, J. R. (1997). *A comparative analysis of the performance of underprepared African-American students and graduation/retention rates at two-year colleges.* Doctoral dissertation, Ann Arbor, MI: University Microfilms.

14

Reading Tests

⇜❧❧⇝

Rona F. Flippo
Fitchburg State College

Jeanne Shay Schumm
University of Miami

Due to the rapid growth of college reading assistance programs throughout the United States, assessing the reading abilities and reading needs of entering college students has become a fairly standard practice. As many as 30% of students in 2-year institutions and 18% of students in 4-year institutions are in need of remediation in reading (Boylan, Bonham, Bliss, & Claxton, 1992). Despite critics from government, academia, and the general public who maintain that remedial reading courses at the college level are expensive and indicative of lower academic standards (e.g., Williams, 1998), most public and many private institutions of higher education continue to provide academic support for underprepared students. Indeed, 99% of 2-year public, 52% of 4-year public, and 34% of 4-year private institutions offer at least one remedial reading course (U.S. Department of Education, 1995).

Reading tests are the most common type of assessment instrument used to determine who needs such programs. Many postsecondary institutions, even those with open admissions policies, require incoming students to take tests as part of the admissions process. Reading tests are often among the exams administered. The extent to which reading tests are used varies from institution to institution and from state to state; some states require all students entering postsecondary schools within the state system of higher education to take reading tests (Abraham, 1987; Ross & Roe, 1986; Wood, 1988).

Although we believe that reading tests are and should be only a part of reading assessment, their widespread use (and often misuse) warrants exclusive attention. This chapter focuses on the use, selection, and limitations of reading tests for various assessment purposes. (Readers seeking information on program evaluations should see Boylan, Bonham, Winter, & George, chap. 13, this volume.)

The prevalence of reading tests in postsecondary institutions is not solely attributable to their use as assessment instruments. Reading tests are popular largely because they provide data for the institution's academic profile of its students and thus provide a standard against which stability or change in the student body can be measured. In this way, reading tests can influence high-level administrative decisions. They are given serious consideration in determining the staffing and programmatic needs for academic assistance and other retention initiatives, which, in turn, influence decisions about institutional budgeting and enrollment management.

In addition, reading tests have been found to have a predictive value similar to that of such robust measures as the Scholastic Aptitude Test (SAT) and the American College Test (ACT). Consequently, they hold significant standing alongside these more traditional admissions criteria (Carney & Geis, 1981; Malak & Hageman, 1985; Noble, 1986). Having found their way into the decision-making process—as part of the institution's academic profile and as a possible predictor of academic success—reading tests, for good or bad, are here to stay.

Reading tests are certainly not free of problems, however. Practitioners are cautioned about the pitfalls of misusing these tests, particularly when the tests are designed to serve as a basis for evaluating student progress or program effectiveness. Research studies on college populations, particularly programmatic and instructional research studies, traditionally use reading tests as dependent variables, and their findings should be evaluated with caution.

Ideally, college reading tests should asses readers' ability to deal with the academic demands of college-level coursework—in other words, the ability to derive, synthesize, and sustain meaning from lengthy texts that vary in content, vocabulary, style, complexity, and cognitive requirements (Smith & Jackson, 1985). The long-standing concern associated with most reading tests is that they may not adequately reflect the actual reading demands of academic coursework (Valencia, Hiebert, & Afflerbach, 1994). Consequently, their use as the definitive tool for assessing reading performance among college populations and for designing and evaluating programs to address performance deficiencies has been questioned (Wood, 1988). This chapter delineates several critical issues related to the shortcomings of conventional reading tests. Our purpose in raising these issues is to engage college reading practitioners and administrators in the kind of deliberation that is needed to make informed decisions about test selection. We examine test specifications, technical and structural considerations, and the types and purposes of many available tests to help practitioners make optimum use of these resources. An appendix of selected commercial tests with test specifications appears at the end of this chapter to guide practitioners in selecting appropriate tests.

ORIGINS OF COLLEGE READING TESTS

The need to evaluate students' reading abilities is not a new phenomenon. In the early 1900s, there was a sweeping movement in the United States to develop measures for sorting students into ability tracks for college admission and for promotion purposes.

Readence and Moore (1983) traced the history of standardized reading comprehension tests, noting that reading tests grew out of a movement to assess skill levels. The original reading tests followed one of three formats: asking students to solve written puzzles, reproduce a passage, or answer questions. Burgess (1921), Kelly (1916), and Monroe (1918) developed tests comprised of written puzzles. These puzzles demanded reasoning skills and painstaking adherence to specific directions. Starch (1915) developed a reading test that required students to read a passage for 30 seconds and then write everything they could remember. Students were allowed all the time that they needed for this exercise. The scorer did not count any words they wrote that were not related to the text (either incorrect or new information). A test developed by Gray (1919) required students to read a passage and then write or retell its content. He eventually added questions to the test.

Thorndike (1914), a major proponent of having students answer questions, saw the need for more objective and convenient measures of students' abilities. To that end, he developed the Scale Alpha for students in Grades 3 through 8. The test consisted of a series of short paragraphs with questions of increasing difficulty. The question—answer format appeared reasonable on several counts:

- Answers could be scored quickly and objectively.
- Questions could tap information at various levels.
- Questioning was a common school activity.
- Questioning was adaptable to the multiple-choice format that became popular during the 1930s.

Questioning continued to gain popularity because it seemed to offer educators the most convenient, economical, and objective format for assessing comprehension. By the 1930s, it was the predominant means for making such assessment.

Researchers in the 1930s had already investigated the shortcomings of tests and the testing process in general (Bloom, Douglas, & Rudd, 1931; Eurich, 1930; Robinson & McCollom, 1934; Seashore, Stockford, & Swartz, 1937; Shank, 1930; Tinker, 1932). By the 1940s researchers were questioning reading tests—specifically the validity of these tests (Bloomers & Lindquist, 1944; Langsam, 1941; Robinson & Hall, 1941; Tinker, 1945).

These concerns have not abated. Kingston (1955) cited the weaknesses of standardized reading assessments noted in early studies. Triggs (1952) stated that assessment of reading ability is limited by the "scarcity of reliable and valid instruments on which to base judgments" (p. 15). Farr and Carey (1986) charged that neither reading tests nor the ways in which they were used had changed significantly in the past 50 years, although advances were being made in the areas of validity and reliability measurement. Since that time, publishers of standardized tests have responded to many criticisms discussed in the literature and the use of alternative assessment techniques has become more widespread. Yet despite initiatives to reform assessment procedures, norm-referenced and criterion-referenced tests are still the primary tools of choice for most developmental reading programs. As Ryan and Miyasaka (1995) explained, "reports about the demise of traditional approaches to assessment are premature" (p. 9).

SELECTING THE APPROPRIATE TEST

To choose the best test for a given circumstance, college reading and study skills instructors must be aware of the different types of tests that are available. Several choices exist, including survey versus diagnostic tests, formal versus informal tests, instructor-made versus commercial tests, and group versus individual tests. Once they know what their options are, instructors can assess their purposes and the skills they want to test in order to select the most appropriate mix of instruments.

Types of College Reading Tests

Survey and Diagnostic Tests.   College reading tests are generally broken down into two broad categories: the *survey test* (or *screening instrument*), which is meant to provide information about students' general level of reading ability, and the *diagnostic test*, which is meant to provide more in-depth information about students' specific reading strengths and weaknesses (Kingston, 1955). Both types of tests have a place in the college reading program.

Since the advent of open-door admissions in the 1960s, colleges have been accepting a greater number of students with a wider range of reading abilities than ever before. A screening instrument allows colleges to provide reading assistance services early on to those who need them. Despite the fact that without further probing screening instruments provide little more than a general idea of reading ability or achievement, they do provide a fast way of broadly screening students to see if they need the assistance of the college reading specialist.

Once students have been identified as needing reading or learning skills assistance, in-depth diagnosis is needed to determine the proper course of instruction (Flippo, 1980a, 1980c). Thus, valid diagnostic measures of reading abilities are important. Of course, even with the best available tests, the results will not yield all the answers. The information gleaned from these tests must be analyzed and interpreted by a knowledgeable reading specialist and combined with other student evaluation data.

Formal and Informal Tests.   Within the two broad categories of reading tests, survey and diagnostic, many different types of tests exist. One way of classifying tests is as *formal* or *informal*. Formal tests are usually standardized instruments with norms that provide the examiner with a means of comparing the students tested with a norm group representative of students' particular level of education and other related factors. This comparison, of course, is valid only to the extent to which the characteristics of the students being tested resemble those of the norm group.

Informal tests, which are usually teacher-made, do not provide an outside norm group with which to compare students. These informal tests are usually criterion referenced—that is, the test maker has defined a certain passing score or level of acceptability against which individual students' responses are measured. Students' scores are compared to the criterion (rather than to the scores of an outside norm group of students). Again, the results are valid only to the extent to which the criteria reflect the reading skills and strategies students actually need to accomplish their own or their instructors' goals.

Instructor-Made and Commercial Tests. Another way of classifying tests already alluded to, is as *teacher-made* or *commercially prepared* tests. This distinction refers to whether a test has been developed locally by a teacher, department, or college, or whether a publishing or test development company has prepared it.

When appropriate commercially prepared tests are available, colleges usually use one of those rather than going to the expense and trouble of developing their own. After evaluating the available commercial tests, however, colleges (or reading specialists) may decide that none of these materials adequately tests the reading skills and strategies they want to measure. In these cases, a teacher-made or department/college-made test is developed.

Group and Individual Tests. The final way of classifying reading tests is as *group* or *individual* tests. These terms refer to whether the test is designed to be administered to a group of students during a testing session or to one student at a time. Most college reading programs rely primarily on group tests because they are perceived to be more time-efficient given the large number of students to be tested.

Most survey tests are designed and administered as group tests. Diagnostic tests can be designed either for group administration or for individual testing, and most diagnostic tests can be used both ways. Similarly, formal, informal, teacher-made, and commercially prepared tests can all be designed specifically for either group or individual administration, but sometimes can be used both ways.

Matching the Test to the Purpose

As the breakdown of test categories shows, the purpose of testing should determine the type or types of tests selected or developed. Therefore, a key question to ask when the issue of testing arises is "What purpose are we trying to accomplish with this testing?" Although this question may sound trivial at first, the answer is not as simple as it seems. Guthrie and Lissitz (1985) emphasized that educators must be clear about what decisions are to be made from their assessments, and then form an appropriate match with the types of assessments they select.

Three major purposes cited for testing college students' reading ability are to conduct an initial screening, to make a diagnostic assessment, and to evaluate the effectiveness of the instruction resulting from the assessment. The purpose of screening is often twofold: (a) to determine if the student has a reading problem or a need for reading assistance, and (b) to determine placement in the appropriate reading course or in special content courses or sections.

Diagnostic testing examines the various skill areas in greater depth and determines the relative strengths and weakness of the reader in performing these skills. This type of assessment provides an individual performance profile or a descriptive account of the reader's abilities that should facilitate instructional planning based on individual needs.

Evaluation of the instruction's effectiveness has two functions: (a) to assess individual students' progress and determine appropriate changes in teaching or remediation, and (b) to assess or document the overall success of the college reading program and identify needed changes.

If the required function of testing is gross screening to determine whether students need reading assistance, testers should probably select an appropriate instrument from the available commercially prepared standardized group survey test. If the screening is to be used for placement, the college should probably develop instruments to measure students' ability to read actual materials required by the relevant courses. If the purpose of testing is diagnostic assessment, an appropriate instrument should be selected from the commercially prepared group or individual tests, or one should be developed by the instructor or the college. Finally, if the purpose for testing is to evaluate the effectiveness of the instruction or the program, an appropriate instrument may be selected either from among the commercially available tests or tests developed by the instructor or college.

Guthrie and Lissitz (1985) indicated that although formal, standardized reading tests are helpful for placement or classification of students as well as for program accountability purposes, they do not provide the diagnostic information vital to making informed decisions about instruction. Consequently, using such tests "as a basis for instructional decisions raises the hazard of ignoring the causes of successful learning, which is the only basis for enhancing it" (p. 29). On the other hand, they note that although informal assessments such as teacher judgments and observations are helpful to the instructional process, they are not necessarily satisfactory for accountability or classification purposes.

One note of caution: If a college elects to develop its own test, it should do so with the expertise of a testing and measurement specialist. Such tests must undergo rigorous review and field testing by the content and reading faculty involved. Colleges must be prepared to commit the necessary resources to this effort. It is not in the realm of this chapter to describe the process of developing a test; however, given the faults of so many existing commercial tests, colleges wishing to develop their own tests should enlist as much expertise and use as much care as possible.

What Should Be Tested?

In addition to determining the purpose of testing, college reading and study strategy instructors must address a second question before selecting a reading test: "What reading skills and strategies should be tested for this population?" Again, the answer to this question is not as obvious as it may seem. In fact, after years of research and discussion, reading authorities still do not agree on this point (Flippo, 1980b).

The exit criterion for many developmental reading programs is satisfactory performance on a standardized reading test. In such cases, instruction focuses on teaching reading subskills that are included on the exit test. Other developmental reading programs, guided by a constructivist view of reading instruction, focus on teaching of reading strategies, content area reading, and reading–writing connections (Mulcahy-Ernt & Stewart, 1994; Simpson, 1993).

Those who administer and teach in college reading programs must make a decision on the basis of their particular situation. They must define the reading skills, strategies, and theory relevant for student success in their college courses and determine the reading needs of the population they serve before selecting the most appropriate tests for their program (Flippo, 1982b). If an appropriate test is not available, the college should develop its own test rather than use an evaluation instrument that is poorly suited to the program's purposes, theory of reading, and students.

REVIEW OF THE LITERATURE

The literature related to reading tests for college students raises a number of important issues. It is important for college reading instructors to understand these issues and what the literature says about them in order to clarify their assessment needs and the criteria for selecting the most appropriate tests for their programs. Some of the literature reviewed refers to groups other than college reading students. These studies were included because they appear germane to problems and issues involved in the testing and diagnosis of college students' reading.

One very basic but sometimes overlooked question the literature addresses is "What is reading?" Early reading tests were largely atheoretical, with no grounding in a consensus of what was to be measured. This fact, however, did not deter researchers from going about the business of measuring reading, despite the lack of a theoretical basis for defining it.

The major problem identified by researchers reviewing early reading tests was the lack of agreement regarding the nature of the reading process. As Cronbach (1949) stated, "no area illustrates more clearly than reading that tests having the same name measure quite different behaviors" (p. 287).

The assumptions behind standardized tests are threefold: that these tests provide a standardized sample of an individual's behavior; that by observing this sample we are able to make valid inferences about the students; and that appraising certain aspects of reading abilities give us insight to overall reading achievement. However, if we cannot agree on the essential skills involved, we cannot agree on the measurement of reading (Kingston, 1955).

Issues in the Literature

Among the many issues cited in the literature, four specifically affect reading programs for college students. The first is the debate about whether reading is a product or a process. The definition practitioners accept for reading will influence the instruments that they select to evaluate students. The second issue relates to the particular demands of college-level reading. The third issue concerns the specific needs of special populations of college students. Finally, researchers raise the issue of how college reading tests should be norm-referenced.

Product Versus Process.   Since the 1940s, researchers have debated the question of what can be measured in reading. One group suggests that reading is a product. This group includes Gates (1935), who investigated reading testing through the skills approach; Clymer (1968) and Wolf, King, and Huck (1968), who explored the taxonomy approach; Cleland (1965), Kingston (1961), Robinson (1966) and Spache (1962), who studied the models approach; and Farr (1969), who researched the measurement approach.

By far the most product-oriented research has been conducted using factor analysis. Using this model, researchers attempted to isolate the factors that make up reading to determine whether reading is composed of a number of discrete skills that can be measured separately or if it is a more generalized, pervasive skill that cannot be subdivided into bits and pieces.

Factor-analytic researchers identified a variety of subskills they thought could be measured separately (Burkart, 1945; Davis, 1944, 1947, 1968; Hall & Robinson, 1945; Holmes, 1962; Holmes & Singer, 1966; Lennon, 1962; Schreiner, Hieronymous, & Forsyth, 1969; Spearritt, 1972). Although the research has identified from 1 to 80 separate factors that can be measured, agreement is centered somewhere between 2 and 5 factors. Yet researchers cannot agree what these factors are (Berg, 1973).

Another group of researchers using the factor-analytic model concluded that reading cannot be divided into separate subskills that can be neatly measured. Instead, they suggest reading is a global skill (Thurstone, 1946; Traxler, 1941). One of these researchers, Goodman (1969), suggested that reading is a form of information processing that occurs when a reader selects and chooses from available information in an attempt to decode graphic messages.

Early attempts to study reading as a process begin with Huey (1908), followed by the works of Anderson (1937), Buswell (1920), and Swanson (1937). More recent research into reading as a process includes work by Freedle and Carroll (1972), Gibson and Levin (1975), Goodman (1968, 1976), Kintsch (1974), Schank (1972), Smith (1973, 1978), and Winograd (1972).

The influence of research on reading as a process has had a strong influence on college-level reading instruction. Increasingly, an emphasis has been placed on teaching students reading–study strategies rather than discrete, isolated reading subskills (Nist & Diehl, 1994; Schumm & Post, 1997). Indeed, some movement toward measuring reading as a process is evident. Most reading measures continue to be group-administered, multiple-choice, paper-and-pencil tests that (at least at face value) deal primarily with the products of reading. This is due largely to teachers' and administrators' demands for tests that are easy to administer, score, and interpret. Yet a careful reading of technical manuals indicates that many publishers of commercial tests have made attempts to address concerns registered by those who advocate assessment reform and greater attention to reading as a process (e.g., Johnston, 1984; Squire, 1987; Valencia & Pearson, 1987).

Advocates of a more process-oriented approach to reading assessment frequently push for the use of standardized tests as one of many measures (Valeri-Gold, Olson, & Deming, 1991). In an attempt to more accurately and authentically document student progress in reading and to get students more engaged in the assessment process, portfolio assessment has been included in many developmental reading programs (Hasit & DiObilda, 1996; Schumm, Post, Lopate, & Hughes, 1992; Valeri-Gold et al., 1991).

Demands of College-Level Reading.
A second issue raised in the literature relates to the special demands of college-level reading. Two primary demands are the need to read sustained passages of text and the need to relate prior knowledge to text being processed.

Regarding the first of these needs, Perry (1959) warned: "The possession of excellent reading skills as evidenced on conventional reading tests is no guarantee that a student knows how to read long assignments meaningfully" (p. 199). For this reason, Perry developed an instrument that used a college reading assignment to assess the reading and study strategies of students at Harvard University.

Most current reading tests measure only minimal skills such as vocabulary, reading rate, and comprehension without attempting to evaluate long-term memory of material or the comprehension of longer text. Smith and Jackson (1985), echoing Perry, maintained that testing students' ability to handle college-level text requires the use of longer passages taken directly from college textbooks.

Research on the effect of prior knowledge demonstrates that comprehension is heavily influenced by what students already know (Anderson, Reynolds, Schallert, & Goetz, 1977; Carey, Harste, & Smith, 1981; Drabin-Partenio & Maloney, 1982). Simpson (1982) concluded that diagnostic processes for older readers needs to consider both their prior knowledge and their background information; few instruments are available to serve those objectives.

Johnston (1984) cautioned against assuming it is possible to construct a reading comprehension test with scores immune to the influence of prior knowledge. Prior knowledge is an integral part of the reading process; therefore, any test on which prior knowledge did not affect performance would not measure reading comprehension. The alternative is to concede that prior knowledge can be responsible for biasing the information the evaluator gains from reading comprehension tests and to factor that bias into the interpretation of the results.

Special Populations of College Students.

A third concern registered in the literature is the inappropriateness of many reading tests for special populations of college students particularly students with learning disabilities and students from culturally and linguistically diverse backgrounds.

As a consequence of federal legislation, increasing numbers of students with learning disabilities (LD) are attending postsecondary institutions (Mangrum & Strichart, 1988, 1997; Vogel, 1994). Traditional tests may be inappropriate for students with disabilities in that they are frequently not normed for this population. Moreover, time constraints and group administration may put undue pressure on students with learning disabilities (Baldwin et al., 1989).

The United States is among the most culturally and linguistically diverse nations in the world and that diversity is being represented in the postsecondary student population. For decades standardized tests have been criticized for their cultural bias and their inappropriateness for non-English language background students (Fradd & McGee, 1994). Obviously, non-English language background students may have difficulty with the semantic and syntactic demands of test passages. Typically students who are learning English are not included in the norming population for standardized tests. In addition, students from diverse cultural backgrounds may not have had the opportunity or experiences needed to obtain prior knowledge of passage topics or to develop strategies for preparing for and taking standardized tests (García, 1994). Because of these and other issues, the use of standardized tests for making placement or other instructional decisions for non-English language background students has been questioned (Fradd & McGee, 1994).

Norm-Referenced and Criterion-Referenced Tests.

A fourth issue raised in the literature is the question of test norms. Until fairly recently, instructors had no real choice about whether to use a norm-referenced instrument or a criterion-referenced one, as none of the latter was commercially available for the college population. Anderson (1972) reminded instructors that norm-referenced tests are intended to rank students and discriminate maximally among them whereas criterion-referenced tests are intended to determine students' level of skill and knowledge.

Popham (1975) recommended norm-referenced tests as the best measures available for looking at one student in relation to others of similar age and educational level. Maxwell (1981), however, encouraged institutions to develop their own norms based on the performance of students on their own campuses. (Once again, the expertise of a testing and measurement specialist would help in developing local norms.)

Problems Cited in the Literature

In addition to raising the four major issues surrounding reading assessment, the literature cites numerous problems in assessment. One such problem is the lack of expertise of many college reading instructors in the area of testing, which results in the misuse of reading tests and in attempts to match readers' assignments to grade equivalencies. Another problem is the technical deficiencies found in many reading tests used for the college population. A third problem is the lack of available, appropriate tests.

Misuse of Reading Tests.   Perhaps the most critical problem cited in the literature is college reading instructors' lack of expertise in the testing of reading (Flippo, 1980; 1980b). In a survey of 300 college reading instructors, Goodwin (1971) found that 60% used the standardized reading test administered to their junior college students at the beginning of the term as a diagnostic instrument. However, the four tests they most often reported using were, in fact, survey tests. Only 27% of the instructors correctly reported that their tests measured reading achievement rather than diagnosing specific skills needs.

Ironside (1969) noted that although survey tests can be appropriately used for prediction, screening, and comparison, they are inappropriate for assessing achievement or performance. Support of Ironside's theory is found in studies by Anderson (1973), Brensing (1974), Feuers (1969), Florio (1975), Freer (1965), Rice (1971), Schoenberg (1969), Taschow (1968), and Wright (1973).

On the other hand, some studies and program descriptions have reported success in using survey tests for diagnostic and achievement purposes (Anderson, 1971; Bloesser, 1968; Cartwright, 1972; Stewart, 1970). Experimenting with a cut-time administration of the Nelson–Denny Reading Test (NDRT), Creaser, Jacobs, Zaccarea, and Carsello (1970) suggested that the test may be useful for screening, prediction, diagnosis, and assessment. Most researchers, however, caution against using survey tests for diagnosis.

The NDRT is the test most widely used by college reading instructors in the United States (Carsello, 1982; Sweiger, 1972). A nationwide survey by Sweiger found that the Diagnostic Reading Test was the next most popular test. These tests, as well as others, are often used incorrectly. Goodwin (1971) and Sweiger both conducted national surveys showing that college instructors used survey instruments to test the broad skills of comprehension and vocabulary. (As noted previously, however, many of the instructors thought these tests were meant to be diagnostic.) Surveys in Georgia (Lowe & Stefurak, 1970) and Florida (Landsman & Cranney, 1978), plus a survey of 588 institutions in the southeastern United States (Gordon & Flippo, 1983), support the studies by Goodwin and Sweiger. In addition, Van Meter (1988) found that of the 90% of community and junior colleges in Maryland that used the NDRT 40% reported using it (inappropriately) for diagnostic purposes.

Matching Assignments to Grade Equivalencies. A problem that has plagued reading researchers for years is the attempt to match readers to text through the use of grade equivalencies determined from students' test results. As one cause of this problem, Daneman (1982) pointed to the two foci of standardized reading tests: one focus is on differentiating readers with the goal of predicting their success, and the other is on measuring the difficulty of the text with the goal of determining whether the material will be comprehended by its intended audience. In 1981, the International Reading Association (IRA) issued a statement warning against the misuse of grade equivalencies. Nevertheless, the majority of the college reading tests used today allow the instructor to convert students' reading scores to grade equivalencies.

Readability formulas allow educators to convert test passages into grade equivalencies. The problem occurs when instructors assume that students' scores on a standardized reading test can be matched to the grade equivalencies of text as measured by readability formula. Bormuth (1985) concluded that it is currently impossible to match readers to materials economically and efficiently.

The real problem with attempting this match occurs at two levels of reading. In the early grades, attempts to match students to materials on the basis of their standardized reading test scores do not succeed because readability formulas underestimate the ability of young readers to comprehend elementary materials. The opposite problem occurs when an instructor attempts to match high school seniors and college freshmen to texts; students' reading ability is generally overestimated at this level. Carver (1985a, 1985b) cited this problem with the Degrees of Reading Power Test, which came out in 1983. Dale and Chall (1948) observed this phenomenon in their readability formula early on; Chall (1958) warned that all readability formulas suffer from the same problem.

Researchers have concluded that none of the 50-plus readability formulas is a perfect predictor of readability. These formulas neglect three essential components of reading comprehension: text considerateness or friendliness (Armbruster & Anderson, 1988; Singer & Donlan, 1989), the information-processing demands of the text, and the readers' processing characteristics (Daneman, 1991).

Technical Problems. Another problem noted in the literature is the incidence of technical deficiencies in reading tests. Test validity has been the concern of numerous researchers. Farr (1968) concluded from his study of convergent and discriminate validity that total test scores are more valid and more reliable than subtest scores. Since then, however, Farr and Carey (1986) noted some advances in the technology of testing. They indicate that in recent years test developers have done a better job of fine-tuning their tests.

Benson (1981) reminded instructors that validity extends beyond test content to the structure of the test, including item wording, test format, test directions, and item readability. Researchers encourage test users to evaluate not only validity but also reliability, usability, and normative data (Gordon, 1983; Schreiner, 1979; Webb, 1983).

Lack of Appropriate Tests.   A third problem cited in the literature is the need for better and more appropriate tests for college students (Flippo, 1980a, 1980b). A number of studies have found that most available tests do not assess all necessary dimensions of reading behavior. These include studies by Alexander (1977), Coats (1968), Cranney and Larsen (1972), Janzen and Johnson (1970), Ketcham (1960), Kingston (1965), Pardy (1977), Phillips (1969), and Tittle and Kay (1971). In addition, as noted earlier, many reading authorities argue that current tests completely fail to assess the more important process dimensions of reading.

Many specific suggestions and criticisms concerning the appropriateness of postsecondary reading tests appear in the literature, from both the product and the process perspective. For instance, Ironside (1969) called for diagnostic tests that would measure subskills and provide interpretation of the resulting information for the instructor. Farr (1969) suggested tests that would give information on higher reading skills such as interpretation, critical reading, and comprehension of the author's intent. Tittle and Kay (1971) implied a need for special reading tests that could adequately measure the lower half of the achievement distribution, where judgments about remediation and reading needs are most often made.

Raygor and Flippo (1981) noted the need for tests that allow for relative item success on at least half the test items. They suggested that one way of judging the appropriateness of a reading test for a given population was students' ability to finish at least half the test correctly, which would indicate an appropriate level of difficulty.

The flaws of existing tests have been widely documented. Evans and Dubois (1972) and Flippo (1980c, 1982a) expressed concern that the tests being used for underprepared students are not diagnostic. Kerstiens (1986b) was troubled about the number of time-critical standardized tests. He indicated that these timed tests are not appropriate for finding out the true reading abilities of students—particularly the lower achieving developmental college students with whom they are frequently used. Ahrendt (1975) called for more diagnostic standardized reading tests and for tests that would measure reading achievement in specific subjects. In building a rationale for the use of computer technology in assessment, Wainer (1990) called for tests that required less administration time, included items at an appropriate level of difficulty for individual students, and required minimum time for administration and scoring.

After studying the NDRT, Chester, Dulin, and Carvell (1975) suggested changes in comprehension questions. Raygor and Flippo (1981) also examined the NDRT and found that the test was much too difficult for college students with significant reading problems. Van Meter and Herrman (1986–1987) reviewed the literature and concurred with the Raygor and Flippo findings. In addition, a study by Noble (1986) indicated that reading skill as measured by the NDRT (Forms C and E) could be predicted with moderate accuracy from the American College Test social studies, reading, and English usage subtests, suggesting that if the ACT were used initially for college admissions purposes, additional NDRT data would not be necessary.

Summary of the Literature

In reviewing the literature on reading tests generally, and college reading tests specifically, three themes continue to surface. First and foremost, researchers are unable to agree on what reading is or how to measure it. Second, college reading instructors need to be better informed about reading tests and their uses. Finally, although some improvements and alternatives have been offered in recent years, there is a scarcity of appropriate reading tests for college students, particularly for students from diverse cultural and linguistic backgrounds and students with learning disabilities.

Some years ago, Farr (1968) concluded that reading evaluation is far behind other aspects of the field. He called for new reading tests, refinement of reading tests currently on the market, and the application of theory and empirical assumptions about reading to the evaluation of reading. Farr and Carey (1986) concluded that after almost 20 years little has changed. The needs Farr cited in 1968 and 1986 are particularly relevant to the testing of college-level reading. Indeed, some changes have been made in the past 10 years in the revision of the theoretical orientation and format of individual tests. In some cases computer technology has been employed for their administration and scoring. Nonetheless, educators of developmental reading students at the college level still are hungry for more refined and instructionally appropriate assessment tools specifically designed for the students they teach.

EVALUATING COMMERCIAL GROUP TESTS

Given the issues and problems surrounding reading tests reported in the literature, it is safe to say that there is a need not only for new and revised reading tests for college students but also for more appropriate selection of the tests that are available. Although this chapter does little to meet the first need, we make recommendations to help college reading instructors make informed choices from among the more recent commercially available tests. To accomplish this task, the appendix contains a selective review of commercially available group tests that were published or revised in 1980 or later. These tests include those that are commonly used for college reading programs (as reported in the literature) and other tests that seem to be applicable to college populations.

The purpose of this test review is to help practitioners select the most appropriate tests for their specific program purposes and populations. Although we acknowledge that many reading researchers consider the currently available commercial tests to be weak, inappropriate, or limited, we also acknowledge that college reading instructors still need to assess large numbers of students. Until better commercial tests are available, these instructors must either choose from the currently available instruments or revise or design their own assessments with the support and assistance of appropriate college personnel or test developers. The recommendations of such researchers as Guthrie and Lissitz (1985) and Farr and Carey (1986) are our prime motivators. These researchers maintain that until new instruments are developed, research needs to concentrate on how to use current tests effectively and avoid the most flagrant misuses.

A number of reading tests that traditionally have been used with college students in the past are not included in this review. These include the NDRT, Forms A and B (1960); the McGraw-Hill Basic Skills Reading Test (1970); the Davis Reading Test (1961); the Diagnostic Reading Tests (1947); the Cooperative English Tests–Reading (1960); and the Sequential Tests of Educational Progress: Reading (1969). The first four tests were excluded from the review because they are out of print. The last two tests were excluded because they are no longer available as separate tests; both are now part of multiple-test booklets. Blanton, Farr, and Tuinman (1972) reviewed all of these tests, except the McGraw-Hill, up to the most current revisions available at that time.

The present chapter contains an updated version of Flippo and Cashen's 1991 review of commercially available college-level reading tests (see Flippo, Hanes, & Cashen, 1991). We did not include several measures included in this earlier review because they are currently out of print or being phased out by the publisher. The reader is referred to Flippo and Cashen (1991) for comprehensive reviews of the following: California Achievement Test, Level 5 (1970); California Achievement Test, Levels 19, 20 (1985); Degrees of Reading Power (1983); Gates-MacGinite Reading Tests, Level F (1978); Iowa Silent Reading Tests, Level 2 (1973); Iowa Silent Reading Tests, Level 3 (1973); Minnesota Reading Assessment (1980); Nelson-Denny Reading Test, Forms C and D (1973); Reading Progress Scale, College Version (1975); Stanford Diagnostic Reading Test, Blue Level (1976); Stanford Diagnostic Reading Test, Blue Level (1984). Also not included in the current review are state tests such as the New Jersey College Basic Skills Placement Test and the Florida College Level Academic Skills Test (CLAST), both basic skills tests and individually administered tests (e.g., the Diagnostic Achievement Test for Adolescents [Newcomer & Bryant, 1993]; Gray Oral Reading Tests—Diagnostic [Bryant & Wiederholt, 1992]; Woodcock-Johnson Psycho-Educational Battery, Revised [Woodcock & Johnson, 1996]).

Practitioners still using one of the dated instruments should consider the more up-to-date tests reviewed in the appendix. Although we acknowledge deficiencies and problems with all of these commercial instruments, we suggest that the newer instruments are probably more appropriate than their dated counterparts. Farr and Carey (1986) supported this recommendation.

The reviews included in the appendix were done by directly examining each test and the information presented in the test manuals. Each of the tests listed has been reviewed to provide the following information:

- name and author(s) of the test
- type of test
- use(s) of the test
- skills or strategies tested
- population recommended
- overall theory of reading
- readability and source of passages
- format of test/test parts
- testing time
- forms
- levels
- types of scores
- norm group(s)
- date of test publication or last major revision
- reliability
- validity
- scoring options

- cost
- publisher
- weaknesses of the test
- strengths of the test

Careful analysis of this information should help practitioners select the most appropriate tests for their given situations and populations. We do not endorse any of these tests in particular. In fact, we find them all deficient in assessing most college reading needs and lacking in the components we believe are most important relating to reading. Our purpose is simply to present practitioners with detailed information regarding the commercially available choices to enable them to make the most informed decisions possible.

Normative Considerations

Most of the tests reviewed in the appendix are norm-referenced. This means that *norms*, or patterns typical of a particular group, are employed to make comparisons between students. Comparisons are often made using percentiles, stanines, or grade equivalents. Test publishers usually report the procedures used to norm their instrument in the test manual. This information includes a description of the norming group in terms of age, sex, educational level, socioeconomic status (SES), race, geographical setting, and size.

Peters (1977) reminded us that without this information, it is impossible to determine whether the test results are applicable to the population to be tested. For example, if all students to be tested are college freshmen from a low socioeconomic rural population, the use of a test that was normed with high school students from an upper middle class urban area would have to be questioned. Even if the norm group and the group tested are comparable, the normative data must be current. For example, a group of college freshmen tested in the 1950s might differ from the same population tested in the 1990s. Therefore, unless both the test and the normative data are continually updated, validity becomes questionable.

Reliability Considerations

Test reliability, usually reported in reliability coefficients, is a measure of how consistently a test measures whatever it is measuring. A test is considered reliable to the extent that students' test scores would be the same each time they took the test (assuming, of course, that no learning would take place between test administrations and that the students would remember nothing about the test at the next administration). If a test is highly reliable, we can assume that test scores are probably accurate measure of students' performance rather than a fluke. The coefficient of stability, or a report of test—retest reliability, is an indication of this stability in performance over time.

Most reading tests also report other types of reliability. One of these is *internal consistency reliability*, which measures the relationship between items on a test and looks at the consistency of performance on the various test items. Internal consistency is usually calculated with the Kuder-Richardson KR–20 or KR–21 formulas or by using split-half reliability. With the split-half method, reliability is computed by dividing the test into two parts and comparing or correlating scores on the parts.

Another type of reliability reported for many reading tests is the *coefficient of equivalence* (also called *parallel forms reliability*, or *alternate forms reliability*). This method is used when a test has two forms. To compute reliability, both forms are given to the same sample group, and then the scores are correlated.

Of course, no test can be 100% reliable. Variability is inevitable when dealing with human beings. The higher the reliability coefficient for a test, however, the more confident we can be that the test accurately measures students' performance. Testing and measurement authorities advise that one way to determine whether a particular test's reliability score is acceptable is to measure it against the highest score attained by a similar test. As Brown (1983) explained, "the reliability of any test should be as high as that of the better tests in the same area" (p. 89). However, Brown also indicates that performance measures with reliability values of .85 to .90 are common. Peters (1977) noted that .80 or higher is a high correlation for equivalent, parallel, or alternate form reliability.

On a final note, users must remember to analyze what a given test actually measures. Even if a test is highly reliable, if it does not measure the appropriate skills, strategies, abilities, and content knowledge of the students to be tested, it is of no value.

Validity Considerations

A test is considered valid to the extent that it measures what the test user is trying to measure. If a test measures the skills, strategies, abilities, and content knowledge that the college or program deems important for a given population's academic success, it is a valid instrument. If the test also measures extraneous variables, its validity is weakened proportionately. A test cannot be considered valid unless it measures something explicitly relevant both to the population being tested and to the purpose of the testing. Of course, a test that is not reliable cannot be considered valid.

As pointed out earlier, validity considerations must extend beyond content validity to include appropriateness of the test's structure and materials. Item wording, test format, test directions, length and readability of passages, and content materials must all be analyzed to determine their appropriateness for the given population and the purposes of the testing.

Test developers and publishers use different terminology to describe the validity of their tests. This terminology actually describes different types of validity. Type of validity is usually a function of the way the test publisher determined that the test was valid for a given purpose. It is important for test users to know something about the different types of validity in order to understand the terminology reported in test manuals.

Often test publishers report only one or two types of validity for their tests. One type of validity cannot be generalized to another. However, if you know why you are testing, what you are testing for, and the needs of the population being tested, you can usually determine the validity of a test even when given limited information. Of course, as Peters (1977) pointed out, reading instructors should demand appropriate validity documentation in test manuals. If an instrument does not provide validity information, it should not be used; purchasing such a test only perpetuates the assumption made by some test publishers that this information is of little importance.

Types of Validity.   According to Brown (1983), the numerous types of validity generally fall into three main classes: *criterion-related validity*, *content validity*, and *construct validity*.

The basic research question for the criterion-related validity measure is "How well do scores on the test predict performance on the criterion?" (Brown, 1983, p. 69). An index of this predictive accuracy, called the "validity coefficient," measures the validity of the particular test. What is of ultimate interest is the individual's performance on the criterion variable. The test score is important only as a predictor of that variable, not as a sample or representation of behavior or ability. An example of criterion-related validity is use of the SAT to predict college grade point average (GPA). Concurrent validity and predictive validity are two types of criterion-related validity often noted in test manuals.

Concurrent validity refers to the correlation between test scores and a criterion measure obtained at the same (or nearly the same) time; therefore, it measures how well test scores predict immediate performance on a criterion variable. Predictive validity examines the correlation of test scores with a criterion measure obtained at a later point in time.

The most frequently used method of establishing criterion-related validity is to correlate test scores with criterion scores. A validity coefficient is a correlation coefficient; the higher the correlation, the more accurately the test scores predict scores on the criterion task. Thus, if the choice is between two tests that are equally acceptable for a given population and purpose, and one test has a validity coefficient of .70 while the other has a validity coefficient of .80, the test user should choose the latter. According to Peters (1977), a test should have a validity coefficient of .80 or above to be considered valid. Any coefficient below this level, he says, should be considered questionable.

The basic question researched for content validity is "How would the individual perform in the universe of situations of which the test is but a sample?" (Brown, 1983, p. 69). The content validity of a test is evaluated on the basis of the adequacy of the item sampling. Because no quantitative index of sampling adequacy is available, evaluation is a subjective process. In evaluating this type of validity, the test score operates as a sample of ability. An example of content validity is use of an exam that samples the content of a course to measure performance and ability in that course.

Face validity is often confused with content validity. A test has *face validity* when the items seem to measure what the test is supposed to measure. Face validity is determined by a somewhat superficial examination that considers only obvious relevance, whereas establishing content validity entails thorough examination by a qualified judge who considers subtle as well as obvious aspects of relevance.

The basic question researched for construct validity is "What trait does the test measure?" (Brown, 1983, p. 69). Construct validity is determined by accumulating evidence regarding the relationship between the test and the trait it is designed to measure. Such evidence may be accumulated in various ways, including studies of content and criterion-related validity. As with content validity, no quantitative index of the construct validity of a test exists. An example of construct validity is the development of a test to define a trait such as intelligence. Congruent validity, convergent validity, and discriminant validity are all types of construct validity that are cited in test manuals.

Congruent validity is the most straightforward method of determining that a certain construct is being measured. Congruence is established when test scores on a newly constructed instrument correlate with test scores on other instruments measuring a similar trait or construct. Convergent and discriminant validity are established by determining the correlation between test scores and behavioral indicators that are aligned theoretically with the trait (convergent validity) or that distinguish it from opposing traits (discriminant validity). For example, we would expect that scores on verbal ability tests would correlate highly with observed performance on tasks that require verbal skills. On the other hand, we would expect a low correlation between scores on manual ability tests and verbal behaviors, because these traits, in theory, are distinct. Ideally, if convergent validity is reported, discriminant validity is also reported.

Brown (1983) emphasizes that validity evidence is always situation-specific. Therefore, any test will have many different validities. It must be remembered that validity is always established for a particular use of a test in a particular situation. As you review tests for possible use in your college reading program, always consider the particular situation and how the test is to be used.

Passage Dependency.   Although not usually mentioned in testing and measurement texts as an aspect of validity, the passage dependency of a test should be considered by reading test users. According to the more traditional testing and measurement perspective, if students can answer test items by recalling prior knowledge or applying logic without having to read and understand the passage, the test items are passage-independent, and the validity of the results should be questioned.

Reading instructors who adhere to this perspective would not want students to be able to answer test questions by drawing on past experience or information. That would defeat the instructors' purpose in conducting a reading assessment. They would argue that if test items are well constructed, students should have to read and understand the test passages in order to correctly answer questions based on those passages.

Of the commercial tests reviewed for this chapter, those that utilize a cloze procedure appear to be the most passage dependent. Cloze assessment is a method of determining a student's ability to read specific textual materials by filling in words that have been deleted from the text. Reading tests using the traditional model—a brief paragraph followed by multiple-choice questions—appear to be less passage-dependent, as answers to questions are sometimes available from the examinees' background knowledge or reasoning ability.

Practitioners can best determine the passage dependency of a reading test by conducting their own studies of the reading materials. In these studies, the same test questions are administered to two groups of examinees; one group takes the test in the conventional manner with the reading passages present, while the other group attempts to answer the items without the reading passages.

In contrast to the more traditional test perspective, some reading researchers consider it desirable to allow prior knowledge to affect reading assessment (Johnston, 1984; Simpson, 1982). In addition, Flippo, Becker, and Wark (chap. 9, this volume) noted the importance of logic as one of the cognitive skills necessary for the test taking success of college students.

Test users must decide for themselves the importance of prior knowledge, logic, and passage dependency as each relates to the measurement of reading comprehension. We recommend that practitioners learn as much as possible about any test they plan to use so they can more accurately analyze their results and better understand all the concomitant variables. As we know from psycholinguists' work with miscue analysis (analysis of word recognition deviations from text), some traits that are traditionally considered undesirable may not be undesirable at all. Miscues, for instance, may actually show reading strengths. Similarly, college students' use of logic or prior knowledge while taking a test may provide practitioners with insights into students' ability to handle textual readings.

Readability Considerations

In the appendix we use traditional readability formulas (Fry, 1977; Raygor, 1979) to compute the approximate readability of test passages whenever test publishers did not furnish this information. Nevertheless, we want to point out the limitations of these formulas. Traditional readability formulas consider only sentence and word length, with the assumption that the longer the sentence and the longer the words in the sentence (or the more syllables per word), the more difficult the passage is for the reader. However, we believe that other factors such as the inclusion of text-considerate or text-friendly features (e.g., headings/subheadings, words in boldface type, margin notes) also contribute to comprehensibility of text (Armbruster & Anderson, 1988; Singer & Donlan, 1989). These factors are less tangible and therefore more difficult to quantify and measure.

Those reviewing tests and materials for use in formal or informal assessment should consider several readability factors in addition to sentence and word length: (a) the complexity of the concepts covered by the material, (b) students' interest in the content, (c) students' past life experience with the content, (d) students' cognitive experience with the content, and (e) students' linguistic experience with the syntax of the material.

OPTIMIZING THE USE OF COMMERCIAL TESTS

If standardized, norm-referenced reading tests are to be used, they should be selected and used wisely. College reading professionals can use a number of strategies to maximize the usefulness of these commercially prepared group tests and achieve a better fit with local needs. We offer several suggestions that are both practical and timely. These ideas show promise in providing practitioners with additional ways of comparing tests, administering tests, and interpreting results.

Moreover, these suggestions address several of the issues and concerns raised in the literature, offering some resolution for the local setting. We recommend four strategies: (a) conducting item analyses to determine the appropriateness of test content and level of difficulty, (b) adjusting administrative time constraints, (c) developing local norms, and (d) using scaled scores.

Item Analysis

Reading tests that do not measure the content taught in reading courses may be inappropriate for evaluating program success. One way to determine the match between reading tests and reading courses is to analyze test items against course objectives. This technique is time-consuming, but it may be helpful. Alexander (1977) recommended that learning assistance personnel take the reading test, examine each item to determine the skill or concept being tested, and compile a checklist of skills and concepts by item. They should compare the checklist with the objectives taught in the reading course. If the instructors think it is important to select an instrument on the basis of its match to reading course objectives, they can analyze several reading tests in this way to find the test with the closest match.

Although this strategy may provide a viable way of evaluating program effectiveness, we caution practitioners that the content of many college reading courses themselves may not match the actual reading needs of college students. Unless the content and objectives of the reading course closely match the reading needs of the students in their regular college classes, this type of item analysis is not worth the time it takes.

Wood (1989) suggested that test items be reviewed to examine the extent to which they represent real college reading. We strongly support this type of item analysis. Items should cover a variety of sources and subjects, be of adequate length, and reflect a level of difficulty typical of college reading assignments. Esoteric topics, according to Wood, prohibit students' use of prior knowledge and make tests unnecessarily difficult. Although practitioners are unlikely to find a perfect representation of actual college reading, this kind of review provides a good way of making relative comparisons among tests.

Raygor and Flippo (1981) suggest that practitioners analyze students' success rate on each item to determine the appropriateness of standardized reading tests for local populations. We concur. Some tests may be too difficult and some too easy to discriminate adequately among the full range of student performance. Analyzing the relative success rates (i.e., percentage of items answered correctly) of several widely used instruments, Raygor and Flippo found that the best discrimination occurs when approximately half of the students respond to at least 50% of the test items correctly. When tests meet this criterion, scores tend to be more normally distributed. Deficient readers as well as highly skilled readers are more likely to be identified under these circumstances.

Tests on which most students have a success rate of 50% or higher may be too easy and tend to discriminate only among the lower performance ranges. On the other hand, tests on which most students have lower than a 50% success rate may be too difficult and will discriminate only among the more highly skilled readers (Raygor & Flippo, 1981). Practitioners should analyze possible test choices and select those that discriminate best for their populations.

Time Constraints

Several studies report that the time constraints imposed by many reading tests result in dubious performance scores for certain populations of college students. Developmental students have been found to have a slower response rate on timed tests, which may amplify relative performance discrepancies on time-critical reading tests (Kerstiens, 1986a, 1986b, 1990). Adult students, culturally and linguistically diverse students (Fradd & McGee, 1994), and students with LD (Baldwin et al., 1989) also appear to be penalized by time-critical factors inherent in standard test administration.

Davis, Kaiser, and Boone (1987) examined test completion rates among 8,290 entering students in Tennessee's community, 4-year, and technical colleges. The test used for the study was the Reading Comprehension Test of the Tennessee State Board of Regents. Performance differences in age and race were found in all three types of institutions. Adult students (those 22 years of age and older) demonstrated lower completion rates than their younger counterparts. Davis recommended extending the test time allotted for completion to remove the performance bias that works against students.

Stetson (1982) reported that pretest and posttest comparisons can be misleading. She used pretesting and posttesting to determine the effectiveness of programs designed to increase reading rates, and found that gains in posttest performance reflected an increase in the number of items attempted rather than an improvement in ability. By adjusting posttest scores to reflect accuracy levels based on pretest completion rates, she found that her students actually did worse on vocabulary and comprehension posttests than they had on the pretests. Test efficiency appeared to decrease with increased attention to rate or speed of response.

It may be of value to practitioners in the developmental setting to compare completion rates on posttests with those on pretests. If considerable discrepancies exist, it may well be worth investigating test efficiency to guard against artificial score inflation. Adjusting raw posttest scores on the basis of pretest completion rates (the farthest point to which the student progressed on the initial testing) allows for a more direct comparison of pre- and posttreatment performance.

Local Norming

The match between the norm-reference group on a standardized test and the college group being tested is critical to test interpretation. When the norm group and the college population are dissimilar, test results have no basis for comparison. Some test publishers provide norms that are aligned with the characteristics of certain local populations, particularly in urban areas; practitioners should inquire about the availability of these norms when national norms are not appropriate. Otherwise, developing local norms is strongly recommended.

Developing local norms requires the redistribution of local scores to simulate a normal curve. Raw scores can then be reassigned to standard units of measurement such as stanines or percentile rankings. Most test manuals and basic statistics texts provide the necessary information about normal distributions to guide the redistribution of local raw scores. For example, raw scores that account for the lowest and highest 4% of the range of scores can be reassigned to the first and ninth stanines, respectively. It is essential to use as large a data set as possible when establishing the local norm group. Repeated administration over time—for instance, scores for all incoming freshmen over 3 to 5 consecutive years—are preferable to ensure adequate representation.

Two other important points should also be considered. First, although the calculations involved in developing local norms may be straightforward, it is advisable to seek the assistance of professionals trained in psychometrics or educational measurement. Second, practitioners must keep in mind that local norms, once established, are meaningful only in making relative judgments about students at their own institutions.

Use of Scaled Scores

More local research is encouraged to assess the long-term changes in students' reading abilities, particularly those changes resulting from intervention by developmental programs. The selection of reading tests may change in response to new local conditions or because of periodic revisions (new editions) of commercially available tests.

Because reevaluation is necessary to keep up with these changes, preserving old records is important. However, valuable data can be lost by preserving the wrong source of performance measures or scores. Keeping raw scores alone on record is not useful. It is far better to retain raw scores along with scaled scores, which sustain their usefulness despite changes of instrumentation or revised editions of formerly adopted instruments. (We have already warned against the use of grade equivalent scores; these scores are misleading and have virtually no comparative value.)

Raw scores have value for measuring individual changes in performance on the same or equivalent forms of tests (e.g., pre- and posttesting). Because they are more sensitive to variations in performance than scaled scores, they can capture smaller (but still meaningful) gains. Raw scores, however, are meaningless when comparing performance on different tests. Normalized scaled scores, such as percentile rankings and stanines, are less sensitive to variations in performance because of the wider bands of scores forced into the comparison scales. Unequal differences between the rankings or stanines at either end of the scales and those in the middle range are also likely. However, the advantage of scaled scores is that they can be used effectively to make comparisons across groups and across tests.

Standard scores are the best alternatives for record keeping. They represent the conversion of raw scores to a form that ensures equal differences among converted values by comparing an individual student's score to the rest of the distribution of scores. They are also the most useful scores for longitudinal studies of performance. Like normalized scaled scores, they can be used for making comparisons with other standardized, norm-referenced tests as well as with revised versions of the same test. Most test publishers report test scores in terms of standard scores, percentile rankings, and stanines.

EVALUATING INFORMAL READING ASSESSMENTS

Because of the large number of students who participate in college reading programs, most programs limit their testing to standardized group instruments. However, we should point out that carefully designed informal reading assessments appropriate for college students can provide more diagnostic information and probably more useful information than any of the formal group tests currently available. Informal measures as well as other artifacts of college reading and writing tasks can serve as artifacts in student assessment portfolios (Schumm et al., 1992; Valeri-Gold et al., 1991).

Informal reading inventories (IRIs) are particularly useful in pinpointing a reader's strengths and areas where improvement is needed. However, using individual IRIs with college students presents two problems: (a) they are time-consuming to administer and analyze, and (b) few commercially available individual IRIs are appropriate for college populations. Although time consuming, an individual IRI may be appropriate for students exhibiting unusual or conflicting results on other assessments, or for students indicating a preference for more diagnosis. The practitioner or program director has to decide when it makes sense to administer an individual IRI. This decision may have quite a lot to do with the philosophy of the program. Certainly, few reading authorities would deny the power of the IRI as a diagnostic tool. It may well be that the level of qualitative analysis one can get from an IRI is worth the time it takes.

In our review of tests for this section, we searched for commercially prepared IRIs that might be appropriate for the college population. We found two commercially available IRIs that contain passages and scoring information through the twelfth-grade level and may therefore be adapted for use with college students: the Bader Reading and Language Inventory (1998) and the Burns/Roe Informal Reading Inventory (1993).

A third IRI, the Secondary and College Inventory (Johns, 1990) is available for secondary school and colleges. Because this instrument was designed for use through the freshman college level, it should be examined by any college program interested in an IRI. Those interested in using a commercially available IRI should consult Jongsma and Jongsma (1981) for a listing of recommendations, and Pikulski and Shanahan (1982) for a critical analysis of the IRI and other informal assessment measures.

Given the dearth of commercial instruments designed for the college population, a program that seriously desires to use an IRI should consider designing its own. Although most program-developed assessments have some flaws, the positive aspects should far outweigh the negative. A college could develop an assessment using actual reading materials from the students' introductory courses. Cloze procedures and written retellings can be used for more qualitative analyses. An institution-developed IRI or cloze procedure would be most desirable in that it would provide both an assessment of students' ability to read materials for their required courses and a powerful tool for qualitative diagnosis.

Many reading texts include directions for constructing an IRI, analyzing the results, and using retellings. In addition, Pikulski and Shanahan (1982) are recommended for information on the IRI and cloze as diagnostic tools, Smith and Jackson (1985) are recommended for information on the use of written retellings with college students, and Flippo (1997); Glazer, Searfoss, and Gentile (1988); and Valeri-Gold et al. (1991) are recommended for a discussion and examples of other informal techniques.

In addition to IRIs, other informal measures that tap reading attitudes, habits, and reading-related study skills are those that can be included in an assessment portfolio. Some standardized tests (e.g., the Stanford Diagnostic Reading Test and COMPASS) offer such measures as supplemental material. Other measures are available commercially such as The Learning and Study Strategies Inventory (LASSI; Weinstein, Schulte, & Palmer, 1987), are included as parts of developmental reading textbooks (e.g., Atkinson & Longman, 1988; Nist & Diehl, 1994; Schumm & Post, 1997), or can be developed by practitioners based on local needs.

SUMMARY OF FINDINGS AND ANALYSIS

In 1991, Flippo et al. reviewed reading tests commonly used in college reading programs. Here, we compare the findings of the Flippo et al. review with the current analysis highlighting areas of change and new outcomes that emerged. Next, we continue with implications of the conclusion of the current analysis for assessment and instruction followed with specific recommendations for reading practitioners. (See Table 14.1 for a concise summary of our conclusions, implications, and recommendations.) Finally, we present avenues for future research in the area of assessment at the postsecondary level.

TABLE 14.1
Reading Tests: Conclusions, Implications, and Recommendations

Conclusions	Implications	Recommendations
No one test will meet the needs of all programs and all student populations.	Programs need to utilize more than one assessment instrument to determine the reading needs of their differing populations.	College reading practitioners should be knowledgeable about the various appropriate screening and diagnostic assessments and continue to explore the use of portfolio assessment in college reading programs.
Few reading tests are normed on entering and undergraduate college students.	Most reading tests in use are inappropriate for many entering and undergraduate college students and may result in students being inappropriately placed in college reading courses. Most of the research on college reading has been conducted with tests that were not appropriately normed for the college population.	Colleges and universities should compile their own data and develop local norms. College reading programs should not rely on the outcomes of studies using tests that are inappropriately normed for the college population.
None of the standardized tests uses extended passages of the type college students are required to read in their textbooks.	Instruments in use do not test the type of reading typically required of college students.	Tests are needed with material that more accurately resembles college-type reading and assignment length.
Most standardized tests reviewed are survey instruments.	Few tests are available to diagnose individual college students' reading strengths and weaknesses.	Colleges should construct their own diagnostic assessments.
Some tests represent a subskill orientation, others a more holistic view of reading.	Reading tests may or may not be compatible with a particular reading program depending on the program's theoretical orientation and instructional practices.	Practitioners need to examine potential tests carefully to make certain that the test is an appropriate measure for the instructional program. Publishers need to continue to explore ways to represent a more holistic view of reading in tests.
The technical information for most of the tests reviewed is adequate, however it is not readily available to practitioners.	Many test users never see or read the technical information.	Test publishers should provide "executive summaries" of technical information in a format that is useable and readily available to practitioners.

TABLE 14. 1 (Continued)

Conclusions	Implications	Recommendations
Publishers have been more attentive to test instruction in areas of test bias and to the needs of students whose test performance is inhibited by time constraints.	Although some strides have been made, additional research and development of appropriate measures is warranted.	Practitioners need to examine test materials carefully to make certain that the test is an appropriate measure for the particular student population. Publishers need to continue to develop measures that accurately gauge the reading strengths and challenges of all readers.
The use of technology for scoring of tests is readily available. The use of technology to improve the quality of student assessment is still in early stages.	Some strides have been made in the area of technology, however these innovations have not been implemented for a variety of reasons including budgetary factors and professional development of staff.	Continued research and development of tools for computer-assisted interactive assessment is needed. Professional development for practitioners in technology for assessment purposes is needed as well.

Conclusions

The overall conclusion drawn by Flippo et al. (1991) in their review of college reading tests was more and better reading tests are needed to evaluate the range of abilities and needs of college students. This finding was particularly prophetic given the burgeoning numbers of academically, culturally, and linguistically diverse students entering institutions of higher education in recent years. Although some strides have been made in revisions of existing measures, surprisingly few new instruments are available. Unfortunately, the overall finding of the present review is that there is still a dearth of adequate, comprehensive reading assessment tools appropriate for college levels students.

Our findings mirror the Flippo et al. review in several additional ways. Flippo et al. concluded that (a) no one available test was sufficient for the needs of all programs and all student populations, (b) few reading tests are normed on entering and undergraduate college students, (c) none of the standardized tests used extended passages of the type college students are required to read in their textbooks, and (d) most standardized tests are survey instruments. These findings are still true.

On the other hand, some overall changes have been observed. The Flippo et al. review indicated that most tests reviewed defined and tested reading as a set of discrete skills. Although some tests still hold to a subskill orientation, other publishers have made attempts to have test items reflect more of a holistic orientation. The Degrees of Reading Power (1995) continues to view reading as a process and measures reading using a cloze format and has added an advanced level to tap higher level reading processes. Other instruments such as the California Reading Test and Stanford Diagnostic Reading Test have revised test items to reduce "subskill" language and include more processing and reading strategy language. Still others, such as the Gates-MacGinite Reading Tests appear at face value to have changed very little, but the promotional and orientation materials do recognize reading as a more global, strategic process.

Despite decades of debate, there is still no agreement among reading educators as to whether reading is a global process or a series of discrete skills (Simpson, 1993). Indeed, many in the reading field advocate a more balanced perspective to reading assessessment, selecting from the most appropriate assessments available from various points of view (Flippo, 1997). Measuring reading as a discrete set of skills using standardized measures is certainly more manageable to interpret to policymakers and administrators. In other words, assessments using more traditional models of the reading process have their proponents—and increasing numbers in many parts of the country. Nonetheless, experimentation with more student-centered, strategy-oriented, holistic assessment procedures continues among publishers and individual practitioners. Before selecting a reading test, reading practitioners should have an in-depth understanding of the reading process, including knowledge of the various models of reading. Only after they have adopted a reading model that reflects their own definition of reading and institutional goals should they select a reading test.

Another change we noted was that technical information for most of the tests reviewed was improved. Most measures do have extensive technical manuals, however, most are still not readily available in the test administration manuals and must be ordered separately at additional cost.

More attention has been placed to diverse student needs. Test administration manuals and promotional materials are more attentive to the needs of individuals with disabilities, students who speak English as a second language, and culturally diverse students. In a few cases, students with diverse needs were included in the norming population. Most attended to test bias (gender or cultural) in test development stages. Although additional strides in addressing special student needs are warranted, a few initial steps have been made.

Finally, more attention has been placed on technology. Ostensibly, the COMPASS, an adaptive measure using computer technology, is on the cutting edge using individualized test administration (see appendix). Most measures have more machine and microcomputer scoring to streamline scoring time and to generate more detailed and varied student and institutional reports.

Implications

The implications of our general conclusions are straightforward. College programs will need to find or develop several assessment instruments to evaluate their different populations. The use of assessment portfolios is a practice that needs to be further developed. The instruments currently in use (although improved over previous versions) do not measure the types of reading required of most college students. Therefore, the results of these tests provide little information concerning students' abilities to handle the necessary college reading requirements.

Improved diagnostic measures continue to be an ongoing need for the college community. The COMPASS is a standardized group test that is currently available for diagnosing college students' strengths and weaknesses. Technical data on the instrument are still forthcoming and the COMPASS does represent a subskill orientation. Although promising, this instrument would not meet the needs of many institutions.

Because of budgetary or time constraints, many users of tests in college reading programs do not purchase or read the separately published technical information. Test users thus may be unaware of the norming, reliability, validity, and other technical information concerning these tests. Even abbreviated executive summary-type information about the merit of measures would be helpful to practitioners and administrators in materials that are readily available to them.

Although some strides have been made in terms of development of instruments that are appropriate for diverse populations, more work needs to be done. It is imperative that selection of tests is made with individual student needs in mind. Moreover, interpretation of test scores needs to be sensitive to issues related to gender, culture, and language as well as the particular needs of returning adult learners.

Finally, use of technology in the assessment of students at the college level is still in its adolescence (if not in its infancy). Development of measures using technology needs to be continued as well as the necessary professional development for administrators and instructors.

Recommendations

In light of the conclusions and implications of our review of the tests and the literature, we offer eight recommendations for reading practitioners. These recommendations are culled (with minor modifications) from the Flippo et al. review (1991). Once again, although some advancements in the area of assessment at the college level have been made, progress is sluggish at best.

First, college reading practitioners should use a variety of assessments on which to base their decisions. Each of these assessments should be appropriate to the students, the purpose of testing, and the tasks that are to be evaluated. To be able to determine such appropriateness, practitioners need to be better informed about the different types and uses of available reading tests (Goodwin, 1971; Gordon & Flippo, 1983; Landsman & Cranney, 1978; Lowe & Stefurak, 1970; Sweiger, 1972). Gordon and Flippo found that many college reading practitioners were not actively involved in research or professional associations, and only infrequently presented papers or attended conferences. This lack of involvement in, and awareness of, current developments in the field is a primary reason for the ill-informed decisions that are made about tests. The internet allows for more interaction among colleagues through e-mail and listserves. Technology now offers the opportunity to access to professional information previously denied individuals who could not attend professional conferences for whatever reason.

The second recommendation is that college and university reading programs compile their own data and develop their own norms. The tests most available and most often used usually have inappropriate or inadequate norms for diverse college populations.

We suggest that college reading practitioners take responsibility for developing local norms based on data collected over a period of 3 to 5 years. This is particularly important given the wide range of student composition from region to region.

In addition, practitioners need to be aware that many studies in the field of college reading used tests that were either inappropriate or inappropriately normed for the college population. They must consider this fact when utilizing the results of these studies. It may be that if the instrument or the norming is inappropriate, the study should not be considered at all.

Third, college reading professionals need to ensure that new tests are developed that more accurately reflect college-type reading in both content and length. To accomplish this task, they need to work with test publishers, test development contractors, and other college faculty members. Publishers of reading tests might be more apt to develop appropriate instruments or revise existing ones if college reading professionals encouraged them by asking for new instruments, providing samples of what would be more appropriate, and choosing not to purchase the less appropriate tests currently available. Test publishers should be provided with prototypes of the materials and questions college students face in their introductory courses.

The impact on publishers would be greater if community colleges and universities in a given area or system joined efforts to work with publishers and contractors. The consortium should also contact test development contractors, such as Educational Testing Service, to discuss development of more appropriate screening and diagnostic instruments. (These companies specialize in developing tests specific to the needs of those contracting with them.) Once again, prototypes should be provided, and representatives from each postsecondary institution in the consortium should work with the contractor in developing the new instruments. Costs and expertise could be shared among participating institutions. This strategy allows the development of tests that evaluated appropriate college reading requirements using appropriate content and length of materials.

Our fourth recommendation is that professionals develop more informal, campus-specific diagnostic instruments for their populations. Several examples of this type of development were noted earlier. For instance, Smith and Jackson (1985) used students' retellings to make assessments. Perry (1959) used students' assignments to diagnose reading problems. Guthrie and Lissitz (1985) noted that the use of students' answers to questions, discussion, and written essays are all helpful diagnostic tools for instructional decision-making purposes.

We recommend that practitioners developing their own instruments concentrate on assessments designed to diagnose the strengths and needs of students using appropriate college-related skills and strategies. Assessments must present students with reading tasks that are accurate examples of the strategies we wish to test. We must also have enough accurate examples of each of the strategies and skills we wish to measure so we can determine which of them, if any, are causing problems for the students. Finally, we must test students' use of these different strategies and skills with the types of materials they are required to handle.

Our fifth recommendation relates to administrators and practitioners who elect to use a commercial instrument. Some tests on the market represent a subskill orientation; others a more holistic perspective. It is imperative that the assessment tools are aligned with the philosophy and instructional practices of the college reading program as much as possible. Careful examination of the instruments themselves is mandatory. Promotional materials often do not provide sufficient information.

Our sixth recommendation is that test publishers provide adequate and pertinent technical information (norming, reliability, and validity data) in the manual for administering the test. This information should be presented in a clear and complete fashion and should be provided at no additional cost to those considering adopting a test. Although we feel that it is best to put all the information in one manual, when more than one manual is published for a test, the technical information should always be cross-referenced to make it usable. Technical information should be presented in an executive summary form with straightforward explanations for those who may not have advanced training in tests and measurements.

Our seventh recommendation pertains to issues related to relevance of measures for various student populations. Although some advancement has been made in terms of attention to cultural bias and adequate norming of tests in terms of representing a wide range of student groups, more work is yet to be done. Publishers need to continue to develop measures that accurately gauge the reading strengths and challenges of all students.

Finally, we recommend continued research and development of technological tools to improve the accuracy, individualization, and efficiency of assessment. The promise of computer assisted interactive assessment is strong—the actuality and accessibility is yet to be actualized. Moreover, professional development for practitioners in technology for assessment purposes is needed.

Future Avenues of Research

Our review of the literature indicated not only a dearth in new measurement instruments, but also a dearth in literature reviewing college reading tests and indeed in the area of college reading itself. It is clear that research in the area of college level reading is imperative.

Based on our analysis of the situation, we support the development of new tests designed to evaluate the reading tasks and strategies necessary for success in college. Such tests should utilize passages and require tasks and strategies comparable in difficulty and length to introductory-level college reading assignments. In essence, we think that decisions about students should be based on assessments and procedures appropriate to college reading and to each specific group of students to be evaluated. We see a need to reexamine totally the reading assessment of college students, including both formal and informal methods of assessment.

Many of our previous recommendations, if carried through, represent future directions for research and planning. In addition, we see several other avenues for future research in this area.

1. We endorse the type of item success rate study used by Raygor and Flippo (1981) and the item analysis approach recommended by Wood (1989) as possible means of determining the appropriateness of any given test for an institution's different college populations. College reading practitioners should conduct studies like these in their own institutions before deciding on any test for their students.

2. The effects of time constraints on special populations of college students warrant continued study in the local setting. Investigations into the relative completion

rates of minority, nontraditional, and developmental student groups may indicate that adjustments are needed in the time allocated to complete tests (Abraham, 1987; Kersteins, 1986a, 1986b, 1990). Practitioners should consider the test scoring technique used by Stetson (1982) to control for the possible situation of increased completion rates at the expense of test efficiency, particularly in pretest/posttest type studies evaluating individual student progress.

3. Research is needed to systematically investigate the actual reading needs of college students. To date, several studies have been conducted at different types of institutions to clarify the amount and type of reading required of undergraduate college students. Researchers in these studies asked both professors and their students exactly what reading was required for the students to succeed in their courses. Results of these studies have been reported by Orlando, Caverly, Flippo, and Mullen (1987); Orlando, Caverly, Flippo, and Mullen (1988); Orlando, Caverly, Mullen and Flippo (1986); Orlando, Caverly, Swetnam, and Flippo (1989); and Orlando, Flippo, and Caverly (1990). More such studies, done on a large-scale basis, could provide test developers with a more appropriate set of reading tasks and strategies than those evaluated by currently available tests.

4. Many decisions regarding the admittance, placement, instruction, and retention of college students have been made on the basis of studies that used tests researchers have called "inappropriate." New studies are necessary to evaluate these decisions as well as the studies and tests used to reach them. If the tests were inappropriate, the results of the studies were probably invalid, and the decisions based on them are thrown into question. Some of the best research should come from the local setting. Practitioners are encouraged to promote research efforts at their home institutions and to document their findings to share at professional meetings and in publications.

5. Johnston (1983), Peters (1977), and Valencia and Pearson (1987) suggested a more interactive approach to assessment. Interactive assessment models should be investigated and tested with the college population to determine the feasibility of this more time-consuming approach. In particular, research using computer technology for interactive assessment (e.g., Byrnes et al., 1991; Shermis, Wolting, & Lombard, 1996; Smittle, 1993) is warranted.

APPENDIX:
COMMERCIALLY AVAILABLE TESTS REVIEWED

CALIFORNIA ACHIEVEMENT TEST, FIFTH EDITION (CAT/5), LEVELS 20 AND 21/22, 1992 EDITION

Test/Author(s)

California Achievement Test (CAT/5)

Type of Test

Survey, formal, standardized, norm-referenced, criterion-referenced

Use(s) of Test

Initial screening. The test is designed to measure achievement of basic reading skills commonly found in state and district curricula.

Skills/Strategies Tested

1. Vocabulary
2. Reading comprehension

Population Recommended

Levels 20/21 (grade ranges 10.6 to 12.9) were designed to measure the achievement of senior high school students, they can be used as a screening instrument for entering college students, particularly students entering 4-year institutions. Level 20 (grade ranges 9.6 to 11.2) might be more appropriate for vocational/technical students.

Overall Theory of Reading

The goal of the CAT/5 was to reflect changes in theory and practice in literacy instruction. The previous (1985) edition of the CAT reflected a subskills orientation to reading instruction and assessment. The influence of constructivist theory as well as the whole-language/literature-based curriculum movement are reflected in this edition. Examples of changes made from previous editions include: an emphasis on strategies rather than skills, less focus on trivial elements of text, passages extracted from trade books, and in-depth mastery of vocabulary.

Readability/Source of Passages

Vocabulary level is carefully controlled to ensure that words selected are appropriate to each test level. This was accomplished by reference to Dale and O'Rourke (1981) and Harris and Jacobson (1982). The Dale and Chall (1948) and Fry (1977) formulas were used to control for readability level. Passages for the reading comprehension section were selected to represent a wide range of narrative and expository text and to represent both contemporary and traditional literature.

Format of Test/Test Parts

The test consists of two parts: vocabulary and comprehension. The vocabulary section contains 40 items. Thirteen items measure knowledge of synonyms, antonyms, and homonyms. Each word is presented in minimal context (e.g., usual *uneasiness*), with a choice of four answers. For words in context, paragraphs are presented in cloze format with three to five words omitted. Four alternatives are offered for each option. Three items measure knowledge of word derivations. The question stem asks, "which modern word comes from the original word." Four alternatives are offered. Four items are designed to measure word connotations. The student selects from one of four alternatives the best word to complete a sentence. Students are given a prompt that is designed to elicit a specific word connotation. Multiple meanings of words are examined with eight items. For each item, two sentences are presented with missing words. Four alternatives are given for each item. The student chooses the word that best completes both sentences.

The comprehension section consists of seven reading selections designed to measure information recall, meaning construction, form analysis, and meaning evaluation. The section includes 50 items, each with four answers. The readings include plays, poetry, biography, and informational text. The section tests recall of facts, character analysis, summarization, forms of writing, author intent, and purpose.

Testing Time

Vocabulary: 20 minutes; Reading Comprehension: 50 minutes.

Forms

The CAT/5 is available in two versions: as a complete battery or as a survey. The survey is an abbreviated form of the CAT/5 and yields only normative scores. The complete battery is available in two equivalent and parallel forms (A and B).

Levels

Levels are available for kindergarten through high school. Level 20: Grades 8.6 to 11.2. Level 21/22: Grades 10.6 to 12.9.

Types of Scores

Scale scores, grade equivalents, normal curve equivalents, percentiles, stanines, objective performance objectives, and anticipated achievement scores

Norm Group(s)

A total of 109,825 students Grades K–12 participated in the standardization of this measure. Tests were administered in April and October of 1991. The following demographics were considered in selecting the sample population: geographic region, community type (e.g., rural, town, small city, city, large city).

Date Published or Last Revised

1992

Reliability

The publishers offer a 696-page technical report on national standardization, validity, and reliability. Kuder-Richardson Formula 20 reliability coefficients were computed. For Level 21/22 these ranged from .81 to .90 for vocabulary and from for .75 to .93 for comprehension. Alternate-form reliability coefficients were calculated only through Grade 11 and ranged from .70 to .85 for vocabulary and from .55 to .82 for comprehension.

Validity

To construct the CAT/5, developers examined state and district curriculum guides, textbooks, instructional programs, and other norm- and criterion-referenced assessment tools. The goal was to construct a measure that would more closely reflect trends in reading/language arts instruction (i.e., holistic approaches, literature-based approaches). In addition, the CAT/5 was reviewed extensively during the development stage to detect cultural or gender bias.

Scoring Options

Machine scoring
• Compu Scan
Hand scoring
• Scoreze
• Compu Scan with hand-scoring stencils

Cost

Secondary Examination Kit
    complete battery: $35.95
    survey: $32.35
Reusable test booklets (30)
    complete battery: $94.65
    survey: $86.55
Answer sheets
• machine-scored
    Compu Scan (30)
        complete battery or survey: $30.80
• hand-scored
    Scoreze (25)
        complete battery or survey: $22.75
Stencils (3)
    complete battery: $40.50
    survey: $27.05

Publisher

CTB/McGraw-Hill, 2500 Garden Road, Monterey, CA 93940-5380

Weaknesses of the Test

1. The test was not designed for use with college students. No scores are provided for them, not even extrapolated scores.
2. The comprehension section does not resemble college-level reading in terms of content.
3. Although the comprehension passages are somewhat longer than in other standardized tests, the passage length does not resemble typically college-level reading assignments..
4. Norms for extended-time administration are not available.

Strengths of the Test

1. Items in the comprehension section of the CAT/5 reflect more attention to reading as a process than in previous versions.
2. Items in the vocabulary section of the CAT/5 reflect more attention to depth of vocabulary understanding than in previous versions.
3. A Locator Test consisting of 20 vocabulary items is available to provide a reliable way to match students with appropriate test levels.
4. Supplemental materials to assess students' writing, listening, and speaking proficiency are also available.

DEGREES OF READING POWER (DRP), STANDARD AND ADVANCED FORMS, 1995 EDITION

Test/Author(s)

Degrees of Reading Power (DRP)

Type of Test

Survey, formal, standardized, criterion-referenced

Use(s) of Test

1. To evaluate the current level of students' achievement in reading
2. To determine the most difficult prose a student can use with instructional assistance and as an independent reader
3. To measure the growth in the ability to read with comprehension
4. To place students in developmental reading courses at the college level

Skills/Strategies Tested

Reading comprehension

Population Recommended

Although college students are not including in the norming population, the publishers do recommend the use of the DRP to place college students in developmental reading programs and to document student progress in reading. In addition, the publishers point out that because the DRP is untimed, it is a more appropriate measure for students with disabilities and students who speak English as a second language. Because all information needed to complete cloze passages is included in the passage, culturally dependent prior knowledge is not a factor in this measure that would inhibit the performance of culturally diverse students.

Overall Theory of Reading

First published in 1983, the DRP provides an alternative to traditional standardized testing. The DRP measures a student's ability to derive meaning from connected prose text. The text is written at different levels of difficulty or readability. The purpose of the DRP is to measure the process of reading rather than to measure individual subskills such as main idea or author purpose. The primary and standard DRP tests are designed to examine surface-level comprehension. The Advanced DRP tests are use a modified format of the primary and standard versions to tap higher level reasoning based on the reading of text. In all DRP test levels, for students to answer questions correctly, they must read and comprehend the text pertaining to those items.

Readability/Source of Passages

The readability of passages is measured on a scale ranging from 0 to 100 DRP units, rather than in grade equivalencies. In practice, commonly encountered English text runs from about 30 DRP units at the easy end of the scale to about 85 DRP units at the difficult end. Bormuth's (1969) mean cloze formula and a set of standardized procedures are used to derive DRP units. The test consists of expository passages organized in ascending order according to passage difficulty.

Format of Test/Test Parts

The DRP is modified cloze test. Each passage is a prose selection of progressive difficulty. Standard DRP test items are created by the deletion of seven words in each passage. The student selects the most appropriate word from the five options provided for each blank. Forms G–4, H–4, G–2, and H–2 have 70 items each. The standard DRP tests incorporate the following characteristics:

1. The test passage must be read and understood for students to respond correctly. That is, the sentences containing the blanks will make sense with each of the options when read in isolation. However, when the surrounding text is taken into account, only one response is plausible.
2. Regardless of the difficulty of the passage, all response options are common words.
3. Item difficulty is linked to text difficulty.

The advanced DRP tests consist of prose passages. Each paragraph in the test passages have the final sentence deleted. Students must read and understand the paragraph to make a determination about which of 4 alternatives best completes the paragraph. The advanced tests each include a total of 24 items. The student must analyze the paragraph and its component propositions to determine which alternative is most logical.

Testing Time

Untimed. Reports from colleges (both 2- and 4-year) using the DRP indicate that the majority of those tested complete the test in approximately 1 hour. (Note: Students are urged to stop when the test no longer is comprehensible; guessing is not encouraged.)

Forms

The standard DRP is available in two forms at each of four sublevels. The forms and levels most appropriate for college students are: G–4 and H–4 (Grades 7 through 9) and G–2 and H–2 (Grades 9 through 12+). The advanced DRP is available in two forms at each sublevel: T–4 and U–4 (Grades 6 through 9) and T–2 and U–2 (Grades 9 through 12).

Levels

The DRP is available in three general levels: primary (Grades 1 through 3), standard (Grades 3 through 12), and advanced (Grades 6 through 12+). Each of the three general levels is also divided into sublevels. The advanced level, most appropriate for college students, is subdivided into two sublevels: Grades 6 through 9 and Grades 9 through 12+. The primary and standard level tests are designed to assess construction of meaning. The advanced level tests are meant to tap higher level reasoning.

Types of Scores

Raw scores, reading levels (independent, instructional, frustration), percentiles, stanines, normal curve equivalents

Norm Group(s)

As in previous versions of the DRP, the measure college students were not included in the norming population.

Date Published or Last Revised

1995

Reliability

The publishers offer a 181-page technical report on national standardization, validity, and reliability. Kuder-Richardson Formal 20 reliability coefficients were computed. Of the 72 reliability coefficients computed, 52 were greater than or equal to .95. The range of reliability coefficients was .93 to .97.

Validity

The publisher suggests that because of the design of the test (i.e., the student who comprehends the prose should be able to answer items correctly), the DRP is unambiguously a measure of ability to read with comprehension. Be definition, this is the central validity issue of a reading test.

Scoring Options

Machine scoring:
• DRP/NCS answer sheets purchased from publisher and returned for scoring
Hand scoring:
• scoring stencils (available from publisher).

Cost

Classrooms Sets (30)—Includes practice materials, tests booklets, answer sheets, and administration procedures
    Standard DRP: $135
    Advanced DRP: $125
Scoring key: $14
Scoring software (PC or Macintosh compatible): $46.95
Scoring and reporting (per student): $1.85

Publisher

DRP Services, Touchstone Applied Science Associates, 4 Hardscrabble Heights, P.O. Box 382, Brewster, NY 10509-0382

Weaknesses of the Test

College students were not included in the norming population.

Strengths of the Test

1. A real attempt has been made to develop a state-of-the-art, nonthreatening reading test representing reading as a holistic process.
2. The untimed administration of the test is an asset for students with disabilities and students who are of non-English language background.
3. An attempt to have answers evolve from the context of passages minimizes demands on prior knowledge—a feature particularly important for culturally diverse students.
4. Independent and instructional reading levels can be determined.
5. The publisher suggests that the students' reading level (in DRP units) can be matched to textbook readability (also in DRP units). Indeed, the publisher also offers four volumes of *Readability of literature and popular titles* in which literature for both children and adult is listed with DRP units. Software for identifying books is also available.

GATES–MACGINITIE READING TESTS, LEVEL F (3RD EDITION), 1989

Test/Author(s)

Gates–MacGinitie Reading Tests (3rd Edition); Level 10/12
MacGinitie, W. H. and MacGinitie, R. K.
Note: A revised version of the Gates–MacGinite Reading Tests is currently in development. The revised version is scheduled for availability in 2001.

Type of Test

Survey, formal, standardized, norm-referenced

Use(s) of Test

1. Initial screening
2. To assess progress and make changes as appropriate

Skills/Strategies Tested

1. Vocabulary
2. Reading comprehension

Population Recommended

Neither the author nor the publisher of the test in any way represent it as an instrument suggested for postsecondary school students. The sample for norming of the instrument did not include beyond Grade 12. Therefore, the norming tables for Grade 12 students should not be used as anything more than an indication of possible problems in reading. Institutions should develop their own local norms.

Overall Theory of Reading

According to the administrator's summary for the Gates–MacGinite Reading Tests, the measure is based on a model that views reading as, "complex, constructive, interactive, strategic, and learnable" (p. 3). Although the comprehension section yields only one score, the passages do represent a variety of language styles, content areas, and topics. Questions are both literal and inferential.

Readability/Source of Passages

Comprehension passages include narrative, expository, and setting text representing the following content categories: fiction, social science, natural science, arts, and poetry. A range of readability levels is included in each level and form of the Gates–MacGinitie Reading Tests. At the 10/12 Levels, readability of passages ranges from 5.0 to 13.0. Readability of passages was determined using three formulas: Dale and Chall (1948), Fry (1985), and Harris and Jacobson (1982).

Format of Test/Test Parts

The vocabulary test has 45 items. It uses words in brief context, each followed by five single-word choices. The student is to select the word that most nearly matches the test word in meaning. The comprehension test has 48 items, with passages of varying lengths (all are fairly short), followed by completion-type questions with four possible short alternatives, requiring an explicit or implicit understanding of information in the passage. A variety of narrative and nonnarrative passages as well as poetry is included.

Testing Time

Vocabulary: 20 minutes; Reading Comprehension: 35 minutes

Forms

Two equated forms (K and L)

Levels

Nine levels are available with one level (10/12) that may be adaptable for some college populations.

Types of Scores

Percentile ranks, normal curve equivalent scores, stanines, grade equivalents, extended scale scores

Norm Group(s)

Norms for Level 10/12 were obtained in 1987–1988. Approximately 77,000 students were included in the sample for standardization. Geographic region, district enrollment, and socioeconomic status (SES) of the community were considered in selecting the sample.

Date Published or Last Revised

Third edition, 1989

Reliability

Kuder-Richardson Formula 20 reliability coefficients were computed. These ranged from .89 to .93 for vocabulary and from .87 to .94 for comprehension.

Validity

Relatively little validity information is provided in the technical manual. Studies correlating the Gates–MacGinite Reading Tests with other tests and with course grades were conducted. In both cases correlations were high. In addition, statistical analyses for bias were conducted to eliminate items that had potential cultural or gender bias. In addition, a panel of experts representing a range of ethnicities reviewed items to detect elements of bias. Although extended-time norms are not provided, the technical report does provide data regarding completion rates.

Eighty percent of the Grade 12 students in the norming population were able to complete the vocabulary and comprehension subtests in the allotted time.

Scoring Options

Hand scoring:
• hand-scorable answer sheet test booklets that include answer keys
Matching scoring:
• for local scanning

Cost

Reusable Test Booklets (35): $70
Self-Scorable answer sheets (35): $45
Mark Reflex answer sheets (100): $69
Trans-Optic answer sheets (250): $205
Scoring Key for Hand-Scorable: $5

Publisher

Riverside Publishing Company, 425 Spring Lake Drive, Itasca, IL, 60143-2079

Weaknesses of the Test

1. The Gates–MacGinitie Reading Tests were not designed to be used with college students.
2. The vocabulary test uses words only in minimal context, which would have been more appropriate for college students.
3. The passages on the comprehension test are particularly short. We would prefer much longer selections more representative of the length of materials for entering college students.
4. The test validity information provided is limited.

Strengths of the Test

1. Overall test development and norming procedures were done with care, indicating potential for a quality instrument that measures what it has been designed to measure, and no more. The procedures used to develop this test provide us with a sense of the integrity of this instrument.
2. The comprehension test evaluates explicit and implicit comprehension from passages selected from a variety of basic content areas.
3. The manual for scoring and interpretation includes instructional suggestions for students whose reading comprehension or vocabulary scores are low.

NELSON–DENNY READING TEST (NDRT), FORMS E AND F, 1980

Test/Author(s)

Nelson–Denny Reading Test, Forms E and F
Brown, Bennett, and Hanna

Type of Test

Survey, formal, standardized, norm-referenced

Use(s) of Test

Primary use: Initial screening
- to identify students who may need special help in reading
- to identify superior students who could profit from placement in advanced/accelerated classes

Secondary uses:
- predicting success in college courses
- diagnosing strengths and weaknesses in vocabulary, reading comprehension, and reading rate

Skills/Strategies Tested

1. Vocabulary
2. Comprehension
3. Reading rate

Population Recommended

This test could be used effectively with entering average college students for screening purposes. Due to the difficulty of the reading comprehension passages, students reading more than 2 years below their grade level could become frustrated. The test could also be used for preprofessional and pregraduate students and for students in community reading efficiency courses. For maximum effectiveness, local norms should be developed.

Overall Theory of Reading

The authors list reading comprehension, vocabulary development, and reading rate as the three most important skills in the reading process, noting that they are related, interdependent functions.

Readability/Source of Passages

The first passage is the longest and the easiest, probably because it is used for measuring rate. Two of the other reading selections are written at high school level (Grades 9 to 10), and five are at the college level (three at 13th and two at 17th). Remaining passages are taken from *Scholastic* magazine or textbooks covering the humanities, social science, and science.

Format of Test/Test Parts

The vocabulary section gives 100 words in minimum context (e.g., to *presume*). The comprehension section has eight passages followed by multiple-choice questions with five alternatives. The first passage has eight questions; the rest have four each for a total of 36 questions. For rate, the students read from the first passage of the comprehension section for 1 minute and then mark the point they have reached when time is called.

Testing Time

Regular administration
    Vocabulary: 15 minutes; Comprehension: 20 minutes; Rate: 1 minute*
Cut-time administration (for speed-reading classes, efficient reading classes, and classes with a preponderance of junior/senior students)
    Vocabulary: 11 minutes; Comprehension; 15 minutes; Rate: 1 minute*
*Included in comprehension time

Forms

Two equivalent and parallel forms (E and F). The previous forms and E/F forms are not all parallel and equivalent, and should not be used interchangeably. Each set of forms should be used as a separate test. (Forms C and D can be used as pre- and posttests, as can E and F. However, C and F for example, cannot be used as pre- and posttests, as they are neither equivalent nor parallel.)

Levels

One level is available for Grade 9 through college.

Types of Scores

Standard scores, stanines, percentile ranks, rate equivalents

Norm Group(s)

Three samples were selected: one from the high school population, one from the 2-year college population, and one from the 4-year college and university population. For the college samples, 6,000 students from 41 two-year institutions and 5,000 students from 32 four-year colleges/universities were sampled in November 1979. For both, two criteria were used to select a representative group: Geographic regions and size of institution. The largest percentage of college students come from the west, followed by the midwest; the sample's largest group was from the southwest, followed by the southeast. The largest percentage of college students come schools with more than 5,000 students; the sample's largest group for 2-year colleges was from schools with 1,200 to 5,000 students, and for 4-year institutions from schools with more than 5,000 students. Racial and ethnic characteristics were not part of the sampling basis.

Date Published or Last Revised

This new form of the NDRT was tested in 1979 and published in 1980. Earlier versions were the Nelson–Denny Forms A/B and C/D.

Reliability

This method selected to assess reliability was the administration of two different forms of the test on separate occasions (alternate-form reliability). In all of the sampling, examiners had half of the examinees take Form E while the other half took Form F. Two weeks later, each examinee took the other form. The publisher's results shows the median reliability coefficient for vocabulary to be .92, for comprehension, .77, and for the total score, .91. The median for reading rate was .69.

Validity

The only form of validity measured by the publisher was context dependence. In this study, a sample of 225 college sophomores from two 4-year institutions varying in region and size took part. Half of the examinees took Form E with the reading passages present and next took Form F with its passages absent. The other half took Form E with its passages absent followed by Form F with its passages present. Results are presented in two scores. The Context Dependence Index (CDI) measures the degree to which correct item responses are influenced by the context. It should be positive and significant. The Context Independence Index (CII) measures the degree to which correct examinees can answer the items through previous knowledge or application of logic. It is an undesirable characteristic and should ideally be zero or negative. For the sampling population, the CDI was .29 for Form E and .44 for Form F. The CII was .09 for Form E and .03 for Form F.

Scoring Options

Machine scoring:
• Use NCS 7010 answer sheets
• Set up institutional scoring system
Hand scoring:
• Answer keys are provided in the manual.
• Use MRC answer sheets and make a stencil key for scoring.
Self-scoring:
• Answer sheets are available from the publisher.

Cost

Test booklets (35): $65
Examiner's Manual: $15
Mark Reflex Answer Sheets (scored by publisher; 100): $85
Self-Scoring Answer Sheets (250): $266
Trans-Optic Answer Sheets (for local scanning; 250): $189

Publisher

Riverside Publishing Company, 8420 Bryn Mawr Road, Suite 1000, Chicago, IL 60631

Weaknesses of Test

1. Although time has been allotted to the vocabulary test, the manual states that fewer than one in five students will complete this section unless they are in the last 2 years of college. Thus, time constraints still appear to be a problem.
2. The rate section remains a problem. Only 1 minute is allowed for testing reading rate, and no comprehension check in involved.
3. The difficulty level of reading passages is still a problem for underprepared students.

Strengths of Test

1. The instrument may be a valid measure of the reading efficiency of students in advanced college reading courses or in speed- or efficient reading courses. It might also be used effectively to measure the reading ability of students preparing for graduate study. For these student populations, cut-time administration should be used.
2. A strong attempt was made to norm the revised test on entering college students. The publisher tested 11,000 entering college students. Few other reading survey tests have been normed on a college population; most rely on high school seniors.
3. The test can be administered in a typical college class period.
4. The passages in the reading comprehension section are an attempt to test students' ability to read typical textbook material. However, due to the brevity of all passages except the first, extended reading cannot be measured.

NELSON–DENNY READING TEST (NDRT), FORMS G AND H, 1993

Test/Author(s)

Nelson–Denny Reading Test, Forms G and H
Brown, Fishco, and Hanna

Type of Test

Survey, formal, standardized, norm-referenced

Use(s) of Test

Primary use: initial screening
• to identify students who may need special help in reading
• to identify superior students who could profit from placement in advanced/accelerated classes

Secondary uses:

- predicting success in college courses
- diagnosing strengths and weaknesses in vocabulary, reading comprehension, and reading rate

Skills/Strategies Tested

1. Vocabulary
2. Comprehension
3. Reading rate

Population Recommended

This test could be used effectively with average entering college students for screening purposes. Due to the difficulty of the reading comprehension passages, students reading more than 2 years below their grade level could become frustrated. The test could also be used for preprofessional and pregraduate students and for students in community reading efficiency courses. For maximum effectiveness, local norms should be developed.

Overall Theory of Reading

The authors list reading comprehension, vocabulary development, and reading rate as the three most important skills in the reading process, noting that they are related, interdependent functions.

Readability/Source of Passages

All passages for form G and H of the NDRT were culled from high school and college textbooks (including social science, science, and humanities). As with previous versions, the first passage is the longest and easiest. The technical manual does not include information about passage readability. Using the Raygor Readability Estimate (1979), the first (longest) passage used for reading rate was estimated at a seventh grade readability level. Other passages ranged from 7th to 11th grade level. It appears that this edition of the NDRT is at a lower readability level than previous versions.

Format of Test/Test Parts

The general format this current version of the NDRT is similar to its predecessors due (as the publishers put it) to its widespread acceptance. In response to previous criticisms, however, the number of vocabulary items and number of comprehension passages were reduced to reduce working-time pressures. The vocabulary section gives 80 words in minimum context (e.g., *Pseudo* feelings are). The comprehension section has seven passages followed by multiple-choice questions with five alternatives. The first passage has eight questions; the rest have five each for a total of 38 questions. For rate, the students read from the first passage of the comprehension section for 1 minute and then mark the point they have reached when time is called.

Testing Time

Regular administration:
   Vocabulary: 15 minutes; Comprehension: 20 minutes; Rate: 1 minute*
Extended-time administration:
   Vocabulary: 24 minutes; Comprehension: 32 minutes; Rate: omitted.

Forms

Two equivalent and parallel forms (G and H). The C/D, E/F, and G/H forms are not all parallel and equivalent, and should not be used interchangeably.

Levels

One level is available for Grade 9 through college.

Types of Scores

Standard scores, stanines, normal curve equivalents, percentile ranks, grade equivalents, rate equivalents

Norm Group(s)

Three samples were selected: one from the high school population, one from the 2-year college population, and one from the 4-year college and university population. For the college samples, 5,000 students from 39 two-year institutions and 5,000 students from 38 four-year colleges/universities were sampled in September and October 1991 and 1992. For both, three criteria were used to select a representative group: geographic regions, size of institution, and type of institution (public or private). Samples included students of both genders and represented a wide range of ethnic backgrounds.

Date Published or Last Revised

This new form of the Nelson–Denny was tested in 1991 and 1992 and published in 1993. Earlier versions were the Nelson–Denny Forms A/B, C/D, and E/F.

Reliability

The publishers offer a 58-page technical report on national standardization, validity, and reliability. Kuder-Richardson Formula 20 reliability coefficients were computed. For the vocabulary subtest coefficients ranges from .92 to .94; for the comprehension subtest from .85 to .89. Alternate-form reliability coefficients were .89 vocabulary, .81 for comprehension and .68 for rate.

Validity

Minimal information about test validity is provided in the technical manual. In developing Forms G and H, a content analysis of current textbooks for developmental reading students was conducted to assure the content validity of key test components: vocabulary, comprehension, and reading rate. In addition, statistical analyses and a content analyses by an expert panel were conducted to assure balanced treatment of minorities and genders.

Scoring Options

Machine scoring:
- Use the NCS 7010 answer sheets
- Set up an institutional scoring system

Hand scoring:
- Answer keys are provided in the manual.
- Use MRC answer sheets and make a stencil key for scoring.

Self-scoring:
- Self-Scorable answer sheets are available from the publisher.

Cost

Test booklets (25): $42
Examiner's Manual: $ 4.50
Trans-Optic Answer Sheets (for local scanning; 250): $178
Self-scorable Answer Sheets (250): $302

Publisher

Riverside Publishing Company, 8420 Bryn Mawr Road, Suite 1000, Chicago, IL 60631

Weaknesses of the Test

1. The rate section remains a problem. Only 1 minute is allowed for testing reading rate, and no comprehension check in involved.
2. Length of passages continues to be a concern. Passages do not represent the length of typical college reading assignments.

Strengths of the Test

1. The extended-time administration of this new edition is an attempt to address reviews of previous editions. The extended-time is designed to accommodate English language learners, students with learning disabilities, and returning adults.
2. The test can be administered in a typical college class period.
3. The passages in the reading comprehension section are an attempt to test students' ability to read typical textbook material. However, due to the brevity of all passages except the first, reading of more extended text cannot be measured.
4. Some attention was given in this version to address concerns about working-time pressures through the reduction of vocabulary items and comprehension passages.
5. The readability level appears to be lower than previous editions.
6. Attention to cultural diversity was considered in selecting the norming population.

STANFORD DIAGNOSTIC READING TEST (SDRT),
BLUE LEVEL, 1995 (FOURTH) EDITION

Test/Author(s)

Stanford Diagnostic Reading Test (SDRT-4), Blue Level
Karlsen and Gardner

Type of Test

Diagnostic, formal, norm-referenced, standardized, criterion-referenced

Use(s) of Test

1. Initial diagnostic assessment; identification of student strengths and weaknesses
2. To assess individual progress and make changes as appropriate

Skills/Strategies Tested

1. Comprehension of narrative, expository, and functional text
2. Comprehension competencies including initial understanding, interpretation, critical analysis, and reading strategies
3. Synonyms
4. Scanning

Population Recommended

This test could be used to get a more diagnostic view of each student's reading abilities and inabilities before assigning underprepared students to reading improvement programs. However, this test is recommended only for freshmen in the lower achieving groups in community or junior colleges and in lower division university special admittance programs. The test would probably not discriminate for the more academically able college students; in fact, the authors and publisher have not included college students at all in this new edition.

Overall Theory of Reading

This edition of the SDRT is a complete revision of the previous edition and is intended to reflect changes in reading instruction. According to the technical manual, state and district curriculum guidelines were examined, classroom teachers were interviewed, and the IRA and NCTE were consulted to gauge trends and issues. The focus is more on strategies than subskills; genuine reading materials; and the reading of a variety of text: recreational, textual, and functional. Because the SDRT-4 is a diagnostic test rather than an achievement test, the emphasis is on detecting the needs of lower level readers and thus includes more easy items than achievement tests.

Readability/Source of Passages

Passages were selected to be representative of a range of topics covered in contemporary curriculum (e.g., narrative, expository, biography). Tradebook authors wrote the recreational reading passages. The technical manual did not include readability data. Using the Raygor Readability Estimate (1979) the range of readability levels of passages was 7th to 12th, with an average of eighth grade level.

Format of Test/Test Parts

Comprehension—Nine passages followed by multiple-choice questions with four alternatives (54 items). This subtest has a total of 54 questions. Illustrations are included to help activate interest and prior knowledge.

Vocabulary—30 items, each requiring identification of a synonym from one of 4 choices.

Scanning (32 items)—Students read a one-sentence question followed by four alternatives and then scan a full-page content-related article (with subheadings) to select the correct phrase or word to answer the question.

Testing Time

Reading comprehension: 50 minutes; Vocabulary: 20 minutes; Scanning: 15 minutes

Forms

Two parallel forms (J and K)

Levels

A total of six levels (K–13) are available. One level is available for the college population: Level Blue (Grades 9 through 13)

Types of Scores

Progress indicators, stanines, percentile ranks, scaled scores, normal curve equivalents, grade equivalents

Norm Group(s)

Testing for standardization took place in the fall of 1994 and in the spring of 1995. Nearly 53,000 students served as standardization participants. The technical manual does not report the number of participating students by grade level. Demographic characteristics considered when selecting the sample included geographic region, SES, urbanicity, and school type (public or private). In addition, students with disabilities and students with limited English proficiency were also included in the sample.

Date Published or Last Revised

The fourth edition was published in 1995.

Reliability

Publishers offer a 103-page technical manual that includes information about norming, reliability, and validity. Kuder-Richardson Formula 20 reliability coefficients were computed. These ranged from .84 to .90 on the vocabulary subtest, .91 to .94 on the comprehension subtest, and .88 to .93 on the scanning subtest. Kuder-Richardson Formal 21 reliability coefficients were also computed for subtests, clusters, and subclusters of the SDRT–4. For first-year college students, the subtest cluster scores ranged from .13 to .84 in vocabulary, from .26 to .89 in reading comprehension, and from .87 to .92 in scanning. Interestingly, some of the lowest reliability coefficients were for items related to new to this version of the SDRT: critical analysis and process strategies. In addition, alternative-forms reliability data for the Blue Form were provided in the technical manual: .80 for vocabulary, .71 for comprehension, and .62 for scanning.

Validity

The technical manual indicates that the best way to determine the content validity of the measure is to compare test content with the potential user's curriculum and instructional objectives. Construct validity was determined by correlating SDRT–4 subtests with comparable subtests on the Otis-Lennon School Ability Test, Sixth Edition. However, these correlations were only available through Grade 7. Construct validity was also explored by correlating corresponding subtests of different levels of the SDRT–4. The correlations between the Blue and Brown levels were as follows: Vocabulary—.75, Comprehension—.78, Scanning—.72.

Scoring Options

Hand scoring: Use Hand-Scorable Test Booklets and purchase stencil keys from the publisher.
Machine scoring: Use Machine-Scorable answer folders and send the test folders to the Harcourt Brace Educational Measurement Central Scoring Services for scoring.

Cost

Manual for Interpreting; $17
Norms Booklet: $40
Test Booklets (25): $63
Hand-Scorable answer documents (25): $23
Machine-Scorable answer documents (35): $29
Stencil for Hand-Scoring answer documents: $17

Publisher

The Psychological Corporation, 555 Academic Court, San Antonio, TX 78204

Weaknesses of the Test

1. Validity data cannot be generalized to the lower ability college freshman population.
2. The vocabulary subtest is a test of synonyms. There is no measure of words in context.
3. The passages used for the comprehension subtest are too brief and simple for the needs of most of the college population. There is an emphasis on functional reading (e.g., reading nutrition, labels, job application forms).

Strengths of the Test

1. The skimming subtest is excellent for the college level population recommended.
   The comprehension subtest provides item clusters to yield diagnostic information regarding a student's literal and inferential comprehension and their textual, functional, and recreational reading comprehension.
2. Three optional reading tests are also available: Reading Strategies Survey, Reading Questionnaire (to tap attitudes about reading), and Story Retelling.
3. The publisher also has a *Handbook of Instructional Techniques* that can be purchased separately (although it may or may not be appropriate for the college population).
4. The SDRT–4 was equated statistically with the Stanford Achievement Test Series (ninth edition) and the SDRT (third edition) so that institutions can compare longitudinal data.

THE ACT ASSET STUDENT SUCCESS SYSTEM, 1993

Test/Author(s)

ACT ASSET Student Success System

Type of Test

Screening, norm-referenced, standardized

Use(s) of Test

1. To assess basic skills in reading
2. To screen students for placement in developmental reading courses

Skills/Strategies Tested

Reading comprehension

Population Recommended

Students entering 2-year postsecondary institutions.

Overall Theory of Reading

ASSET was introduced nationally in 1983 to serve as an initial screening instrument for students entering 2-year institutions of higher education. Items in the instrument reflect a traditional standardized testing format with questions relating to reading subskills: main idea, details, sequence, drawing conclusions, vocabulary, and fact/opinion.

Readability/Source of Passages

Passages were selected to represent typical topics of freshman level reading assignments: social science, business, and fiction.

Format of Test/Test Parts

Three passages followed by eight multiple-choice questions (24 items). Multiple-choice questions are divided equally between explicit (referring) and inferential (reasoning) question types. The ASSET also includes mathematics and writing subtests.

Testing Time

25 minutes

Forms

In 1989, Forms B and C1 were put on the market and were phased out in 1994. Currently two forms (B2 and C2; 1993) are available.

Levels

One level is available

Types of Scores

Raw scores, ASSET scale scores (range 23 to 55)

Norm Group(s)

Current forms of ASSET were normed in 1992. A total of 23,334 students were included in the sample. Gender, ethnicity, and educational status (e.g., high school graduate) were the primary considerations in selecting the sample.

Date Published or Last Revised

1993

Reliability

Publishers offer a 116-page technical manual and includes information about norming, reliability, and validity. Kuder-Richardson Formula 20 reliability coefficients were computed for the reading subtest. These coefficients were .78 for both forms B2 and C2. Test–retest reliability were .80 for Form B2 and .76 for Form C2. Equivalent-forms reliability was .74 (Form B2 administered first) and .73 (Form C2 administered first).

Validity

Publishers discuss validity of the instrument in terms of measuring educational knowledge and skills and course placement. In terms of measuring educational knowledge and skills, the publishers refer to their instrument development procedures. Content validity of ASSET was determined by gathering input from representative college faculty in writing test items. Extensive review was conducted to eliminate ethnic or gender bias. Course placement data in reading were used to track student success in history, psychology, and biology. The publishers do not provide data on placement in remedial or developmental reading courses.

Scoring Options

Machine or microcomputer scoring:
• Require SCANTON or NCS answer document
Self scoring:
• Include self-carboning Educational Planning form and answer sheet

Cost

Test Booklets (25): $32.50
Microcomputer Answer Documents: $2.25 to $2.75 per student depending on volume.
Self-score or machine-score answer sheets: $2.40 to $2.90 per student depending on volume.
Technical Manual: $10
ASSET Success Folder (100): $70

Publisher

ACT, 2201 North Dodge Street, P.O. Box 168, Iowa City, IA 52243-0168

Weaknesses of the Test

1. Although the passages in the current versions are longer than in previous forms, their length (about 375 words) is not representative of typical college reading assignments.
2. The limited number of passages (three) and the subskill orientation of test items provide a restricted picture of student performance in reading. This is a screening instrument only.

Strengths of the Test

1. The ASSET test has the ability to screen large numbers of students in a short period of time.
2. The test also includes supplementary materials that are useful in student advising (e.g., career assessments, study skills assessments).
3. Institutional reports and individual student profiles provide valuable information for advising and keeping track of student placement, tracking underprepared students, and retention data.

4. Braille and large-type versions are available for students with vision impairments.
5. Publishers caution about potential misuse of the instrument. In particular they point out that ASSET is not designed for admission screening but rather for advising and placement. Publishers do not provide grade equivalent scores and caution users not to interpret ASSET scores as such.

COMPUTERIZED ADAPTIVE PLACEMENT ASSESSMENT AND SUPPORT SYSTEM (COMPASS), 1994

Test/Author(s)
ACT Compass

Type of Test
Adaptive, screening, diagnostic, norm-referenced, standardized

Use(s) of Test
1. To determine student strengths and weaknesses in reading
2. To screen students for placement in developmental reading courses

Skills/Strategies Tested
Reading comprehension and vocabulary

Population Recommended
Students entering postsecondary institutions.

Overall Theory of Reading
COMPASS utilizes computer technology (adaptive testing) to circumvent the historic dilemma of inappropriate standardized test levels. As the publishers explained, "The basic concept of adaptive testing is to 'adapt' the selection of test items to the goal of testing" (p. 2-2). Adaptive tests include a large pool of test items, a system for gauging student level of performance online, a procedure for selecting appropriate test items, and for termination of examination. Thus, testing time and test composition varies from student to student. Items in the instrument reflect a traditional standardized testing format with questions relating to reading subskills: main idea, details, sequence, drawing conclusions, and fact/opinion. vocabulary is tested as one component of reading comprehension in the placement test, but also tested as vocabulary in abbreviated context in the diagnostic test.

Readability/Source of Passages

Passages were selected from existing literature or written to represent typical topics and level of freshman level reading assignments: social science, humanities, natural sciences, fiction, and practical reading.

Format of Test/Test Parts

The Reading Comprehension Placement Test consists of a pool of 41 reading passages, approximately 200 words long. For each passage there are five items: two explicit (referring) and three inferential (reasoning). Prior knowledge questions are also included. These questions do not impact the students' scores, but rather are there to provide descriptive information about the potential impact of prior knowledge on the students' reading. The placement test includes both multiple choice (five alternatives) and text highlighting items. The text highlighting items require students to highlight the source of the answer in the passage text on the computer screen.

The Reading Comprehension Diagnostic Test has the same basic format as the placement test. It includes more passages (a pool of thirty 200-word passages) and taps specific reading subskills: main idea, details, and drawing conclusions. A Vocabulary Diagnostic Test consists of 100 items that require students to select the best word to complete a sentence. COMPASS also includes mathematics and writing subtests.

Testing Time

Because of the adaptive nature of COMPASS testing time and test content vary. For the placement test, administrators can determine minimum and maximum number of passages to be administered as well as an accuracy parameter. Examiners can also determine the type of passages (e.g., fiction, social sciences). For the diagnostic test, a proficiency-estimation model is used. In this case the test administrator determines the minimum and maximum number of items as well as specifications for a standard error of proficiency estimate.

Field testing of the COMPASS Reading Placement Test indicate that on the average students complete 3.84 passages and spend an average of 17.68 minutes taking the test. Completion of the demographics information takes another 10 to 20 minutes.

Forms

One form with an extensive item pool

Levels

One level is available

Types of Scores

Scoring depends of the test administration options selected. A 0 to 100 scale is used to represent the percentage of entire item pool items that the examinee would be predicted to have answered correctly.

Norm Group(s)

The Reading Test was normed with a sample of 1,058 students in Spring 1994 and 2,855 students in Fall 1994. Gender, ethnicity, age, geographic region, and urbanicity were considered in selection of postsecondary institutions and students within those institutions.

Date Published or Last Revised

1994

Reliability

An extensive COMPASS manual is available in a three-ring binder format. This includes a user's guide, software manual, and technical manual. The publishers emphasize that COMPASS is a new testing instrument—constantly in the process of being revised. Information provided in the technical manual is described at "preliminary" and the binder format makes updating more feasible. Publishers explain that conventional reliability indices are not appropriate for adaptive tests in that individual examinees complete items based on different passages. Simulation studies that estimate reliabilities were generated using data from more than 100,000 examinees. Classification accuracy (i.e., classifying students into performance categories) was .86 and marginal reliability (i.e., averaging individual reliabilities across examinees) was .90.

Validity

Publishers discuss validity of the instrument in terms of measuring educational knowledge and skills and making placement decisions. In terms of measuring educational knowledge and skills, the publishers refer to their instrument development procedures. Content validity of ASSET was determined by gathering input from representative college faculty in writing test items. Extensive review was conducted to eliminate ethnic or gender bias. In addition, the publishers point out that using adaptive tests confounds issues of validity in that examinees have highly individualized tests.

Placement data for the COMPASS was sparse and admittedly "in development." The publishers do not provide data on placement in remedial or developmental reading courses.

Scoring Options

Computer scoring

Cost

License Fees: $525 Annual Fee per Campus

Administration Units (costs for generation of student records, placement tests, diagnostic tests, retests): $.90 to $1.10 per unit depending on service desired and ordering volume.
COMPASS Manual: $30
COMPASS Standard Item Set: $10

Publisher

ACT, 2201 North Dodge Street, P.O. Box 168, Iowa City, IA 52243-0168

Weaknesses of the Test

1. Passages are brief (designed to fit on a computer screen) and not representative of typical college reading assignments.
2. The subskill orientation of test items provides one picture of student performance in reading and may be less useful for institutions espousing a more holistic approach to developmental reading instruction.
3. Reliability and validity data are sparse because the instrument is in development.
4. Because of the nature of the instrument, traditional reliability and validity procedures are difficult to compare and are procedures that are unfamiliar to most practitioners and potential users.

Strengths of the Test

1. The primary strength is that COMPASS uses computer technology to alleviate the use of inappropriate test levels to tap knowledge about students' reading.
2. The test includes a prior knowledge component in an attempt to describe, if not control for prior knowledge.
3. Test scores are available immediately due to the use of computer technology.
4. Retesting logistics can be simplified.
5. A COMPASS reader profile is also available to tap students' reading habits. This survey does not impact test scores, but does provide advisors with additional information about reading habits and interests.
6. A variety of individual reading profile and institutional reports are available.

Note
For all tests reviewed, the following applies: The readability of passages was determined by use of the Fry Readability Graph (1977) or the Raygor Readability Estimate (1979), except where otherwise noted; testing time does not include time for passing out materials, giving directions, or rest periods.

ACKNOWLEDGMENTS

We acknowledge the contributions of Madlyn Hanes and Carol Cashen who were coauthors with Rona Flippo of the original version of this chapter, published in 1991 by the International Reading Association. Additionally, special recognition goes to Carol Cashen, who coauthored with Flippo the appendix, reviewing the commercially available tests at the same time.

Special recognition goes to Suzette Ahwee and Whawn Allen, University of Miami students who assisted us with the update of this chapter and appendix.

REFERENCES AND SUGGESTED READINGS

Abraham, A. (1987). *Report on college level remedial/developmental programs in SERB states.* Atlanta: Southland Regional Education Board. (ERIC Document Reproduction Service No. ED 280 369)

ACT ASSET Student Success System. (1993). Iowa City, IA: ACT.

*Ahrendt, K. M. (1975). *Community college reading programs.* Newark, DE: International Reading Association.

Alexander, C. F. (1977). Adding to usefulness of standardized reading tests in college programs. *Journal of Reading, 20,* 288–291.

Anderson, C. A. (1971). Problems of individualization. In F. P. Greene (Ed.), *Reading: The right to participate* (pp. 211–214). Milwaukee, WI: National Reading Conference.

Anderson, C. A. (1973). A study of accountability in the community college reading program. In P. L. Nacke (Ed.), *Programs and practices for college reading* (Vol. 2, pp. 7–11). Boone, NC: National Reading Conference.

Anderson, I. H. (1937). Studies on the eye movements of good and poor readers. *Psychological Monographs, 48,* 21–35.

Anderson, R., Reynolds, R., Schallert, D., & Goetz, E. (1977). Frameworks for comprehending discourse. *American Educational Research Journal, 14,* 367–381.

Anderson, R. C. (1972). How to construct achievement tests to assess comprehension. *Review of Educational Research, 42,* 145–170.

Armbruster, B. B., & Anderson, T. H. (1988). On selecting "considerate" content area textbooks. *Remedial and Special Education, 9,* 47–52.

Atkinson, R., & Longman, D. (1988). *Reading enhancement and development (READ)* (2nd ed). St. Paul, MN: West Publishing.

Bader, L. A. (1998). *BADER reading and language inventory.* Upper Saddle River, NJ: Merrill.

Baldwin, R. S., Murfin, P., Ross, G., Seidel, J., Clements, N., & Morris, C. (1989). Effects of extending administration time on standardized reading achievement tests. *Reading Research and Instruction, 29,* 33–38.

Benson, J. (1981). A redefinition of content validity. *Educational and Psychological Measurement, 41,* 793–802.

Berg, P. C. (1973). Evaluating reading abilities. In W. H. MacGinitie (Ed.), *Assessment problems in reading* (pp. 27–33). Newark, DE: International Reading Association.

*Blanton, W., Farr, R., & Tuinman, J. J. (Eds.). (1972). *Reading tests for the secondary grades: A review and evaluation*. Newark, DE: International Reading Association.

Bloesser, R. E. (1968). *Study skills project*. Cupertino, CA: Foothill Junior College District. (ERIC Document 022 437)

Bloom, M. E., Douglas, J., & Rudd, M. (1931). On the validity of silent reading tests. *Journal of Applied Psychology, 15*, 35–38.

Bloomers, P., & Lindquist, E. F. (1944). Rate of comprehension of reading: Its measurement and its relation to comprehension. *Journal of Educational Psychology, 15*, 449–473.

Bormuth, J. R. (1969). *Development of readability analyses*. (Final report, OEG-3-7-070052-0326). Washington, DC: U.S. Office of Education.

Bormuth, J. R. (1985). A response to "Is the Degrees of Reading Power test valid or invalid?" *Journal of Reading, 29*, 42–47.

Boylan, H., Bonham, B., Bliss, L., & Claxton, C. (1992, November). *The State of the Art in Developmental Education*. Paper presented at the National Conference in Research in Developmental Education, Charlotte, NC.

Brensing, D. D. (1974). Improvement of the reading abilities of vocational students. *Dissertation Abstracts International, 35*, 4321–4322A. (University Microfilms No. 74-25, 593)

*Brown, F. G. (1983). *Principles of educational and psychological testing (3rd ed.)*. New York: Holt, Rinehart & Winston.

Brown, J. E., Bennett, J. M., & Hanna, G. S. (1980). *The Nelson–Denny Reading Test* (Forms E & F). Chicago, IL: Riverside.

Brown, J. E., Fishco, D. J., & Hanna, G. S. (1993). *The Nelson–Denny Reading Test* (Forms G & H). Chicago, IL: Riverside.

Brown, J. E. Nelson, M. J., & Denny, E. C. (1973). *The Nelson-Denny Reading Test* (Forms C & D). Boston: Houghton Mifflin.

Bruning, R. (1985). Review of Degrees of Reading Power. In J. V. Mitchell, Jr. (Ed.), *The ninth mental measurements yearbook* (pp. 443–444). Lincoln: University of Nebraska Press.

Bryant, B. R., & Wiederholt, J. L. (1992). *Gray oral reading tests—diagnostic*. Austin, TX: Pro-Ed.

Burgess, M. A. (1921). *The measurement of silent reading*. New York: Department of Education.

Burkart, K. H. (1945). An analysis of reading abilities. *Journal of Educational Research, 38*, 430–439.

Burns, P. C., & Roe, B. D. (1993). *Informal reading inventory* (4th ed.). Boston: Houghton Mifflin.

Buswell, G. T. (1920). An experimental study of the eye-move span in reading. *Supplementary Educational Monographs, 17*, 1–105.

Byrnes, M. E., Forehand, G. A., Rice, M. W., Garrison, D. R., Griffin, E., McFadden, M., & Stepp-Bolling, E. R. (1991). Putting assessment to work: Computer-based assessment for developmental education. *Journal of Developmental Education, 14*, 2–8.

California Achievement Test (CAT/5): Reading, E and F, Level 20. (1992). Monterey, CA: CTB/McGraw-Hill.

California Achievement Test (CAT/5): Levels 20 and 21/22. (1992). Monterey, CA: CTB/McGraw-Hill.

Carey, R. F., Harste, J. C., & Smith, S. L. (1981). Contextual constraints and discourse processes: A replication study. *Reading Research Quarterly, 16,* 201–212.

Carney, M., & Geis, L. (1981). Reading ability, academic performance, and college attrition. *Journal of College Student Personnel, 22*(1), 55–59.

Carsello, J. (1982, October). *Tests, workbooks, and books being used in college basic skills programs: The latest survey of college and university programs in the U.S.* Paper presented at the 25th annual conference of the North Central Reading Association, Flint, MI.

Cartwright, H. D. (1972). Individualization of instruction in a reading and study skills center with junior college and/or open door policy students. In F. P. Greene (Ed.), *College reading: Problems and programs of junior and senior colleges* (Vol. 2, pp. 118–122). Boone, NC: National Reading Conference.

Carver, R. P. (1975). *Reading Progress Scale, college version.* Kansas City, MO: Retrace.

Carver, R. P. (1985a). Is the Degrees of Reading Power test valid or invalid? *Journal of Reading, 29,* 34–41.

Carver, R. P. (1985b). Why is the Degrees of Reading Power test invalid? In J. A. Niles & R. V. Lalik (Eds.), *Issues in literacy: A research perspective* (pp. 350–354). Rochester, NY: National Reading Conference.

Cashen, C. J. (1980). A study of the effect of the test environment on the reading comprehension, comprehending, and processing of text by junior high school readers. *Dissertation Abstracts International, 41,* 3503A.

Chall, J. S. (1958). *Readability: An appraisal and assessment.* Columbus: Ohio State University.

Chester, R. D., Dulin, K. L., & Carvell, R. (1975). Mature readers' Nelson-Denny comprehension scores. In G. H. McNinch & W. P. Miller (Eds.), *Reading: Convention and inquiry* (pp. 227–234). Clemson, SC: National Reading Conference.

Cleland, D. L. (1965). A construct of comprehension. In J. A. Figuel (Ed.), *Reading and inquiry* (pp. 59–64). Newark, DE: International Reading Association.

Clymer, T. (1968). What is reading?: Some current concepts. In H. M. Robinson (Ed.), *Innovation and change in reading instruction, Sixty-Seventh Yearbook of the National Society for the Study of Education* (pp. 1–30). Chicago: University of Chicago Press.

Coats, D. F. (1968). The enigma of the survey section of the Diagnostic Reading Test. In G. B. Schick & M. N. May (Eds.), *Multidisciplinary aspects of college adult reading* (pp. 70–78). Milwaukee, WI: National Reading Conference.

College Level Academic Skills Test. (1984). Tallahassee, FL: Department of Education.

COMPASS *(Computerized Adaptive Placement Assessment and Support System).* (1994). Iowa City, IA: ACT.

Cranney, A. G., & Larsen, J. (1972). Compensatory programs for specially admitted freshmen to the University of Florida, 1968-1971. In F. P. Greene (Ed.), *College reading: Problems and programs of junior and senior colleges* (Vol. 2, pp. 38–41). Boone, NC: National Reading Conference.

Creaser, J., Jacobs, M., Zaccarea, L., & Carsello, J. (1970). Effects of shortened time limits on the Nelson-Denny Reading Test. *Journal of Reading, 14,* 167–170.

Cronbach, L. J. (1949). *Essentials of psychological testing.* New York: Harper & Row.

Curtis, M. E., & Glaser, R. (1983). Reading theory and the assessment of reading achievement. *Journal of Educational Measurement, 20,* 133–147.

Dale, E., & Chall, J. S. (1948). A formula for predicting readability. *Educational Research Bulletin, 27,* 11–20.

Dale, E., & Eichholz, G. (1954-1969). *Children's knowledge of words, an interim report* (A Payne Fund Communication Project). Columbus: Ohio State University, Bureau of Educational Research and Service.

Dale, E., & O'Rourke, J. (1981). *The living word vocabulary.* Chicago, IL: World Book-Childcraft.

Daneman, M. (1982). The measurement of reading comprehension: How not to trade construct validity for prediction power. *Intelligence, 6,* 331–345.

Daneman, M. (1991). Individual Differences in reading skills. In R. Barr, M. L. Kamil, P. B. Mosenthal, & P. D. Pearson, (Eds.). *Handbook of Reading Research, 2,* 512–538. New York: Longman.

Davis, B. (1944). Fundamental factors of comprehension in reading. *Psychometrika, 9,* 185–197.

Davis, B. (1947). A brief comment on Thurstone's notes on a reanalysis of Davis' reading tests. *Psychometrika, 11,* 249–255.

Davis, F. B., & Davis, C. C. (1961). *Davis Reading Test.* New York: Psychological Corp.

Davis, B. (1968). Research in comprehension in reading. *Reading Research Quarterly, 3,* 499–545.

Davis, F. B. (1978). Iowa Silent Reading Tests. In O. K. Buros (Ed.), *The eighth mental measurements yearbook* (pp. 1199–1201). Highland Park, NJ: Gryphon.

Davis, T., Kaiser R., & Boone, T. (1987). *Speediness of the Academic Assessment Placement Program (AAPP) Reading Comprehension Test.* Nashville: Tennessee State Board of Regents. (ERIC Document 299 264).

Degrees of Reading Power. (1983). New York: The College Board.

Degrees of Reading Power. (1995). *(DRP): Standard and Advanced Forms.* Brewster, NY: DRP Services.

Derrick, C., Harris, D. P., & Walker, B. (1960). *Cooperative English Tests—Reading.* Princeton, NJ: Cooperative Tests and Services, Educational Testing Service.

Drabin-Partenio, I., & Maloney, W. H. (1982). A study of background knowledge of three groups of college freshmen. *Journal of Reading, 25,* 430–434.

Erwin, T. D. (1981). The Nelson-Denny Reading Test as a predictor of college grades. *Reading Psychology, 2,* 158–164.

Eurich, A. C. (1930). The relation of speed of reading to comprehension. *School and Society, 32,* 404–406.

Evans, H., & Dubois, E. (1972). Community/junior college remedial programs: Reflections. *Journal of Reading, 16,* 38–45.

Farr, R. (1968). The convergent and discriminant validity of several upper level reading tests. In G. B. Schick & M. M. May (Eds.), *Multidisciplinary aspects of college adult reading* (pp. 181–191). Milwaukee, WI: National Reading Conference.

Farr, R. (1969). *Reading: What can be measured?* Newark, DE: International Reading Association.

Farr, R. (1972). Test reviews: Nelson-Denny Reading Test. In W. Blanton, R. Farr, & J. H. Tuinman (Eds.), *Reading tests for the secondary grades: a review and evaluation* (pp. 31– 34). Newark, DE: International Reading Association.

Farr, R. (Coord. Ed.). (1973). *Iowa Silent Reading Tests* (Levels 2 & 3). Cleveland, OH: Psychological Corporation.

*Farr, R., & Carey, R. F. (1986). *Reading: What can be measured?* (2nd ed.). Newark, DE: International Reading Association.

Feuers, S. (1969). The relationship between general reading skills and junior college academic achievement. *Dissertation Abstracts International, 30*, 3186A-3187A. (University Microfilms No. 70-2200).

Filby, N. N. (1978). Iowa Silent Reading Tests. In O. K. Buros (Ed.), *The eighth mental measurements yearbook* (pp. 1196–1197). Highland Park, NJ: Gryphon.

Flippo, R. F. (1980a). Comparison of college students' reading gains in a developmental reading program using general and specific levels of diagnosis, *Dissertation Abstracts International, 41*, 179–180A.

Flippo, R. F. (1980b, Winter). Diagnosis and prescription of college students in developmental reading programs: A review of literature. *Reading Improvement, 17*(4), 278–285.

Flippo, R. F. (1980c). The need for comparison studies of college students' reading gains in developmental reading programs using general and specific levels of diagnosis. In M. L. Kamil & A. J. Moe (Eds.), *Perspectives on reading research and instruction*, pp. 259–263. Washington, DC: National Reading Conference. (ERIC Document 184 061).

Flippo, R. F. (1982a). Do we need differential diagnosis at the college level? Maybe. *Western College Reading Association Journal, 2*(2), 1–3.

Flippo, R. F. (1982b). Organizing for diagnostic instruction in reading lab. *Reading Horizons, 22*(4), 288–291.

*Flippo, R. F. (1997). *Reading assessment and instruction: A qualitative approach to diagnosis*. Fort Worth, TX: Harcourt Brace.

*Flippo, R. F., & Cashen, C. J. (1991). Appendix to chapter 4: Commercially available tests reviewed. In R. F. Flippo & D. C. Caverly (Eds.), *College reading & study strategy programs* (pp. 173–210). Newark, DE: International Reading Association.

*Flippo, R. F., Hanes, M. L., & Cashen, C. J. (1991). Reading tests. In R. F. Flippo & D. C. Caverly (Eds.), *College reading & study strategy programs* (pp. 118–210). Newark, DE: International Reading Association.

Florio, C. B. (1975). An assessment of the effectiveness of remedial reading courses at San Antonio College. *Dissertation Abstracts International, 36*, 2664A. (University Microfilms No. 75-24, 864).

Forsyth, R. A. (1978). Nelson-Denny Reading Test, Forms C and D. In O. K. Buros (Ed.), *The eighth mental measurements yearbook* (pp. 1207–1209). Highland Park, NJ: Gryphon.

Fradd, S. H., & McGee, P. L. (1994). *Instructional assessment: An integrative approach to evaluating student performance*. Reading, MA: Addison-Wesley.

Freedle, R. O., & Carroll, J. B. (1972). Language comprehension and the acquisition of knowledge: Reflections. In J. B. Carroll & R. O. Freedle (Eds.), *Language, comprehension, and the acquisition of knowledge* (pp. 361–368). New York: Wiley.

Freer, I. J. (1965). A study of the effect of a college reading program upon grade point average in Odessa College, Odessa, Texas. *Dissertation Abstracts International, 27,* 601A. (University Microfilms No. 66-6124).

Fry, E. B. (1977). Fry's Readability Graph: Clarifications, validity, and extension to level 17. *Journal of Reading, 21*(3), 242–252.

Garciá, G. E. (1994). Assessing the literacy development of second-language students: A focus on authentic assessment. In K. Spangenberg-Urbschat & R. Pritchard (Eds.), *Kids come in all languages: Reading instruction for ESL students* (pp. 180–206). Newark, DE: International Reading Association.

Gates, A. J. (1935). *The improvement of reading.* New York: Macmillan.

Gibson, E. J., & Levin, H. (1975). *The psychology of reading.* Cambridge, MA: MIT Press.

Glaser, R. (1981). The future of testing: A research agenda for cognitive psychology and psychometrics. *American Psychologist, 36*(9), 923–936.

*Glazer, S. M., Searfoss, L. W., & Gentile, L. M. (Eds.). (1988). *Reexamining reading diagnosis: New trends and procedures.* Newark, DE: International Reading Association.

Goodman, K. S. (1968). *The psycholinguistic nature of the reading process.* Detroit, IL: Wayne State University Press.

Goodman, K. S. (1969). Analysis of oral reading miscues: Applied psycholinguistics. *Reading Research Quarterly, 5,* 9–30.

Goodman, K. S. (1976). Reading: A psycholinguistic guessing game. In H. Singer & R. Ruddell (Eds.), *Theoretical models and processes of reading* (2nd ed., pp. 497–508). Newark, DE: International Reading Association.

Goodwin, D. D. (1971). Measurement and evaluation in junior college reading programs. *Junior College Research Review, 6,* 1–3.

Gordon, B. (1983). A guide to postsecondary reading tests. *Reading World, 23,* 45–53.

*Gordon, B., & Flippo, R. (1983). An update on college reading improvement programs in the southeastern United States. *Journal of Reading, 27,* 155–163.

Gray, W. S. (1919). Principles of method in teaching reading as derived from scientific investigation. In *Eighteenth yearbook of the National Scoiety for the Study of Education.* Chicago, IL: National Society for the Study of Education.

*Guthrie, J. T., & Lissitz, R. W. (1985, Summer). A framework for assessment-based decision making in reading education. *Educational Measurement: Issues and Practice, 4,* 26–30.

Hall, W. E., & Robinson, F. P. (1945). An analytical approach to the study of reading skills. *Journal of Educational Psychology, 36,* 429–442.

Harris, A. J., & Jacobson, M. D. (1982). *Basic reading vocabularies.* New York: Macmillan.

Hasit, C., & DiObilda, N. (1996). Portfolio assessment in a college developmental reading class. *Journal of Developmental Education, 19,* 26–31.

Holmes, J. A. (1962). Speed, comprehension, and power in reading. In E. P. Bliesmer & R.C. Staiger (Eds.), *Problems, programs, and projects in college-adult reading* (pp. 6–14). Milwaukee, WI: National Reading Conference.

Holmes, J. A., & Singer, H. (1966). *The substrata factor theory.* Washington, DC: U.S. Government Printing Office.

Huey, E. B. (1908). *The psychology and pedagogy of reading.* Cambridge, MA: MIT Press.

Ironside, R. A. (1969, March). *Who assesses reading status and progress–tests, teachers, or students?* Paper presented at the twelfth annual meeting of College Reading Association, Boston.

Janzen, J. L., & Johnson, E. F. (1970). *The use of reading tests for entrance and placement testing in a community college.* Calgary, Alberta: Mount Royal College.

Johns, J. (1990). *Secondary and college inventory.* DeKalb: Northern Illinois University.

*Johnston, P. H. (1983). *Reading comprehension assessment: A cognitive basis.* Newark, DE: International Reading Association.

*Johnston, P. H. (1984). Prior knowledge and reading comprehension test bias. *Reading Research Quarterly, 14,* 219–239.

*Jongsma, K. S., & Jongsma, E. A. (1981, March). Test review: Commercial informal reading inventories. *The Reading Teacher, 34*(6), 697–705.

Karlsen, B., Madden, R., & Gardner, E. R. (1976). *Stanford Diagnostic Reading Test, Blue Level.* New York: Psychological Corporation.

Karlsen, B., & Gardner, E. R. (1995). *Stanford Diagnostic Reading Test, Blue Level.* San Antonio, TX: Psychological Corporation.

Karlsen, B., Madden, R., & Gardner, E. R. (1984). *Stanford Diagnostic Reading Test, Blue Level (3rd ed.).* New York: Psychological Corporation.

Kelly, F. J. (1916). The Kansas Silent Reading Tests. *Journal of Educational Psychology, 7,* 69–80.

Kerstiens, G. (1986a). A testimonial on timed testing: Developmental students and reading comprehension tests. In M. P. Douglass (Ed.), *Fiftieth Yearbook of the Claremont Reading Conference* (pp. 261–267). Claremont, CA: Claremont Graduate School.

Kerstiens, G. (1986b, April). *Time-critical reading comprehension tests and developmental students.* Paper presented at the annual meeting of the American Educational Research Association. San Francisco, CA.

Kerstiens, G. (1990). A slow look at speeded reading comprehension tests. *Research in Developmental Education, 7*(3), 1–6.

Ketcham, H. E. (1960). Reading tests and college performance. In O. J. Causey (Ed.), *Research and evaluation in college reading* (pp. 63–66). Fort Worth, TX: Texas Christian University Press.

Kibby, M. W. (1981). Test review: The Degrees of Reading Power. *Journal of Reading, 24,* 416–427.

Kingston, A. J. (1955). Cautions regarding the standardized test. In O. Causey & A. J. Kingston (Eds.), *Evaluating college reading programs* (pp. 11–16). Forth Worth, TX: Texas Christian University Press.

Kingston, A. J. (1961). A conceptual model of reading comprehension. In E. Bliesmer & A. J. Kingston (Eds.), *Phases of college and adult reading.* Milwaukee, WI: National Reading Conference (pp. 100–107).

Kingston, A. J. (1965). Is reading what the reading tests test? In A. L. Thurston (Ed.), *The philosophical and sociological basis of reading* (pp. 106–109). Milwaukee, WI: National Reading Conference.

Kintsch, W. F. (1974). *The representation of meaning in memory.* Hillsdale, NJ: Lawrence Erlbaum Associates.

Landsman, M. B., & Cranney, A. G. (1978). Training and activities of Florida community college reading teachers. *Florida Reading Quarterly, 14,* 17–22.

Langsam, R. S. (1941). A factorial analysis of reading ability. *Journal of Experimental Education, 10,* 57–63.

Lennon, R. T. (1962). What can be measured? *The Reading Teacher, 15,* 326–337.

Lowe A. J., & Stefurak, D. W. (1970). The college reading improvement programs of Georgia: 1969-1970. In G. B. Schick & M. M. May (Eds.), *Reading: Process and pedagogy* (Vol. 2, pp. 118–124). Milwaukee, WI: National Reading Conference.

MacGintite, W. H. (1978). *Gates-MacGintite Reading Tests, Level F* (2nd ed.). Boston: Houghton Mifflin.

MacGinitie, W. H., & MacGinitie, R. K. (1989). *Gates-MacGinitie Reading Tests (3rd ed.): Level 10/12.* Itasca, IL: Riverside.

Malak, J. F., & Hageman, J. N. (1985). Using verbal SAT scores to predict Nelson scores for reading placements. *Journal of Reading, 28,* 301–304.

Mangrum, C. T., & Strichart, S. S. (1988). *College and the learning disabled student* (2nd ed.). Philadelphia: Grune & Stratton.

Mangrum, C. T., & Strichart, S. S. (Eds.); (1997). *Peterson's colleges with programs for students with learning disabilities* (4th ed.). Princeton, NJ: Peterson's.

Maxwell, M. (1981). *Improving student reading skills.* San Francisco, CA: Jossey-Bass.

Mitchell, Jr. (Ed.), *The ninth mental measurements yearbook* (p. 1037). Lincoln, NE: University of Nebraska Press.

Monroe, W. S. (1918). Monroe's Standardized Silent Reading Tests. *Journal of Educational Psychology, 9,* 303–312.

Mulcahy-Ernt, P., & Stewart, J. P. (1994). Reading and writing in the integrated language arts. In L. M. Morrow, J. K. Smith, & L. C. Wilkinson (Eds.), *Integrated language arts: Controversy to consensus* (pp. 105–132). Boston: Allyn & Bacon.

Nelson, M. J., Denny, E. C., & Brown, J. I. (1960). *Nelson-Denny Reading Test (Forms A & B).* Boston: Houghton Mifflin.

Newcomer, P. L., & Bryant, B. R. (1993). *Diagnostic achievement test for adolescents* (2nd ed.). Austin, TX: PRO-ED.

New Jersey Department of Higher Education Basic Skills Council. (1992). *New Jersey College Basic Skills Placement Test.* Trenton, NJ: Author.

*Nist, S., & Diehl, W. (1994). *Developing textbook thinking* (3rd ed.). Lexington, MA: D. C. Heath.

Nist, S. L., Mealey, D. L., Simpson, M. L., & Kroc, R. (1990). Measuring the affective and cognitive growth of regularly admitted and developmental studies students using the Learning and Study Strategies Inventory (LASSI). *Reading Research and Instruction, 30,* 44–49.

Noble, J. (1986, Summer). Estimating reading skill from ACT assessment scores. *College and University, 61*(4), 310–317.

Orlando, V. P., Caverly, D. C., Flippo, R. F. & Mullen, J. (1987, May). *Reading demands of college students in history and psychology classes.* Paper presented at the 32nd annual convention of the International Reading Association, Anaheim, CA.

Orlando, V. P., Caverly, D. C., Flippo, R. F., & Mullen, J. (1988, November 29–December 3). *Reading and studying in college: A follow-up.* Paper presented at the thirty-eighth annual meeting of the National Reading Conference, Tucson, AZ.

Orlando, V. P., Caverly, D. C., Mullen, J. & Flippo, R. F. (1986, December). *Text demands in college classes: An investigation.* Paper presented at the thirty-sixth annual meeting of National Reading Conference, Austin, TX.

*Orlando, V. P., Caverly, D. C., Swetnam, L., & Flippo, R. F. (1989). Text demands in college classes: An investigation. *Forum for Reading, 21*(1), 43–48.

Orlando, V. P., Flippo, R. F., & Caverly, D. C. (1990, May). *Meeting text demands in college classes.* Paper presented at the 35th annual convention of International Reading Association, Atlanta.

Pardy, M. (1977). A comparative study of the effects of the use or misuse of sustained silent reading on reading skill proficiency and self-concepts of college students engaged in a traditional diagnostic prescriptive program. *Dissertation Abstracts International, 38,* 5957A. (University Microfilms No. 7802921)

*Perry, W. G., Jr. (1959). Students' use and misuse of reading skills: A report to the Harvard faculty. *Harvard Educational Review, 29,* 193–200.

Peters, C. W. (1977). Diagnosis of reading problems. In W. Otto, N. Peters, & C. W. Peters (Eds.), *Reading problems: A multidisciplinary perspective* (pp. 151–188). Reading, MA: Addison-Welsey.

Phillips, G. O. (1969). The relative effectiveness of three instructional approaches upon the reading, study habits and attitudes, and academic performance of disadvantaged black college freshman. *Dissertation Abstracts International, 31,* 1084A. (University Microfilms No. 70-15, 460)

*Pikulski, J. J., & Shanahan, T. (Eds.). (1982). *Approaches to the informal evaluation of reading.* Newark, DE: International Reading Association.

Popham, W. J. (1975). *Educational evaluation.* Englewood Cliffs, NJ: Prentice-Hall.

Rankin, E. F., & Helm, P. (1986). The validity of cloze tests in relation to a psycholinguistic conceptualization of reading comprehension. *Forum for Reading, 17*(2), 46–59.

Raygor, A. L. (1970). *McGraw-Hill Basic Skills Reading Test.* New York: McGraw-Hill.

Raygor, A. L. (1979). *Raygor Readability Estimator.* Rehoboth, MA: Twin Oaks.

Raygor, A. L. (1980). *Minnesota Readability Assessment.* Rehoboth, MA: Twin Oaks.

*Raygor, A. L., & Flippo, R. F. (1981). Varieties of comprehension measures: A comparison of intercorrelations among several reading tests. In G. McNinch (Ed.), *Comprehension: Process and product* (pp. 13–17). Athens, GA: America Reading Forum. (ERIC Document 198 485)

Readence, J. E., & Moore, D. W. (1983). Why questions? A historical perceptive on standardized reading comprehension tests. *Journal of Reading, 26,* 306–313.

Rice, H. D. (1971). A study to determine the effectiveness of a developmental reading program in a community college setting. *Dissertation Abstracts International, 32,* 5573A–5574A. (University Microfilms No. 72–10).

Robinson, F. P., & Hall, P. (1941). Studies of higher-level reading abilities. *Journal of Educational Psychology, 32,* 241–251.

Robinson, F. P. & McCollom, F. H. (1934). Reading rate and comprehension accuracy as determinants of reading test scores. *Journal of Educational Psychology, 25,* 154–157.

Robinson, H. M. (1966). The major aspects of reading. In H. A. Robinson (Ed.), *Reading: Seventy-five years of progress* (Supplementary Educational Monograph No. 96). Chicago, IL: University of Chicago Press.

Ross, E. P., & Roe, B. D. (1986). *The case for basic skills in programs in higher education.* Bloomington, IN: Phi Delta Kappa Educational Foundation.

Ryan, J. M., & Miyasaka, J. (1995). Current practices in testing and assessment: What is driving the change? *NASSP Bulletin, October,* 1–10.

Sadden, L. J., & Reid, J. (1984). The cloze procedure as a reading test. *Journal of Developmental Education, 9*(2), 30–31.

Schank, R. C. (1972). Conceptual dependency: A theory of natural language understanding. *Cognitive Psychology, 3,* 552–631.

Schoenberg, B. M. (1969). The development and evaluation of a program for the teaching of reading in junior college. *Dissertation Abstracts International, 30,* 2861A-2862A. (University Microfilms No. 69–21)

Schreiner, R. (Ed.). (1979). *Reading tests and teachers: A practical guide.* Newark, DE: International Reading Association.

Schreiner, R. L., Hieronymus, A., & Forsyth, A. (1969). Differential measurement of reading abilities at the elementary school level. *Reading Research Quarterly, 5,* 84–99.

*Schumm, J. S., & Post, S. A. (1997). *Executive learning.* Upper Saddle River, NJ: Prentice-Hall.

*Schumm, J. S., Post, S., Lopate, K., & Hughes, M. (1992). Postsecondary student reflection using assessment portfolios: A step toward independence in college level literacy. In P. A. Malinowski & S. D. Huard (Eds.), *Perspectives on practice in developmental education* (pp. 21–23). Canandaigua, NY: New York College Learning Skills Association.

Seashore, R. H., Stockford, L. B. O., & Swartz, B. K. (1937). A correlation analysis of factors in speed of reading tests. *School and Society, 46,* 1180.

Sequential Tests of Educational Progress: Reading (1969). Princeton, NJ: Cooperative Tests and Services, Educational Testing Service.

Shank, S. (1930). Student responses in the measurement of reading comprehension. *Journal of Educational Research, 22,* 119–129.

Shermis, M. D., Wolting, M., & Lombard, D. (1996). Computerized adaptive testing for reading placement and diagnostic assessment. *Journal of Developmental Education, 20,* 18–24.

*Simpson, M. (1982). A diagnostic model for use with college students. *Journal of Reading, 26,* 137–143.

Simpson, M. L. (1993). Cutting edge: Defining the vision of developmental studies programs. *Journal of Developmental Education, 17,* 32–33.

Singer, H., & Donlan, D. (1989). *Reading and learning from text* (2nd ed.). Hillsdale, NJ: Lawrence Erlbaum Associates.

Smith, F. (1973). *Psycholinguistics and reading.* Orlando, FL: Holt, Rinehart & Winston.

Smith, F. (1978). *Understanding reading: A psycholinguistic analysis of reading and learning to read* (2nd ed.). Orlando, FL: Holt, Rinehart & Winston.

*Smith, S. P., & Jackson J. H. (1985). Assessing reading/learning skills with written retellings. *The Reading Teacher, 28*(7), 622–630.

Smittle, P. (1993). Computer adaptive testing: A new era. *Journal of Developmental Education, 17*, 8–12.

Spache, G. (1962). What is comprehension? In E. Bliesmer & R. Staiger (Eds.), *Problems, programs, and projects in college-adult reading.* Milwaukee, WI: National Reading Conference. (pp. 17–19)

Spearritt, D. (1972). Identification of subskills of reading comprehension by maximum likelihood factors. *Reading Research Quarterly, 8*, 92–111.

Squire, J. R. (1987). Introduction: A special issue on the state of assessment in reading. *The Reading Teacher, 40*(8), 724–725.

Starch, D. (1915). The measurement of efficiency in reading. *Journal of Educational Psychology, 6*, 1–24.

State of Florida, Department of Education. (1984). *College Level Academic Skills Test.* Tallahassee, FL: Author.

Stephens, E. C., Weaver, D. R., Ross, G. A., & Edmond, S. B. (1986, Fall/Winter). The cloze procedure as predictor of undergraduate achievement in introductory courses. *Forum for Reading, 18*(1), 32–36.

*Stetson, E. G. (1982). Reading tests don't cheat, do they? *Journal of Reading, 25*, 634–639.

Stewart, E. W. (1970). Reading improvement program for college students. In G. B. Schick & M. M. May (Eds.), *Reading: Process and pedagogy* (pp. 202–207). Milwaukee, WI: National Reading Conference.

Swanson, D. E. (1937). Common elements in silent and oral reading. *Psychological Monographs, 48*, 36–50.

Sweiger, J. D. (1972). Designs and organizational structure of junior and community college reading programs across the country. In F. P. Greene (Ed.), *College reading: Problems and programs of junior and senior colleges* (pp. 1–7). Boone, NC: National Reading Conference.

Taschow, H. G. (1968). A comparative study of a corrective reading program and its effects on two freshman reading groups at Central Oregon Community College. *Dissertation Abstracts International, 29*, 2160A. (University Microfilms No. 69–464)

Thorndike, E. L. (1914). The measurement of ability in reading. *Teachers College Record, 15*, 207–277.

Thurstone, L. L. (1946). Note on reanalysis of Davis' reading tests. *Psychometrika, 11*, 185–188.

Tierney, R. J. (1985). Review of Stanford Diagnostic Reading Test, Blue Level, 1976 edition. In J. V. Mitchell, Jr. (Ed.), *The ninth mental measurements yearbook* (pp. 1463–1464). Lincoln, NE: University of Nebraska Press.

Tinker, M. A. (1932). The relation of speed to comprehension in reading. *School and Society, 36*, 158–160.

Tinker, M. A. (1945). Rate of work in reading performance as measured in standardized tests. *Journal of Educational Psychology, 36*, 217–228.

Tittle, C., & Kay, P. (1971, February). *Selecting tests for an open admissions population.* Paper presented at the annual meeting of the American Educational Research Association, New York. (ERIC Document Reproduction Service No. ED 048 359).

Traxler, A. E. (1941). *Problems of measurement in reading.* Paper presented at the American Council on Education's invitational conference on testing problems, New York.

Triggs, F. O. (1947). *Diagnostic Reading Tests.* Princeton, NJ: Educational Records Bureau.

Triggs, F. O. (1952). *Diagnostic reading tests: A history of their construction and validation.* New York: Committee on Diagnostic Tests.

U.S. Department of Education, National Center for Education Statistics. (1995). *Remedial education in higher education institutions* [Online]. Available: http://www://nces.ed.gov

*Valencia, S., Hiebert, E. H., & Afflerbach, P. (1994). Definitions and perspectives. In S. Valencia, E. H. Hiebert, & P. Afflerbach (Eds). *Authentic reading assessment: Practices and possibilities* (pp. 6–21). Newark, DE: International Reading Association.

Valencia, S., & Pearson, P. D. (1987). Reading assessment: Time for change. *The Reading Teacher, 40*(8), 726–732.

*Valeri-Gold, M., Olson, J. R., & Deming, M. P. (1991). Portfolios: Collaborative authentic assessment opportunities for college developmental learners. *Journal of Reading, 35,* 298–305.

Van Meter, B. J. (1988). A survey of the use of the Nelson-Denny Reading Test in the community/junior colleges of Maryland. *Reading: Issues and Practices, 5,* 78–84.

Van Meter, B. J., & Herrman, B. A. (1986–1987). Use and misuse of the Nelson-Denny Reading Test. *Community College Review, 14*(3), 25–30.

Vogel, S. A. (1994). A retrospective and prospective view of postsecondary education for adults with learning disabilities. In S. A. Vogel & P. B. Adelman (Eds.), *Success for college students with learning disabilities* (pp. 3–20). New York: Springer-Verlag.

Wainer, H. (1990). *Computerized adaptive testing: A primer.* Hillsdale, NJ: Lawrence Erlbaum Associates.

Webb, M. W. (1983). A scale for evaluating standardized reading tests, with results for Nelson–Denny, Iowa, and Stanford. *Journal of Reading, 26,* 424–429.

Weinstein, C. E., Schulte, A. C., & Palmer, D. P. (1987). *Learning and study strategies inventory.* Clearwater, FL: H & H Publishing.

Williams, T. (1998, May 28). New York City college moves to drop remedial education. *The Miami Herald,* p. 8A.

Winograd, T. (1972). Understanding natural language. *Cognitive Psychology, 3,* 1–191.

Wolf, W., King, M., & Huck, G. (1968). Teaching critical reading to elementary school children. *Reading Research Quarterly, 3,* 435–498.

Wood, K. (1988). Standardized reading tests and postsecondary curriculum. *Journal of Reading, 32,* 224–230.

*Wood, K. (1989). Reading tests and reading assessment. *Journal of Developmental Education, 13*(2), 14–19. *Reading Research Quarterly, 3,* 435–498.

Woodcock, R. W., & Johnson, W. B. (1996). *Woodcock-Johnson psycho-educational battery, revised.* Allen, TX: DLM Teaching Resources.

Wright, G. L. (1973). A experimental study comparing the differential effectiveness of three developmental reading treatments upon the rate, vocabulary, and comprehension skills of white and black college students. *Dissertation Abstracts International, 34,* 5811A. (University Microfilm No. 74 6257)

Ysseldyke, J. E. (1985). *Review of the Nelson-Denny Reading Test, Forms E and F.* In J. V. Mitchell, Jr. (Ed), The ninth mental measurements yearbook (p. 1037). Lincoln, NE: University of Nebraska Press.

Author Index

꙳§§꙳

Locators annotated with *n* indicate notes
Locators annotated with *t* indicate tables

A

Abraham, A. A., xiv, xvi, *xvii*, 385, 393, 398, 403, 432, *460*
Abrams, L., 114, 117, *144*
Abuhmaidan, Y. A., 117, *133*
Ackerman, J. M., 160, 161, *166*
ACT ASSET Student Success System, 453, *460*
Actkinson, T. R., 106, *136*
Adams, A., 126, *134*
Adams, E. K., 109, *134*
Adams, S. M., 298, *316*, 349, *356*
Adamson, H. D., 267, *281*
Adelman, C., vii, *x*
Aeschleman, S. R., 126, 127, *140*
Afflerbach, P. P., 269, 289, 404, *471*
Ahrendt, K. M., 414, *460*
Akst, J., 377, *397*
Albinski, E. E., 49, *67*
Aldersley, S., 121, 123, 124, *140*
Alderson, J. C., 274, *281*
Alexander, C. F., 414, 421, *460*
Alexander, P. A., 76, 77, 78, 80, 81, *96*, *98*
Alfaro, L., 301, *313*
Allen, G. J., 239, 242, 243, *252*
Allen, R., 385, 393, *398*
Allison, J., 206, *217*
Almanza, E., 269, *281*
Alting, T., 241, *252*
Altwerger, B., 267, 269, *281*, *283*
Alvarez, M. C., 90, *96*, *101*, 204, 205, 208, 209, 213, *216*, *219*

Amer, A. A., 113, 120, 121, 123, 124, *134*
American Association for Education, 387, 388, *397*
Anastasi, A., 234, 235, 251, *252*
Anderson, B., 227, *254*
Anderson, C. A., 412, *460*
Anderson, D. K., 114, *145*, 295, 296, 300, *319*
Anderson, I. H., 410, 412, *460*
Anderson, J., 385, 393, 395, *397*, 398
Anderson, M. C., 78, 79, *96*
Anderson, O. S., 343, *357*
Anderson, R. C., 46, 48, 55, 67, *71*, 78, 79, 83, 84, *96*, *99*, *101*, *102*, *103*, 110, 120, 127, *134*, *143*, 411, 412, *460*
Anderson, S., 366, 367, 368, 373, *398*
Anderson, T. H., 90, 91, 92, *96*, 105, 109, 118, 125, 126, 128, *133*, *134*, 175, *196*, 413, 421, *460*
Anderson-Inman, L., 303, 304, 309, *310*
Andrews, M. B., 306, *310*
Andriotle, S. J., 208, *216*
Ani, U. N., 44, *72*
Annis, D. B., 109, *134*
Annis, L., 109, 110, 112, 115, 117, *134*, *137*, 305, *310*
Anzul, M., 372, *399*
Aponte, C. F., 242, *252*
Aponte, J. F., 127, *137*, 242, *252*
Appel, A. W., 354, *357*
Applebee, A., 157, 160, *166*
Arani, M. T., 267, *281*
Archambeault, B., 214, 215, *216*

Subject Index

෴

Locators annotated with *f* indicate figures.
Locators annotated with *t* indicate tables.
Locators annotated with *n* indicate notes.